Invitation and Promotion Design

Ideas with Impact

Invitation and Promotion Design

Ideas with Impact

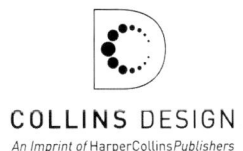

INVITATION AND PROMOTION DESIGN: IDEAS WITH IMPACT
Copyright © 2008 COLLINS DESIGN and **maomao** publications

All rights reserved. No part of this book may be used or reproduced in any manner whatsover,
without written permission except in the case of brief quotations embodied in critical articles and reviews.
For information, address Collins Design, 10 East 53rd Street, New York, NY 10022.

HarperCollins books may be purchased for educational, business, or sales promotional use.
For information, please write: Special Markets Department, HarperCollins*Publishers*,
10 East 53rd Street, New York, NY 10022.

First Edition published by:
maomao publications in 2008
Tallers, 22 bis, 3º 1ª
08001 Barcelona, Spain
Tel.: +34 93 481 57 22
Fax: +34 93 317 42 08
mao@maomaopublications.com
www.maomaopublications.com

English language edition first published in 2008 by:
Collins Design
An Imprint of HarperCollins*Publishers*
10 East 53rd Street
New York, NY 10022
Tel.: (212) 207-7000
Fax: (212) 207-7654
collinsdesign@harpercollins.com
www.harpercollins.com

Distributed throughout the world by:
HarperCollins*Publishers*
10 East 53rd Street
New York, NY 10022
Fax: (212) 207-7654

Publisher:
Paco Asensio

Editorial Coordinator:
Anja Llorella

Editors:
Lou Andrea Savoir
Paz Diman

Art Director:
Emma Termes Parera

Layout:
Gemma Gabarron Vicente

English Translation:
Jay Noden

Library of Congress Cataloging-in-Publication Data

Diman, Paz.
  Invitation and promotion design : ideas with impact / Paz Diman and Lou
Andrea Savoir-- 1st English language ed.
      p. cm.
  Includes bibliographical references and index.
  ISBN 978-0-06-124199-4 (alk. paper)
 1. Invitation cards–Design. 2. Graphic arts. I. Title.

  NC1880.A8313 2008
  741.6--dc22

2008019653

Printed in Spain
First Printing: 2008

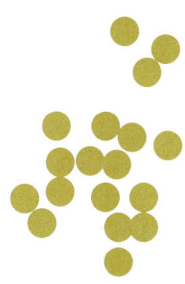

Contents

Introduction   7

Pump up the volume!   10
Flyers, posters, and invitations related to concerts and parties

Care to join us?   84
Pamphlets and brochures for exhibitions, conferences, and theater productions

Remember me?   162
Business cards, brand identity, and more

Introduction

There are over six billion people living in the world today, and as time passes, we continue to globalize. Our constantly evolving technology brings all corners of the globe together like never before. Through these advancements we are able to keep in touch with the countless people we meet, and those that once seemed far away are now at the tips of our fingertips.

We come into contact with so many people each day and learn so many new names and faces we see on a regular basis—what can we do to make sure that we are remembered? How do we remember others? With so much information around us, how do we capture people's attention, so that we do not go unnoticed?

In *Invitation and Promotion Design: Ideas with Impact*, we find these answers through a brilliant compilation of work by over one hundred designers who have asked the same questions. These artists have designed affective pieces, using their distinct tastes and modern outlooks to grab any viewer's attention. Since these concepts are personality driven, each project is able to stand out against boundless and unending competition. Their search for fresh design strategies gives way to a revision of art history, reviving work done by hand, such as art nouveau, kinetic art, minimalism, references to the cinema and famous icons of the consumer culture. However, the key to these successful designs is the innovative and singular viewpoint of the designers themselves, updating previous references and submersing themselves in a markedly contemporary world.

In this book, the material is organized in three chapters so the reader can compare and contrast different proposals that revolve around one theme. Thus, "Pump up the volume!" includes flyers, posters and invitations related to concerts, and parties; "Care to join us?" concerns exhibitions, conferences, theatre productions and prizes; and, finally, "Remember me?" focuses on business cards, good causes, and collective efforts. And since all invitations may lead to great stories, the designers allow us to spy on their personal lives, leaving us with a sentence about the best party experience they've ever had. Of course, there are those who say they have never been invited to any…

Invitation and Promotion Design: Ideas with Impact brings together lucid and ingenious ideas that, despite having their necessary differences, all coincide by paying homage to originality. With this, we can find the inspiration to make any basic message an original and inventive piece of art.

Pump up the volume!

Flyers, posters, and invitations related to concerts and parties

At a party where the only person we knew was the host, my friend Josh and I created fictitious personas for ourselves. Josh was Hans Shoemaker (the speedo-wearing son of German immigrants), and I was Alex Schmitlickey (a zoology writer for the Floridian Gazette). We pulled it off until late in the evening, when the booze caused us to stumble over our stories and forget our names—blowing our ruse.

Jesse LeDoux

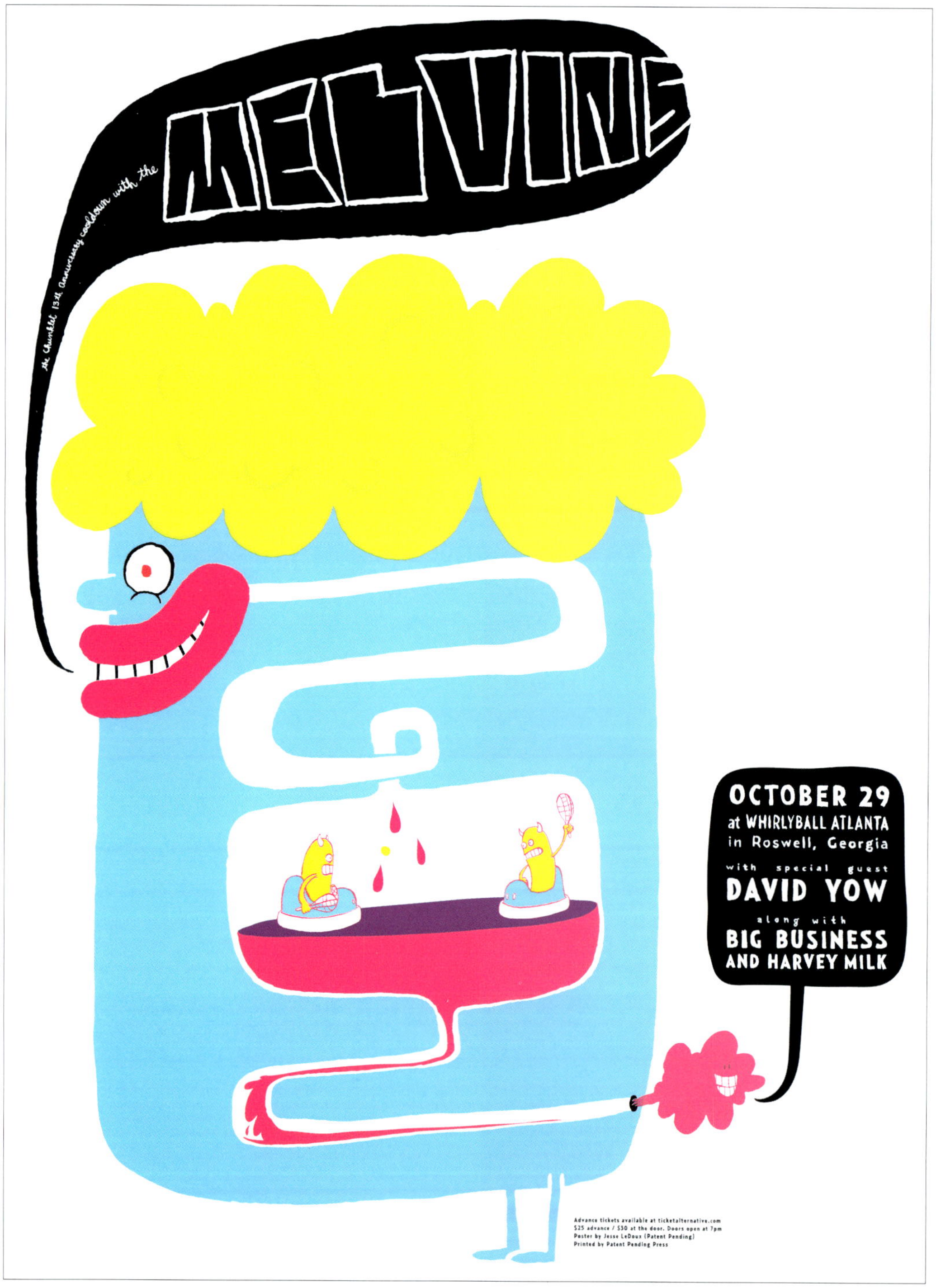

Melvins poster | 2006

Jesse LeDoux/LeDouxville
www.ledouxville.com

This is a promotional poster for a concert that was to take place on a whirlyball* court. The amusing scatological angle takes strength from the explosion of saturated colors.

*A sport played with rackets on bumper cars.

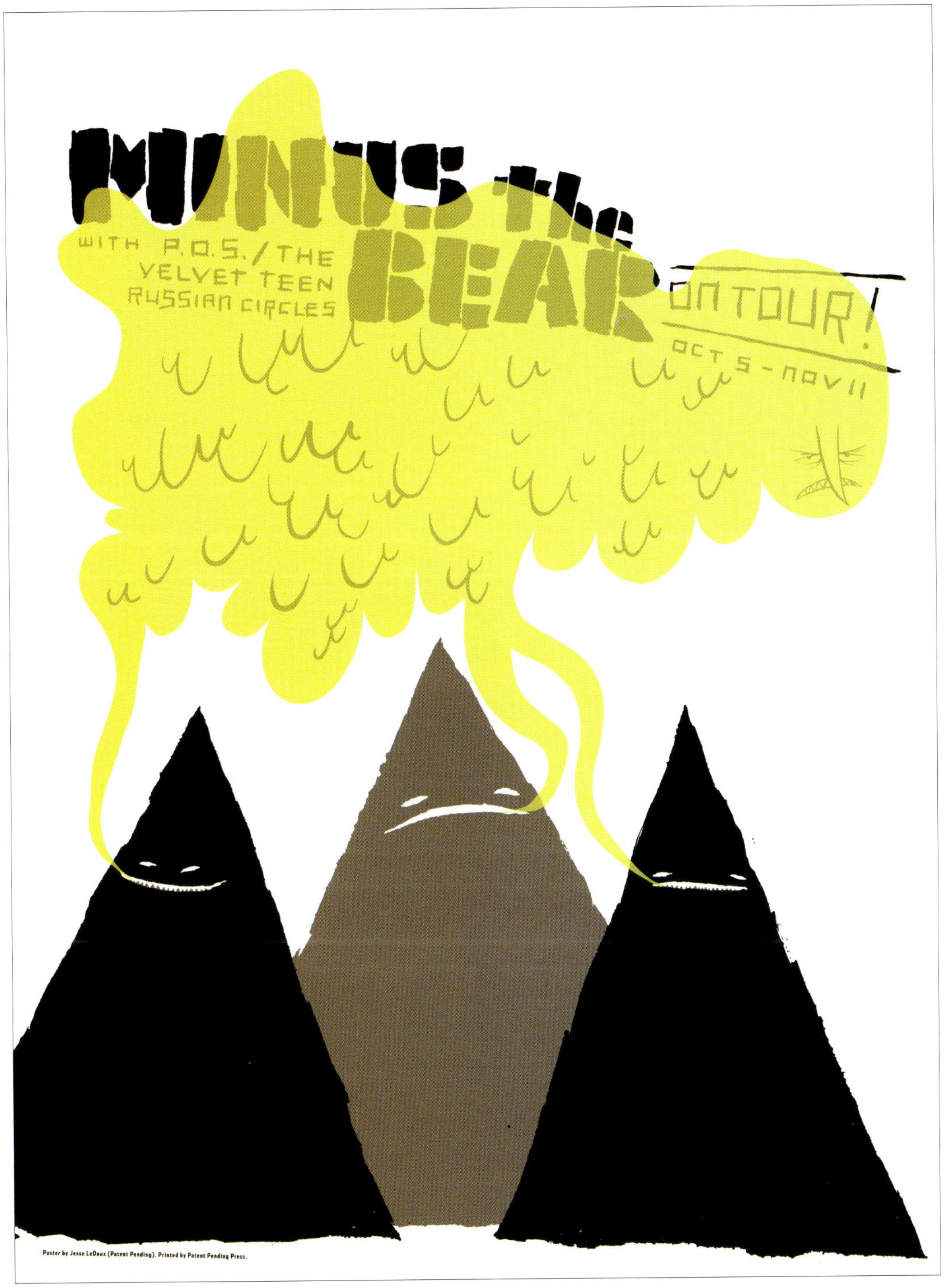

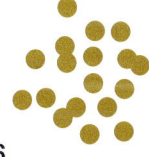

Minus the Bear poster | 2006

Jesse LeDoux/LeDouxville
www.ledouxville.com

The art from the poster has also been applied to a T-shirt and a wallet. From just two colors, LeDoux achieves a brilliant, striking figure, without this detracting from the poster's legibility or practicality.

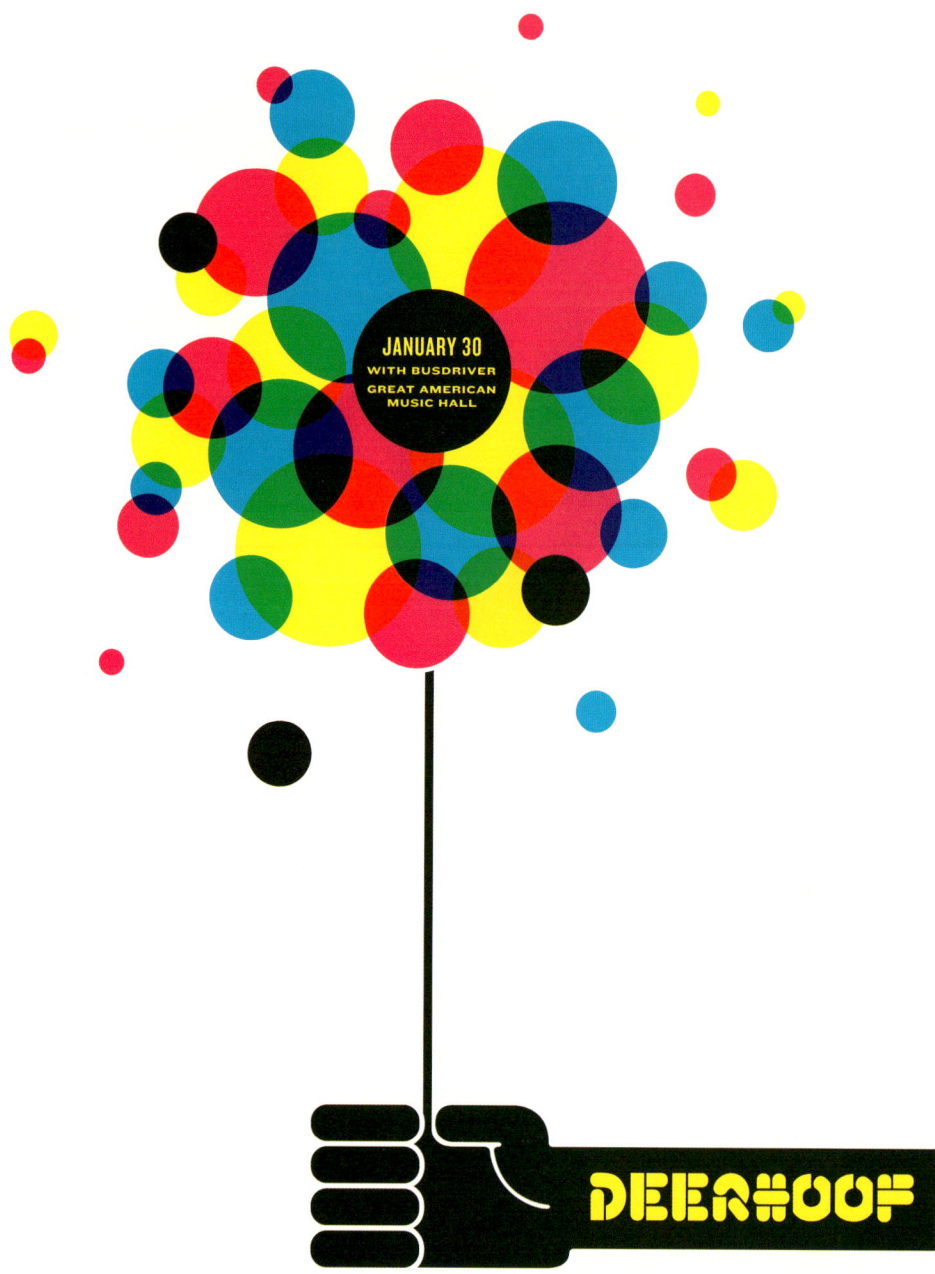

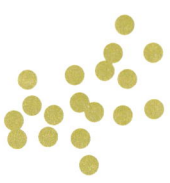

Deerhoof | 2007

Jason Munn/The Small Stakes
www.thesmallstakes.com

For the promotional poster for the group Deerhoof basic forms and pure colors appeal to an intuitive perception. The complement of this initial impression is the figure of the black hand that is outlined on a neutral background.

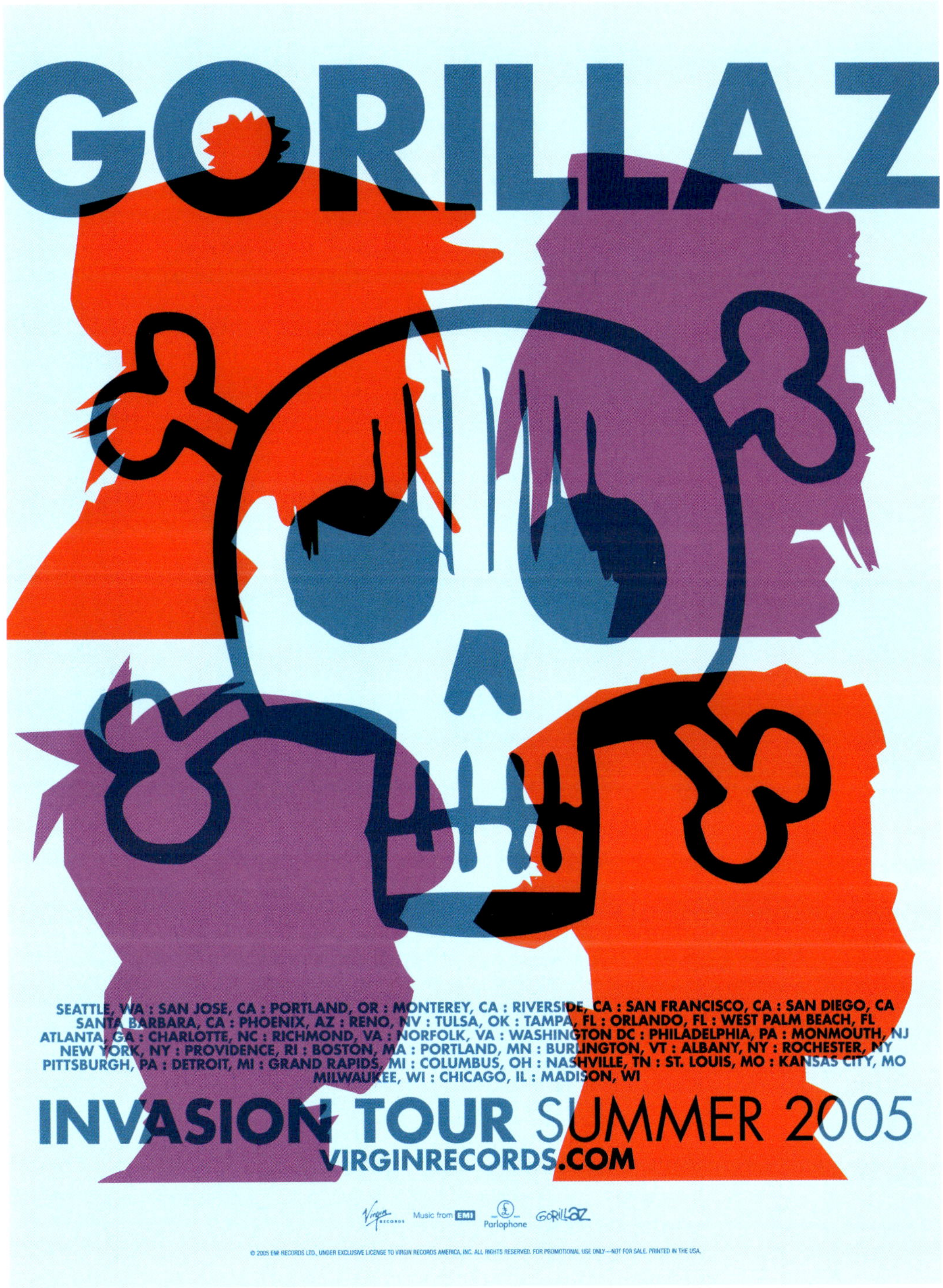

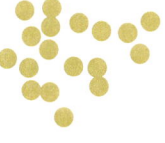

Gorillaz poster | 2005

Illustration: Jamie Hewlett
Design: Mike Joyce/Stereotype
www.stereotype-design.com

The tour poster superimposes the typography and color to create an idea of abstraction and dimension. Through transparency the figure of the characters that identify the group can be observed.

I'd have to say my thirtieth birthday party was pretty fun. We rented out the Screening Room which is a cool old theater with a bar on the balcony in Tribeca. About twenty-five of my friends and I watched The Texas Chainsaw Massacre *(the original of course) while the staff kept pouring the drinks on. Leatherface never looked so good!*

Mike Joyce

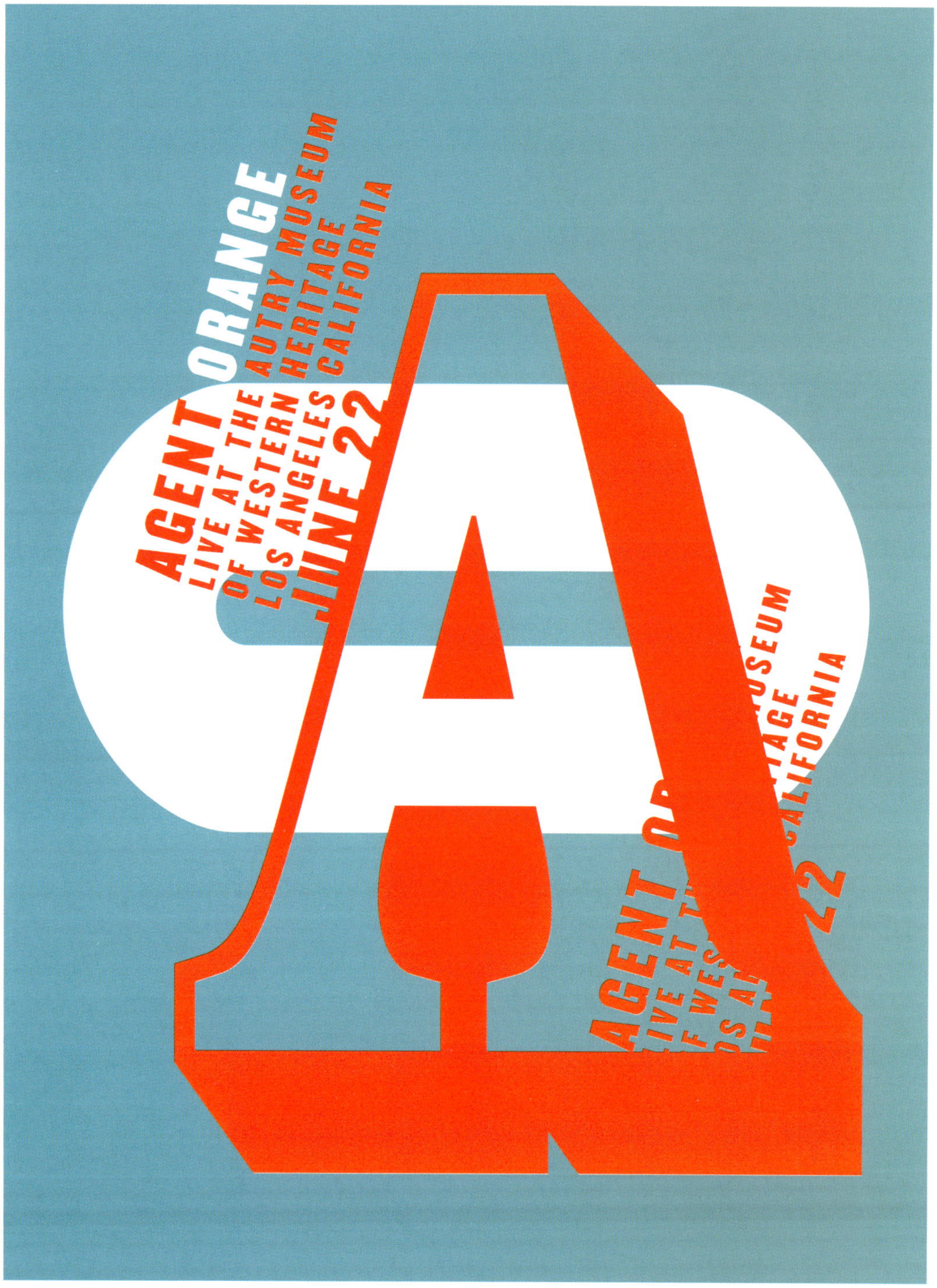

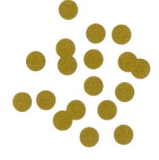

Agent Orange poster | 2004

Mike Joyce/Stereotype
www.stereotype-design.com

How can *surf-punk* be linked with the West? One proposal is to reflect the anxiety and energy of punk in explosive colors, and combine them with typography with wide serifs. This is what this poster does for a concert in the Autrey Museum of Western Heritage.

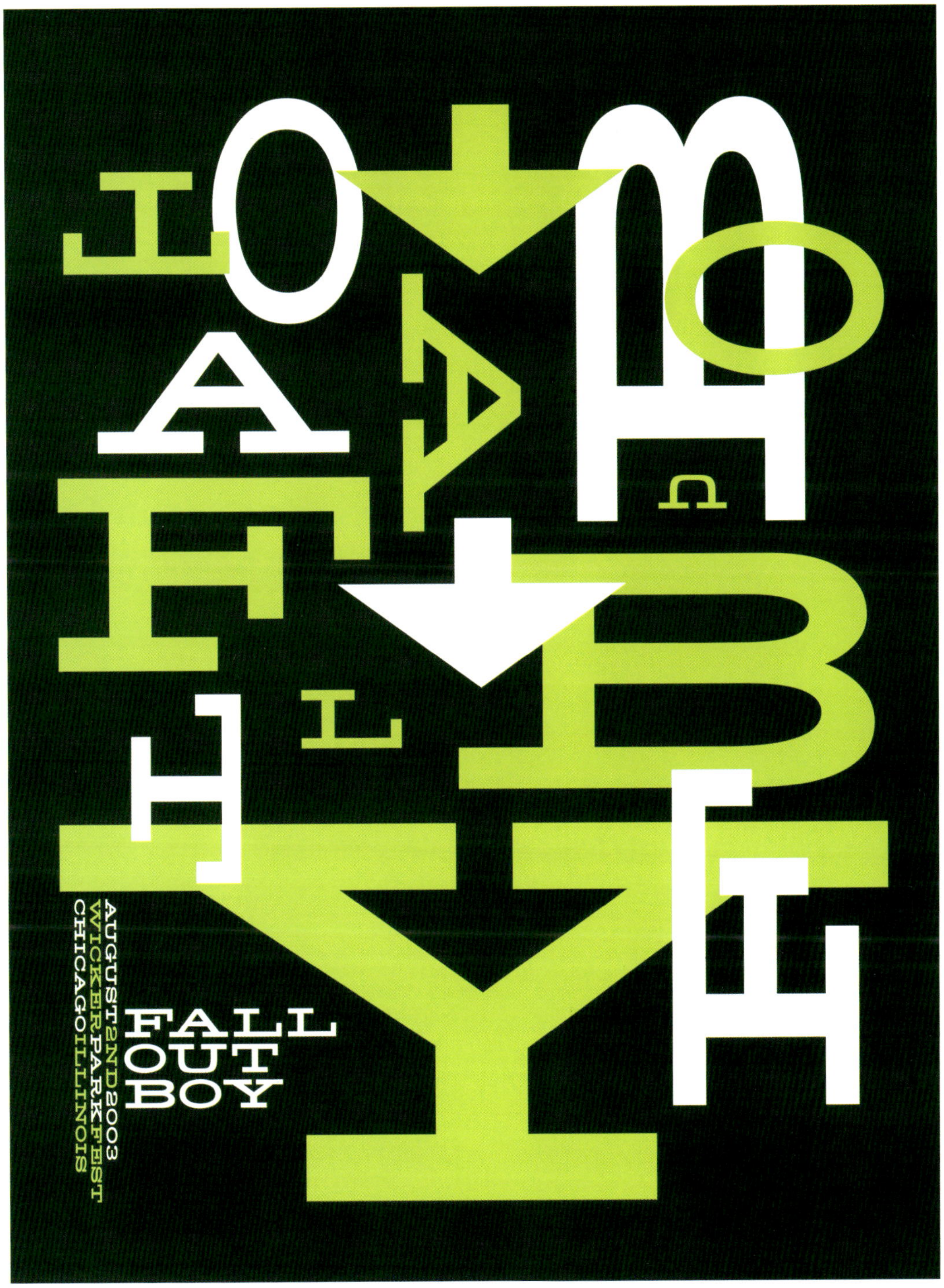

Fall Out Boy poster | 2003

Mike Joyce/Stereotype
www.stereotype-design.com

In an exercise in deconstruction, the name of the band is broken down into separate letters arranged by hand, repeated and in different sizes. The result is a self-promotional poster full of strength, depth and movement.

Back in the days...new year 1989/90.

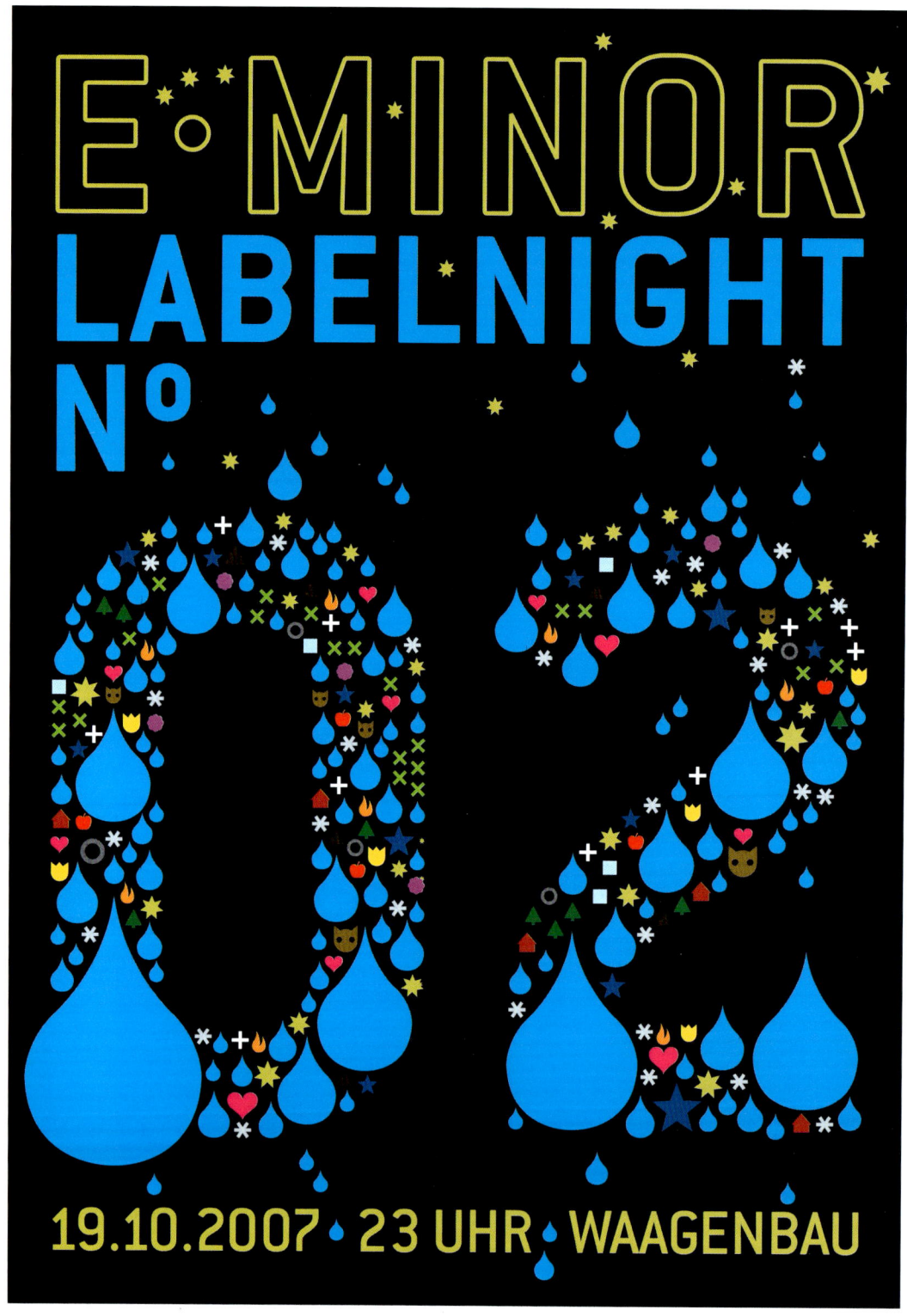

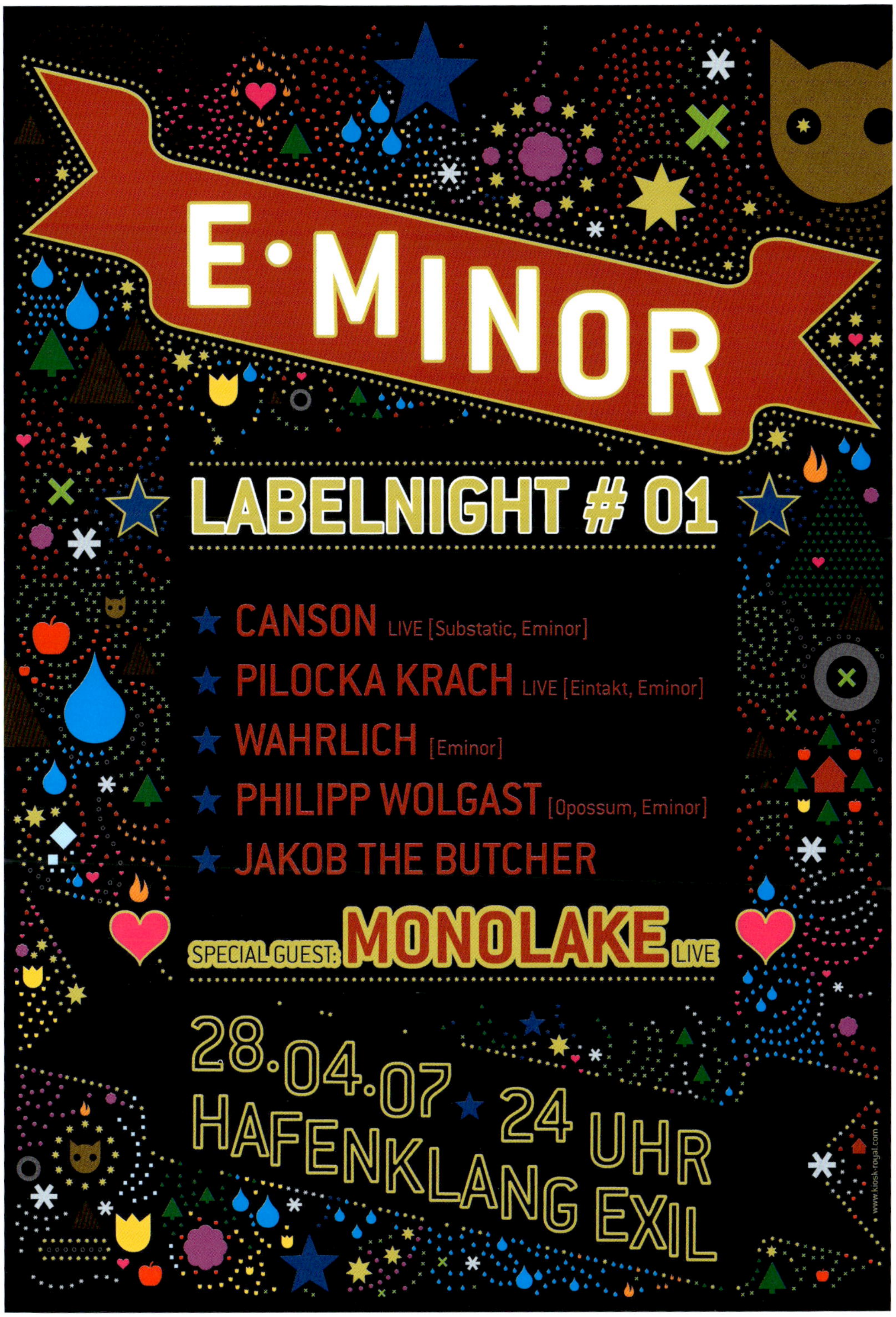

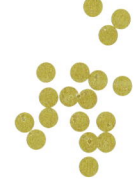

Eminor Labelnights | 2007

Hanna Zeckau/Kiosk Royal
www.kiosk-royal.com

Eminor is a German electronic music record label. They began two years ago, and since then their references have quickly multiplied. All their graphics are based on a system of twenty symbols, and each of them represents the launch of a new record.

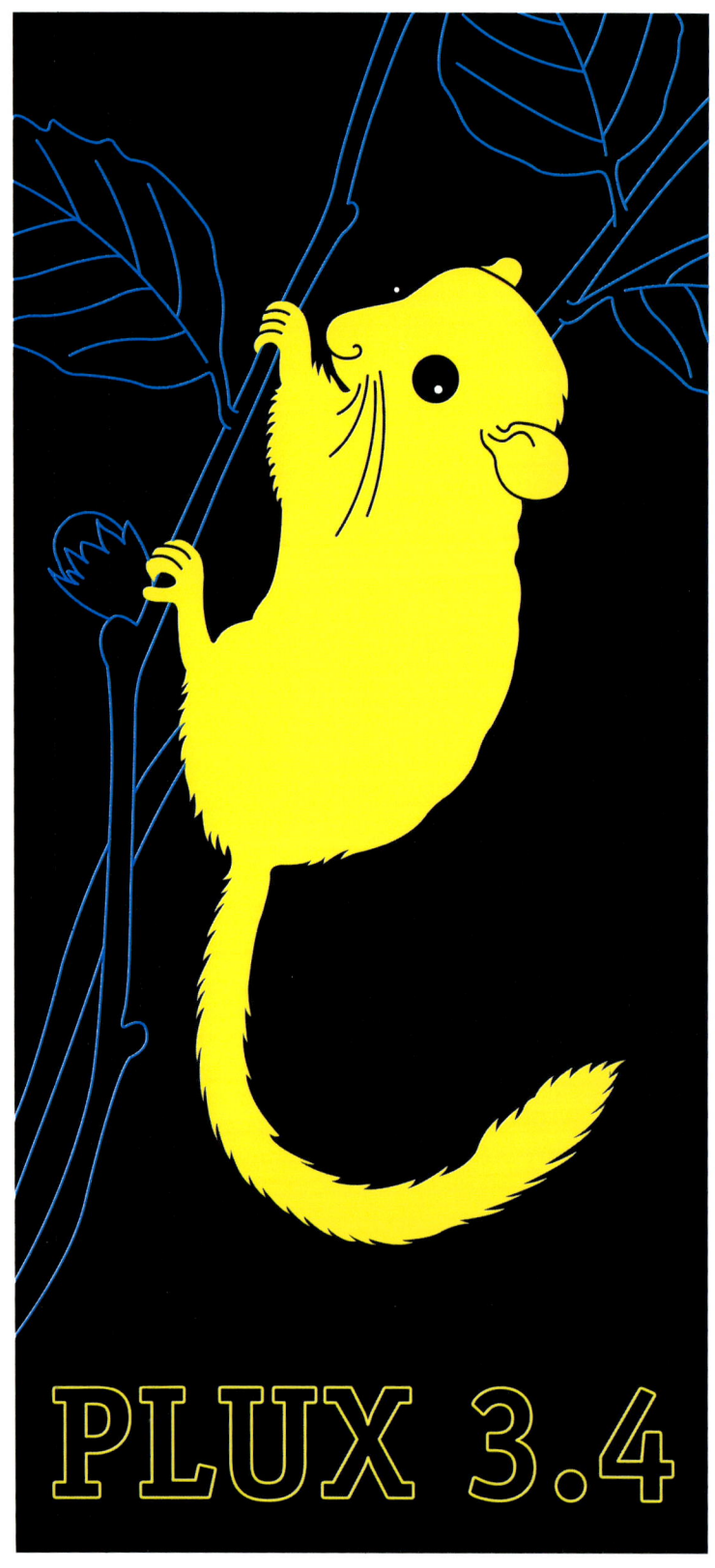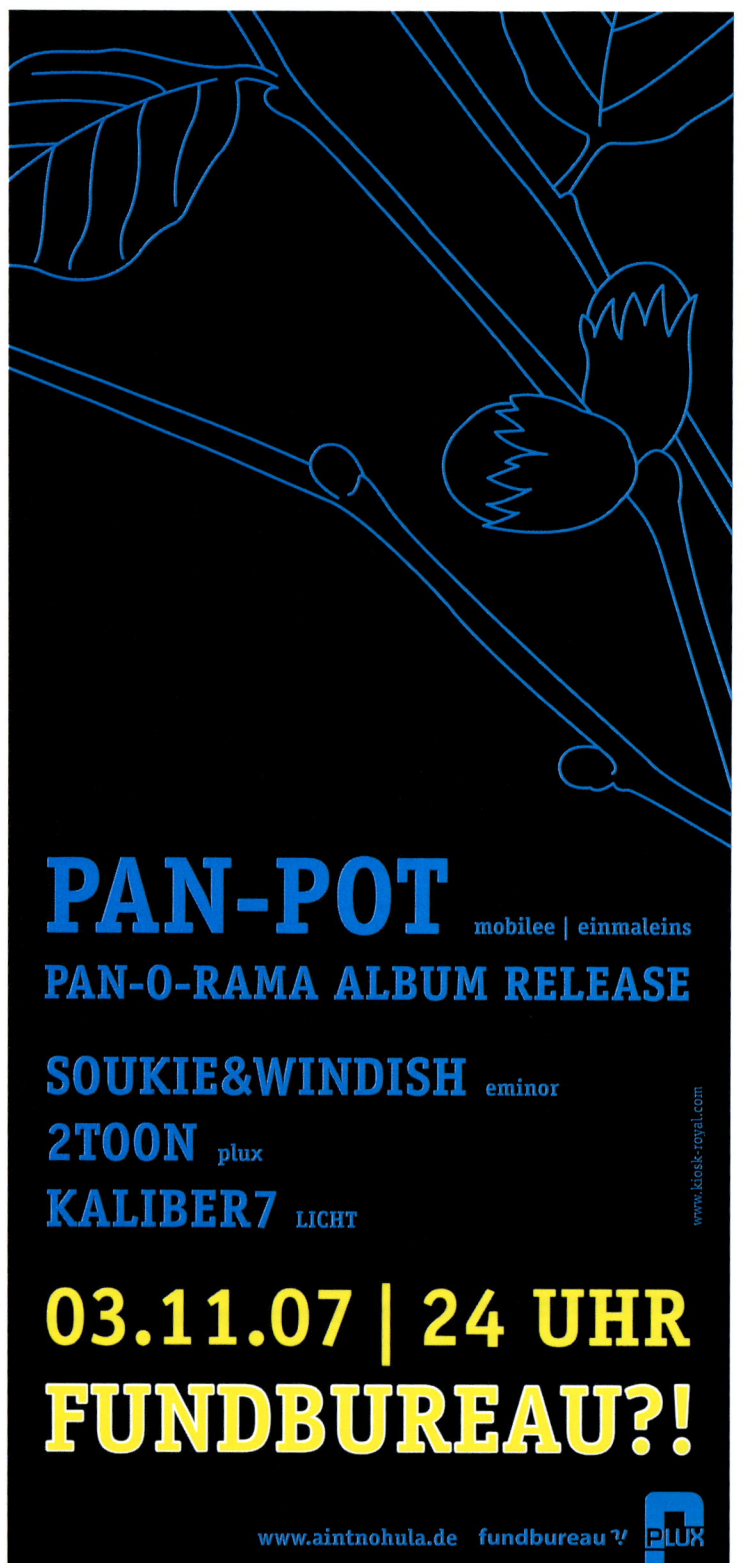

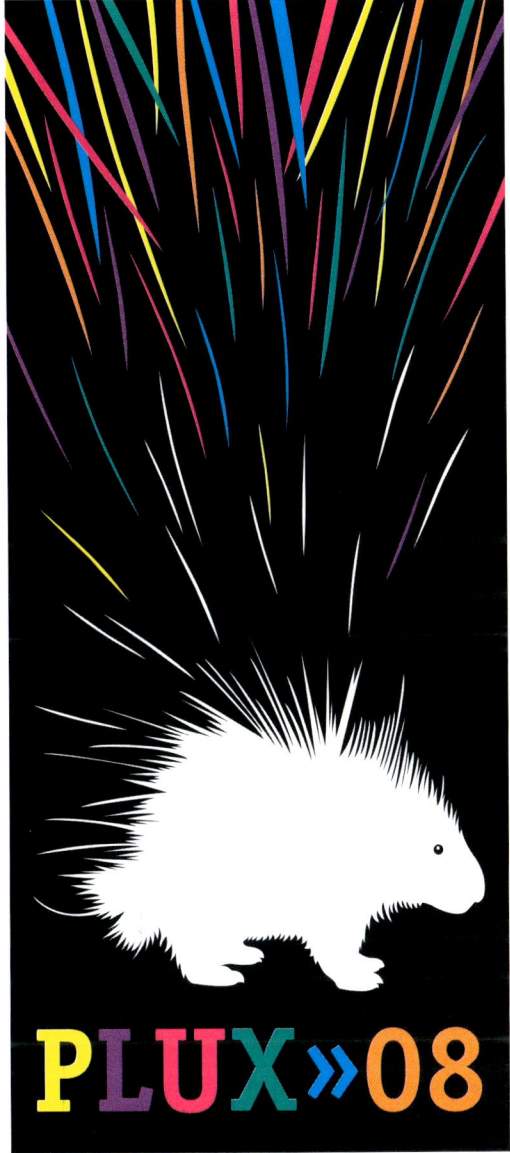
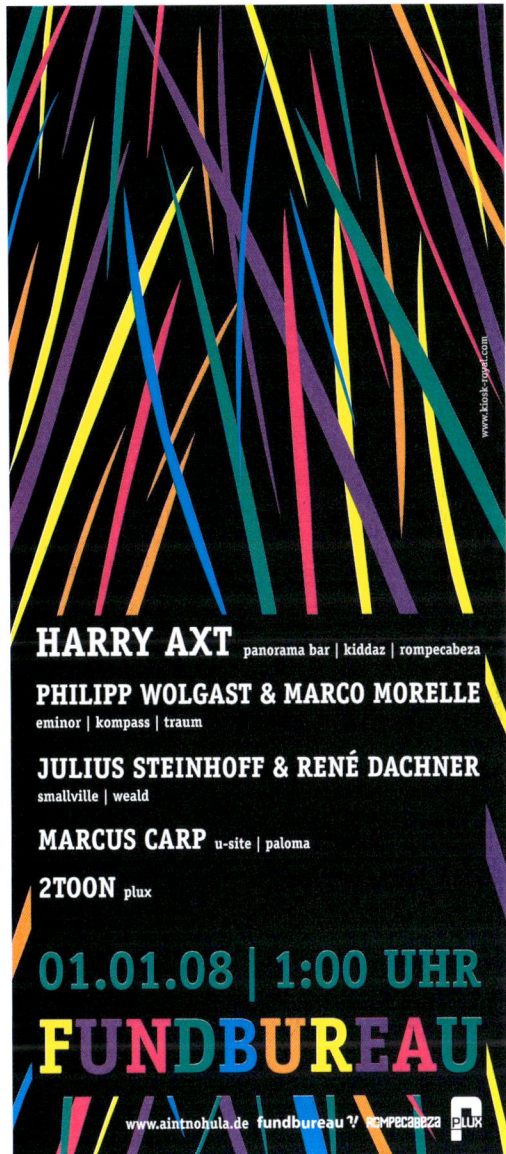

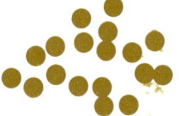

Plux | 2007

Hanna Zeckau/Kiosk Royal
www.kiosk-royal.com

The flyers for the Plux parties found their inspiration in nocturnal animals. The composition is structured from a black background. The contrast this color generates with the patches of bright colors is the strategy used to capture attention.

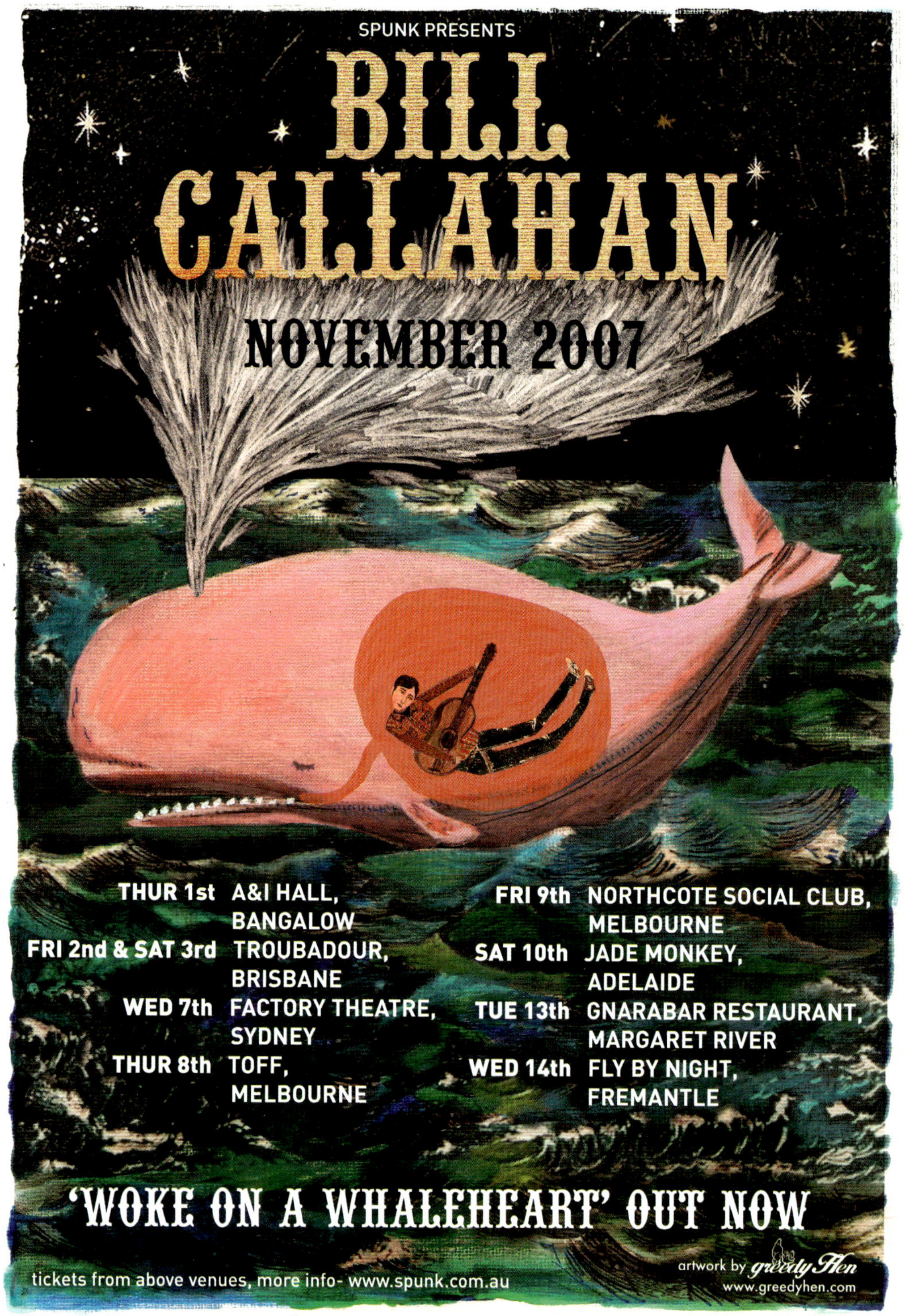

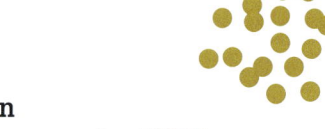

Bill Callahan
Australian tour poster | 2007

Katherine Brickman,
Kate Mitchell/Greedy Hen
www.greedyhen.com

Woke on a Whaleheart is the first album that Callahan has released with his real name. Caught in the center of the poster, and in the heart of the whale, the figure of the musician on a patch of pink makes reference to the title and the art on the album cover.

The best party I ever went to was my fifth birthday party. It was a surprise party, and I was truly surprised. My cake had Star Wars *figures standing in the frosting, I was pretty psyched about this at the time.*

Jason Munn

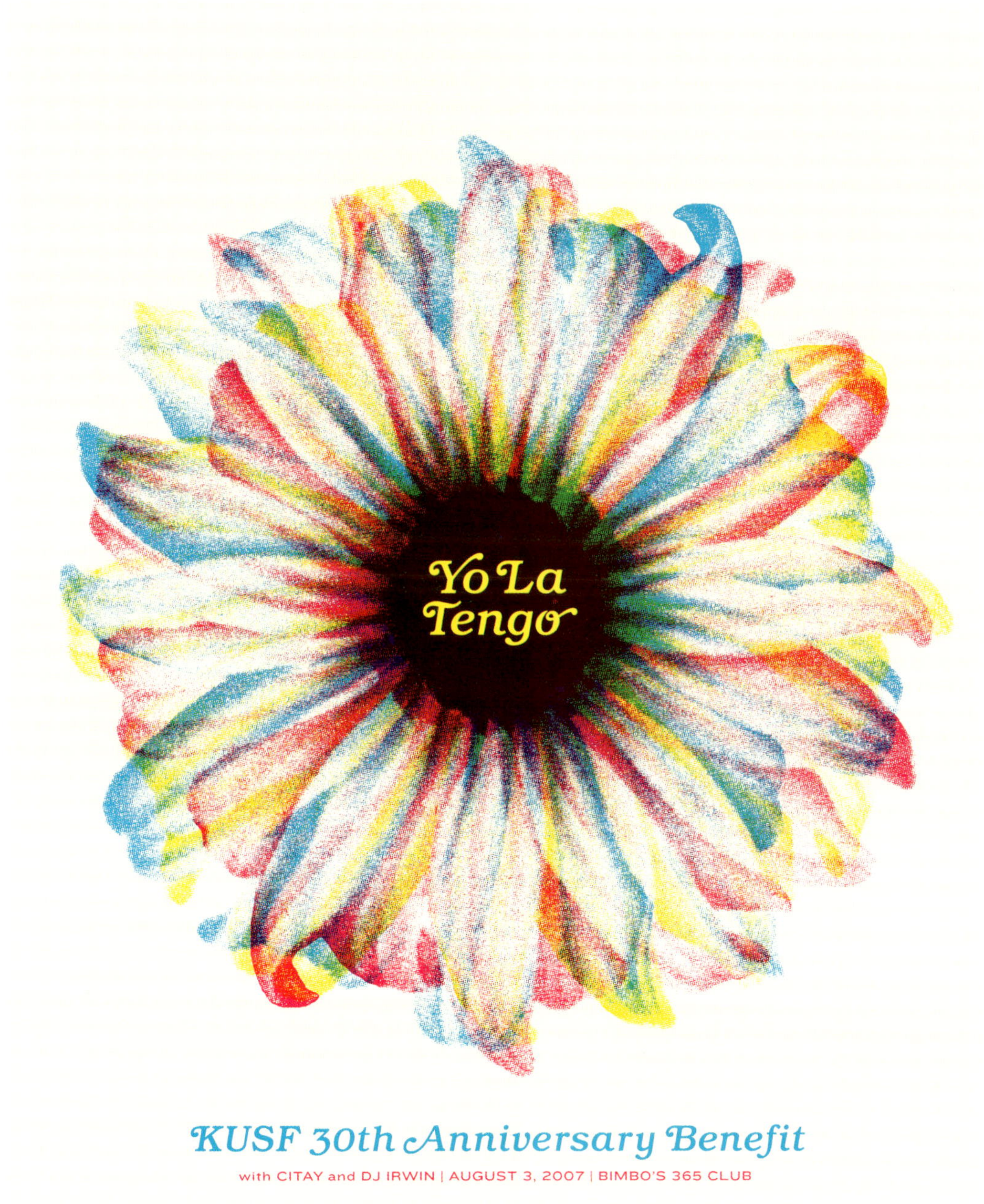

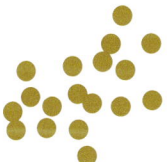

Yo La Tengo | 2007

Jason Munn/The Small Stalkes
www.thesmallstakes.com

This silk-screen print using three colors promotes a concert in San Francisco in aid of a local radio station, KUSF. The vaporous texture of the petals and their diffused shapes direct the focus towards the center, which features the name of the band.

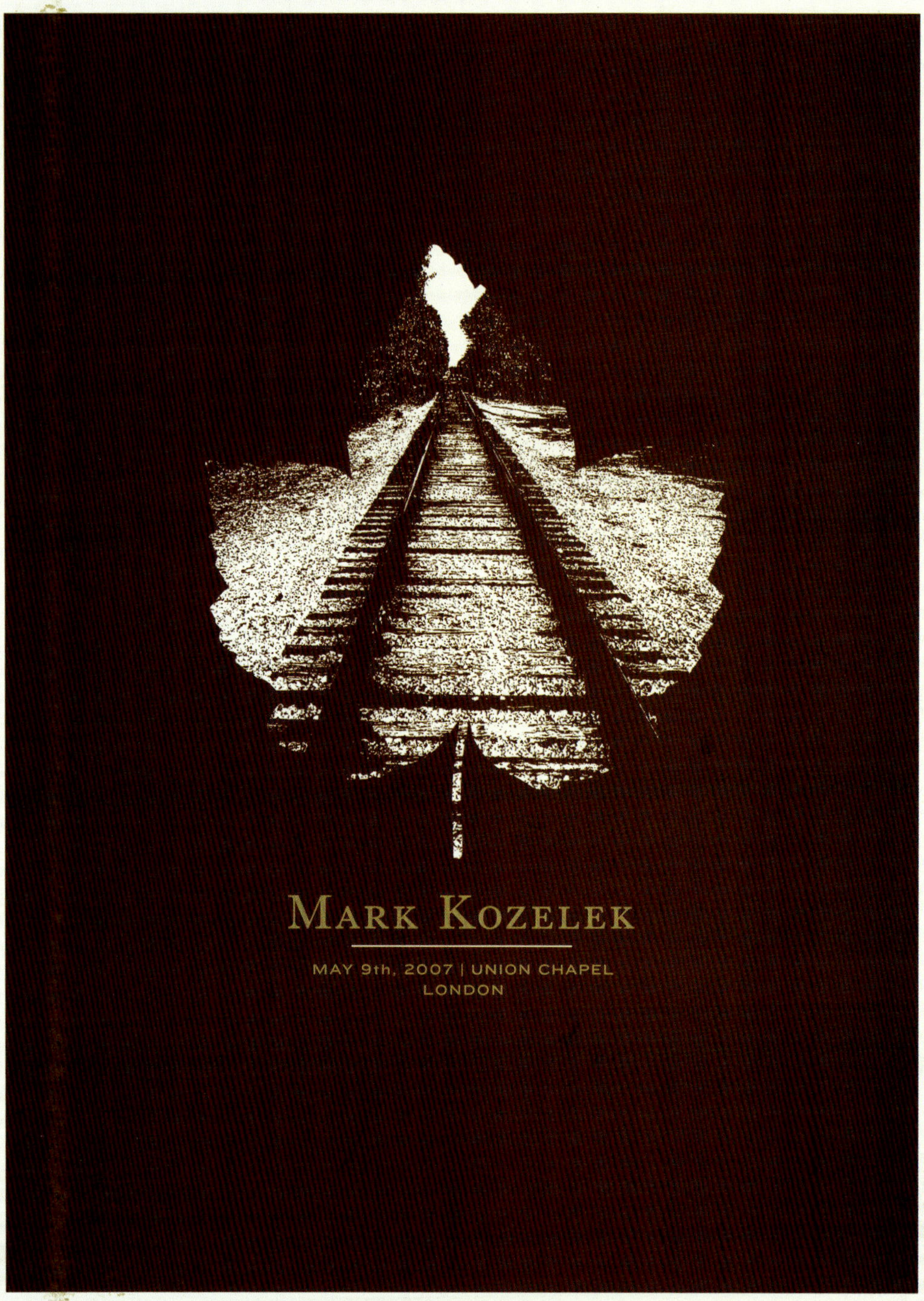

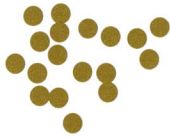

Mark Kozelek | 2007

Jason Munn/The Small Stakes
www.thesmallstakes.com

Folk music is related to folklore, which, in turn, is linked to the earth, with an origin. This poster connects with this essence and transfers it to the brown-nature-humanity trio, which taints it with a comforting nostalgia.

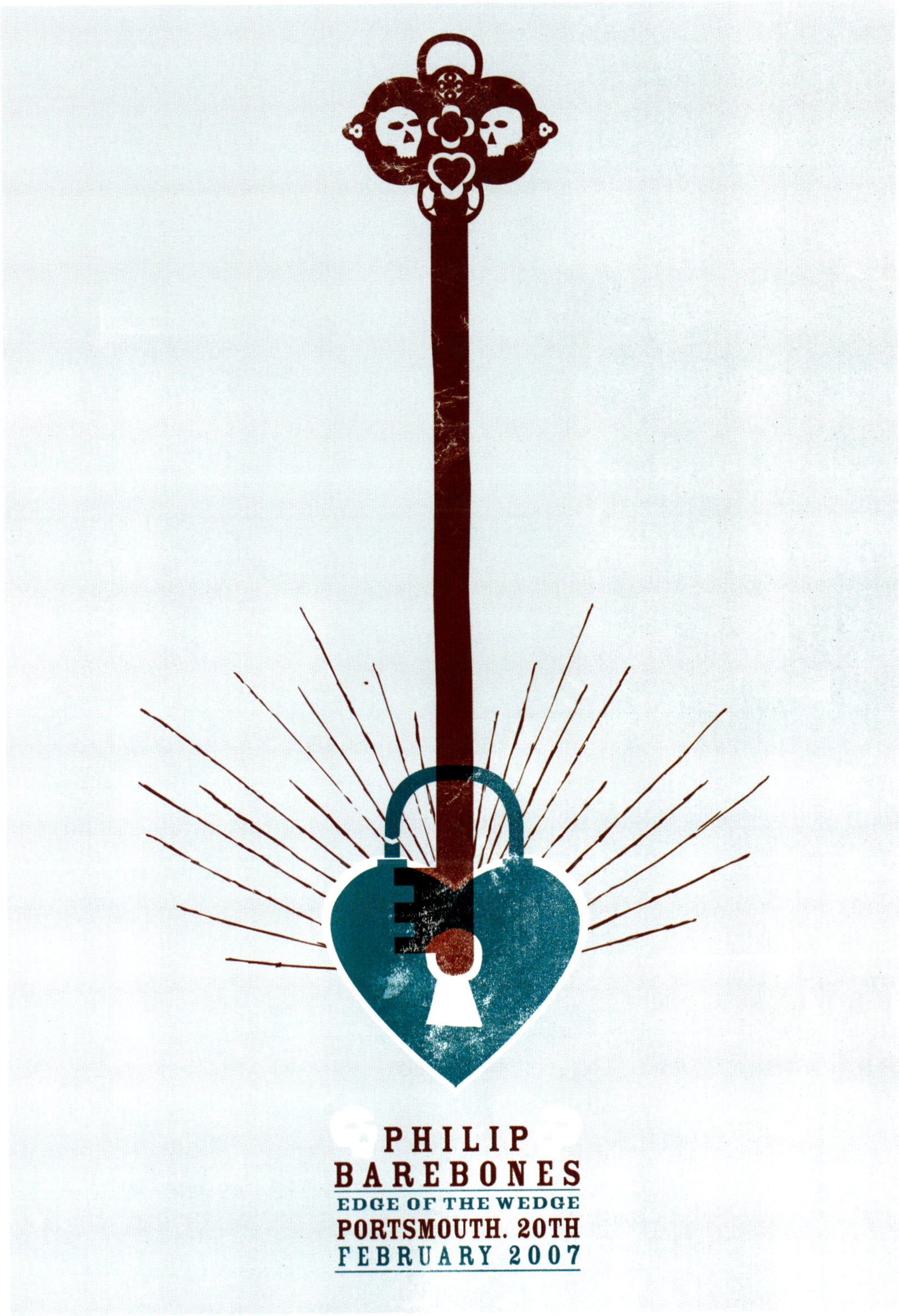

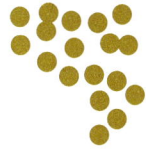

Philip Barebones | 2006

Christopher Gove,
Robert Evans/Telegramme
www.telegramme.co.uk

The design of this silk-screen poster refers to a play on words involving the name of the artist, Barebones, playing with a combination of skulls and hearts. Folk can be both subtle and dark.

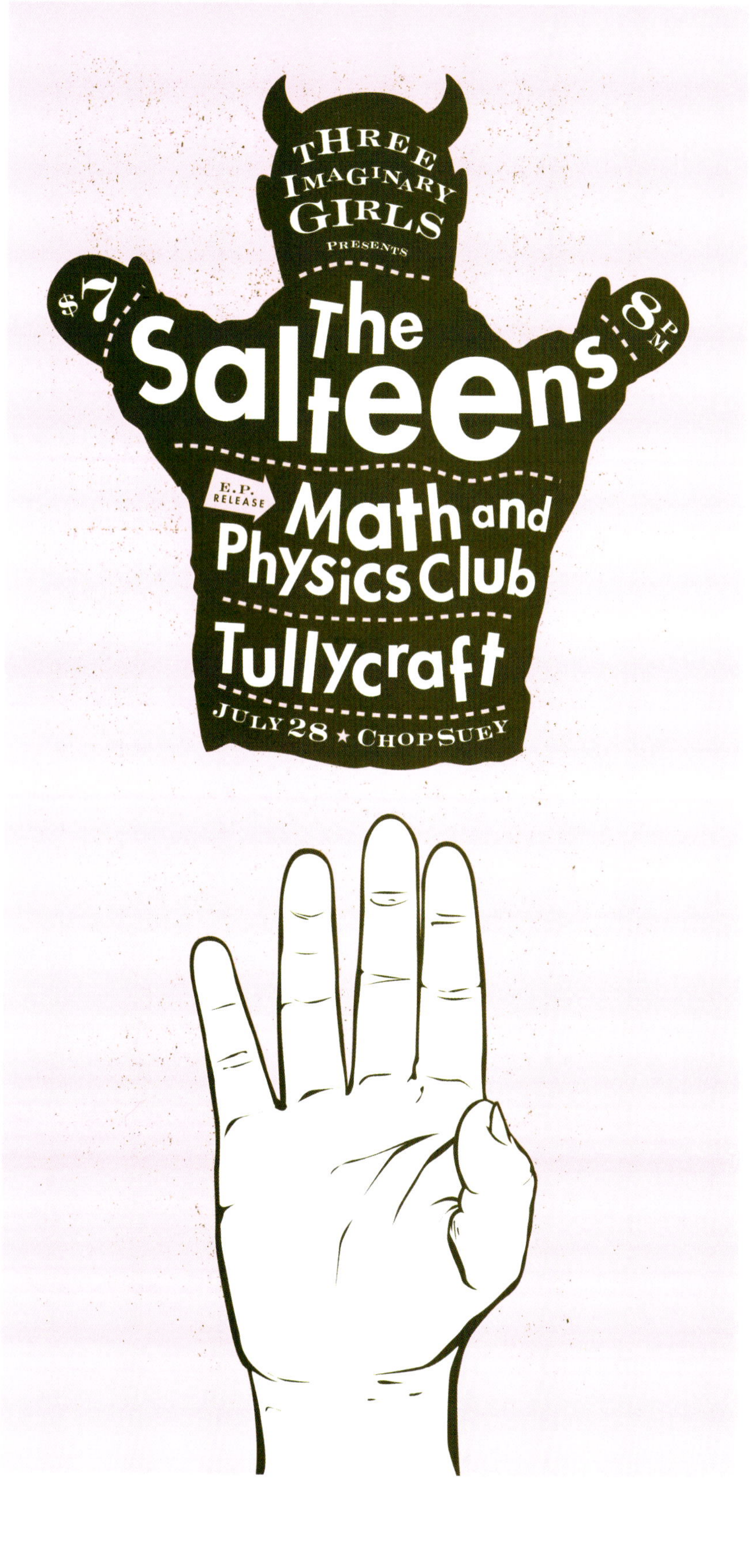

The Salteens poster | 2006

Corianton Hale/Sleep Op Projects
www.sleepop.com

The poster for this concert, where three different groups played, plays with alter egos, represented by the figure of the puppet that covers the hand. The softness of the image is achieved through the use of pastel colors and typography that runs over the base line.

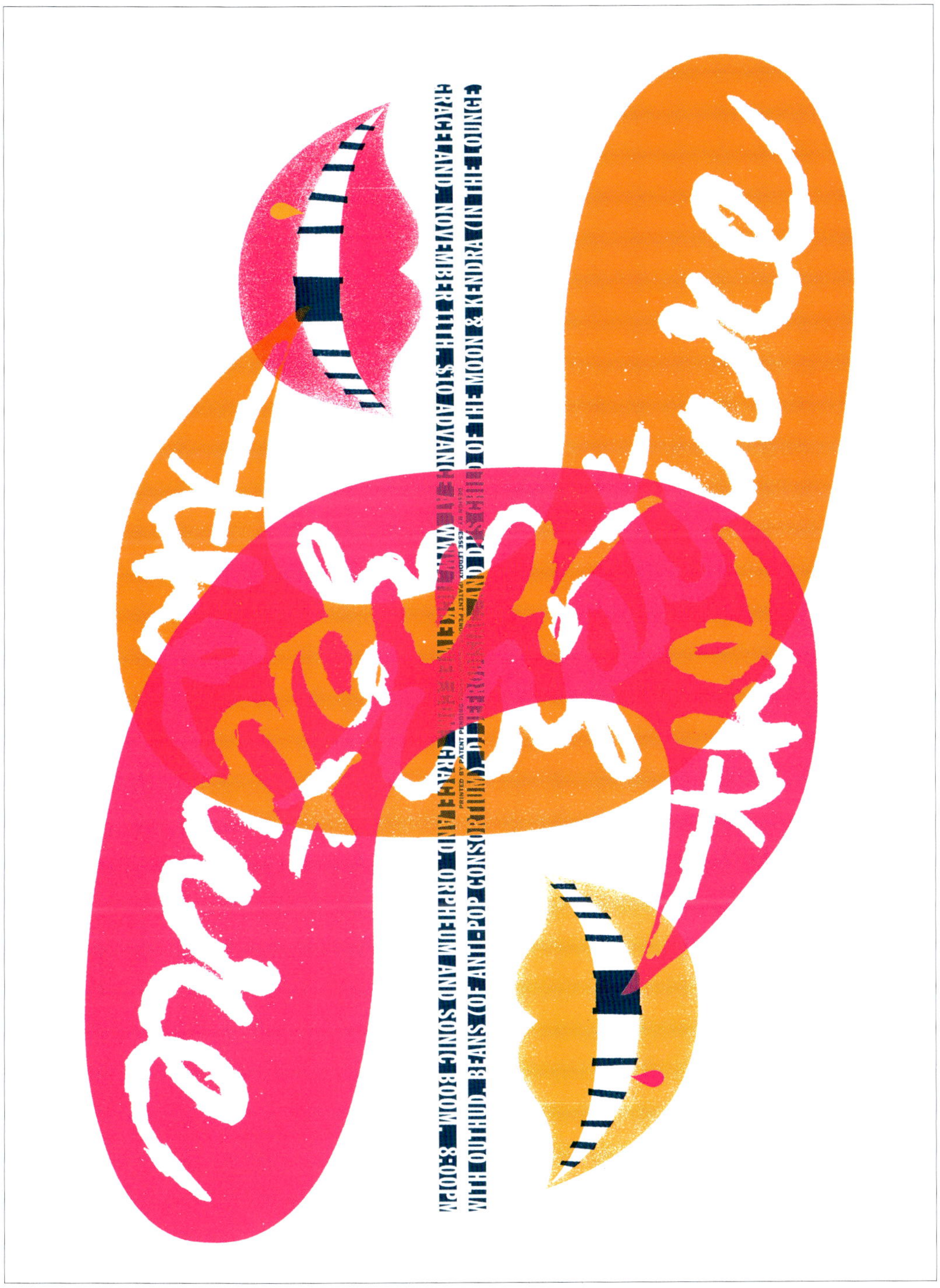

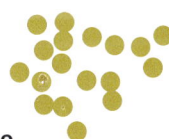

The Rapture poster | 2003

Jesse LeDoux/LeDouxville
www.ledouxville.com

At the time of this tour, everyone was beginning to talk about The Rapture. Two tongues, represented symmetrically in different colors, announce their upcoming concerts.

Unexpected parties, when suddenly everything gets out of control, are the best.

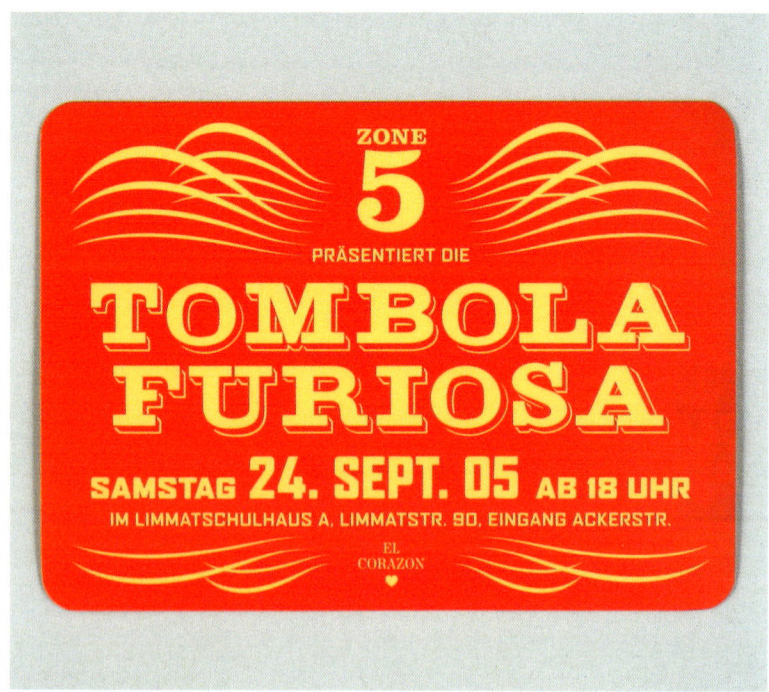
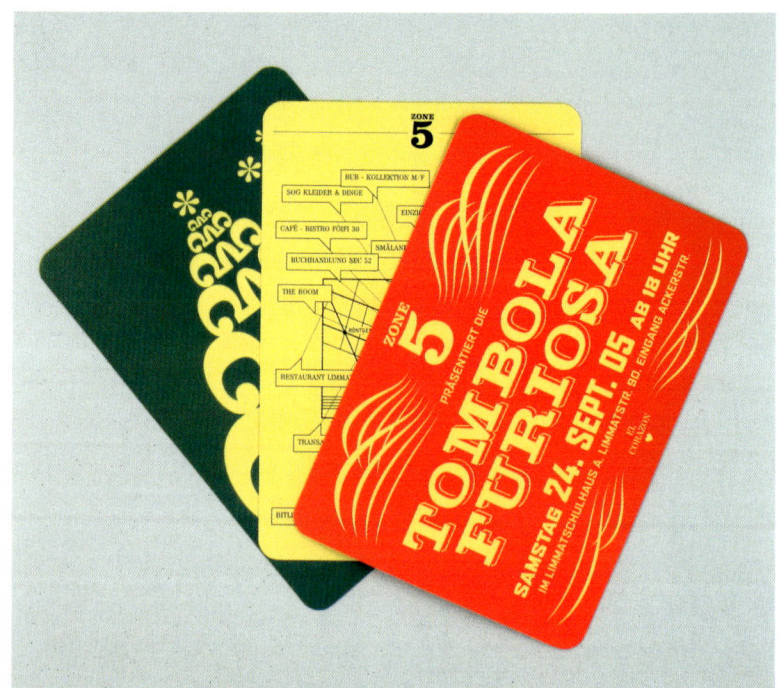
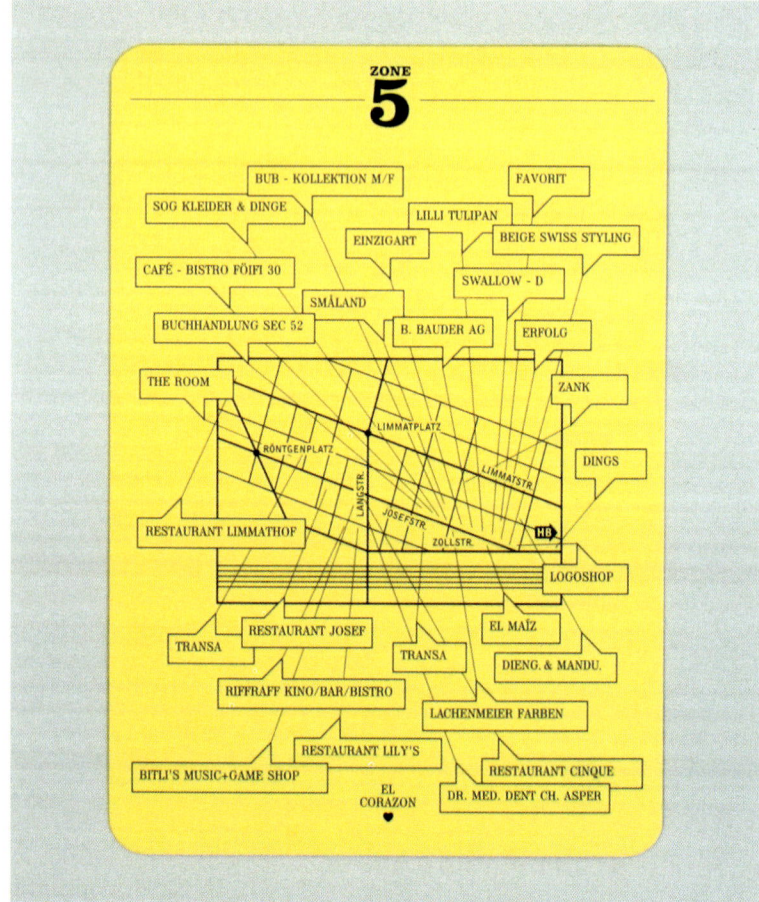
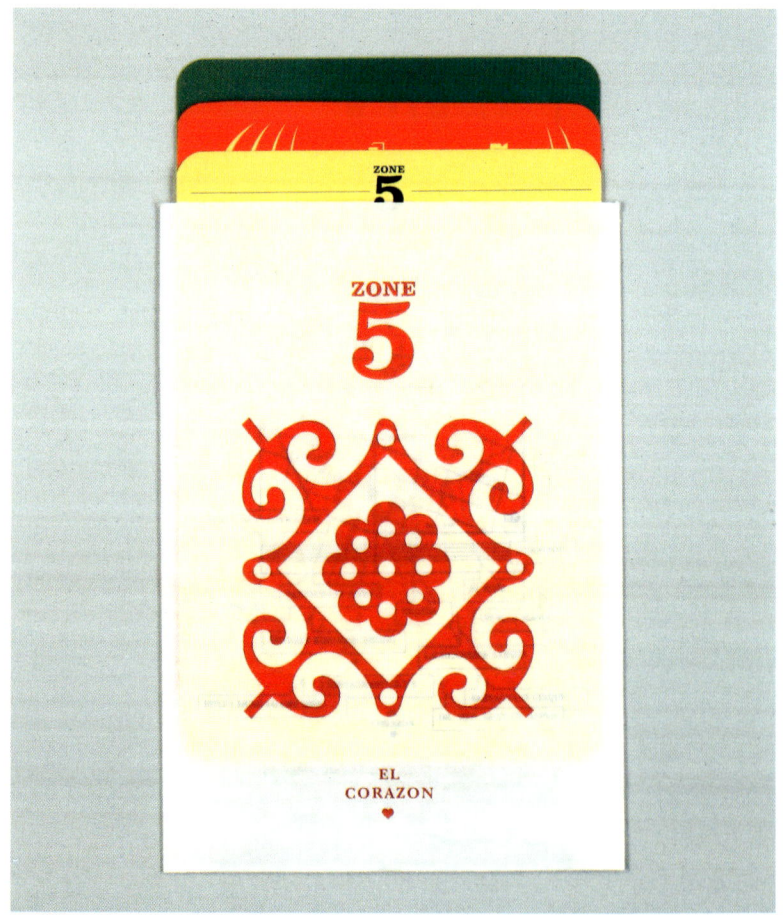

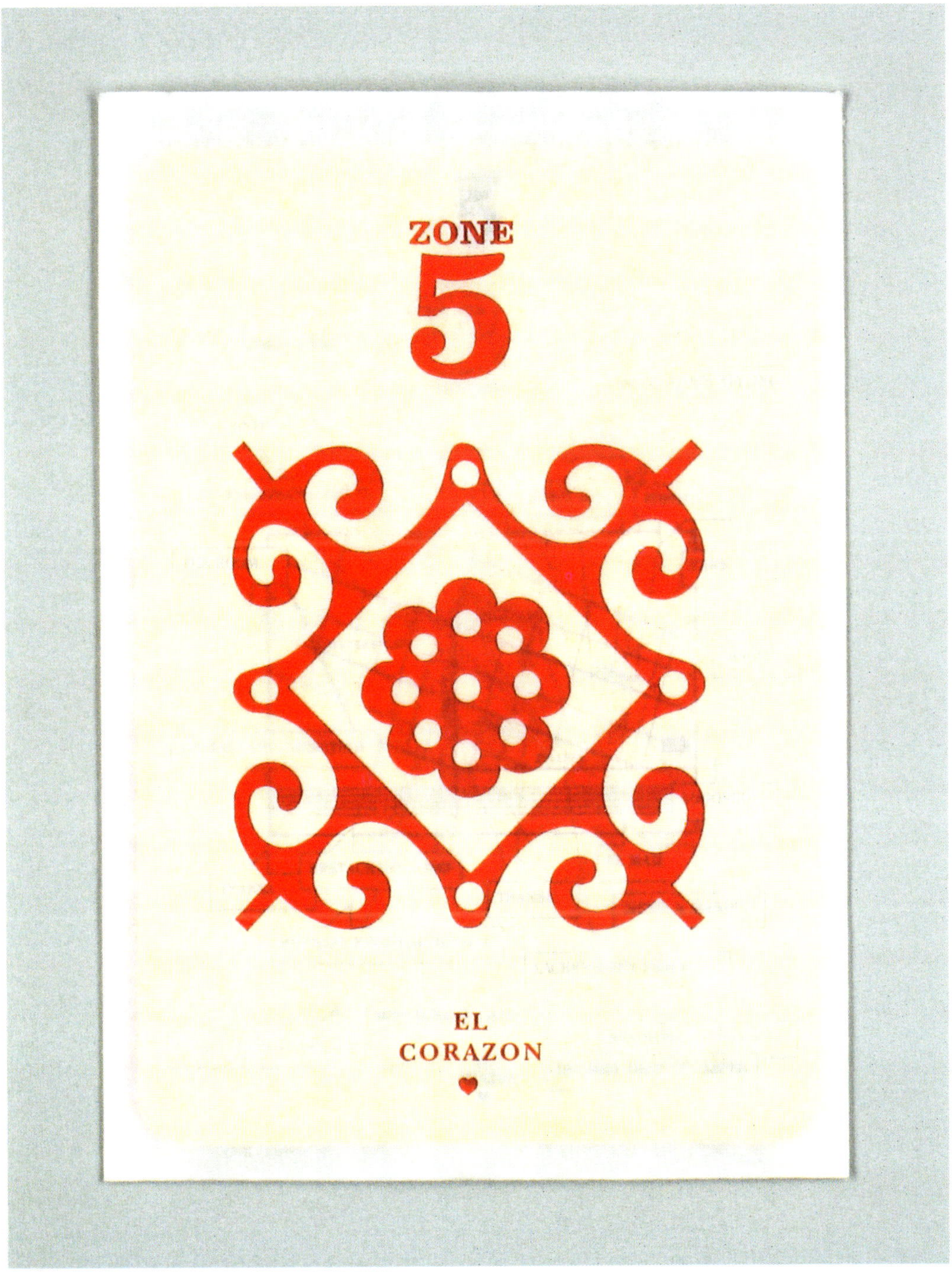

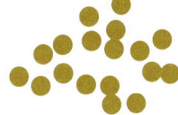

**Zone 5 promotion
card set | 2005**

**Fauxpas Grafik
www.fauxpas.ch**

To promote the Zone 5 in Zurich, Fauxpas designed a small bag for different stores to put their flyers into. The simplicity of the cards, done in a single color, contrasts with the range of colors on the flyers in the stores.

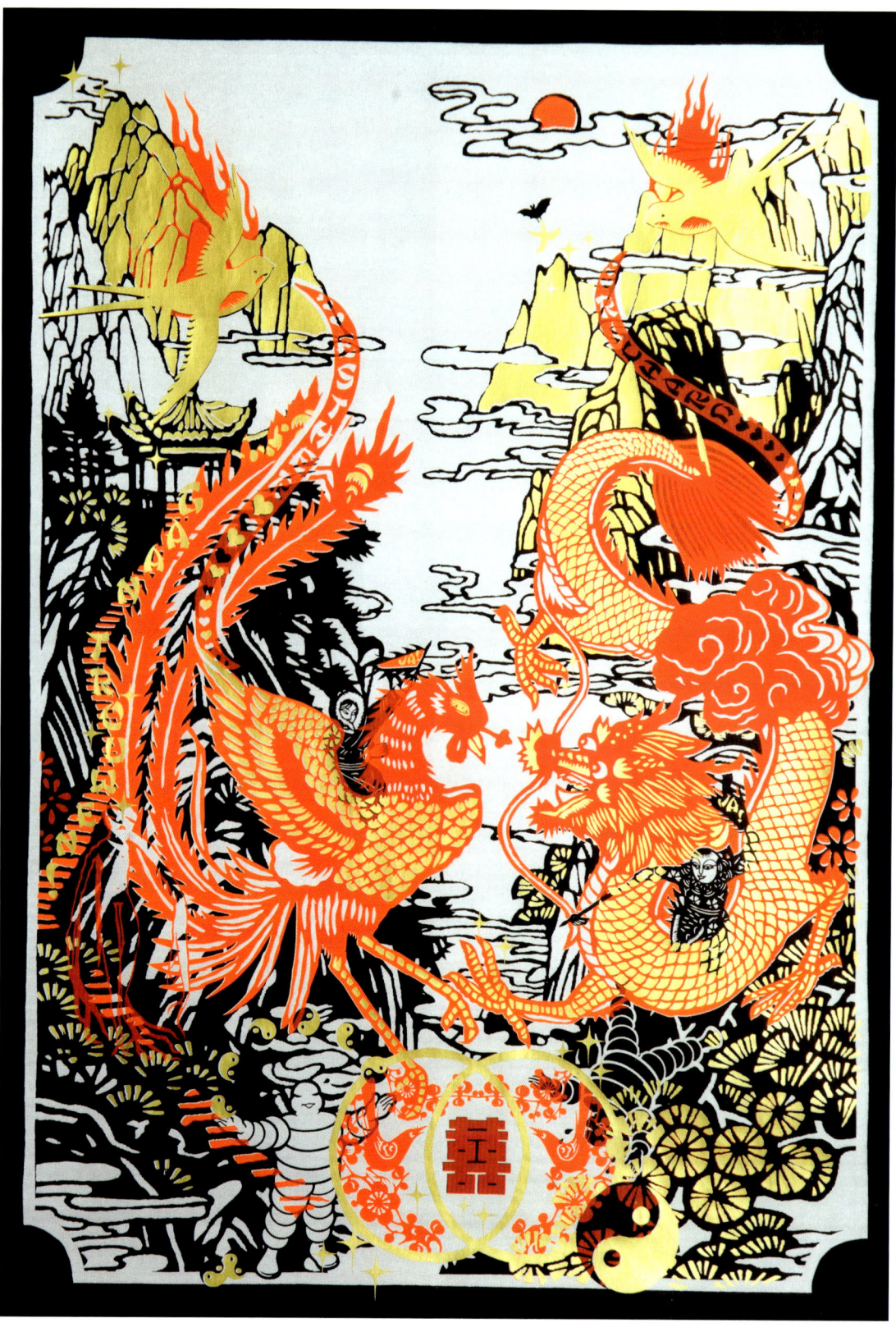

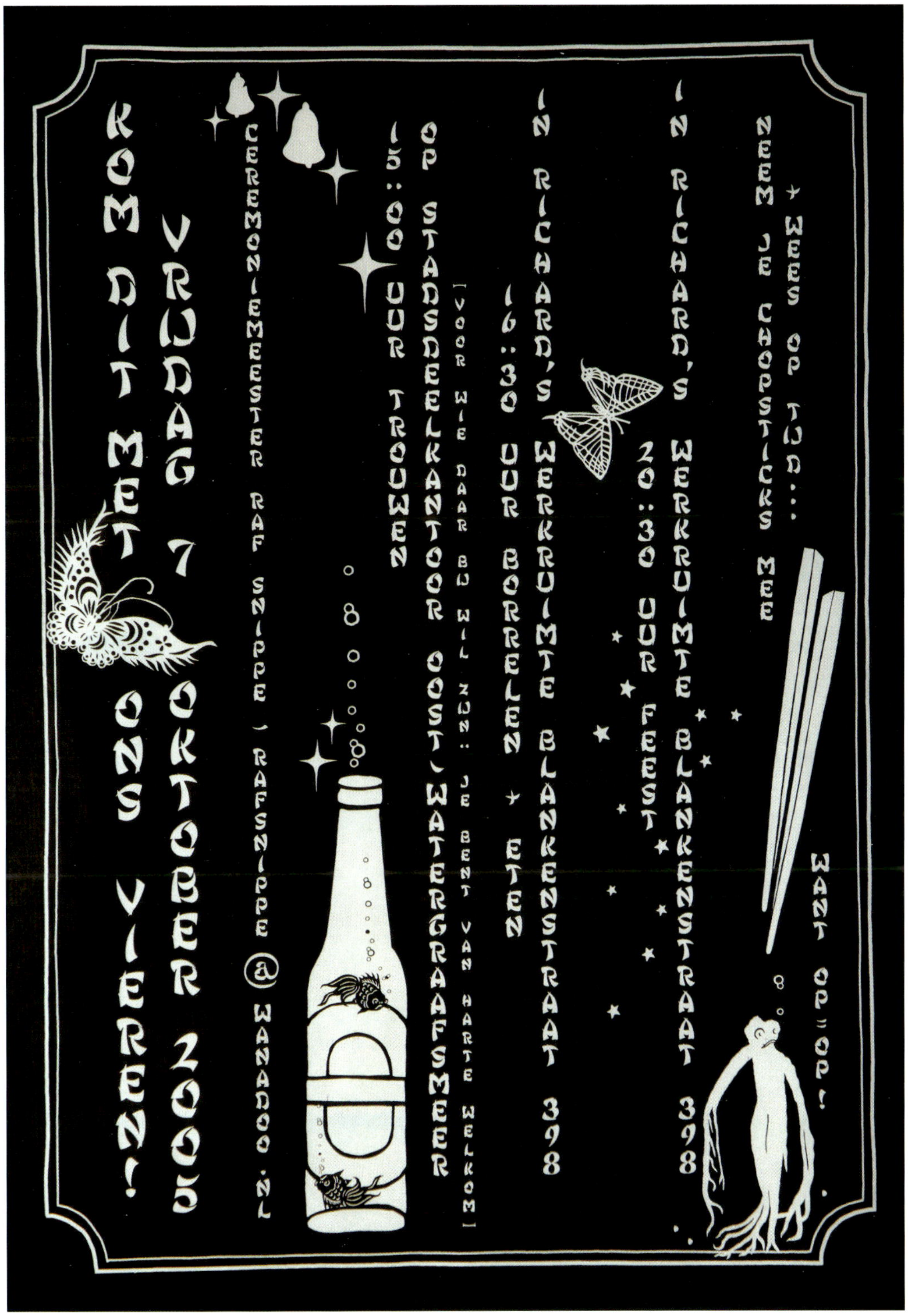

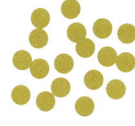

Richard & Esther | 2005

Harmen Liemburg, Kees Maas
www.harmenliemburg.nl

This wedding invitation is inspired by the honeymoon destination: China. The work of Zhang Shuxian, a master in the ancient tradition of paper cutting, combines with icons from the consumer culture, such as the Michelin man.

Going to an animal party and being the only ones dressed as animals was fun!

Hennie Haworth

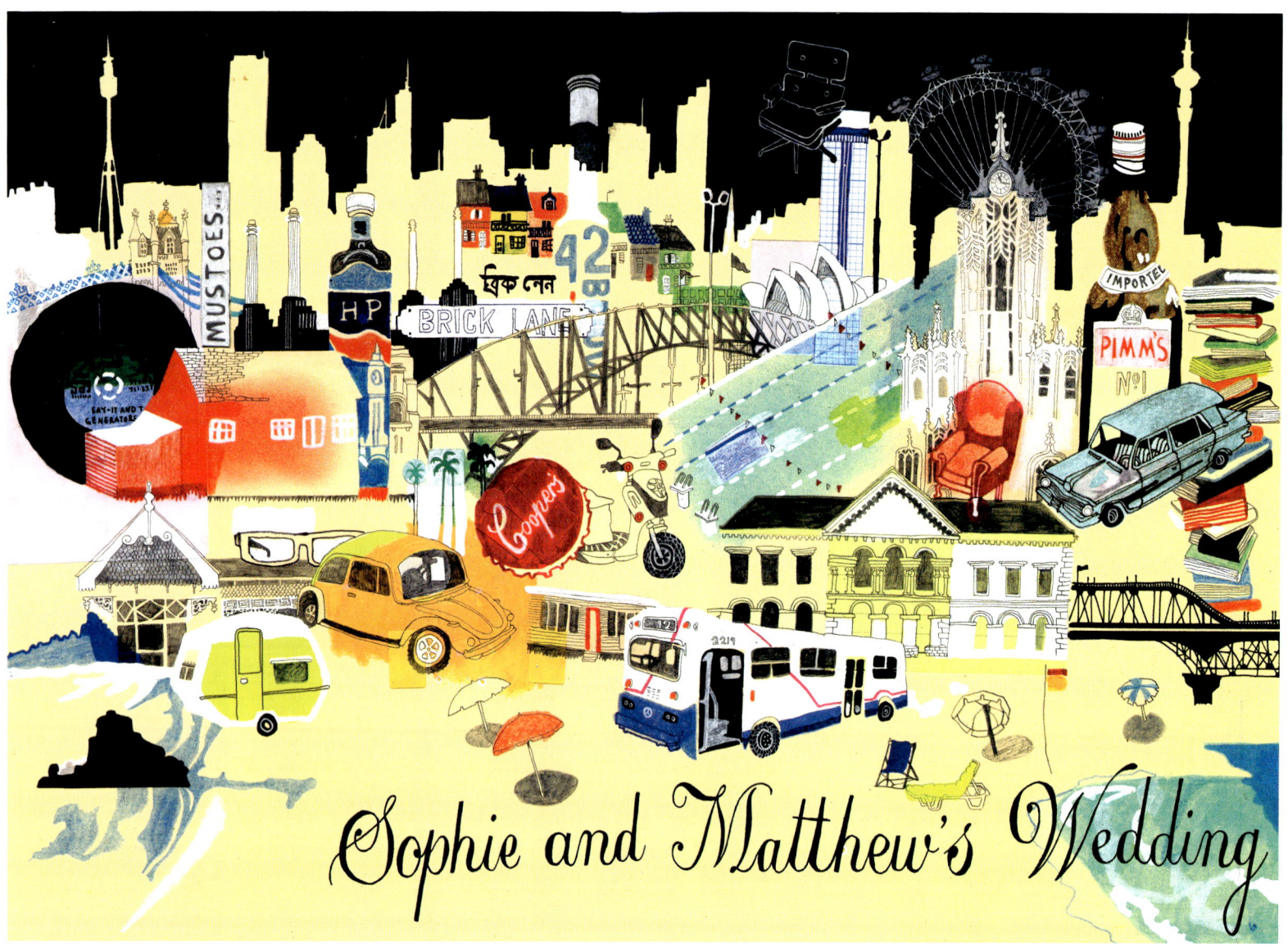

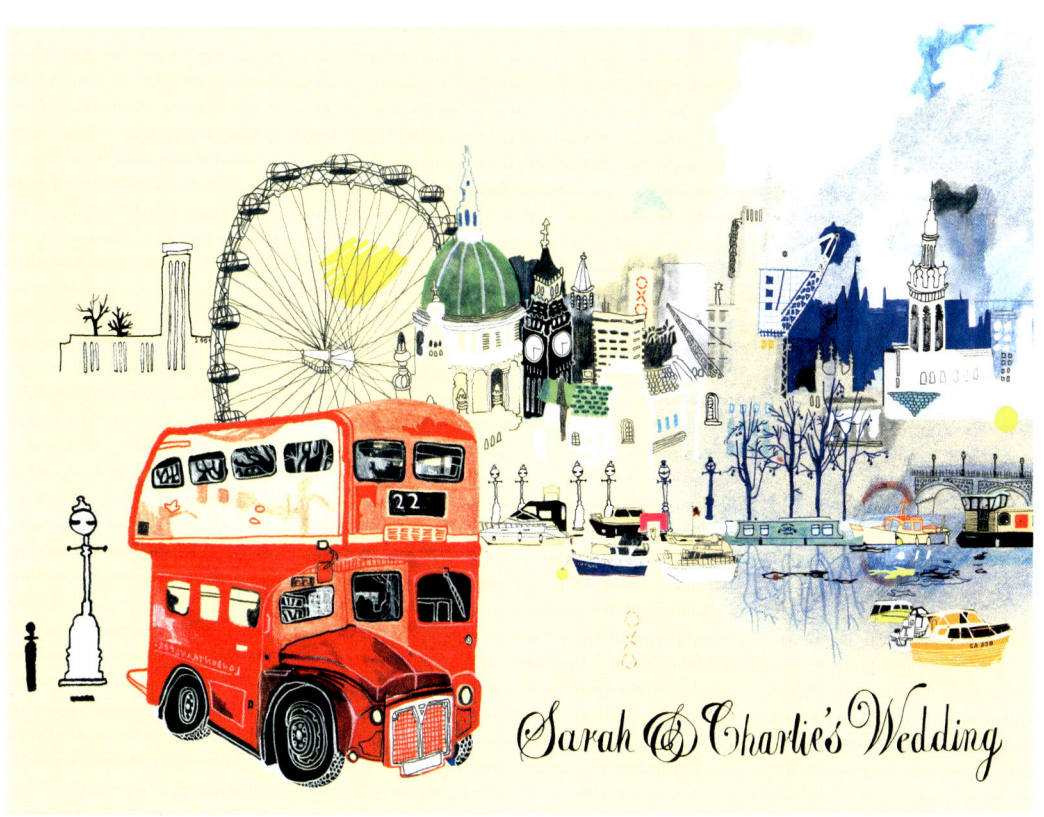

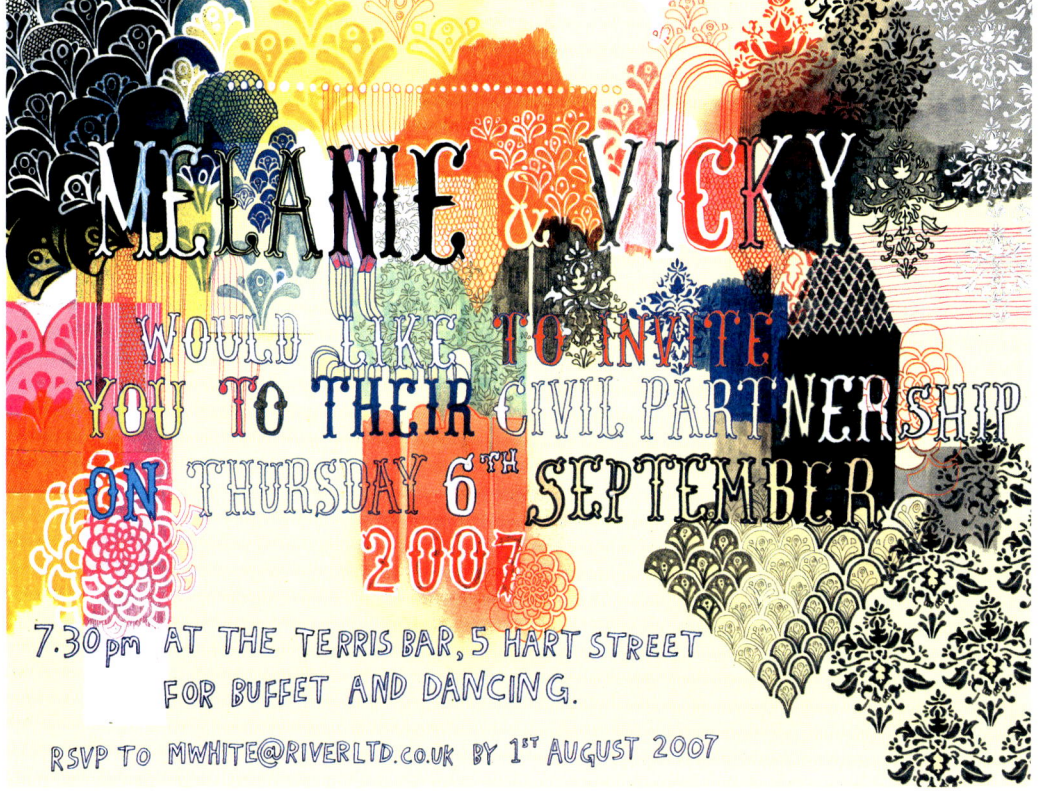

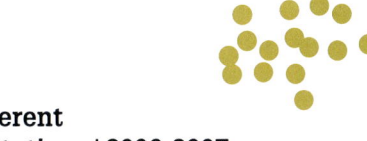

**Different
invitations | 2006-2007**

Hennie Haworth
www.henniehaworth.co.uk

Haworth's vintage multi-color style incorporates personal and significant elements in the lives of the central characters into the invitations. The loud illustrations attract attention and also narrate part of a story.

Last year Nothing: Something: NY leased a private cruise liner, The Queen Mary, and had a party on the open water beneath the Statue of Liberty. Open only to close friends, clients, design compatriots and A-list NYC scenesters. Legends were born...

Nothing: Something: NY

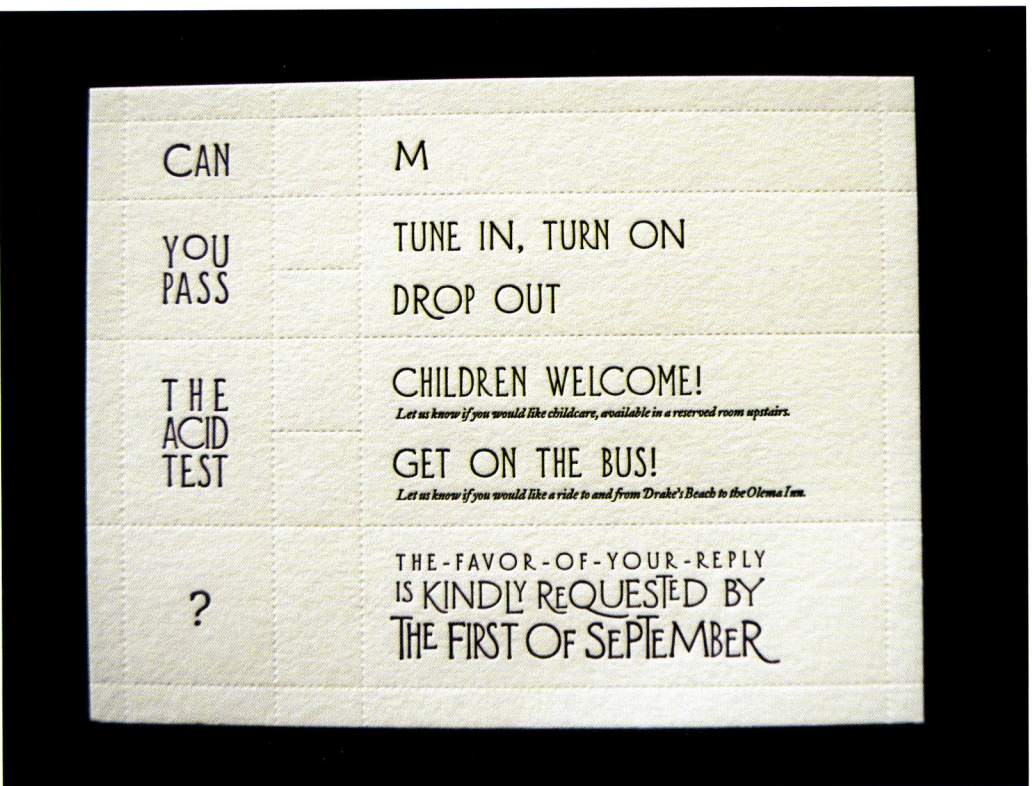

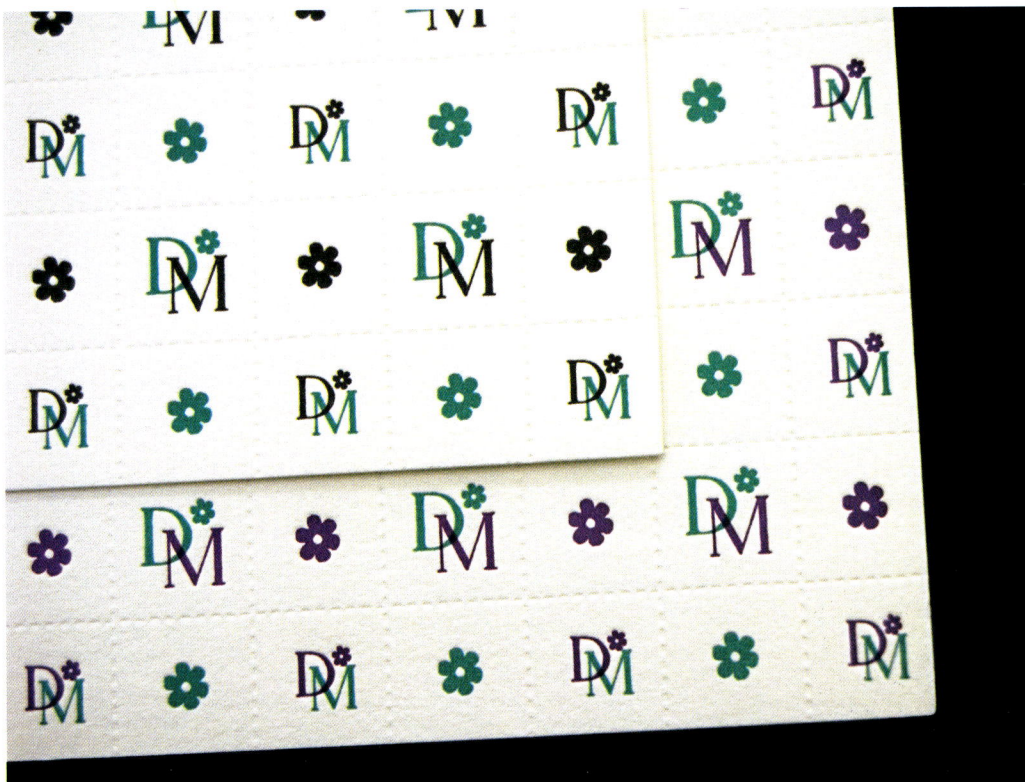

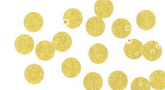

Can You Pass the Acid Test? | 2007

Nothing: Something: NY
www.nothingsomething.com

For a wedding that was to take place in the epicenter of the summer of love, the designers play with the idea of an LSD tab. The sober restriction on the color palette preserves elegance. The typography flirts with the Weimar era.

The best party I've ever been to was a house party at the end of my second year of university. Lots of friends, lots of rum, lots of dancing, and then for some reason I found myself cycling around Brighton at four a.m..

Jez Burrows

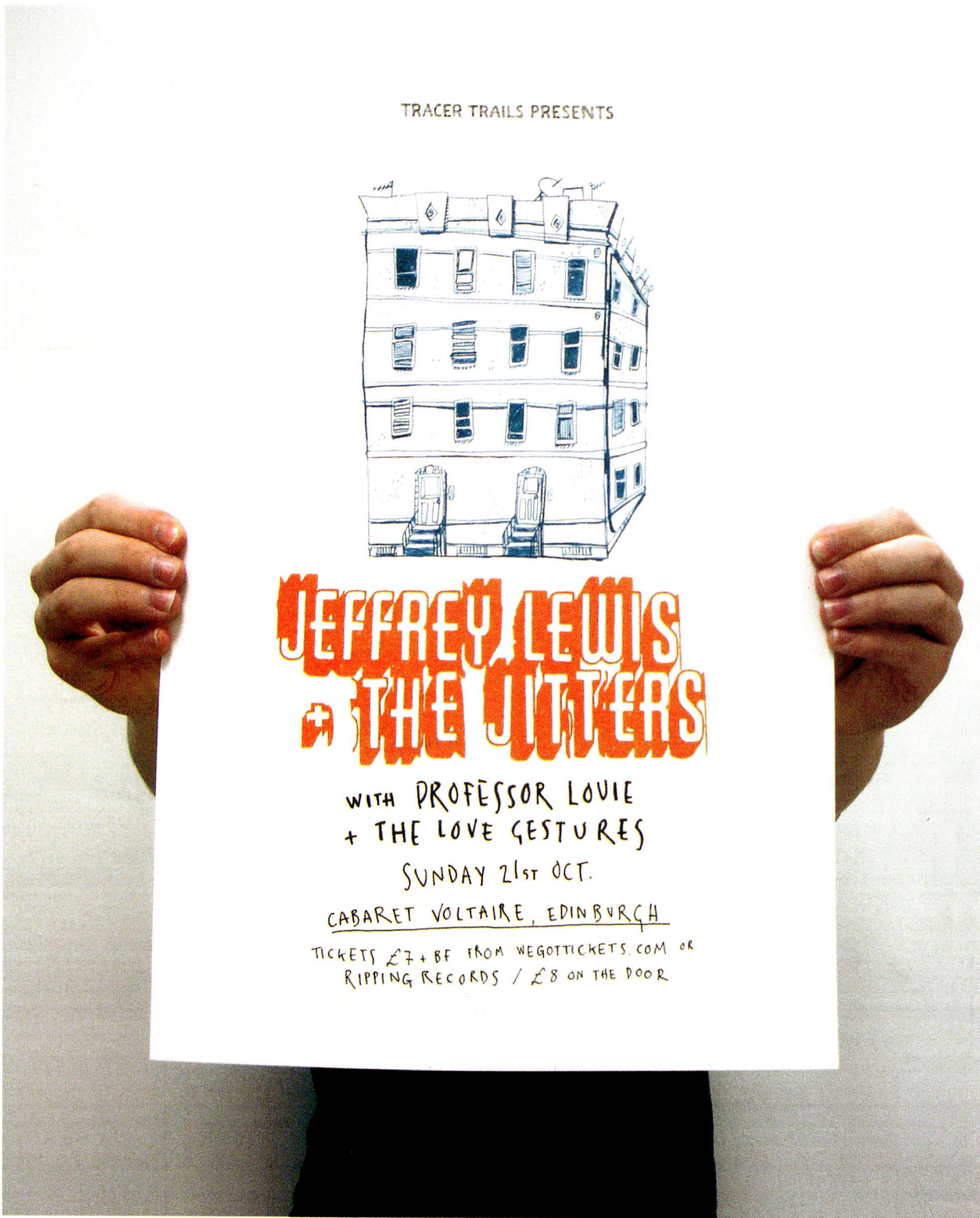

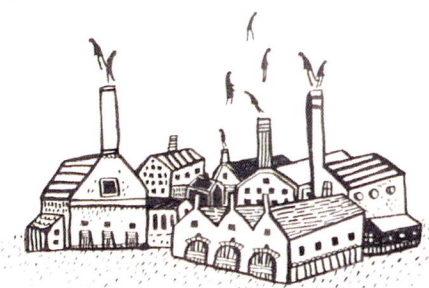

**Tracer Trails
Presents | 2007**

**Sing Statistics
www.singstatistics.co.uk**

Two concert posters are linked by the same aesthetic treatment. Legibility was the key to the poster that contains more information, while the spectacular appearance of the other is achieved through a typographical collage.

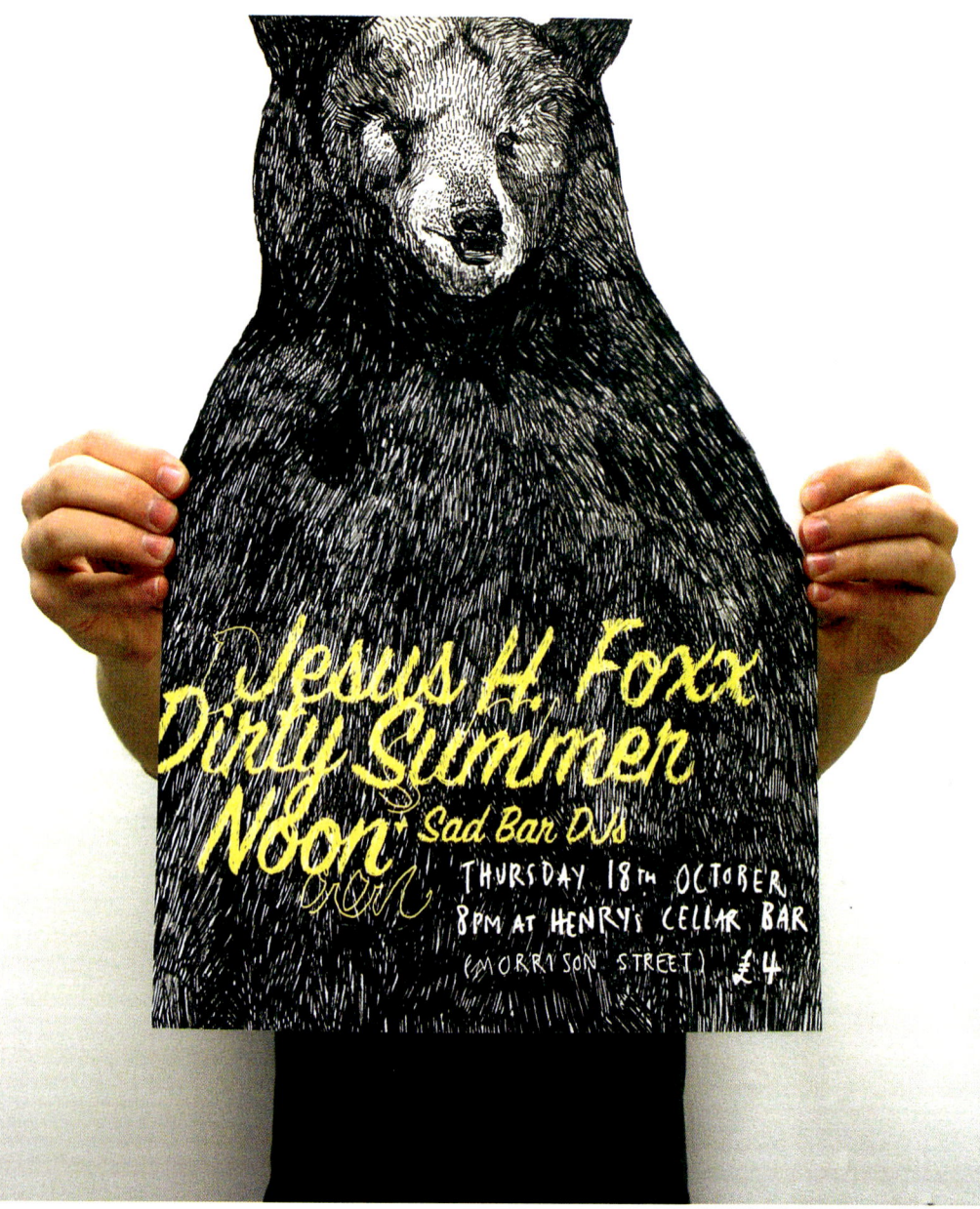

**Jesus H. Foxx
Dirty Summer
Noon | 2007**

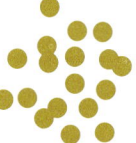

**Sing Statistics
www.singstatistics.co.uk**

To promote a concert a three-dimensional effect was used, inspired by the texture of bear fur. This image combines with the color contrast and brings the piece together through the repetition of the shading from the illustration on the typography.

The best party I've ever been to was... a Christmas tea party in my second year in Edinburgh. Lovely people assembled around a lovely table talking about fictional animals, alarming piercings and hats. Lots of hats.

Lizzy Stewart

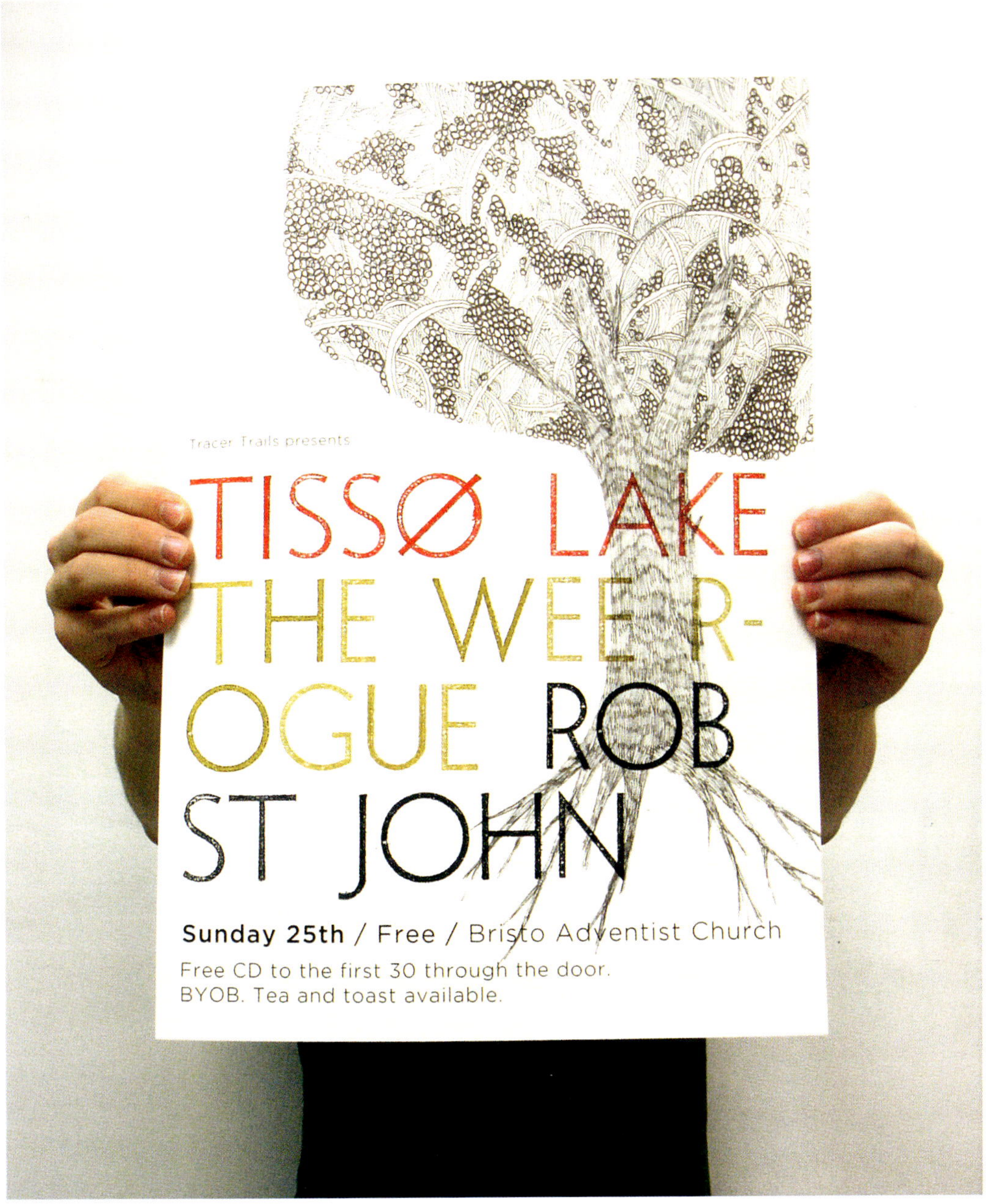

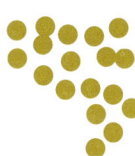

Tisso Lake/The Wee Rogue/Rob St John | 2007

Sing Statistics
www.singstatistics.co.uk

The closeness and collection of cold colors create the right atmosphere for announcing this concert that is to take place in a chapel. They also maintain the necessary balance for the majestic illustration of the tree.

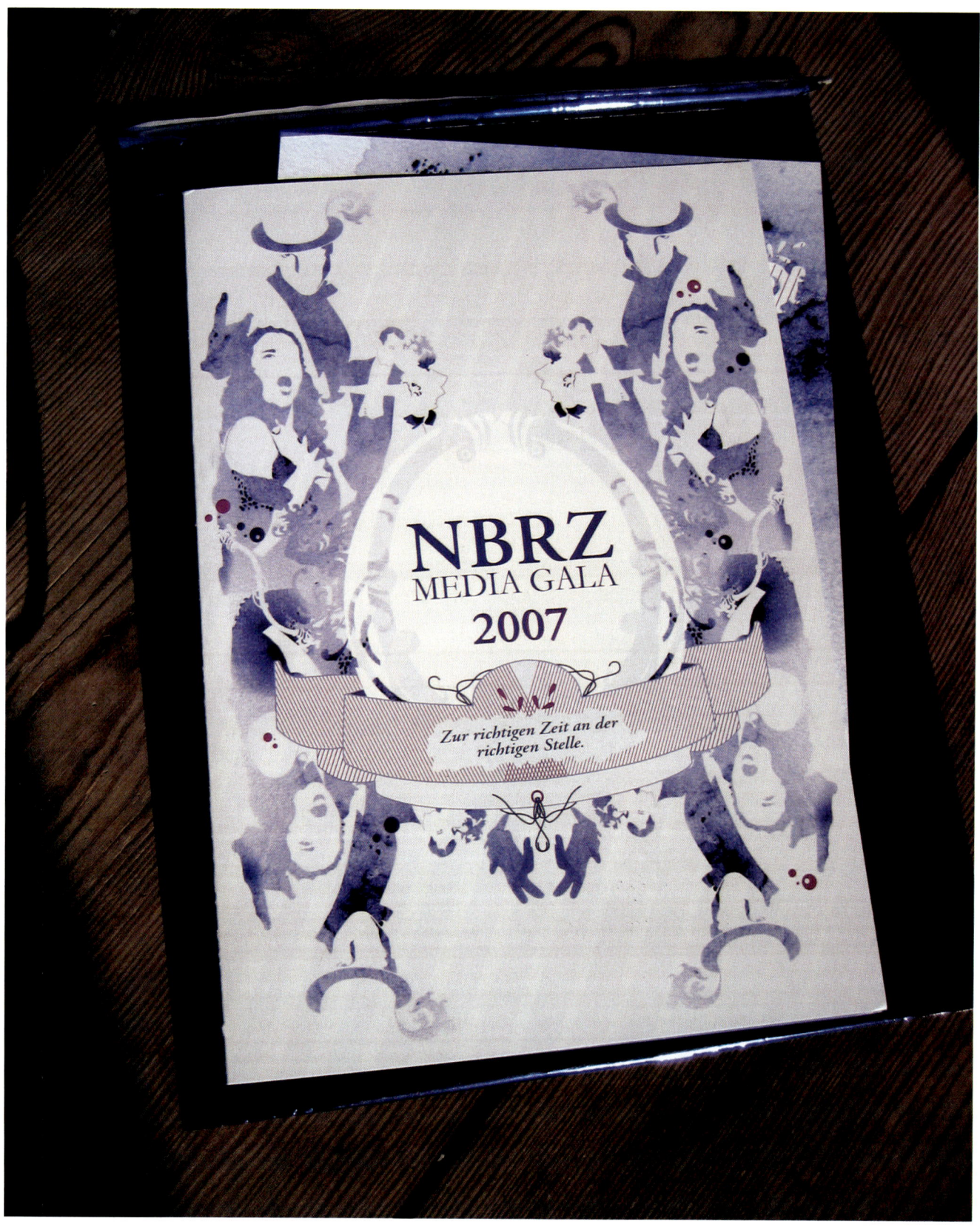

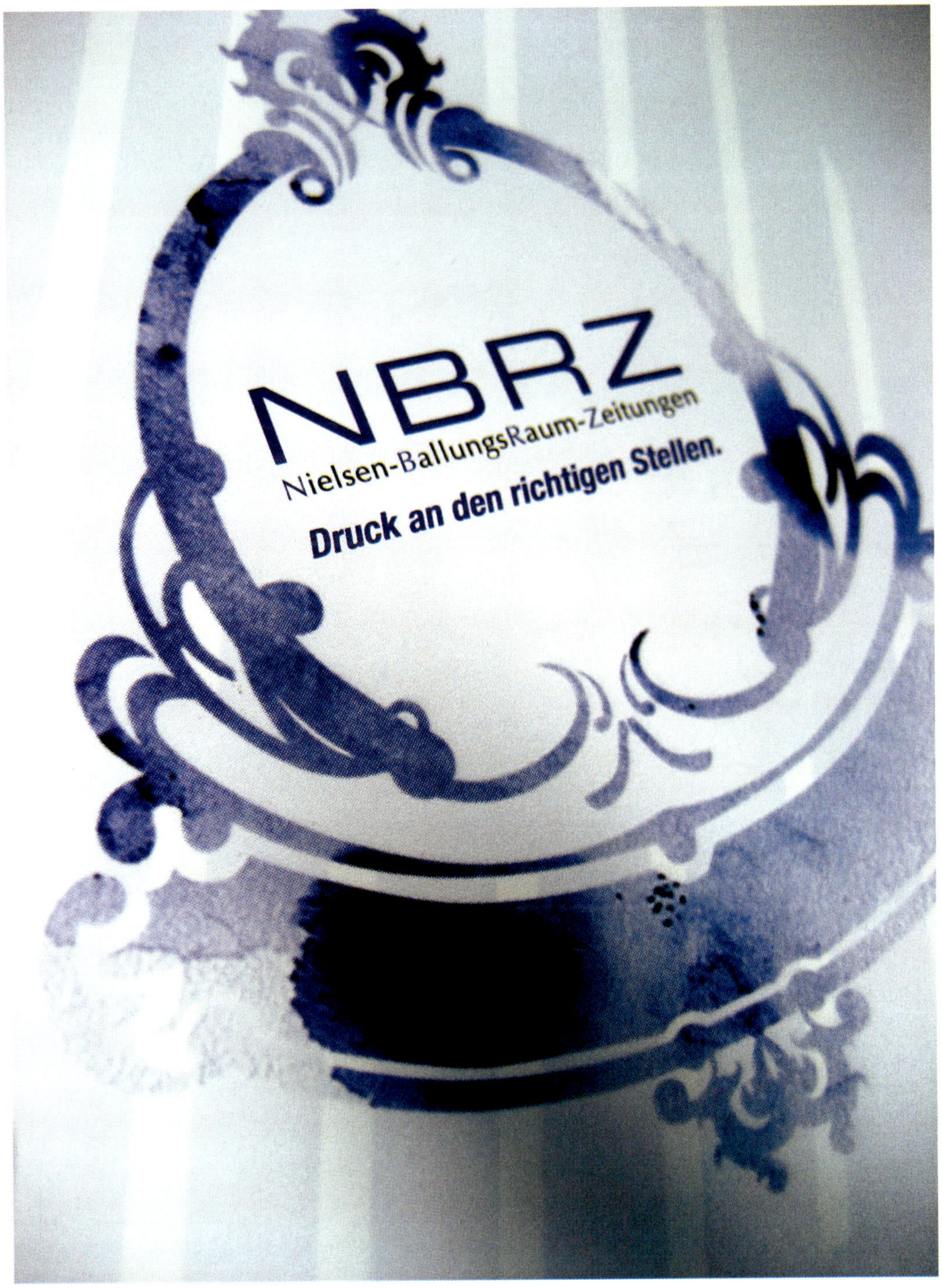

**Mailing for the NBRZ
Media Gala | 2007**

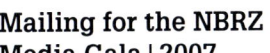

Spoonlight, mamapapacola
www.spoonlight.com

The mailing for the gala should project
the charming effect of people who
are used to being in the spotlight.
Symmetrically arranged, the illustrations
draw invitees' eyes to the center.

My great party was The Day of the Dead at the cemetery in a beautiful small town called Morelia. People were building colorful private altars to honor the deceased, using sugar skulls, marigolds, and the favorite foods and beverages. Scent of flowers, thousand of candle light and families get together full of passion. It was a very spiritual moment to me!

Ignatius Hermawan Tanzil

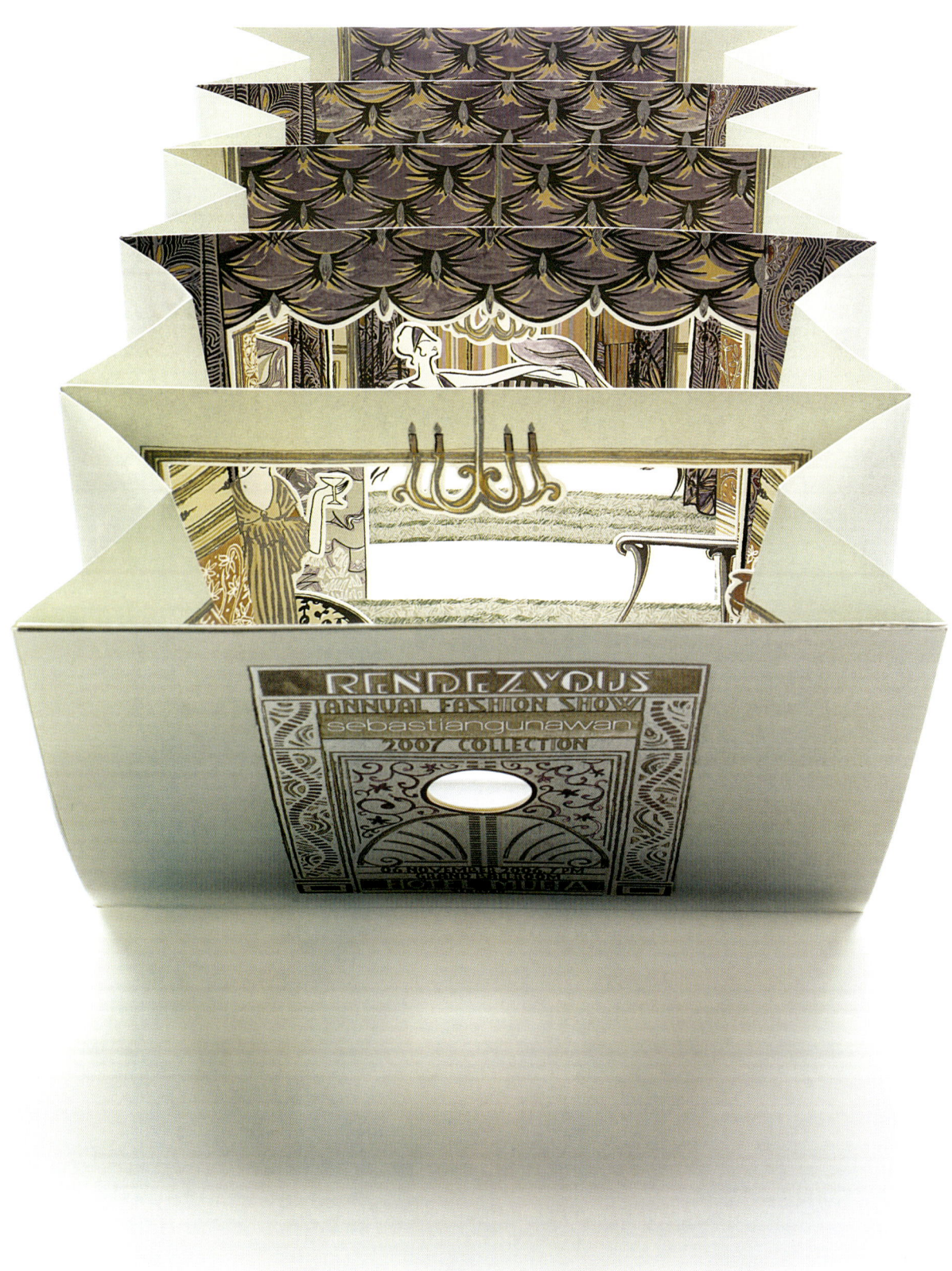

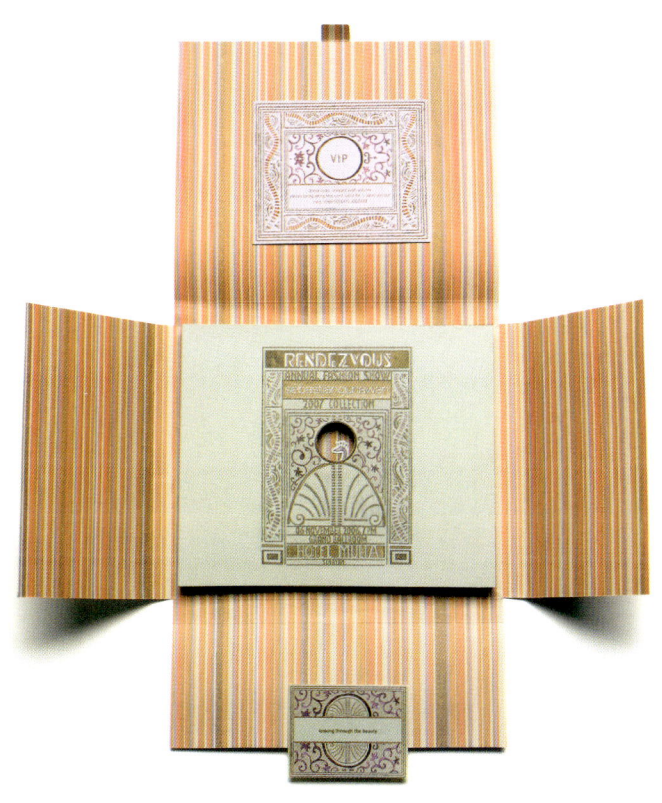

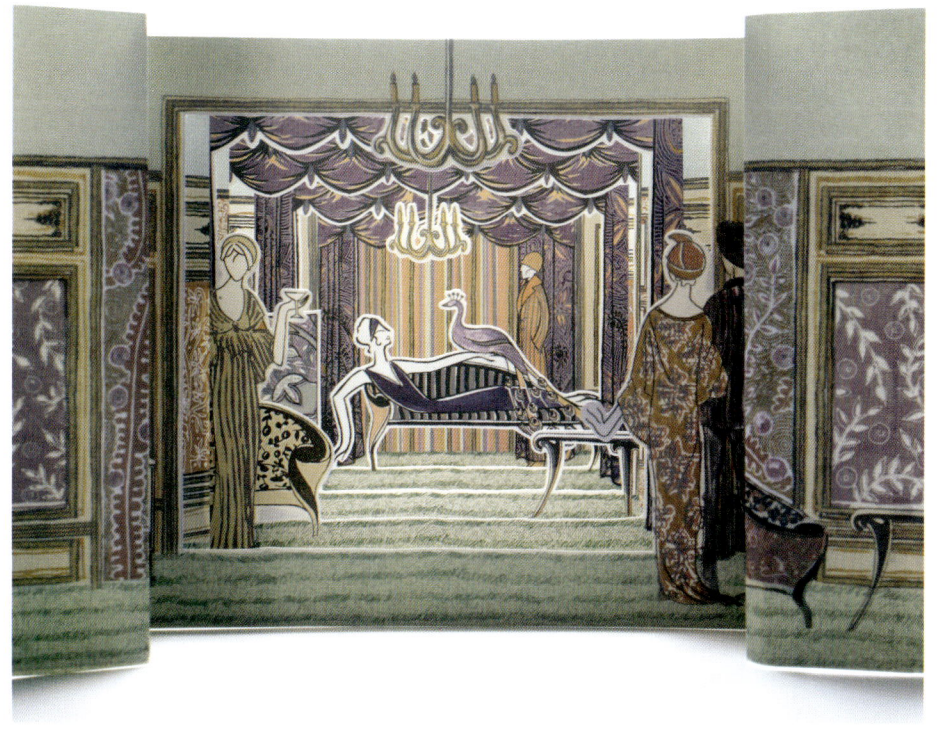

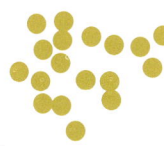

Sebastian Gunawan | 2007

Léboyé
www.leboyedesign.com

A hole in the cover of the invitation to the fashion show reveals a room decorated in an art-deco style. The inspiration comes from the work of Gunawan concerning singularity, femininity and decoration.

41

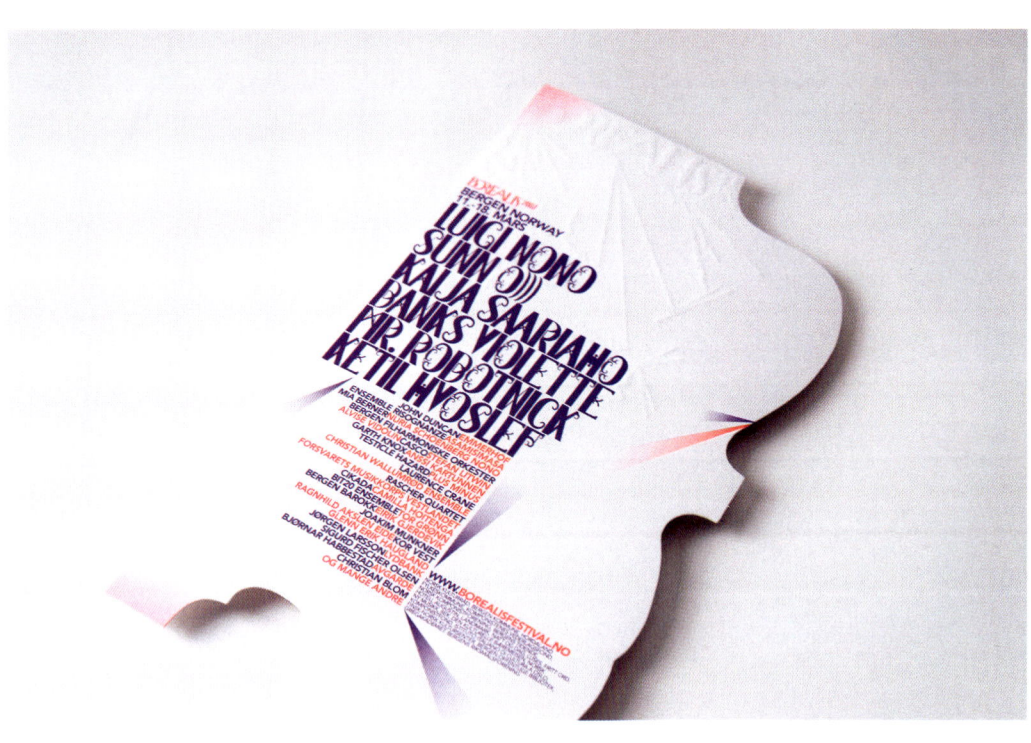
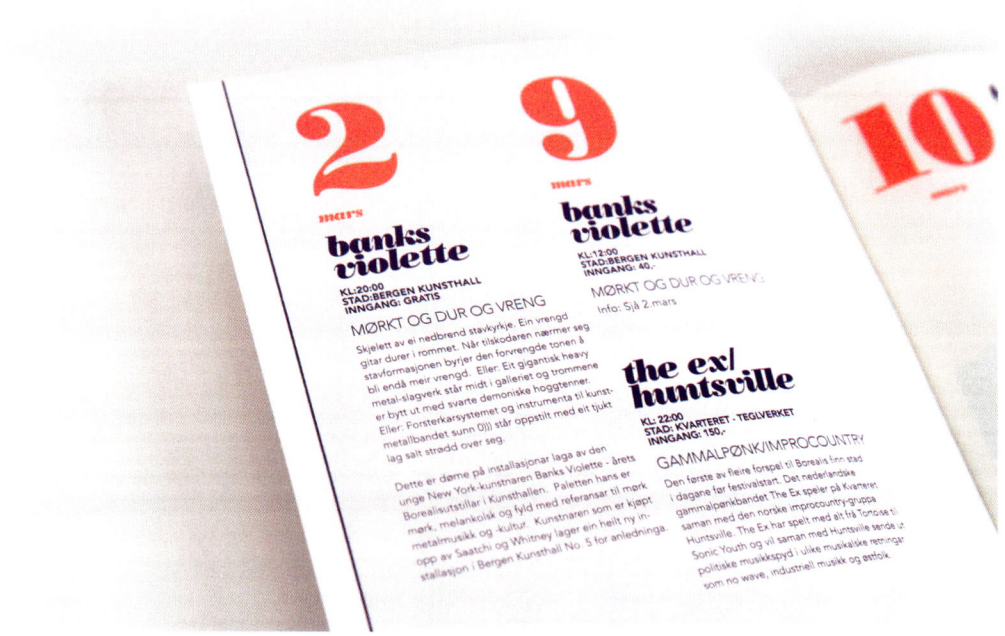

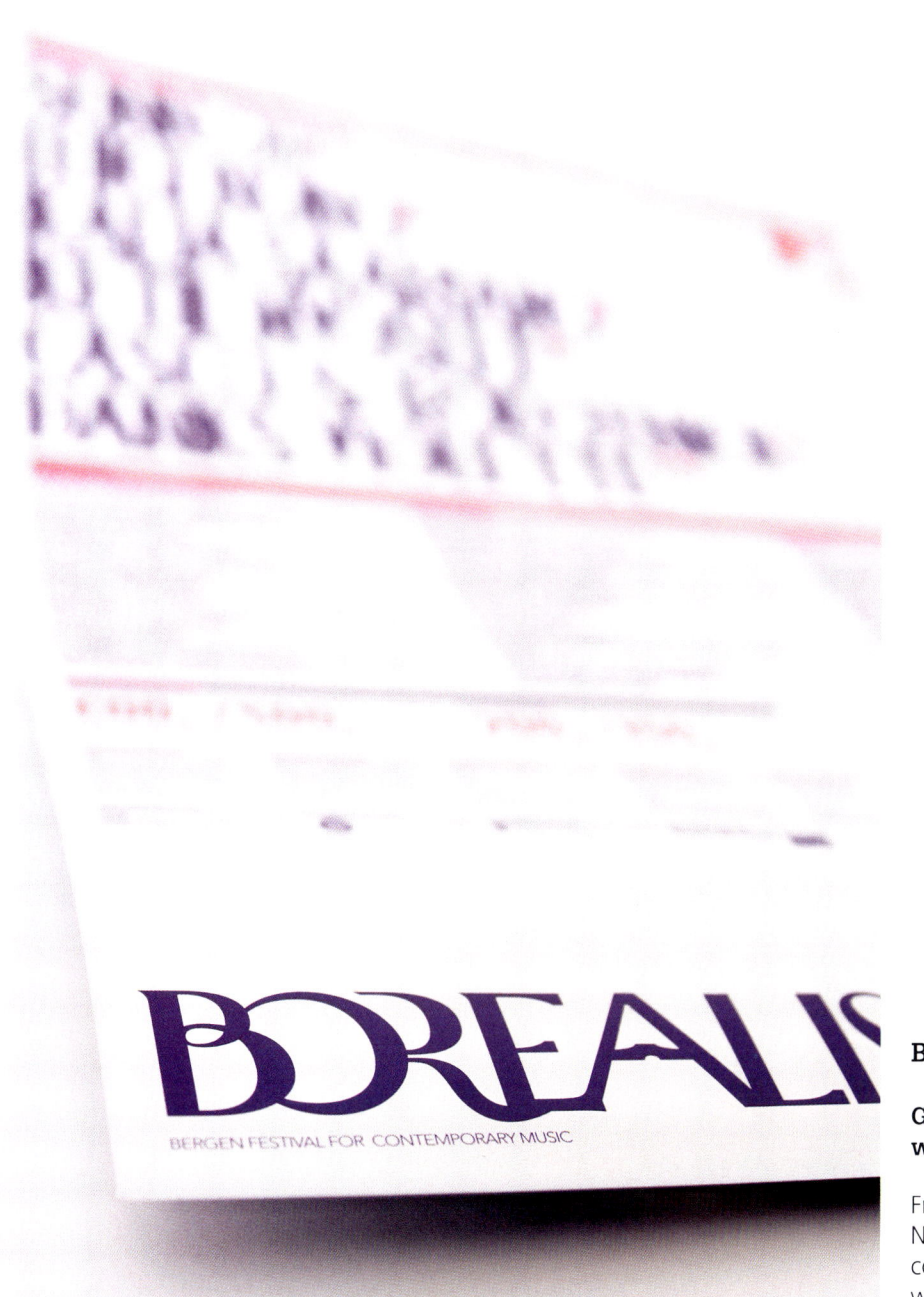

Borealis Festival | 2007

Grandpeople
www.grandpeople.org

From the variety on offer at the Norwegian festival, the work links the country's old traditions and architecture with the variety that Borealis proposes. This is reflected in the use of grotesque typographies with or without finishes.

Opening party of studio 020, Friday 23 July 1999, Amsterdam.

Arjan Groot

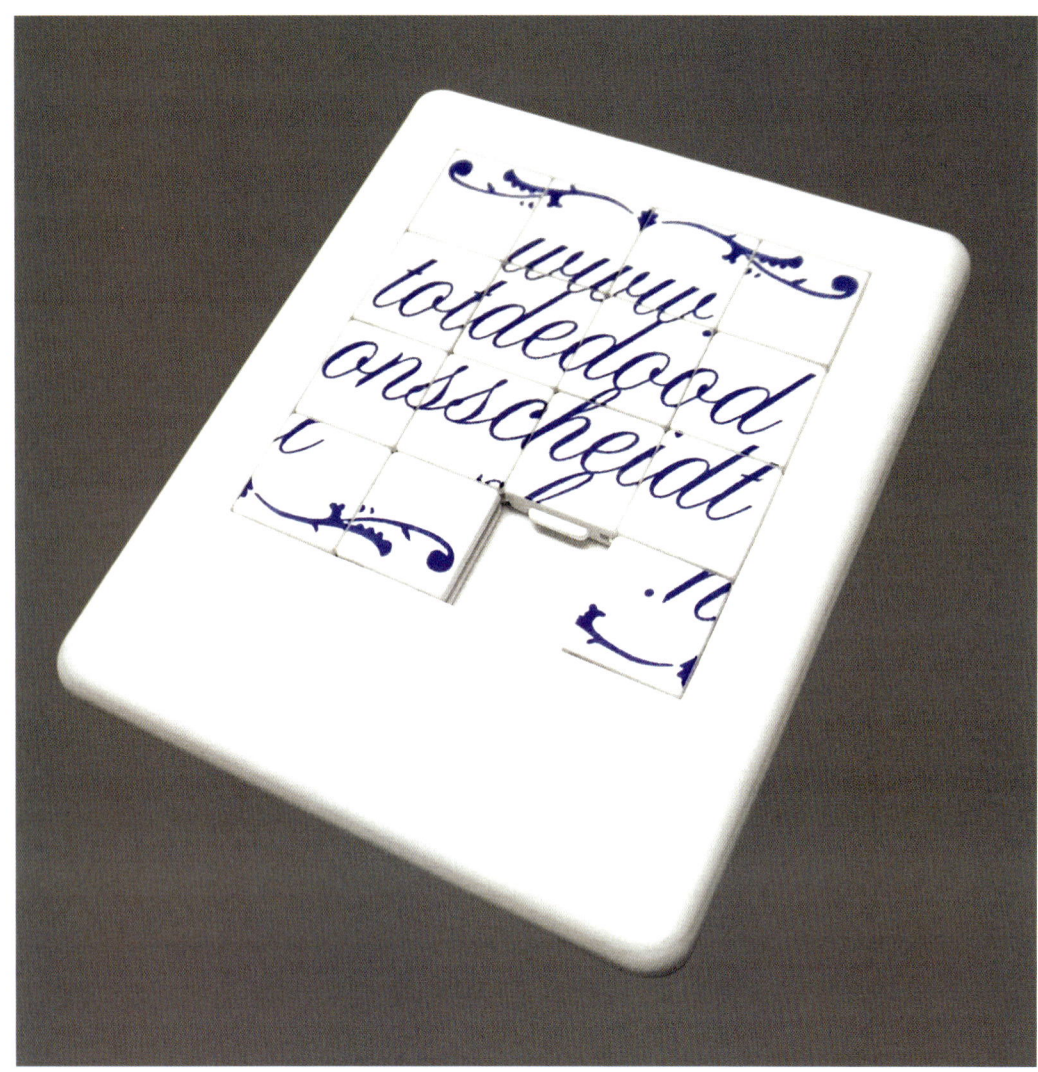

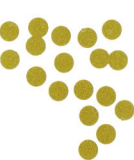

Wedding invitation | 2002

Arjan Groot
www.thecoverup.eu

The wedding invitation is a jigsaw puzzle with mosaic aesthetics. When it has been put together it reads "www.tilldeathdouspart.nl." At this website was all the necessary information regarding the link.

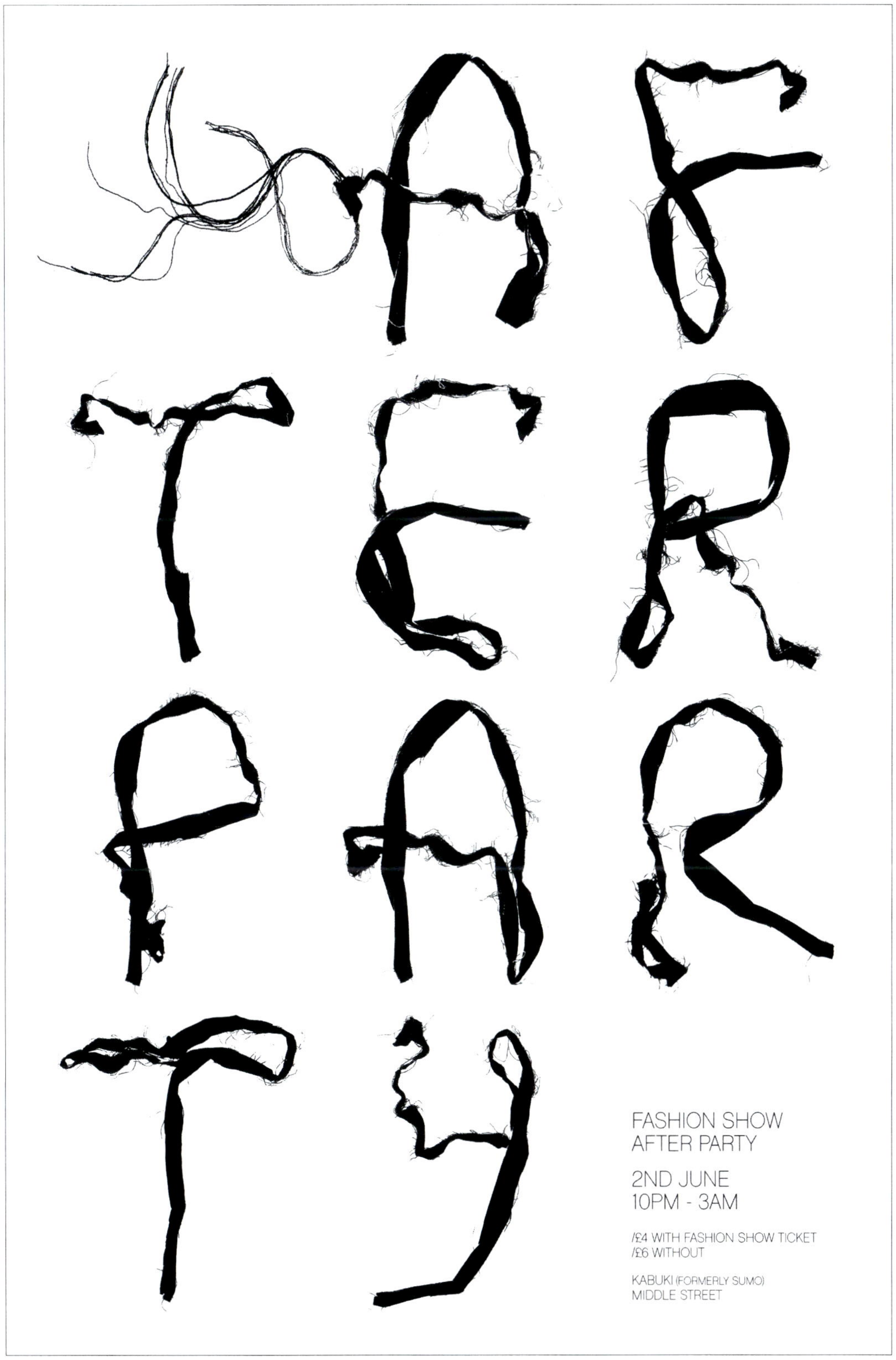

**Fashion Show
After Party | 2007**

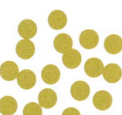

Owen Gildersleeve
www.eveningtweed.com

The base of this poster is the typography made from frayed cloth: the texture highlights the letters as if they were in bold type, as well as making reference to the fashion designers who are organizing the party. The complexity of the typography does not detract from the delicacy.

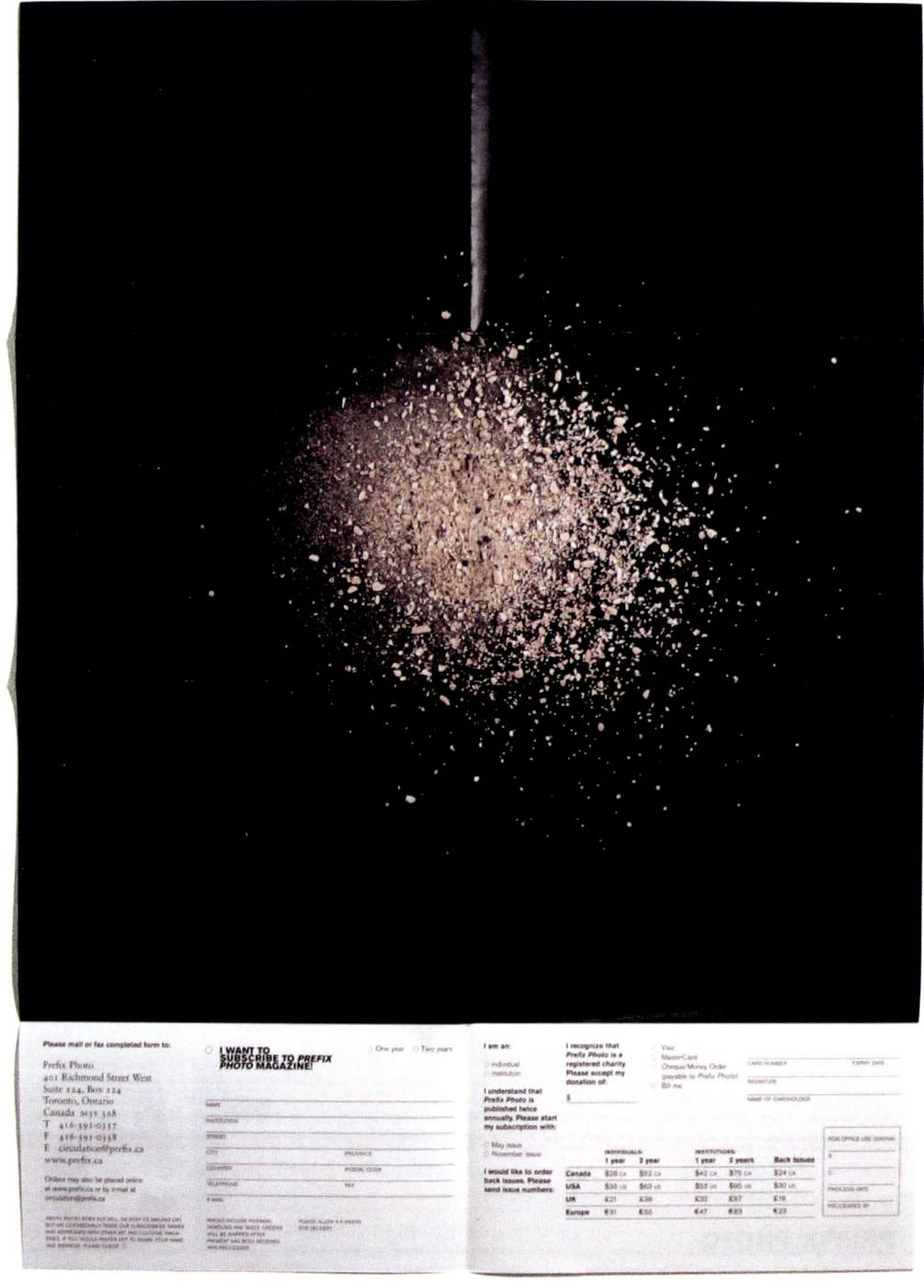

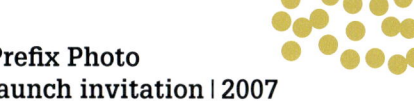

**Prefix Photo
launch invitation | 2007**

Underline Studio
www.underlinestudio.com

When photography appeared, artists knew that the hyper-reality of the camera was impossible to compete with using a brush. This image is the culmination of that representation, although at first sight we may doubt: dust, fireworks or a galaxy?

2002, Washington, eighteenth Street Lounge, Party DJ-ed by Thievery Corporation. We were students at the Portfolio Center attending an AIGA conference. That night Russell kissed for the first time his future wife, Luis actually danced and taught Agi how to do tequila shots, and Agi finally understood what good DJ-ing was about. Bonds were made and the foundation was laid for what would become Lucha.

Lucha Design

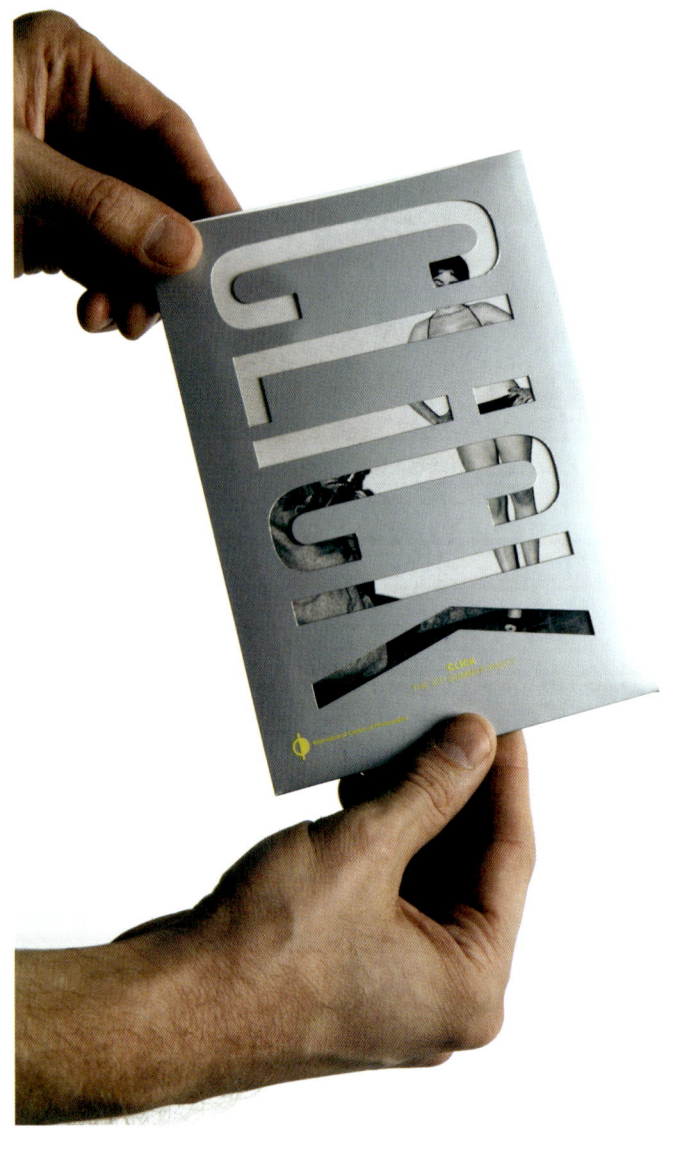
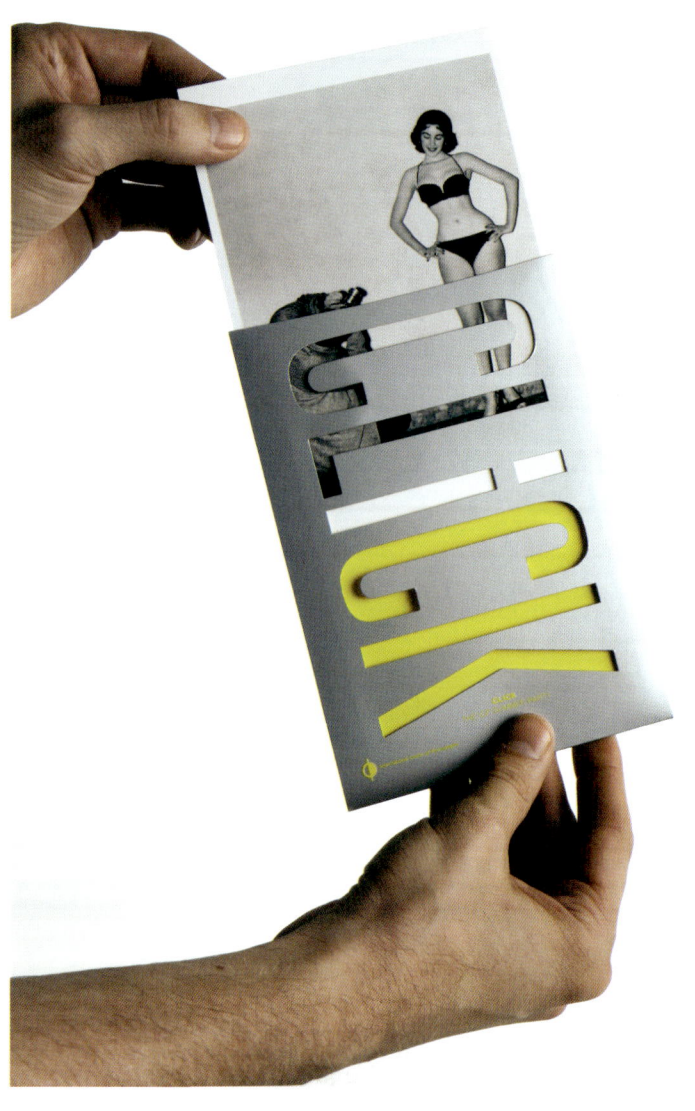

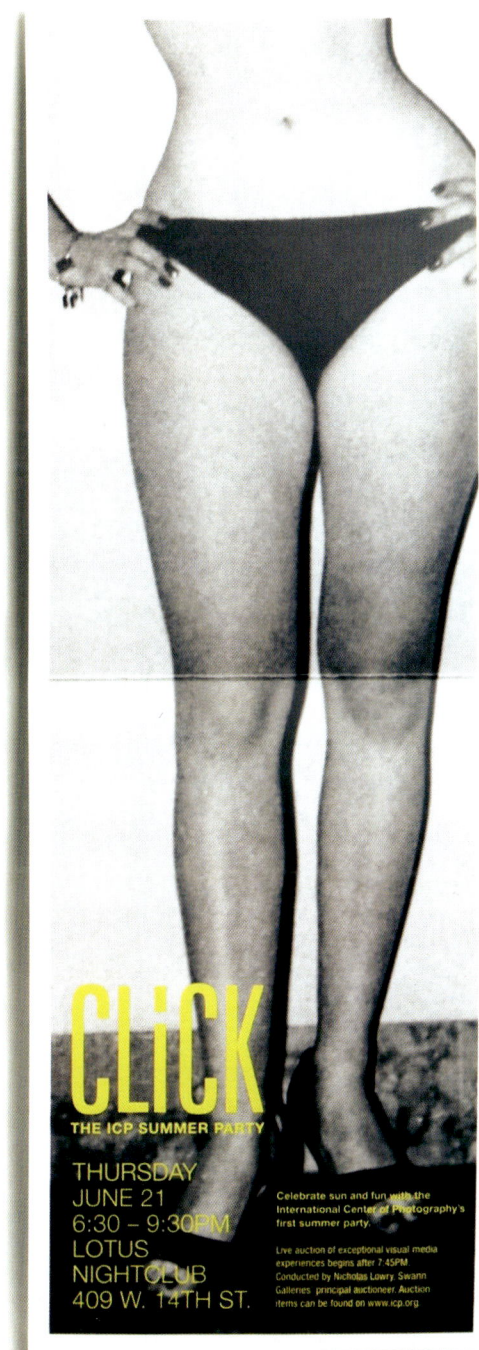

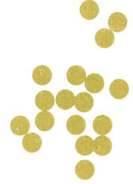

**CLICK: The ICP
Summer Party | 2007**

Lucha Design
www.luchadesign.com

The idea of the party was to make the guests feel like subjects of a photo shoot. From the point of view of the voyeur, the envelope half covers the photo of the invitation, which when taken out also loudly announces the name of the party.

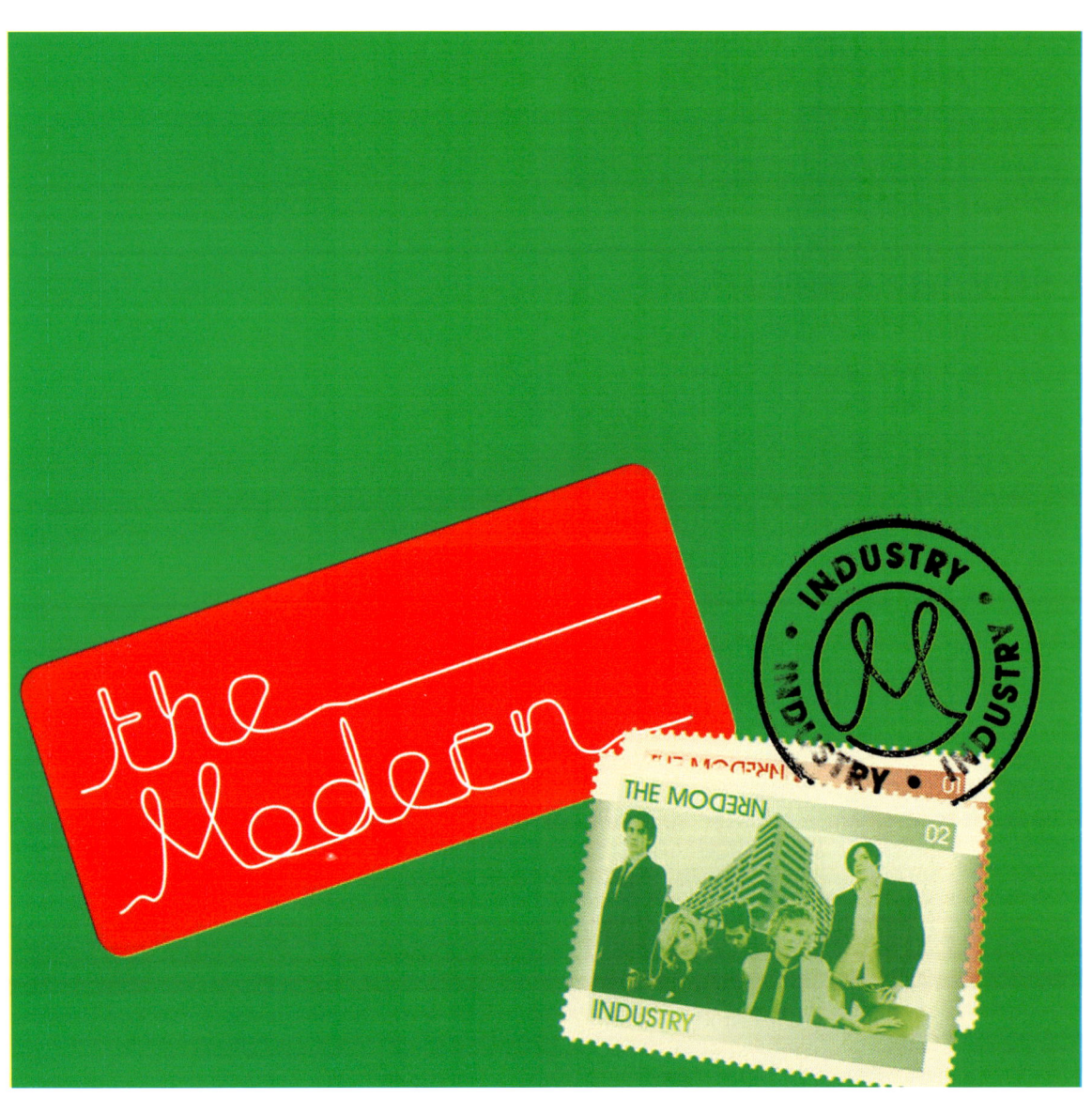

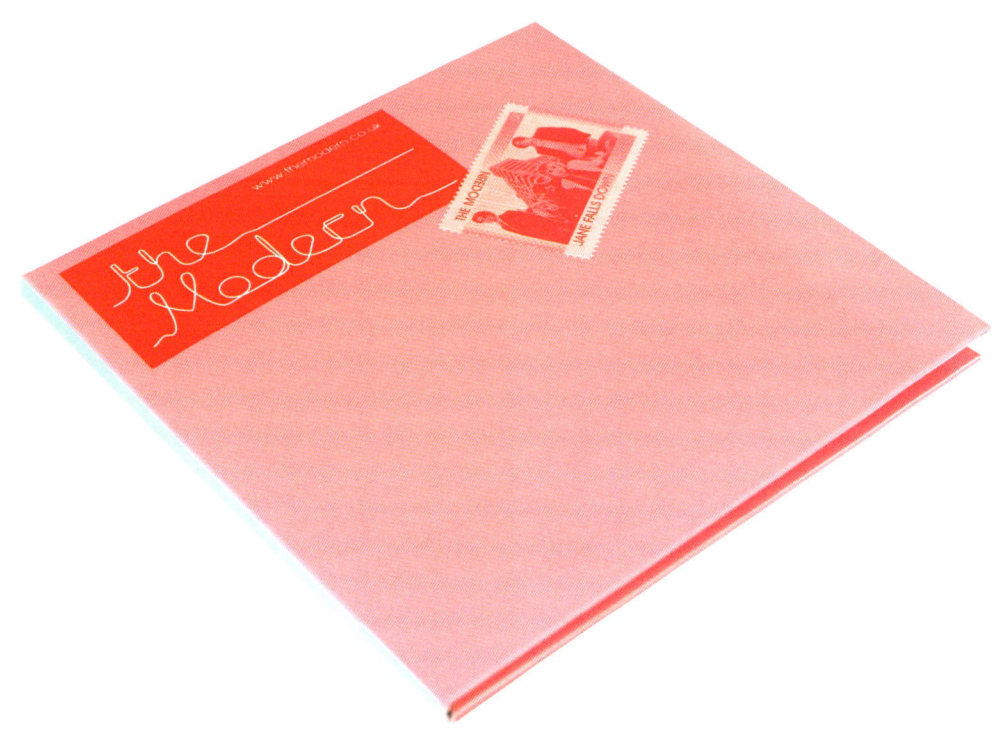

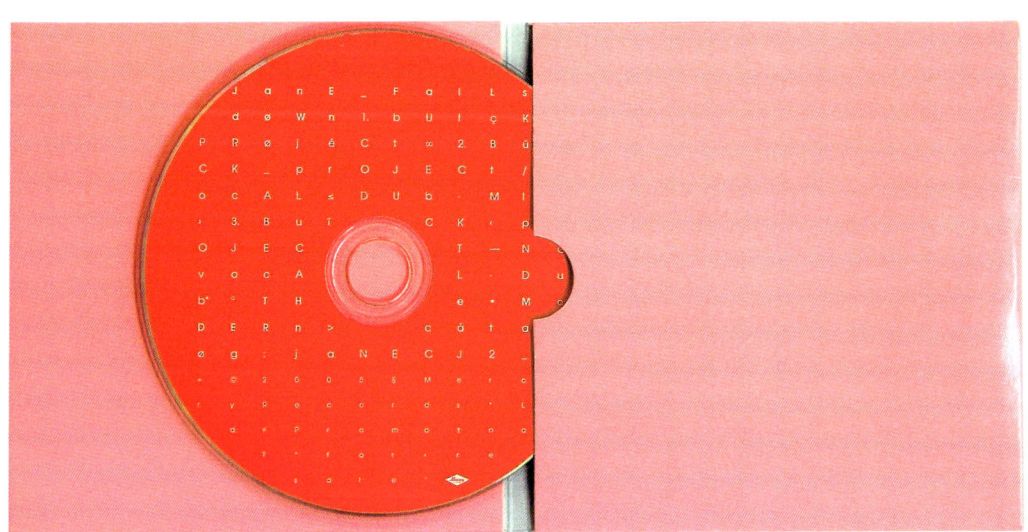

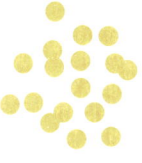

The Modern | 2007

Art direction: Paul West
Design: Paul West, Andy Harvey, Claire Warner/Form
www.form.uk.com

The design of the promotional material of the group, The Modern, arises from the combination of highly diverse elements: the typography of the logo is the vectorial version of a folded piece of wire, and the arrangement and treatment of color fuses with the Bauhaus and the electro.

We don't get out much.

Marcus Walters

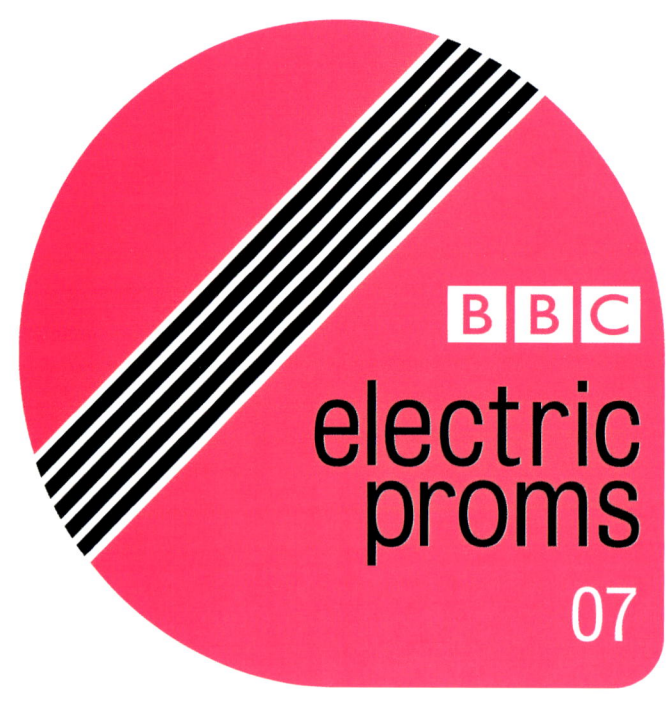

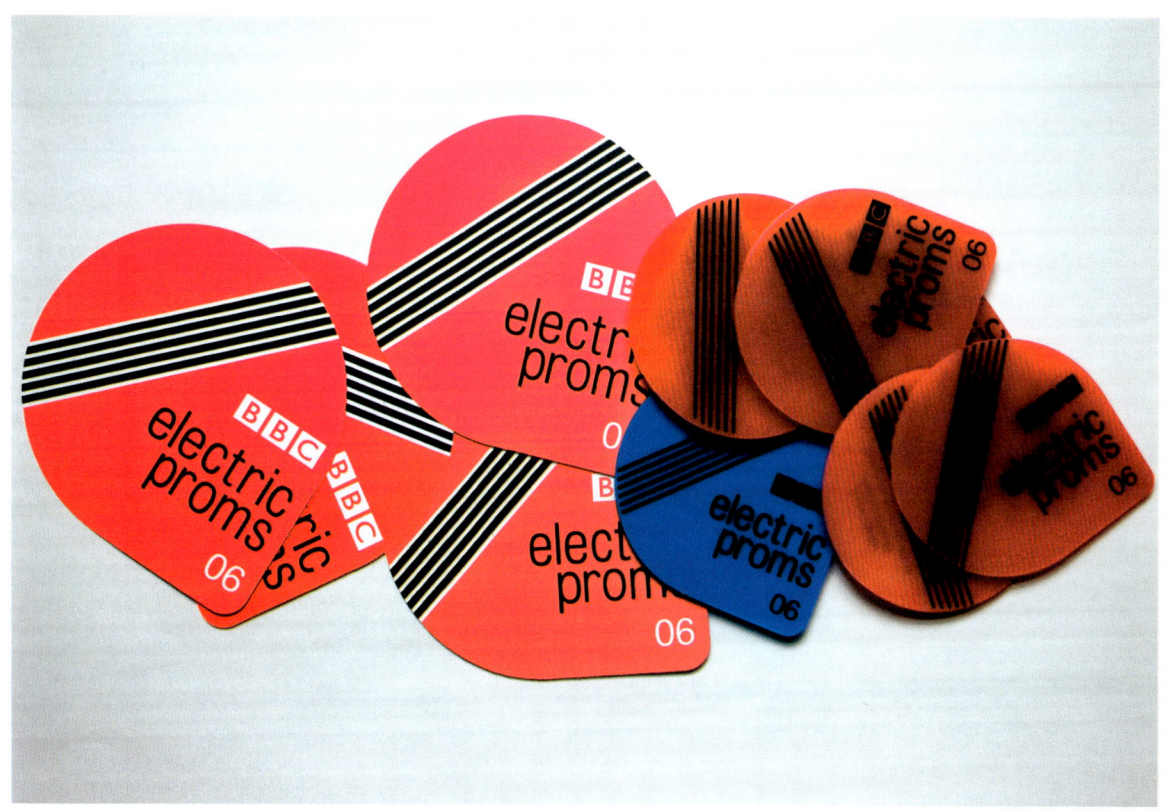

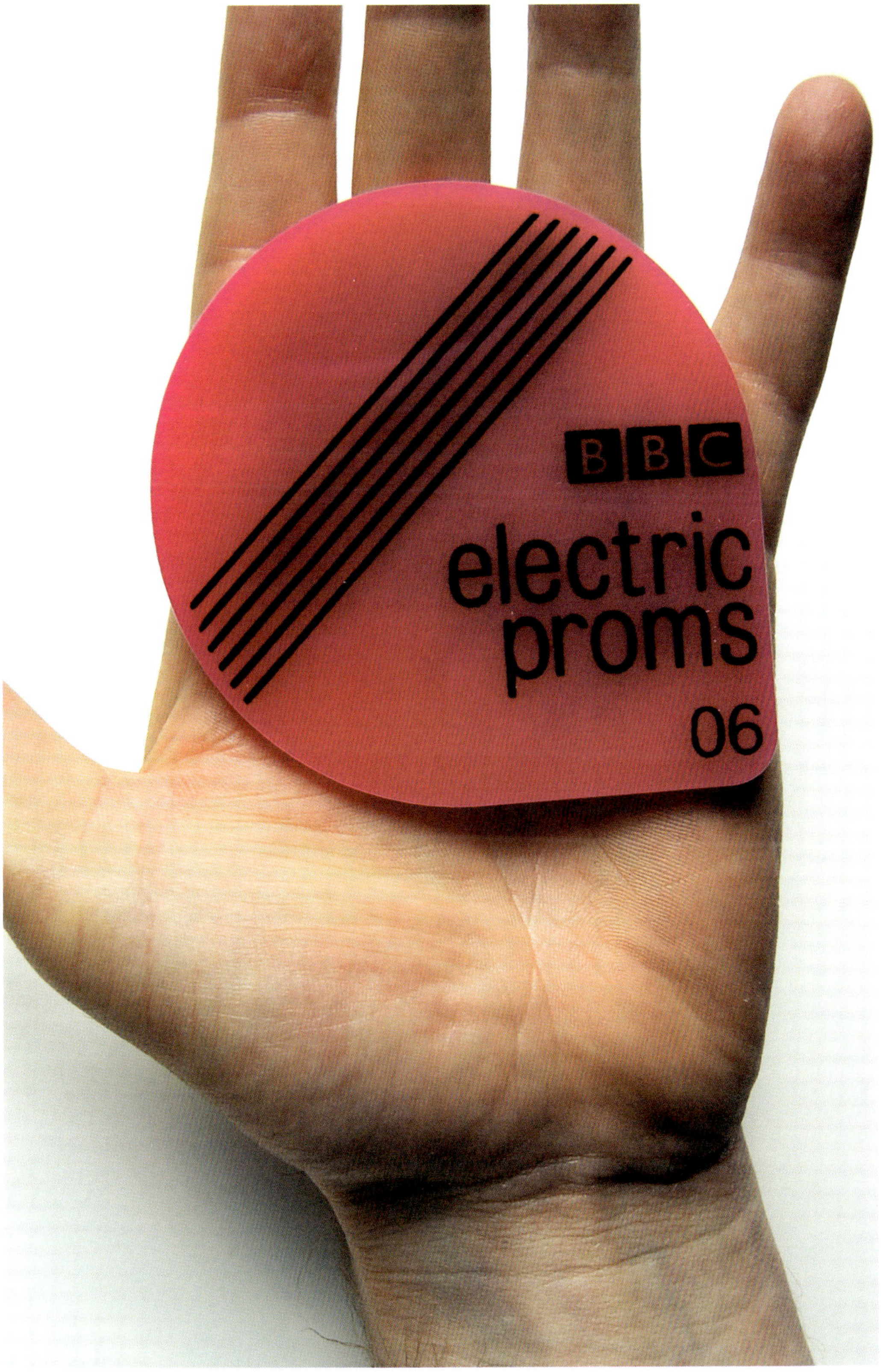

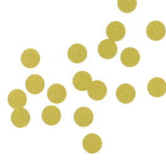

BBC Electric Proms | 2006-2007

New Future Graphic
www.newfuturegraphic.co.uk

The festival had to be promoted without making reference to a particular style of music and showing the connection with the BBC. Inspired by a magnified pick, the solution was to conserve the typography of the company and preserve the visibility of the logo.

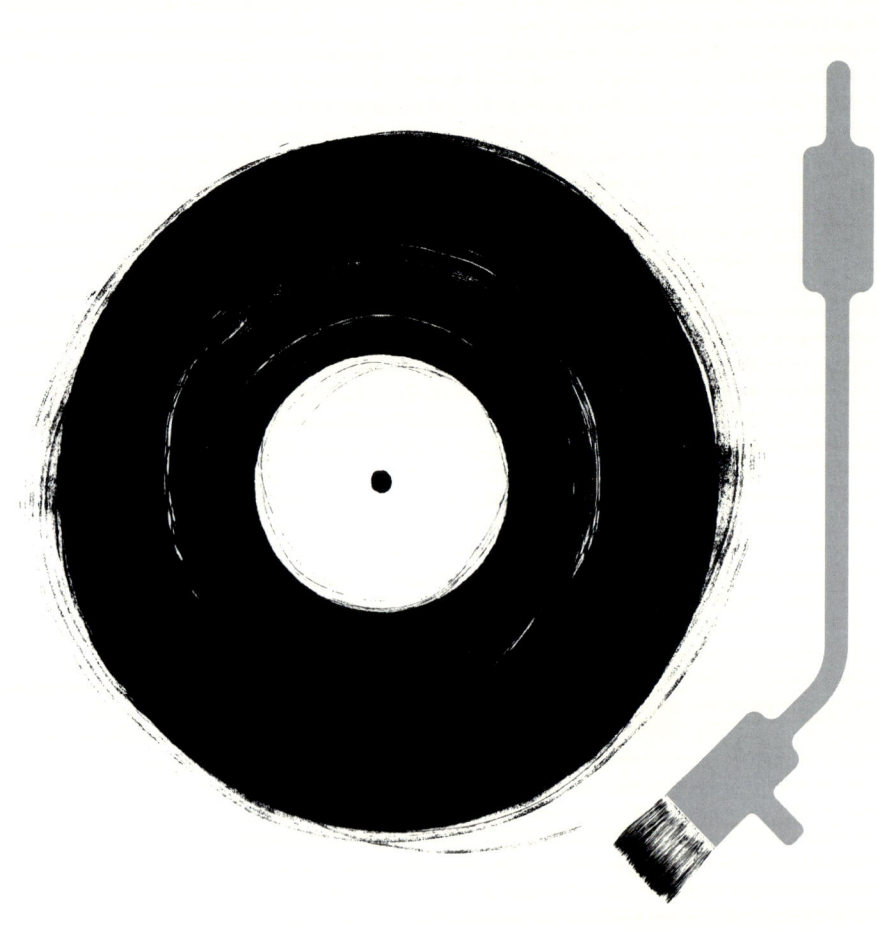

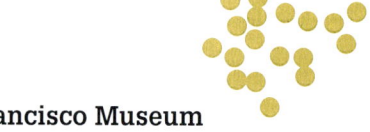

San Francisco Museum
of Modern Art | 2006

Jason Munn/The Small Stalkes
www.thesmallstakes.com

Based on the use of an achromatic scale of retro touches, the poster promotes a night when the museum invites local students to concerts and talks. The shape of the needle from the record player transformed into a paintbrush completes the message.

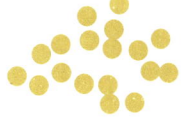

**69 Love Songs
Tribute poster | 2006**

Corianton Hale/Sleep Op Projects
www.sleepop.com

The theme had to make reference to Saint Valentine and to The Magnetic Fields album *69 Love Songs*. The proposal was resolved with a heart made from the names of the groups and by using courier typeface in deep red, the tonic color throughout the work.

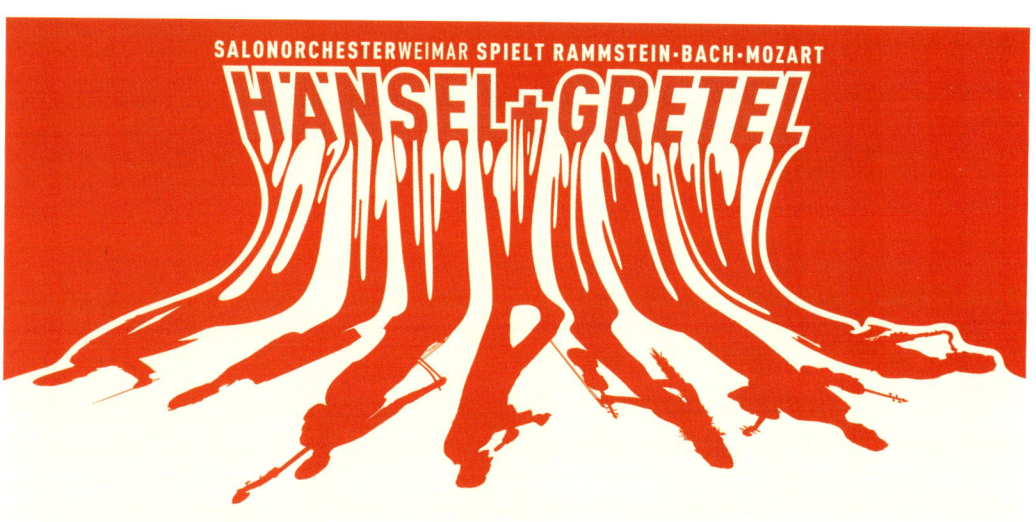

Hänsel + Gretel | 2006

Ariane Spanier
www.arianespanier.com

The Weimar Chamber Orchestra was performing the classic traditional story of Hänsel and Gretel, but interlinking songs by Rammstein with pieces by Mozart and Bach. The bloody shadows of the seven members of the orchestra slide from the typography.

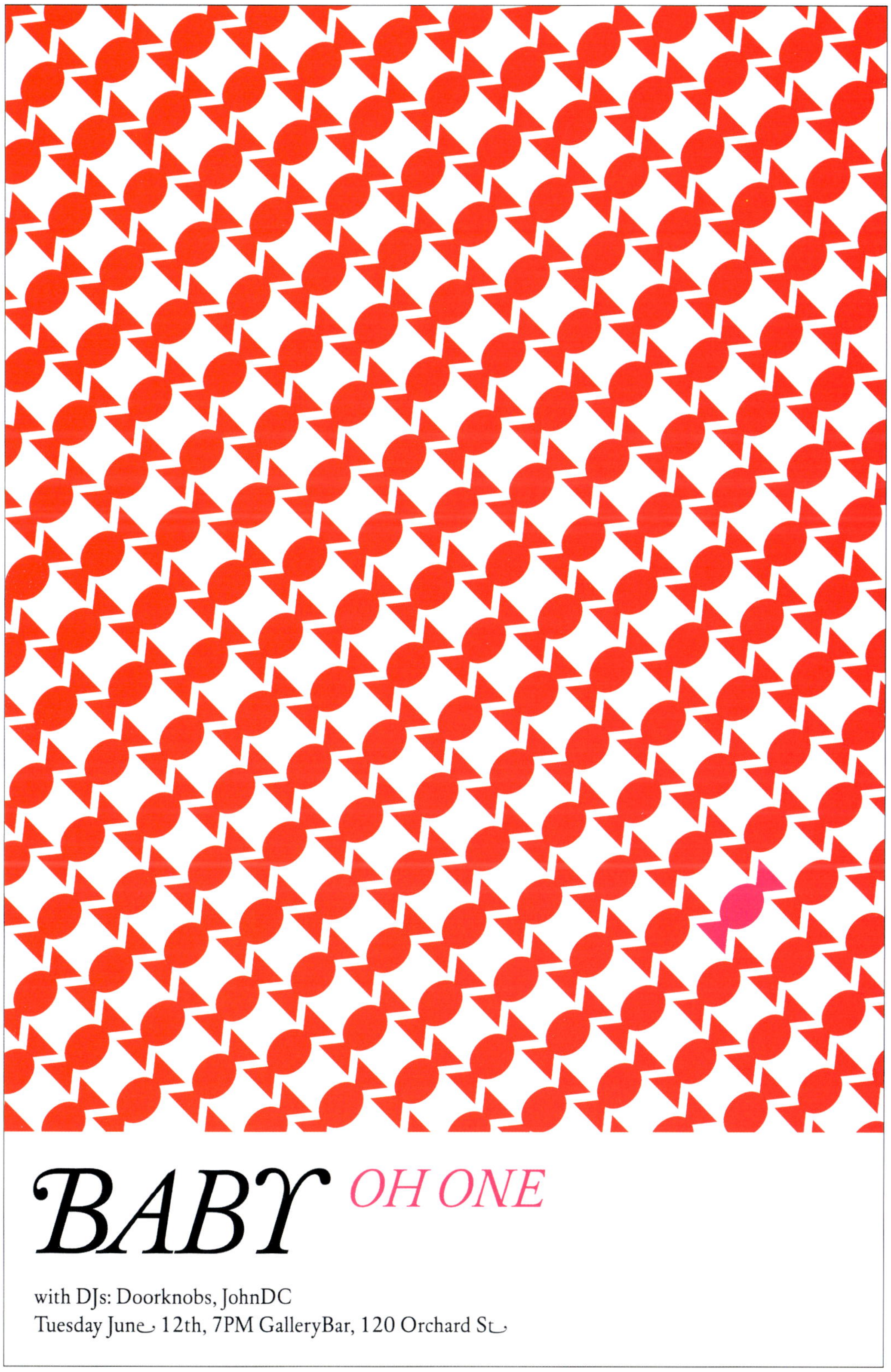

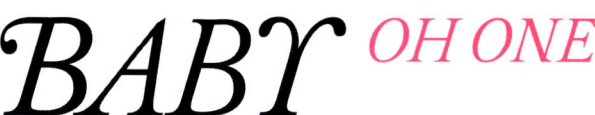

BABY *OH ONE*

with DJs: Doorknobs, JohnDC
Tuesday June 12th, 7PM GalleryBar, 120 Orchard St

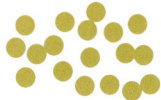

Baby | 2007

Lucha Design
www.luchadesign.com

The commission was to promote a series of monthly parties of "minimal electronic music, but with beautiful, and above all sweet, melodies." The answer was this pattern that links the sweets with the bits.

The best party Greedy Hen has ever been to was the art event of the year, by this we mean the Modified Power Tool Racing! The aim of the day was for each artist to pimp their power tool ready for racing. With two tracks built inside an art gallery, entrants were pitted against each other, the winner moving to the next round. Lots of drinking + cheering × five hours of racing = seriously good times.

Greedy Hen

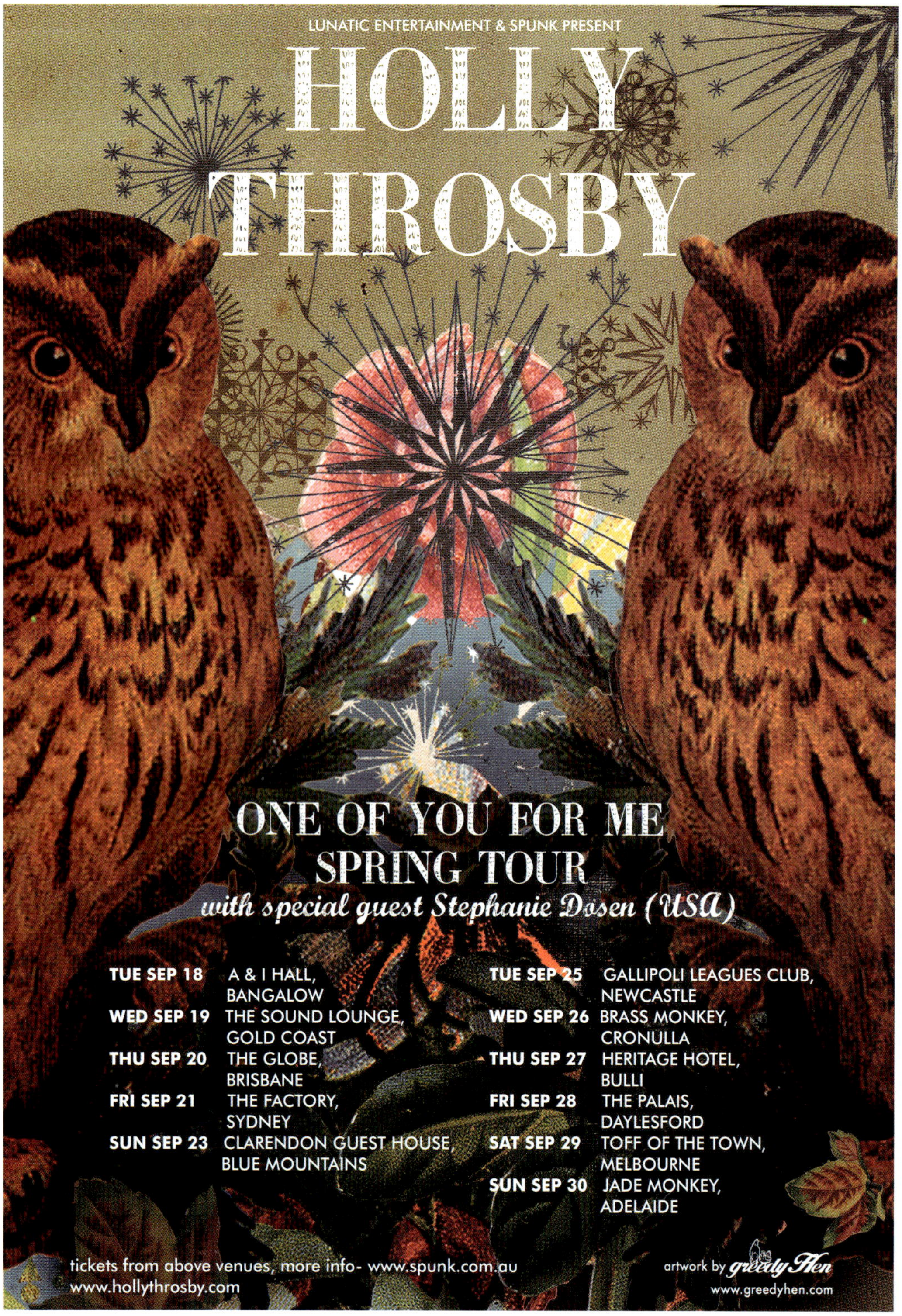

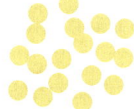

Holly Throsby
One Of You For Me
Australian tour poster | 2007

Katherine Brickman,
Kate Mitchell/Greedy Hen
www.greedyhen.com

Symmetry is the trigger here. Images have been used that evoke this effect: the enigmatic image of two owls staring at each other, while the background repeats kaleidoscopic patterns and fireworks.

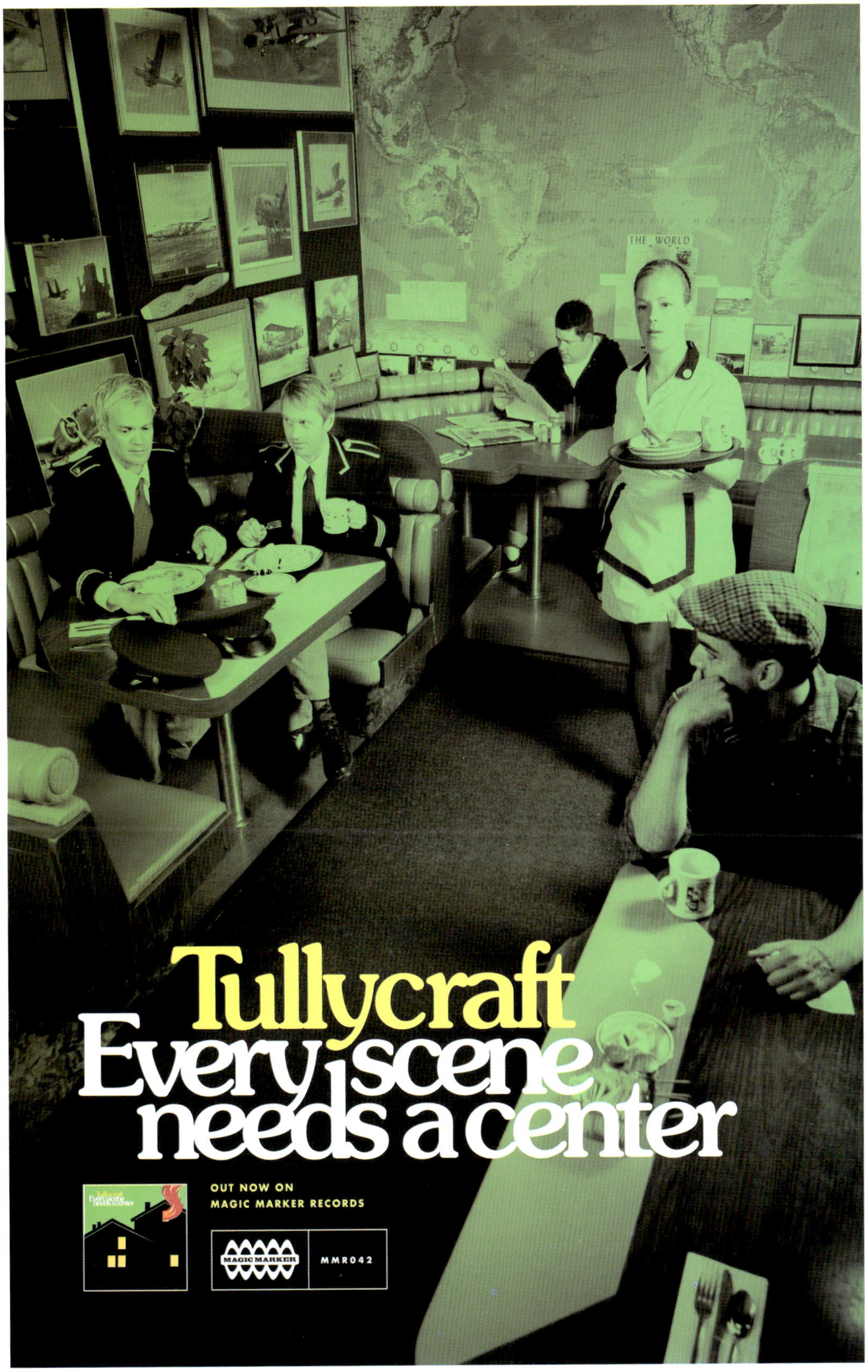

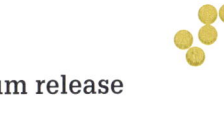

Tullycraft album release poster | 2007

Corianton Hale/Sleep Op Projects
www.sleepop.com

The poster promotes Tullycraft's new album. The photograph of an airmen's bar is tinted green and scattered with yellow typography. The intention is to repeat the color balance from the album cover.

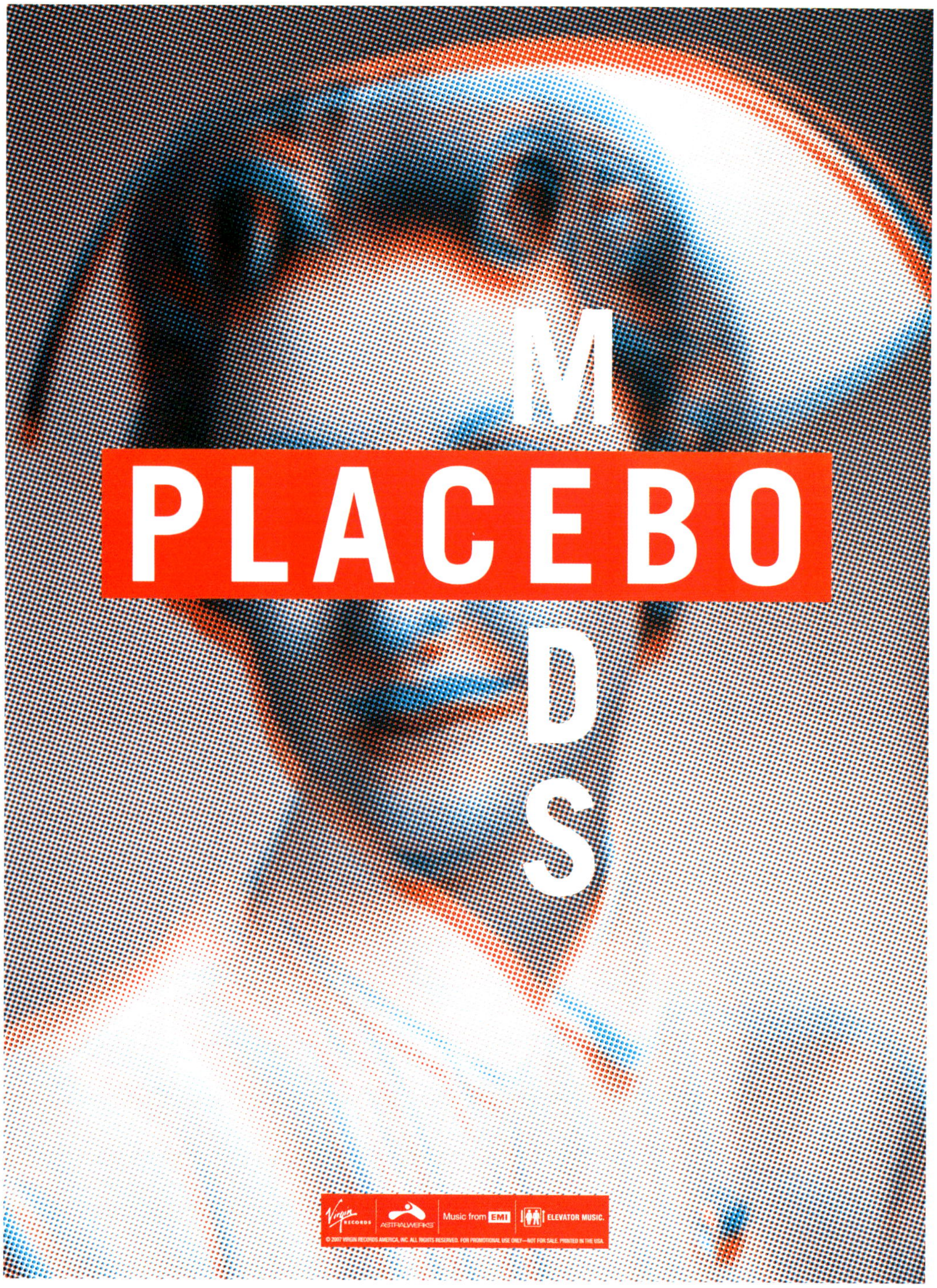

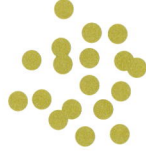

Placebo poster | 2007

Mike Joyce/Stereotype
www.stereotype-design.com

For the masterful irony of one of Placebo's albums entitled *Meds*, the designer works with the classical hospital iconography. The poster that promotes the album uses the asepsis from white and red to generate a feeling of vertigo and dizziness.

Our best party ever, no doubt, was the time we partied like it was 1999 in Austin, Texas. On a whim, we purchased last-minute airfare to see Lyle Lovett ring in the new year and new century, Texas-style. Y2K was the least of our worries as we wandered the streets of Austin in formal wear and euphoria.

Toolbox Creative

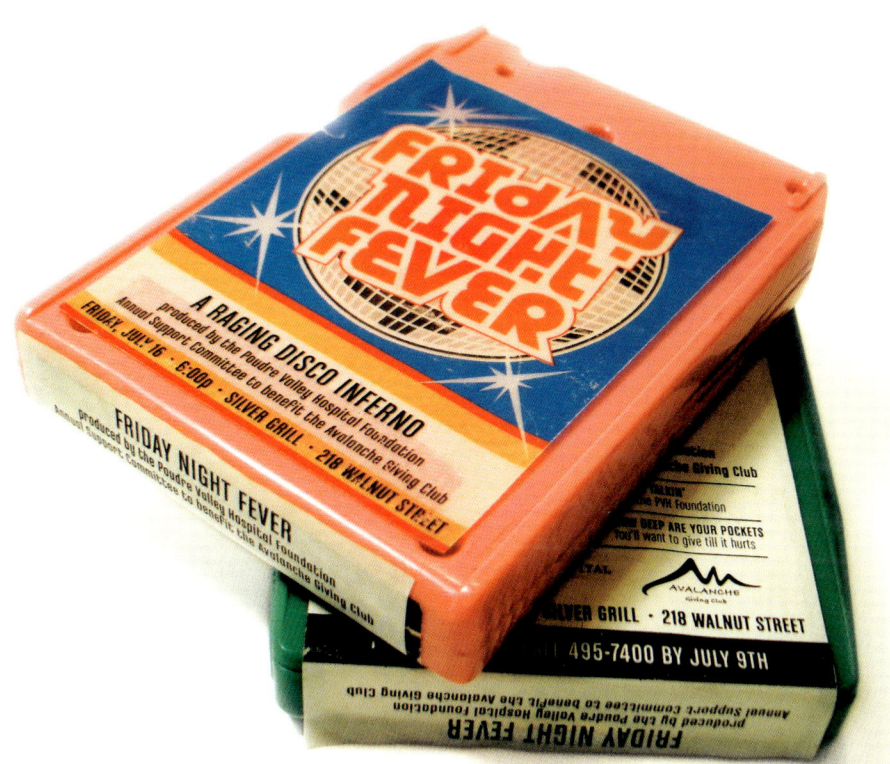

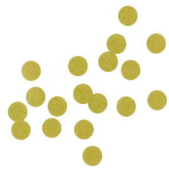

Friday Night Fever fundraiser invitation | 2004

Toolbox Creative
www.toolboxcreative.com

The invitation reflects the disco spirit of the party. The effect of the eight track tapes as a support is reinforced by the classic image of the mirror ball and an interplay of typography and color that copies those from the era.

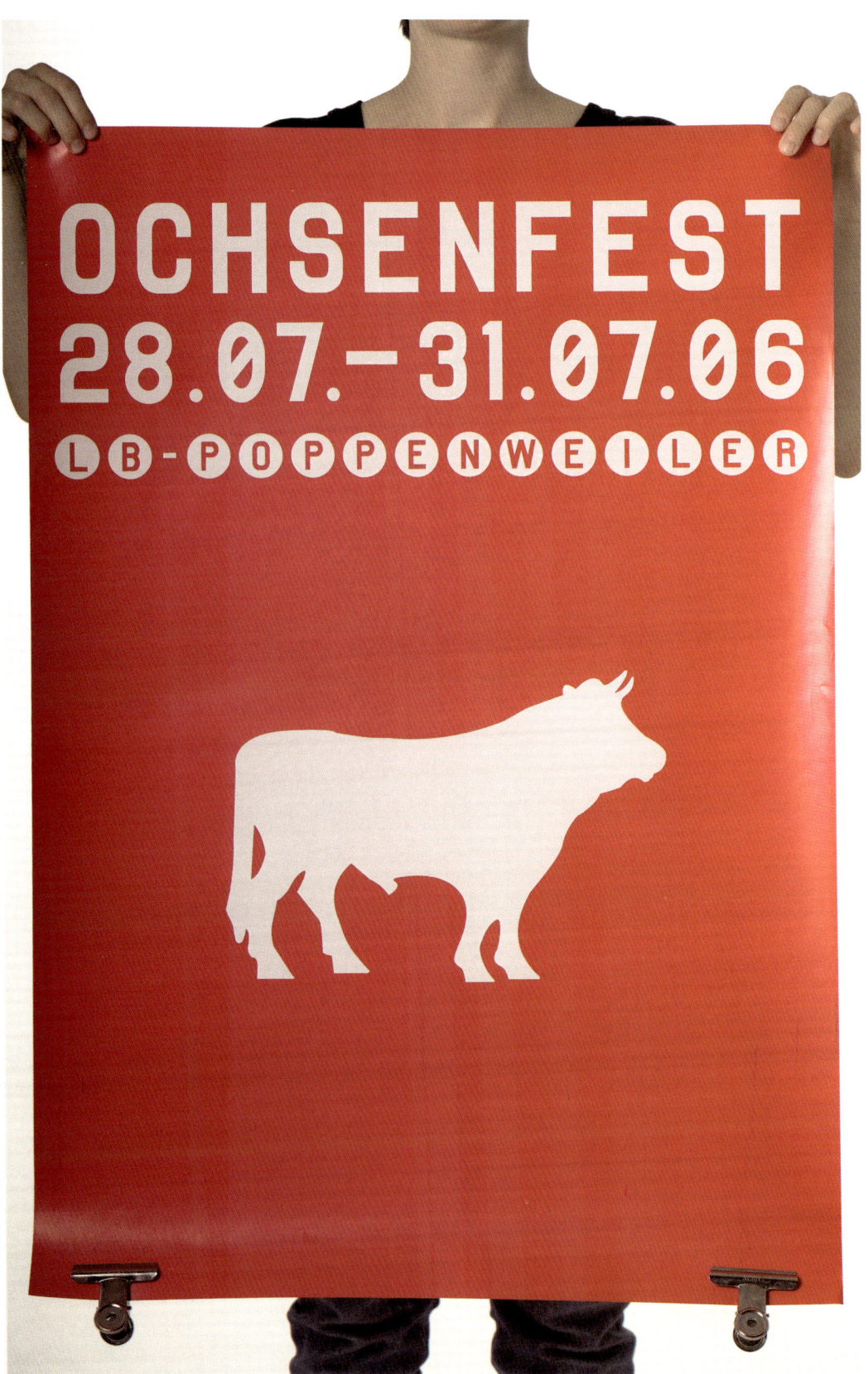

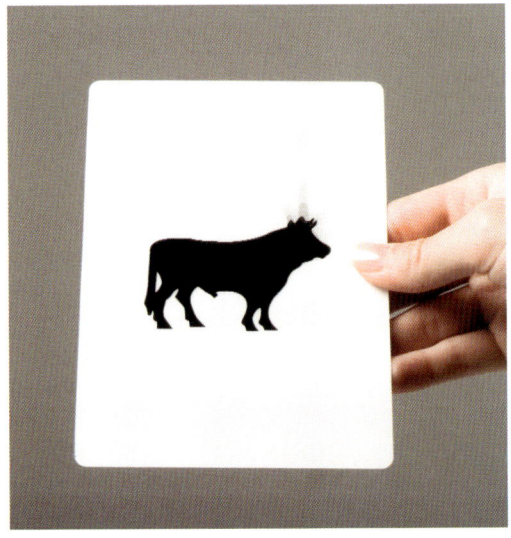 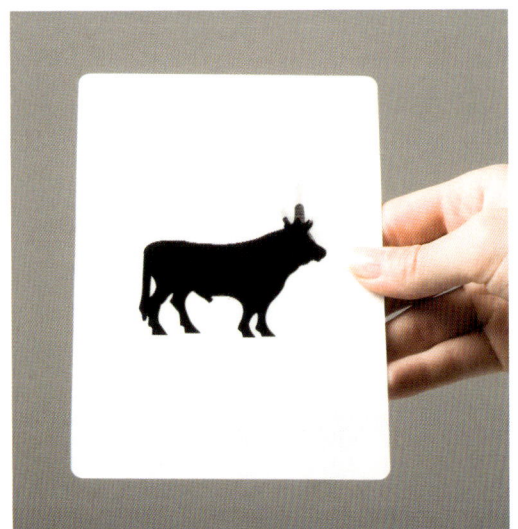
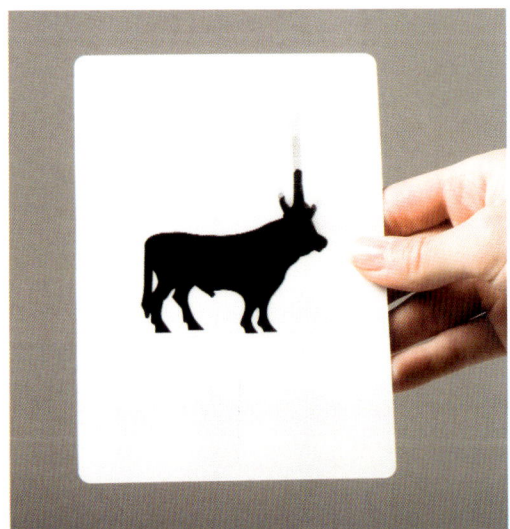 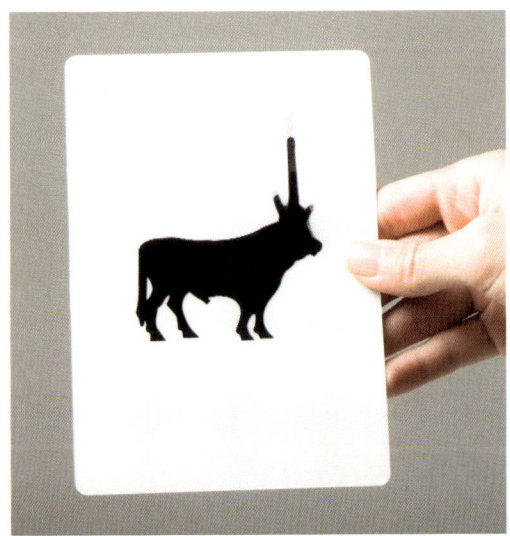
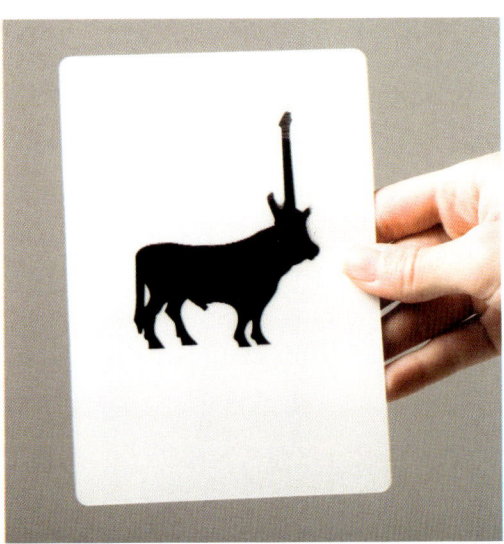 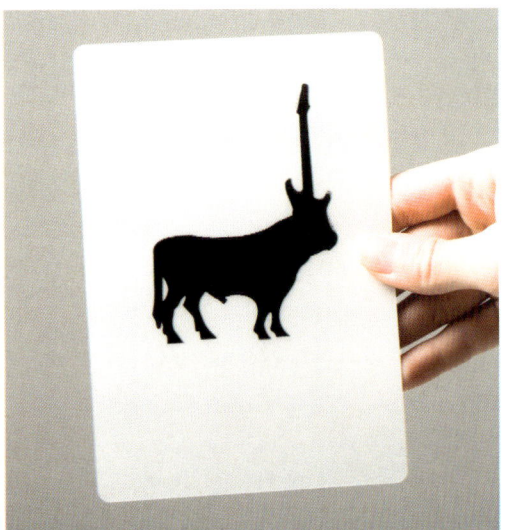

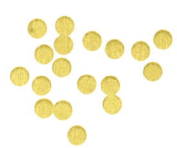

Ochsenfest | 2006

Nicole Jacek
nicolejacek@aol.com

The Ochsenfest festival is becoming less known for its traditional ox grills and now has a reputation for its concerts. The image takes this mutation and projects it as a new logo that joins tradition with modernity.

The best parties are the ones hosted by Drunken Lion Soundsystem. I don't remember a thing. The best parties are always the small ones in the park when it's summer. With my friends and good food and drinks. Too bad this year's summer didn't give us much opportunity to have them.

Denise van Leeuwen

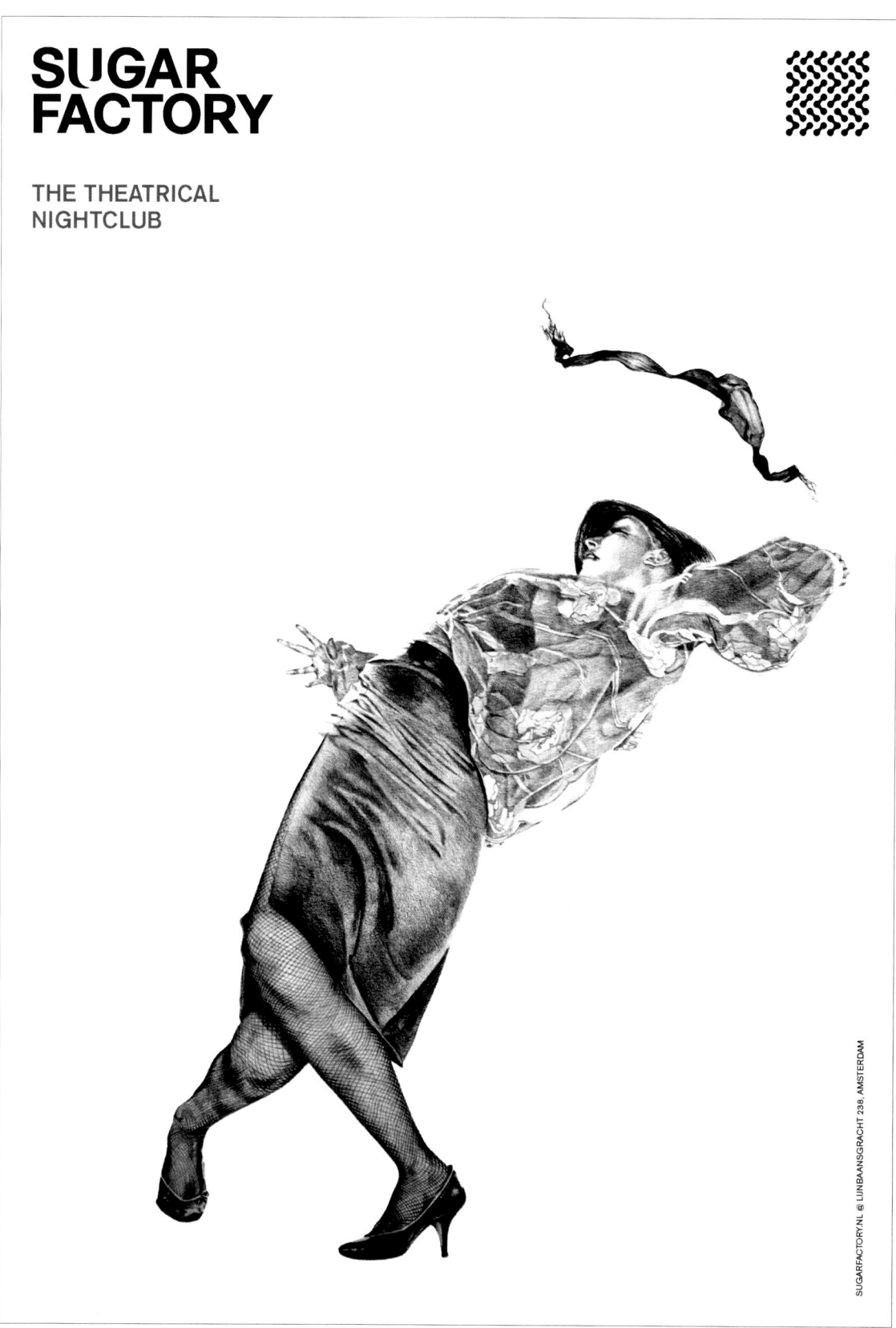

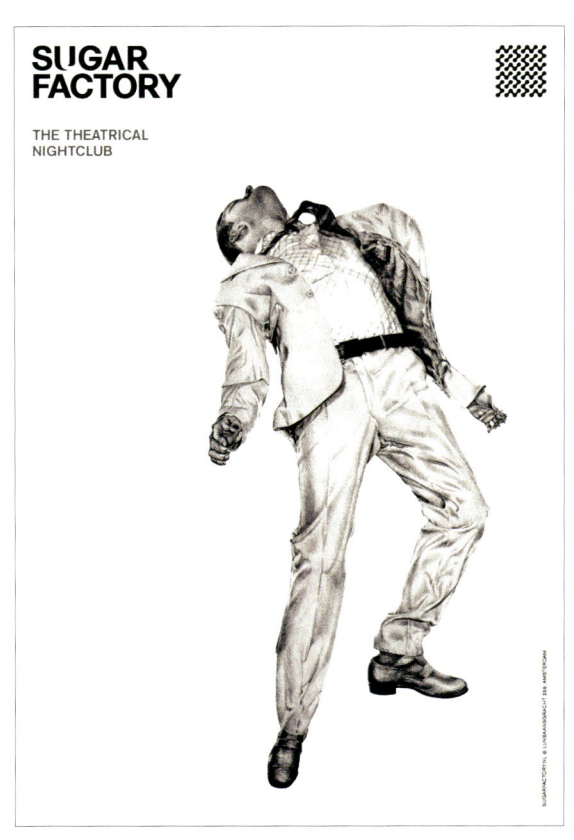

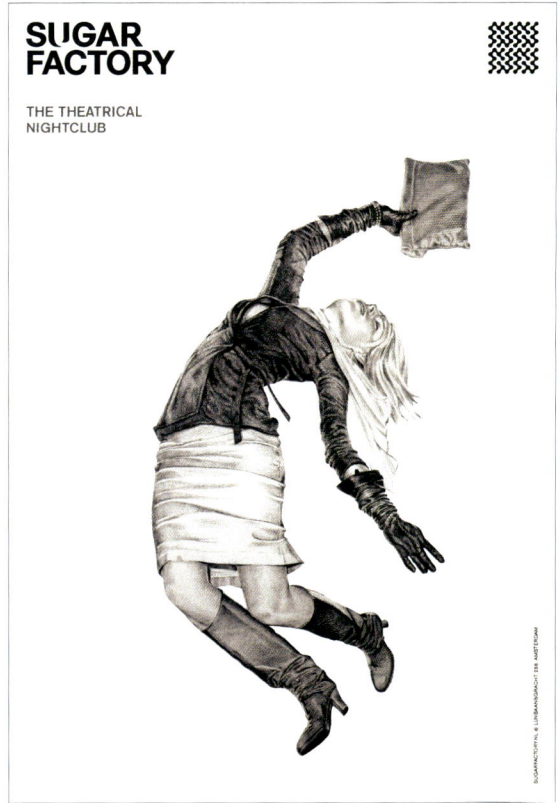

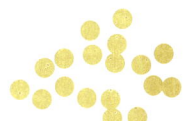

Sugar Factory campaign | 2006

Denise van Leeuwen/CJP
www.denise.dds.nl

Sugar Factory is a disco and also a performance theater. The company, inspired by the work of Robert Longo, enhances this double characteristic with drawings of people in movement, about to fall over. All illustrations have been done in pencil.

Hollywood, 1968, at Blake Edwards's house, really fun!

Grégoire Romanet

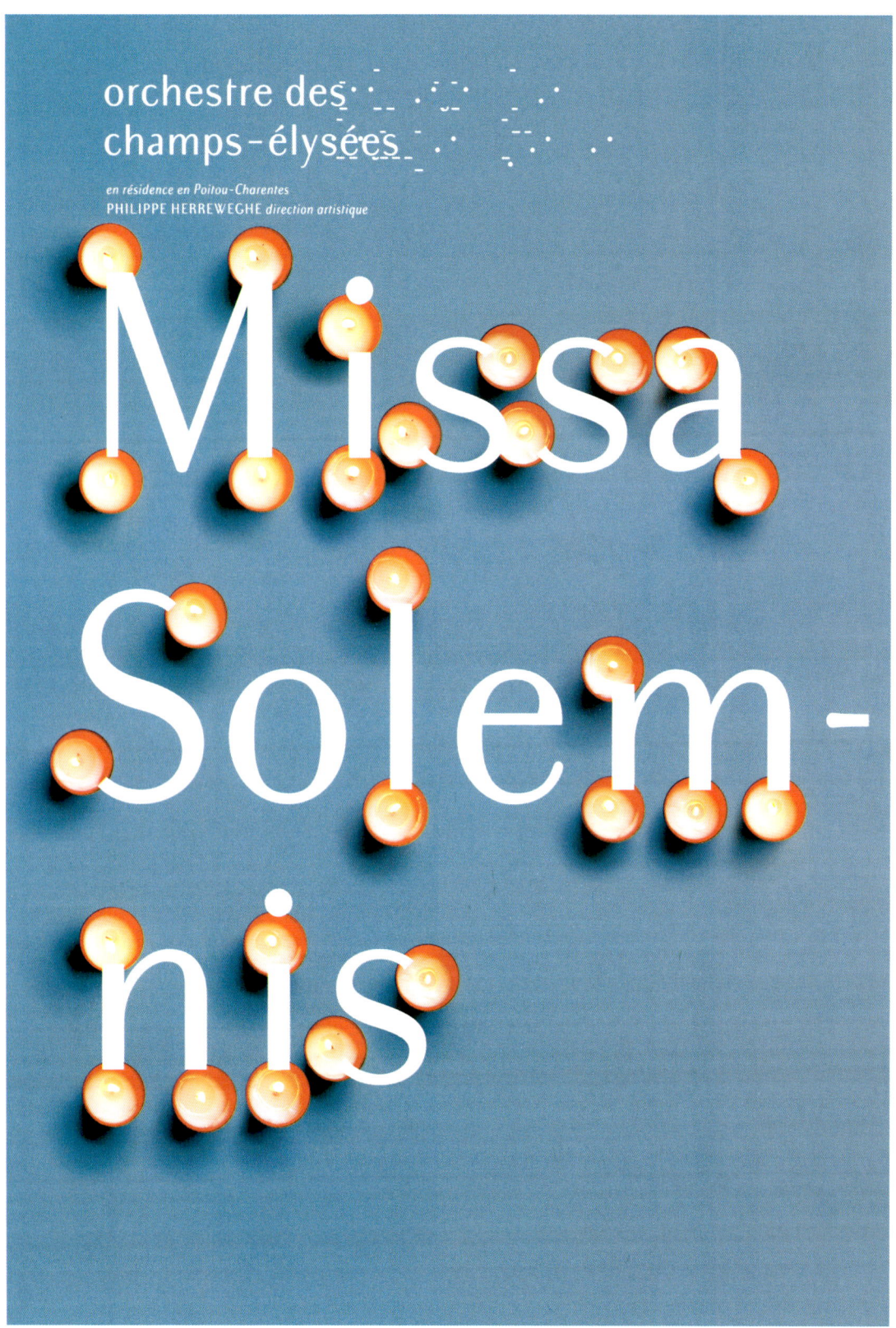

27 janvier 2004 à 20 h, Théâtre Mogador

orchestre des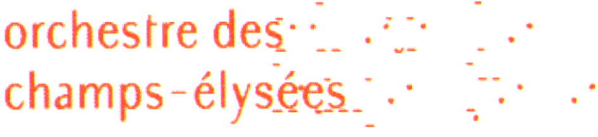
champs-élysées

en résidence en Poitou-Charentes
PHILIPPE HERREWEGHE direction artistique

Missa Solemnis

LUDWIG VAN BEETHOVEN

LETIZIA SCHERRER, MARIANNE BEATE KIELLAND
STEVE DAVISLIM, ALFRED REITER
COLLEGIUM VOCALE GENT
ORCHESTRE DES CHAMPS-ÉLYSÉES
PHILIPPE HERREWEGHE *direction*

Réservations : 0825 000 821 / FNAC, fnac.com
Théâtre Mogador - 25, rue de Mogador - 75009 Paris

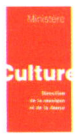 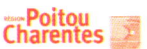 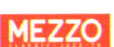 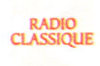 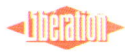

**Orchestre
des Champs-Élysées | 2003-2006**

**Grégoire Romanet, Pierre Bernard/
Atelier de création graphique
gregoire.romanet.free.fr**

The logo had to reflect Beethoven's *Missa Solemnis*, the composer's greatest work. Thus the typography becomes the expressive instrument of the orchestra's musicality: its base and ornaments vibrate over the writing line.

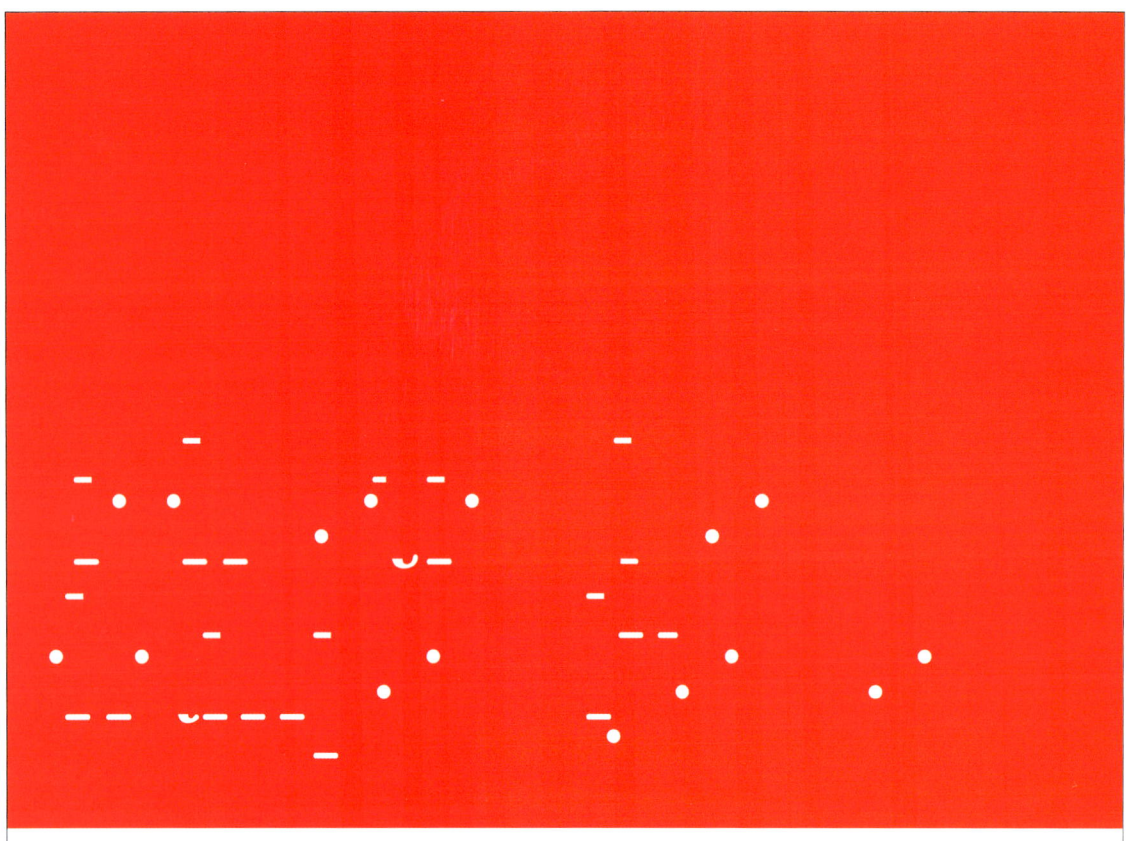

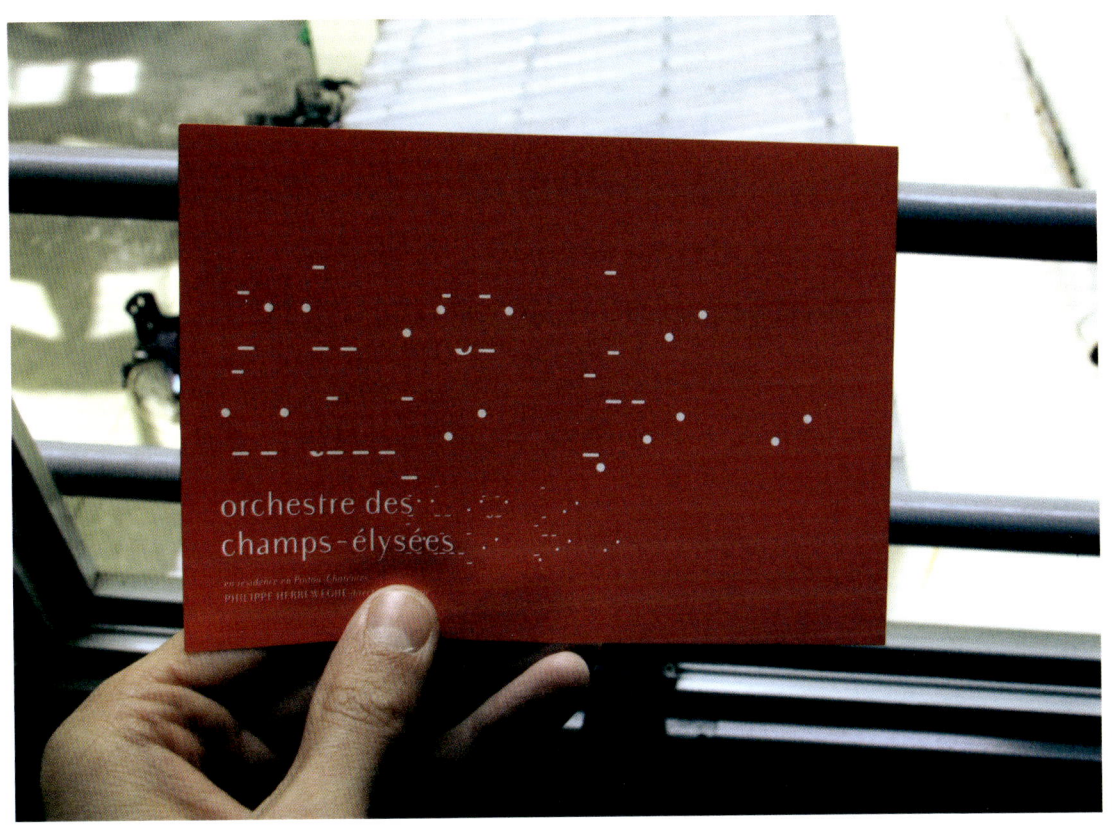
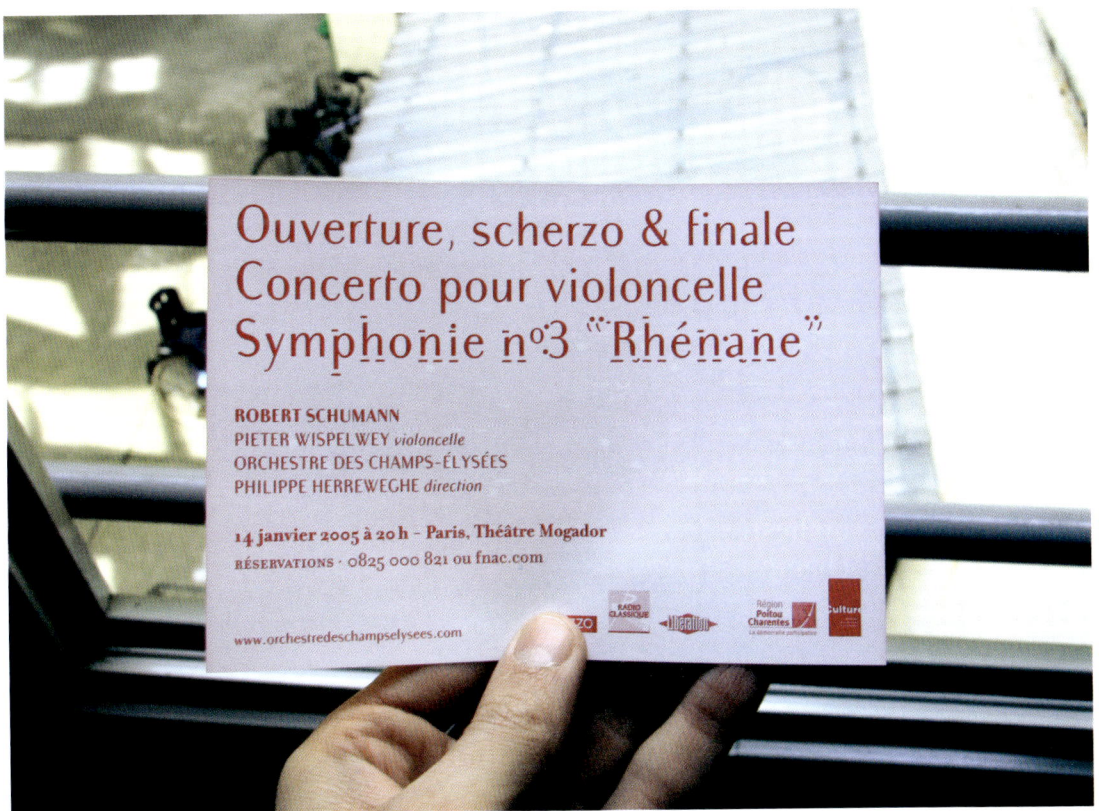

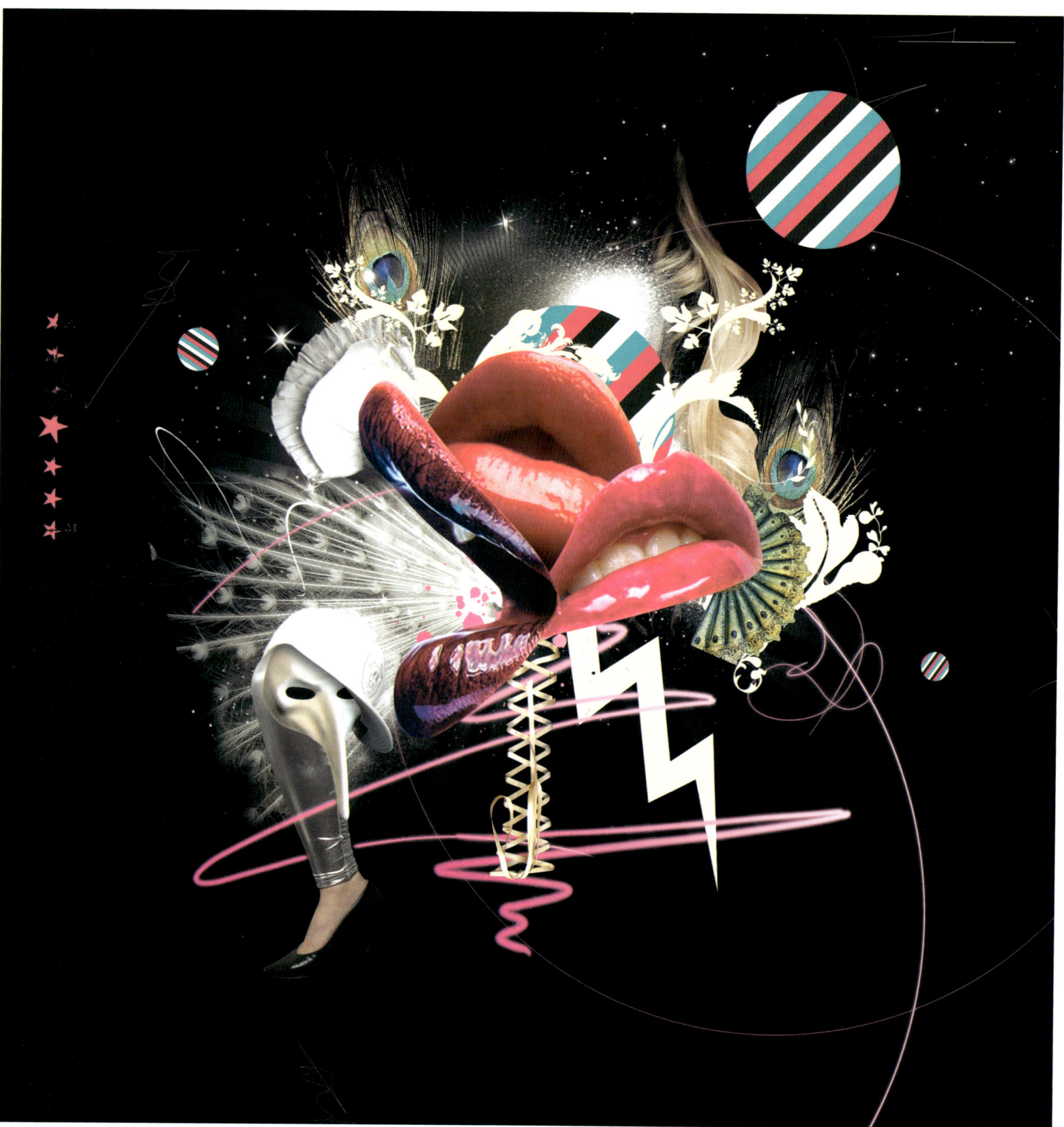

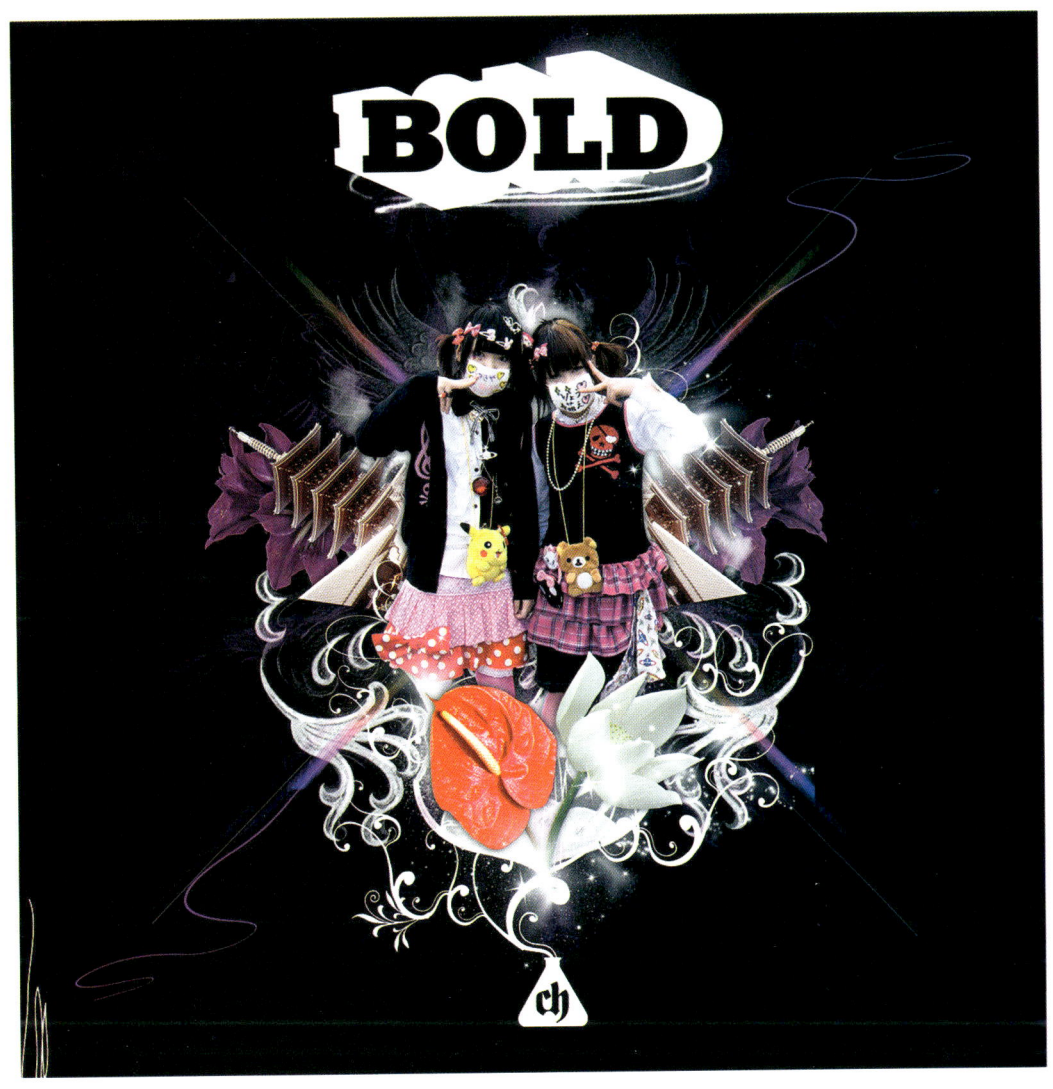

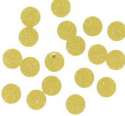

Bold | 2006

Teis Albers/Hypnoteis
www.hypnoteis.nl

From the different thematic proposals of the Bold parties, the illustration expands from the logo as a paradigmatic collage of different elements that connect and balance with use of color.

I've been to lots of parties, but the best are the ones I didn't expect to be. To me the best parties are the ones I'm at with nice friends and have a good time. It doesn't matter if this is at a house party, concert or just in a bar. I love to be at rock concerts, electro dance club night or a sweating hiphop party, as long as there's a good vibe and nice tunes!

Teis Albers

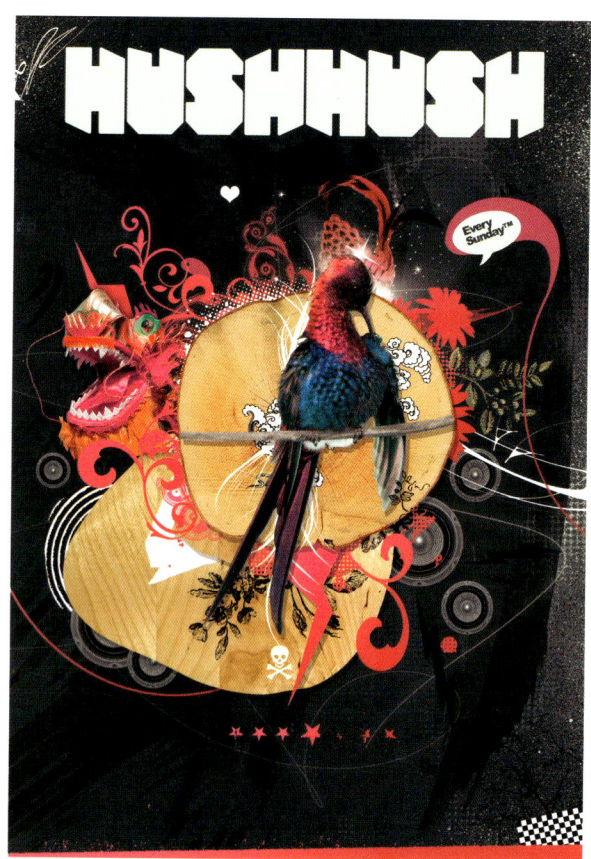
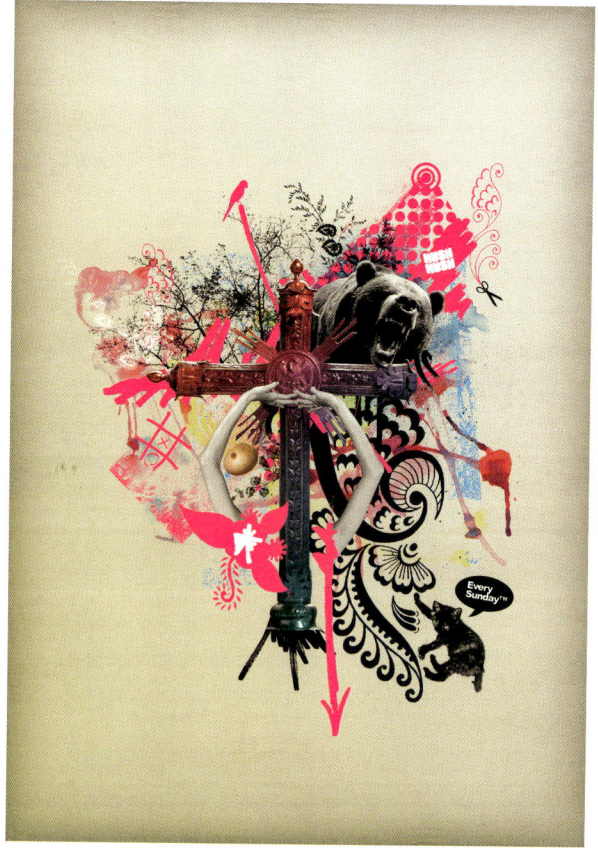
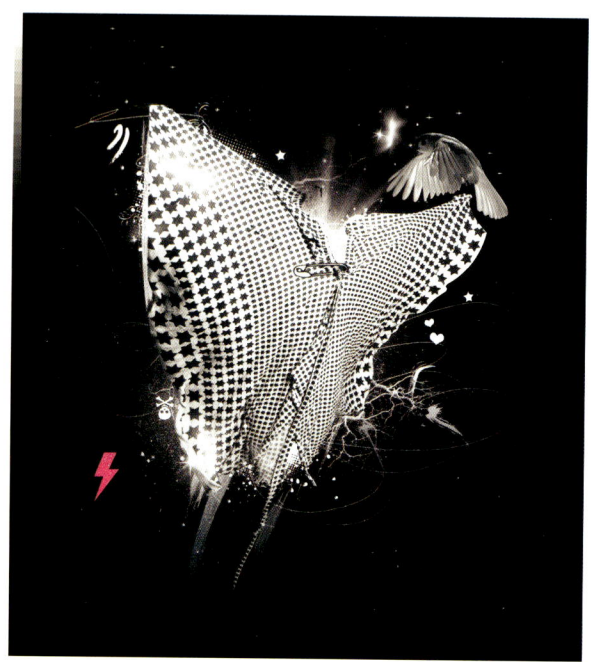
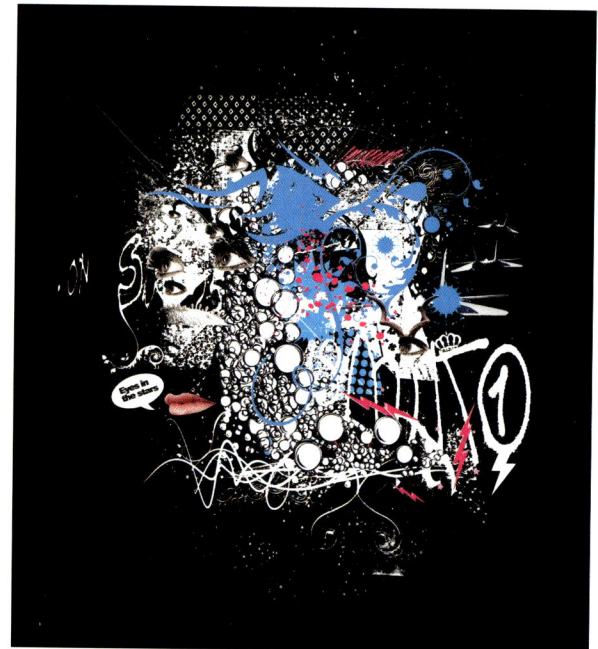

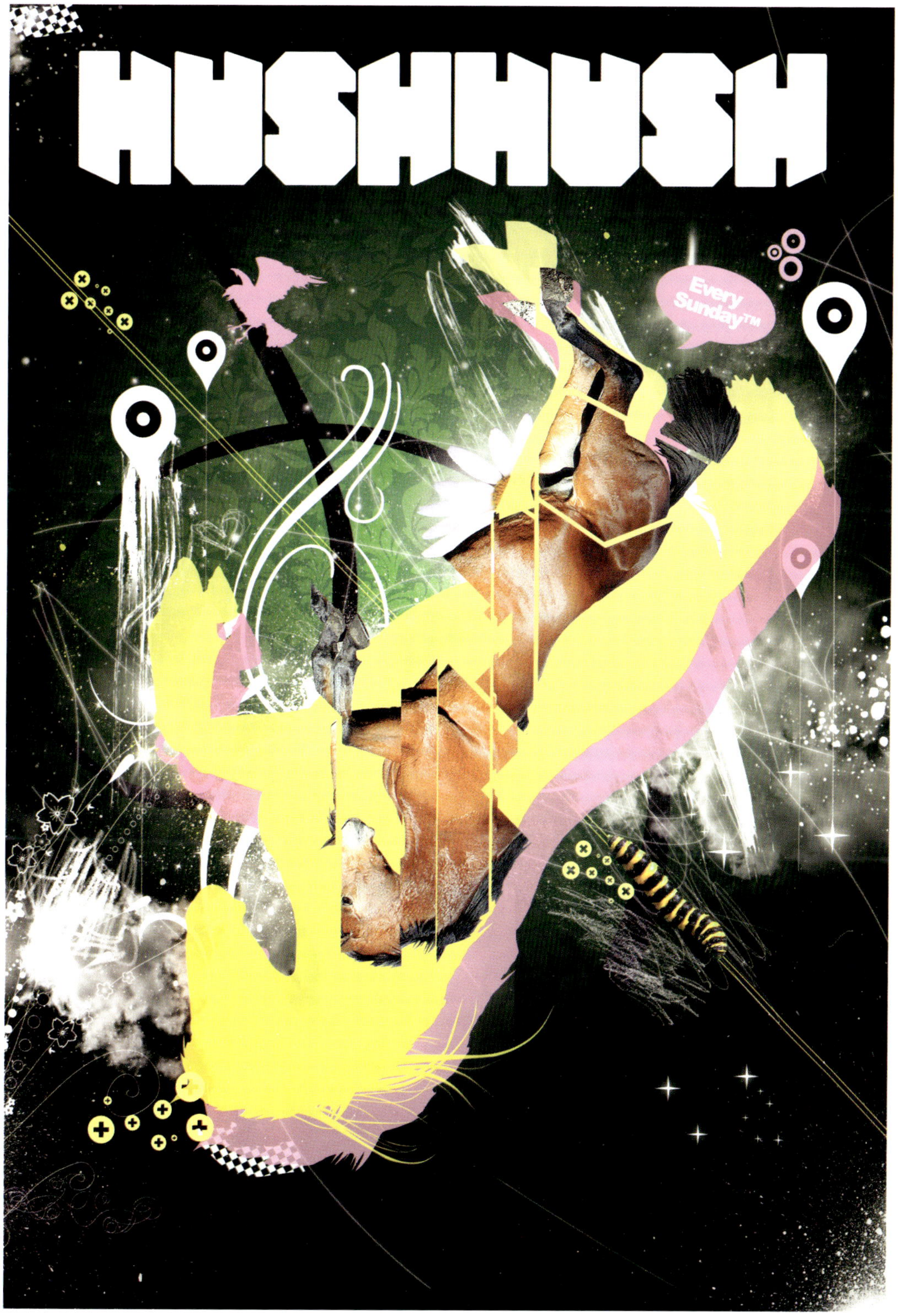

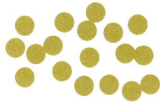

Hush Hush | 2006

Teis Albers/Hypnoteis
www.hypnoteis.nl

The only requirement of the flyer was that it featured the date of the Hush Hush parties, each Sunday. The vectorial treatment of the drawing and the manipulation of the images of the animals are framed within this open requirement.

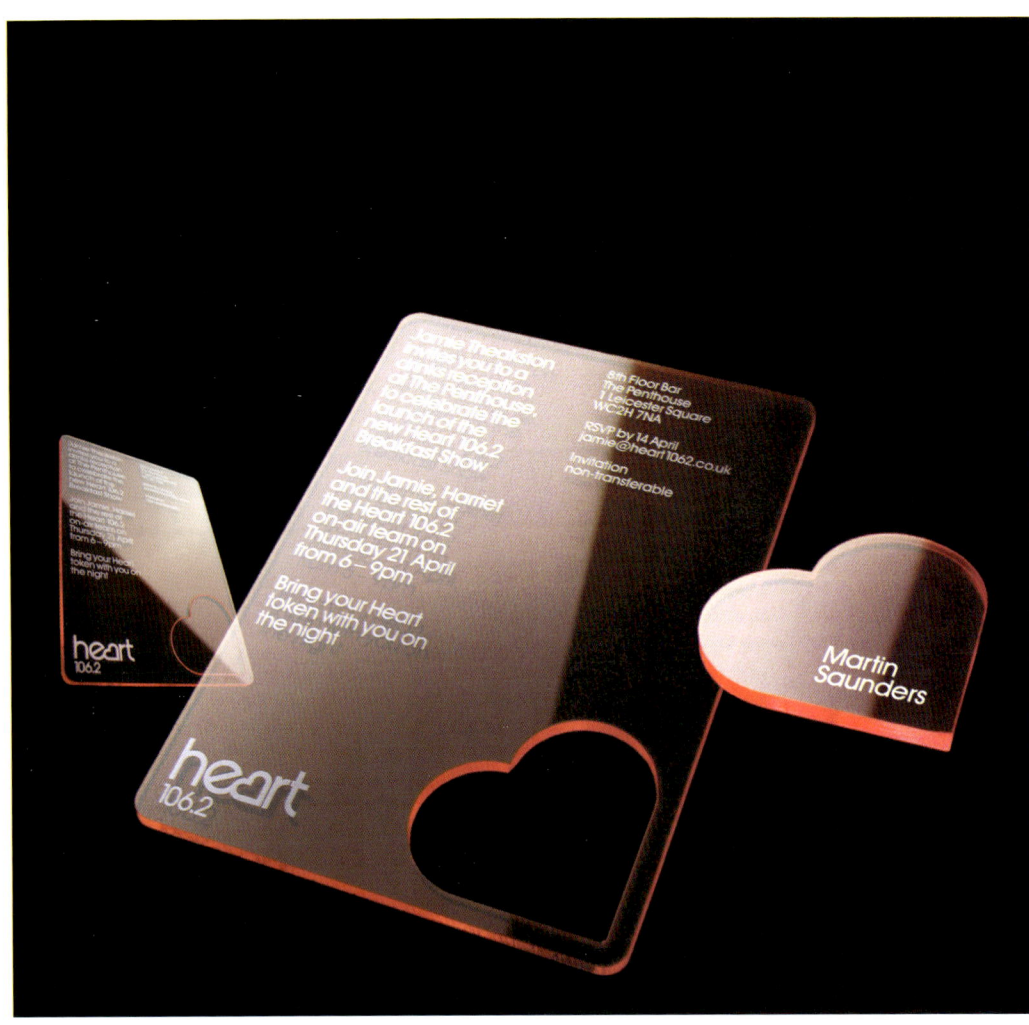

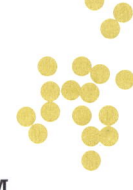

Jamie Theakston Heart FM breakfast show launch party | 2005

BB/Saunders
www.bbsaunders.com

The guests had to take off the heart shape, which functioned as a ticket to the party. As the invitations were taken in, they were put in a bowl, which when full of hearts, transformed into a decorative object.

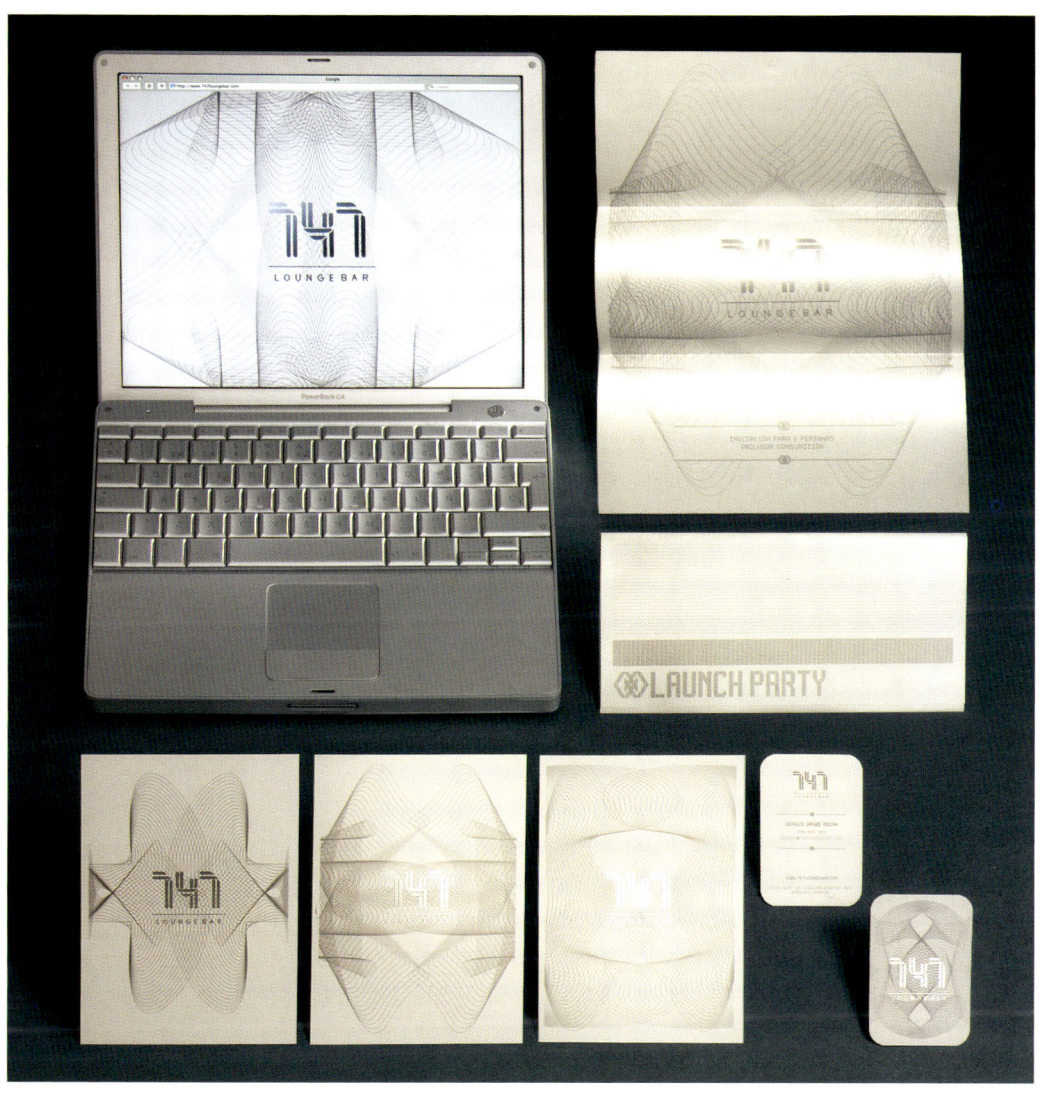

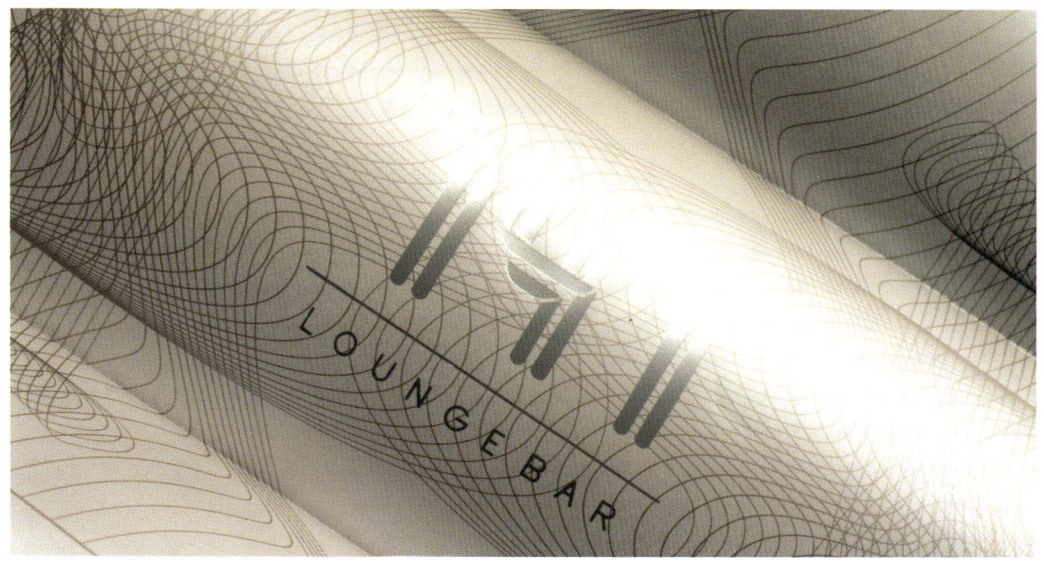

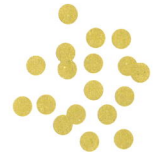

747 Lounge Bar | 2006

Sergio del Puerto/Serial Cut
www.serialcut.com

The 747 is a bar for pilots and air hosts and hostesses close to the airport of Madrid. The typography, the silver shine and the pearly white paper give the piece a technological feel, as well as a modern, sober and refined one.

This should be Cindy Gallop's private B-Day party. I can hardly remember anything except for: half-naked male models, crazy dancing, tons of little snacks, me waking up on my kitchen floor at six a.m.

Tiziana Haug

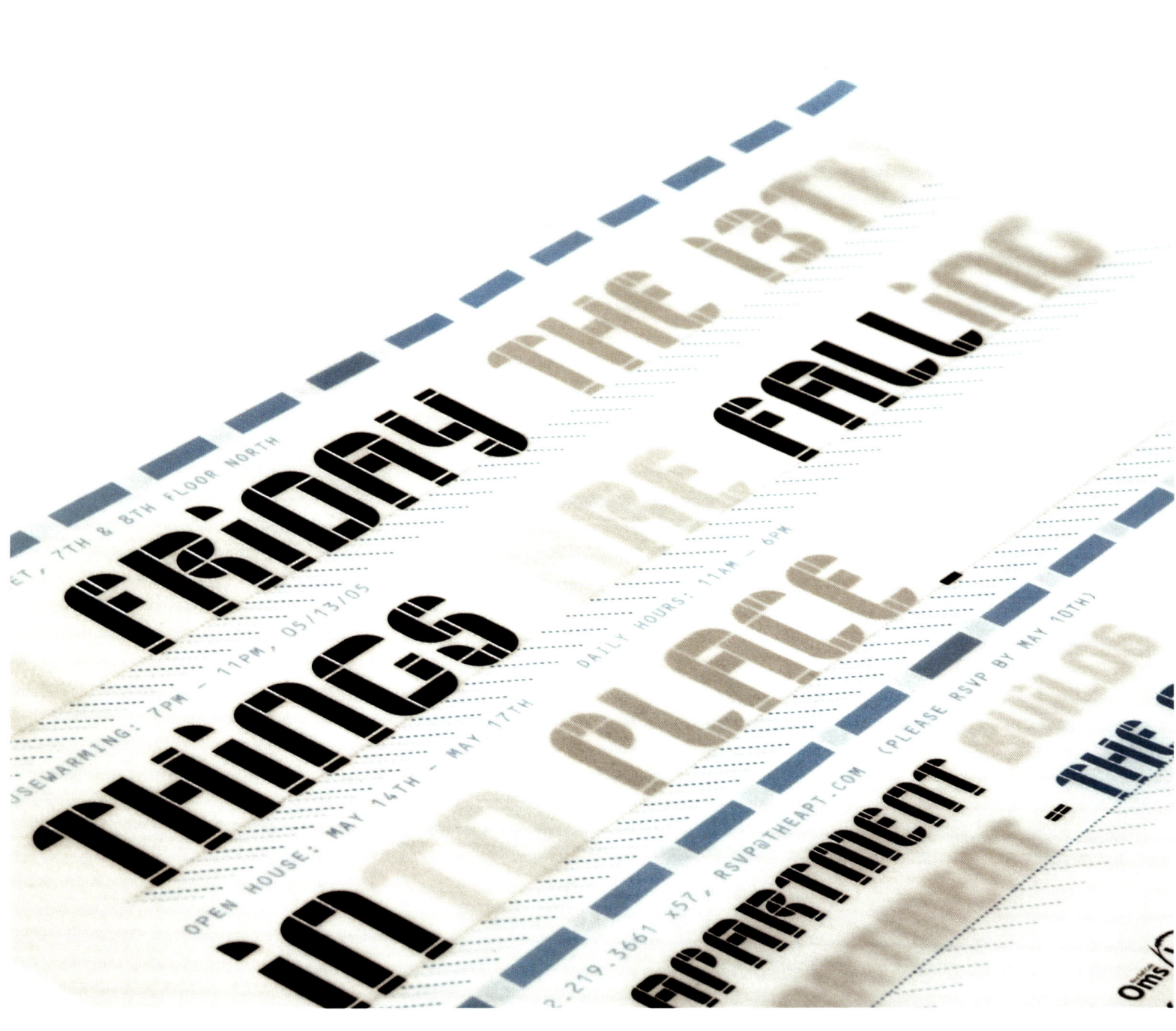

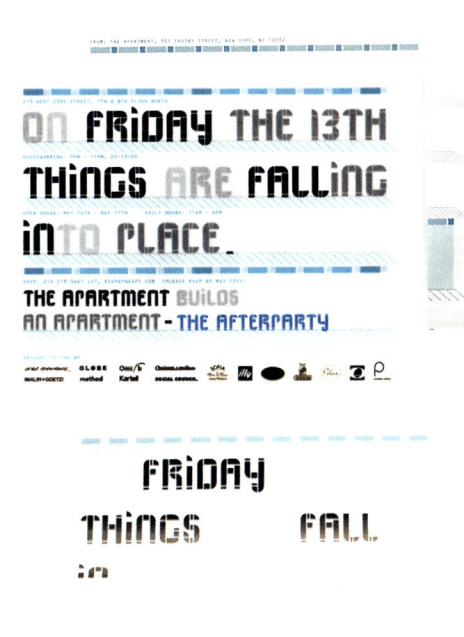
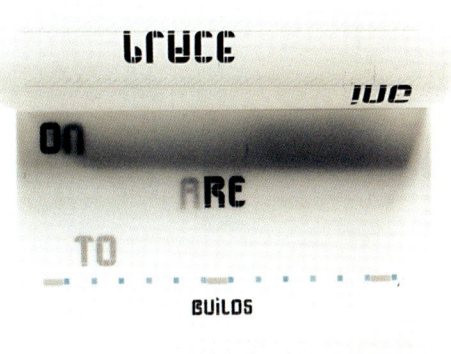
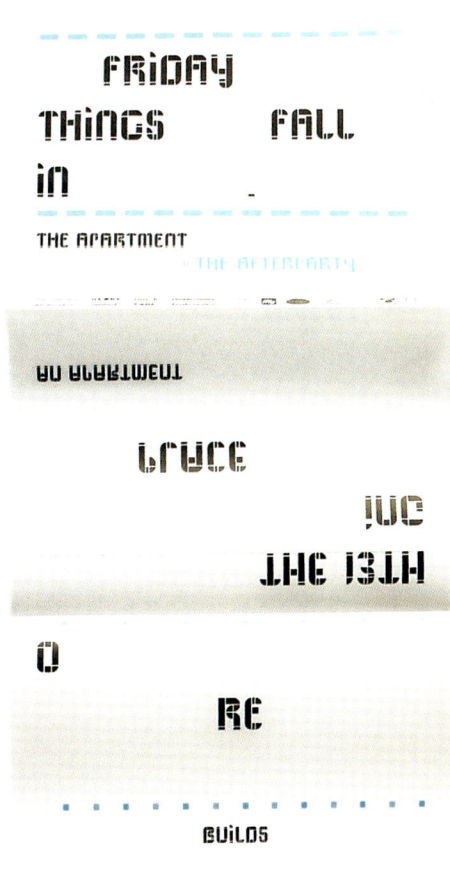
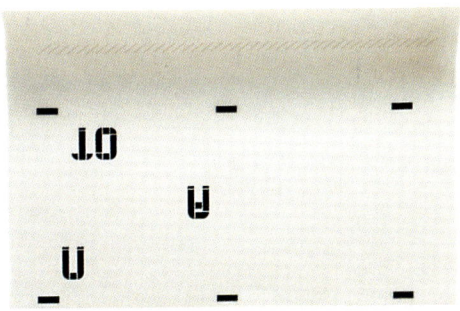
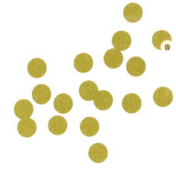

ICFF invitation | 2005

Tiziana Haug/The Apartment
www.inthehabit.com

The party celebrated the transformation of the basketball court of the YMCA into a luxurious loft. The invitation unfolds in four panels, one for each stage of the construction. Once the panels are lined up, all the information can be read.

Maybe the one we had in our old office facilities that resulted in us getting thrown out by the owner of the building, and led us to find our new and brilliant premises.

Grandpeople

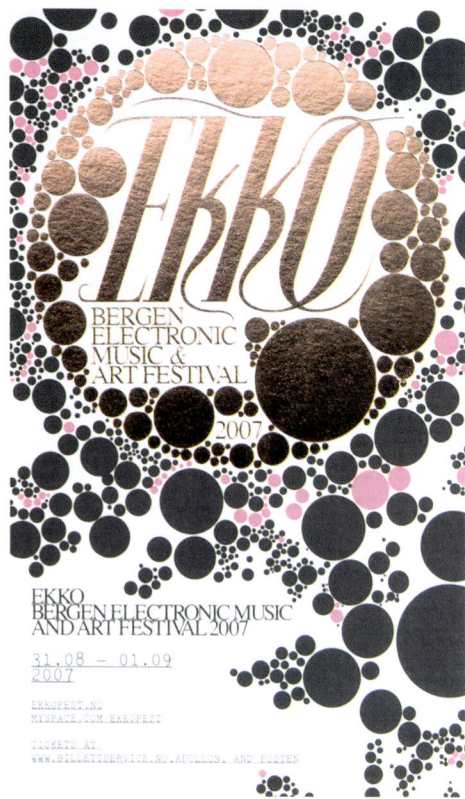
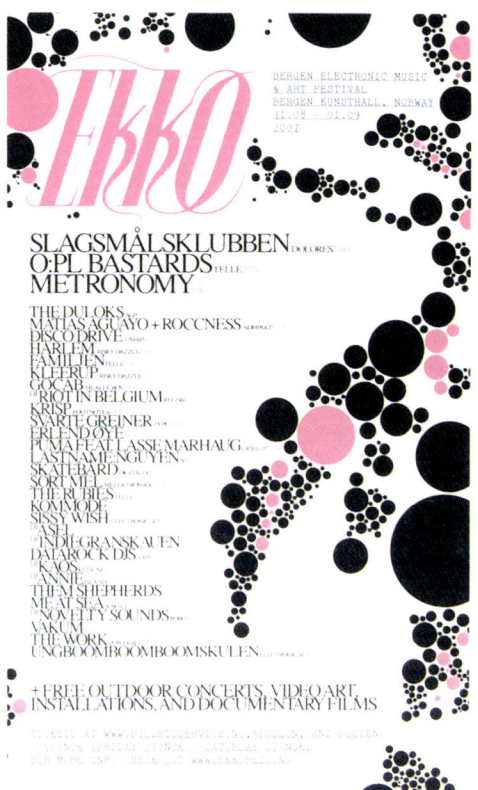
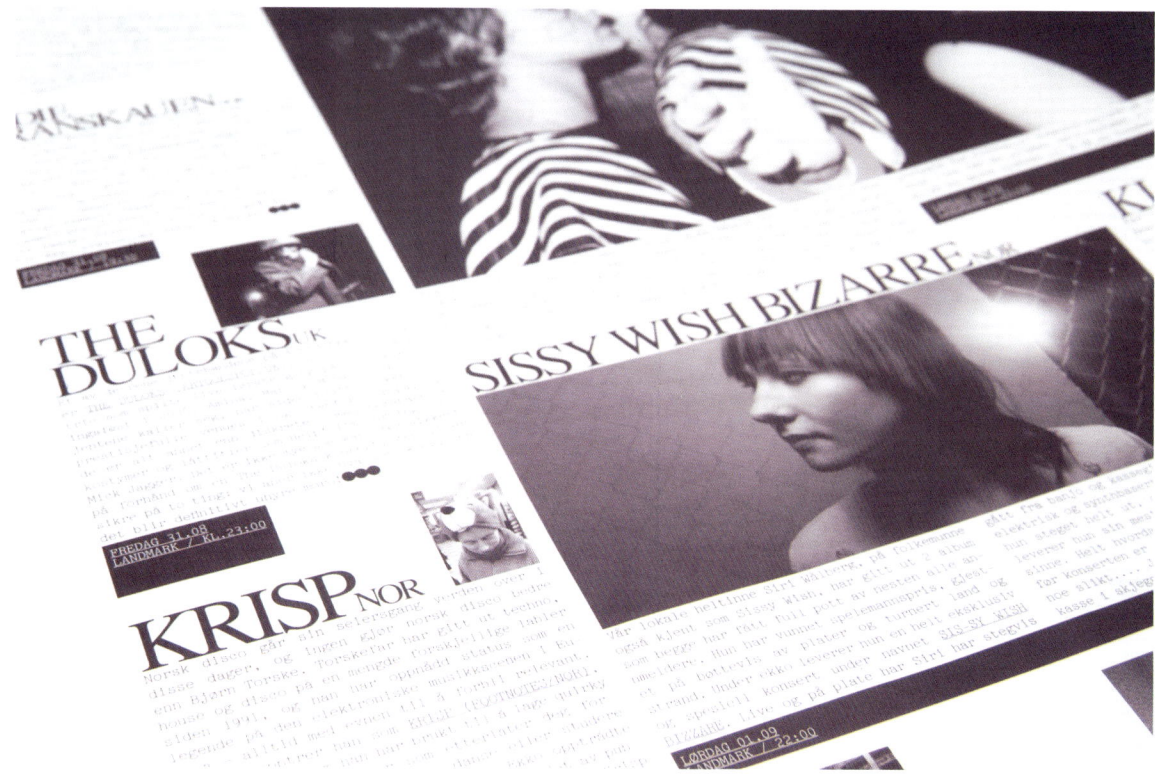

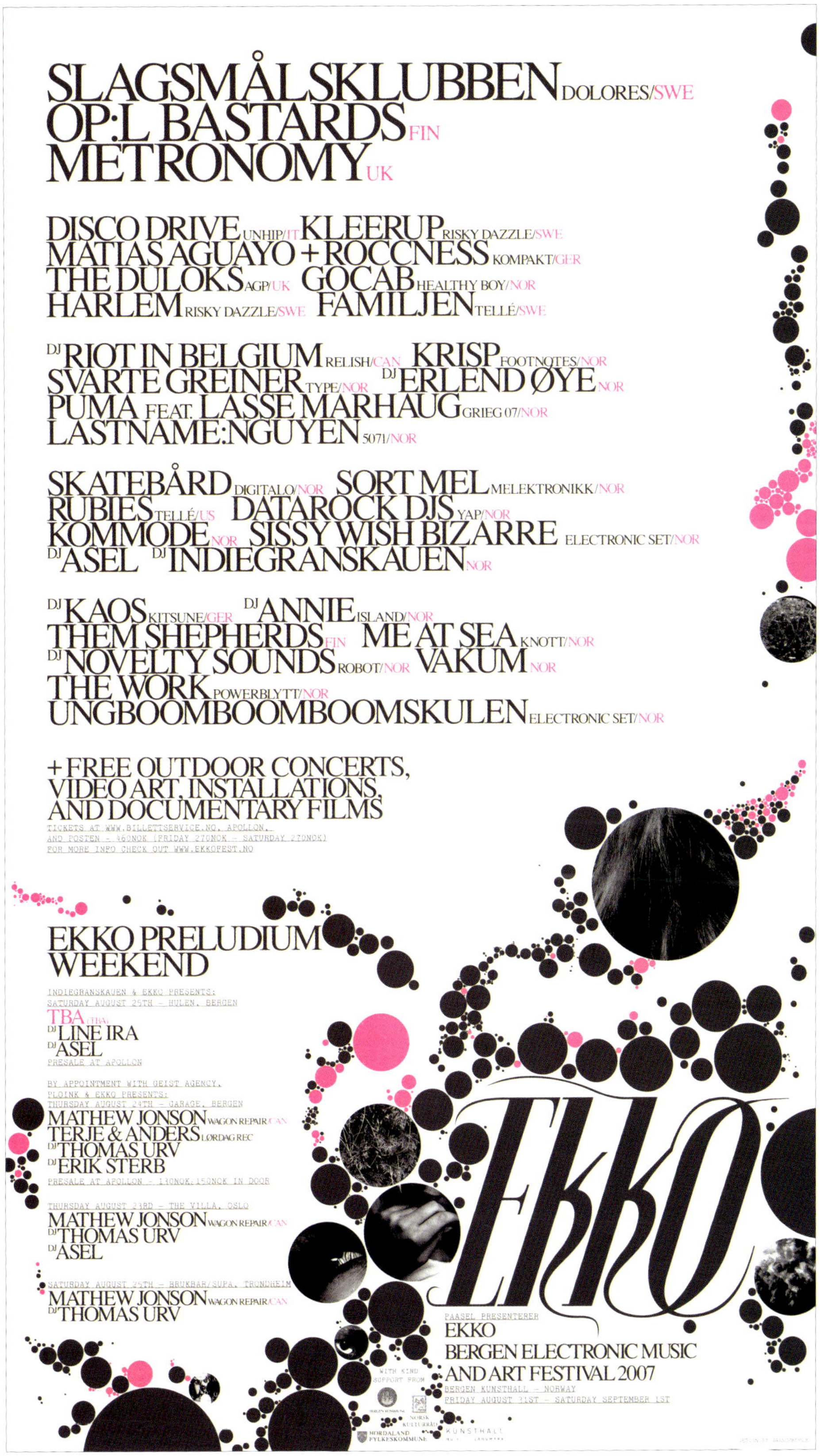

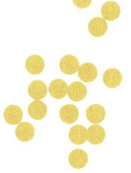

Ekko Festival | 2007

Grandpeople
www.grandpeople.org

Every year, Grandpeople designs the image of this electronic music festival. On this occasion simplicity was the key, carried out through circles and a simple typography. By not using a grid, the result moves between being strict and unsure.

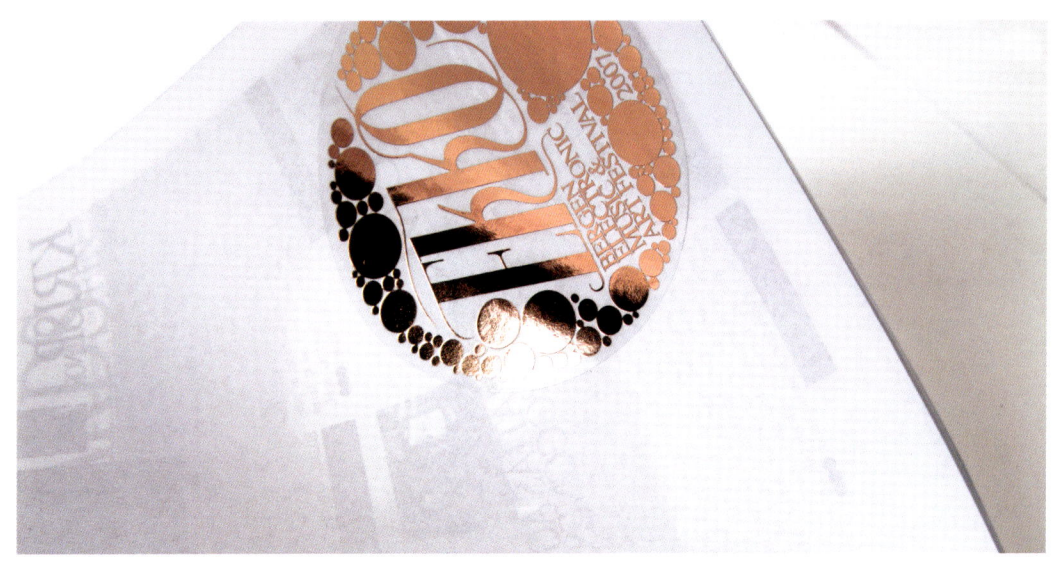

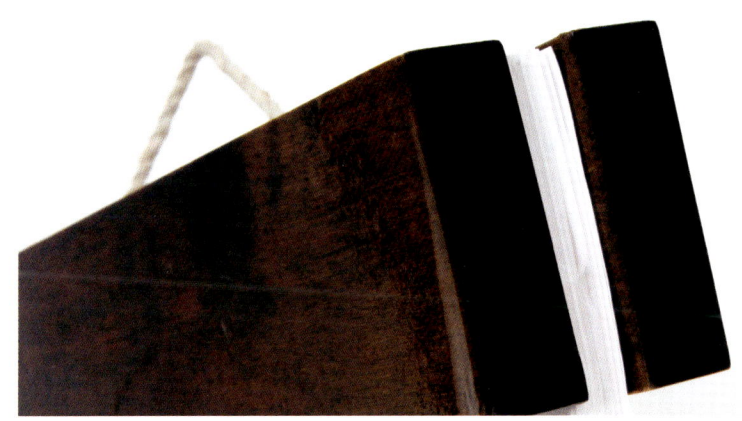

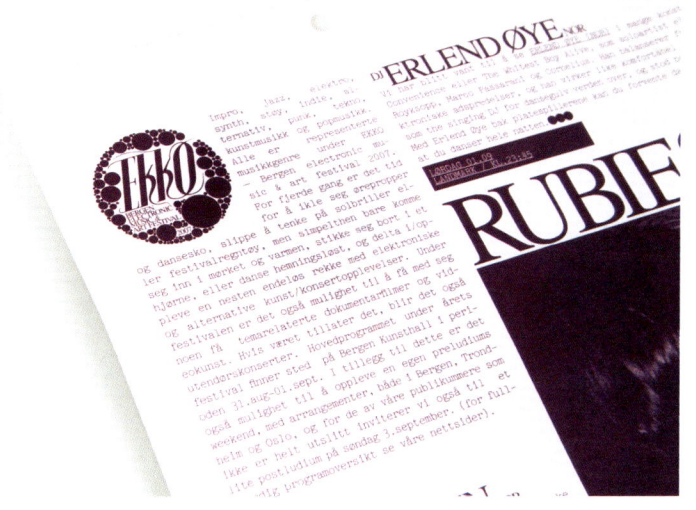

Care to join us?

Pamphlets and brochures for exhibitions, conferences, and theater productions

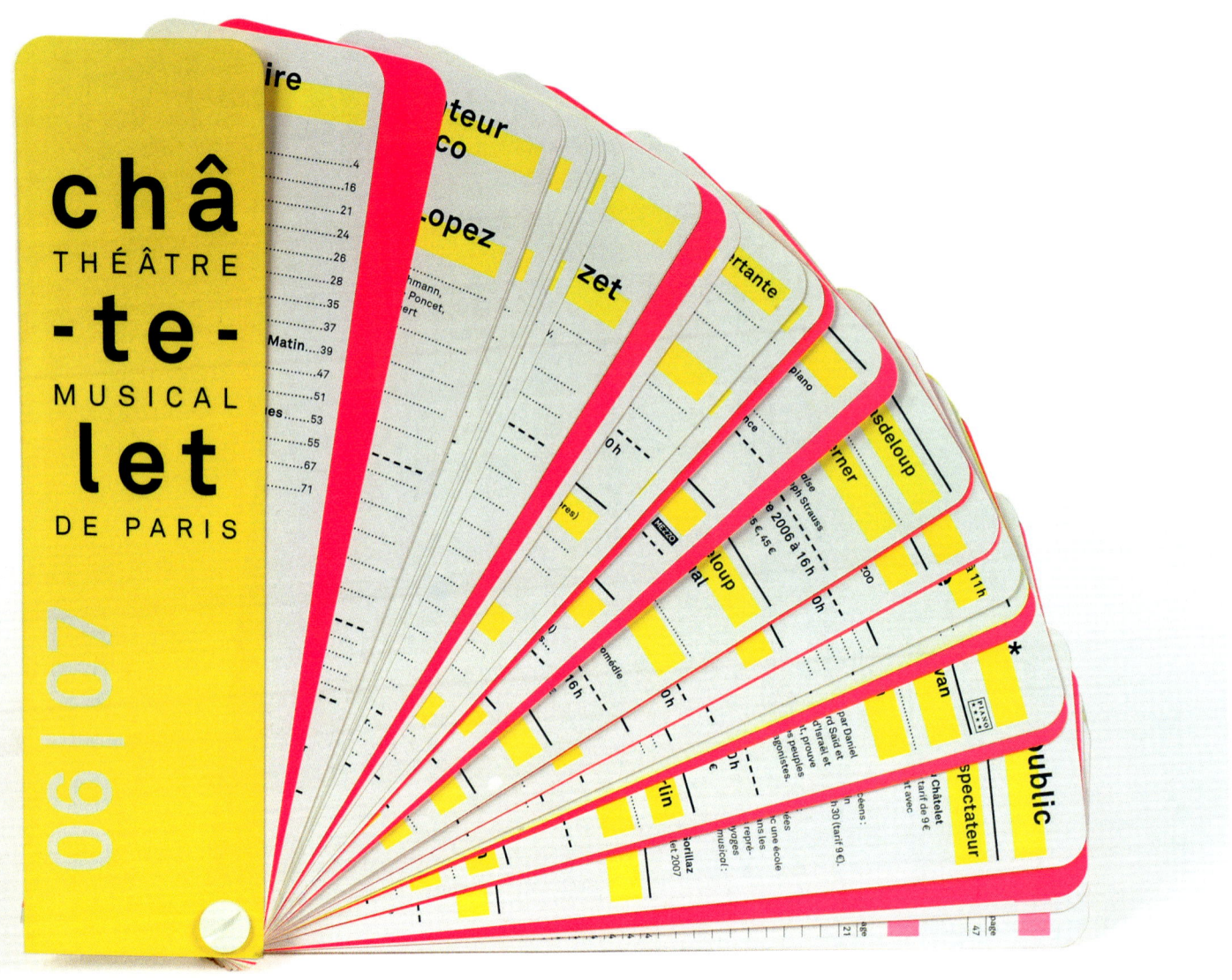

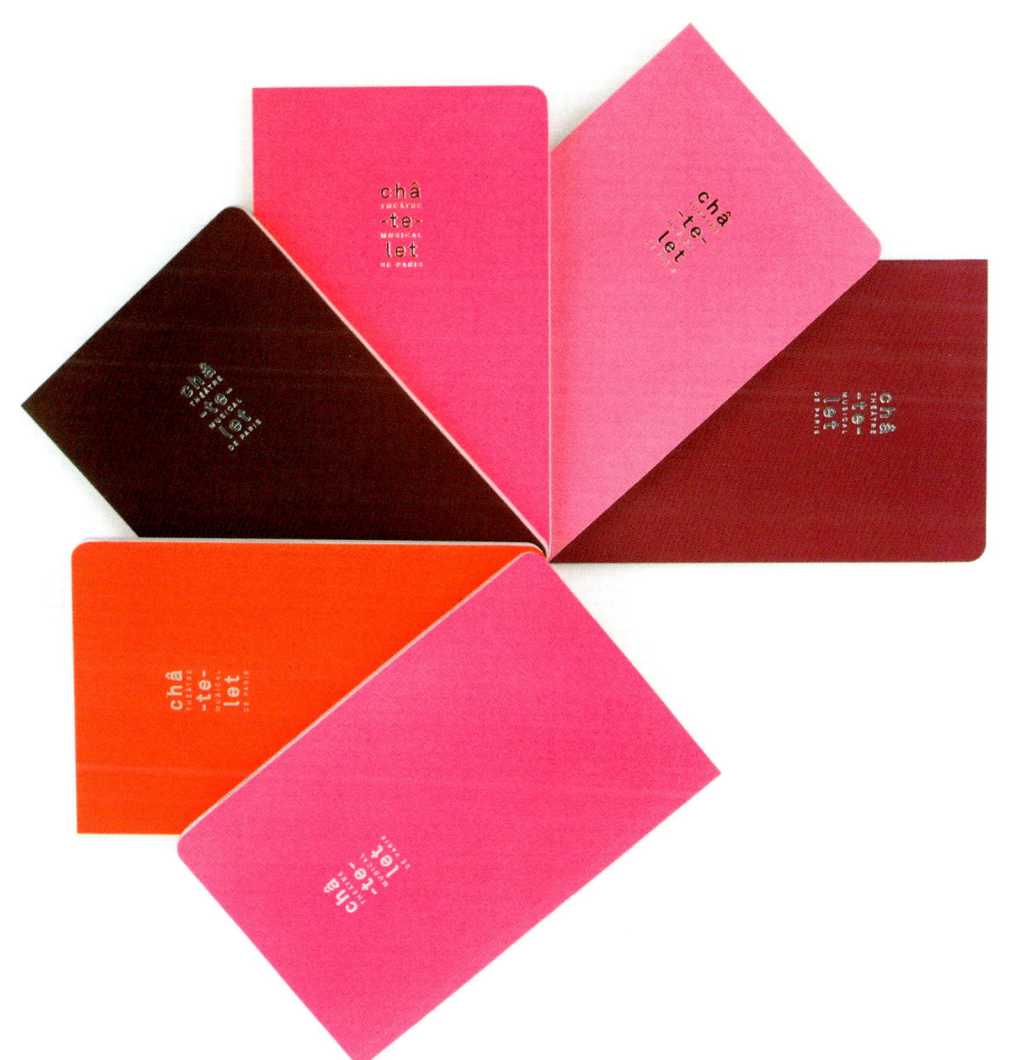

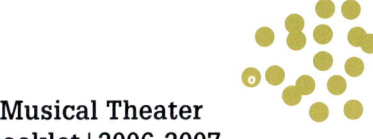

**Châtelet Musical Theater
of Paris booklet | 2006-2007**

Studio Philippe Apeloig
www.apeloig.com

Two concepts are combined: visibility and playfulness. The pieces can be identified by the different shades of pink of the programs, while the diversity of the billboard is reflected in the different possible combinations of the Pantone book.

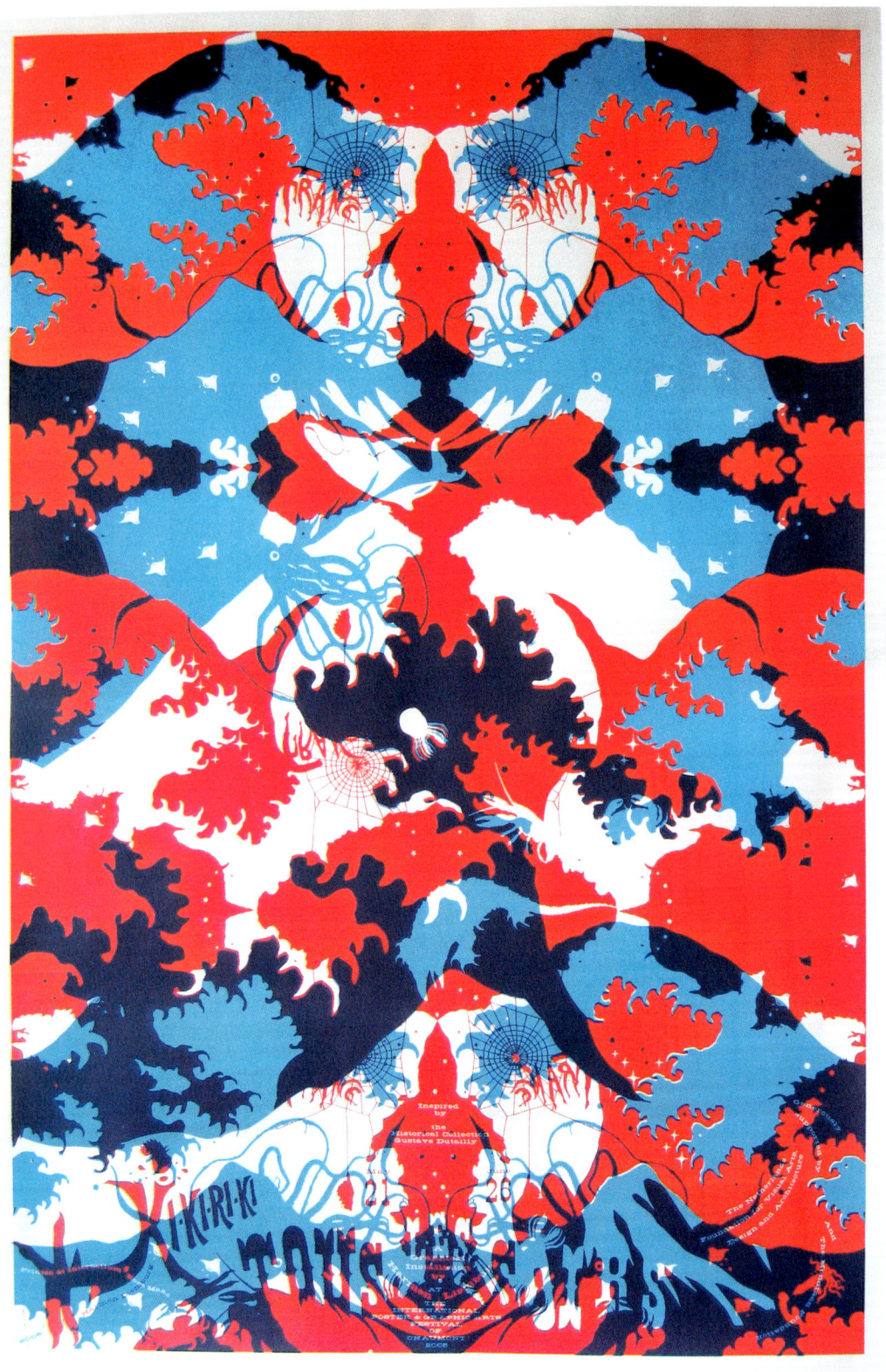

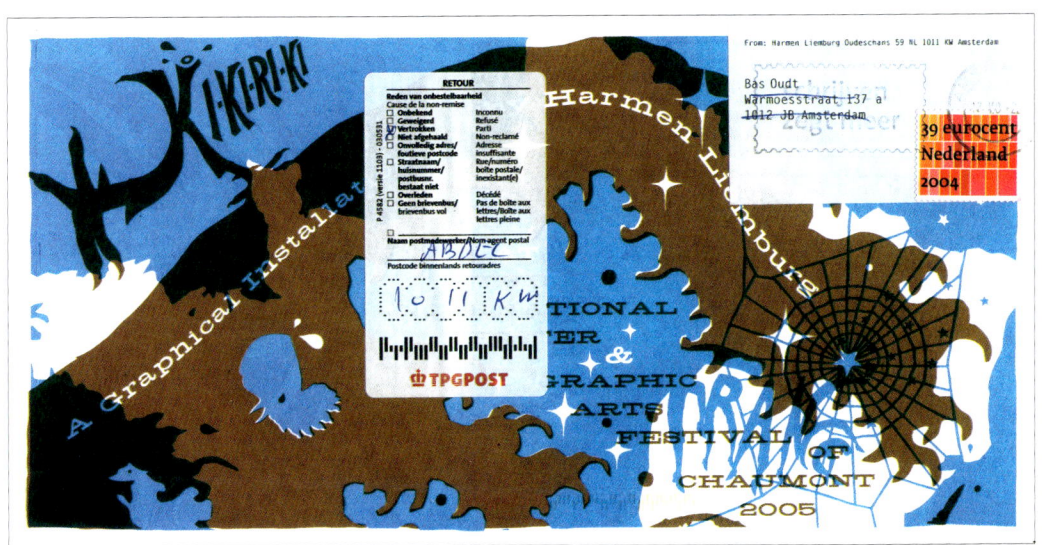

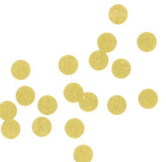

Ki ki ri ki
Tous Les Soirs | 2005

Harmen Liemburg, Kees Maas
www.harmenliemburg.nl

The poster promotes the exhibition at the International Posters and Graphic Arts Festival of Chaumont. The composition acts as a hypertext: it mixes images from the collection of Gustave Dutailly with new graphic elements.

These days I hardly ever dance anymore, but last summer, at my friend Richard's birthday party, a small group of die hards lingered on after all the folks with kids had long left. Of course we got very drunk, somebody played weird old records, and we danced and danced and danced. I think the best thing is when all of a sudden you realize it's early in the morning.

Harmen Liemburg

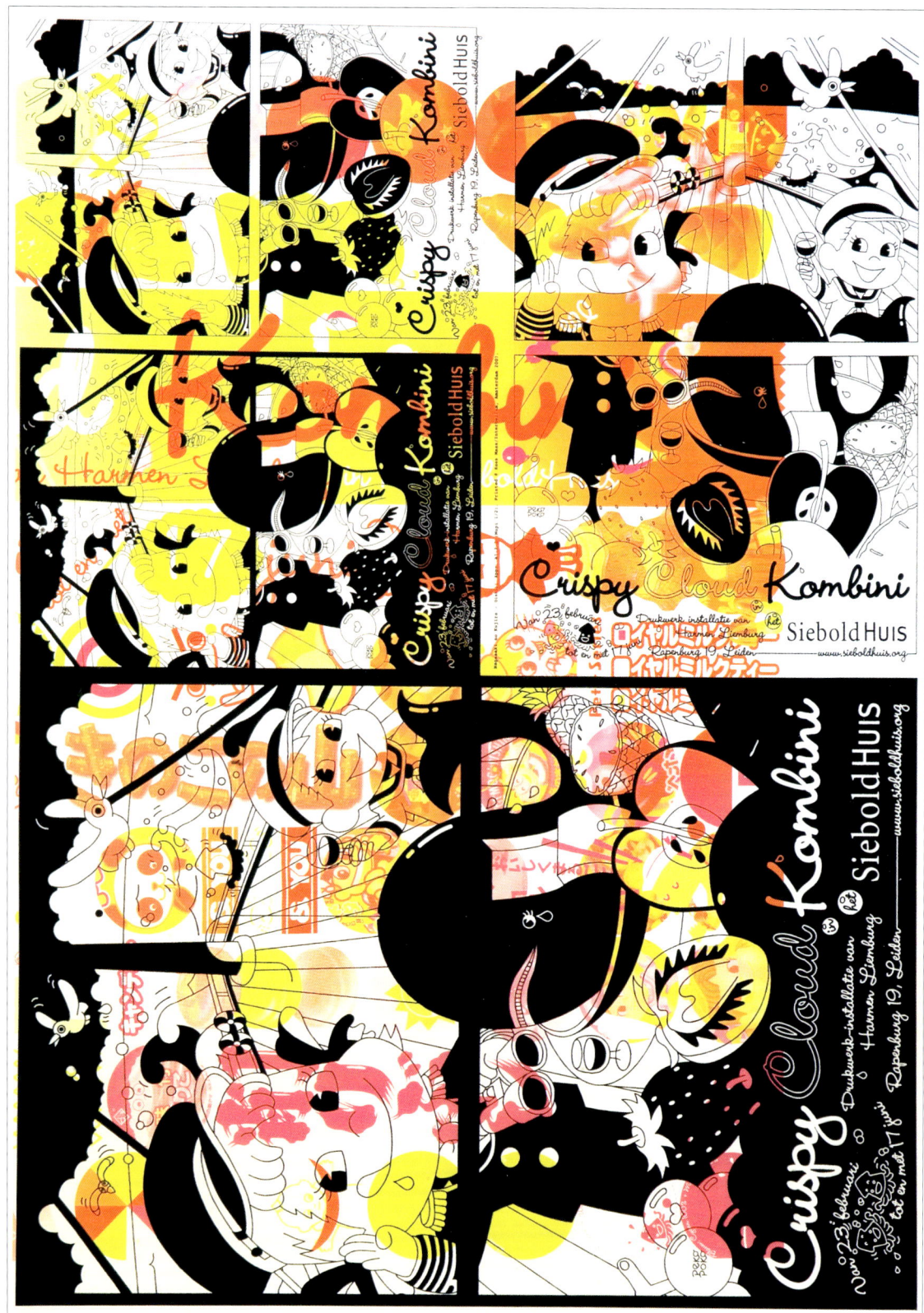

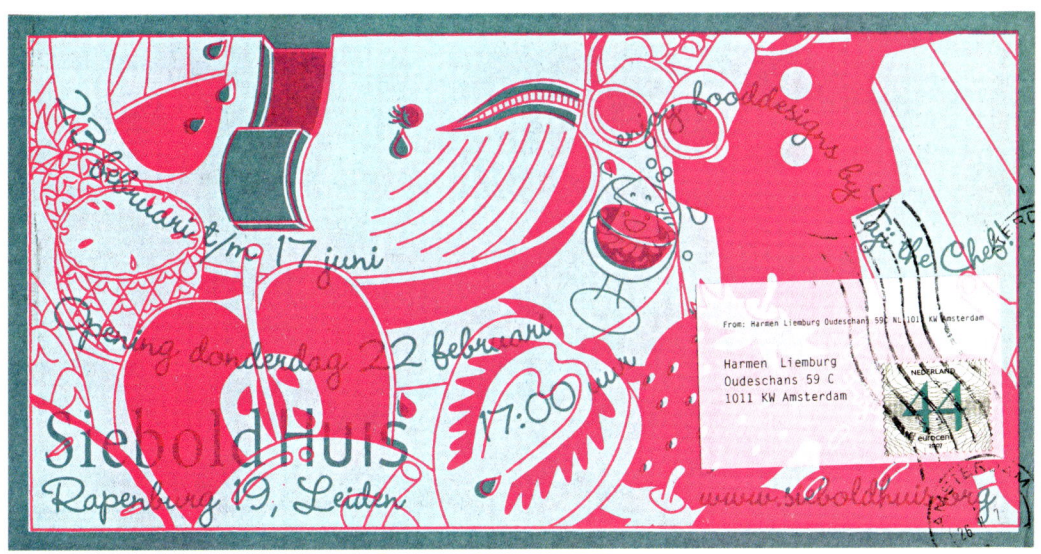

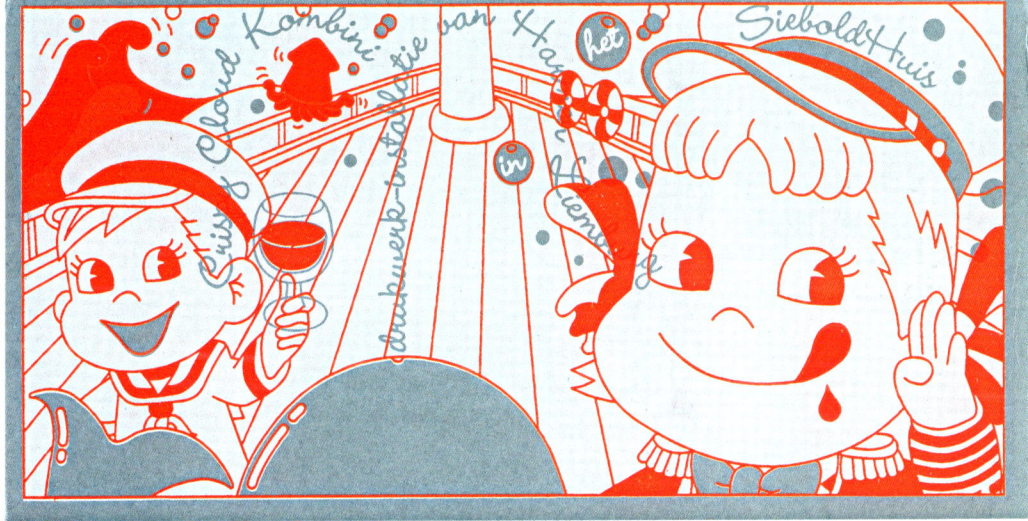

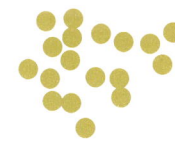

Crispy Cloud Kombini | 2007

Harmen Liemburg, Kees Maas
www.harmenliemburg.nl

The exhibition connected the historic collection of SieboldHuis with contemporary Japanese culture. To resolve the complexity of the message, Japanese sweet wrappers were used, as well as the combination of radically different typographies.

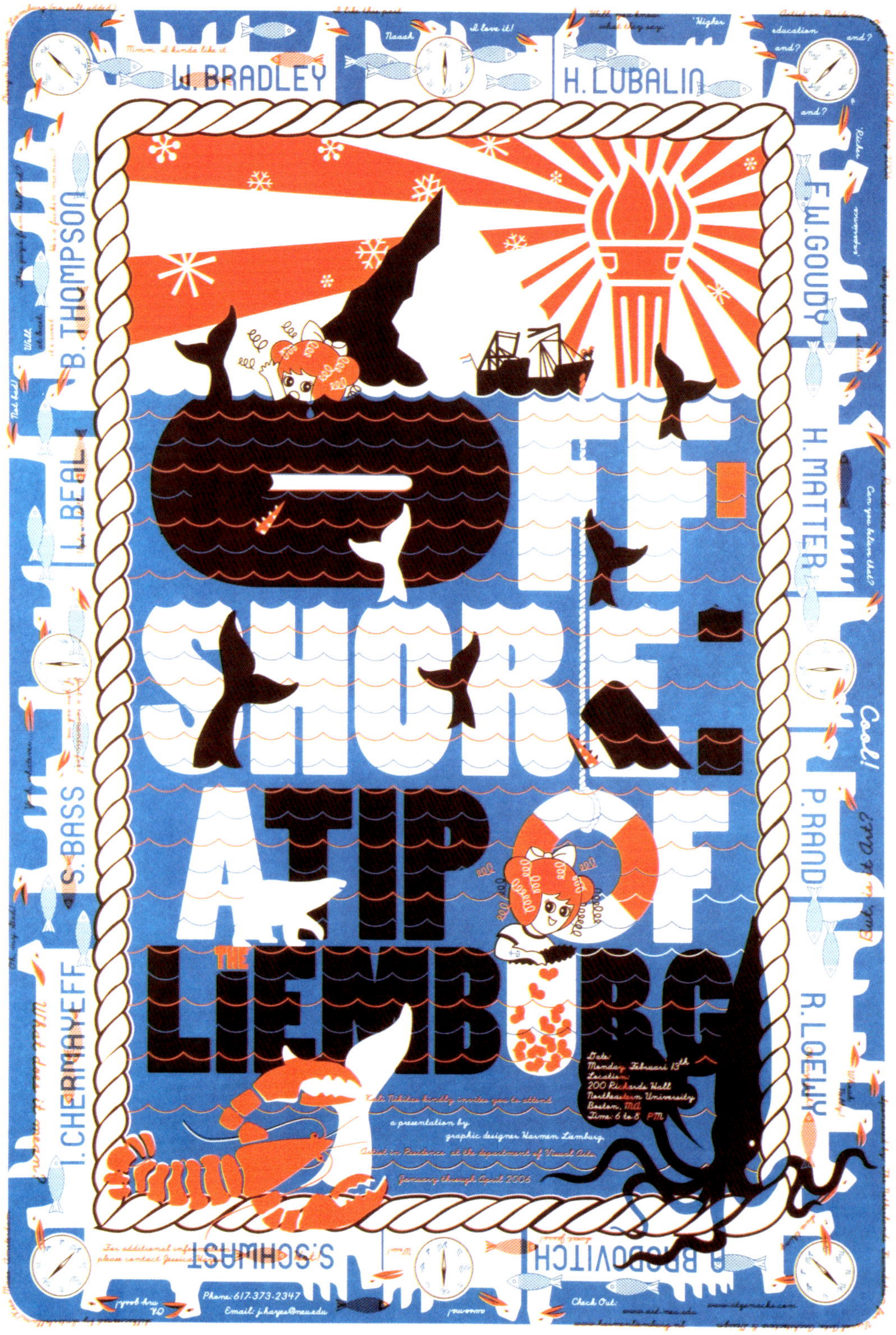

Offshore | 2006

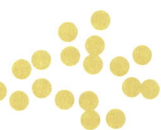

Harmen Liemburg, Kees Maas
www.harmenliemburg.nl

To promote one of their conferences, Liemburg showed a collection of everything that one could find on the coasts of Massachusetts: a whale, lobsters, a flock of seagulls and the logo of the university where the talk was to take place, transformed into a lighthouse.

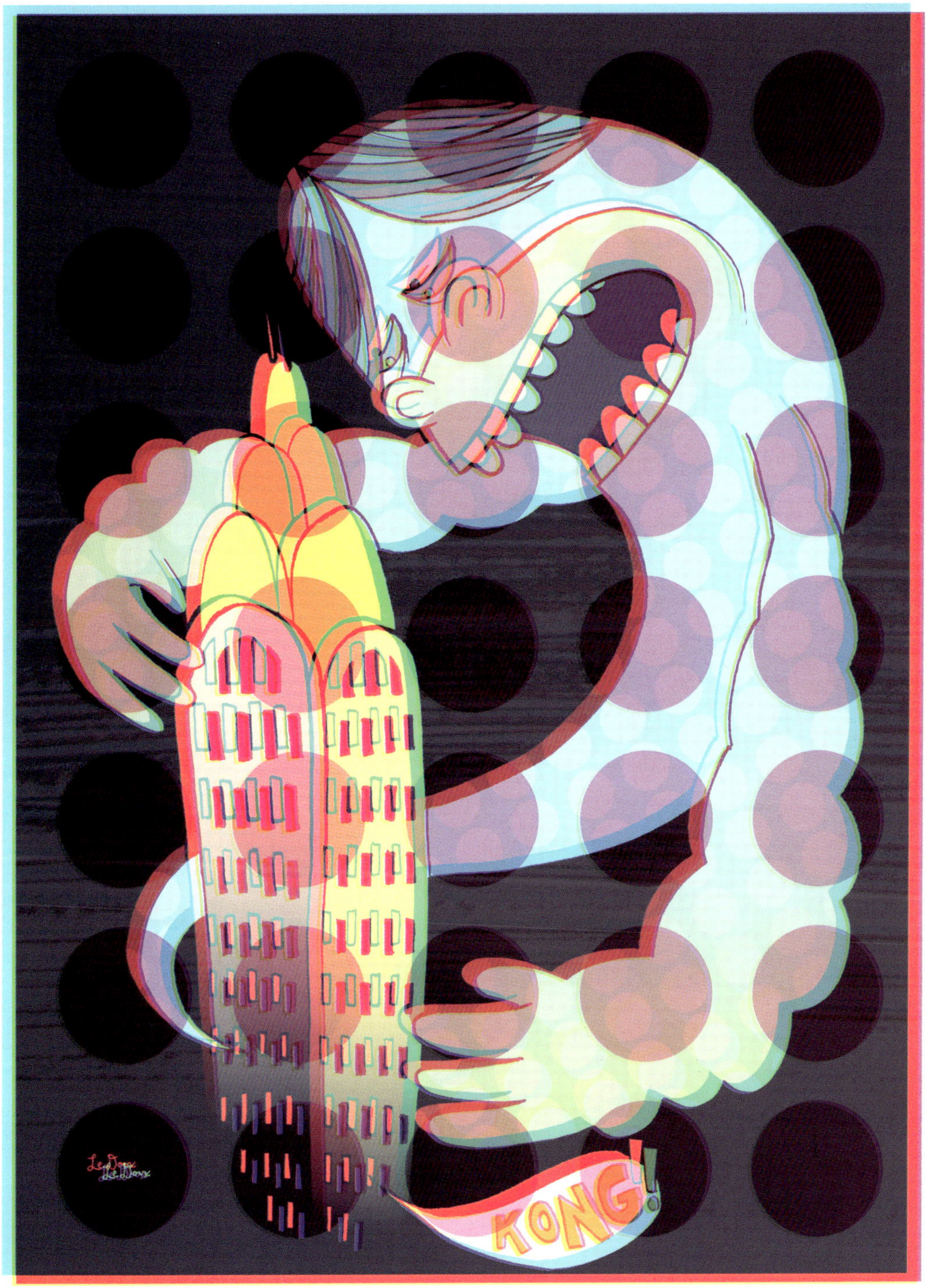

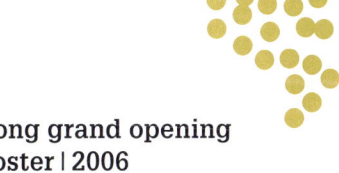

Kong grand opening poster | 2006

Jesse LeDoux/LeDouxville
www.ledouxville.com

The only requirement for promoting the opening of the gallery was that the word "kong" appeared. It could have been "Hong Kong" or even "konga," but the designer chose an outrageously pop version of "King Kong."

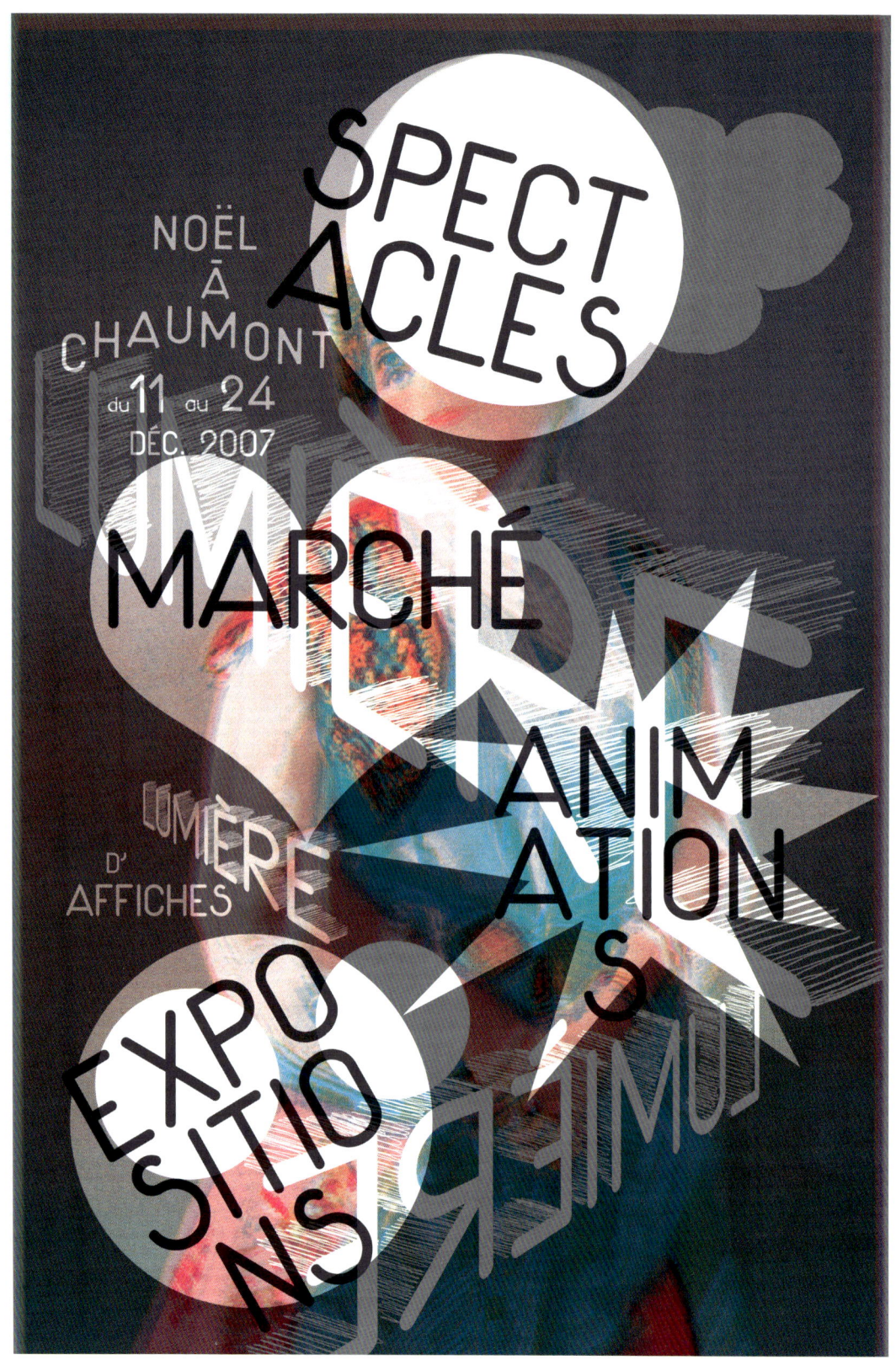

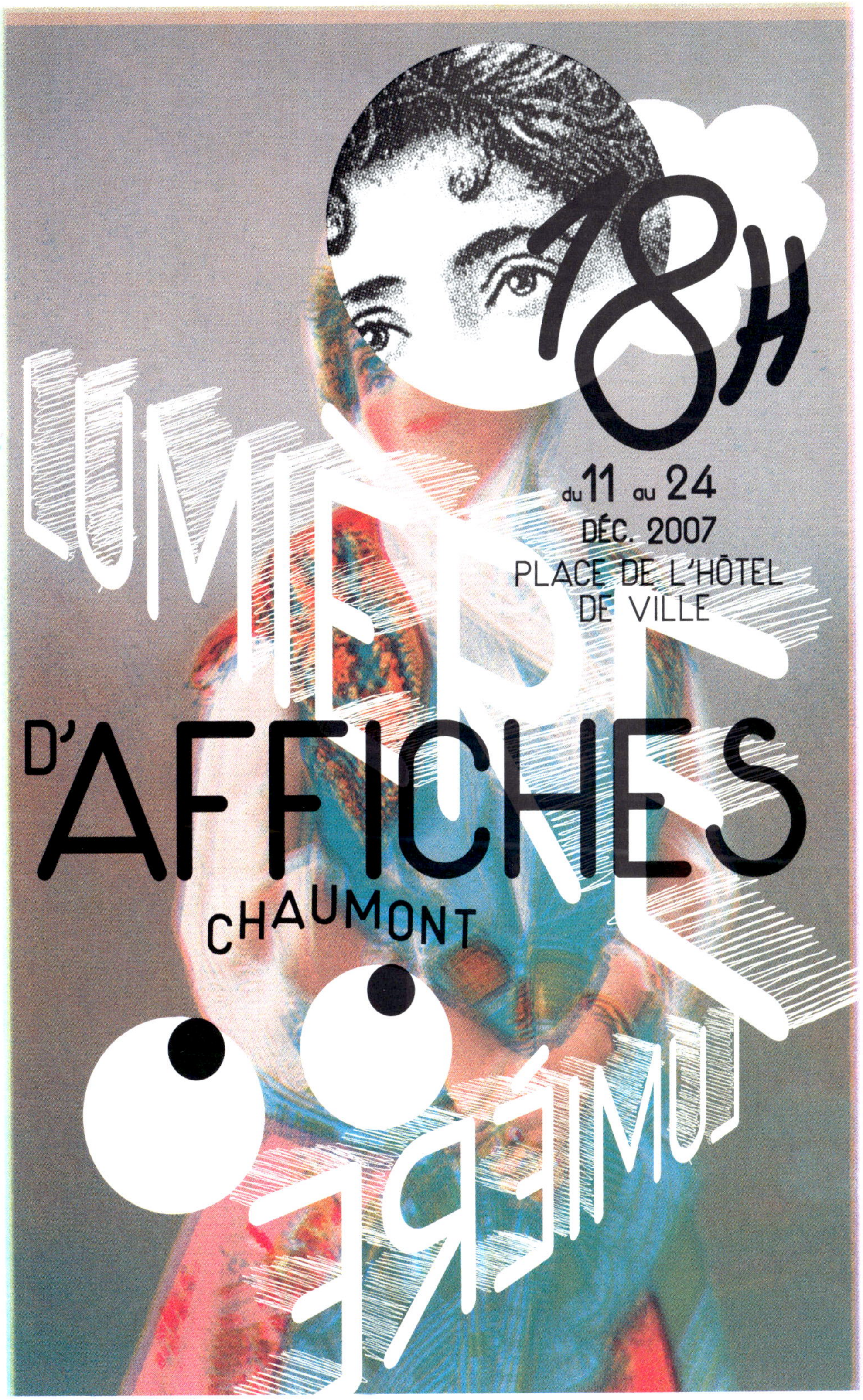

Lumière d'affiches | 2007

Grégoire Romanet
gregoire.romanet.free.fr

The event consisted in the discovery of a poster from the Dutailly collection each day at the same time. Mimicking the old lithographs, the posters explore the focus: in one the image is insinuated, in another a section is cut away and enhanced.

Every new day is the best party I've ever been to.

Corianton Hale

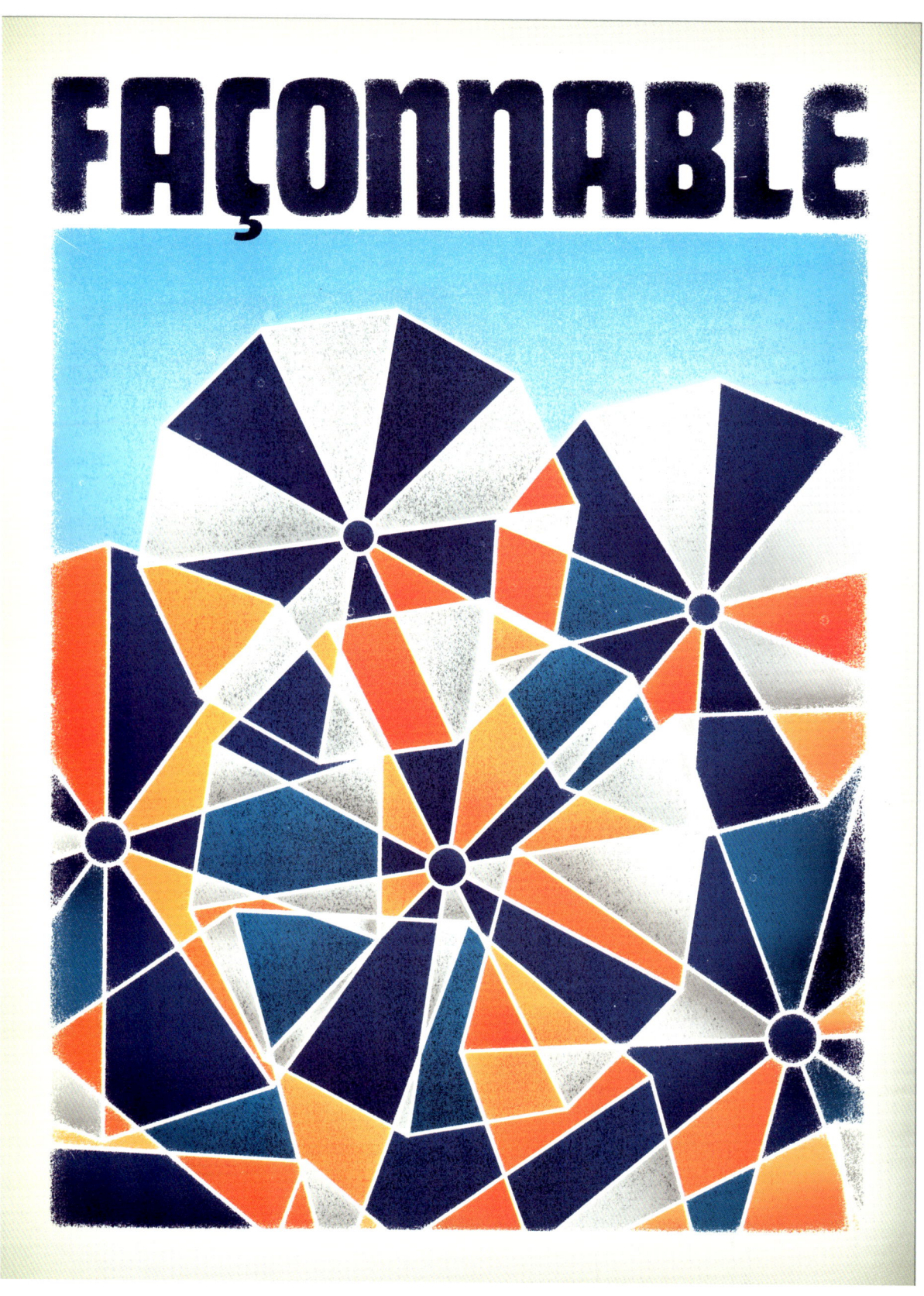

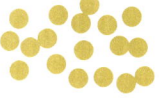

Façonnable | 2005-2006

Corianton Hale/Sleep Op Projects
www.sleepop.com

The Façonnable store had commissioned an identity that could be used during successive campaigns. The whole is achieved through illustrations drawn entirely by hand, the color palette and definitively vintage forms.

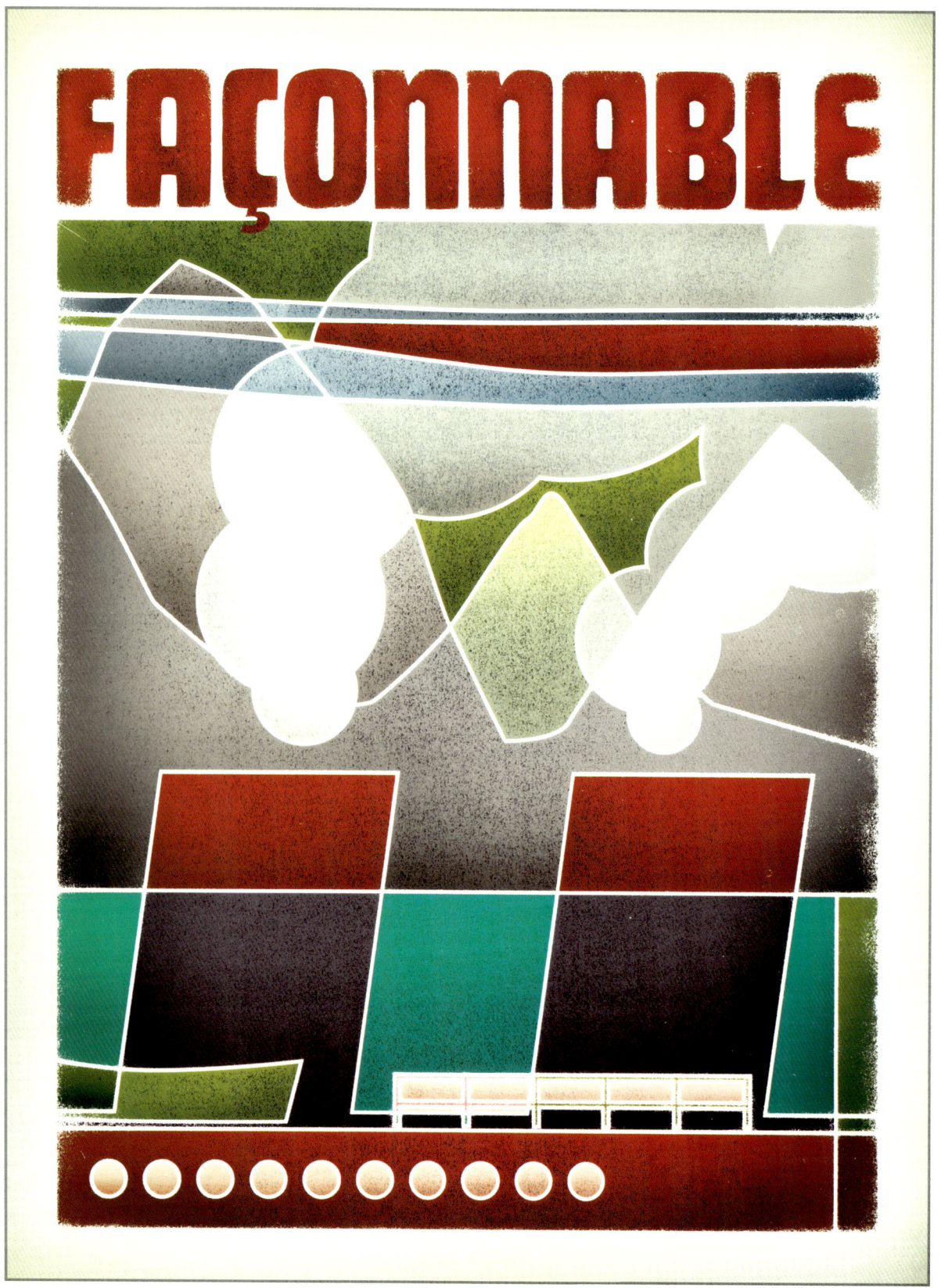

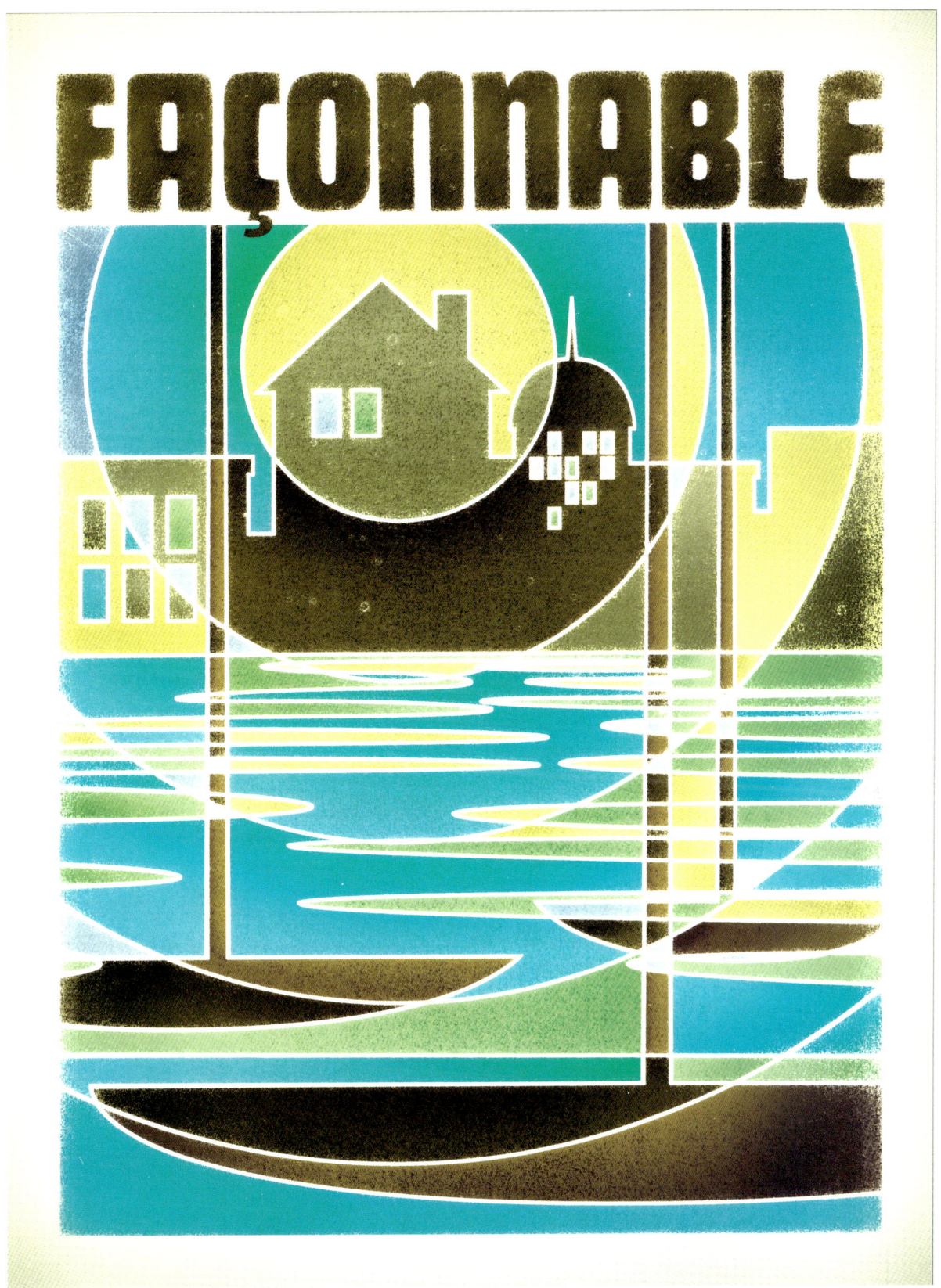

Too many amazing, random parties to count although we are both petrified and excited about this year's Halloween event at design friends LRB's studio. Those guys know how to throw a party. I'm sure there will be some images sneaking onto our site at some point.

Telegramme

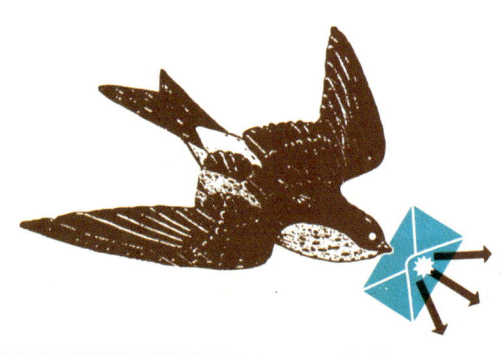
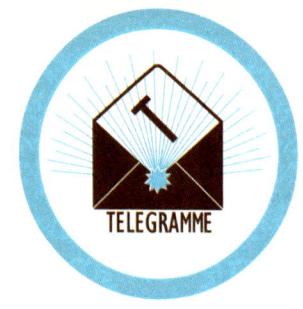

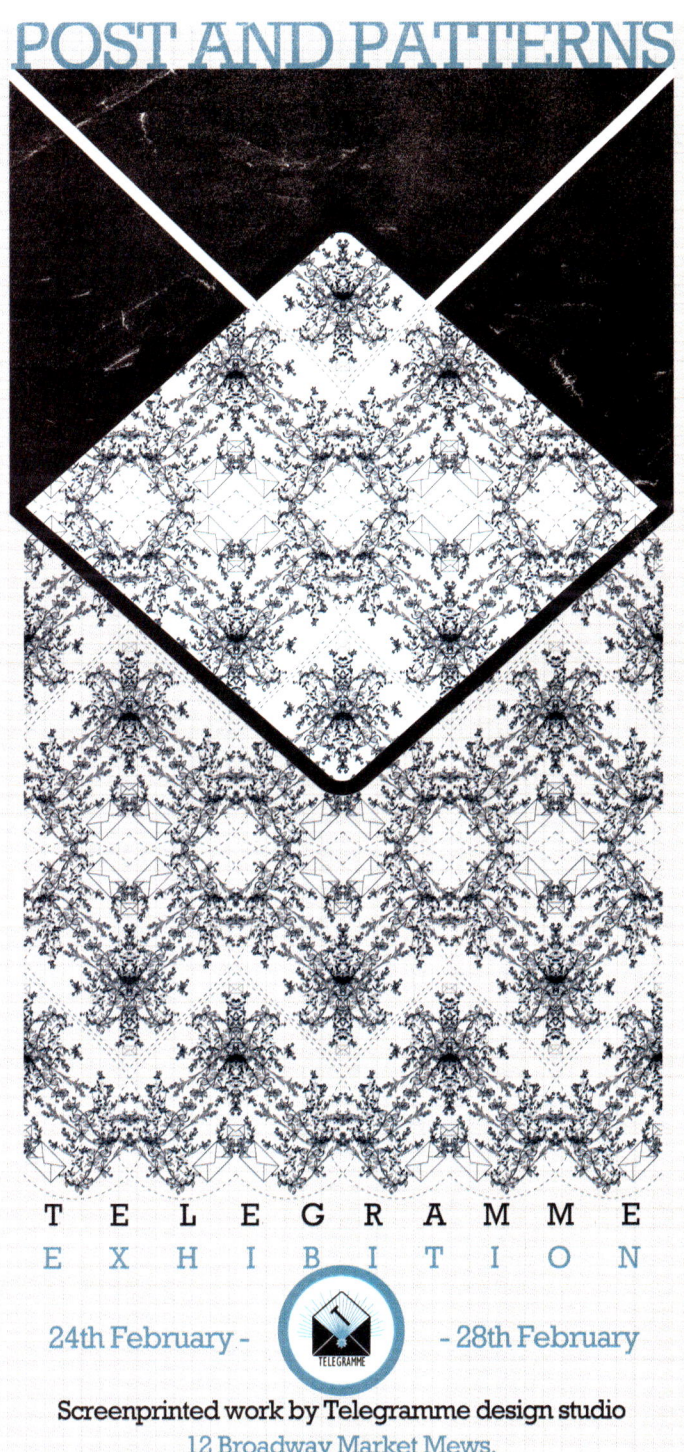

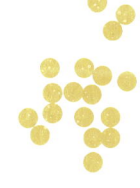

Telegramme exhibition poster and invitation | 2006

Christopher Gove,
Robert Evans/Telegramme
www.telegramme.co.uk

These limited edition posters were sent to different agencies and magazines to promote the new work of Telegramme regarding patterns. The texture of the backgrounds and the combination of light blue with brown evoke the seventies.

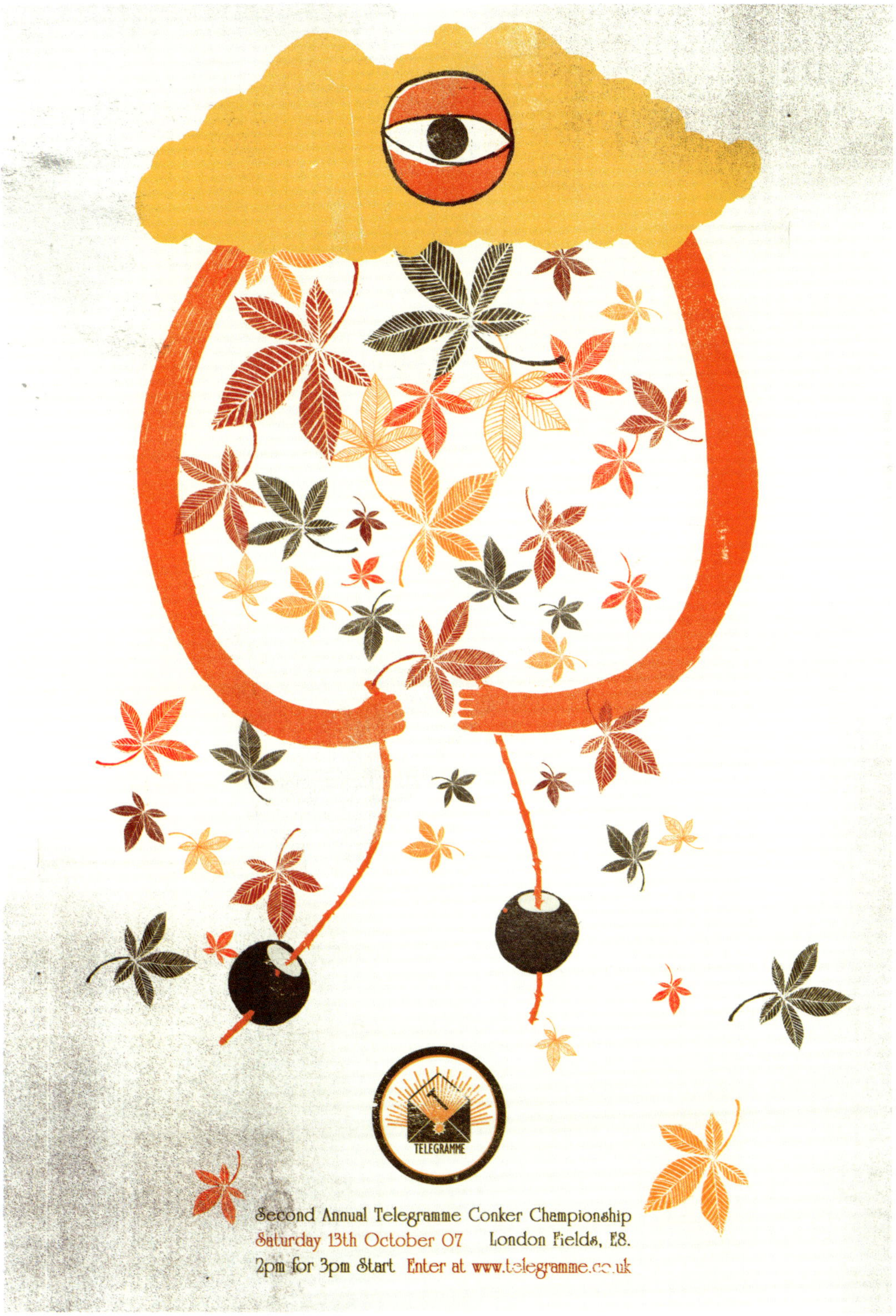

**Telegramme Conker
Championship | 2007**

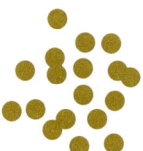

Christopher Gove,
Robert Evans/Telegramme
www.telegramme.co.uk

A conker championship is a traditional game in which the competitors must try to break each other's conkers. Telegramme organizes these championships and this poster, in which a conker appears to be enjoying the game, promotes the initiative.

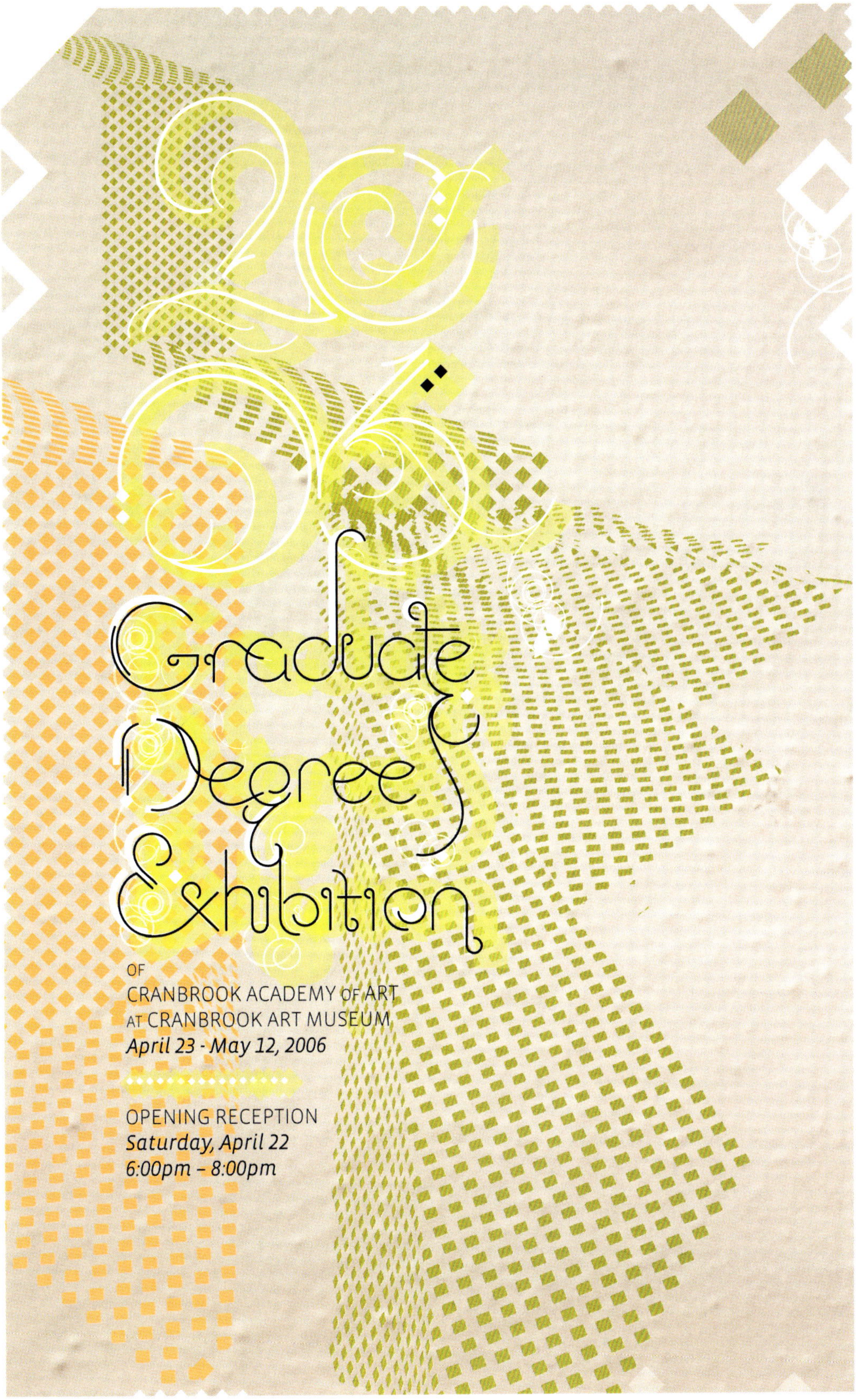

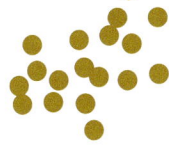

Cranbrook Academy of Art graduate show invitation | 2006

Keetra Dean Dixon/FromKeetra
www.fromkeetra.com

The brief was expeditious: "Make it decorative. And fast!" The interplay of the letter finishes, the year and the different elements fulfil the first requisite. Also, the shades of brown and the texture of the background, similar to card, make reference to recycling.

At my age (almost seventy) I don't go to parties anymore, thank goodness! On the other hand I just had a big party (five hundred and ten people) in New York because I was one who received the AIGA gold medal this year and they held a grand black tie gala for the winners!

Ed Fella

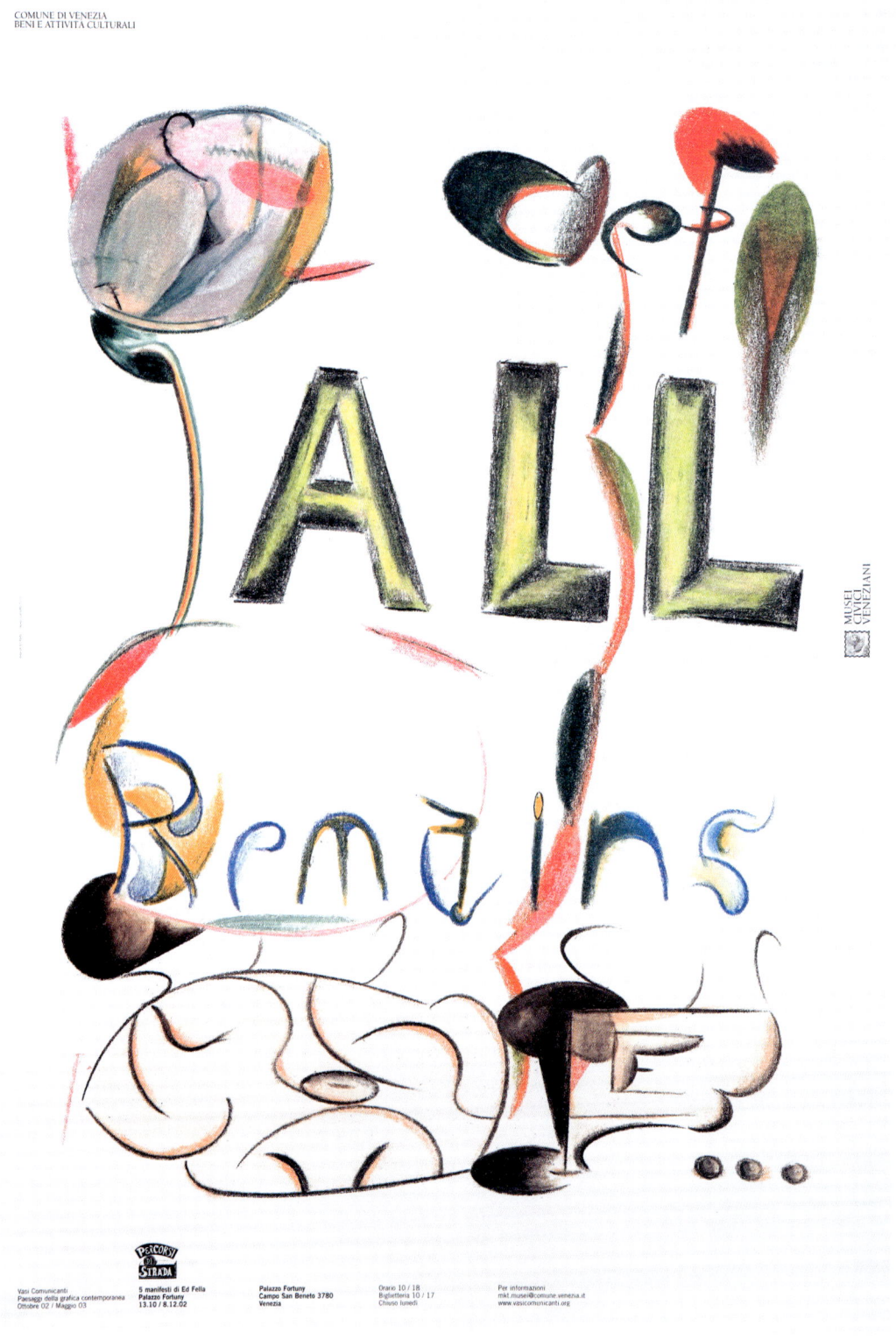

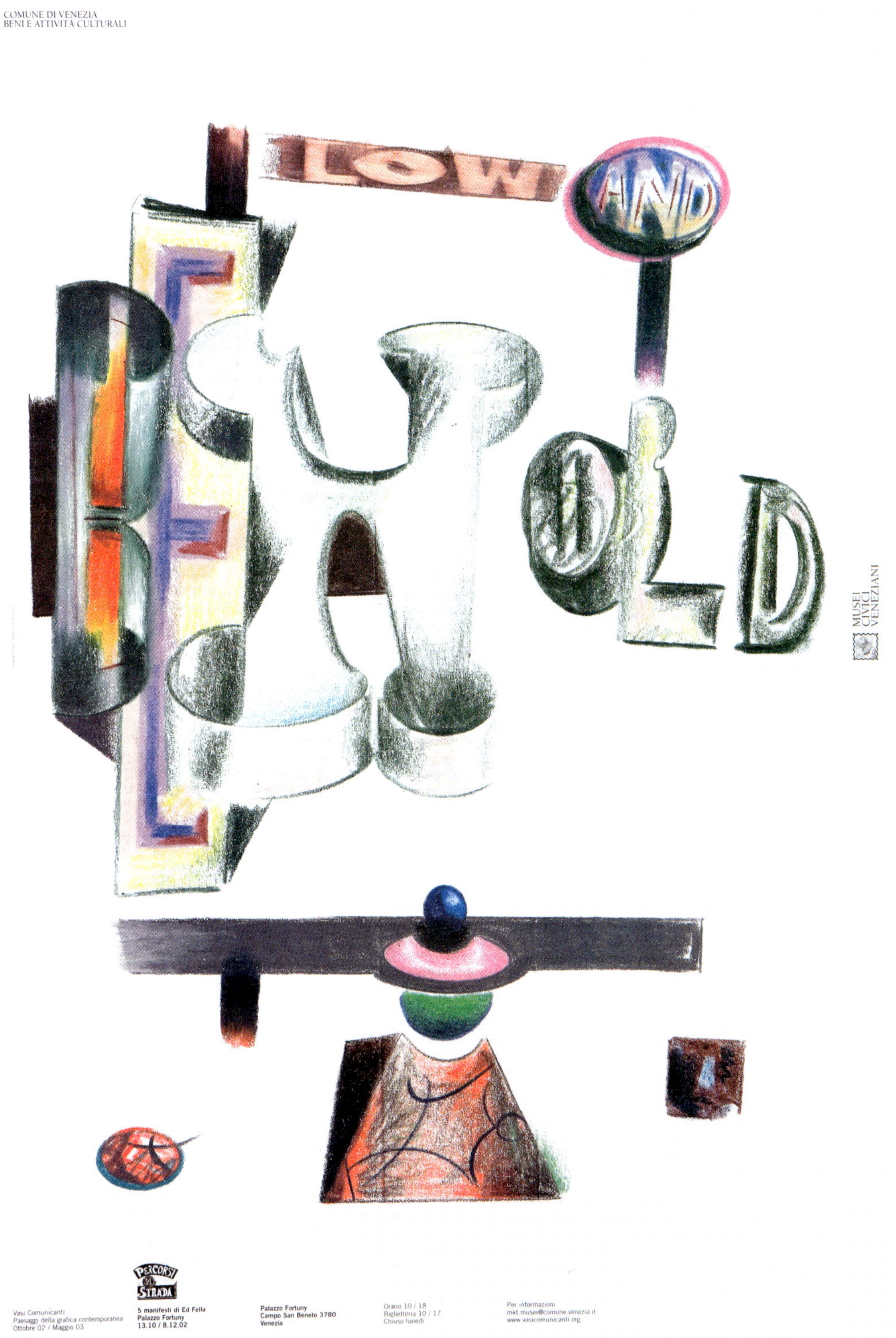

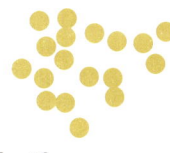

Percosi di Strada: 5 Manifesti di Ed Fella | 2002

Ed Fella
www.edfella.com

The idea was for Venice to be seen subtly, almost as if it were a euphemism. Fella shows us the spirit of the city by using typical colors from Murano glass, but with a more natural essence, which is the result of it being illustrated freehand.

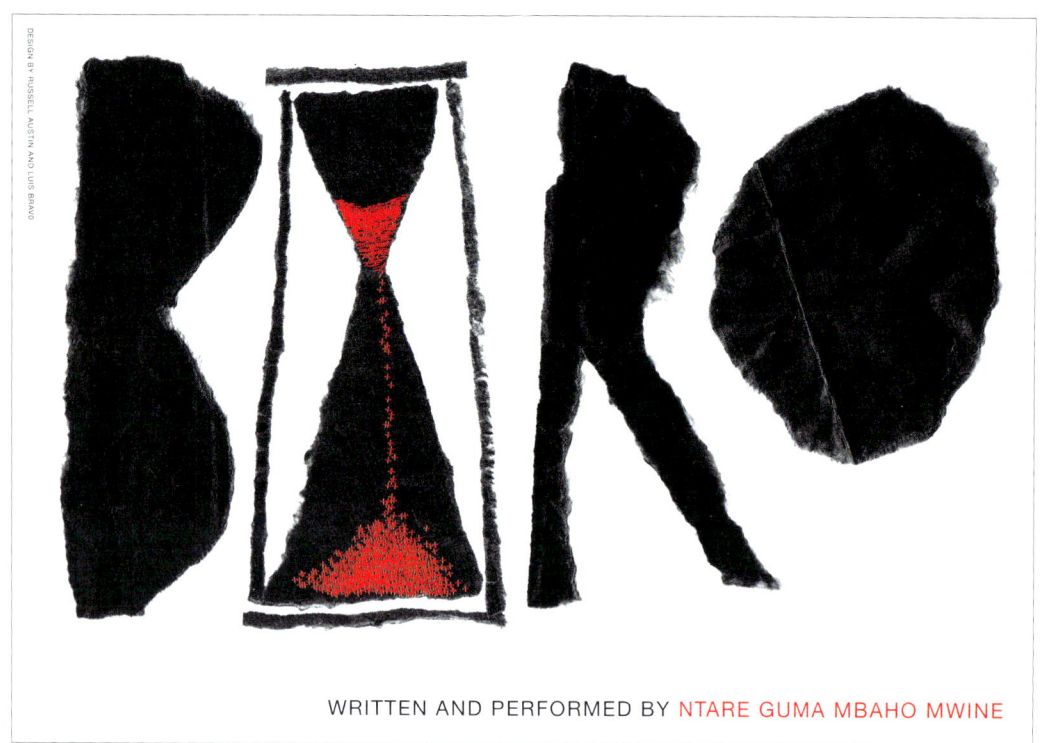

Biro poster | 2005

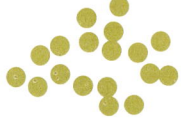

Lucha Design
www.luchadesign.com

In publicizing the theater production, whose title is the name of the main character, the poster makes use of a double function of the symbols, both pictorial and narrative. The rock aesthetics, the sand watch and the positive and negative symbols sum up the story.

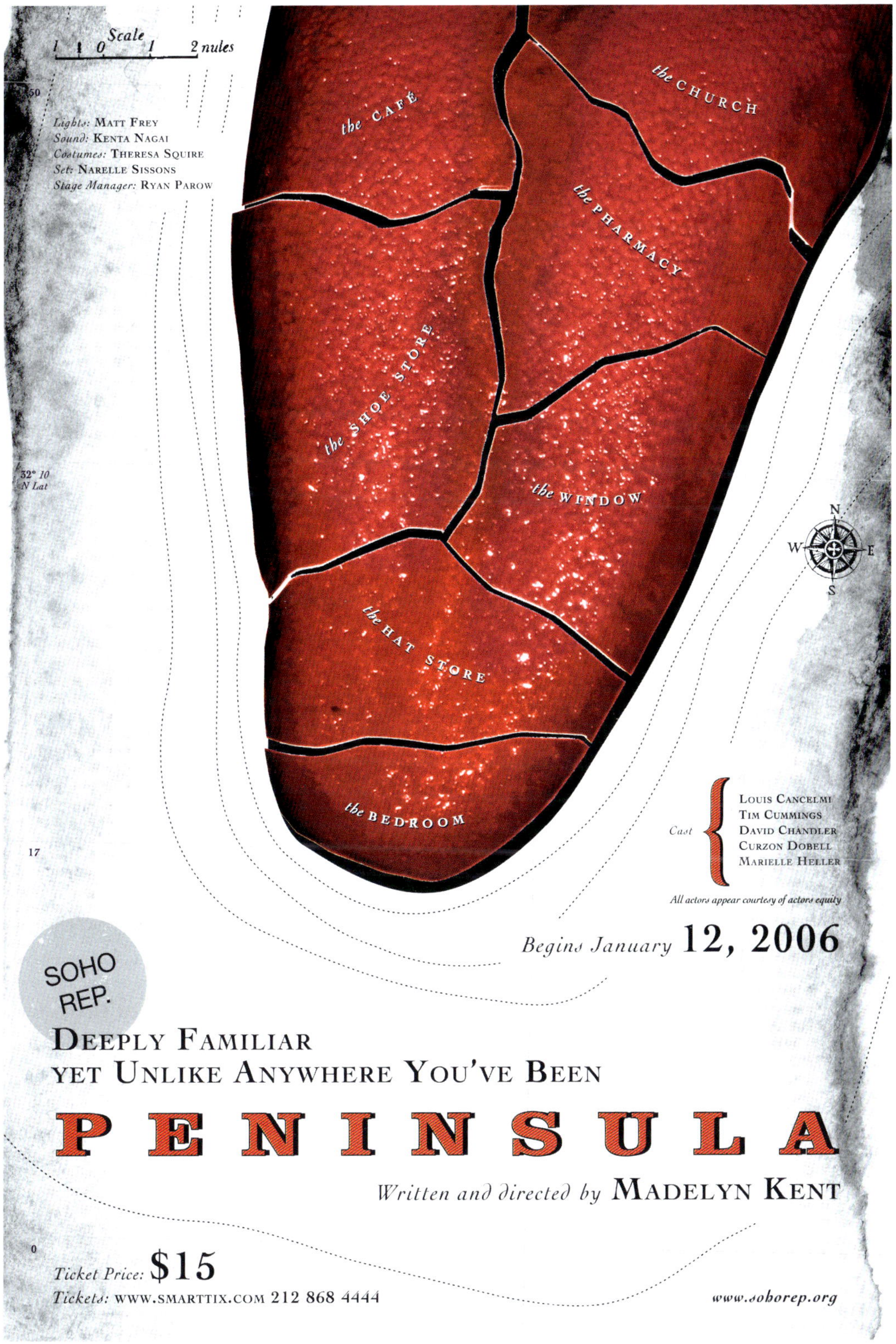

Peninsula poster | 2006

Lucha Design
www.luchadesign.com

This piece attempted to tackle the different treatments of communication, above all, that which is interrupted or broken. The cracked tongue on the poster represents the theme of the work, as well as producing a powerful visual effect.

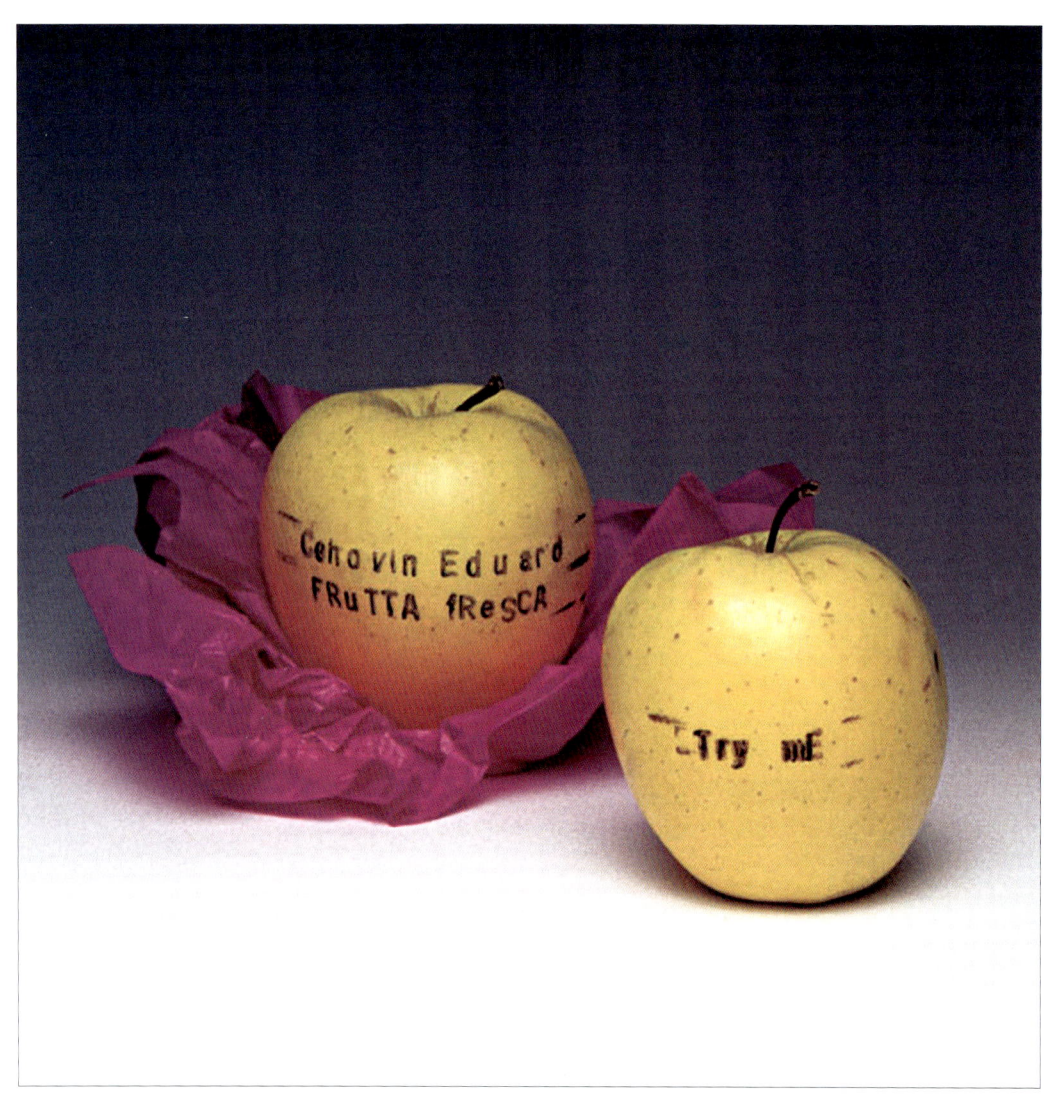

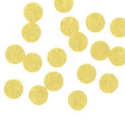

**Frutta Fresca
apple invitation | 2003**

**Eduard Cehovin
www.cehovin.com**

When someone is considered young and a novice, it could be said that they are yet to ripen. The invitation to the young Slovenian designers' exhibition takes this concept and reformulates it: the fruit is already ripe; it can even be bitten into.

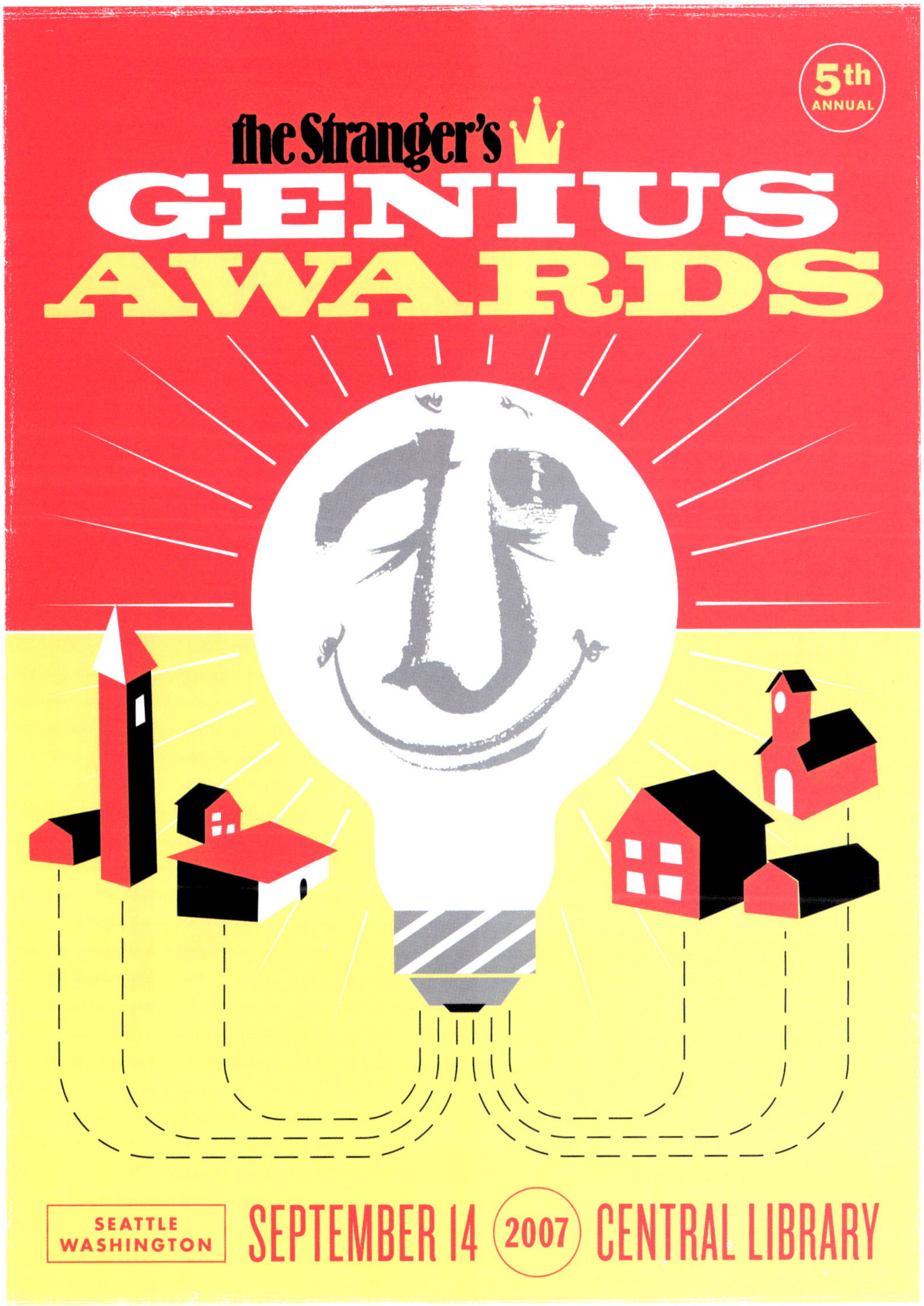

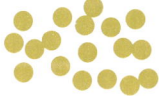

The Stranger's 2007
Genius Awards poster | 2007

Corianton Hale/Sleep Op Projects
www.sleepop.com

The Genius awards are presented by the newspaper *The Stranger* to a member of the community of Seattle who has provided outstanding creative contributions. The illustration sums up, brilliantly and concisely, the idea of this initiative.

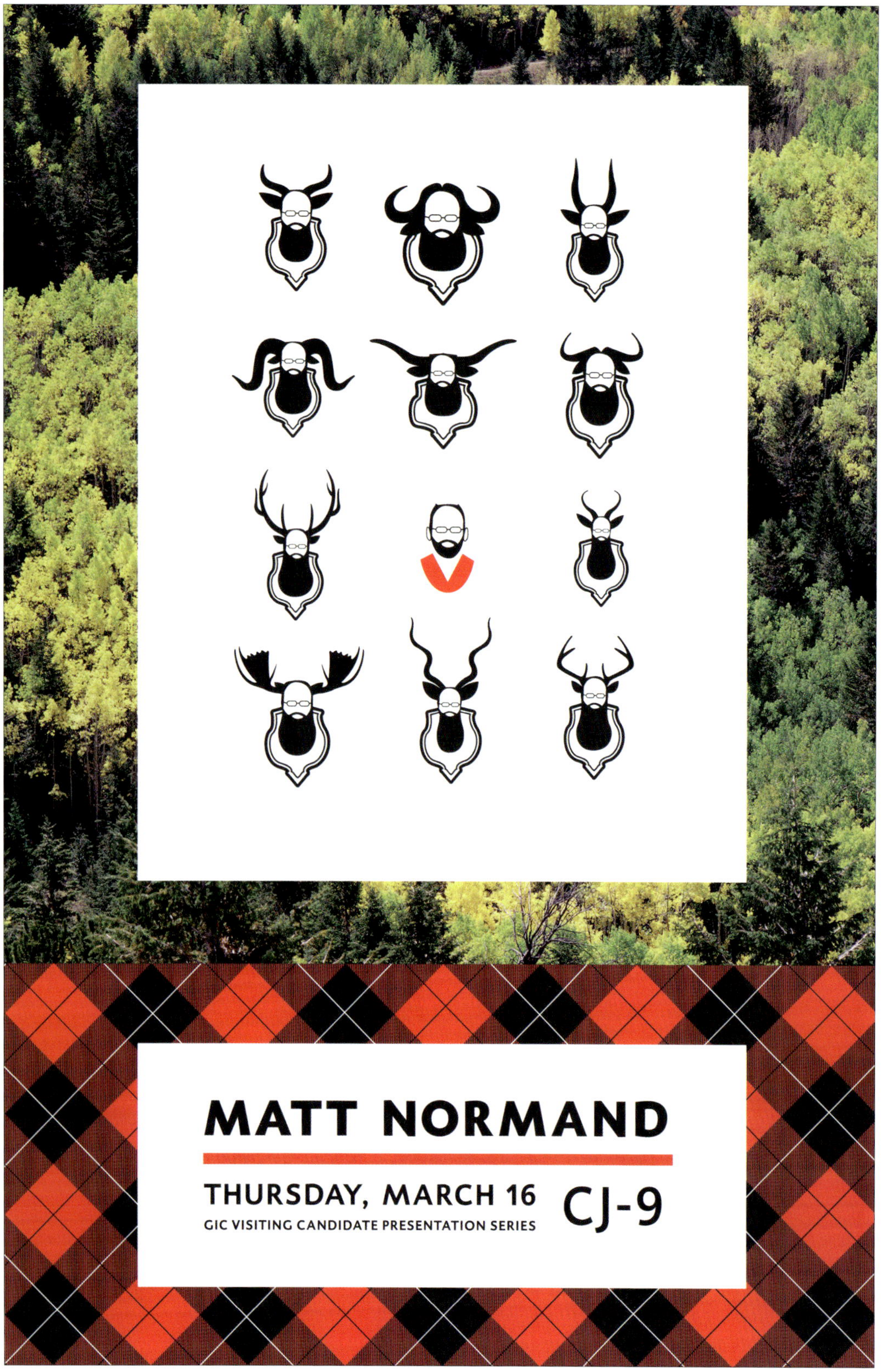

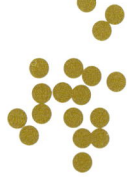

Matt Normand Visiting
Artist poster | 2005

Tyler Lang
www.tylerlang.com

The artist possesses, almost inevitably, a freak nature. The poster presents the artist as different trophy catches, lending greater strength to Matt Normand's outlandishness.

Paco is the name of Heineken's latest aluminium bottle designed by ORA-ITO. For the launch party, the Parisian studio's patio had been carpeted with grass lawn, white rabbits, and two hundred drunk and snobby guests. Paco is also the name of the rabbit that I brought home with me that morning.

Marie Bres-Negretti

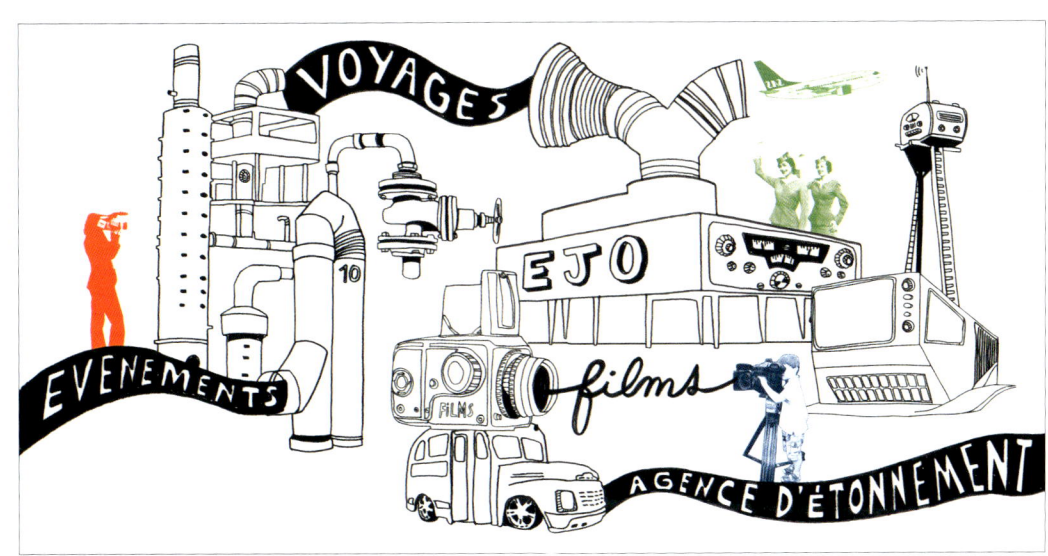

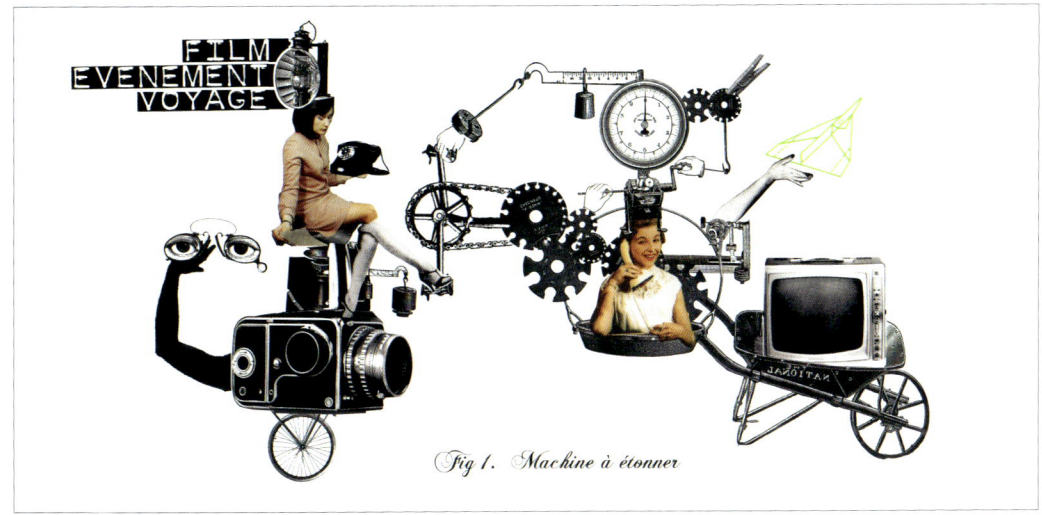

Machine à étonner and The Factory | 2006

Marie Bres-Negretti/La belle Simone
www.labellesimone.com

Transforming expressionist fabrics into pop laboratories, the postcards promote the producers of EJO events. The different aesthetic references that come together in the collage and in the illustration sum up the spirit of the agency.

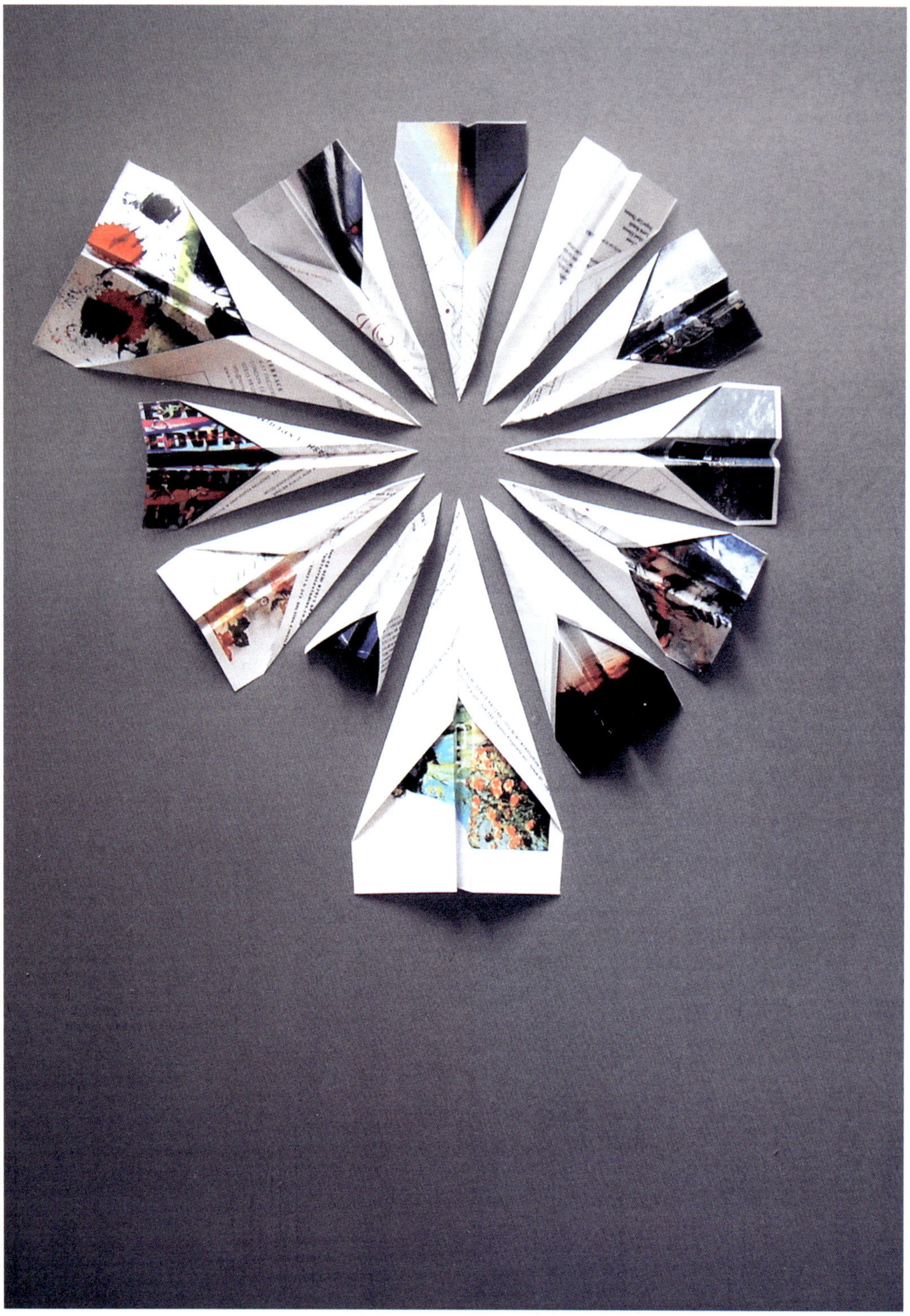

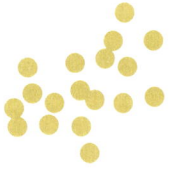

Time Flies | 2006

Ewan Robertson/Oscar & Ewan
www.oscarandewan.co.uk

The flyer promotes a collective exhibition that commemorates the first year of the Terrace gallery. The twelve paper airplanes arranged like a clock are made from the twelve flyers from the past year.

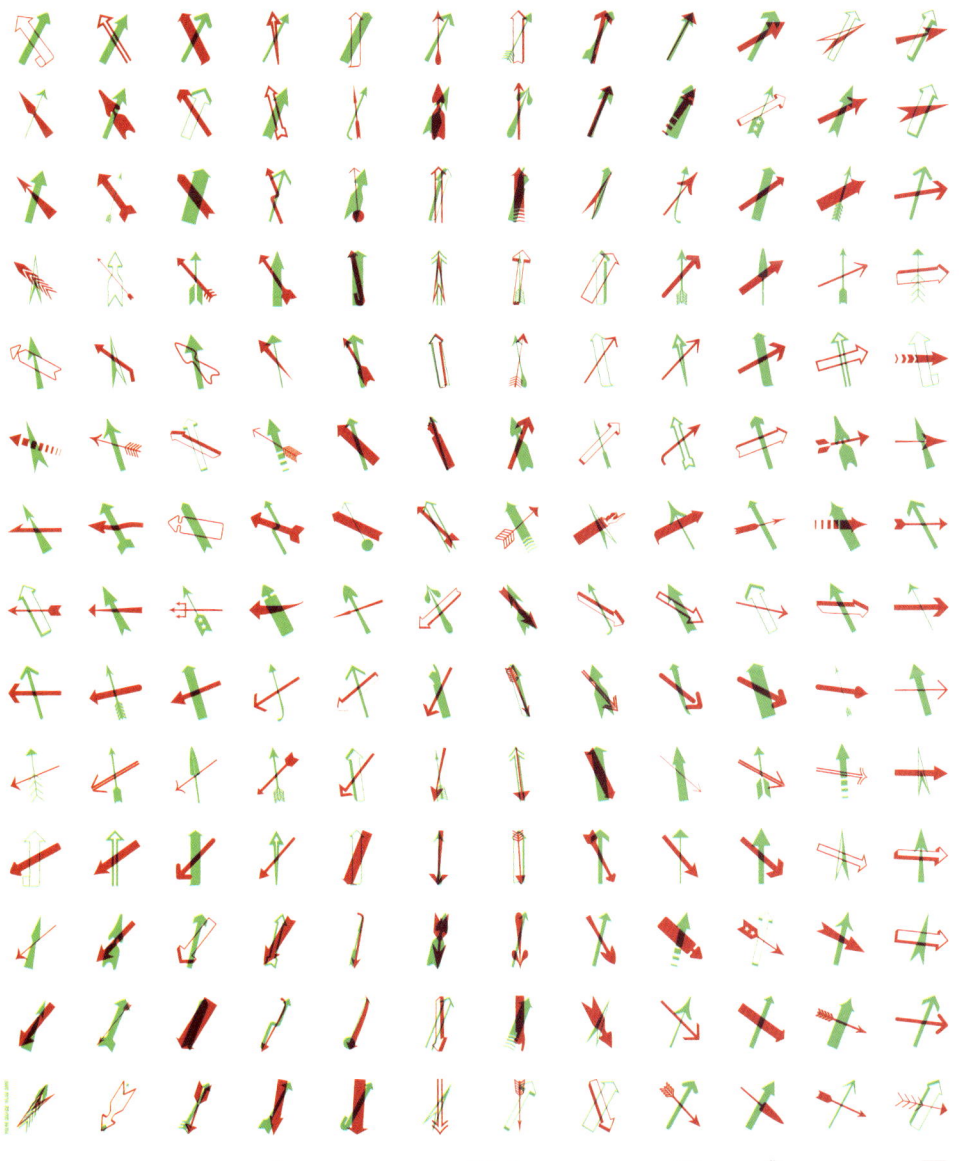

**Forum Laus 03:
Gráfica Reactiva | 2003**

Arjan Groot
www.thecoverup.eu

The theme of the conference was to analyze the capacity of designers and communicators to be dissident in an increasingly globalized world. The arrows represent individuals in the field of communication: it is inevitable that they influence each other.

So good that I can't remember.

Oscar Bauer

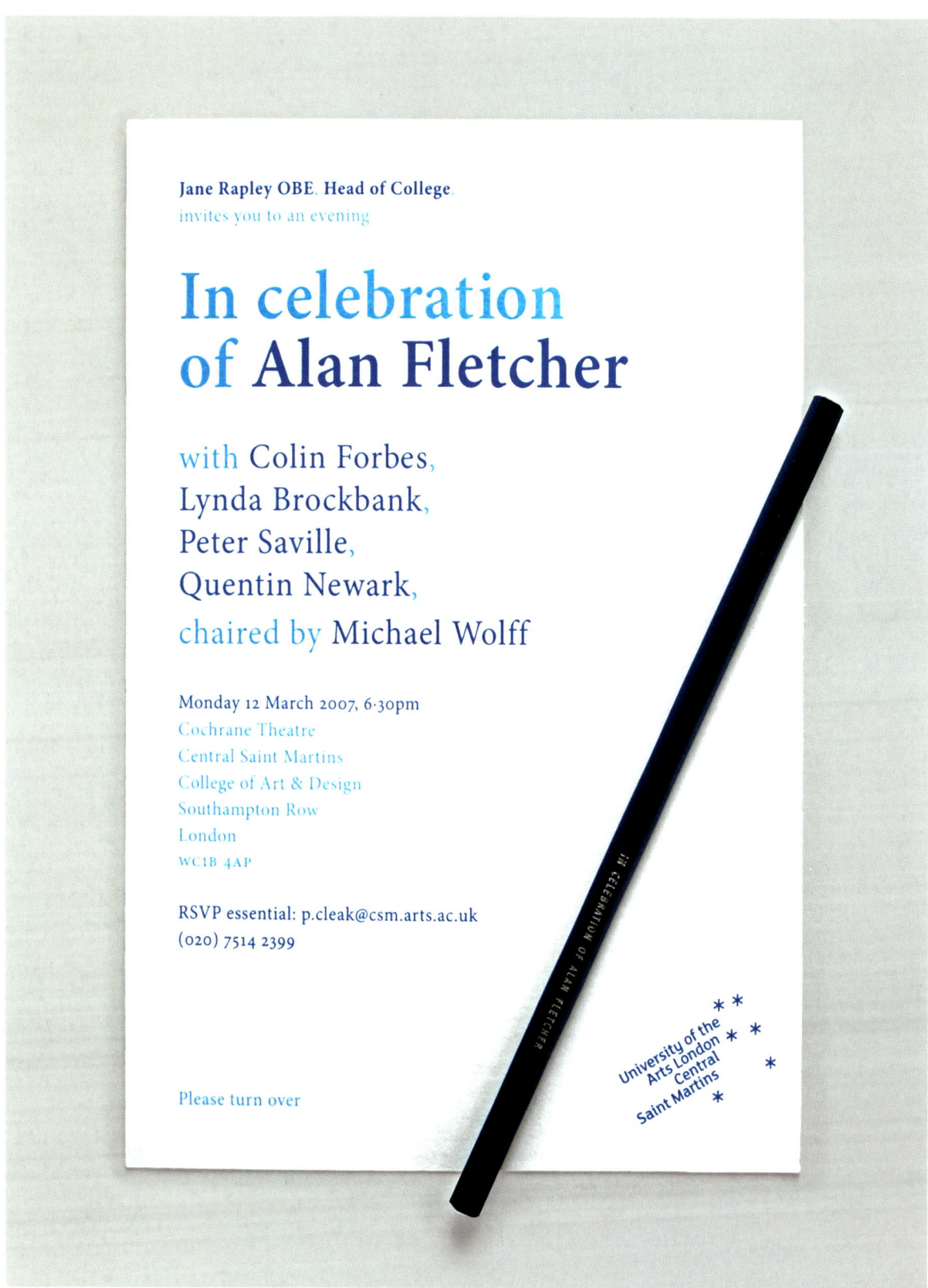

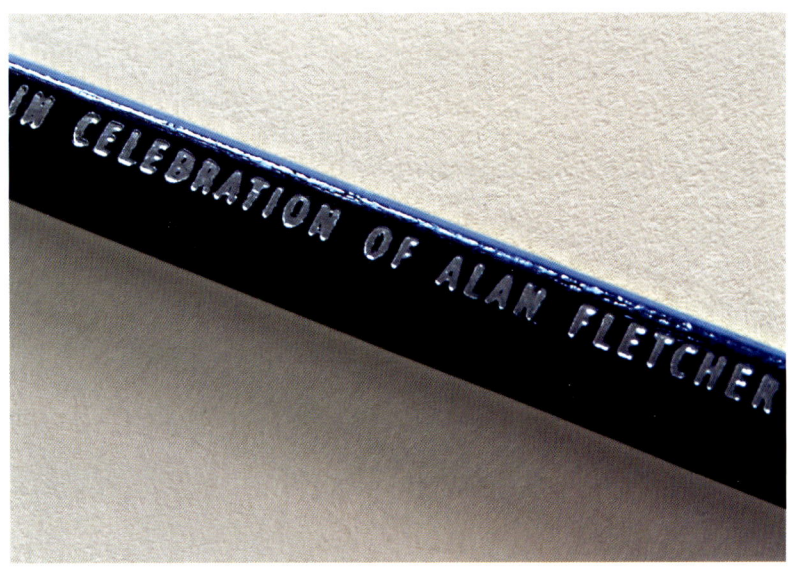

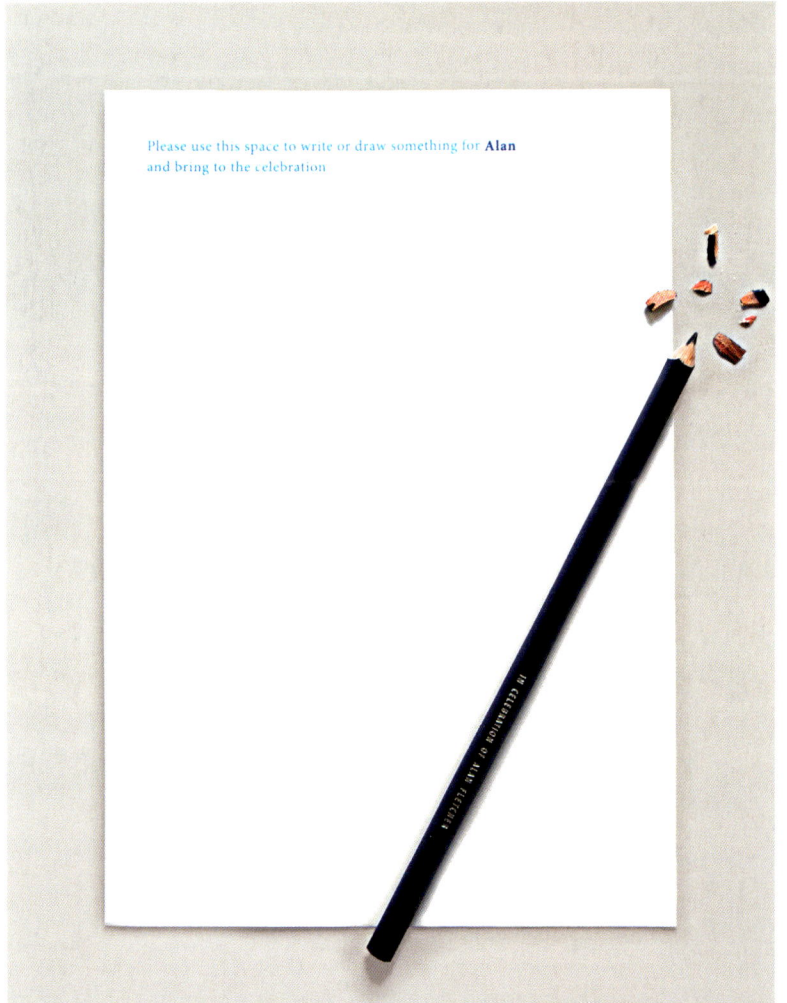

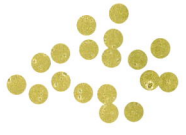

In celebration of Alan Fletcher | 2007

Oscar Bauer/Oscar & Ewan
www.oscarandewan.co.uk/terrace.htm

A minimalist and sober design for a commemorative speech. On the back of the invitations, notes could be written that were later given to the Fletcher family; that way small comments from friends and admirers could be kept.

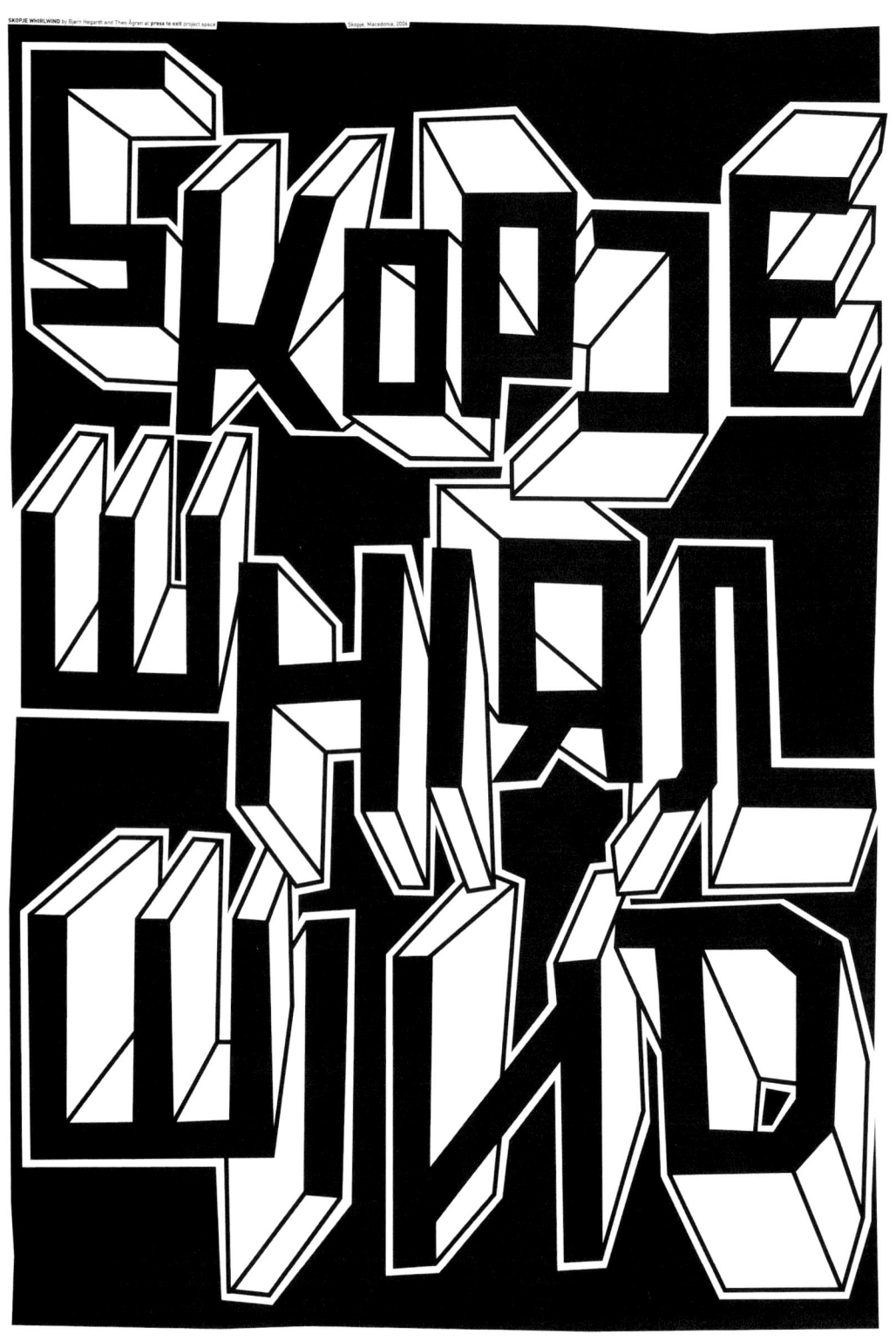

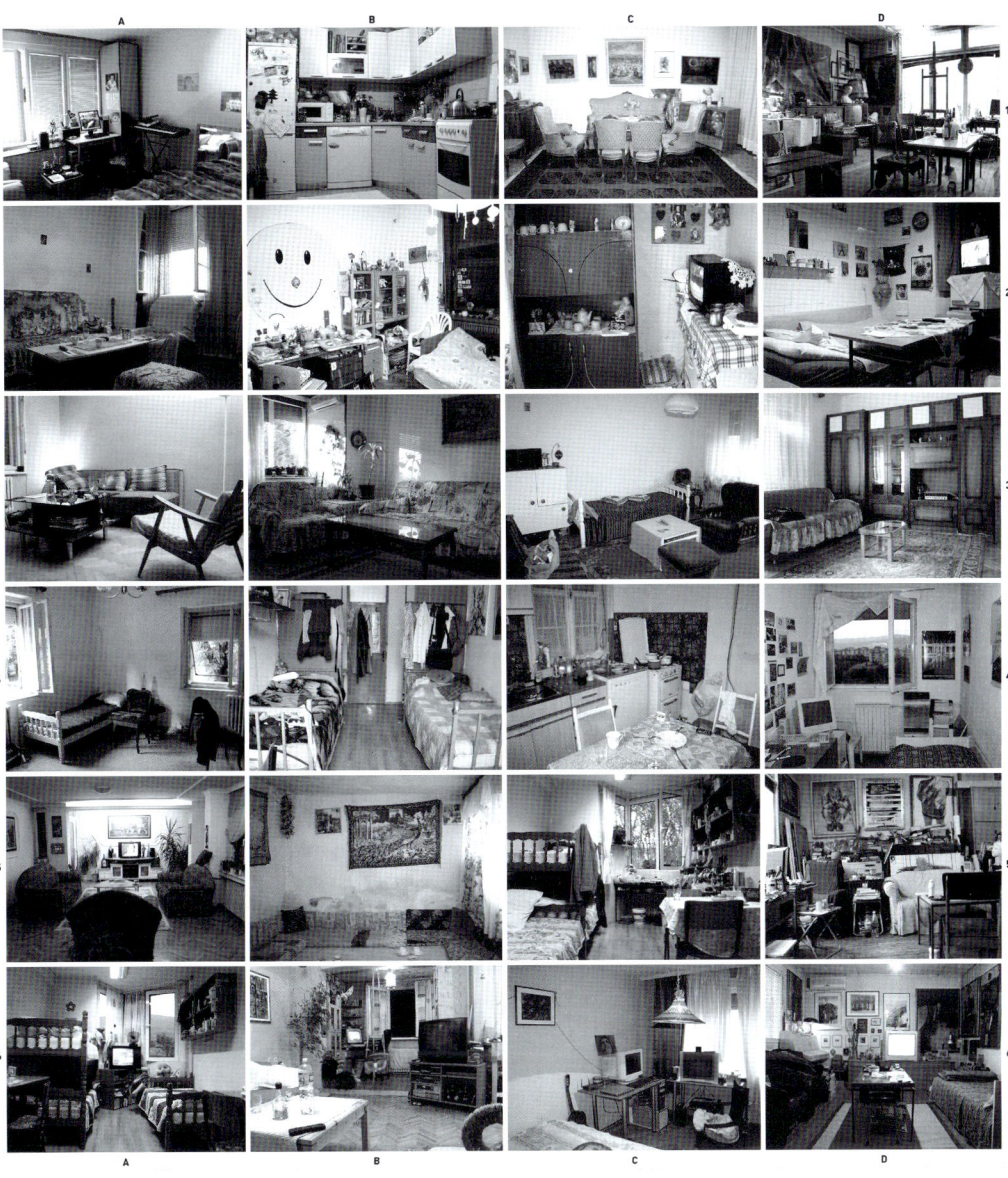

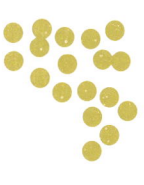

Skopje Whirlwind | 2006

Ariane Spanier
www.arianespanier.com

The format is B1, then folded into B5, and promotes a photography exhibition of houses in Skopje (Macedonia). The typography mixes fonts from Latin and Cyrillic alphabets, approaching linguistic universes.

The party, against which all subsequent parties would be measured, would have to have been the weekend-long shindy for long-time friend and club football captain, Count Farthingham Buckleman VII. Suffice it to say, Seal and The Edge's impromptu duet marked the start of the fourth wind, and old Farthy's debauched mishap with the champagne fountain marked an epic end.

Ryan Dunn

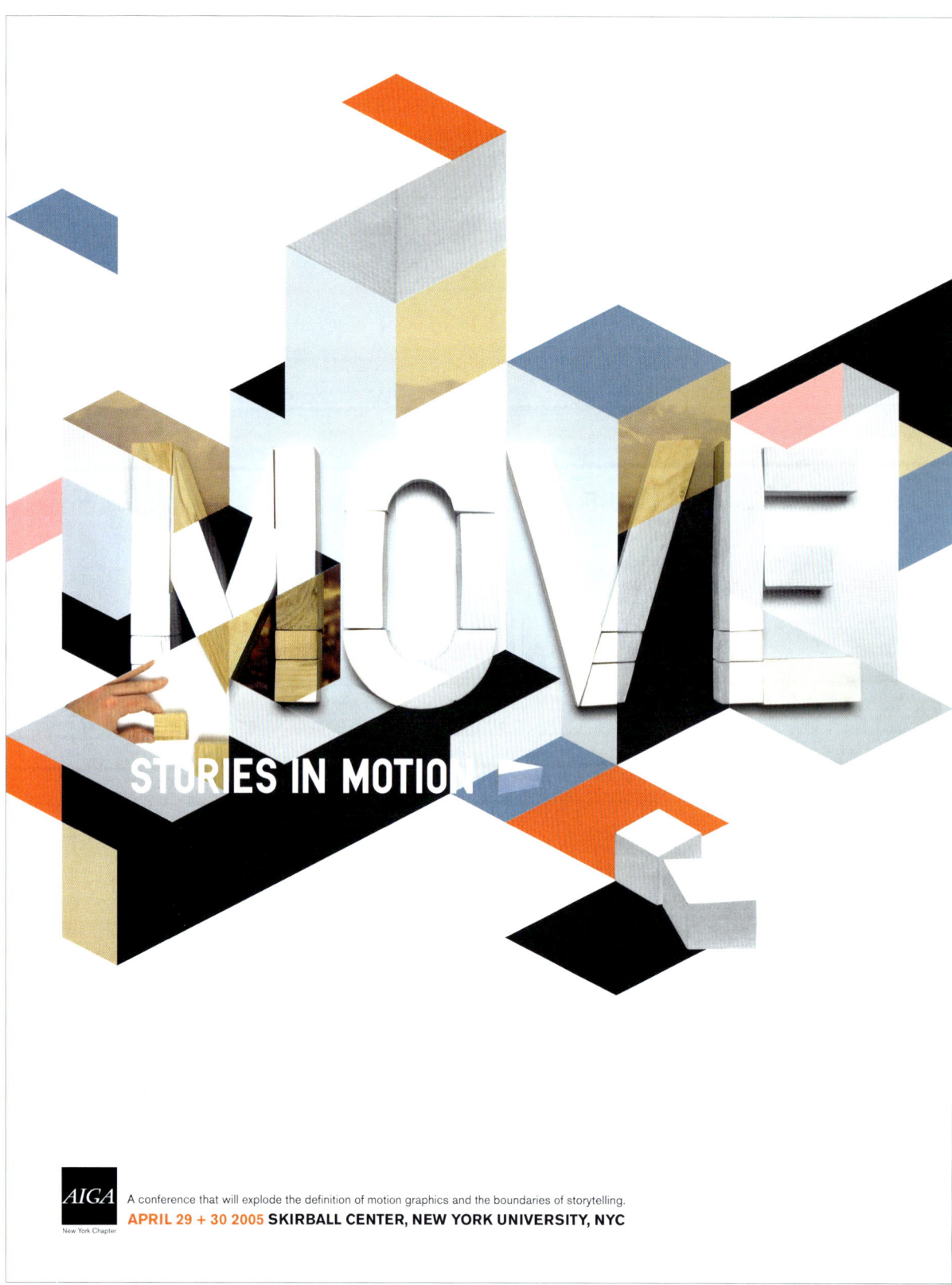

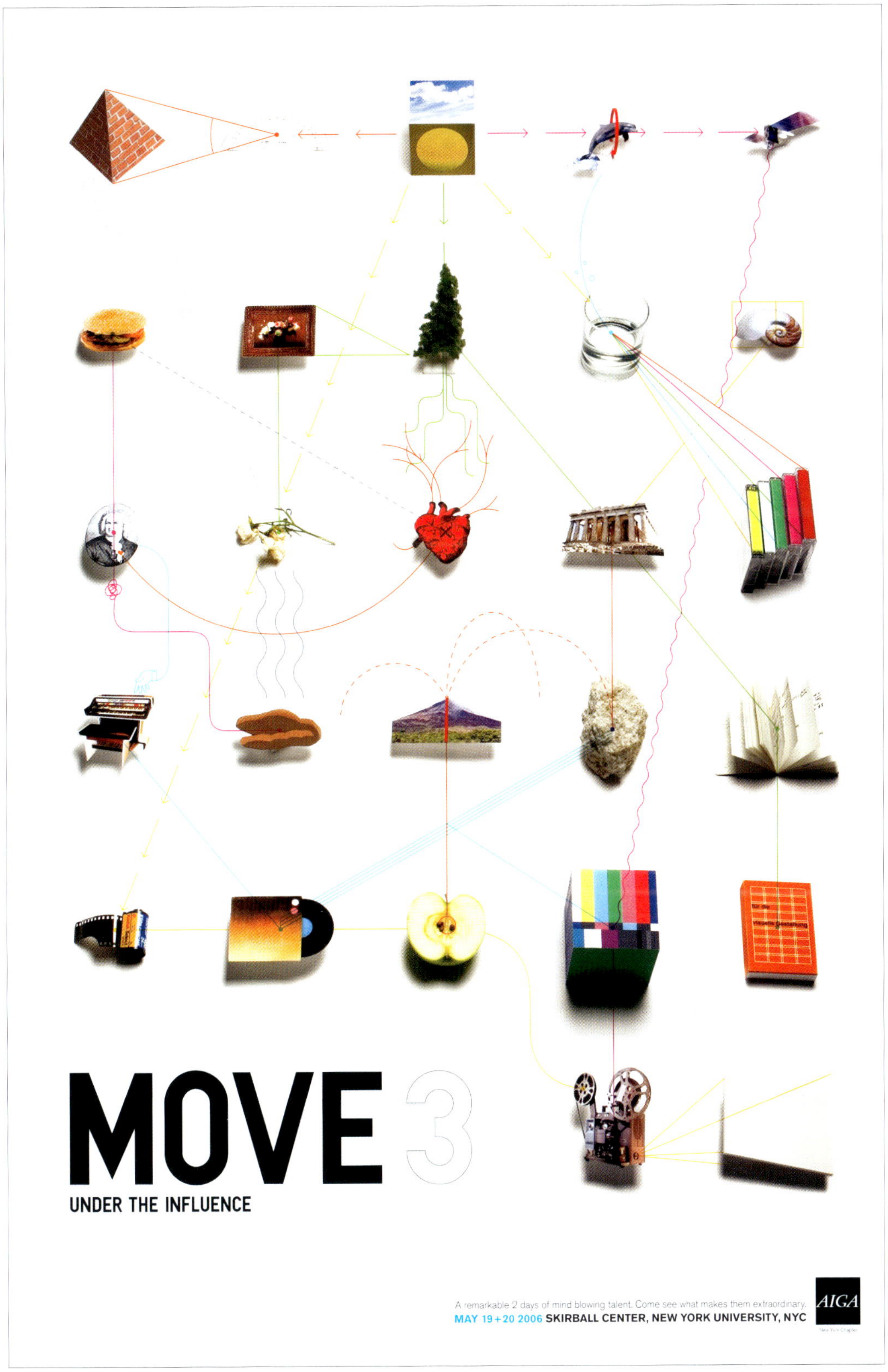

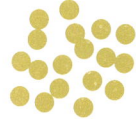

AIGA/NY – Move
conference | 2005-2006

Ryan Dunn, Wyeth Hansen/Labour
www.labour-ny.com

The Move conference, organized by AIGA, investigates the different narrative forms of audiovisual language. The break in the linear aspect that runs through post-modernism is reflected in the arrangement of the elements in both posters.

A tiny penthouse room, rumored to have been abandoned by Grace Jones, stuffed with people warbling in and out of hysterics. The action revolved around a make-your-own-chili buffet and brownies.

Keetra Dean Dixon

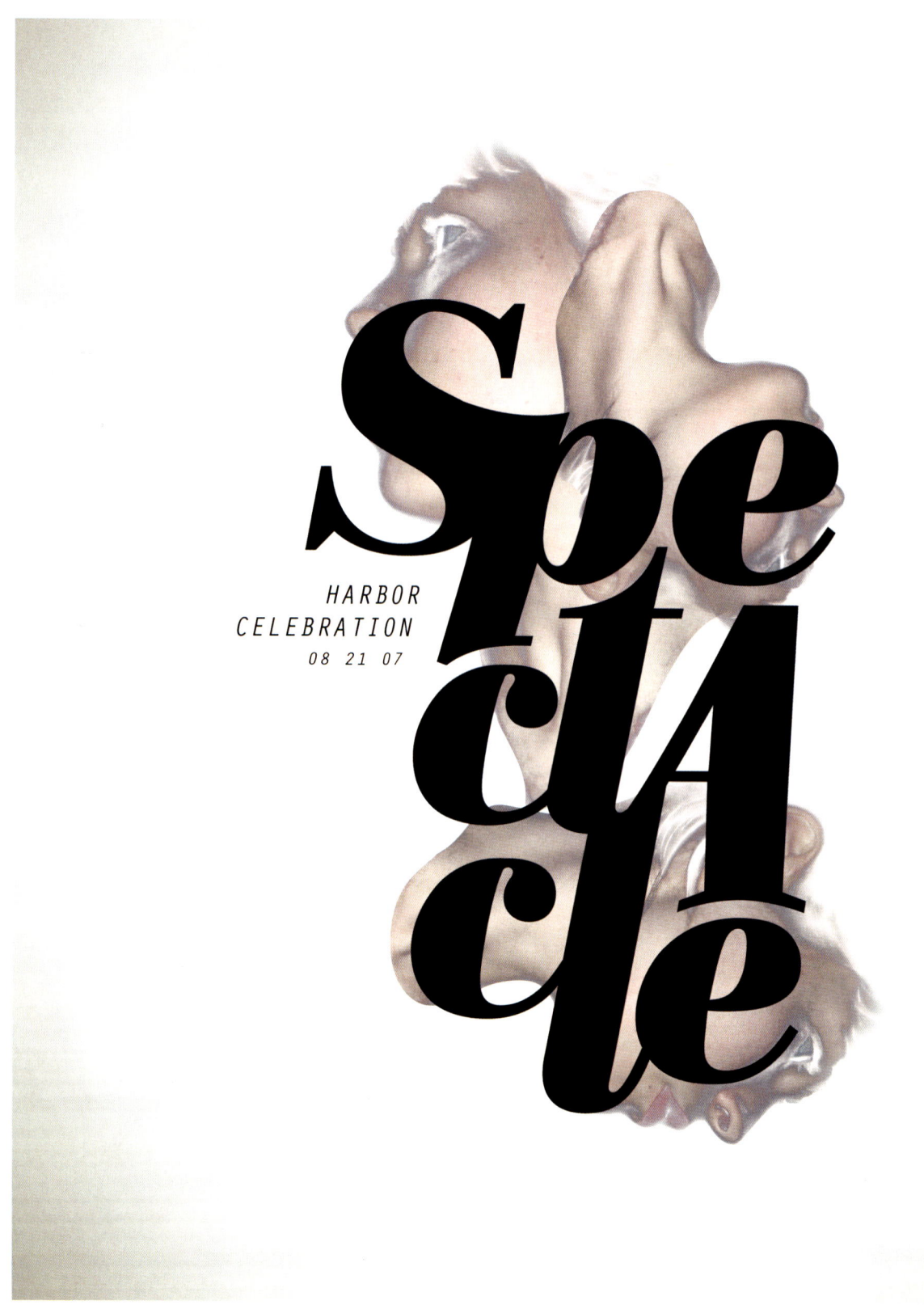

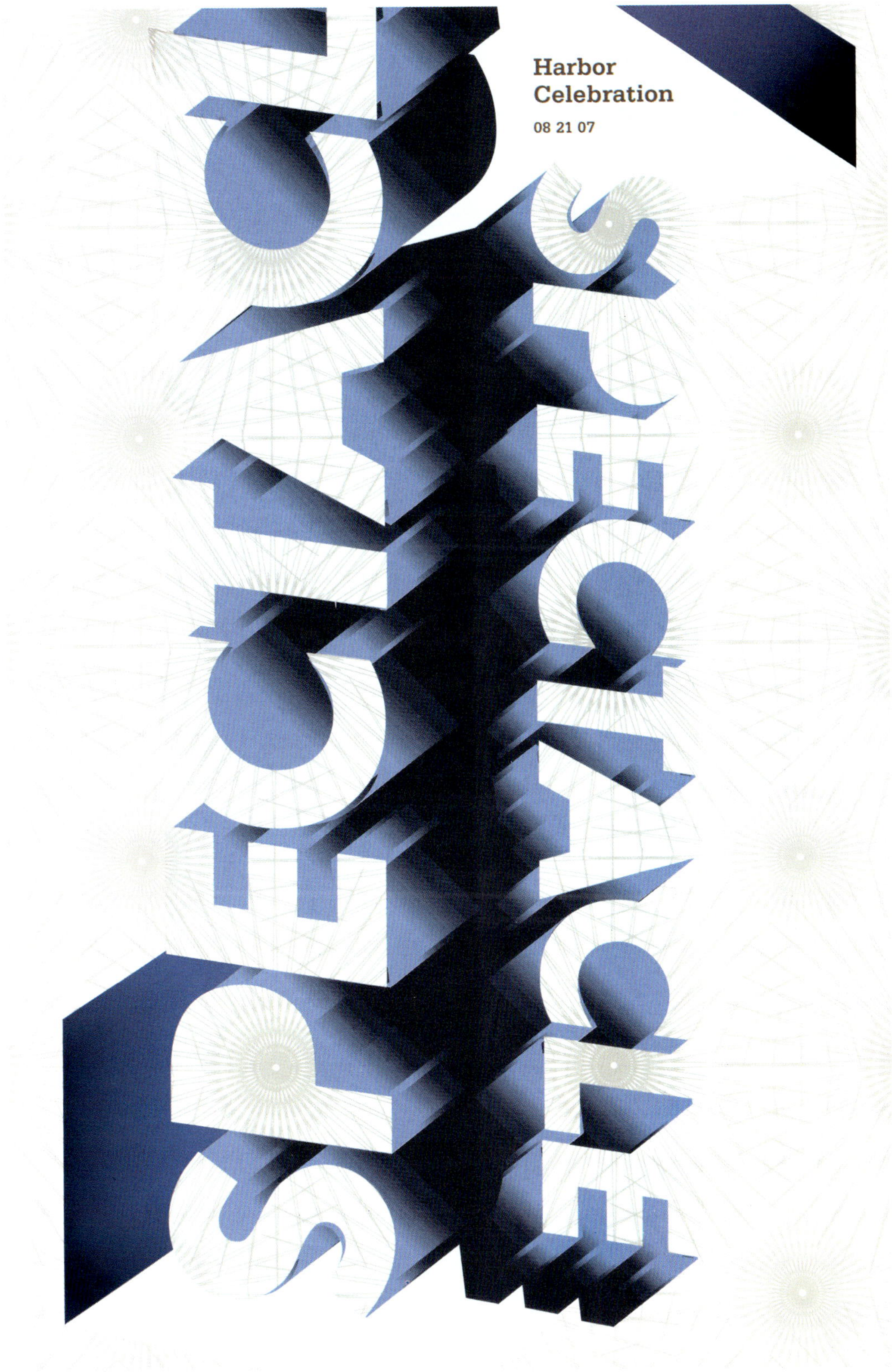

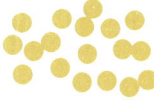

Spectacle | 2007

Keetra Dean Dixon/FromKeetra
www.fromkeetra.com

The posters are an invitation to an event of stage art. The intention was to encapsulate movement in a still image, containing it in the forms, but without forgetting the imposing effect of the audience, even when mute.

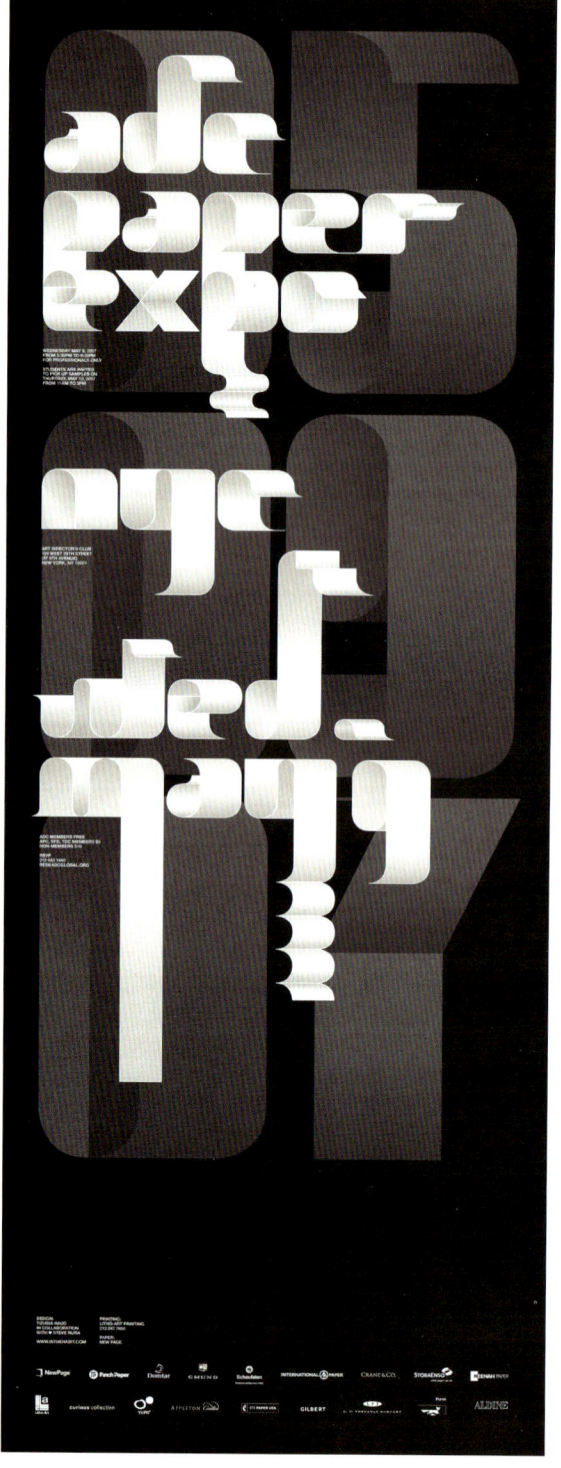

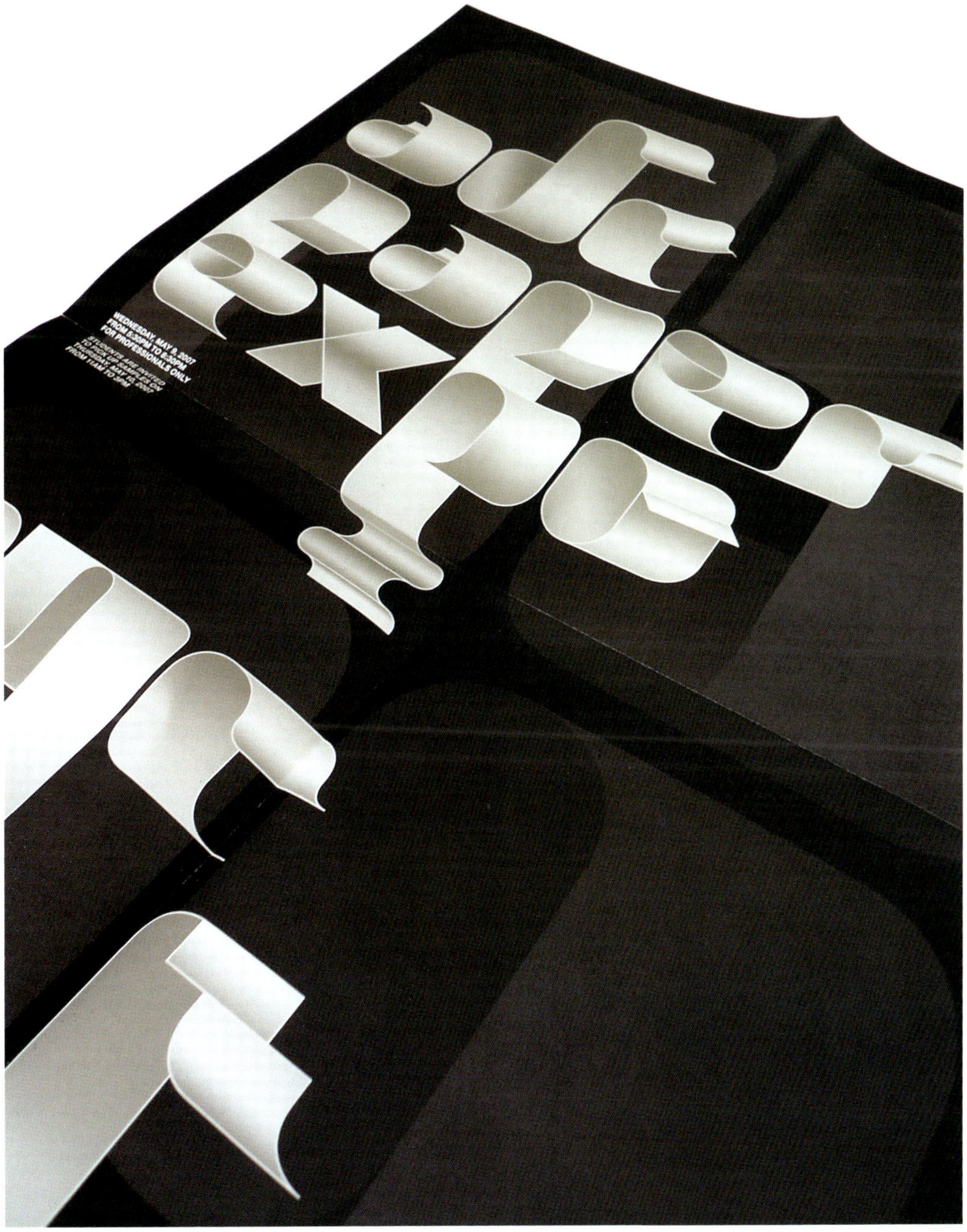

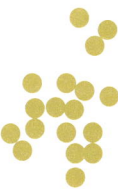

ADC Paper Expo | 2007

Tiziana Haug, Steve Rura/In the Habit
www.inthehabit.com

Instead of a complex design, it was decided to explore different dimensions. Thus, the work with the typography produces the visual effect of a third dimension. The choice of colors gives the impression of outer space.

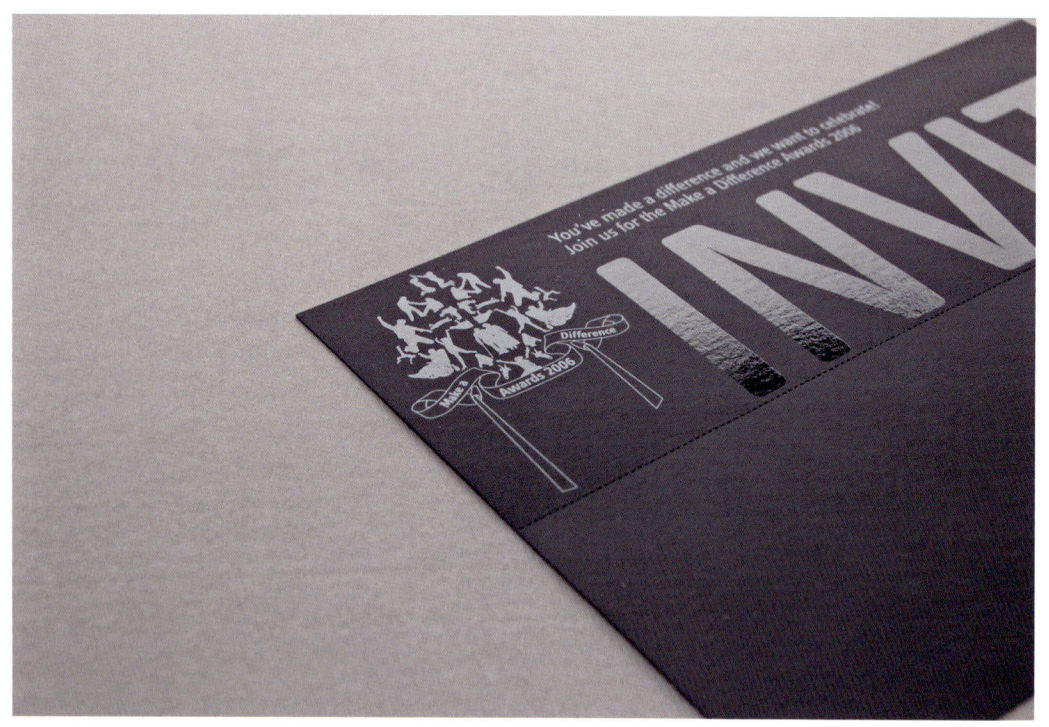

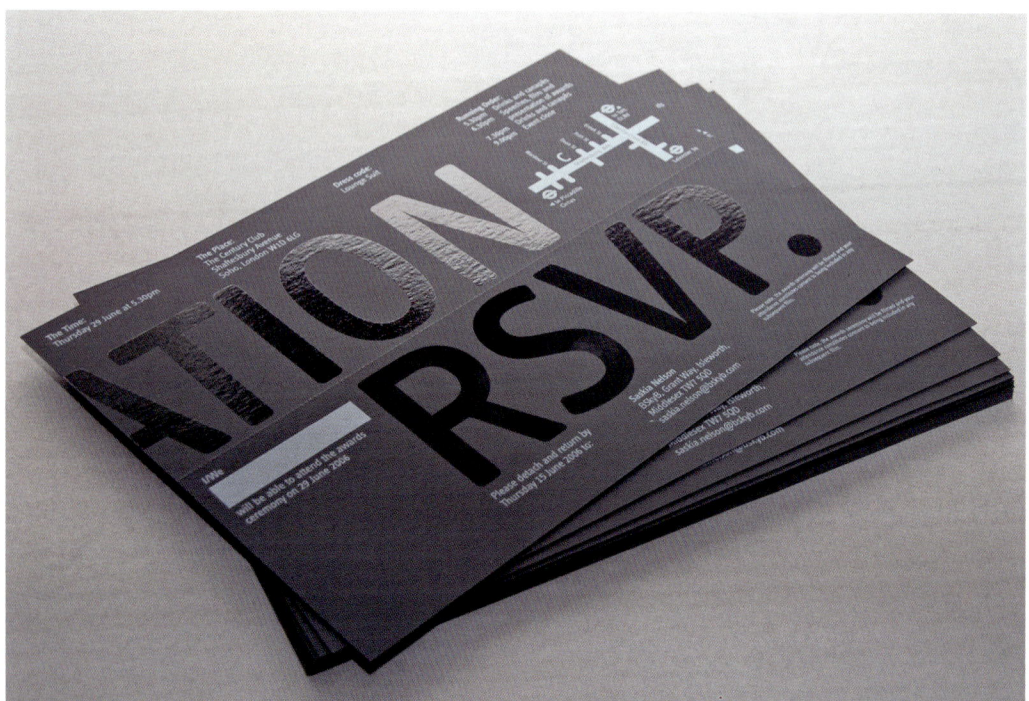

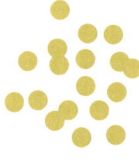

**Sky's Make a Difference
invitations | 2006**

Kent Lyons
www.kentlyons.com

Within a sober frame, the invitation joins distinction with practicality. The shine of the letters adds texture and volume to the completely black background. The RSVP section is die-cut so that it can be easily cut out.

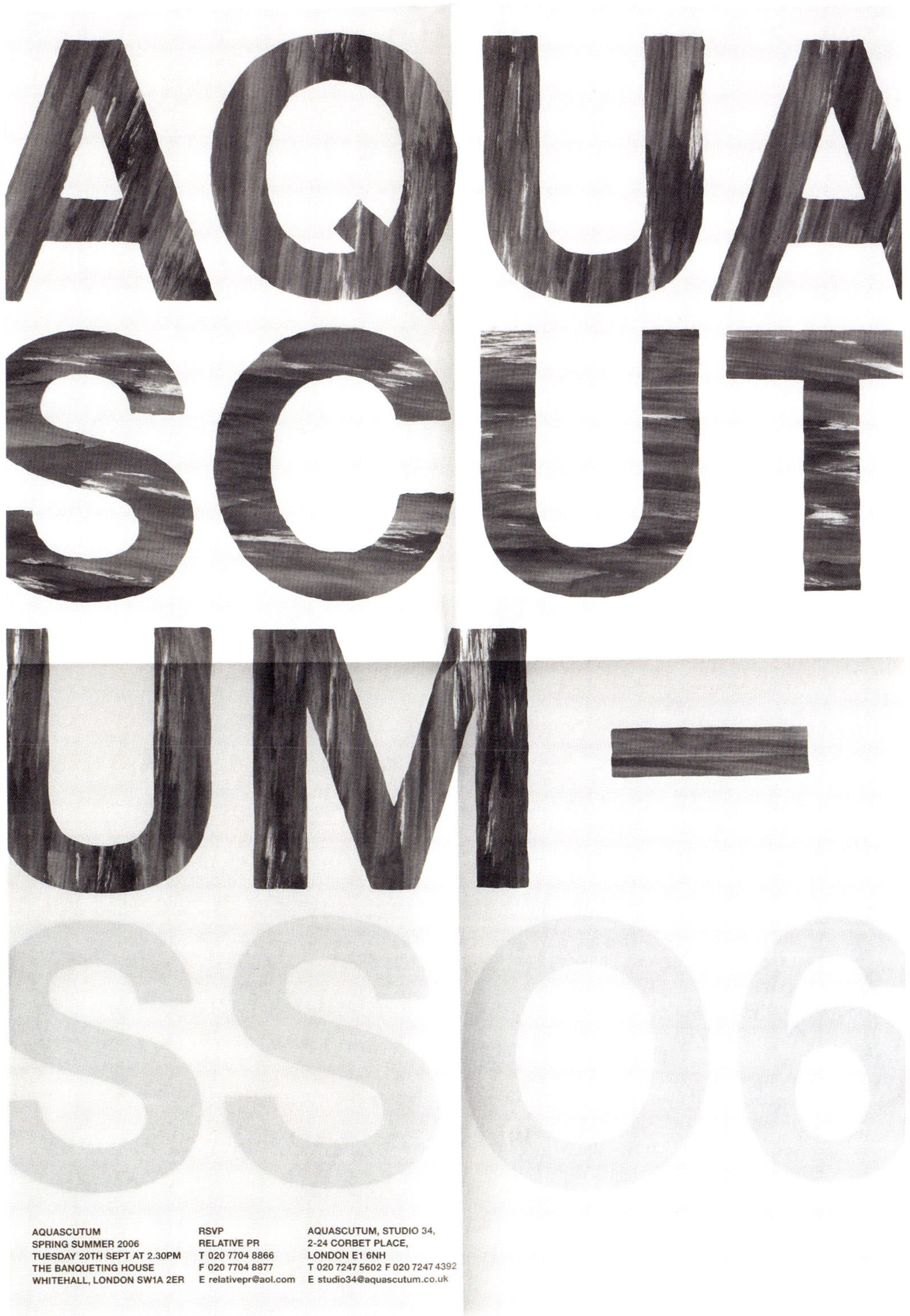

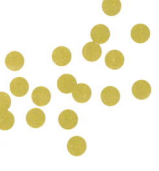

Aquascutum SS06
invitation | 2006

StudioThomson
www.studiothomson.com

Since the collection was inspired by shipwrecks, the invitation was printed on both sides and on Bible paper so that it would look like the sail of a ship. The aquatic texture of the typography consolidates this sensation.

There was a party some time ago for which all women had to dress up as men and all men as women, this party went really wild.

Ariane Spanier

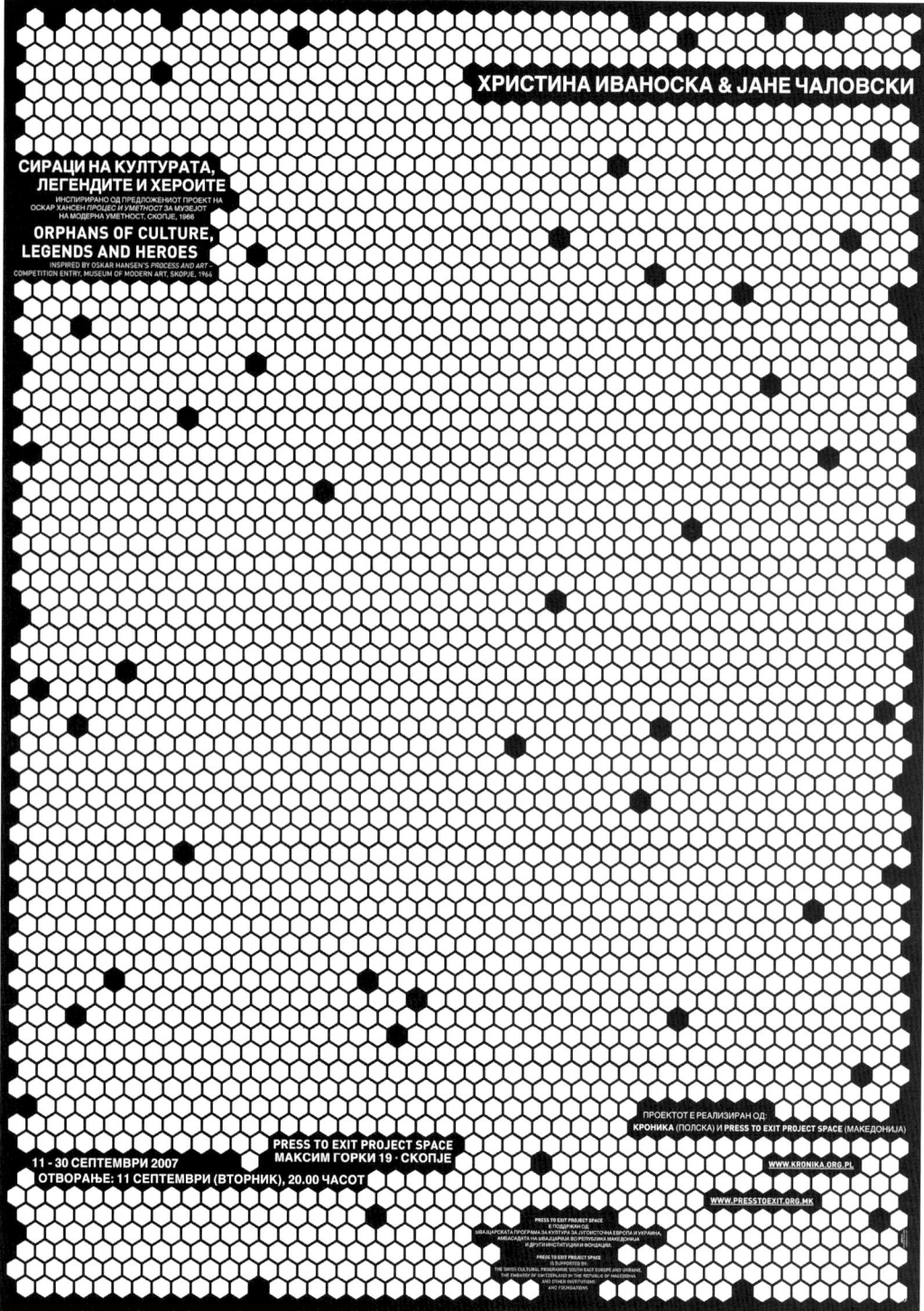

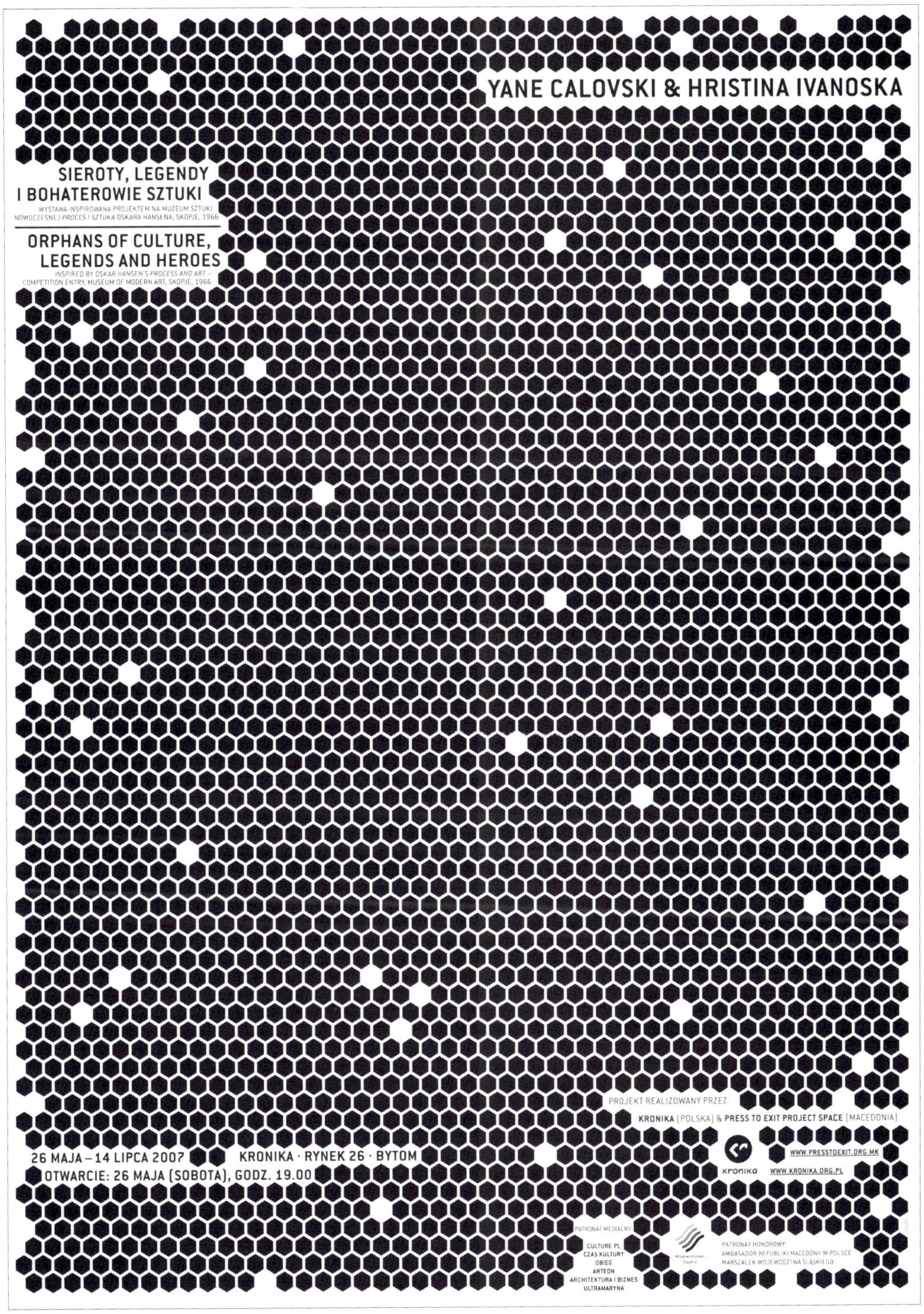

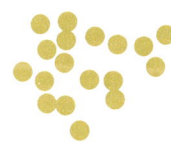

Orphans of Culture | 2007

Ariane Spanier
www.arianespanier.com

The poster is inspired by a modular system proposed by architect Oskar Hansen and brings hexagons back as a graphic element. The positive and the negative, printed on each side, announce the same exhibition in two different cities.

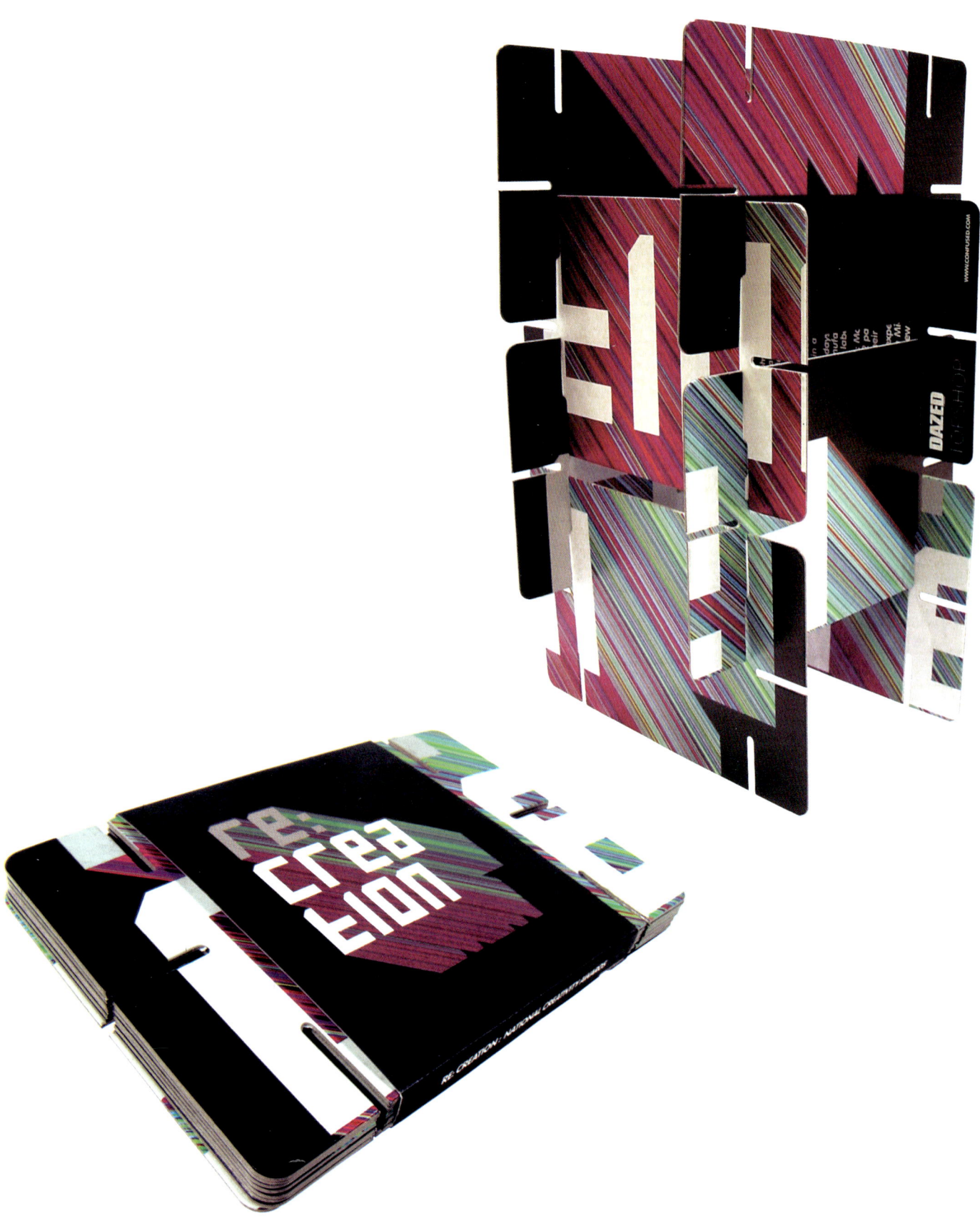

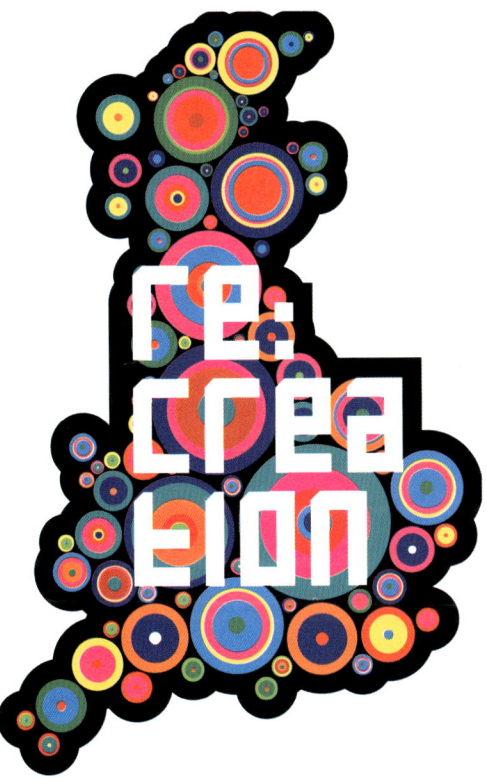
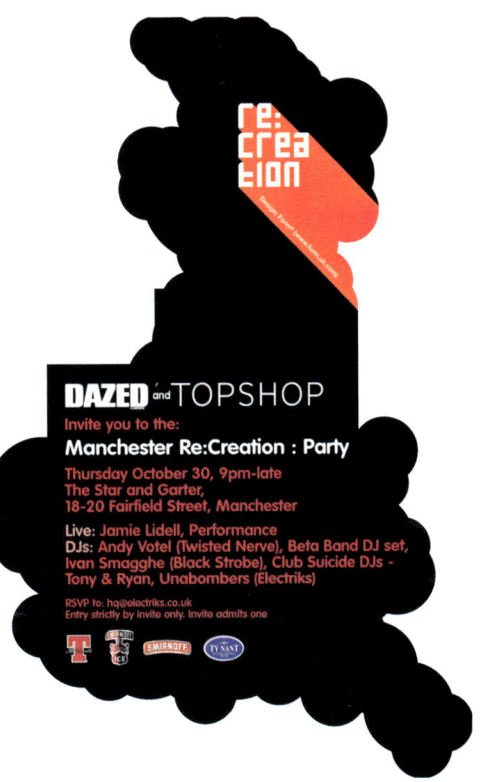
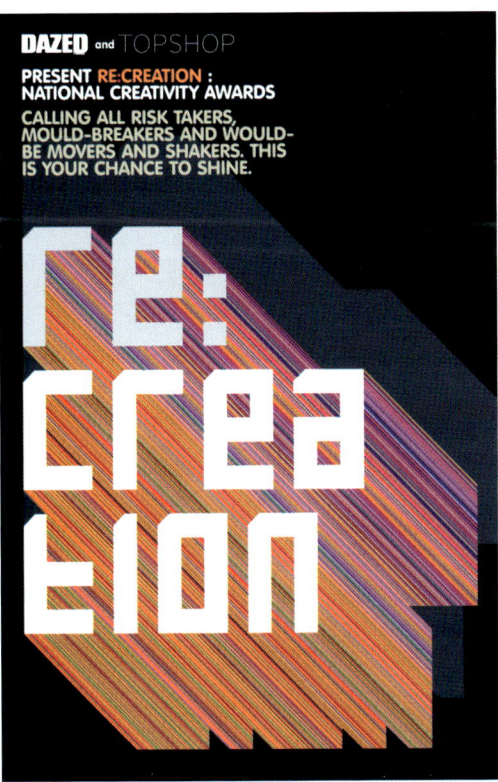
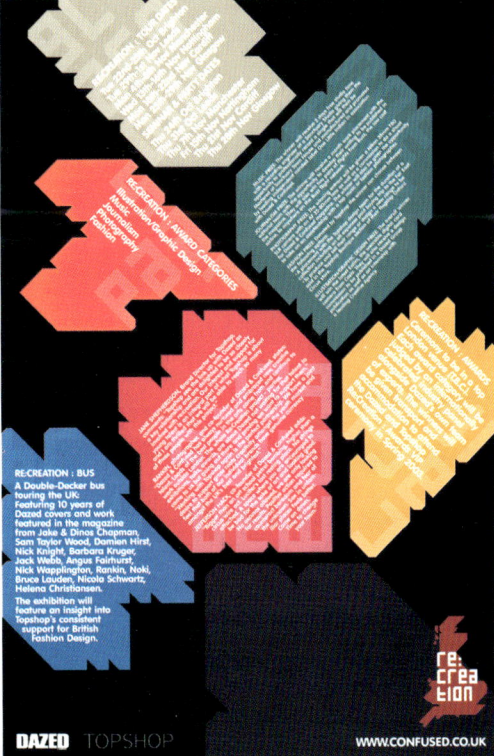

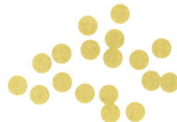

Re:Creation National
Creativity Awards | 2003-2004

Paul West, Paula Benson,
Nick Hard/Form
www.form.uk.com

The invitations, the flyers and the posters experiment with different formats and supports. The logo as leitmotif and reiteration of the same tones helps to associate the graphic materials with the event, despite their differences.

It has to be the Park Studio five year anniversary party where we paraded down Oxford Street on bejewelled elephants with singing ostriches and dancing flamingos!

Park Studio

CELESTE ART PRIZE

FINALISTS' EXHIBITION
23–28 MAY 2006

A NEW PRIZE TO PROMOTE PAINTING IN ITS WIDEST SENSE

£15,000 PRIZE MONEY
The finalists will vote for the overall winners in two sections: **Artist** (£10,000) & **Student Artist** (£5,000)

EXHIBITION VENUE
The Well, Dray Walk
The Old Truman Brewery
off Brick Lane
London E1 6QL

Opening times: 10am–7pm

Nearest tube: Liverpool Street, Aldgate East, Shoreditch

FOR FURTHER INFORMATION
T: +44 (0)20 7701 6679
E: info@celesteartprize.co.uk
www.celesteartprize.co.uk

Goldsmiths UNIVERSITY OF LONDON | THE OLD TRUMAN BREWERY

CELESTE ART PRIZE
Design by www.park-studio.com

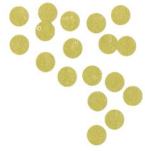

Celeste Art Prize | 2007

Linda Lundin, Nina Nägel/Park Studio
www.park-studio.com

The Celeste Art Prize is a new award which promotes painting that employs the most varied and modern techniques. To fit this into a traditional context without forgetting its peculiarity, a classic frame and singular details were used.

PREEN
by
thornton
bregazzi
autumn
winter
2005/6
___

tuesday
15th
february
3.30pm
___

the
great
hall
___

the
west
stand
___

stamford
bridge
football
stadium

chelsea
village
___

fulham
road
___

sw6
lhs
___

fulham
broadway
tube
___

london
fashion
week
return
bus
service
available
from
front
of
bfc
tent

name
___

block
___

row
___

RSVP
relativepr
@aol.com
___

telephone
020
7704
8866
___

facsimile
020
7704
8877

SPONSORED BY
TOPSHOP

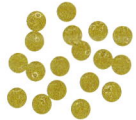

Preen invitation | 2005–2006

StudioThomson
ww.studiothomson.com

The collection has a childlike theme with wide collars and giant buttons. To honor the elements of the collection, the invitation mimics the aesthetics of an old spelling book, marking the letters by the space left between them.

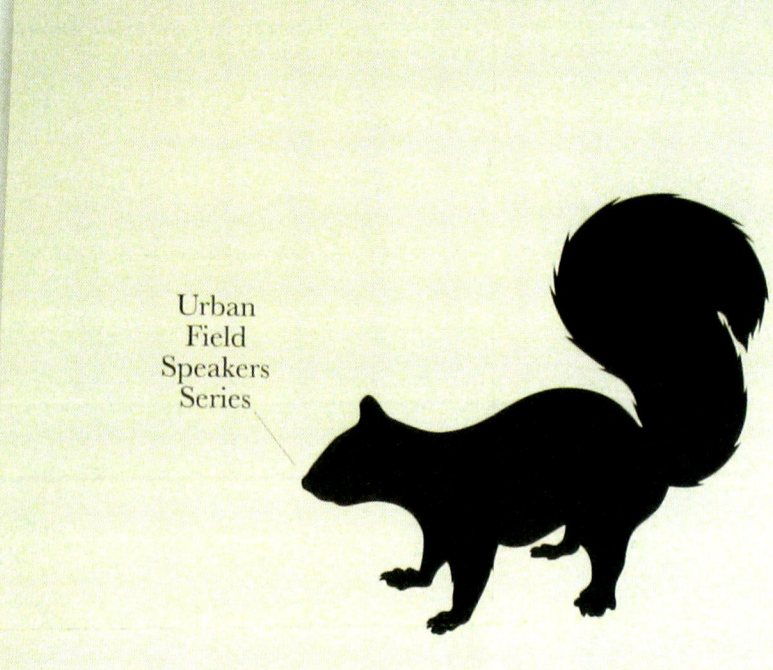

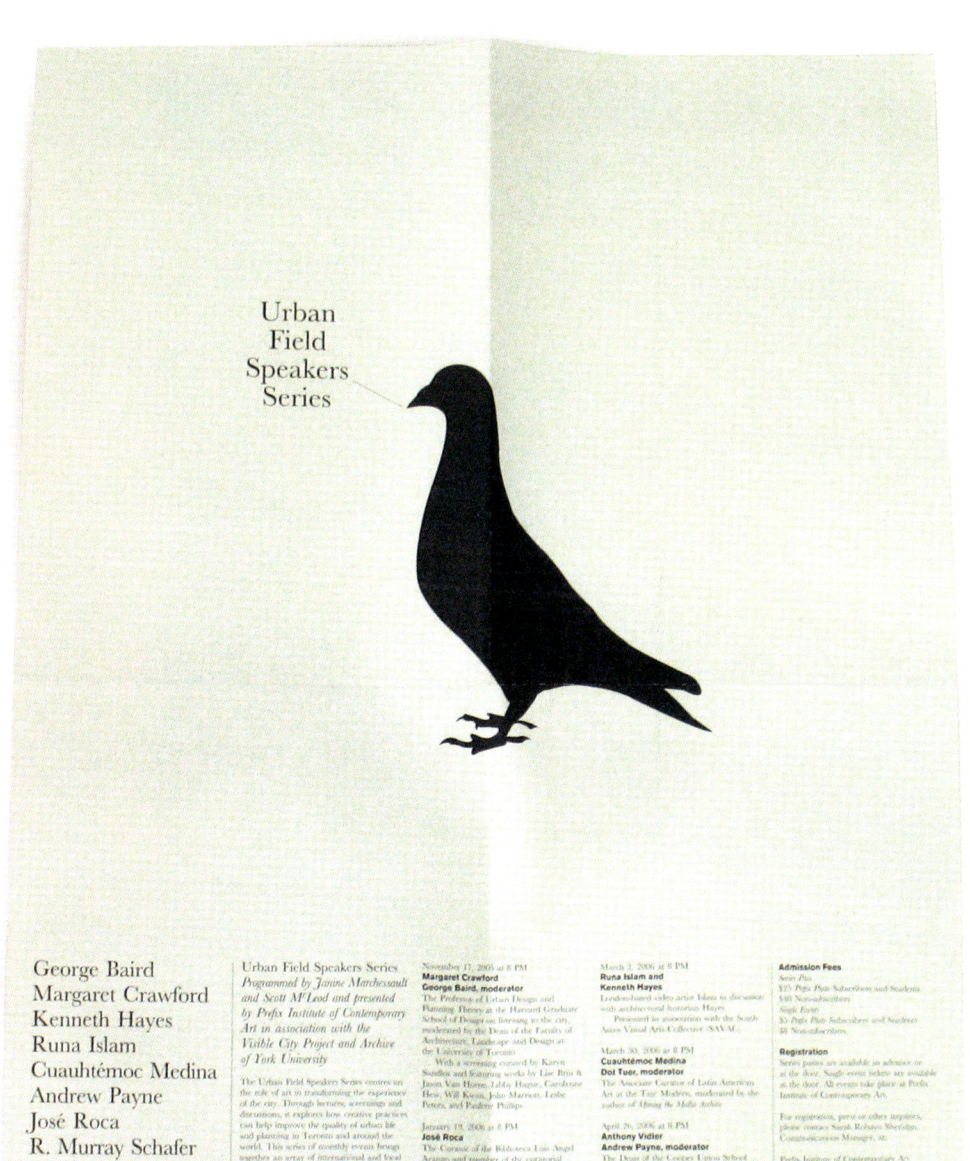

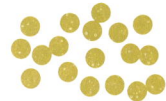

**Urban Field Speakers
Series | 2005-2007**

Underline Studio
www.underlinestudio.com

Inspired by the figure of the orator who speaks in the park, the poster reinterprets the situation and gives the stage to the passing spectators: a pigeon, a squirrel... The feel of the composition is concluded in an attractive design.

The party was during the university trip to Germany, in a small basement club in Berlin.

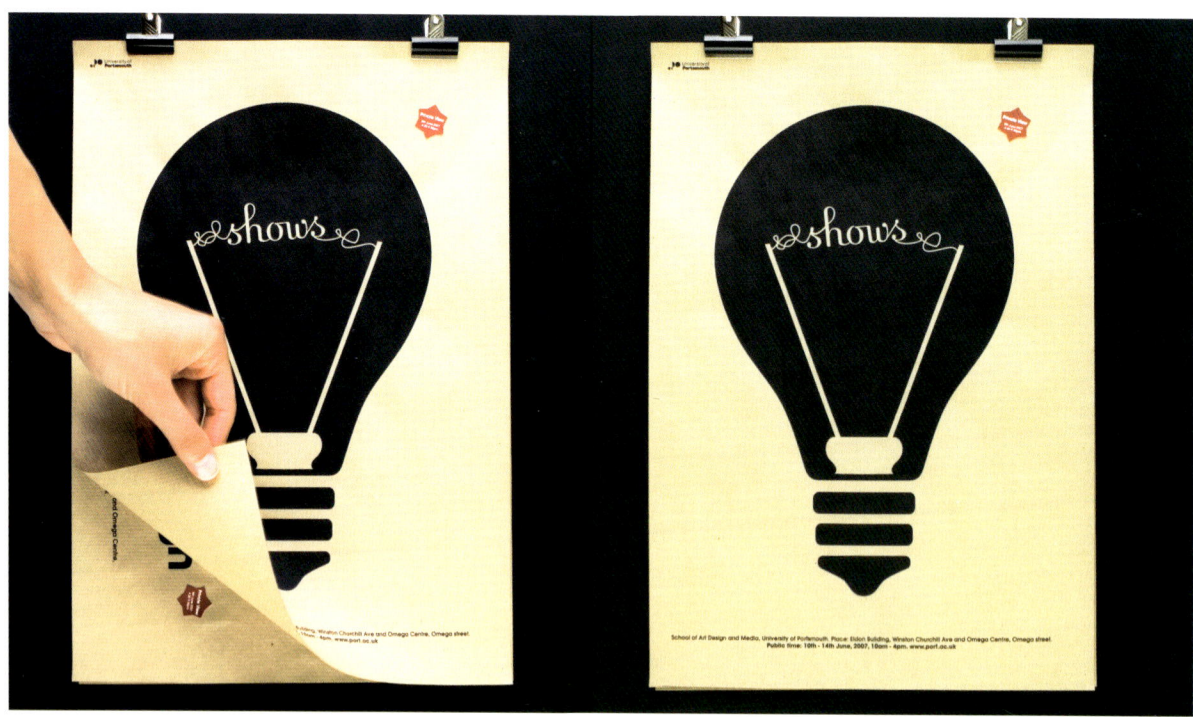

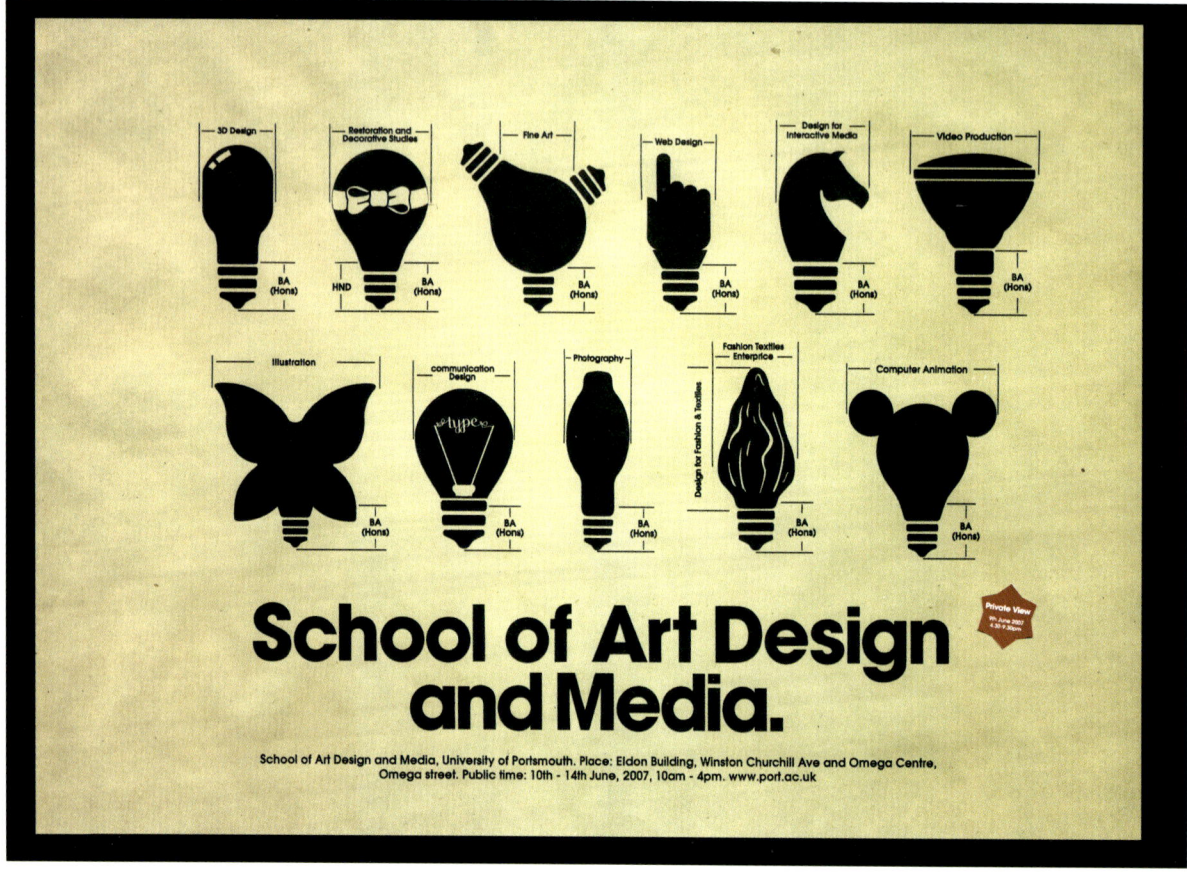

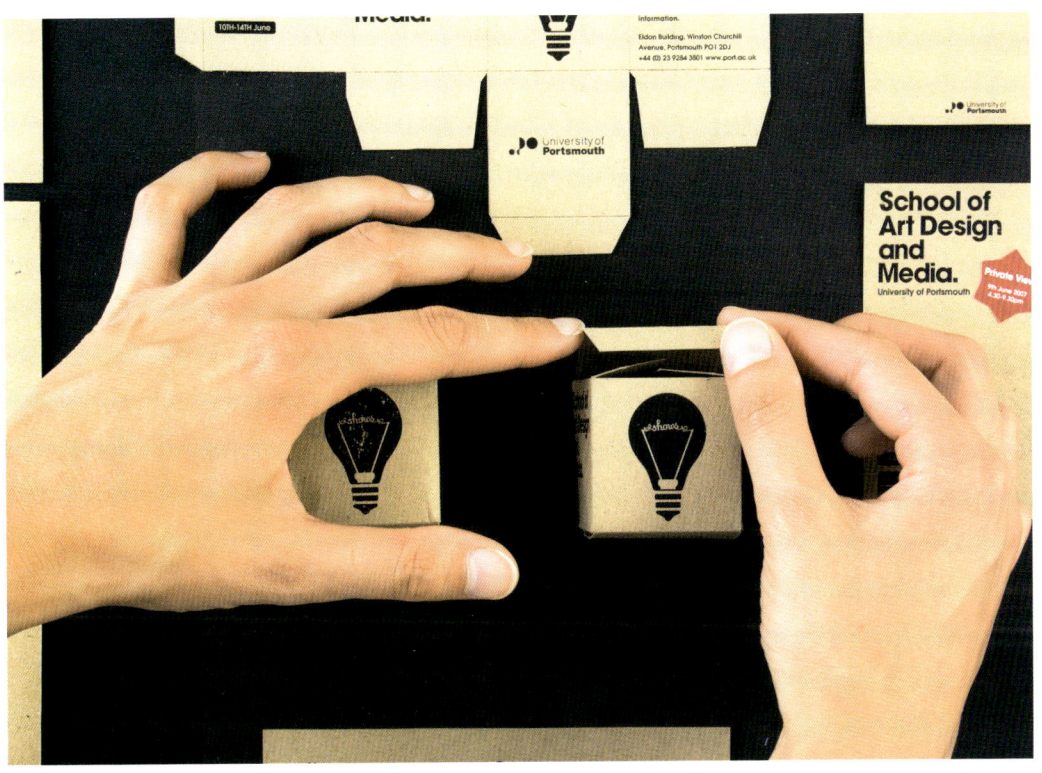

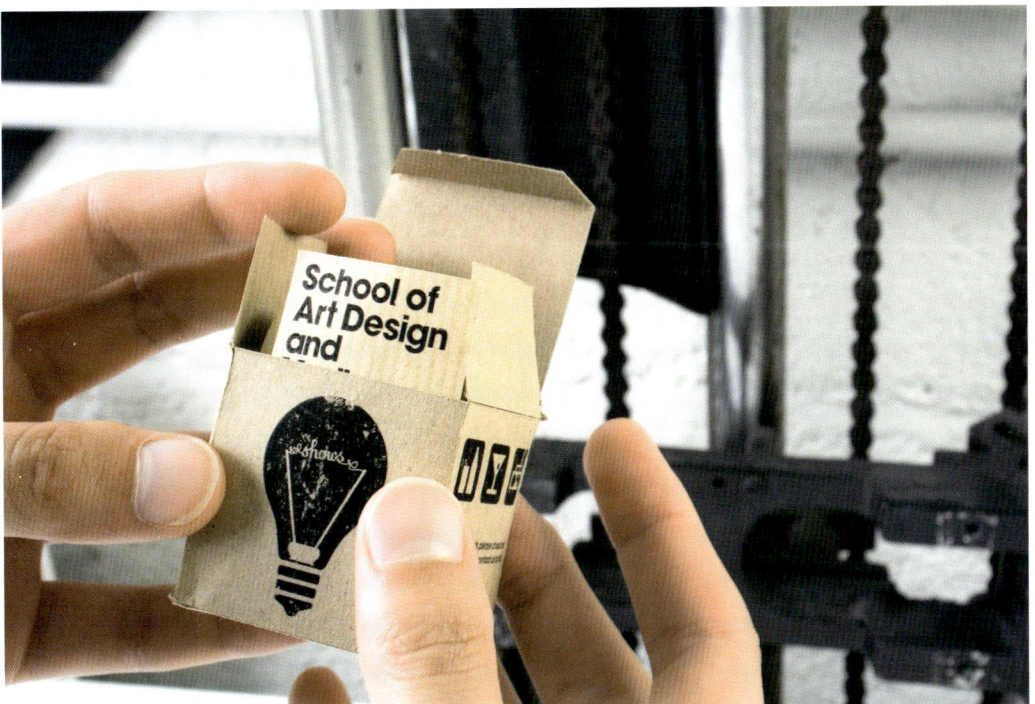

University of Portsmouth summer show promotion | 2007

Shi Yuan
www.shiyuan.co.uk

When a genius has an idea, the bulb lights up. The light bulb is the figure from which everything develops here: it forms the base of the different images that represent the courses at the school and even the invitation imitates its packaging.

I went to a marvelous party. / We played the most wonderful game, / Maureen disappeared / And came back in a beard / And we all had to guess at her name! / We talked about growing old gracefully. / And Elsie who's seventy-four / Said, "A, it's a question of being sincere, / And B, if you're supple you've nothing to fear." / Then she swung upside down from a glass chandelier, / I couldn't have liked it more.

Noel Coward

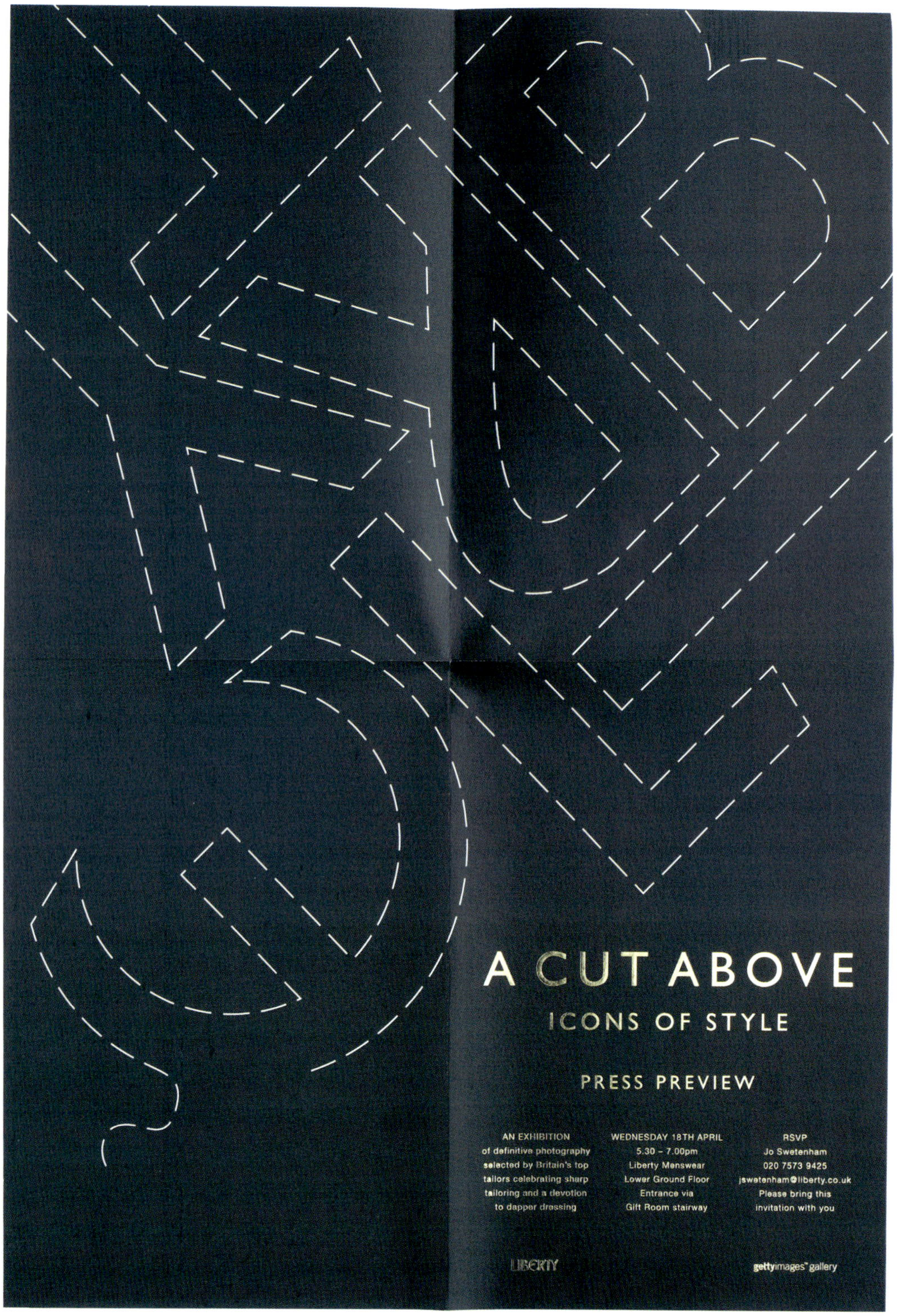

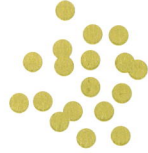

Liberty A Cut Above invitation | 2007

StudioThomson
www.studiothomson.com

The exhibition was on tailoring, so the invitation was designed so that it would look like a tailor's cutting pattern. Despite working from simplicity, the keys here are a clean typography and the delicate layout.

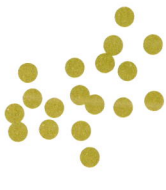

**Liberty Christmas
invitation | 2007**

**StudioThomson
www.studiothomson.com**

Without blocking visibility, white on white was used, making the message stand out from the volume. The intention is to mimic the texture of snow and repeat the theme of the place's decoration, the candelabras.

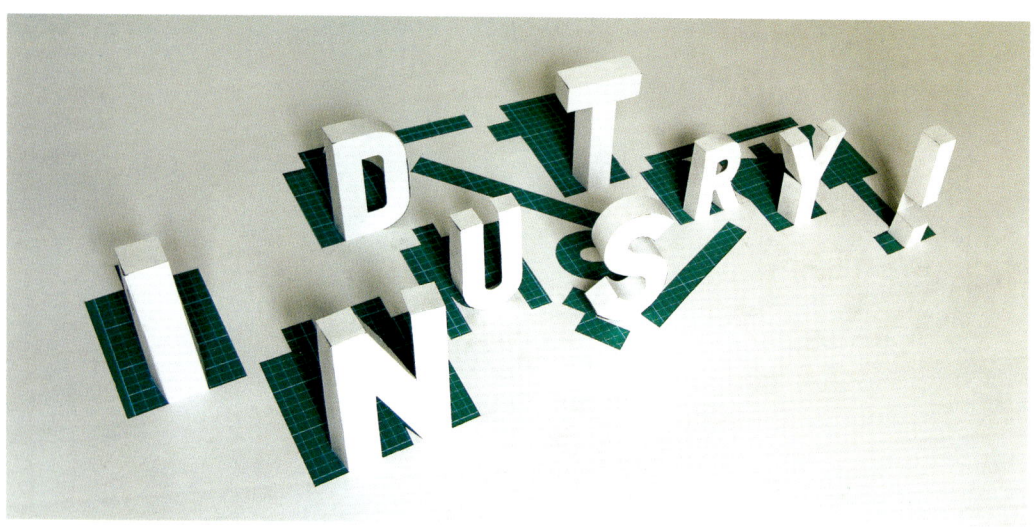

Industry! | 2006

Ariane Spanier
www.arianespanier.com

For an exhibition of three architectural studios from different countries, the letters of the title are constructed as a three-dimensional model using gray card. The form of the cuttings can still be seen, like shadows.

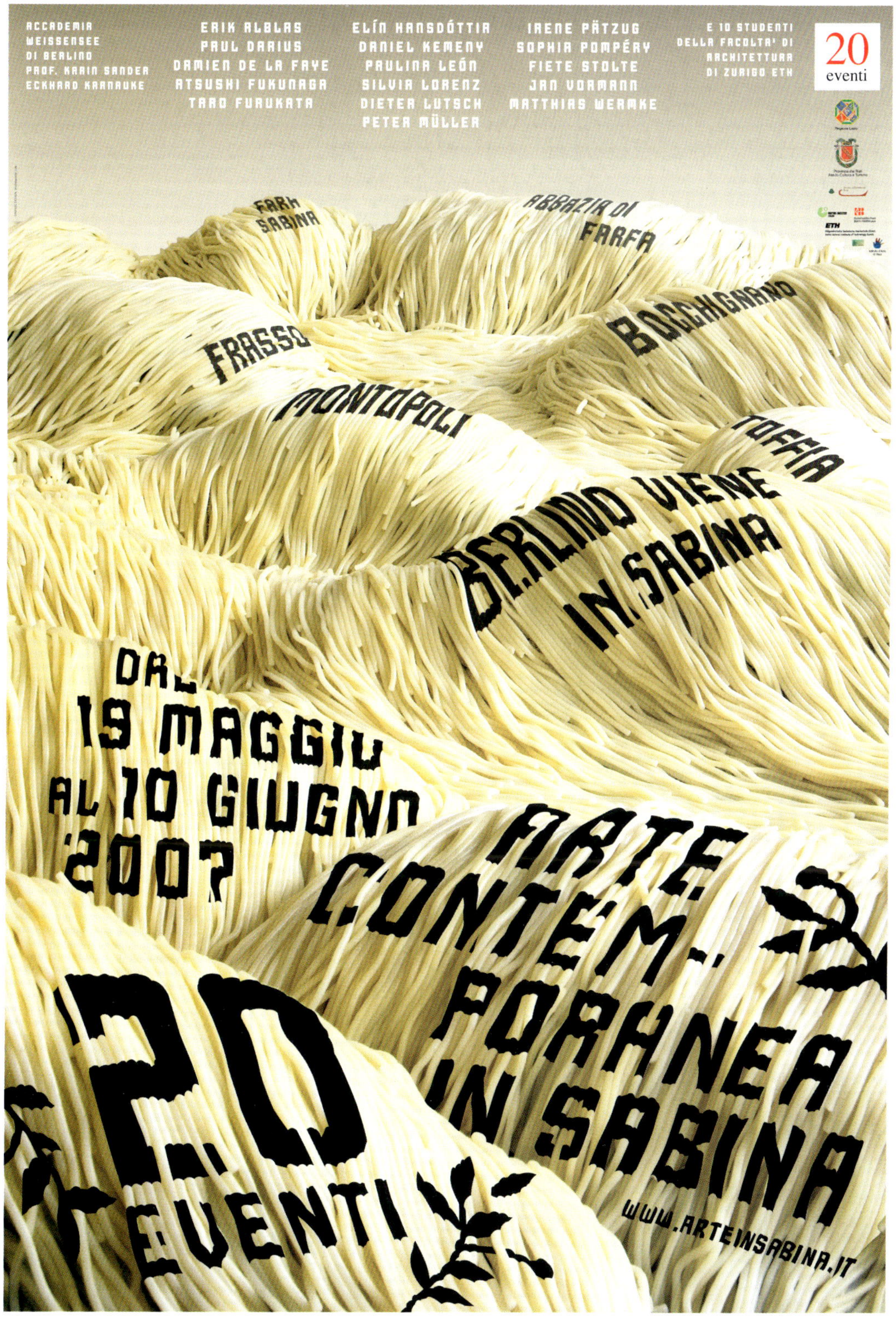

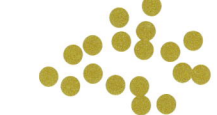

20 Eventi | 2007

Ariane Spanier
www.arianespanier.com

The cliché of spaghetti was used to construct hills, which promoted the exhibition of an academy. The form of the landscape is a tribute to the beauty of Sabina hills, where the exhibition was to take place.

For a party to be the best it has to be memorable for me, and that has to involve fancy dress. A Halloween party where a male friend came as Milla Jovovich in The Fifth Element *with the bandages sticks in the mind for some reason. Not sure if that's the best but I know I won't forget it.*

BB/Saunders

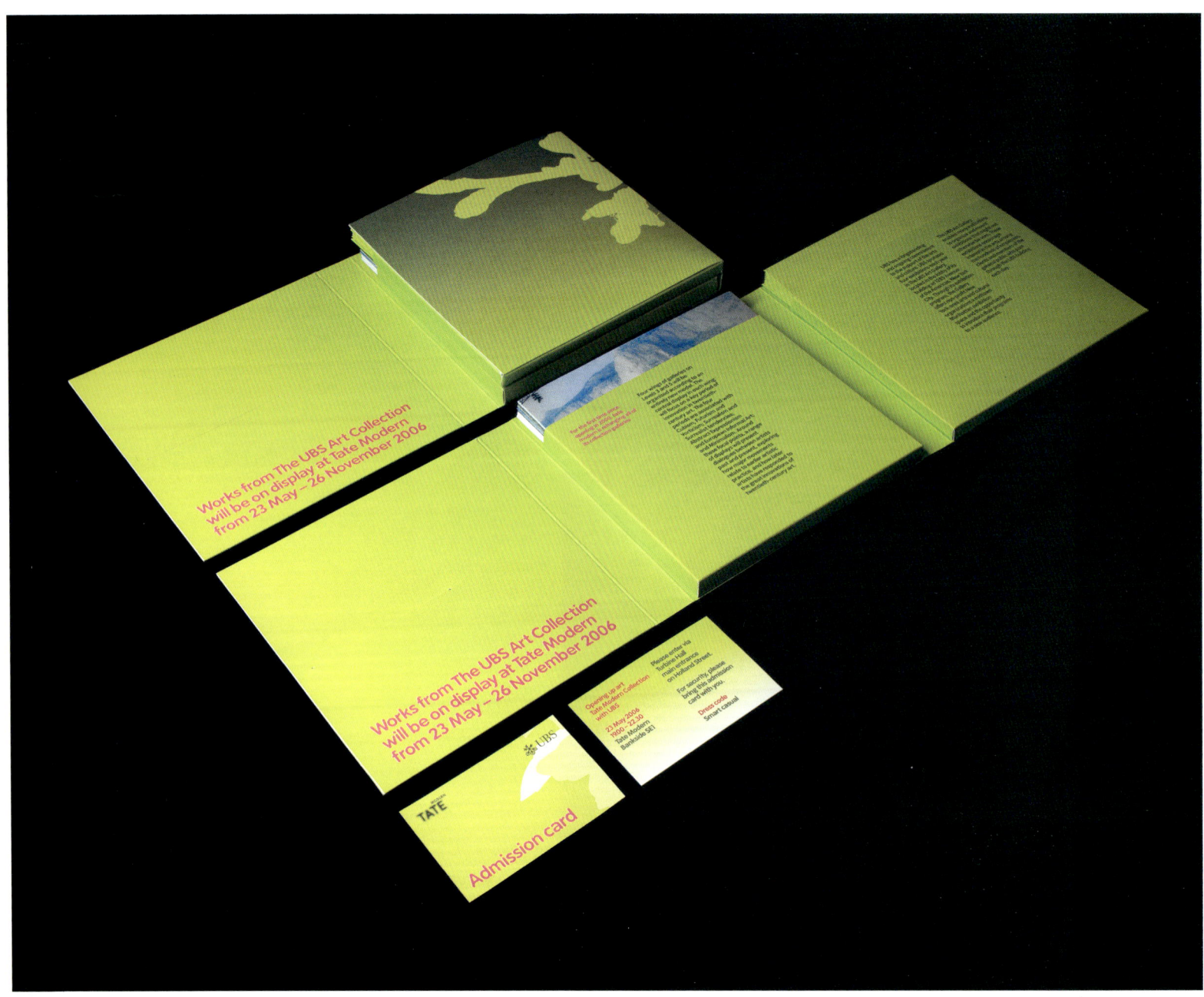

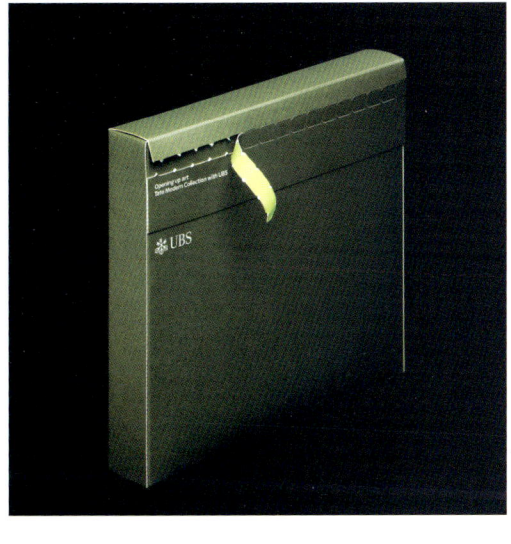
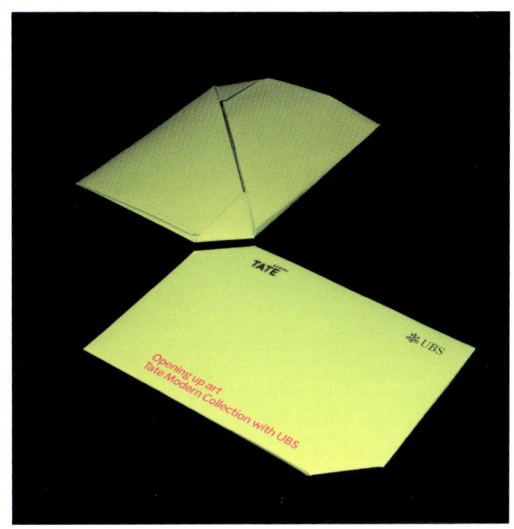
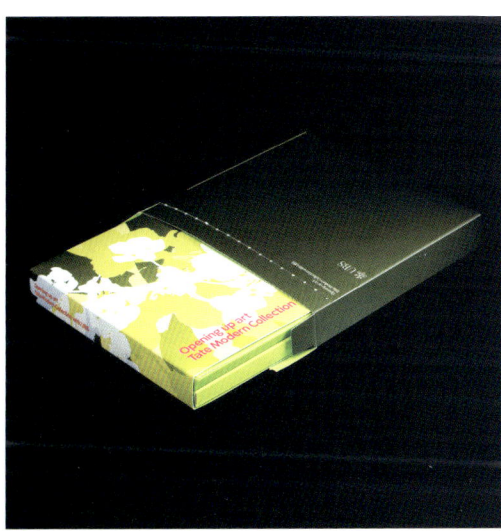
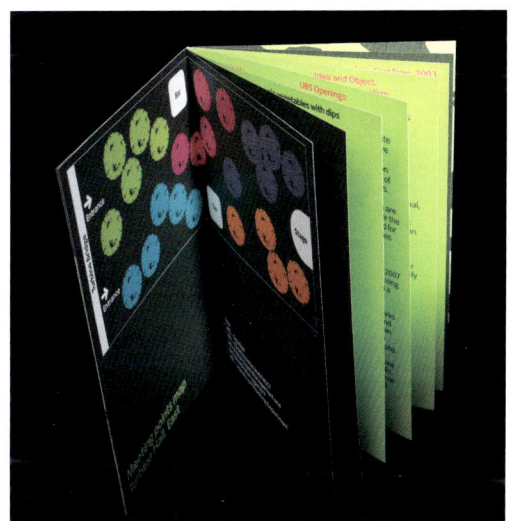
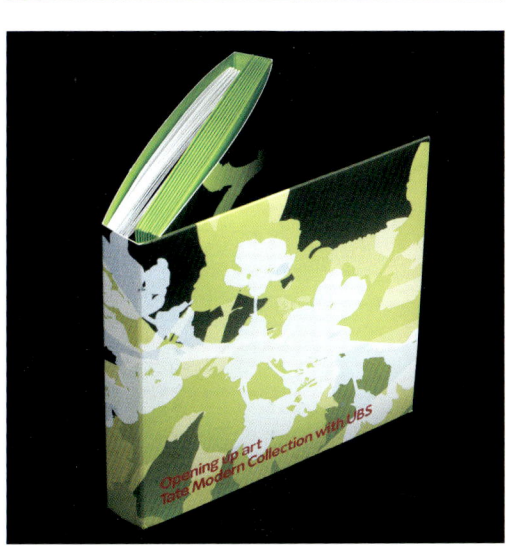
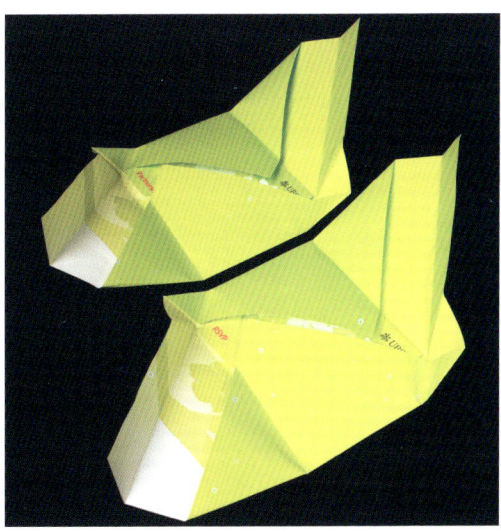
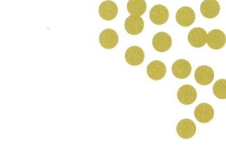

Tate/UBS Opening Up
Art invitation and RSVP | 2006

BB/Saunders
www.bbsaunders.com

The night of the inauguration, the Turbine Hall in the Tate Modern was filled with flowering trees. That is why the form of these trees can be insinuated in the image of the cover, and why different shades of green have been used.

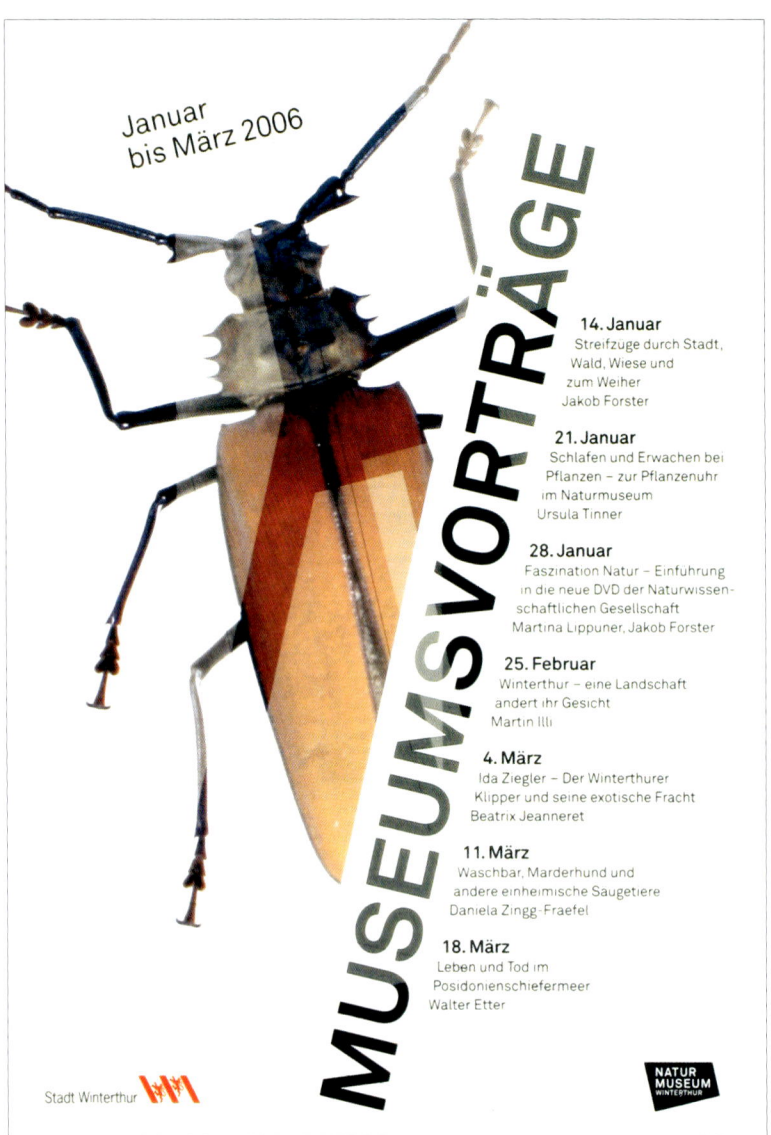
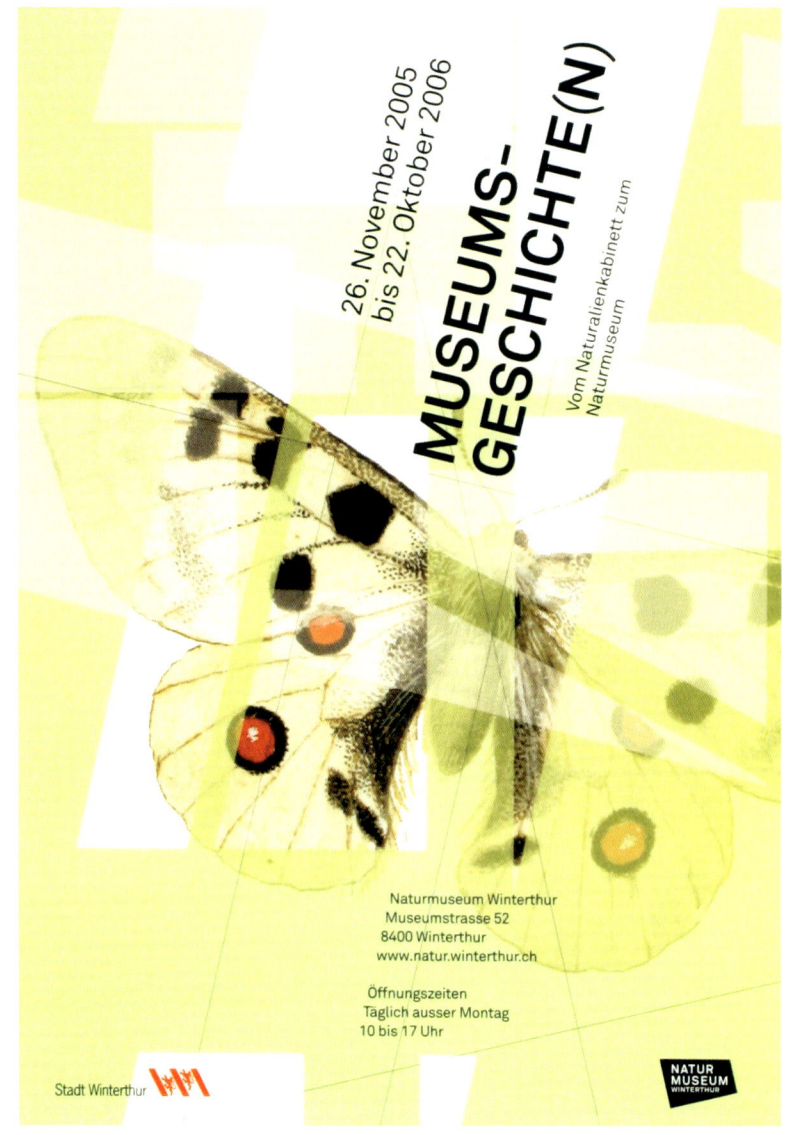

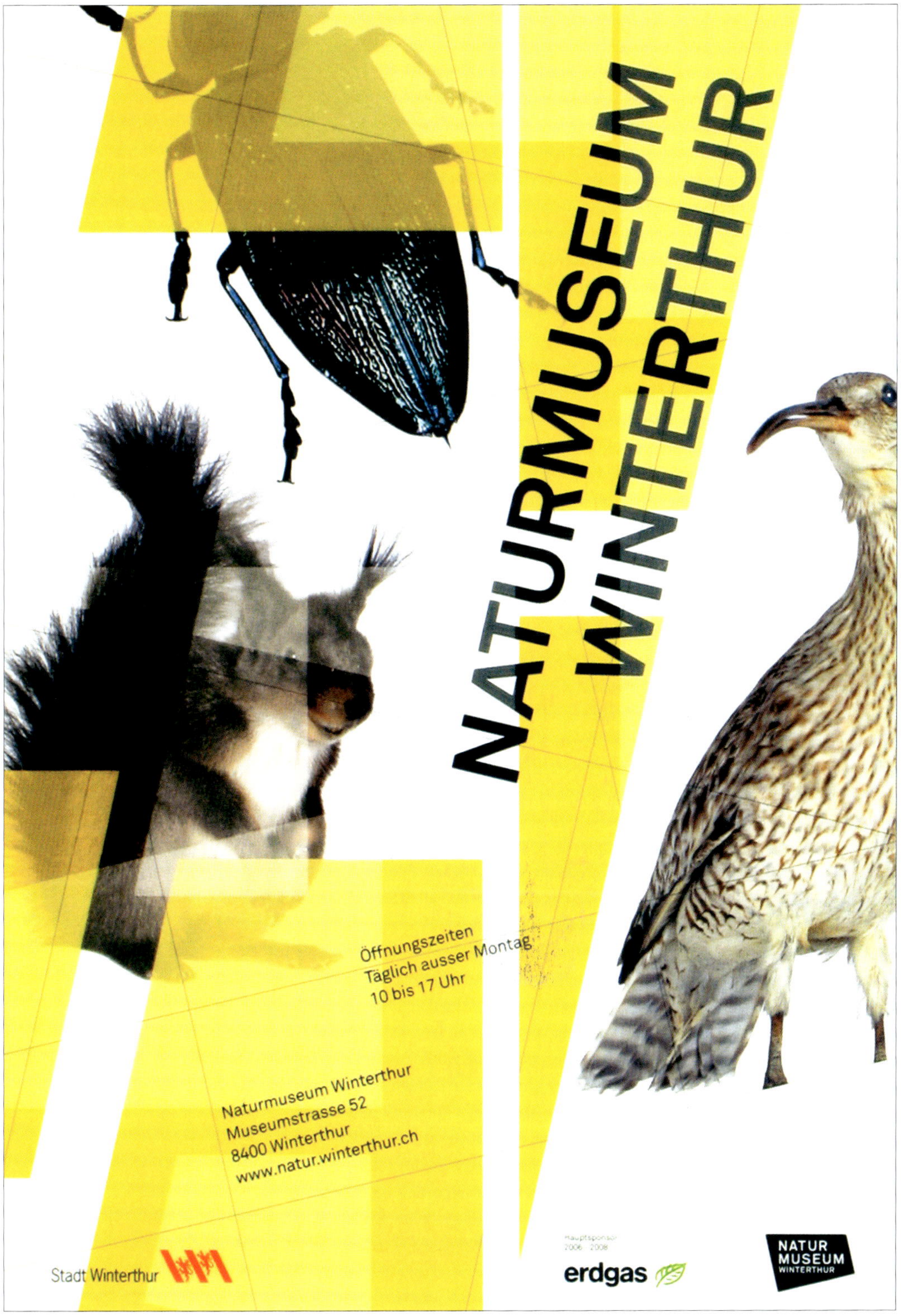

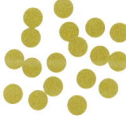

**Naturmuseum Winterthur
cards and posters | 2005**

**Fauxpas Grafik
www.fauxpas.ch**

In accordance with the museum's proposal, part of the insects and animals are hidden: the focus is on the details that can be seen. The typical diagonals of the building are also reflected in the vectorial design.

I was fifteen when I was invited to this afternoon party. The theme was "Black and White." I thought it would be a great idea to dress up as a rabbit. I wore a huge white fake fur jumpsuit and a hood with long ears. Unlike me, the other girls wore sexy short skirts and checkered tops. I was left on my own eating carrot sticks. Nobody danced with me. Not even when I took the rabbit costume off…

Cleo Charuet

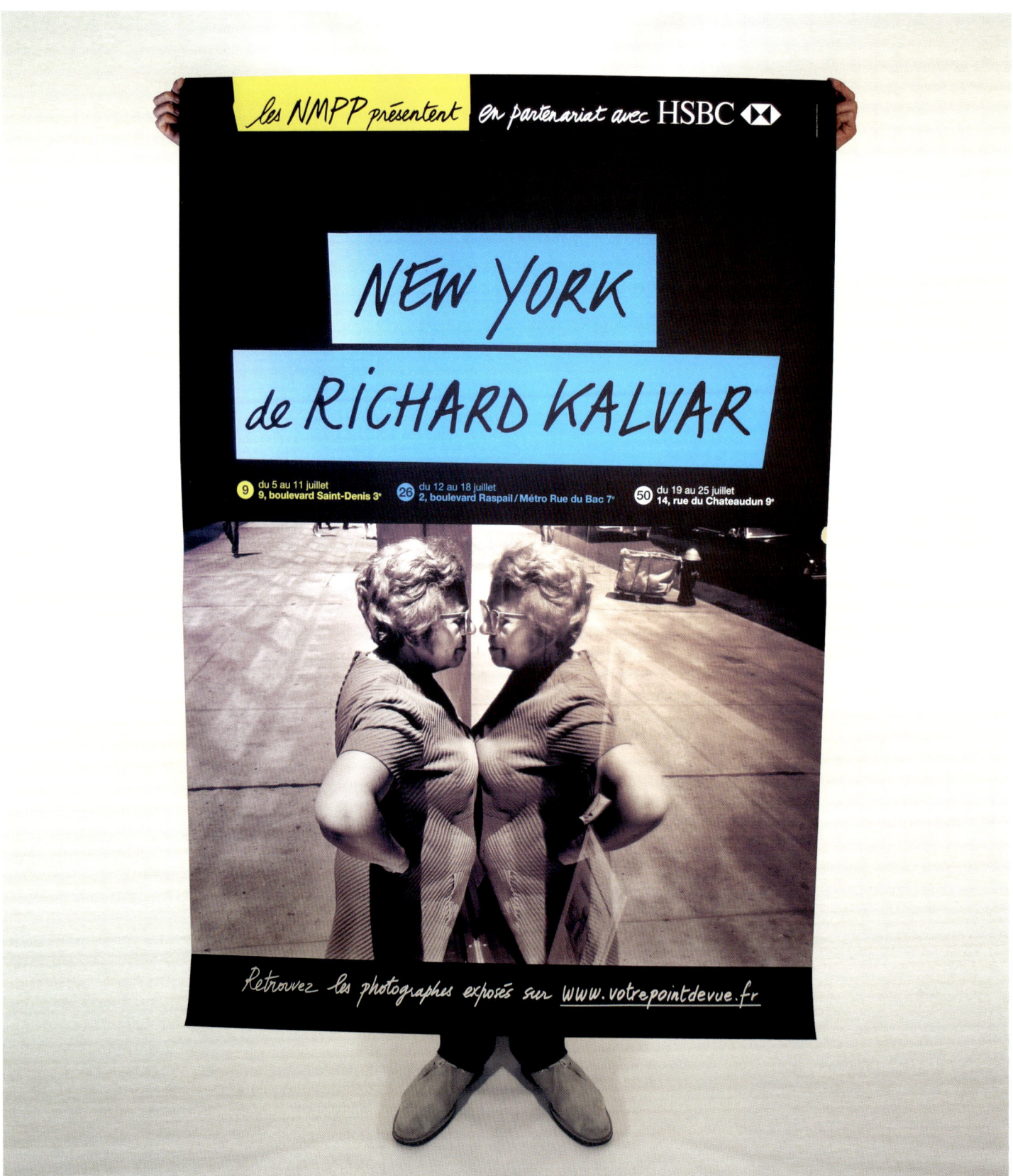

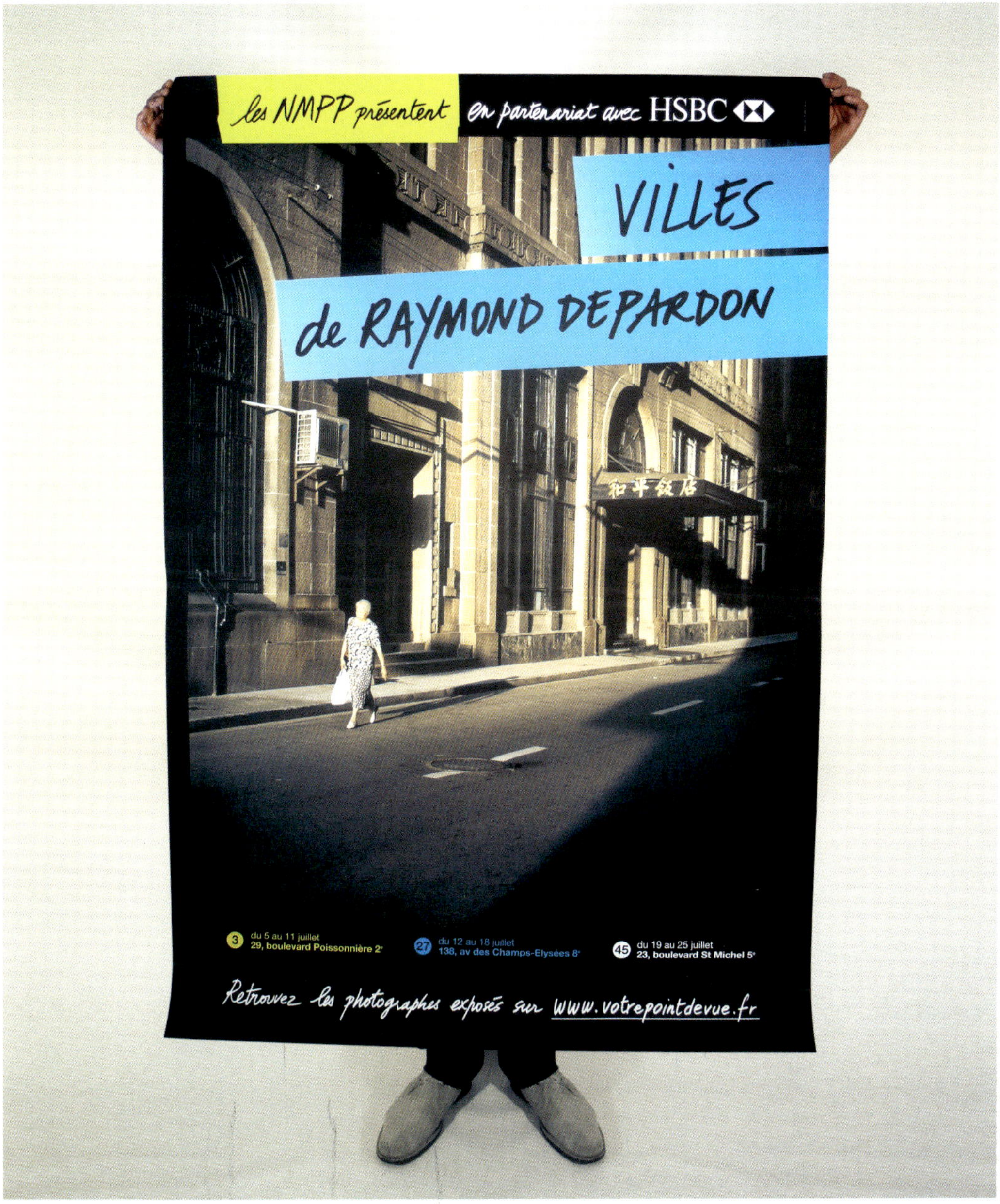

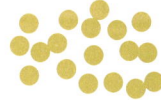

**MAGNUM Photos
à l'affiche/MAGNUM Photos
in the public eye | 2007**

Cleo Charuet/Cleoburo
Assisted by Fred de Brugada Vila
www.cleoburo.com

Without breaking up the space of the photograph, the posters attempt to simulate an unfinished work. The blue forms imitate sticky tape for labeling and organizing material and hand-drawn typography supports the effect of a "work in progress."

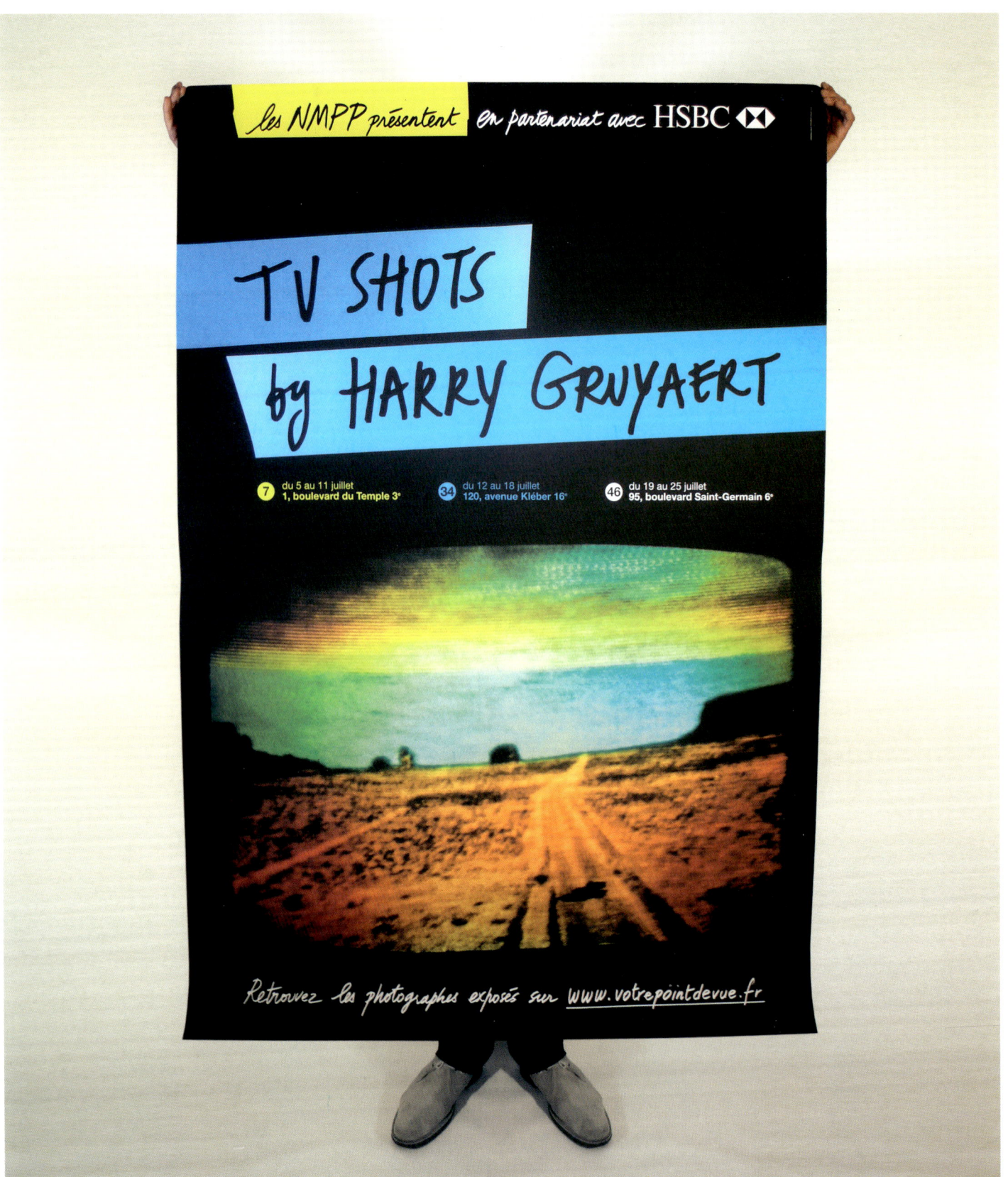

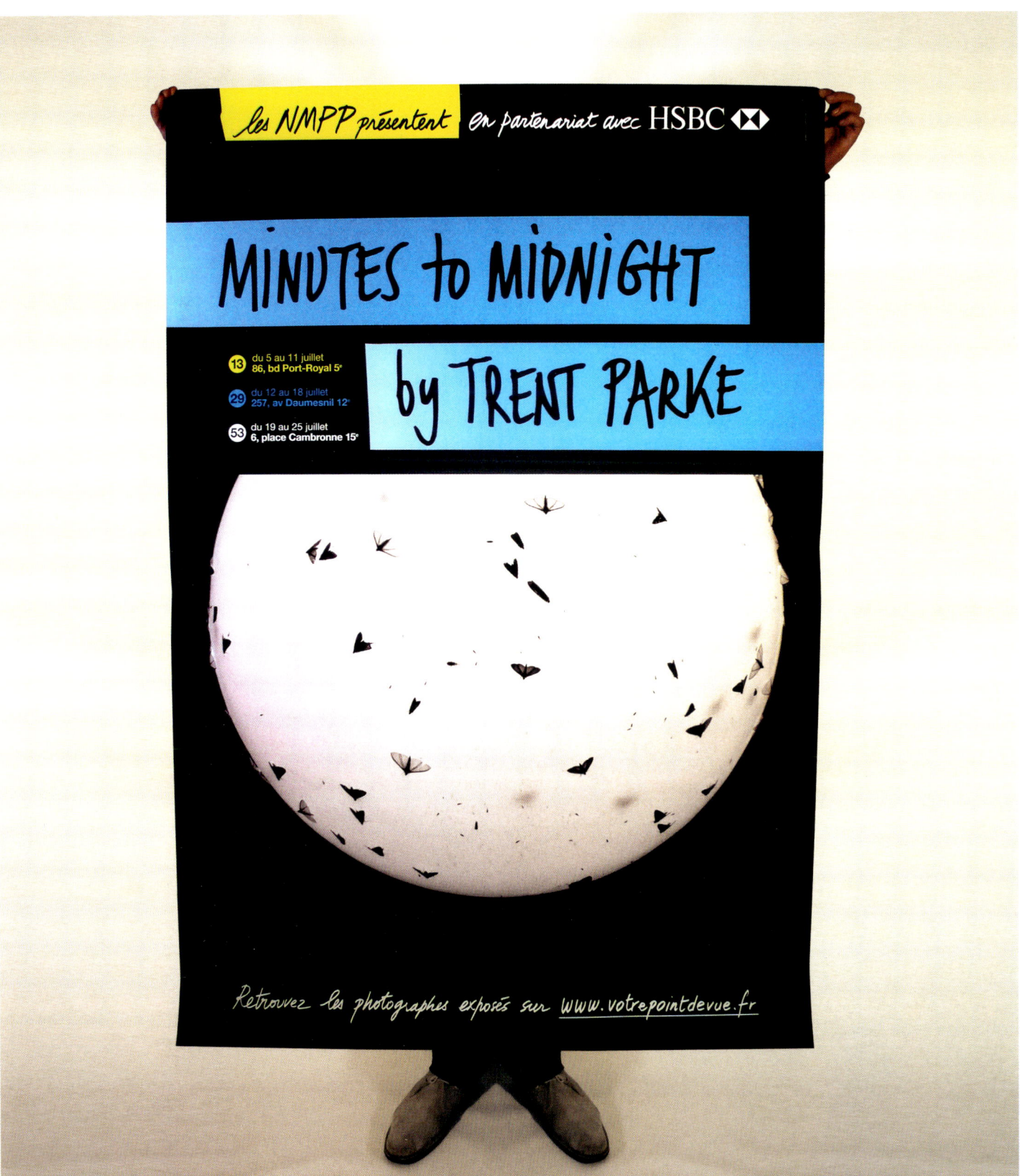

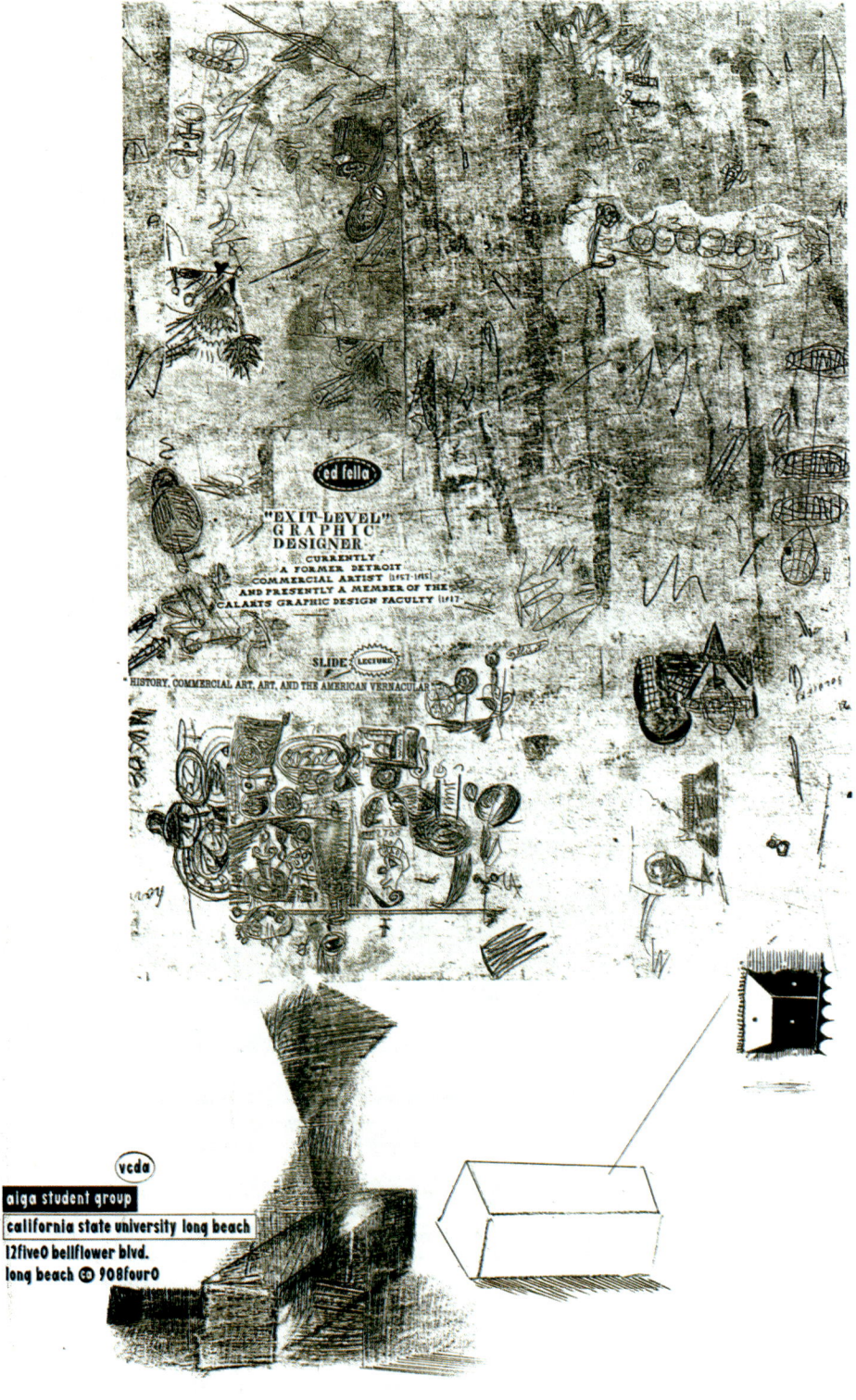

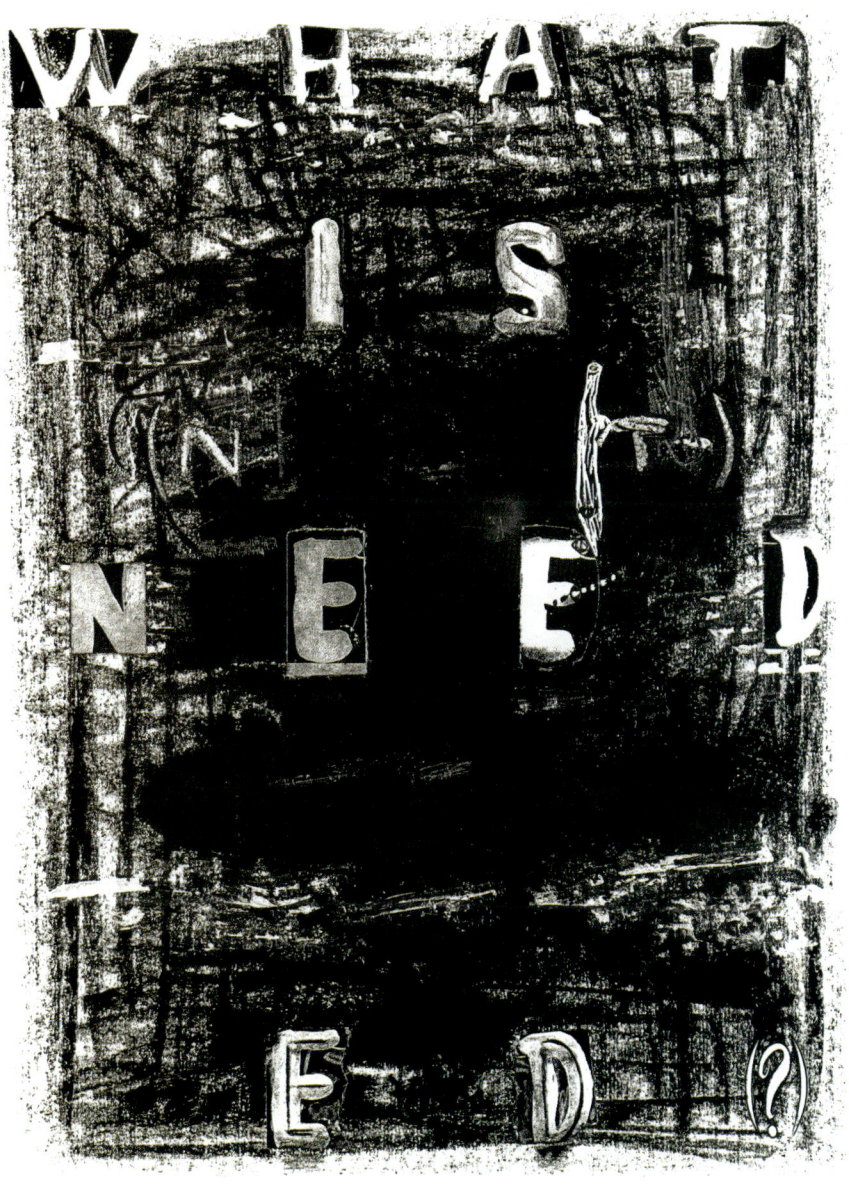

What is need Ed (?)
Fella flyer | 2006

Ed Fella
www.edfella.com

Counter-promotion: as an advertisement a posteriori, the designer only handed out these postcards after the conference had finished. As if it were a draft, the space is covered with scribbles, lines, shadows and marks.

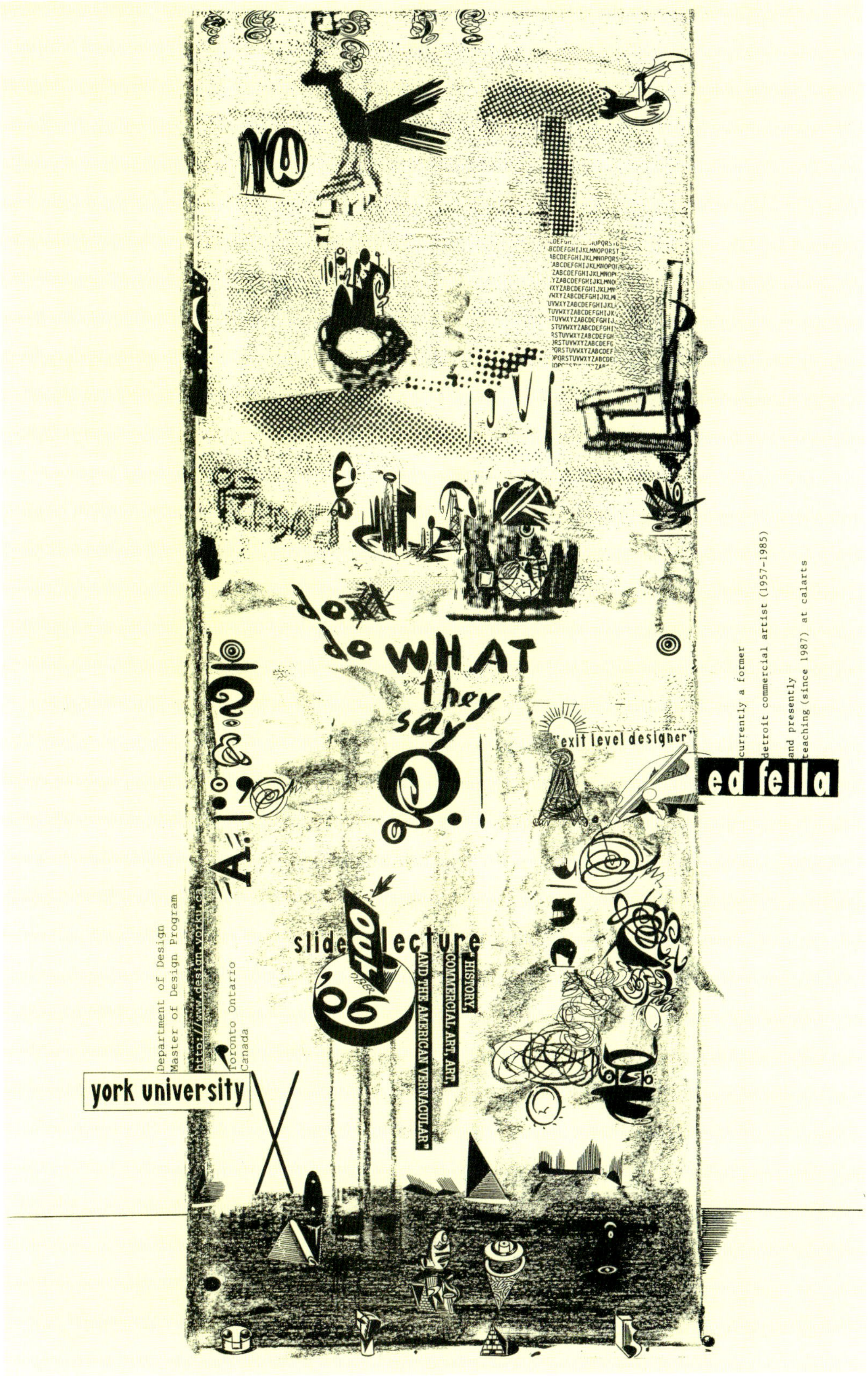

York University | 2006

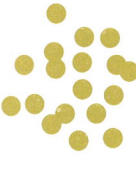

Ed Fella
www.edfella.com

Behind, different pieces of vernacular graphic design. In front, a personal piece of the designer that plays with the idea of a work of art. Good design, according to Ed Fella, is somewhere between these two faces.

We've never been invited to one...

Underline Studio

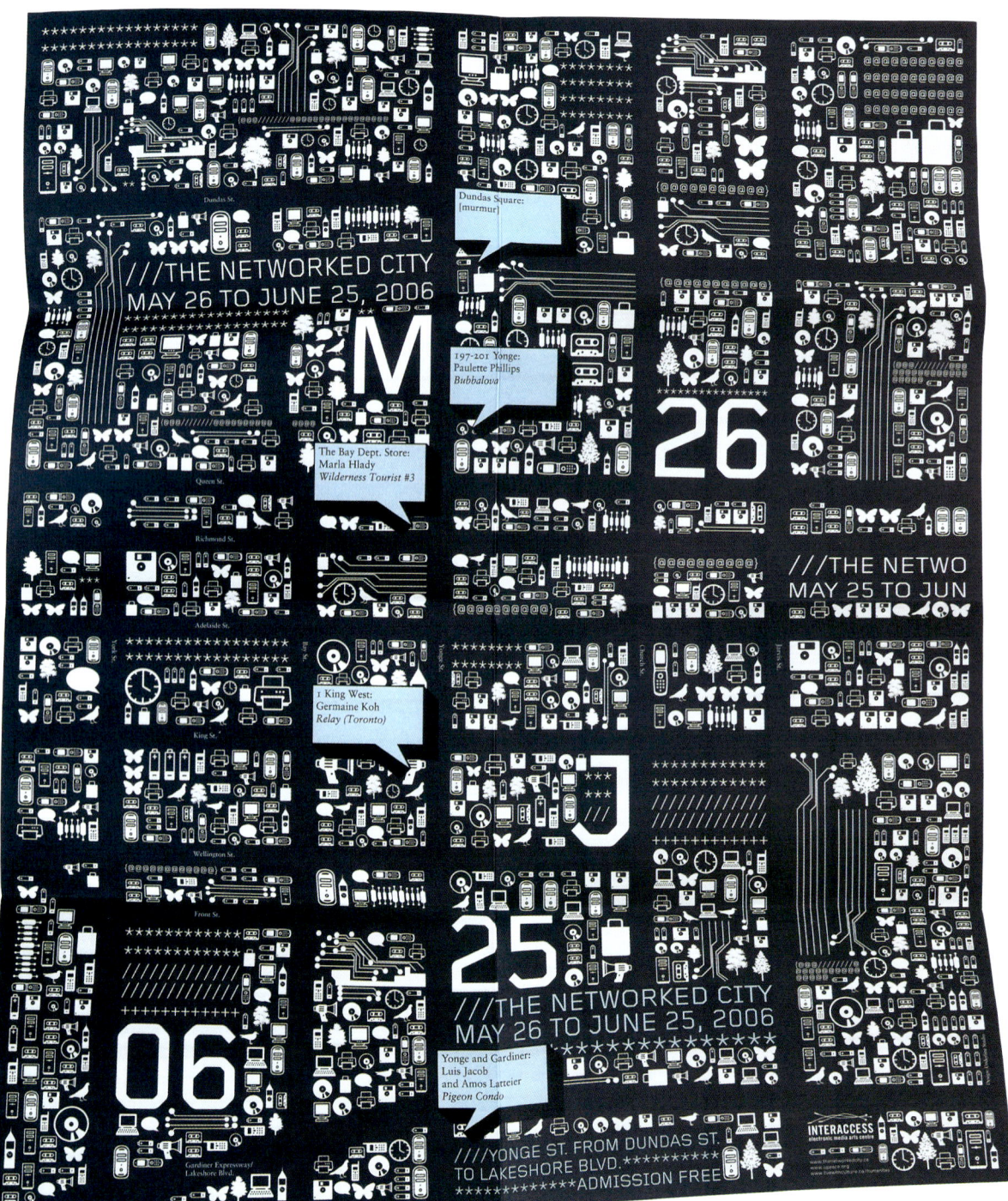

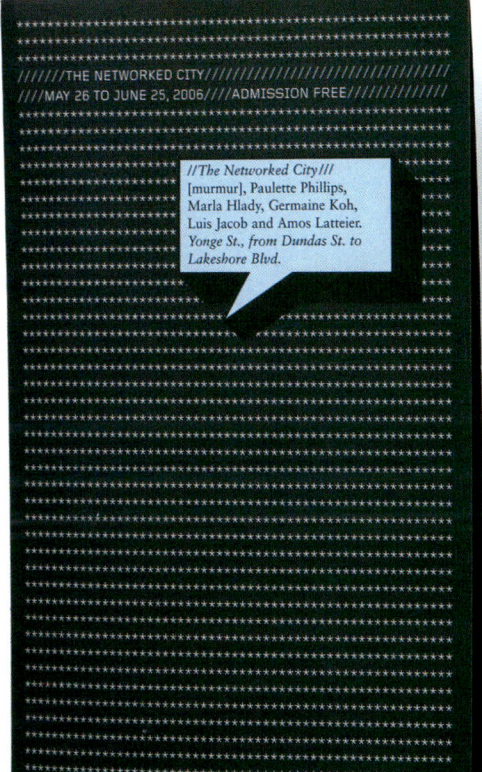
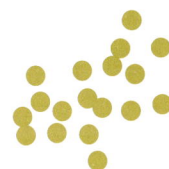

The Networked City | 2006

Underline Studio
www.underlinestudio.com

For a festival of digital art, the poster becomes a map where the different installations can be localized through the city. The city, which was transformed for this event, is represented as a group of digital symbols.

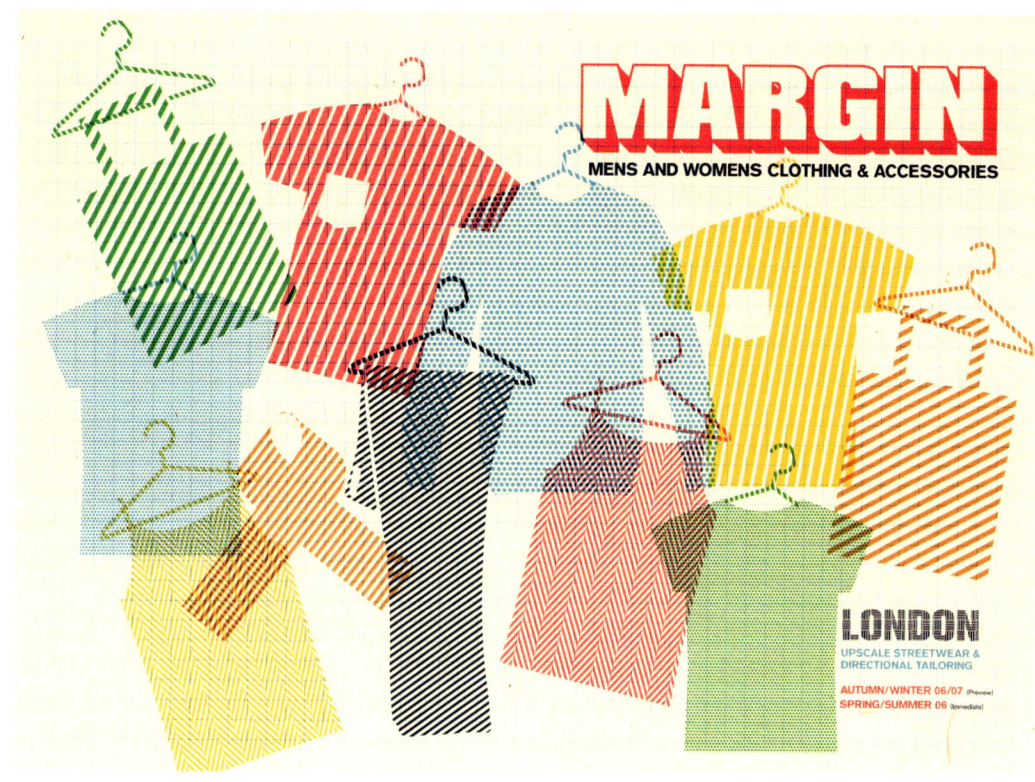

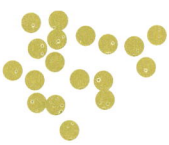

Margin Fashion Trade Show | 2006

New Future Graphics
www.newfuturegraphic.co.uk

For the identity of a new fashion event, the logo recreates patterns and textures that represent the trends of the season without favoring any one in particular. This image is used in advertisements, posters and even on water bottles.

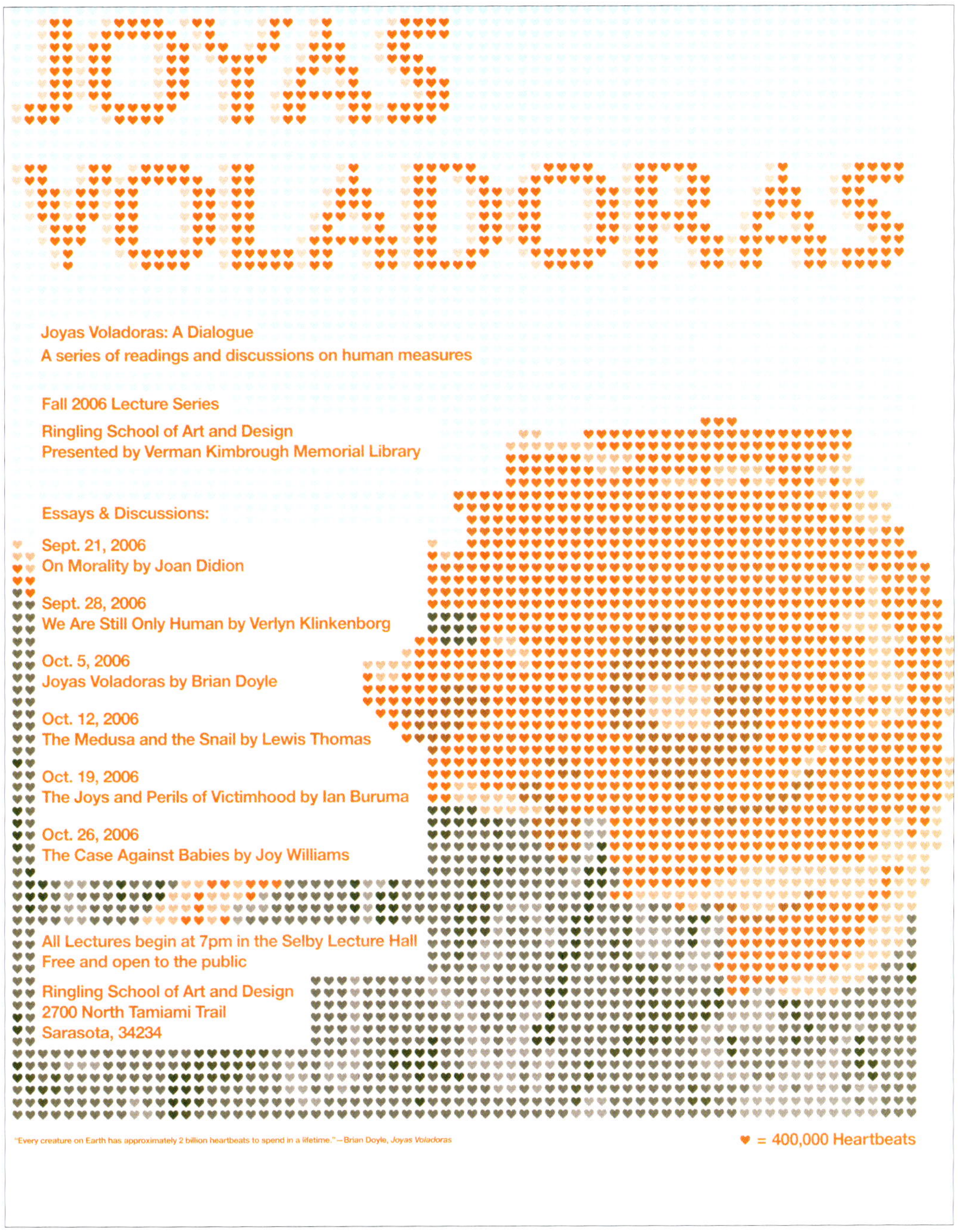

I know how to party. Therefore, I cannot remember the best party I've been to.

Tyler Lang

Joyas voladoras | 2006

Tyler Lang
www.tylerlang.com

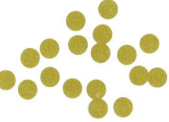

A hummingbird* can only live for two years because of the speed of its heartbeat; a tortoise, over a hundred (its heartbeat is very slow). The hearts that give the poster its form represent the average beats in a human life: two billion.

*Joyas voladoras (meaning "flying jewels") is a common way of refering to hummingbirds in certain Latin American countries.

The day after the best party I have ever been to, I didn't remember at all what I did or what I said during the party, except that I met the man that is the father of my son, today...

Fanette Mellier

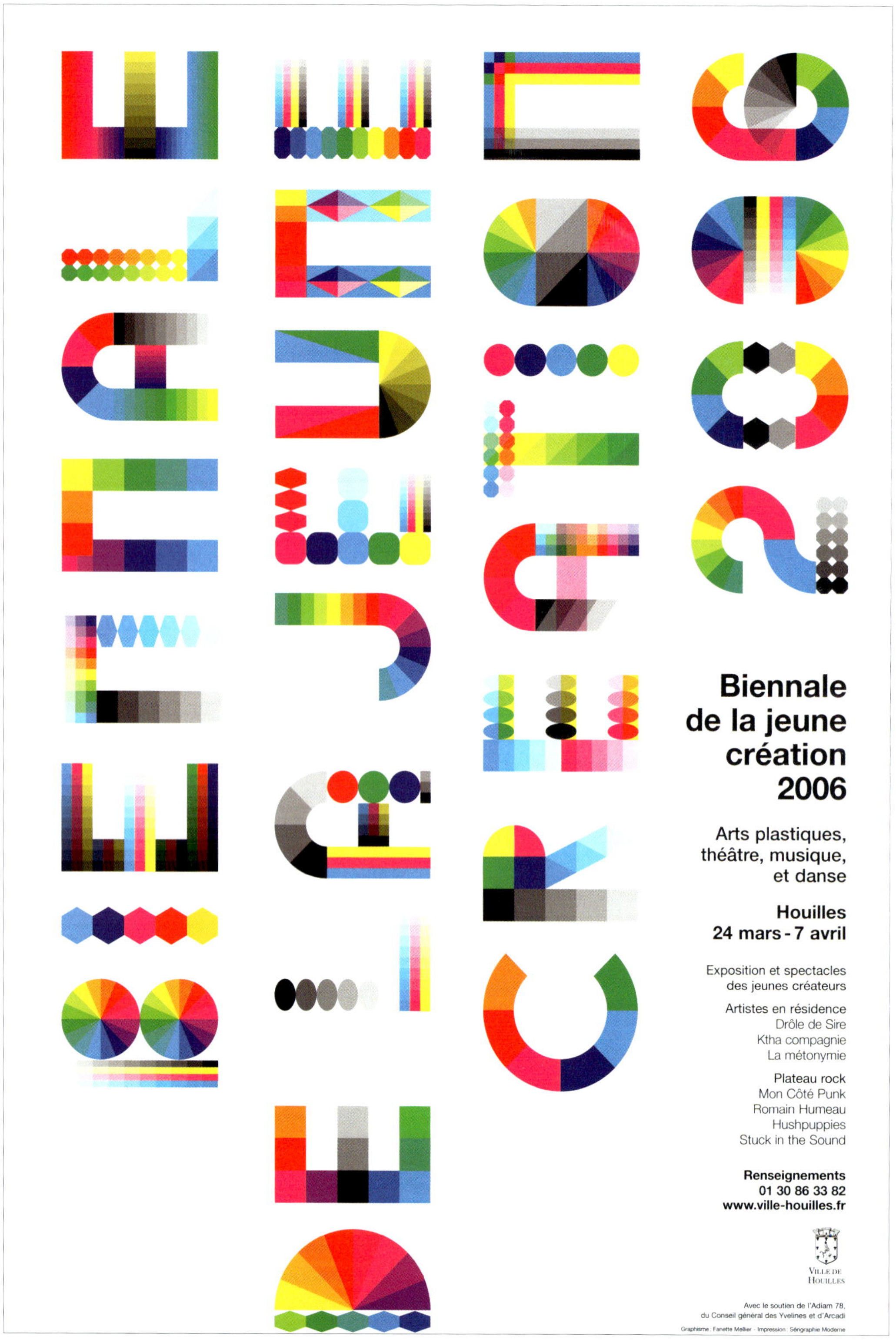

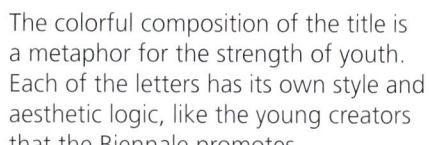

Biennale de la jeune création | 2006

Fanette Mellier
www.fanettemellier.com

The colorful composition of the title is a metaphor for the strength of youth. Each of the letters has its own style and aesthetic logic, like the young creators that the Biennale promotes.

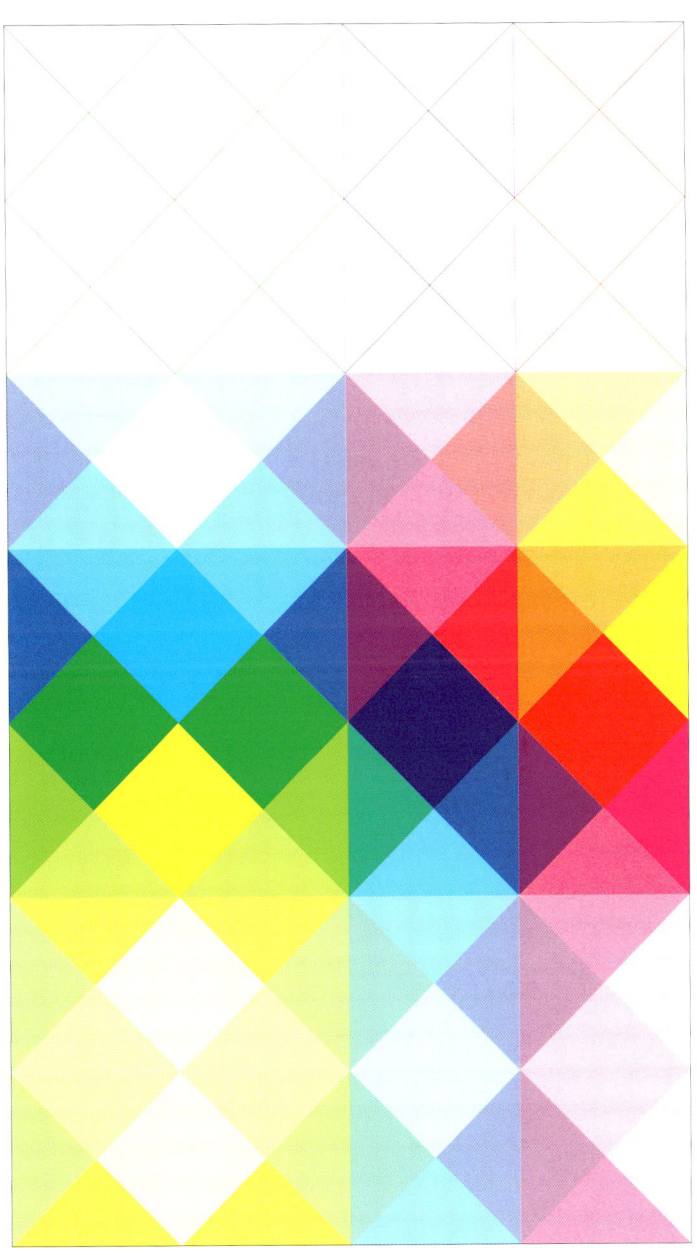
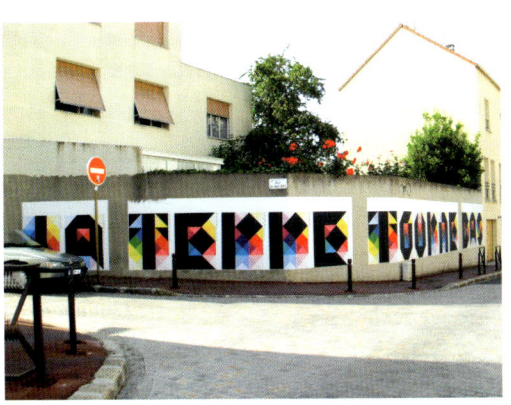
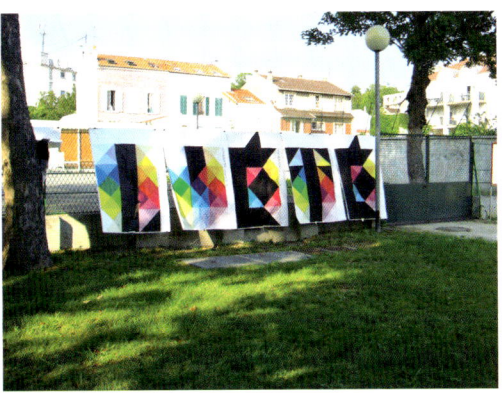
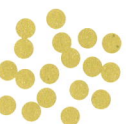

Fontenew | 2007

Fanette Mellier
www.fanettemellier.com

For the festival *Graphics in the Street*, a poster works as a mold for the giant letters that appear when parts of the drawing are covered with black paint. On the image, an unpublished poem by Laure Limongi decorates the streets of Fontenay-sous-Bois.

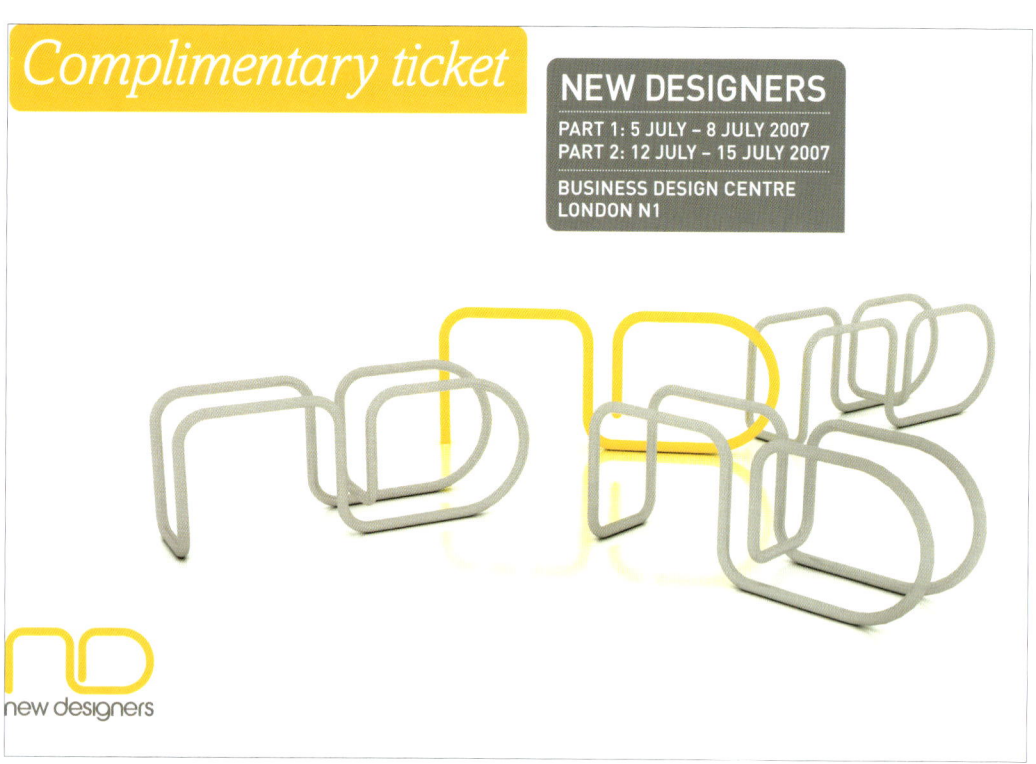

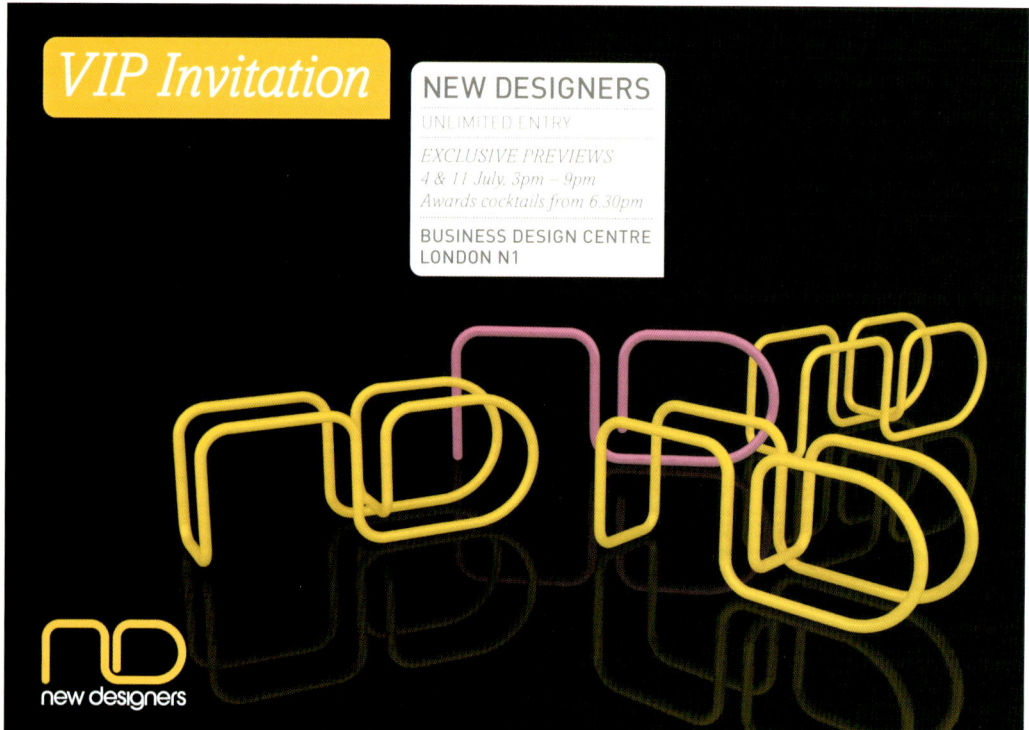

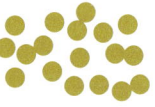

New Designers | 2007

Linda Lundin, Nina Nägel/Park Studio
www.park-studio.com

The work is based on the neon logo of New Designers, which has been twisted to be directly introduced into the digital age. That way, without losing identity, the "rendered" image becomes more up-to-date.

It was around 1996 and I accidentally arrived at one of the biggest raves in London. I drank mushroom tea and found myself dancing for hours with some of the craziest hippest Londoners around a huge plastic totem pole.

Michiel Schuurman

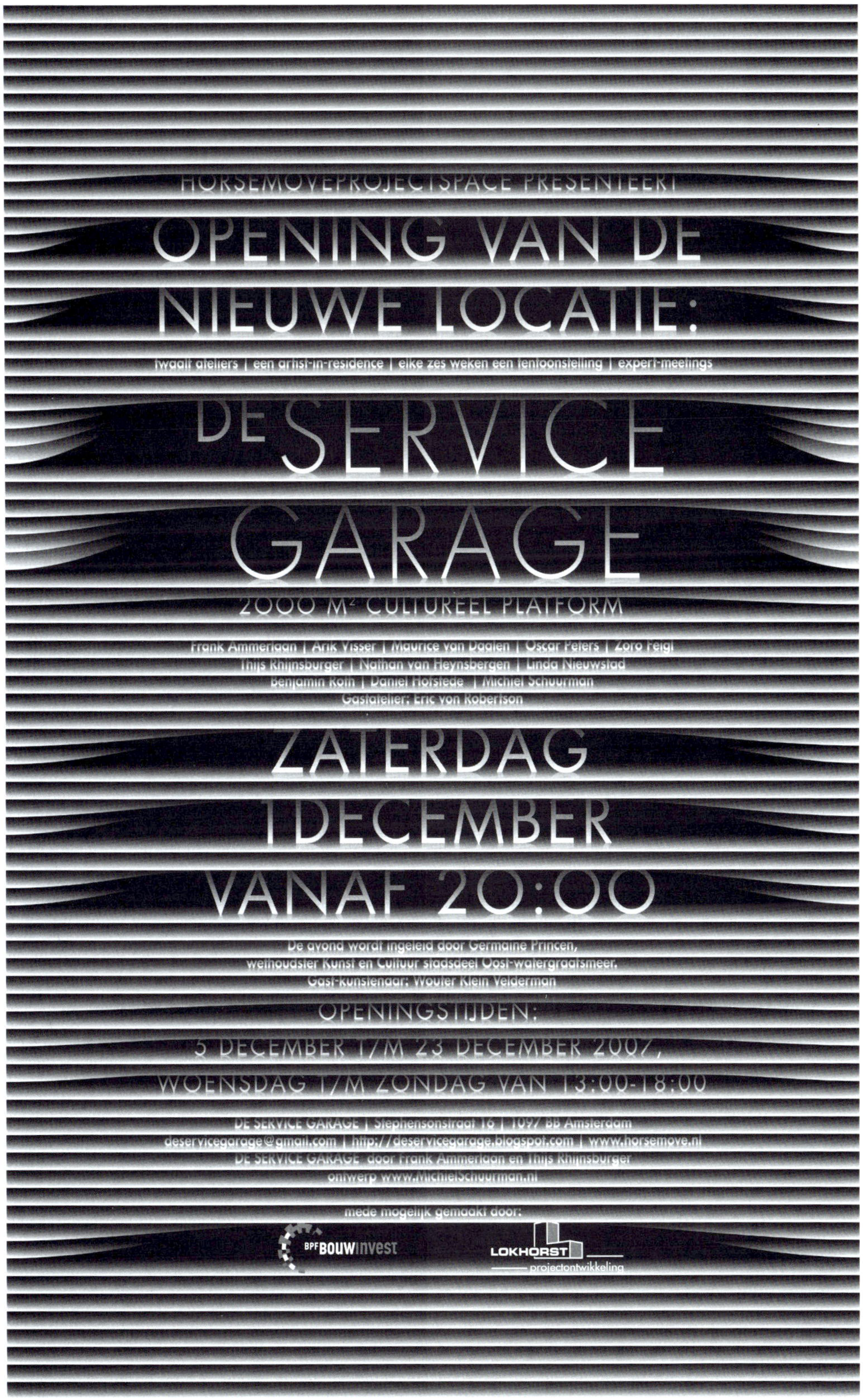

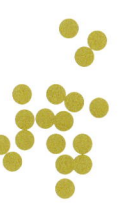

HorseMoveProjectSpace | 2006-till now

Michiel Schuurman
www.michielschuurman.nl

Curiosity can undoubtedly be a powerful weapon. These posters created for the different exhibitions of the gallery attract the attention of the observer thanks to the process of deciphering the message. The project works with kinetic art and psychedelia.

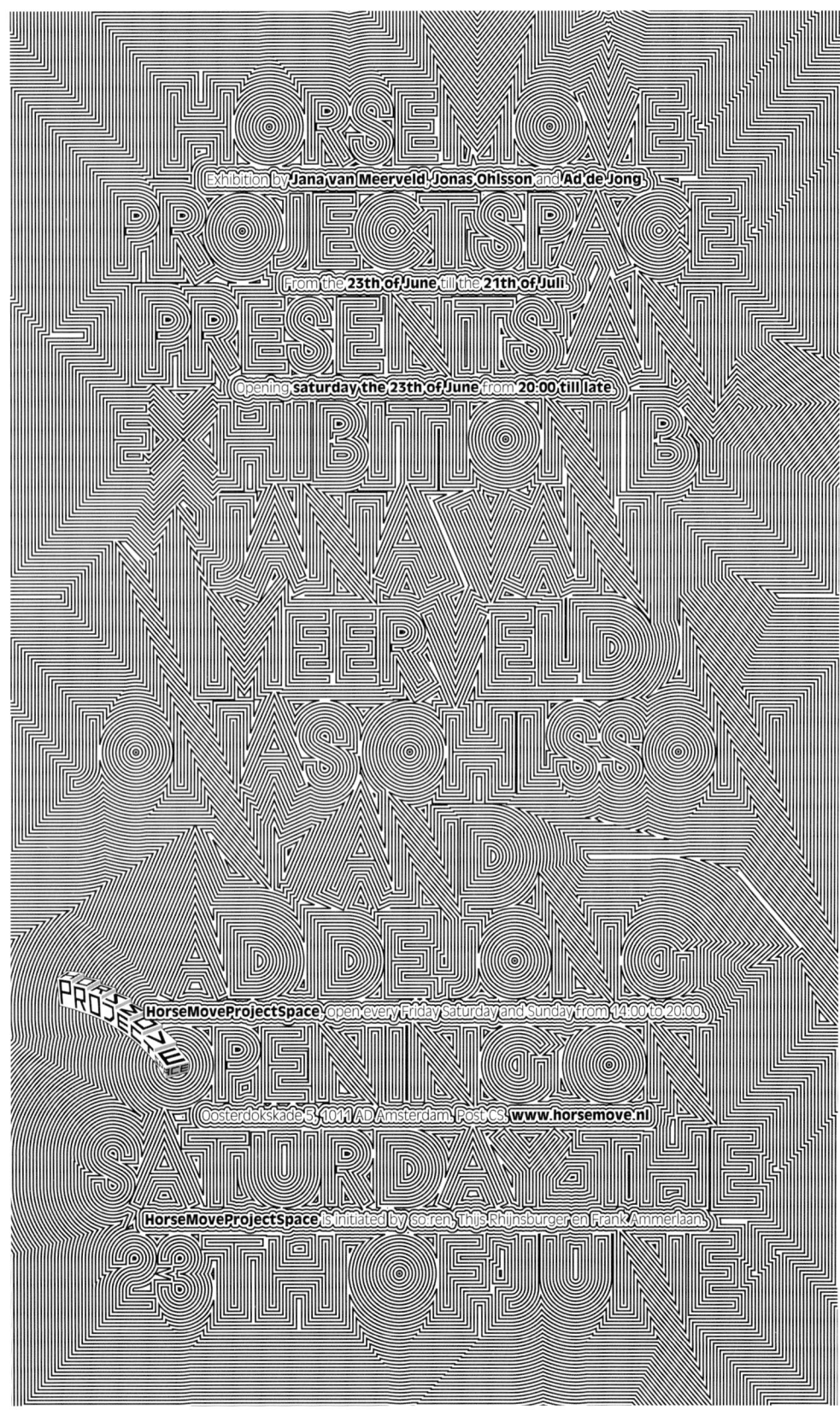

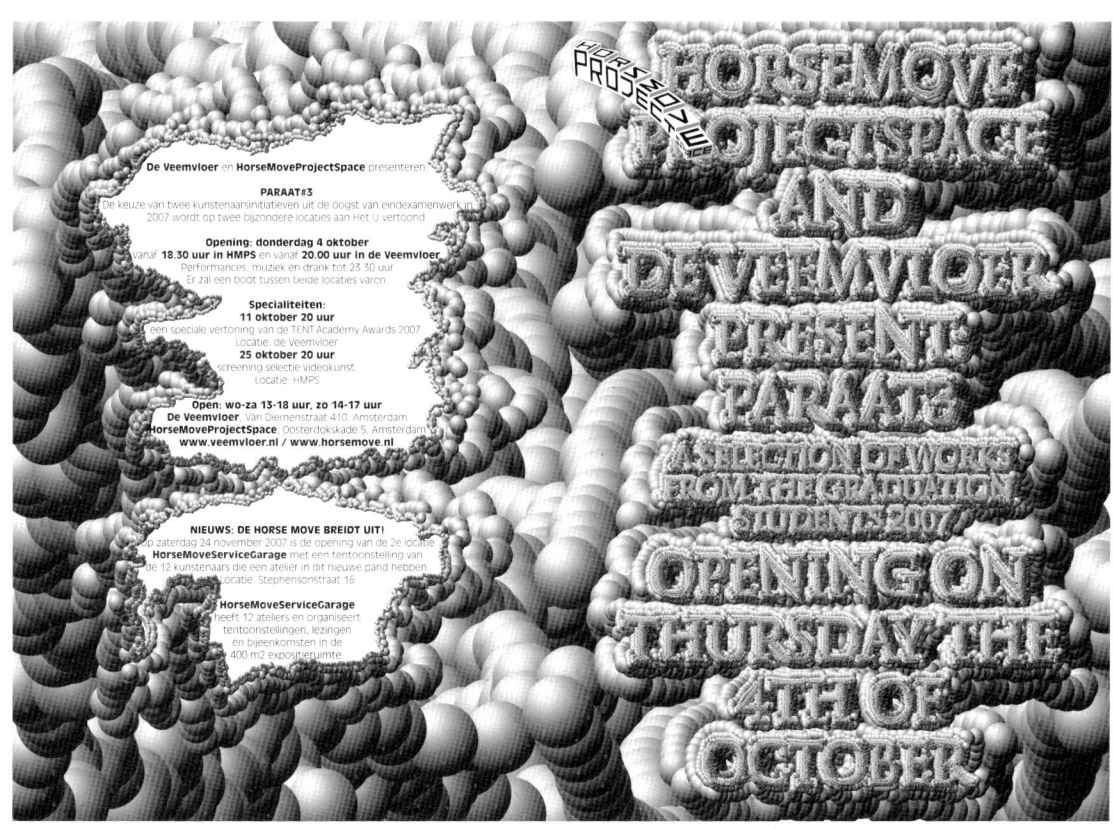

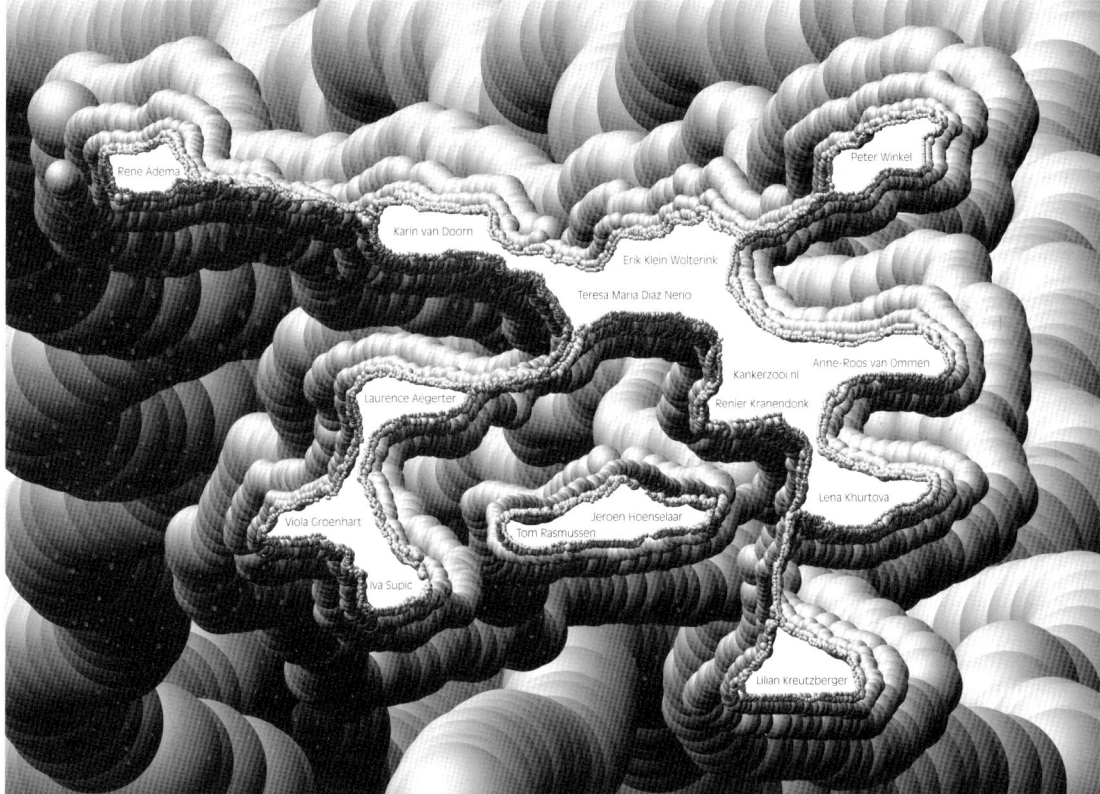

Remember me?

Business cards, brand identity, and more

I crashed a party, found the girl, then found the girl's jealous ex-boyfriend, then "found" the rapidly approaching garden chair he swung at me, ouch.

Jamie Wieck

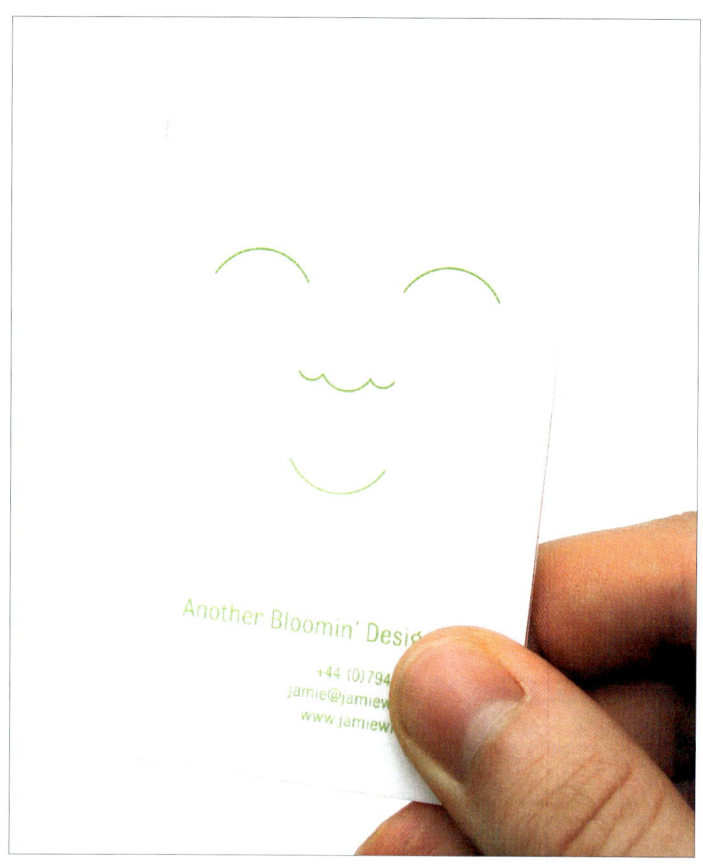
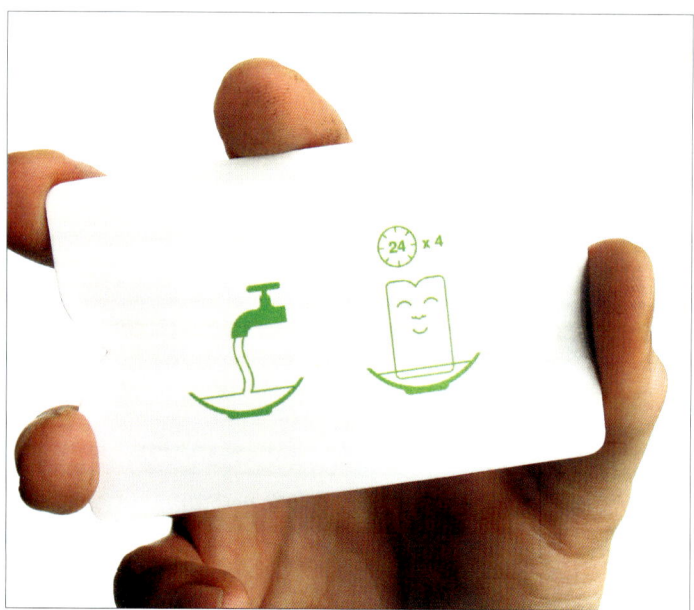
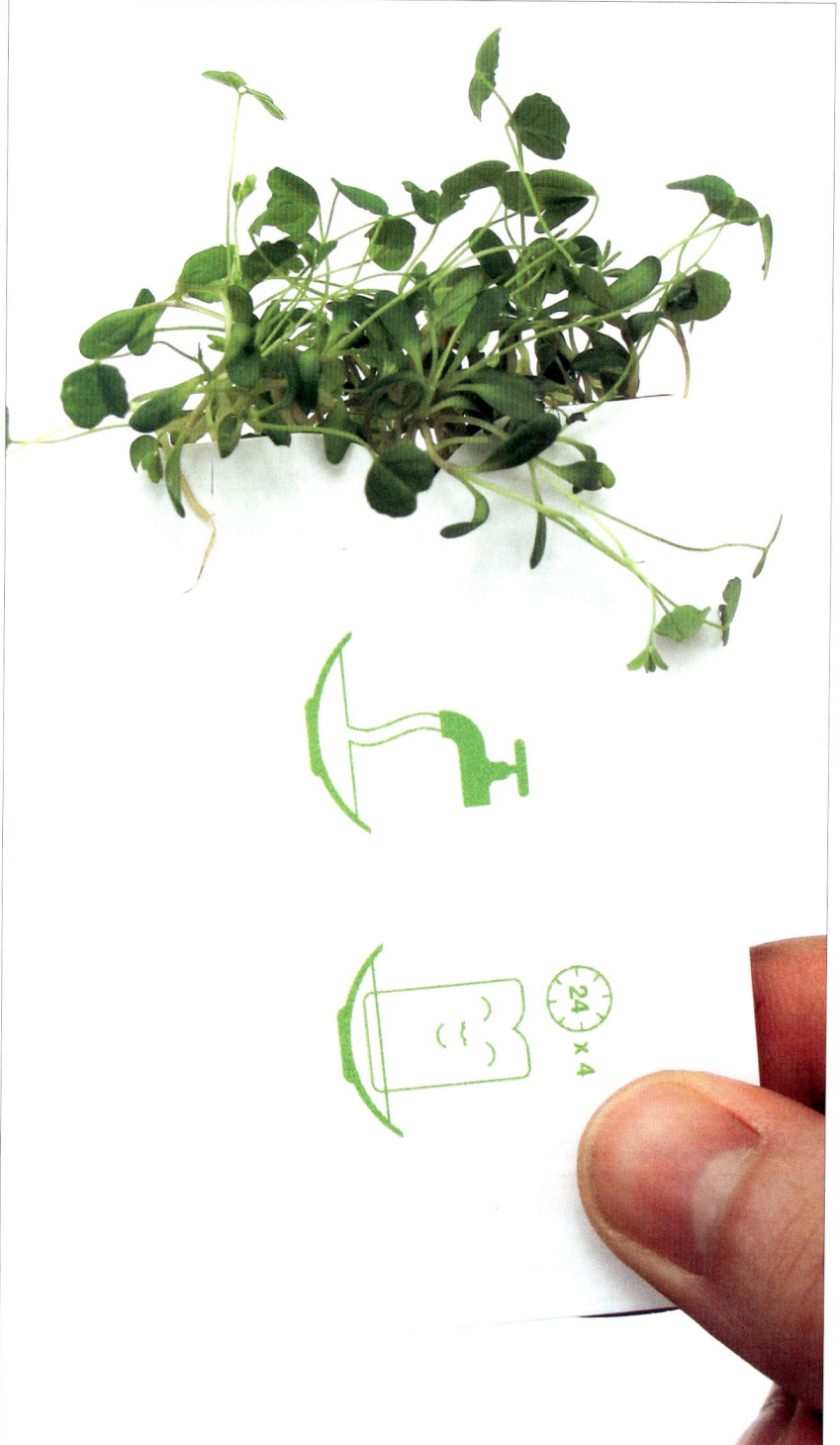

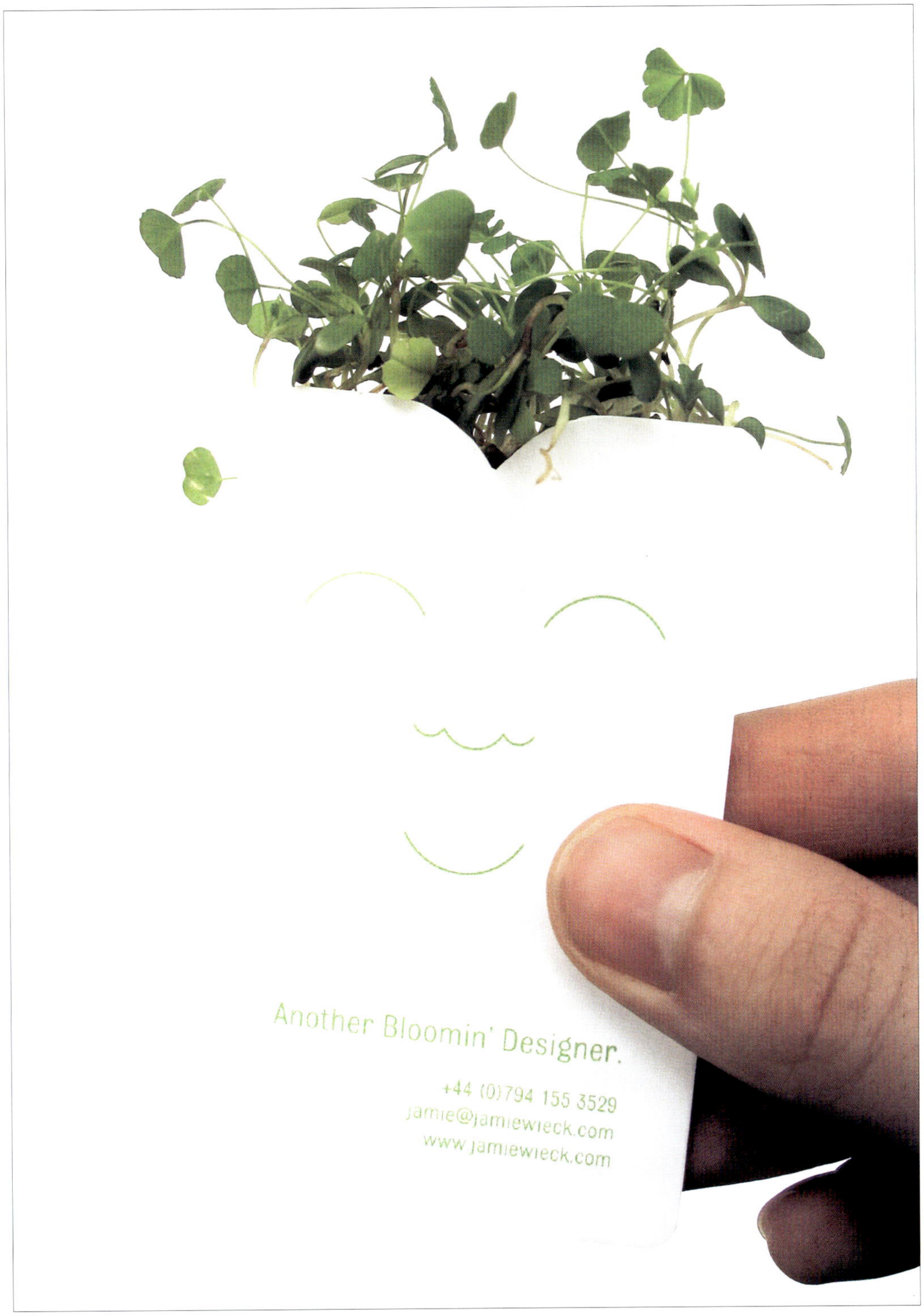

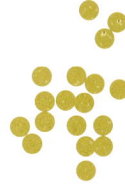

Another Bloomin' Designer | 2007

Jamie Wieck
www.jamiewieck.com

The idea was a business card to have on the table, and not inside your pocket. Like a "mini-greenhouse," inside were alfalfa seeds or watercress that flower (like the designer) when submerged in water.

Irony, it's a funny thing really. I can't remember the best party I've ever been to because I drank too much whilst I was there.

Craig Oldham

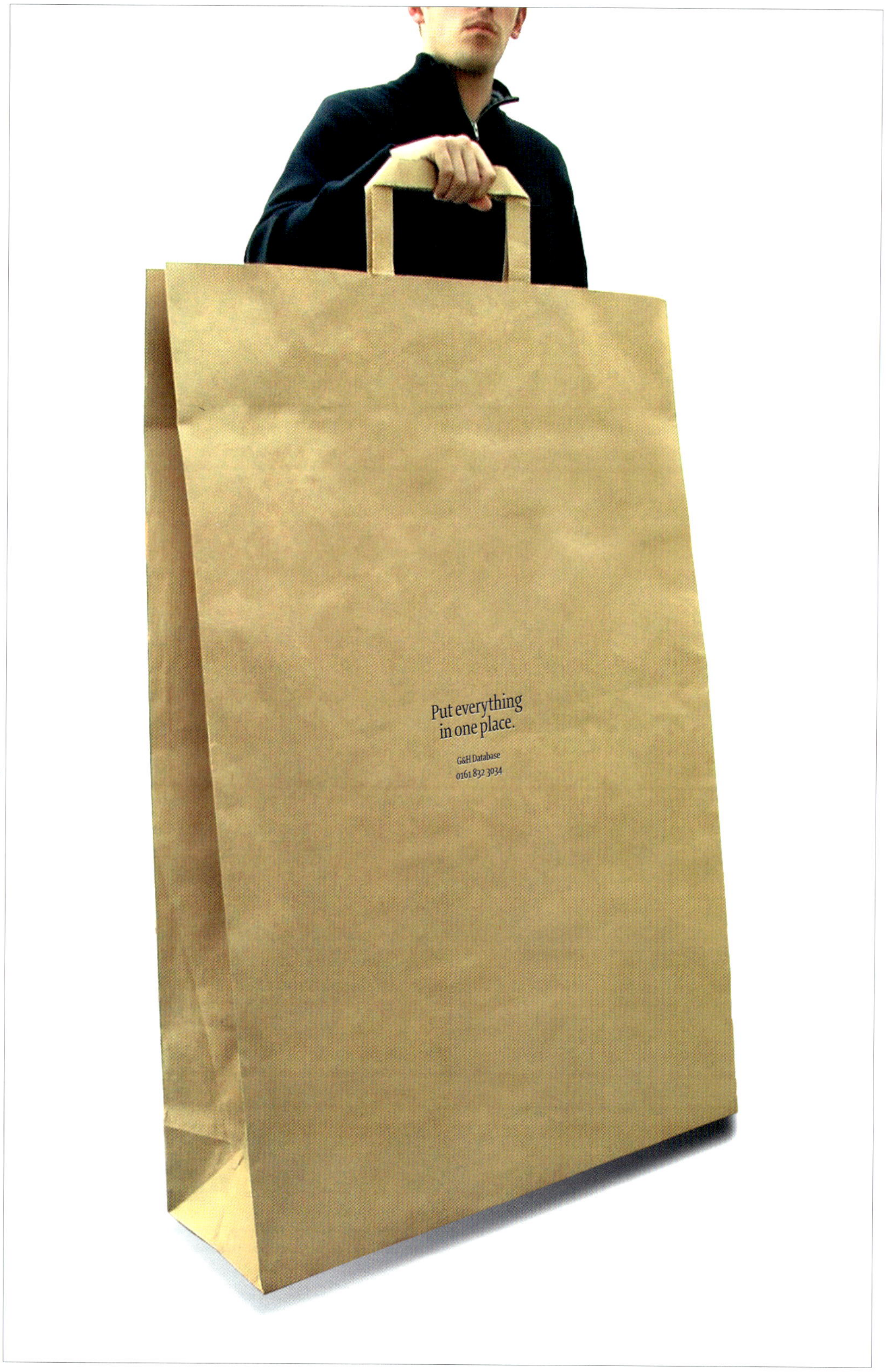

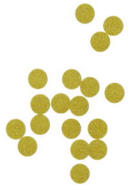

G&H Database Big Bag | 2003

The Chase
thechase.co.uk

This giant bag formed part of a mailing system of Gask & Hawley's, a company who offers storage and data bases. The incredible size of the bag simulates the capacity of the company.

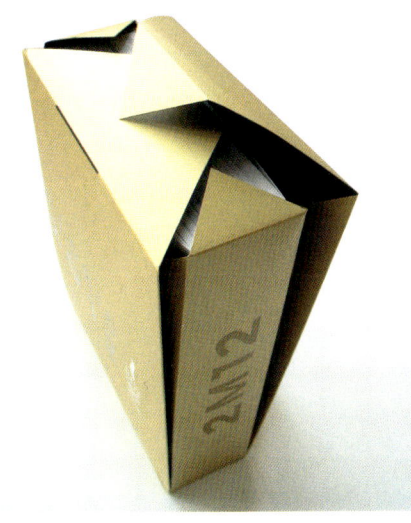
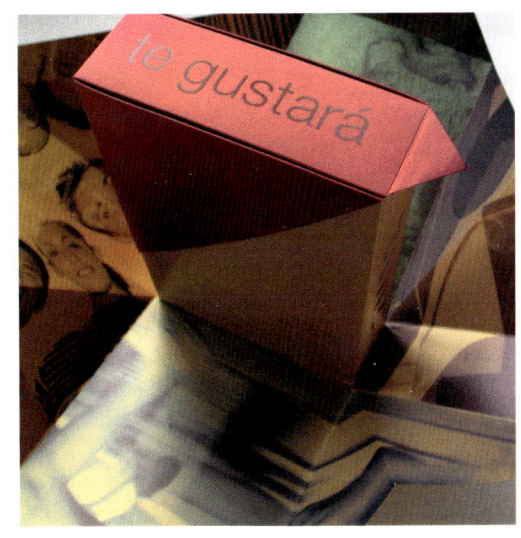
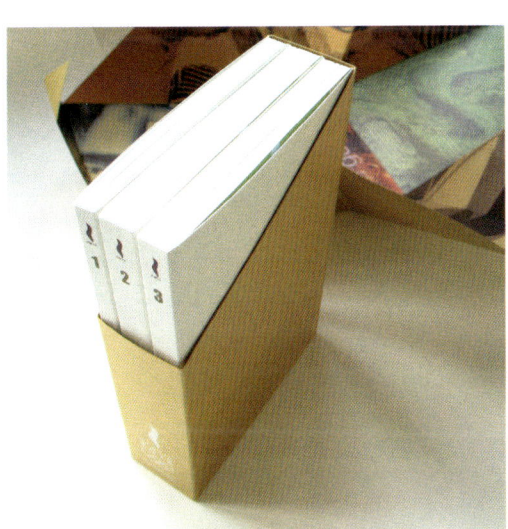
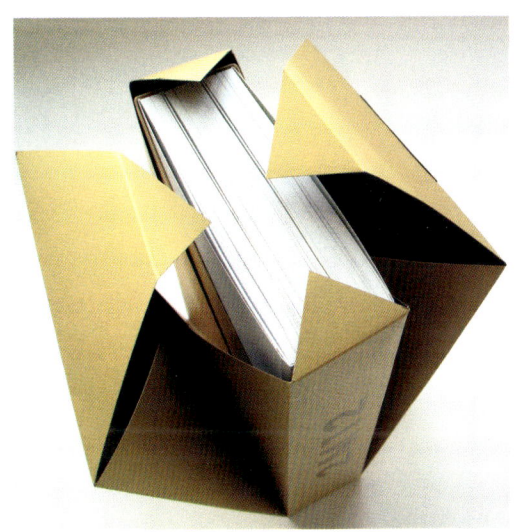
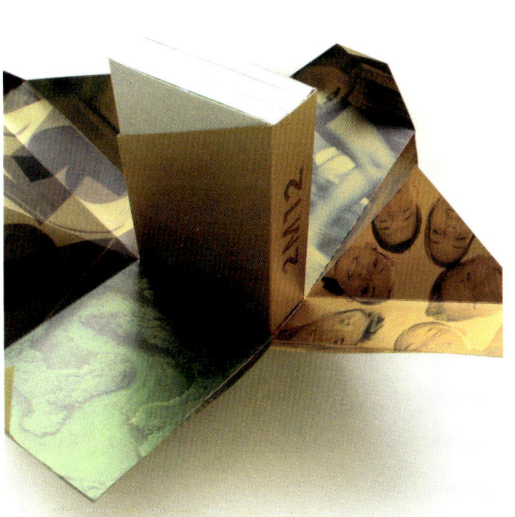
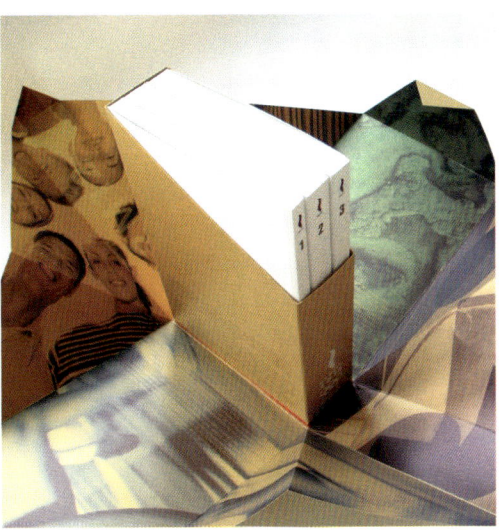

Candidatura Olímpica Madrid 2012 packaging dossier | 2004

Azúamoliné/Estudi Virgili
www.martinazua.com

Considering that a new Olympic regulation prohibits the use of materials that are not cardboard or paper, the folder is presented as a folder enveloped in two sheets of paper. When opened, a mechanism reveals the images and the slogans of the candidature.

Let's just keep it brief and clean and say that it involved a starry night, a crapload of fireworks and an endless bonfire of discarded spray-painted Christmas trees that burst into multi-colored flames once they hit the fire. The rest is up to your imagination.

Duane King

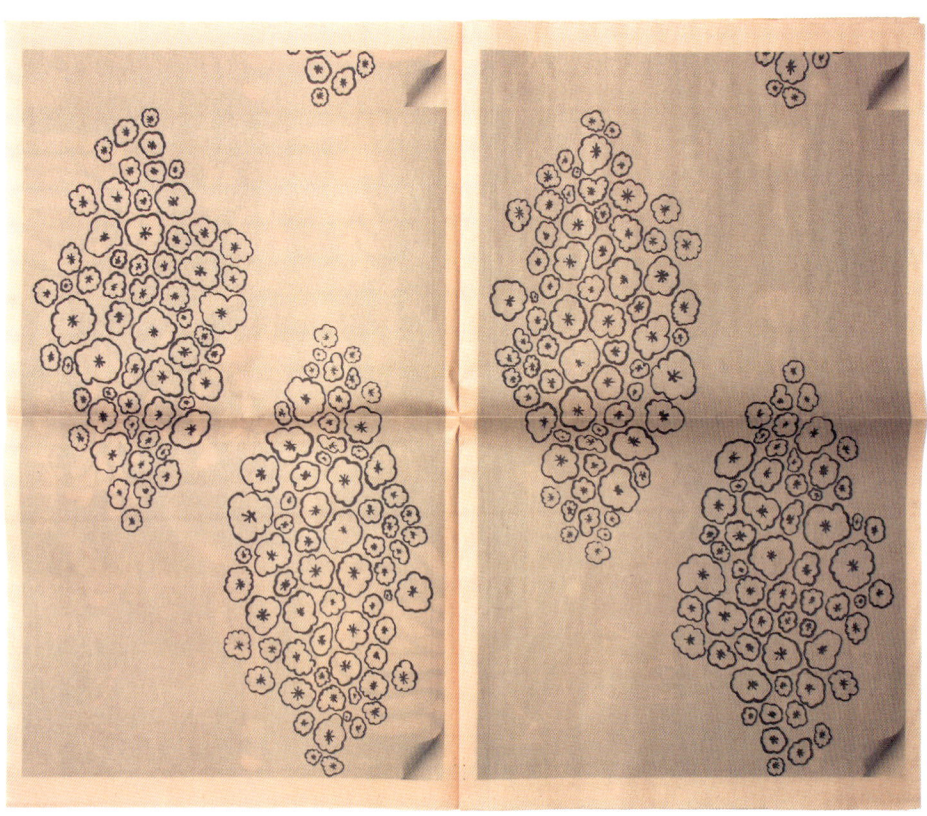

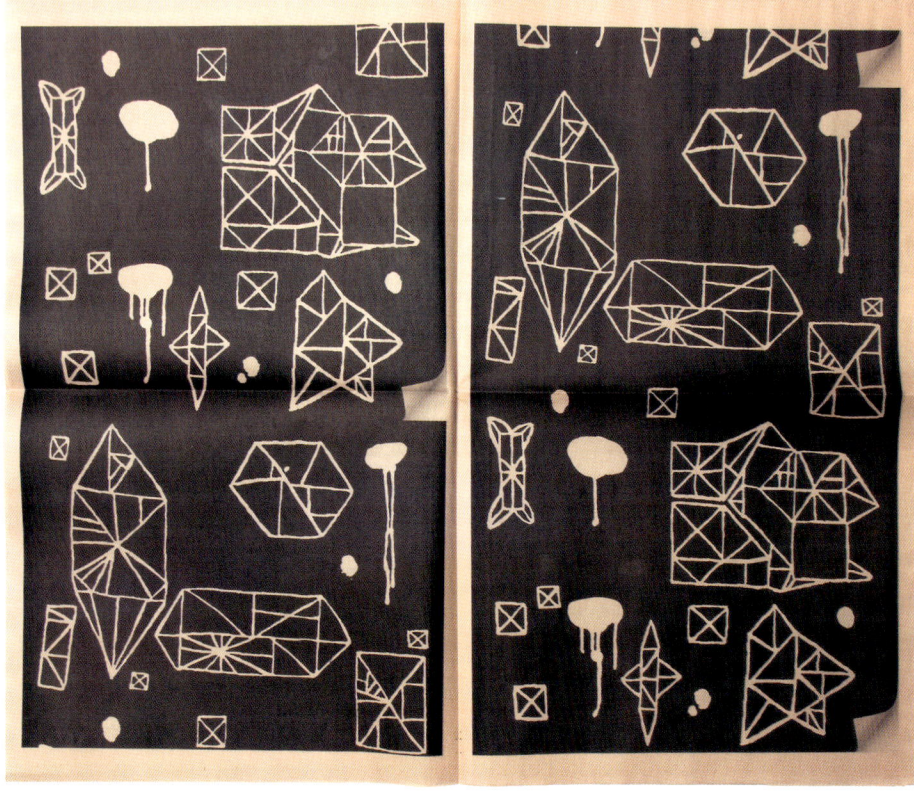

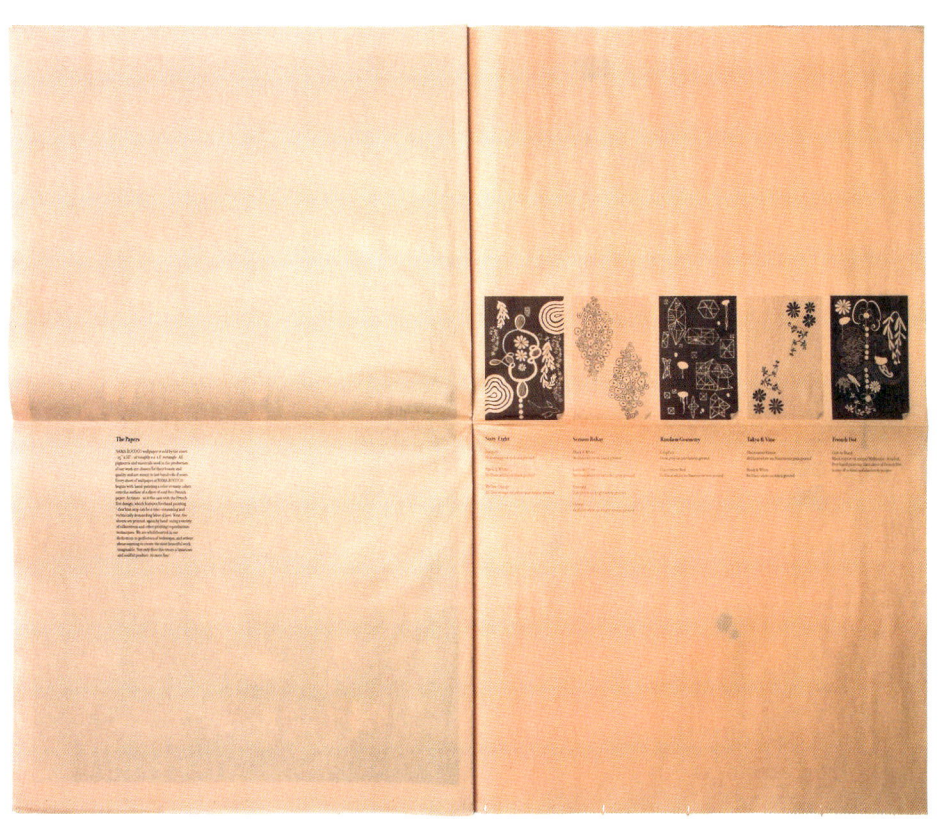
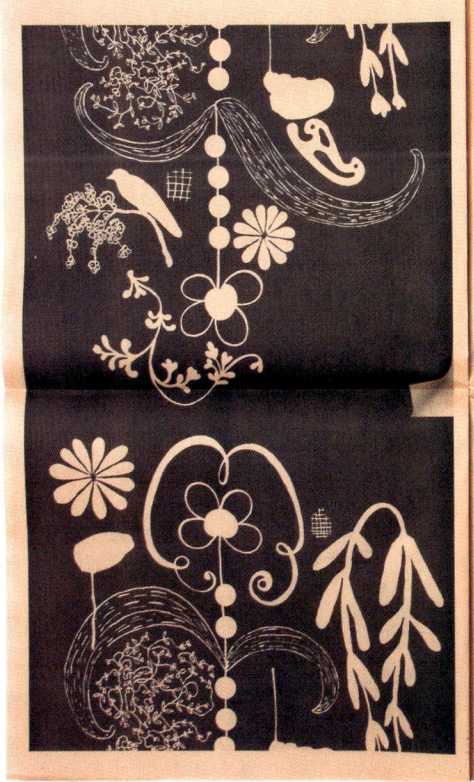
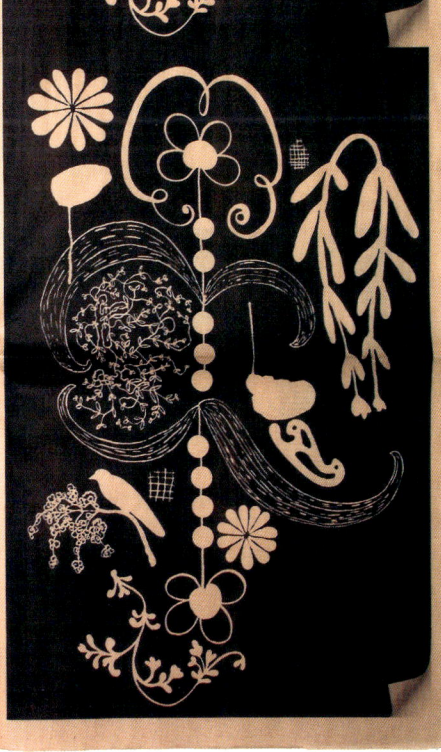
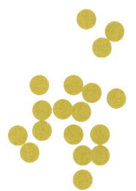

Nama Rococo newsprint promo | 2007

Duane King/BBDK
www.bbdk.com

A support of salmon pink paper, reminiscent of *The Financial Times*, was used to display the sensitivity of the designer: elegant, powerful and a little crazy. The choice of this paper indicates Rococo's love for all that is old.

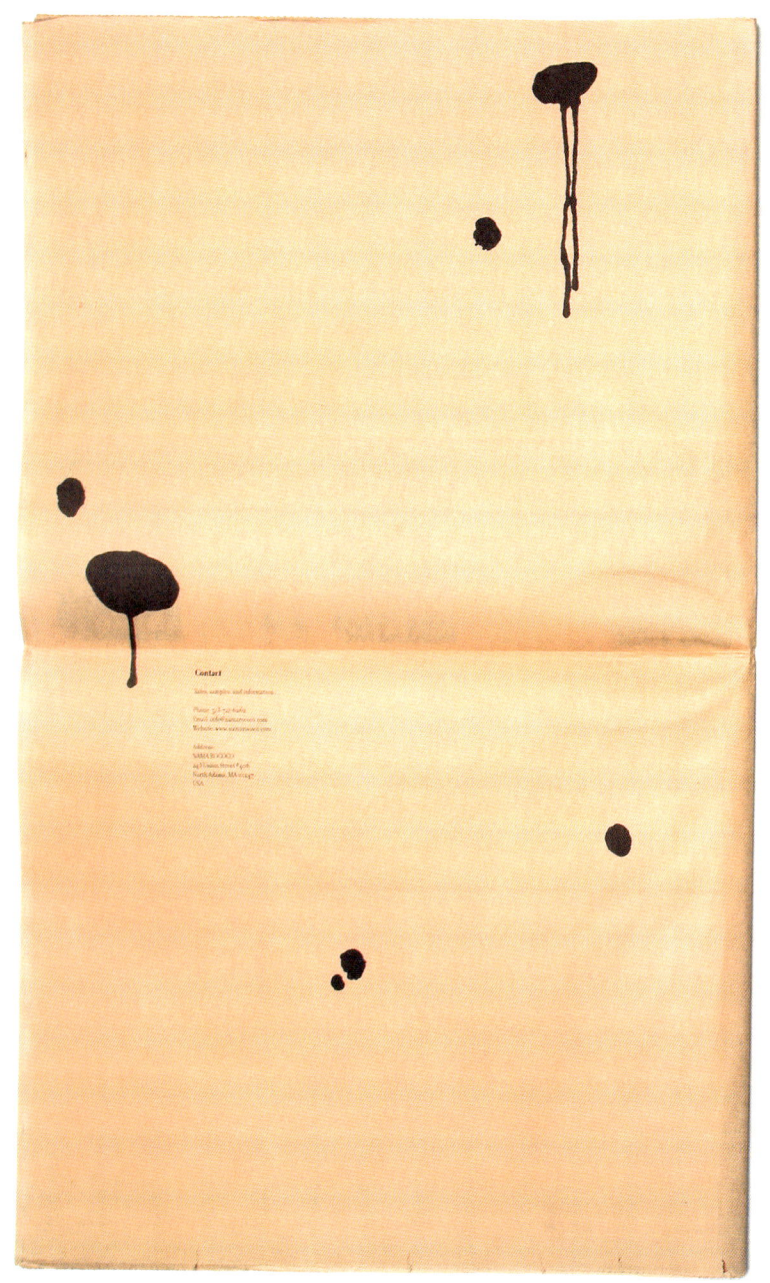
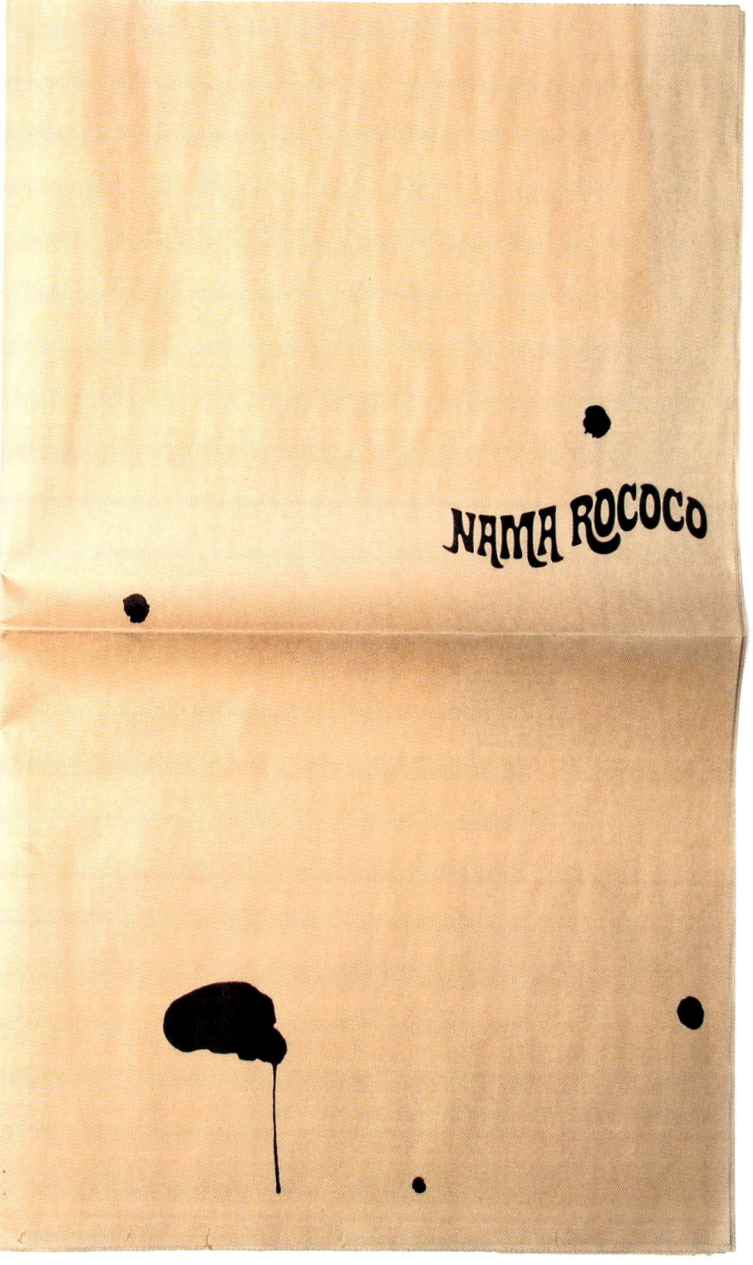

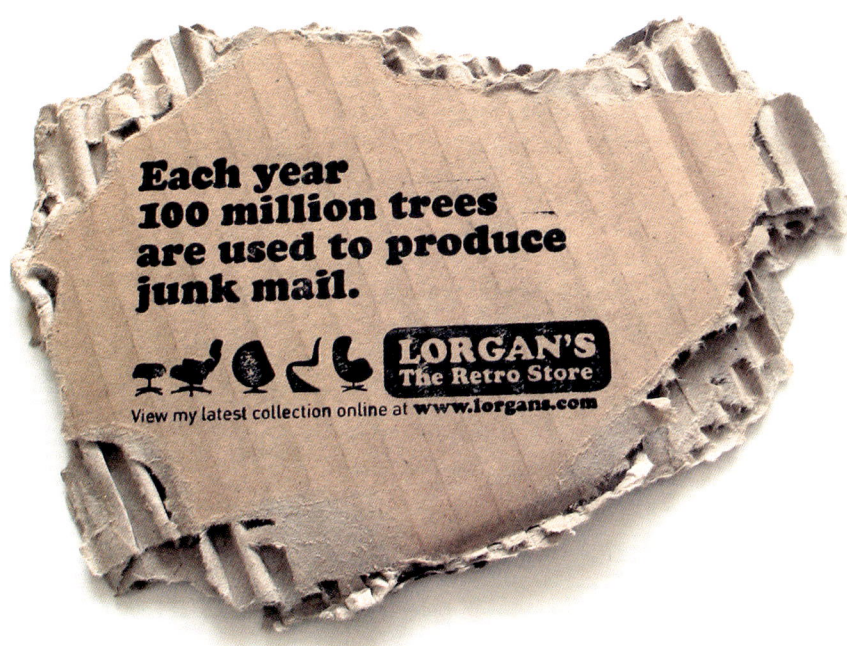

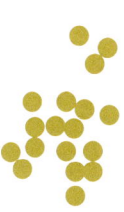

Junkmail | 2006

Kinetic
www.kinetic.com.sg

Each time a new batch of furniture arrived at the store, the boxes were saved to be used as bases for mailing. Thus environmental awareness was promoted along with the brand.

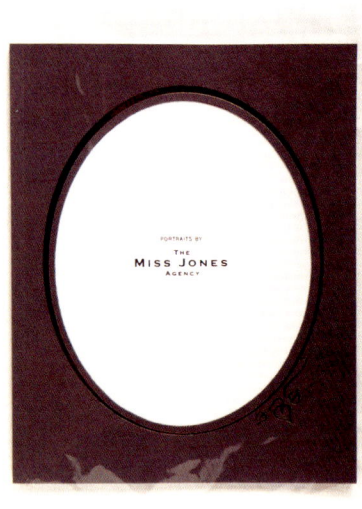
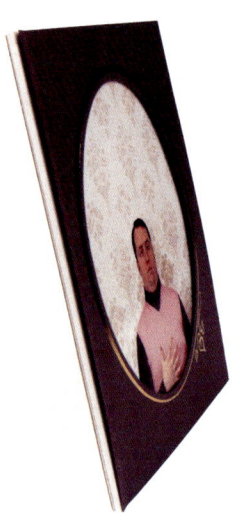
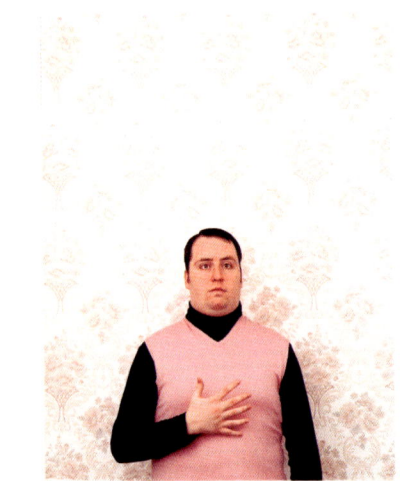
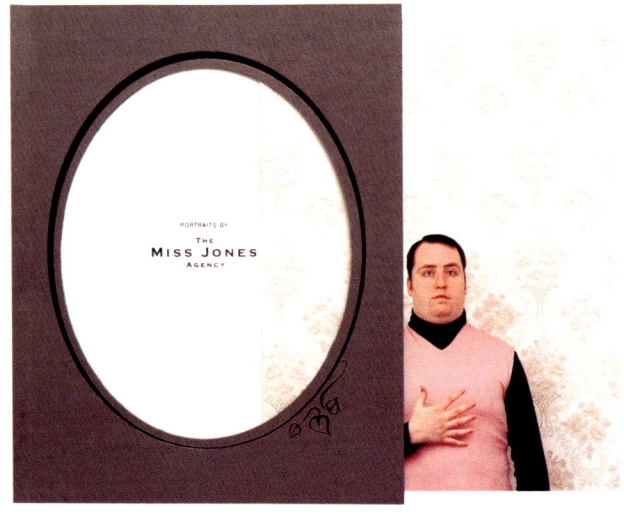

Portraits by The Miss Jones Agency | 2006

The Chase
thechase.co.uk

This book for a photographer's agency folds like a frame. The images of the book, that belong to each of the photographers, can be easily separated and introduced into the frame, so that they can be easily shown.

That would have to be the U'Luvka Vodka Magnum launch party at the Boujis night club in London. We created the invitation and RSVP card to the event, which was a joint collaboration between our clients U'Luvka Vodka, kinky lingerie company Coco de Mer, and hotel owners Mr. & Mrs. Smith.

Aloof Design

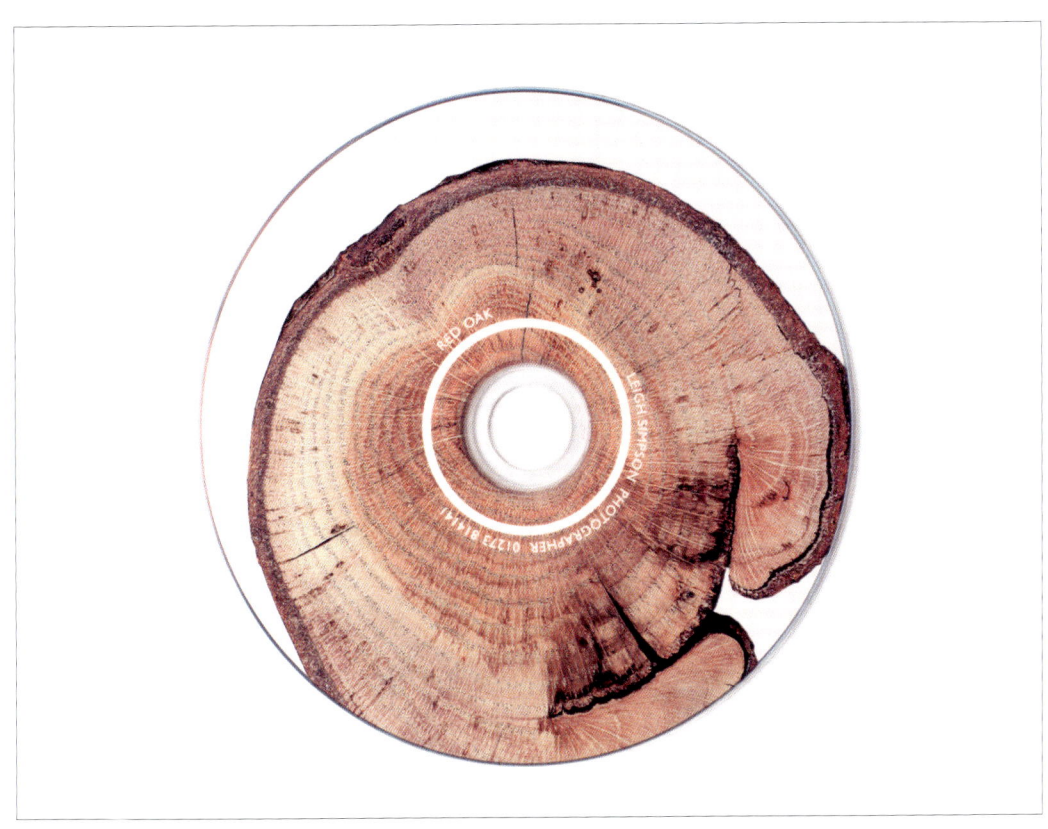

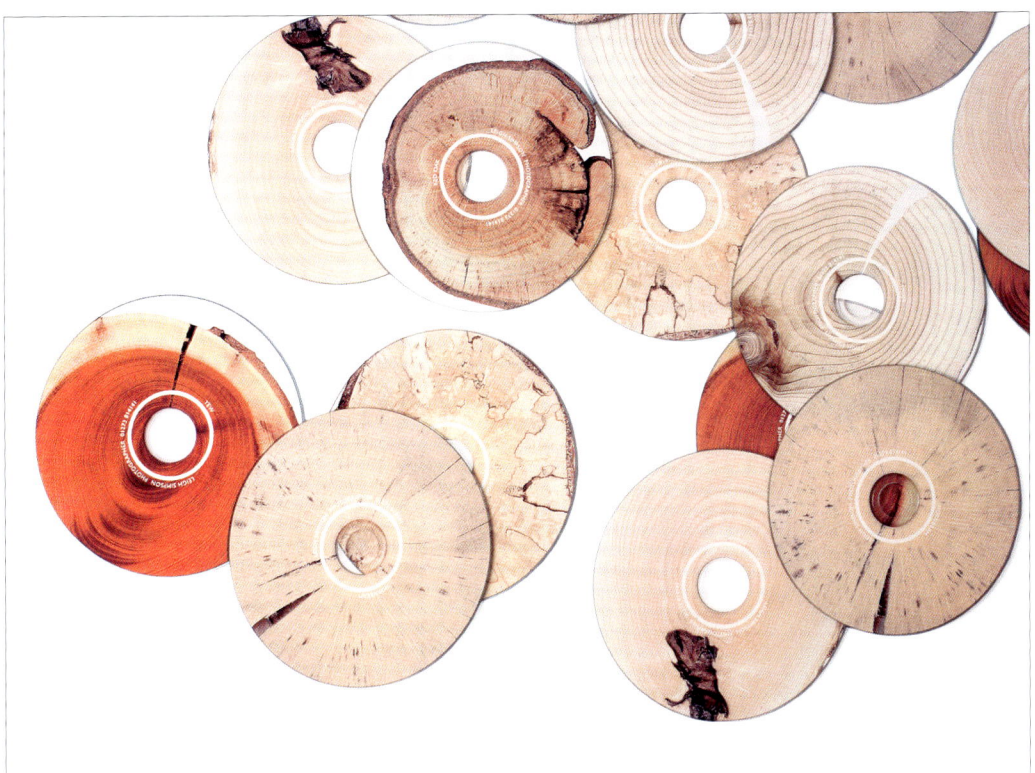

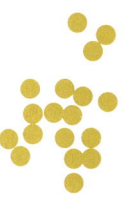

Leigh Simpson Photographer printed CDs | 2005

Aloof Design
www.aloofdesign.com

The natural theme reflects one of the interests of the photographer outside of his professional career. The image of the trunk, in real-size, is lined up exactly with the center of the CD. The lines of the tree reflect the lines of the data stored.

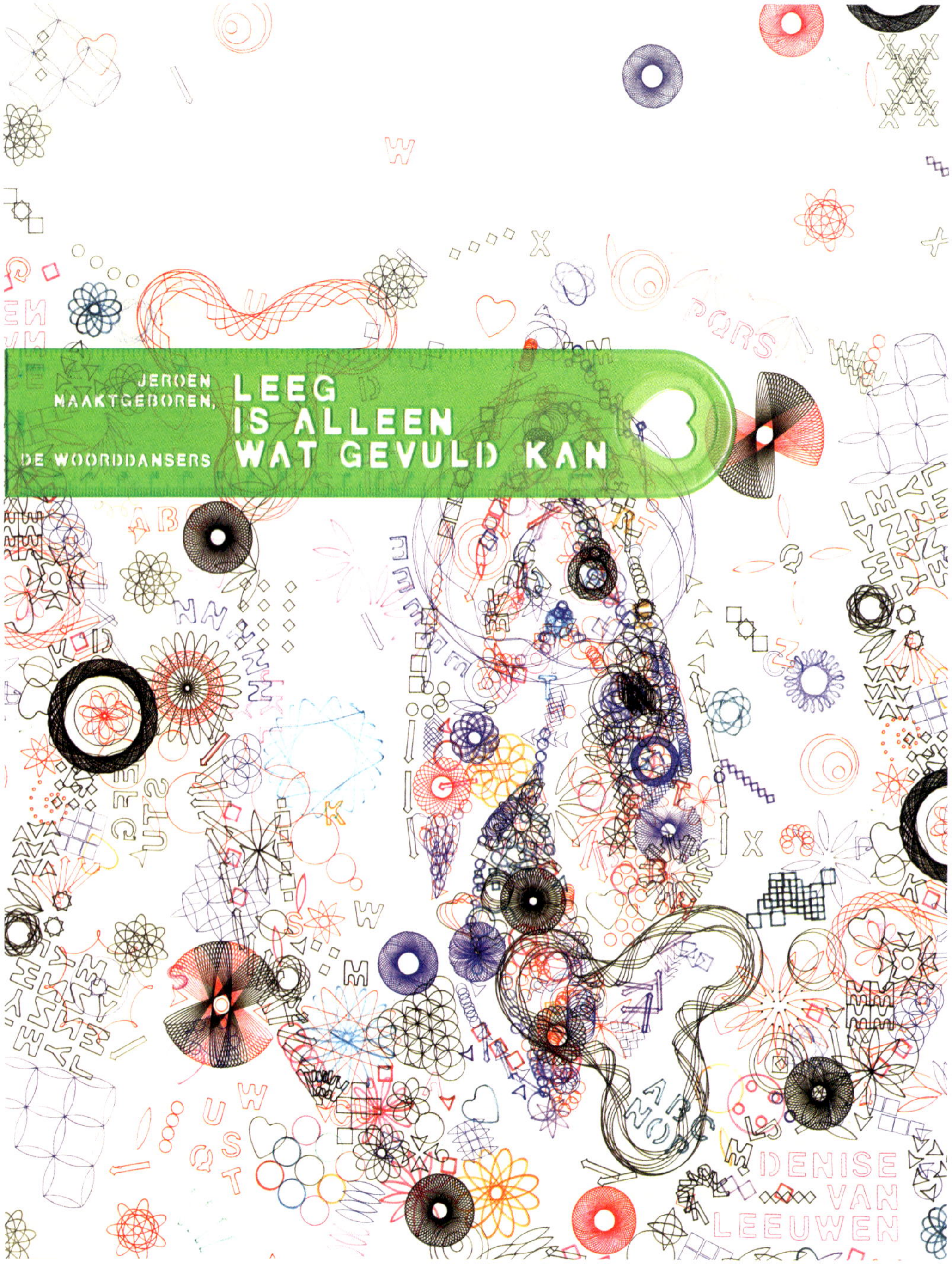

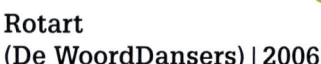

**Rotart
(De WoordDansers) | 2006**

**Poem: Jeroen Naaktgeboren
(De WoordDansers)
Design: Denise van Leeuwen**
www.denise.dds.nl

Joining forces for the purposes of self-promotion can be a good strategy. Designer and poet join in this mission and the result of the collaboration is a poster with something reminiscent of Gustav Klimt in the wheels, atomic forms and letters.

The best party. It was the birthday of a designer friend Curro Claret; in a swimming pool without water, but unexpectedly it started to rain. The menu was based on sardines; it was a disastrous party where everyone had a great time.

Martín Azúa

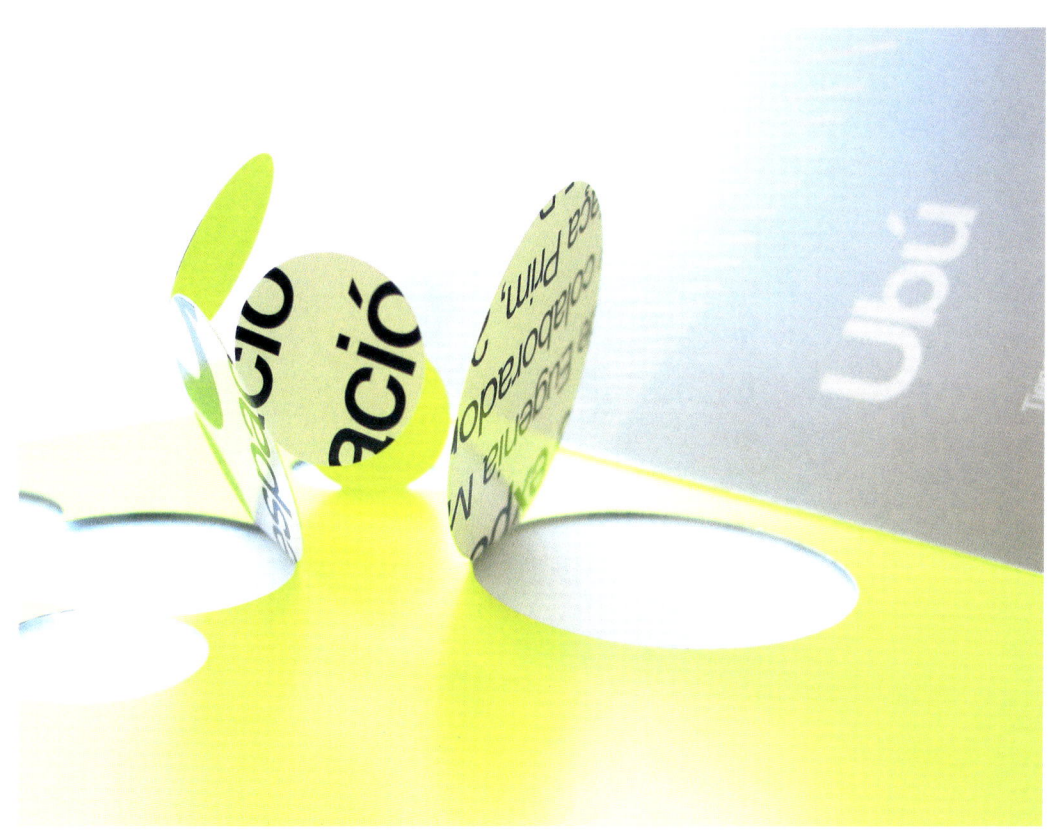

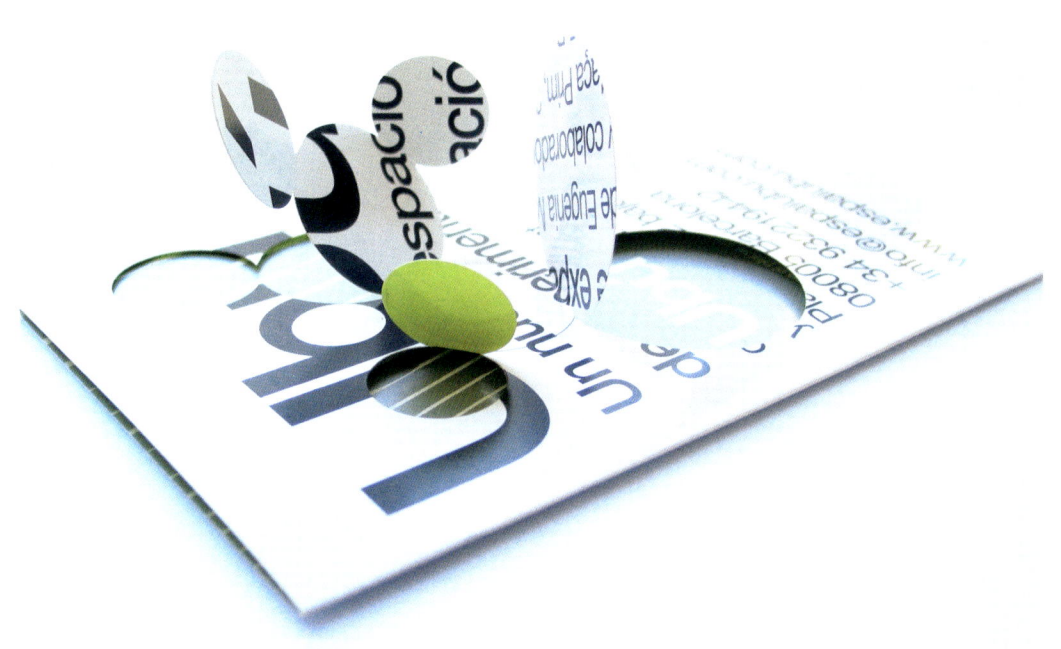

Micro-sculpture invitation | 2004

Azúamoliné
www.martinazua.com

The card for the inauguration of the Ubú gallery is a two-fold stamp. Exploring the transformation of the object and the plane, once the message is read, the card becomes a mini-sculpture displaying the stamp.

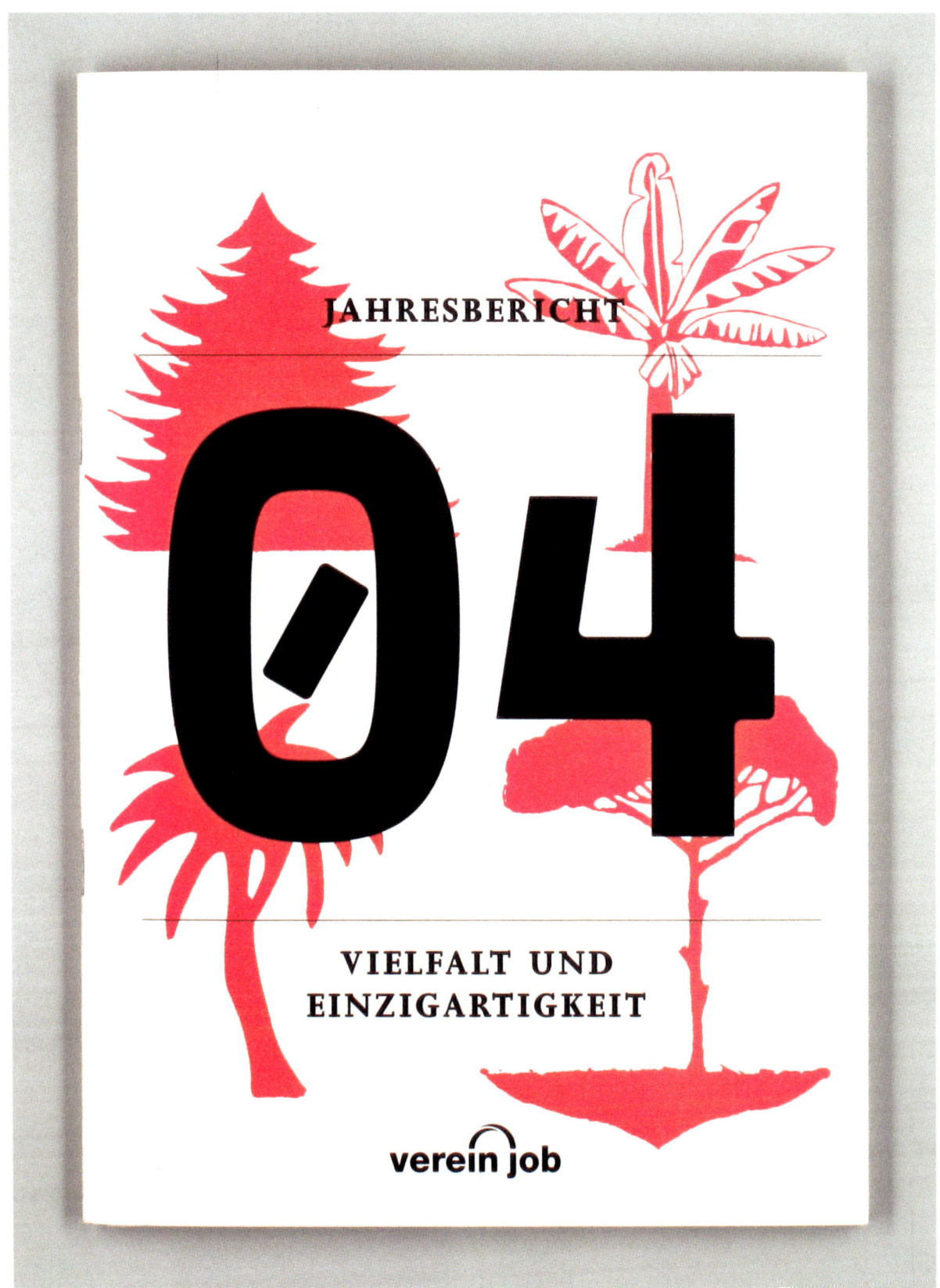

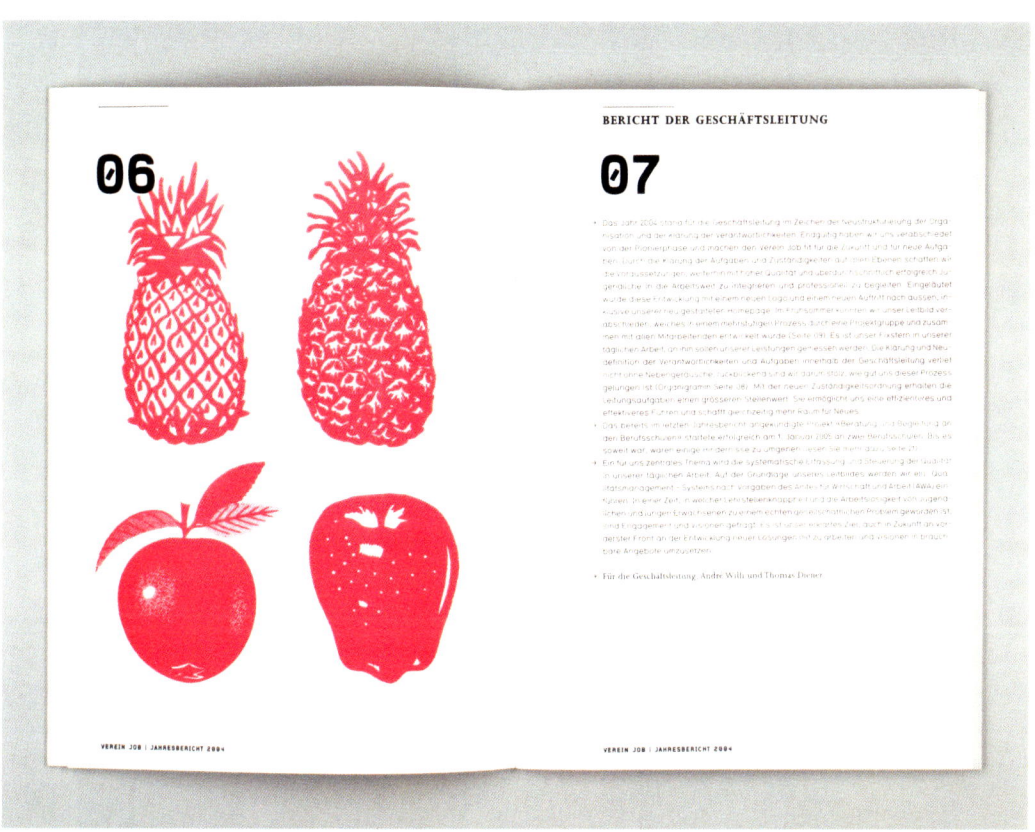

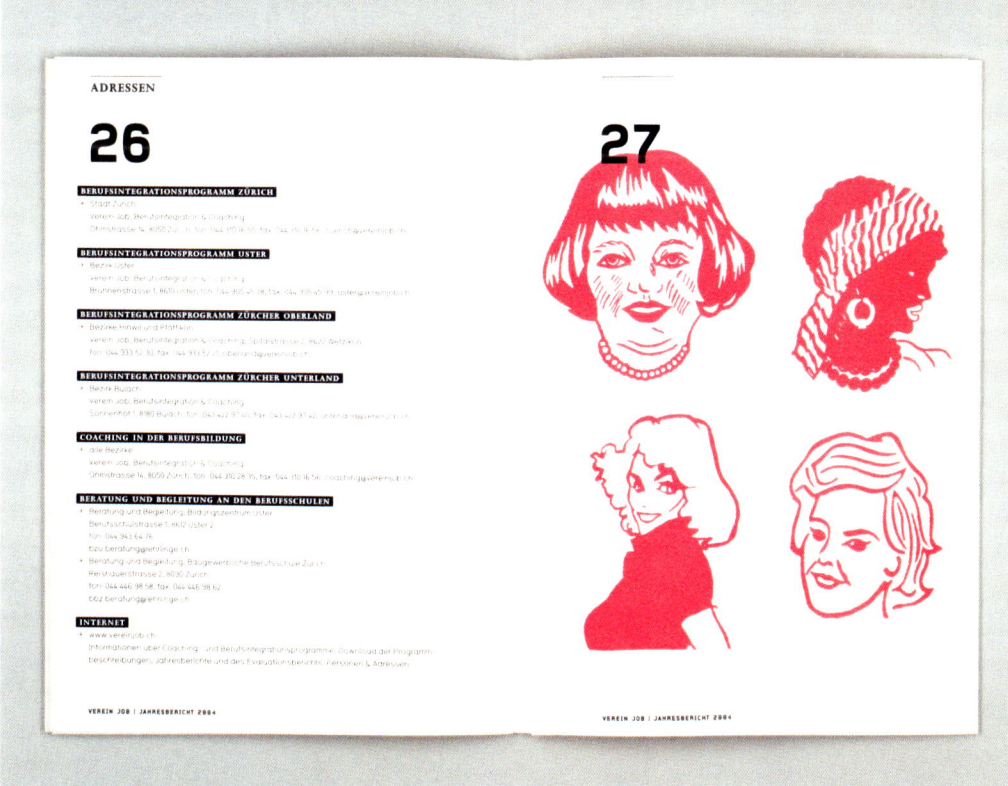

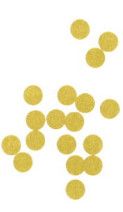

**Verein Job 2004
annual report | 2005**

**Fauxpas Grafik
www.fauxpas.ch**

The themes of the association's report, which deals with integration and employment of young people, were variety and particularities. Diversity and freshness in the typography, as well as the illustration style, support the message.

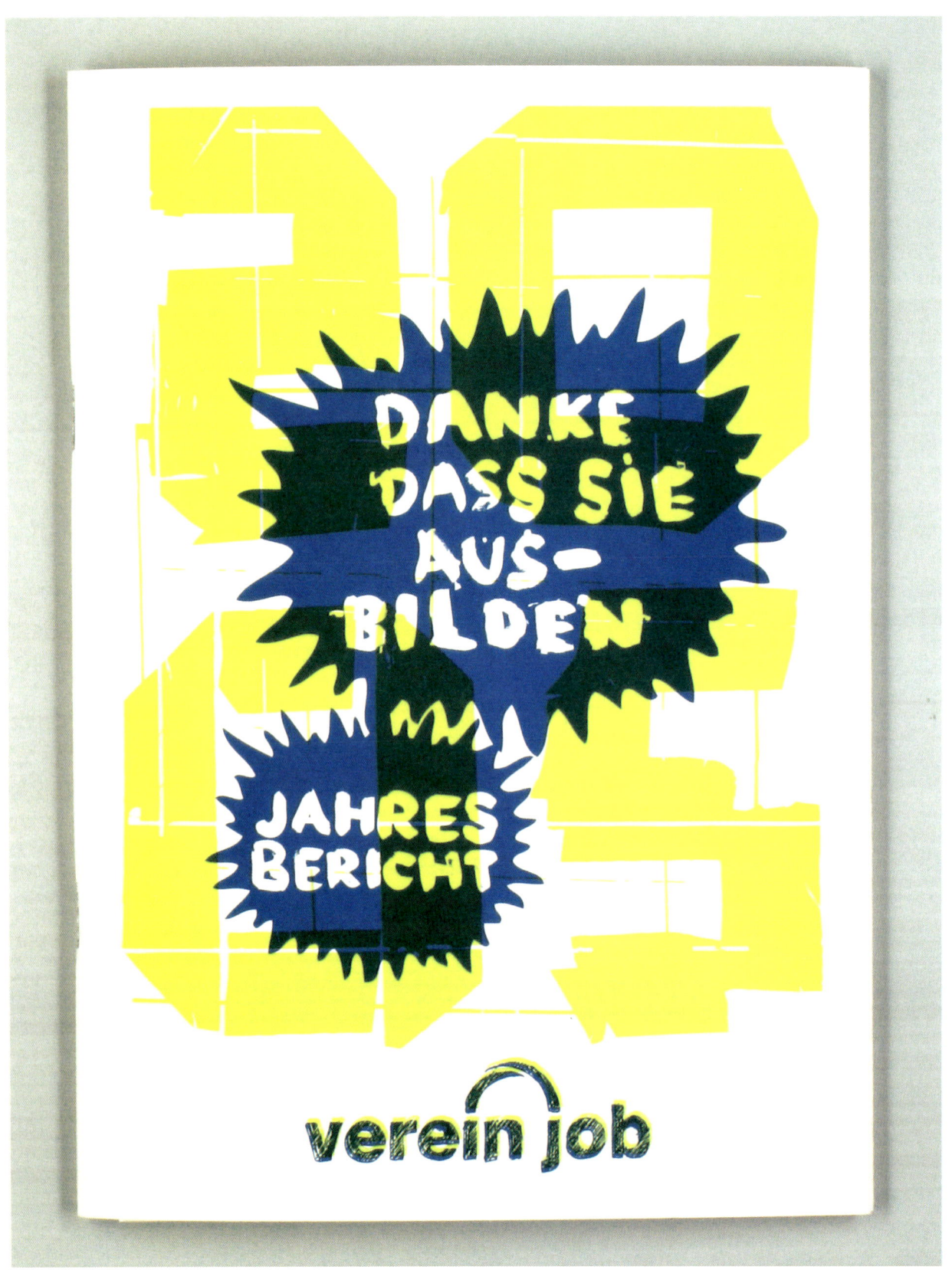

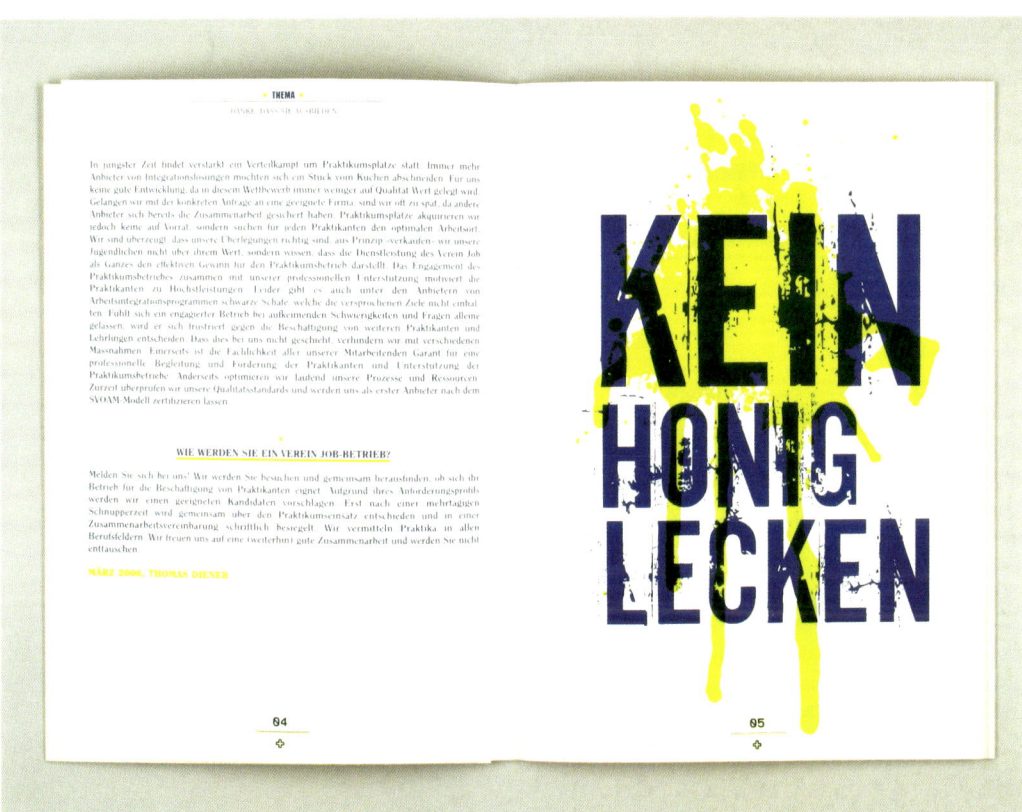
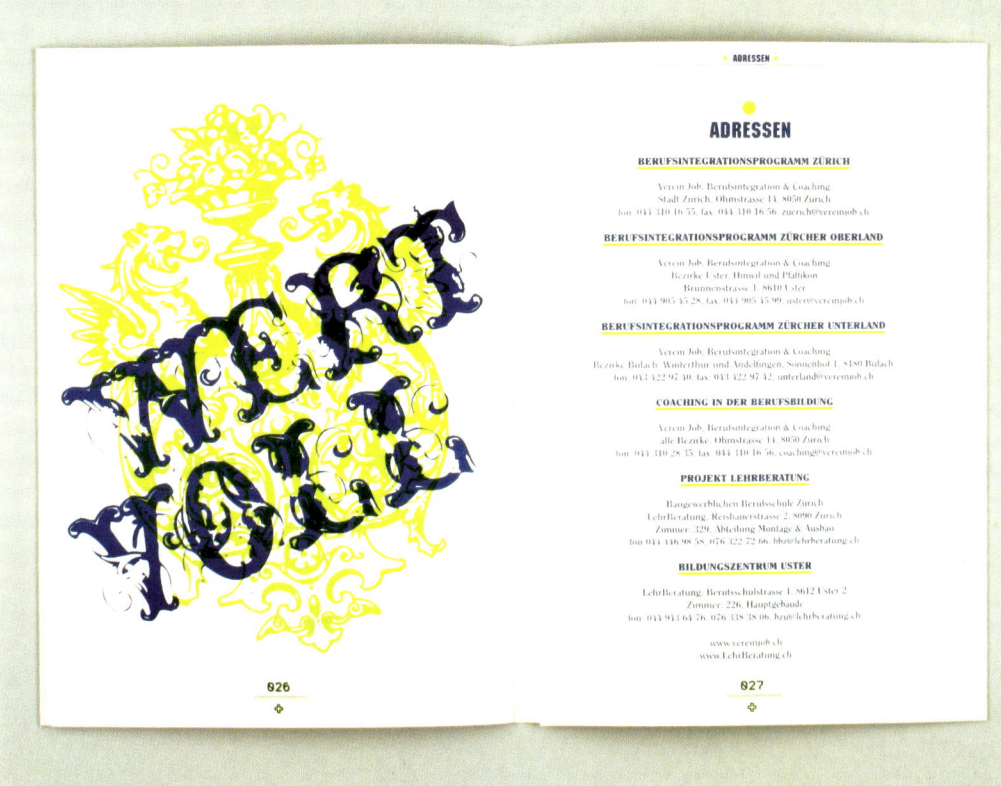

**Verein Job 2005
annual report | 2006**

**Fauxpas Grafik
www.fauxpas.ch**

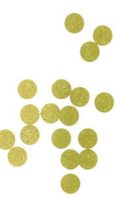

Capturing the attention of young people is one of the most difficult tasks. To do it, the graphics of this report on young people are given character thanks to the work with smudges and extremely modern typographies.

The best party I have been to involved dropping acid on an boat trip to a hidden cove on an island off Hong Kong and spending the night with about twenty friends on a beach. It all got very weird in a good way—I remember the surrounding jungle looked very Jurassic. Yay!!

Fiona Hewitt

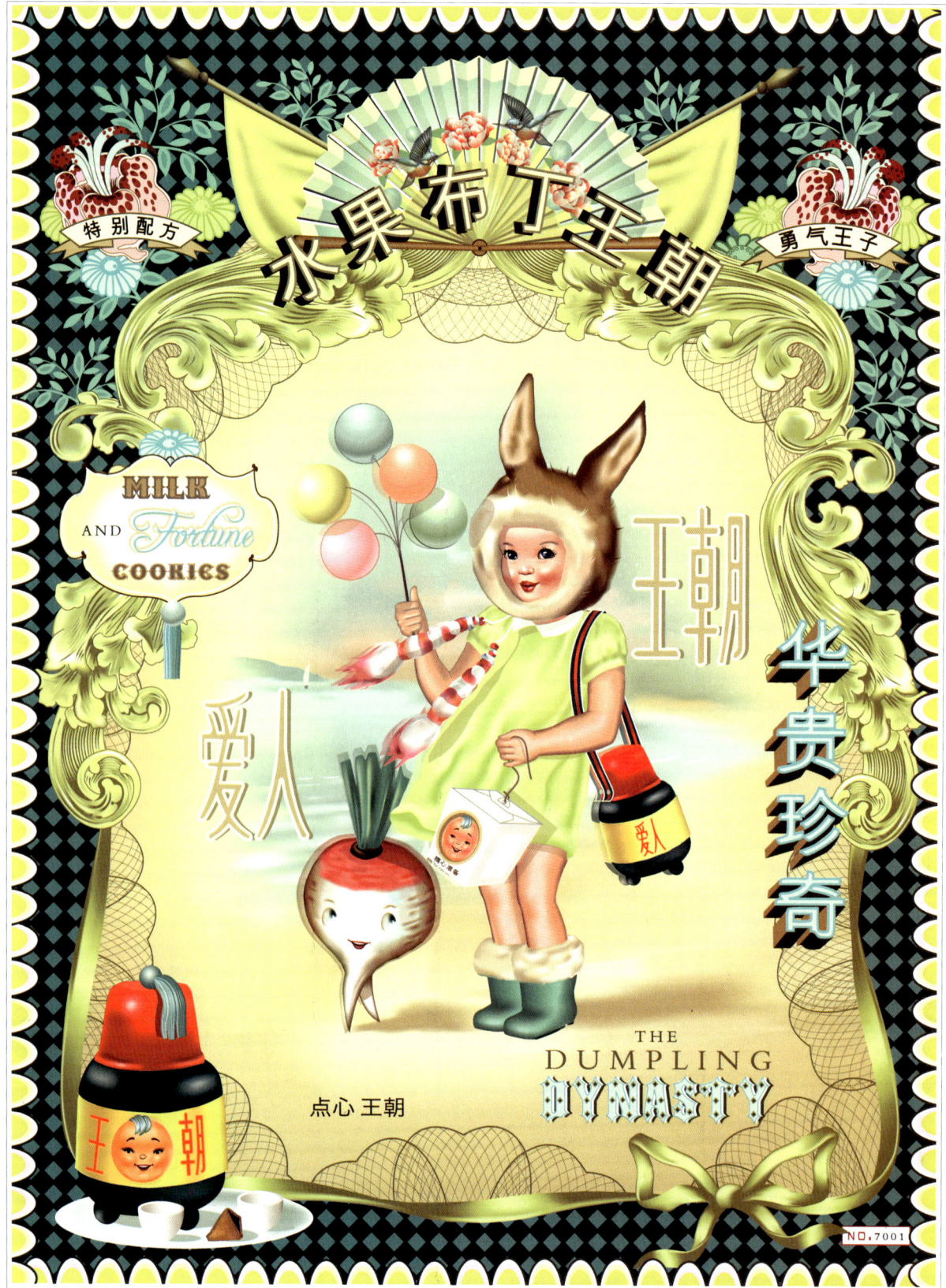

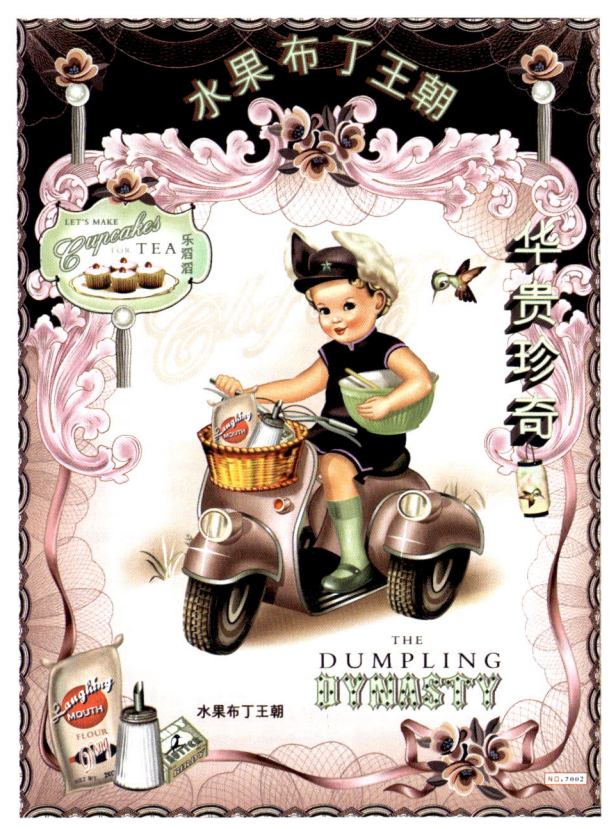

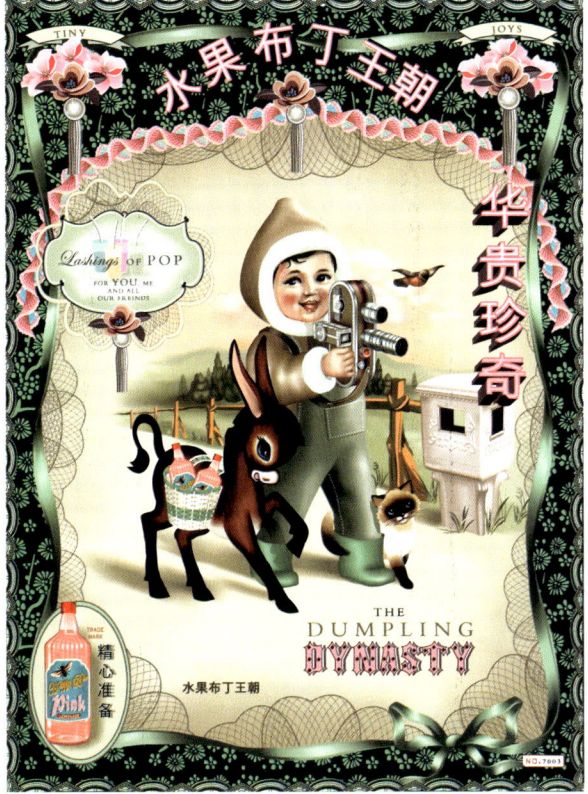

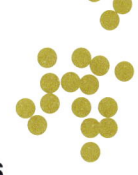

The Dumpling Dynasty | 2006

Fiona Hewitt
www.fionahewitt.com

As a tribute to kitsch communist imagery from the fifties, the image is submerged in icons from yesteryear. Chronicle Books used the illustrations for a set of stationery; then the designers printed them on different articles.

OFFF Festival in Barcelona, celebrated since 2001 annually, an event which brings together the most elite and inspiring artists from various schools of graphic design. The topics of discussion behind each seminar brought me back to the reason for which I came to design and the direction in which I continue.

Sheila Seyfert

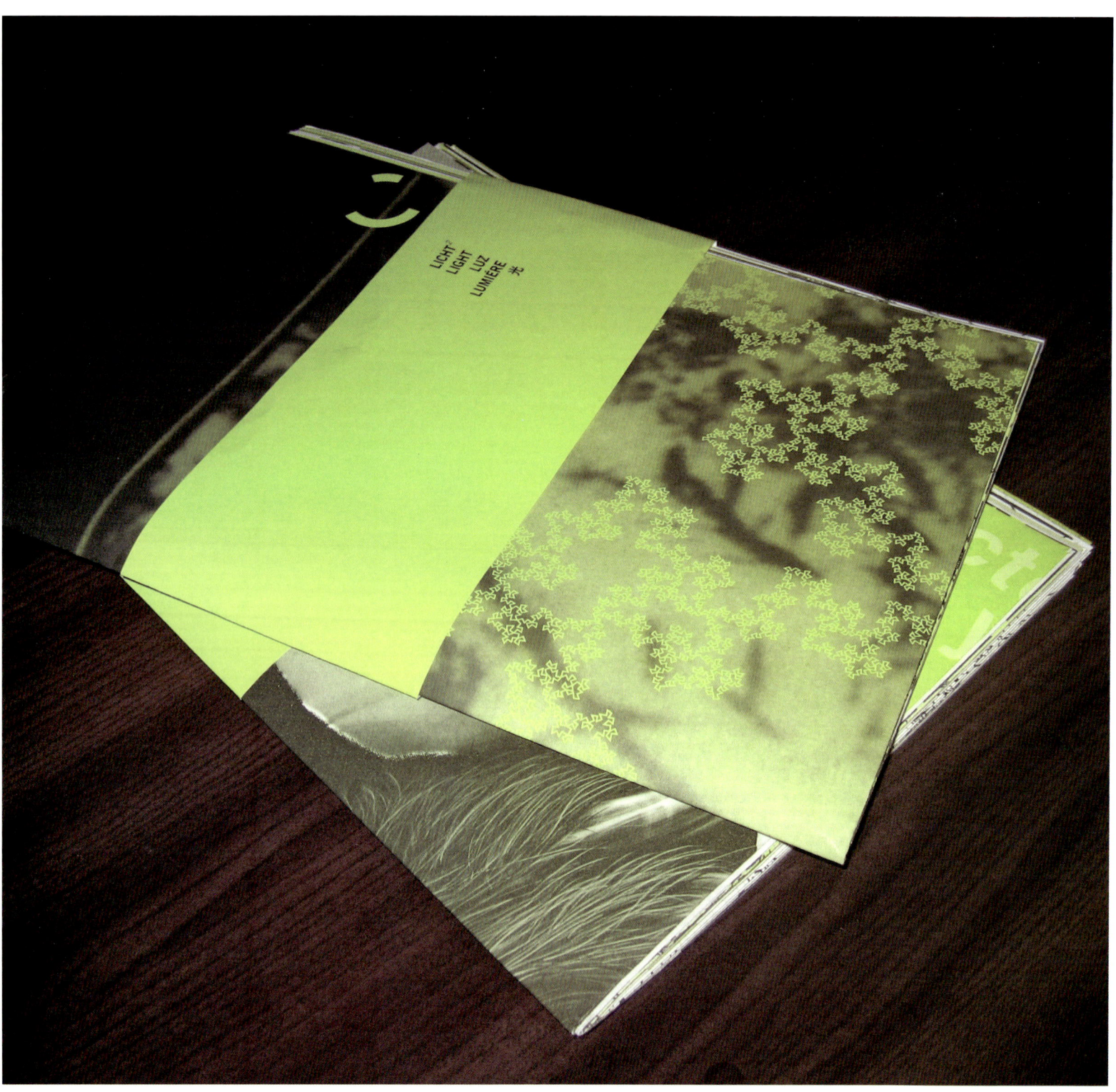

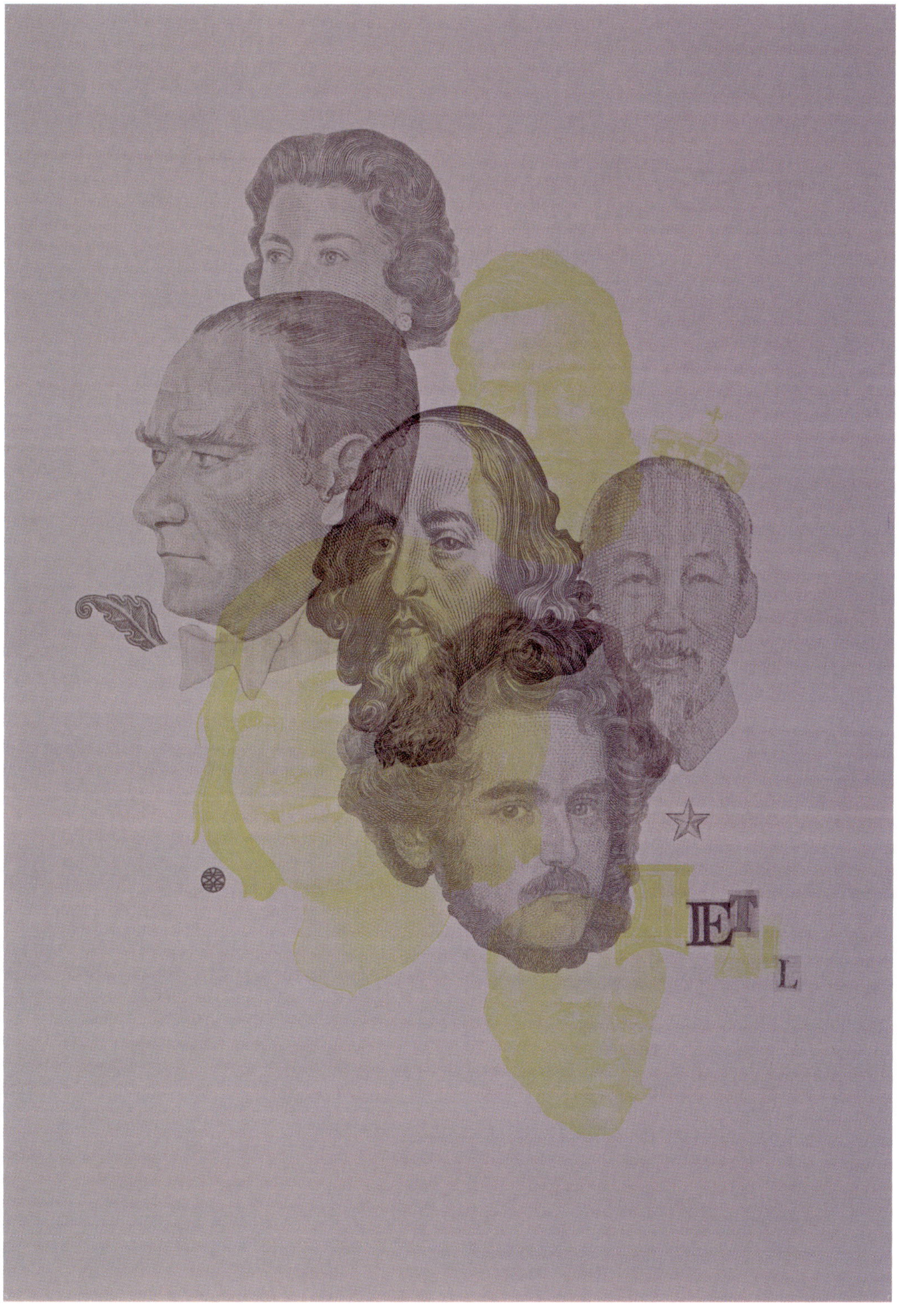

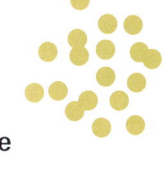

Poster for the magazine
Licht | 2007

Spoonlight
www.spoonlight.com

Die Krieger des Lichts agency invites different artists to collaborate with their magazine. The subject of this issue was detail, and the proposal works with detail from a phantasmagoric angle: one needs to delve into the shadows to recognize the faces in green.

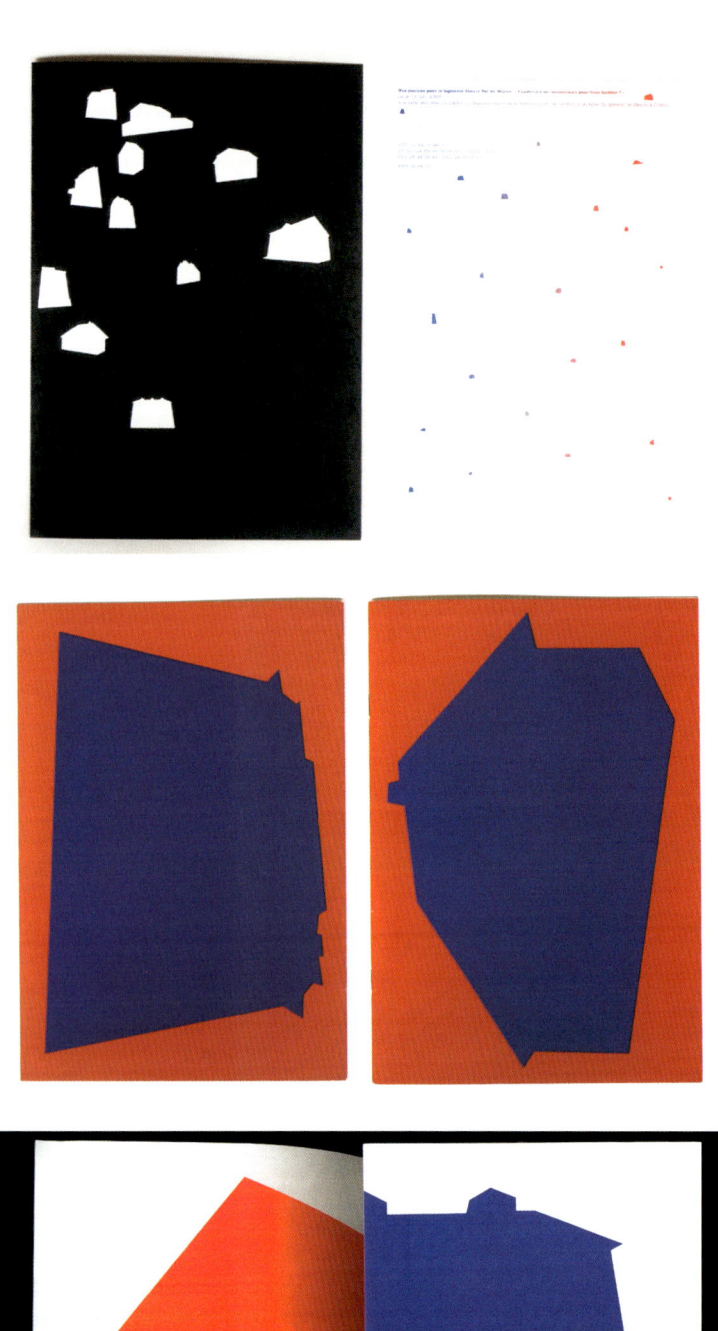

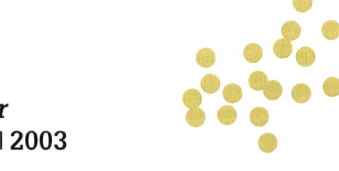

A day for housing | 2003

Fanette Mellier
www.fanettemellier.com

In the graphic identity of a day of political reflection concerning housing, the silhouettes of houses stand out in the background and become a bold image for the spectator. The publicity represents the theme of the debate: "Construct or reconstruct?"

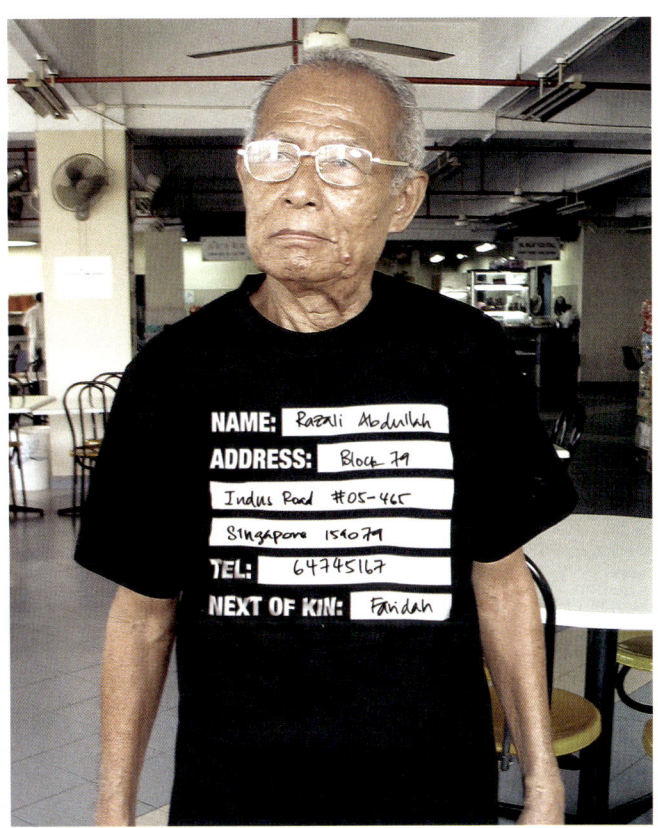

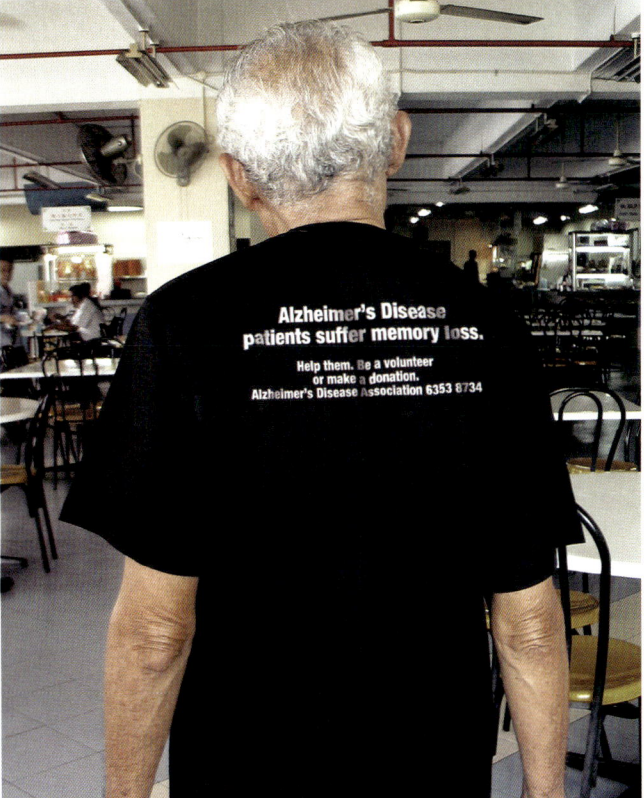

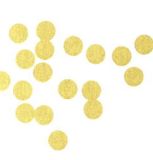

Alzheimer | 2006

Kinetic
www.kinetic.com.sg

Alzheimer's causes the gradual loss of the faculties eventually leading to an extreme situation: no longer recognizing oneself. To raise funds and educate regarding the illness, the T-shirt considers this consequence by simulating an ID card.

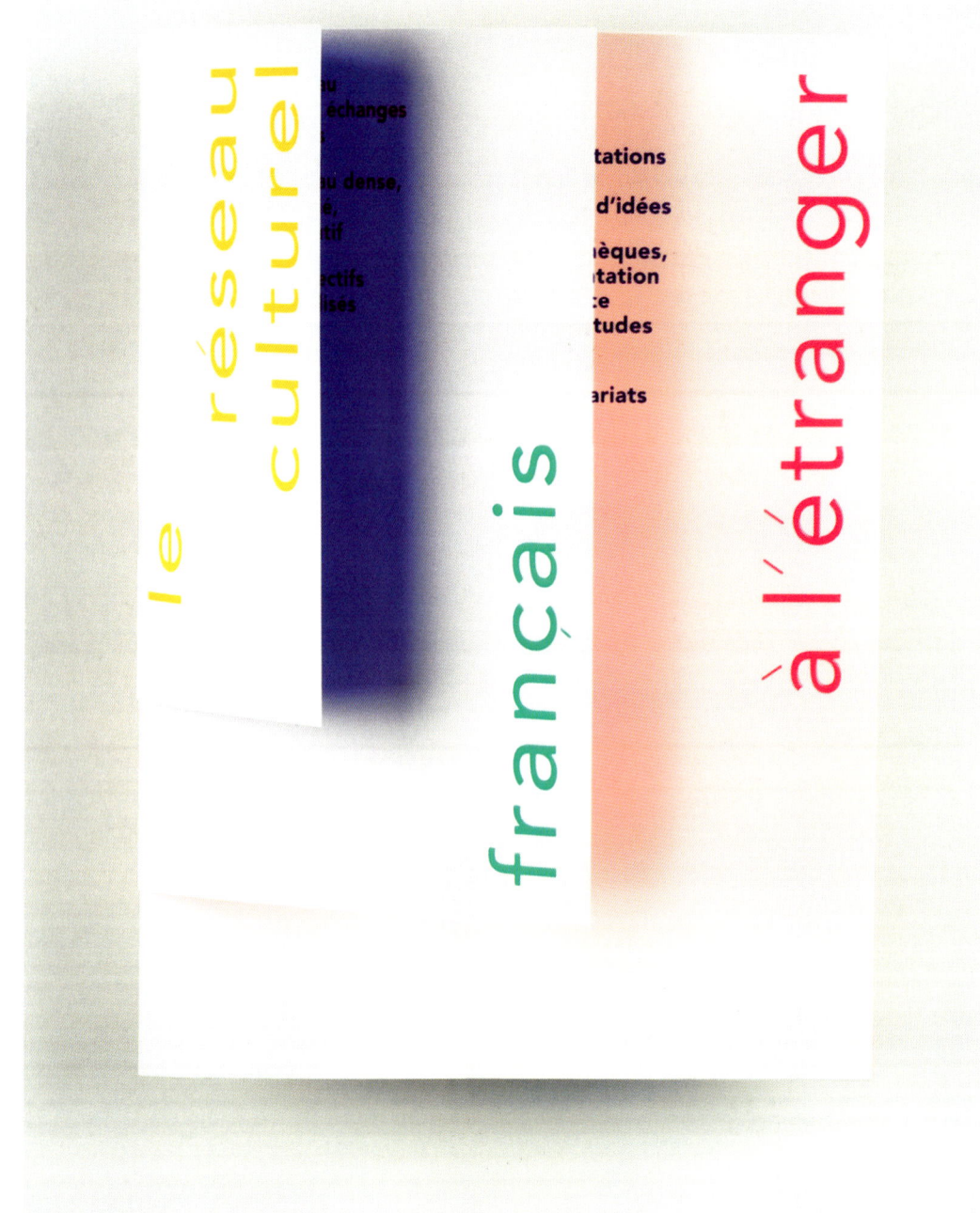

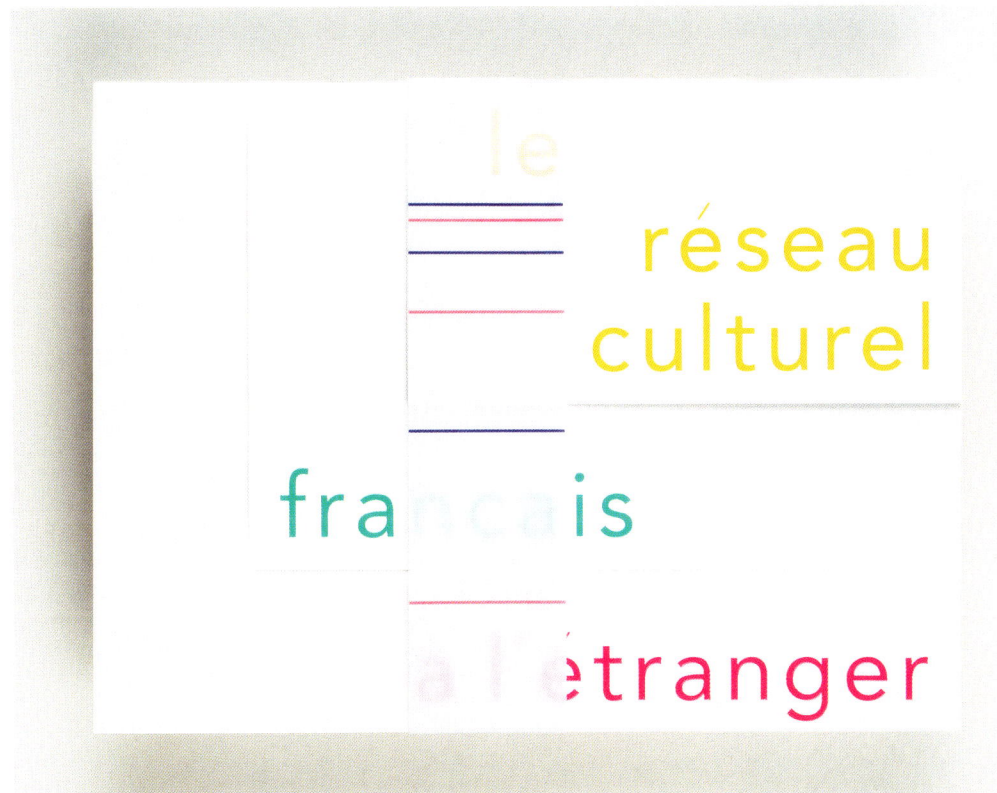

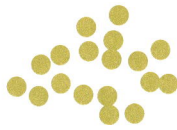

**Le Réseau Culturel
Français à l'Étranger | 2006**

Studio Philippe Apeloig
www.apeloig.com

To promote the French cultural network abroad, the leaflet reinterprets the French flag on the cover. The different sizes and transparencies renovate the institutional image without losing discretion.

There were empanadas and cumbia and a bride and a groom.

Ayelen Carrasco

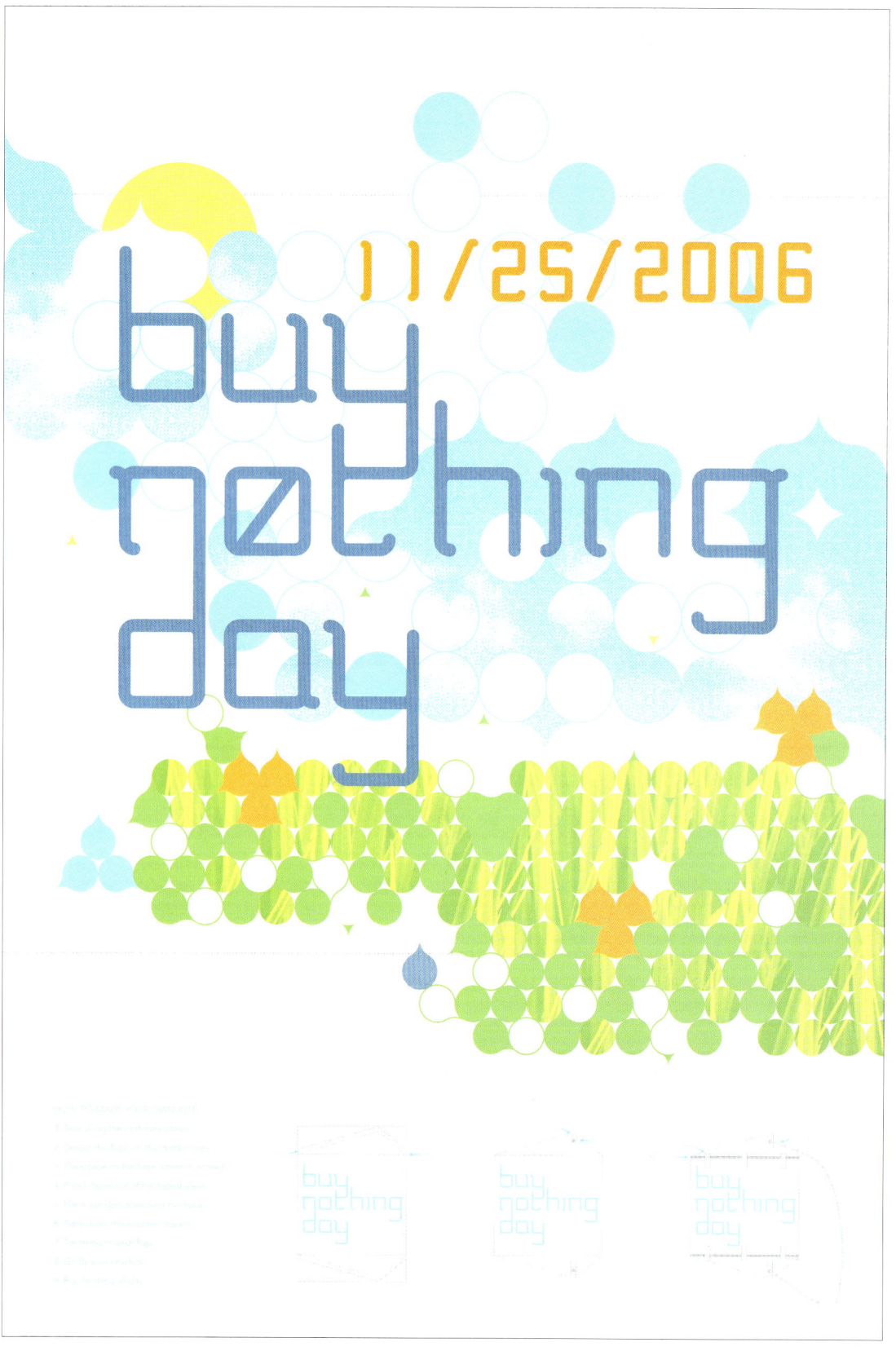

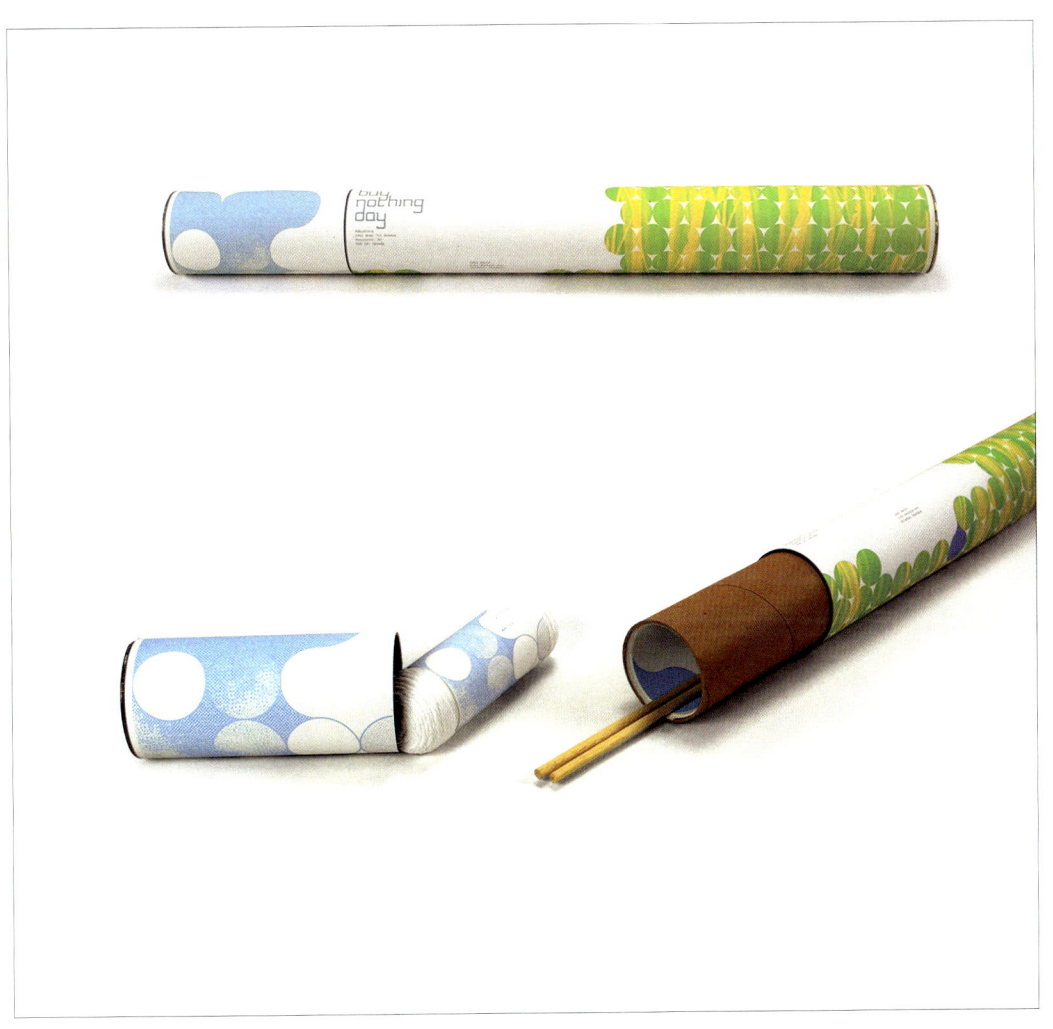

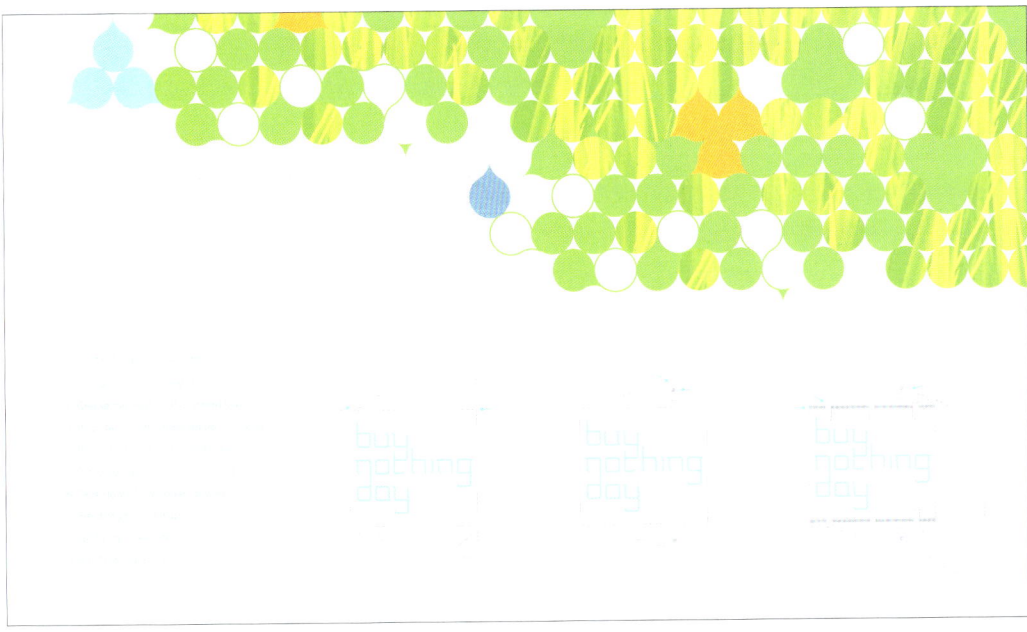

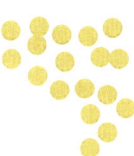

**Buy Nothing Day
poster/kite | 2006**

Ayelen Carrasco
www.ayelencarrasco.com

The poster becomes a kite and promotes the event while being used. The Lanolin typography with its angular structure, created for the project, contrasts with the circular forms repeated throughout the composition.

The best party I've ever been to? I haven't been to one yet.

Tnop Wangsillapakun

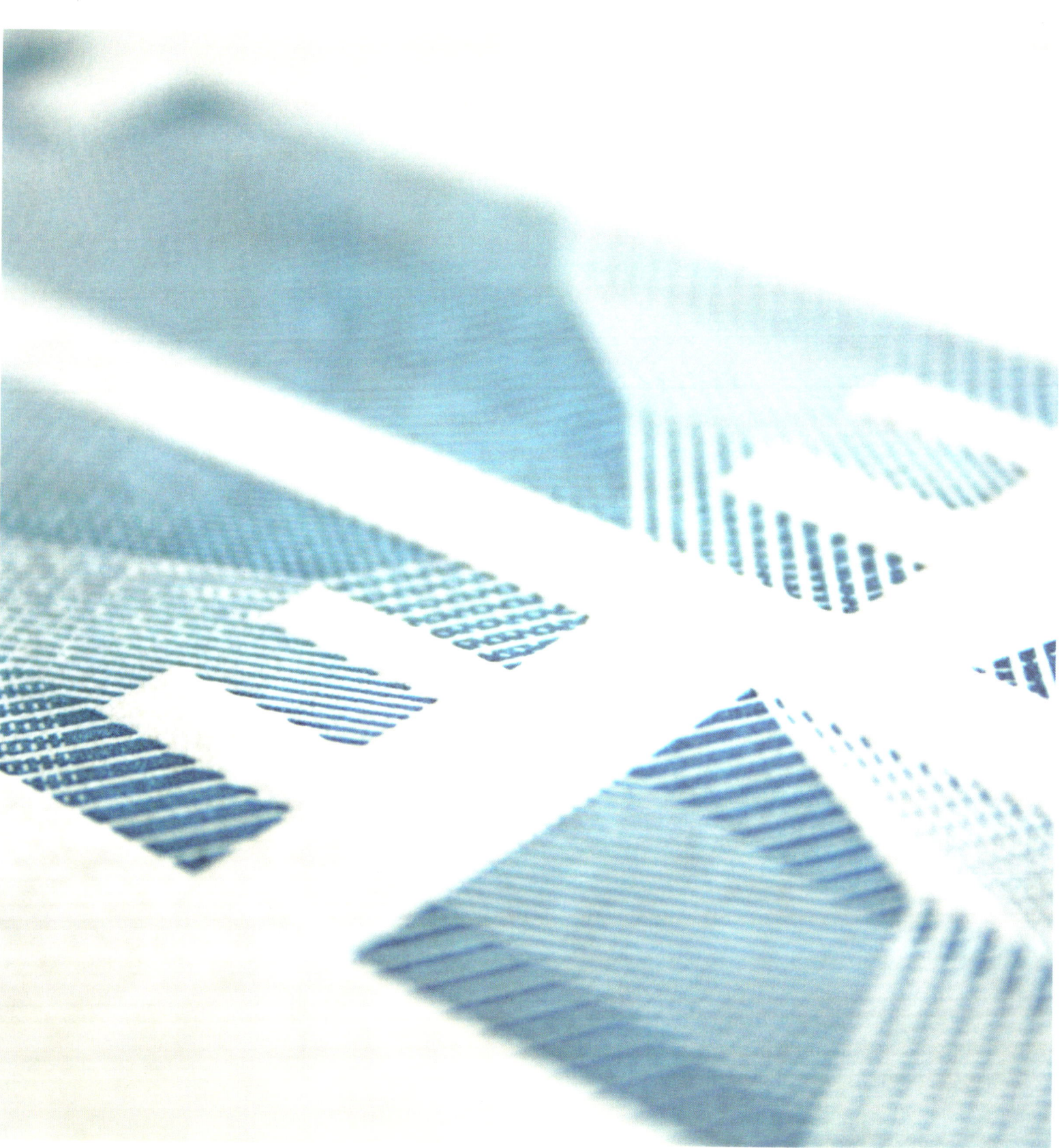

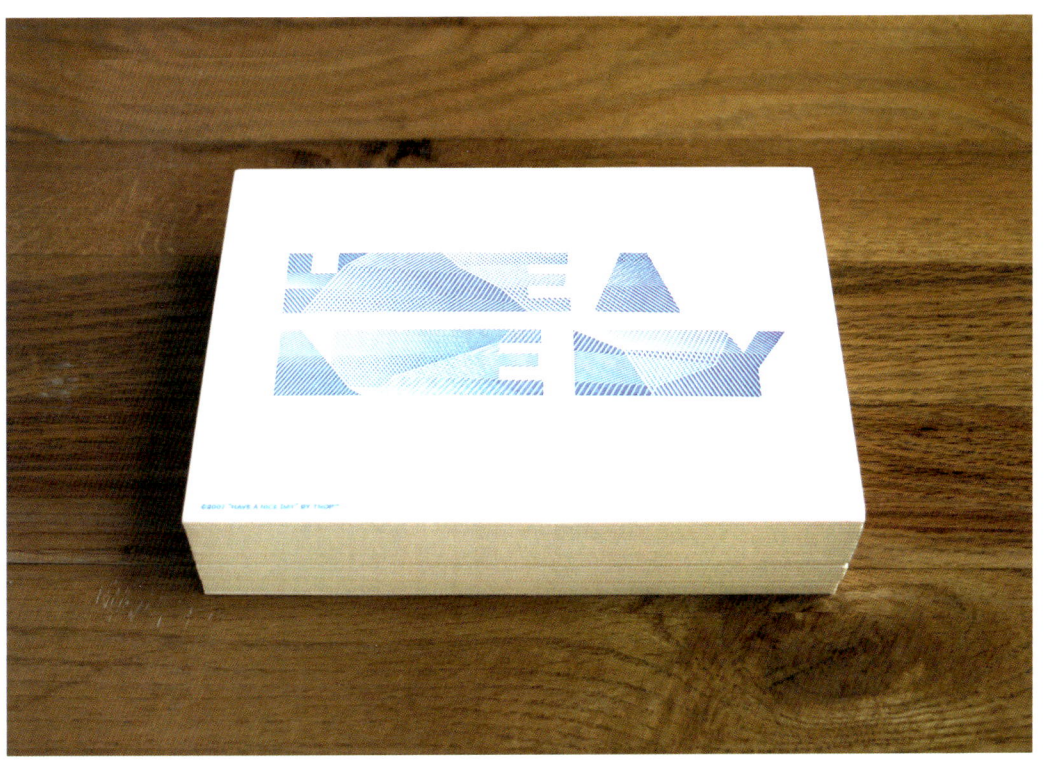

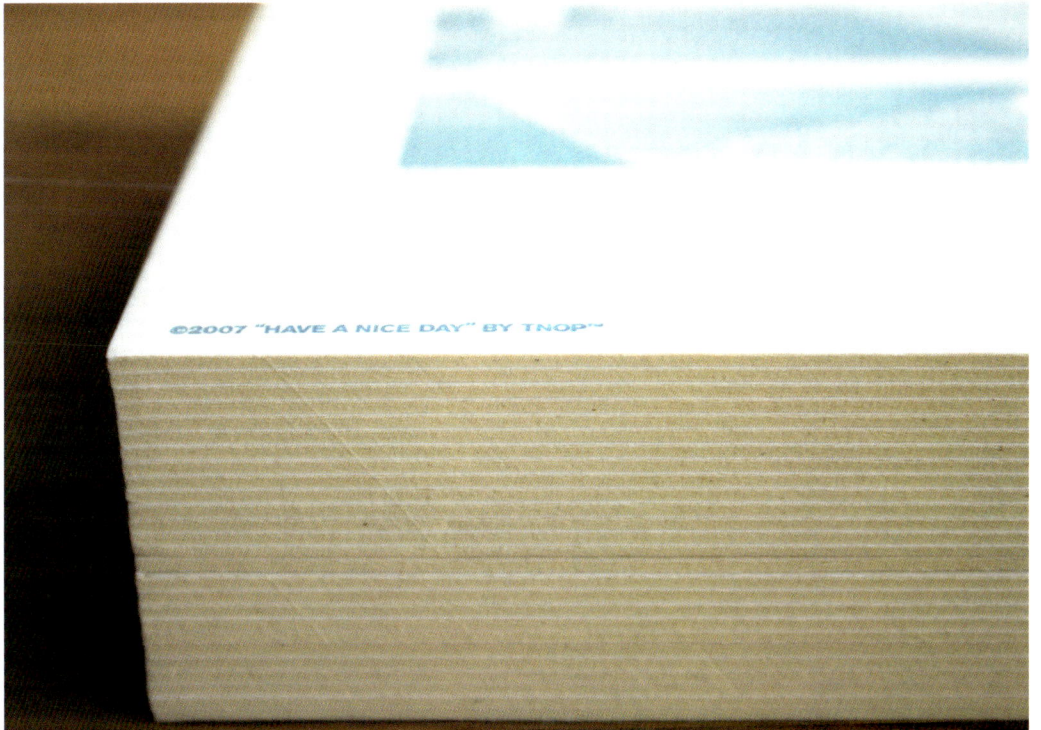

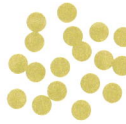

HAVE A NICE DAY
postcard | 2007

Tnop Wangsillapakun/TNOP design
www.tnop.com

Sometimes the hook that retains clients can be based on a simple "hello." These self-promotional postcards done by the studio focus on this idea, with an emphasis on a carefree attitude by using beer mat material as a support.

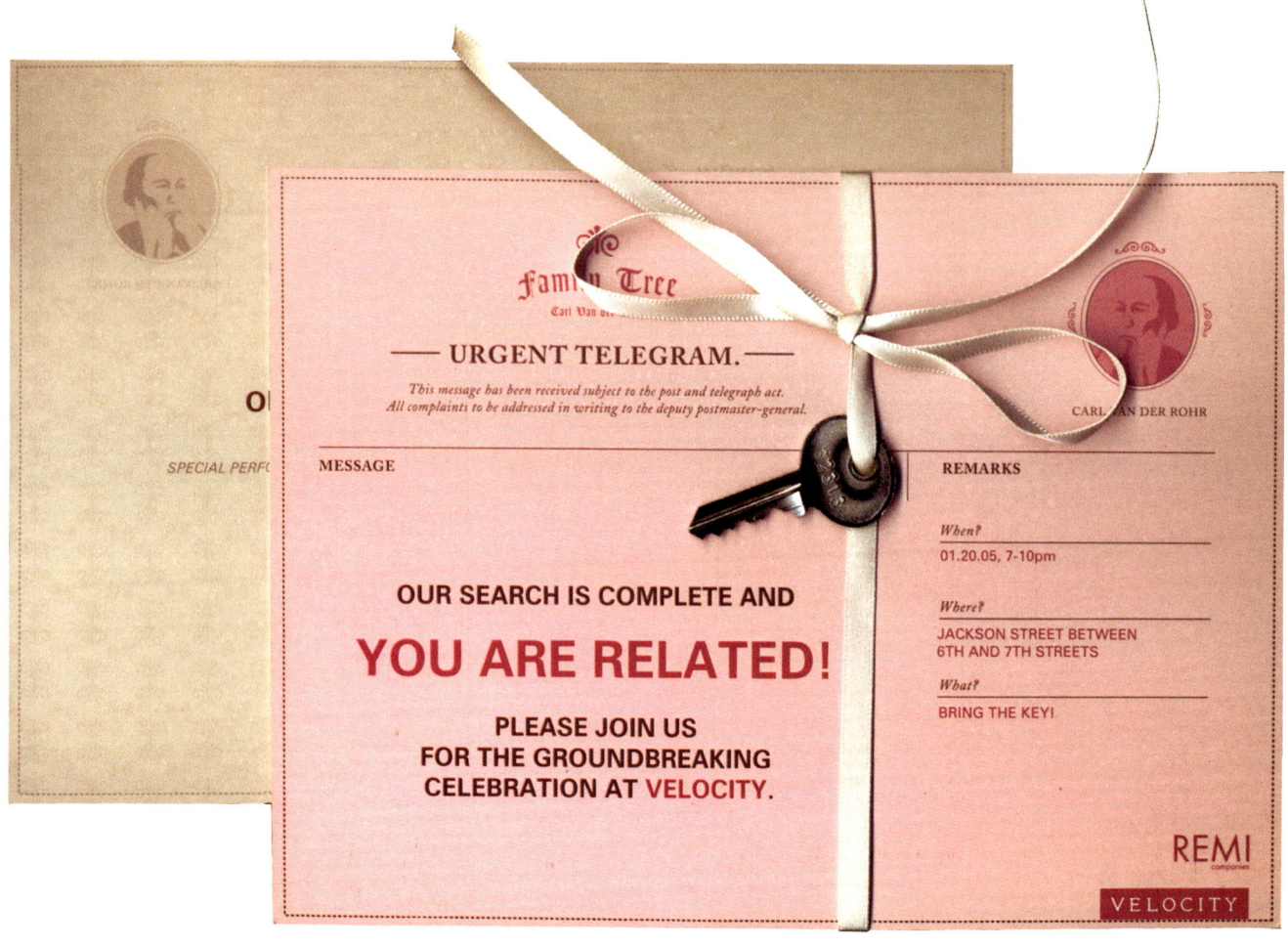

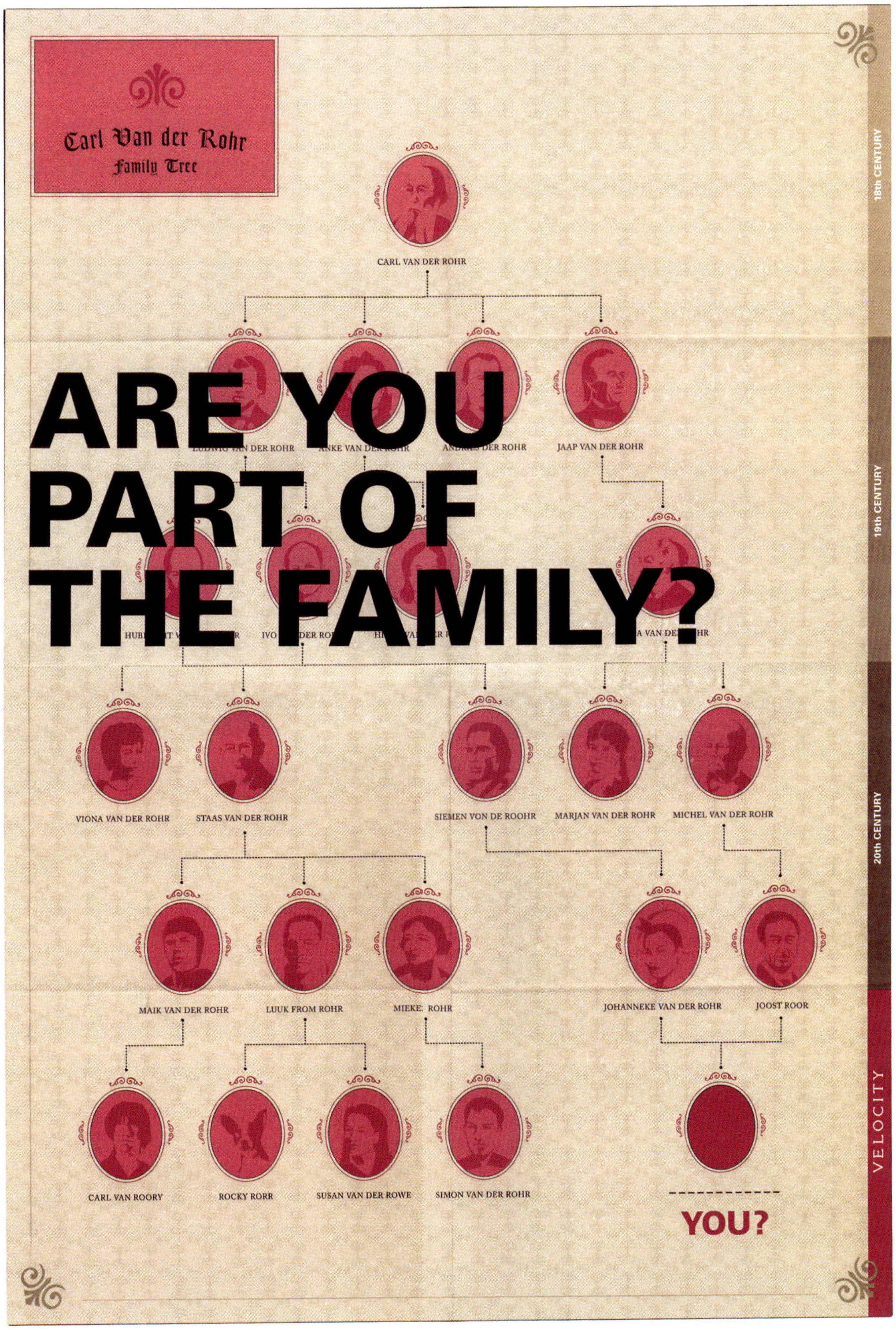

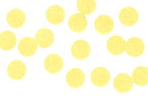

Velocity invitations and poster | 2005

Tiziana Haug/The Apartment
www.inthehabit.com

Velocity, a new condominium, needed an image that would link their traditional architecture with care for interior design. Within both a modern and historical framework, the ornaments and patterns combine with bright, striking colors.

Can't remember the last party I attended? (Think I need to get out more?)

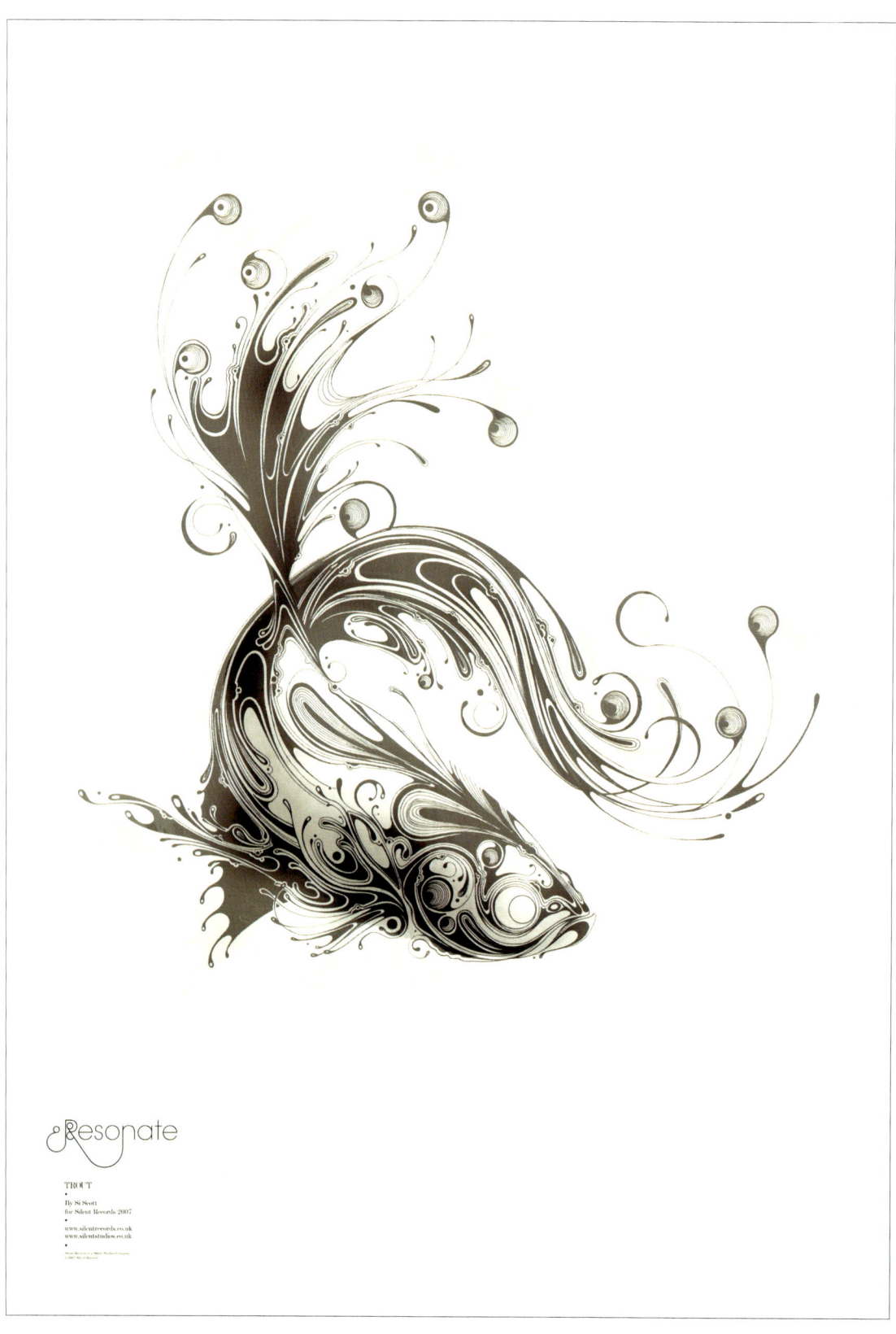

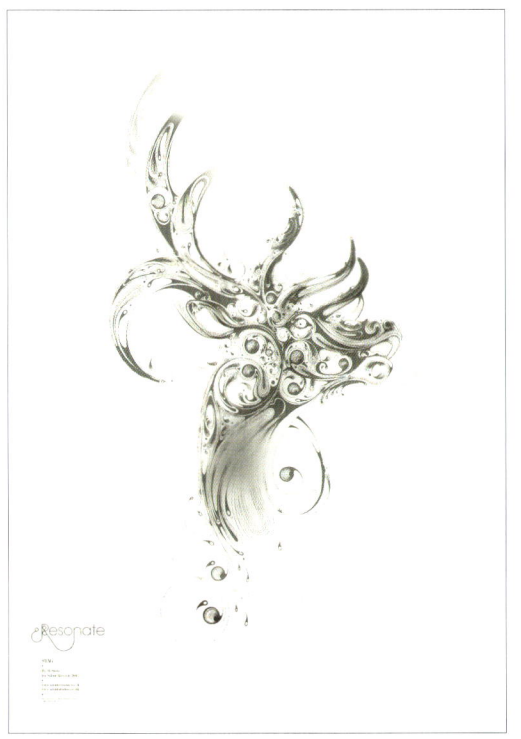
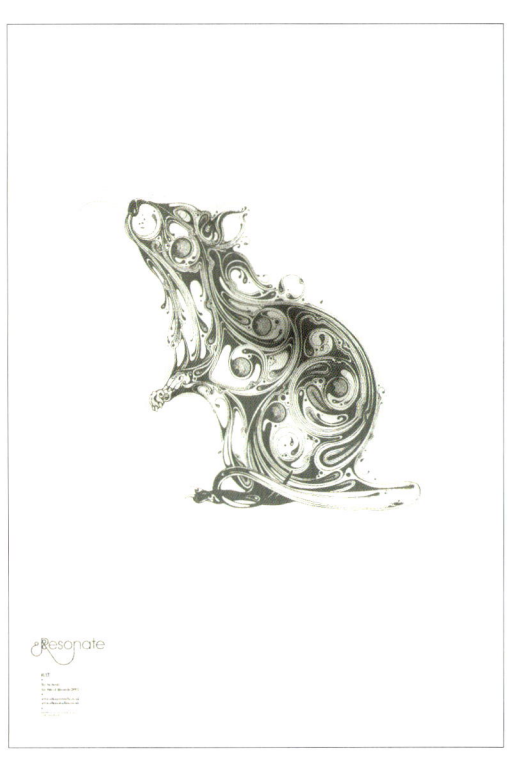
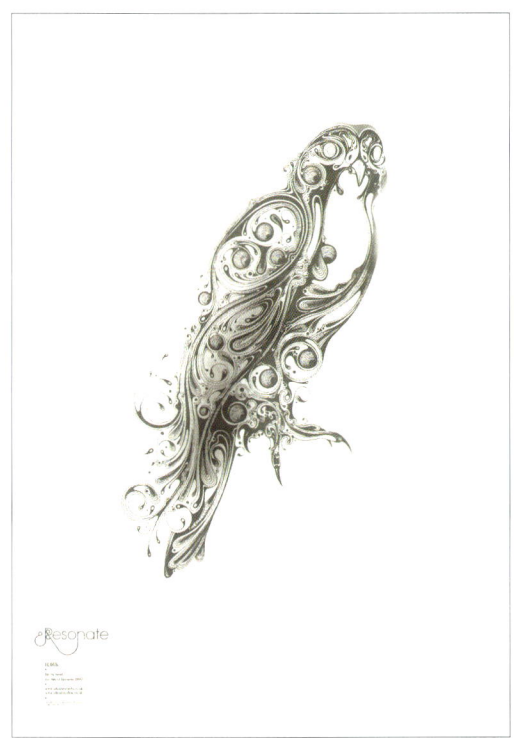
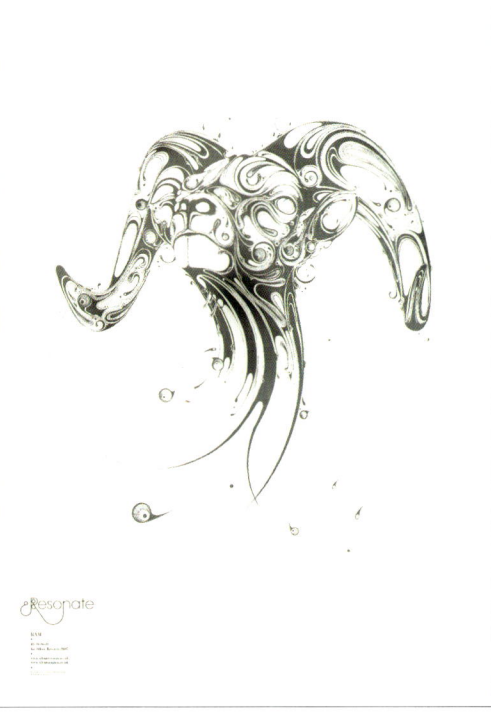

Resonate/Stag/Ram/ Hawk/Rat/Trout | 2007

Si Scott Studio
www.siscottstudio.com

Combining self-promotion with a good cause, each month this series of posters features an animal that lives in the English forests. The vitality of the animals is reflected in the endings, which look like intense, uncontrolled brushstrokes.

The best party or craziest party I have been to was a Crash Worship concert in Salt Lake City, Utah when I was about eighteen or nineteen. It was total chaos and completely illegal: tribal drum music, fireworks in doors, fire, public sex, drinking and much more. I couldn't believe what was going on around me, it made me realize things weren't as rigid as I thought they were which was a very nice feeling to have in Utah.

Nate Williams

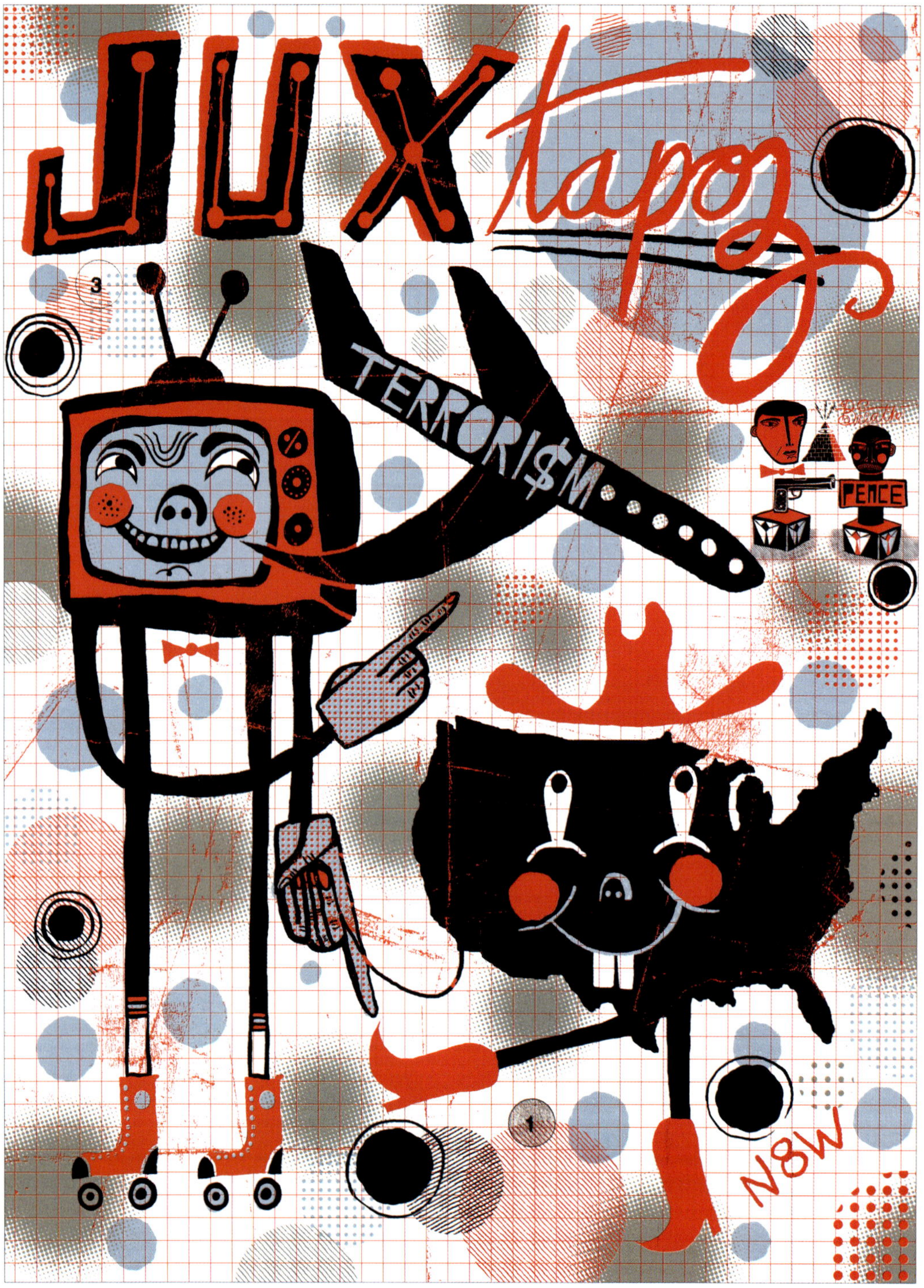

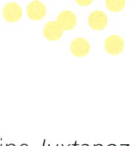

Juxtapoz | 2007

Nate Williams
www.n8w.com

This poster for the magazine *Juxtapoz* is inspired by the lyrics of a song by Operation Ivy: "We have the flag of freedom as we conquer and invade." The features of the caricatures, far from being naïve, communicate the meaning of the phrase.

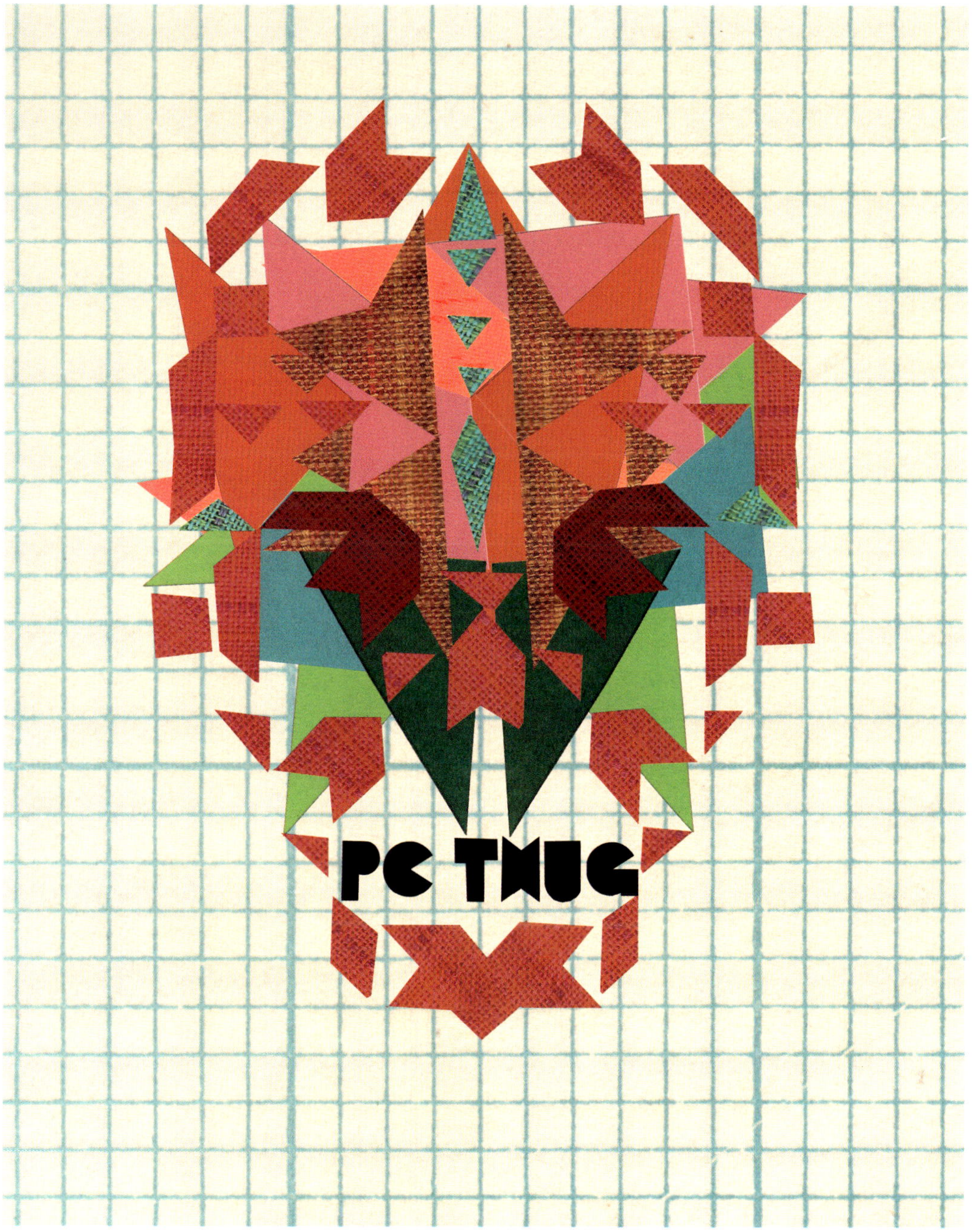

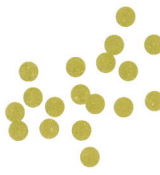

PC Thug DJ poster | 2007

Katherine Brickman,
Kate Mitchell/Greedy Hen
www.greedyhen.com

The poster that promotes DJ PC Thug delves into the paradigm of the eighties and adds to these references and hints of Mexican masks and origami. The textures are created by different pieces of cloth napkins from the fifties.

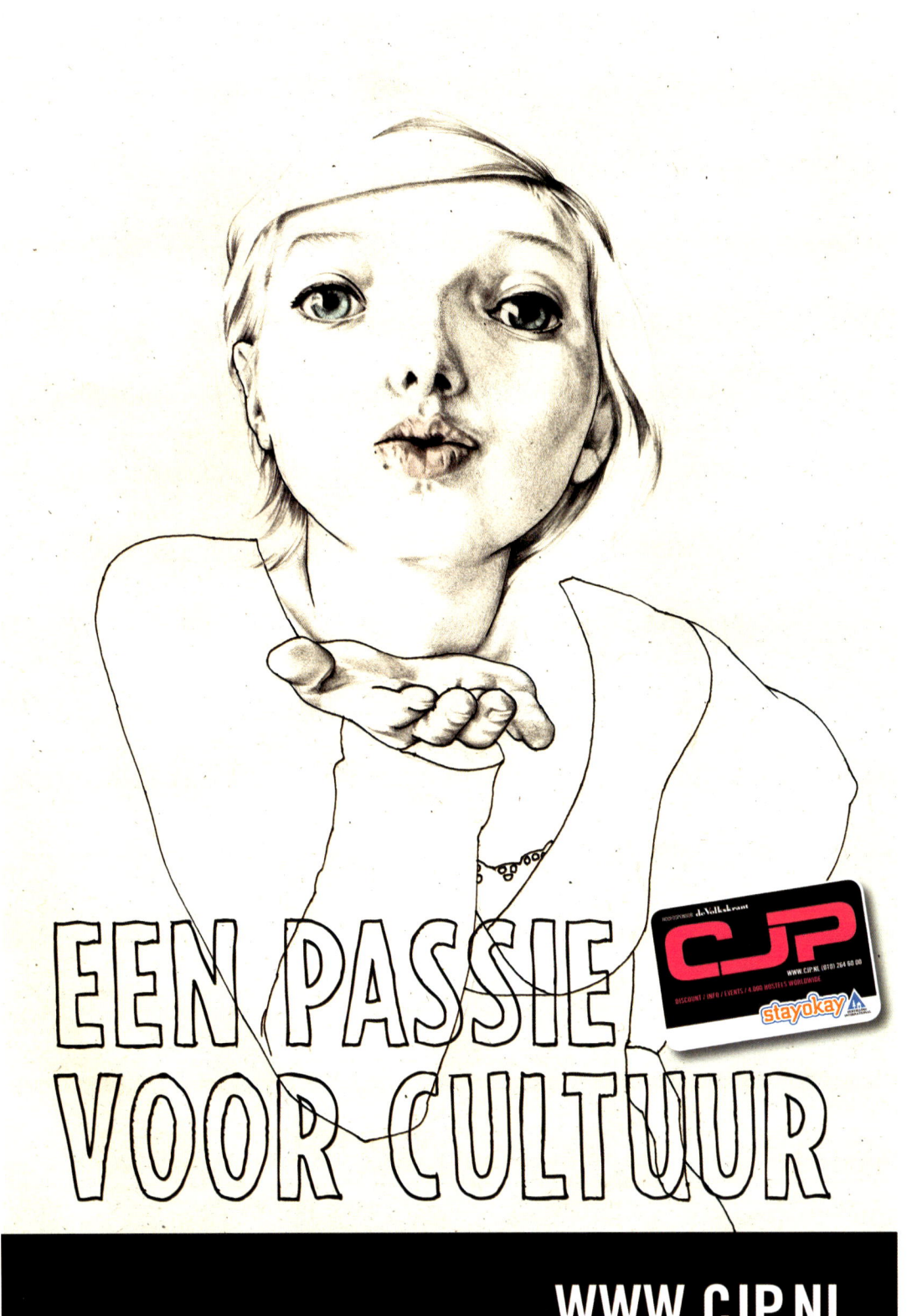

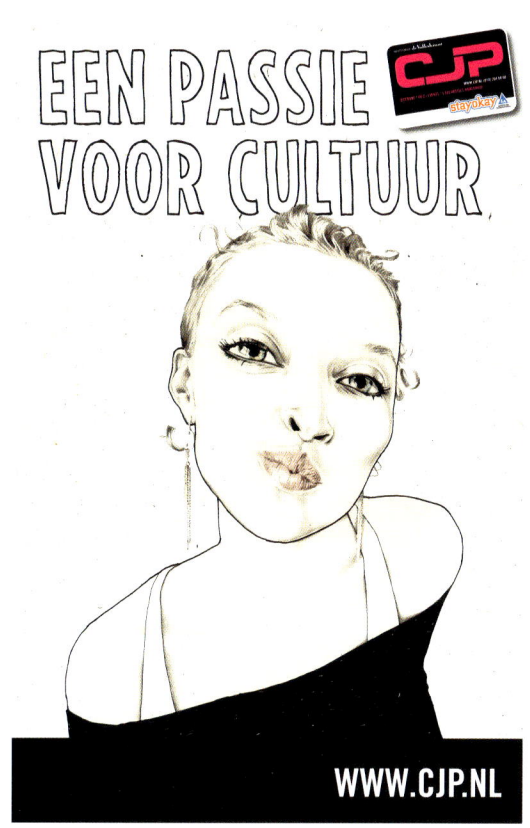

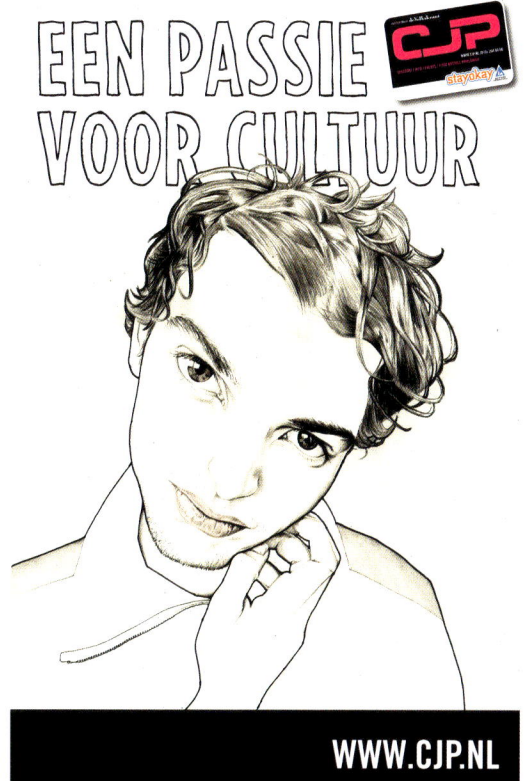

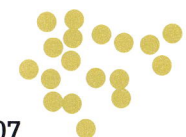

CJP campaign | 2006-2007

Denise van Leeuwen/CJP
www.denise.dds.nl

CJP motivates young people to participate in cultural activities. Leaning toward sensitivity, the illustrations sum up a subjectivity based on gestures and not clothing, returning to the timeless campaign.

I've been to a lot of good parties in Brighton. One that sticks in my mind was a huge free party at Black Rock during the summer. They had a big sound system set up blasting out lots of jungle, dubstep and breaks. In the morning we all went down onto the pebbles to watch the sun rise and then went straight to the pub to drink gin and tonics until the early evening. Good times.

Owen Gildersleeve

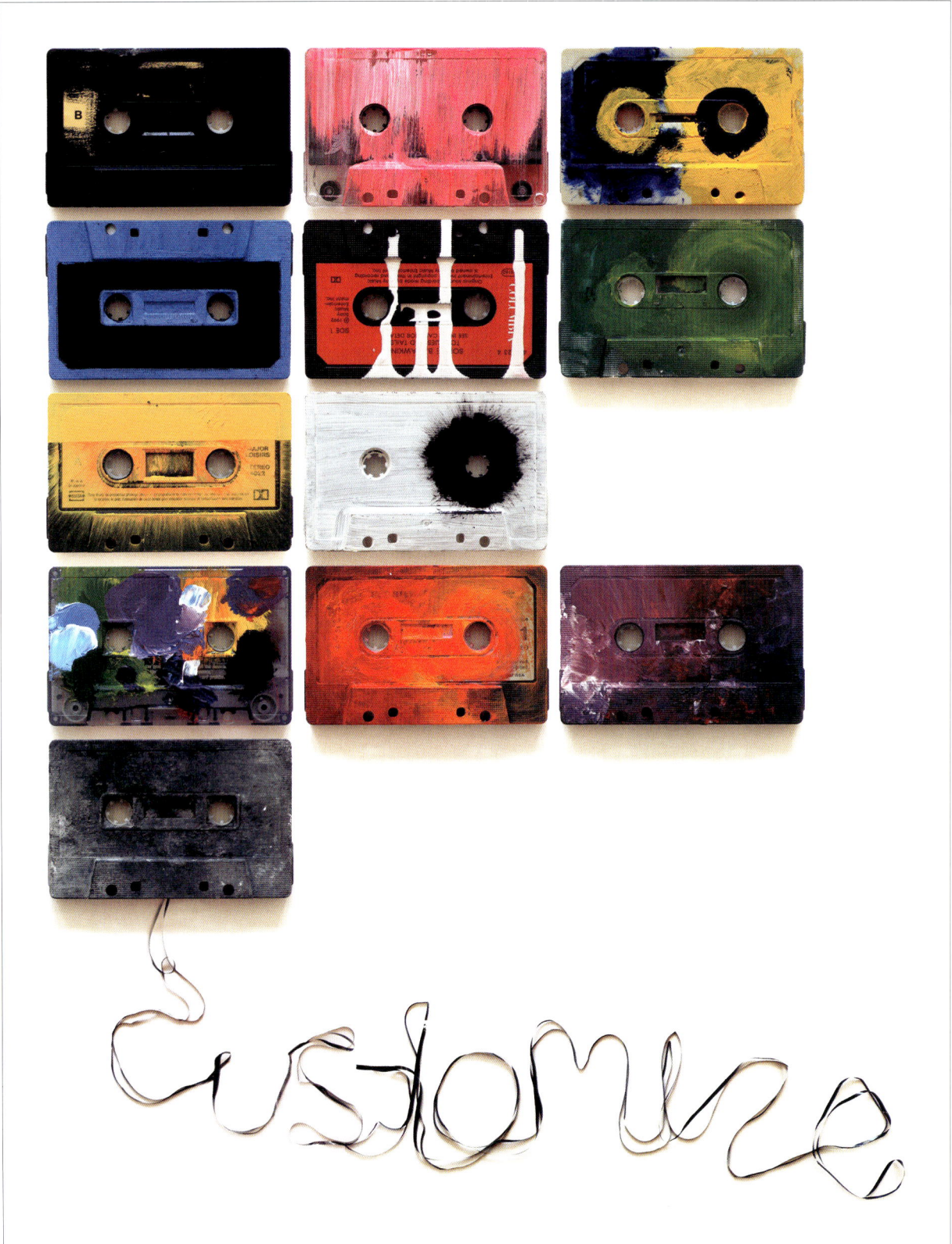

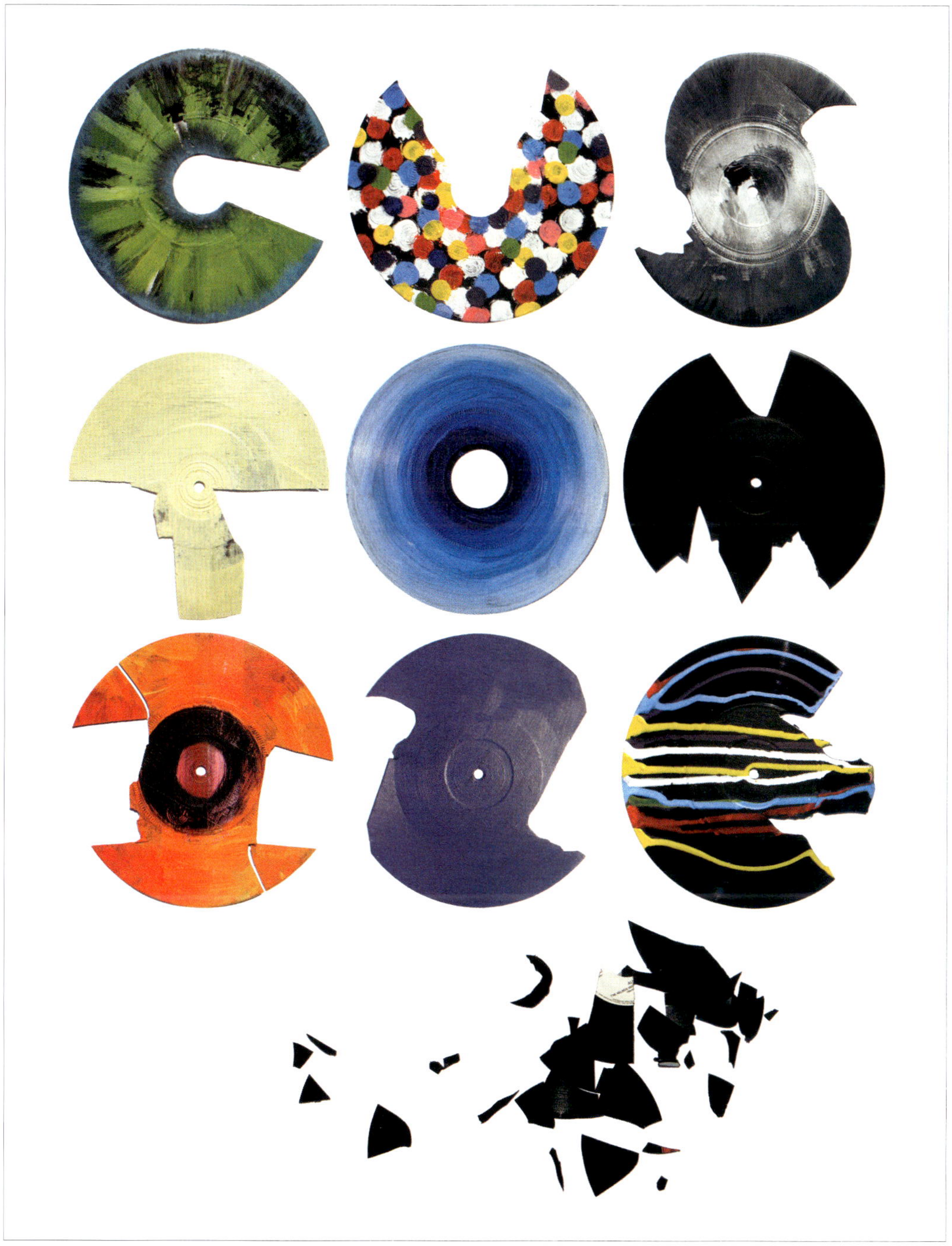

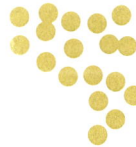

Customize Your Music | 2007

Owen Gildersleeve
www.eveningtweed.com

An unusual vision can also be a good exercise in self-promotion, as is reflected in this poster for Gildersleeve. The experiments in personalization of tapes and records are proof of the designer's passion for music.

An Elvis/Nativity fancy dress party. A cross between The King, and the King of Kings. Some of the wise men got into a scuffle with a shepherd, and were marched out by Elvis, in full Las Vegas rhinestone costume.

Kent Lyons

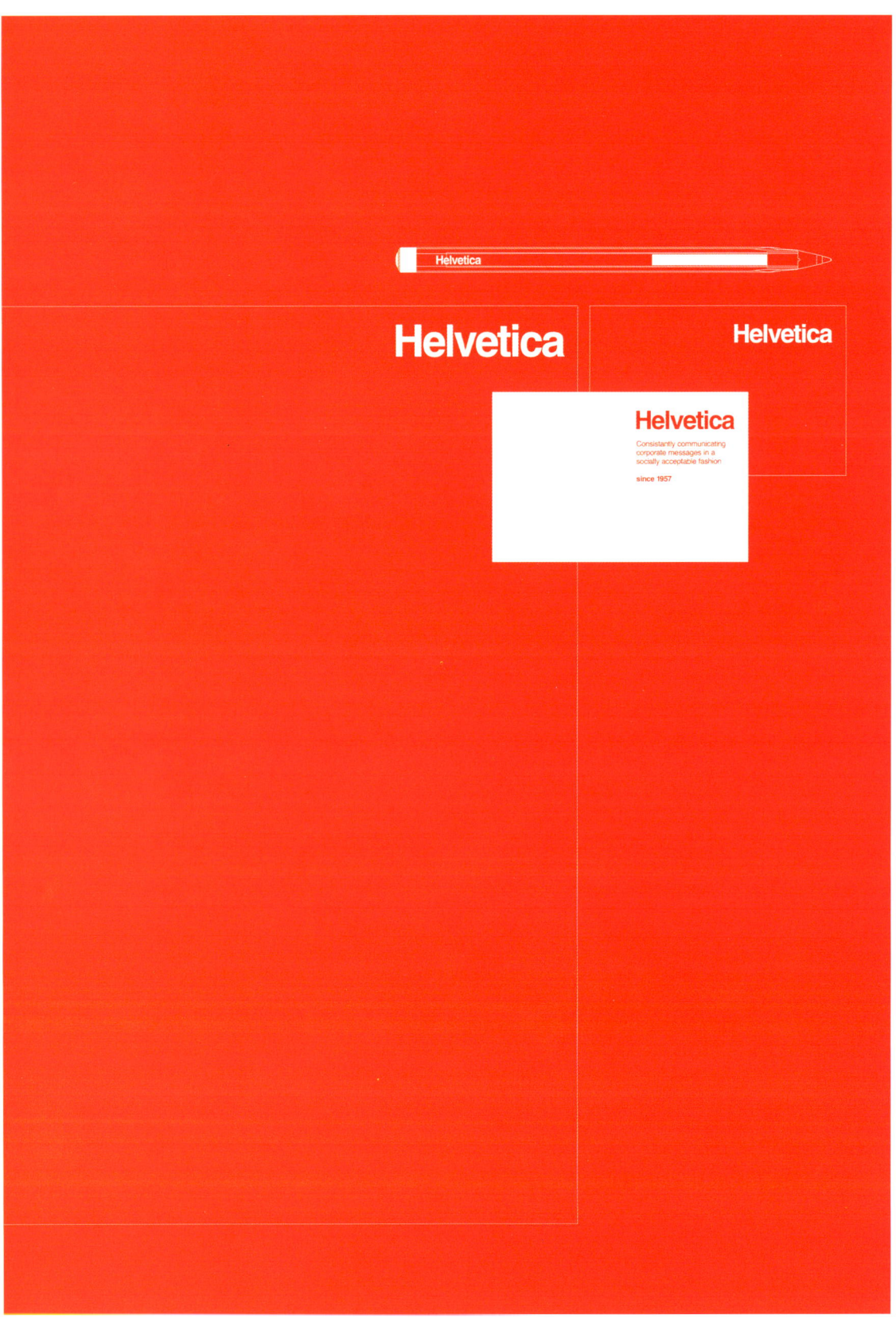

Helvetica posters | 2007

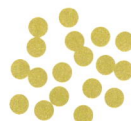

Kent Lyons
www.kentlyons.com

On leaving the exhibition that commemorated fifty years of Switzerland, a strong feeling of anxiety seized Kent Lyons. They returned to the studio and among their tributes to typography were the creation of a brand and "deconstruction" of the myth.

Habit	**Hiccup**
Haddock	**Hide-and-seek**
Haka	**High tide**
Half-asleep	**History**
Half-awake	**Hitchcock**
Hamburger & Chips	**HMS Invincible**
Handbag	**Ho ho ho**
Hand-held	**Holistic**
Handlebar moustache	**Holy of holies**
Hangover	**Homage**
Happy	**Home**
Harakiri	**Homemade**
Hard hat	**Honeybee**
Hard-boiled	**Honky Tonk Women**
Harpoon	**Hospital**
Harry met Sally	**Hostile**
Hawaiian	**Hula-Hoop**
Headphones	**Human**
Heart	**Humble pie**
Hedonism	**Hundreds and thousands**
Helicopter	**Hunger Strike**
Hello? Is This Thing On?	**Hungry Hippos**
Hell's Angel	**Hydrogen bomb**
Helvetia	**Hydropower**
Herbert	**Hyperreality**

Helvetica 50 years of universal language

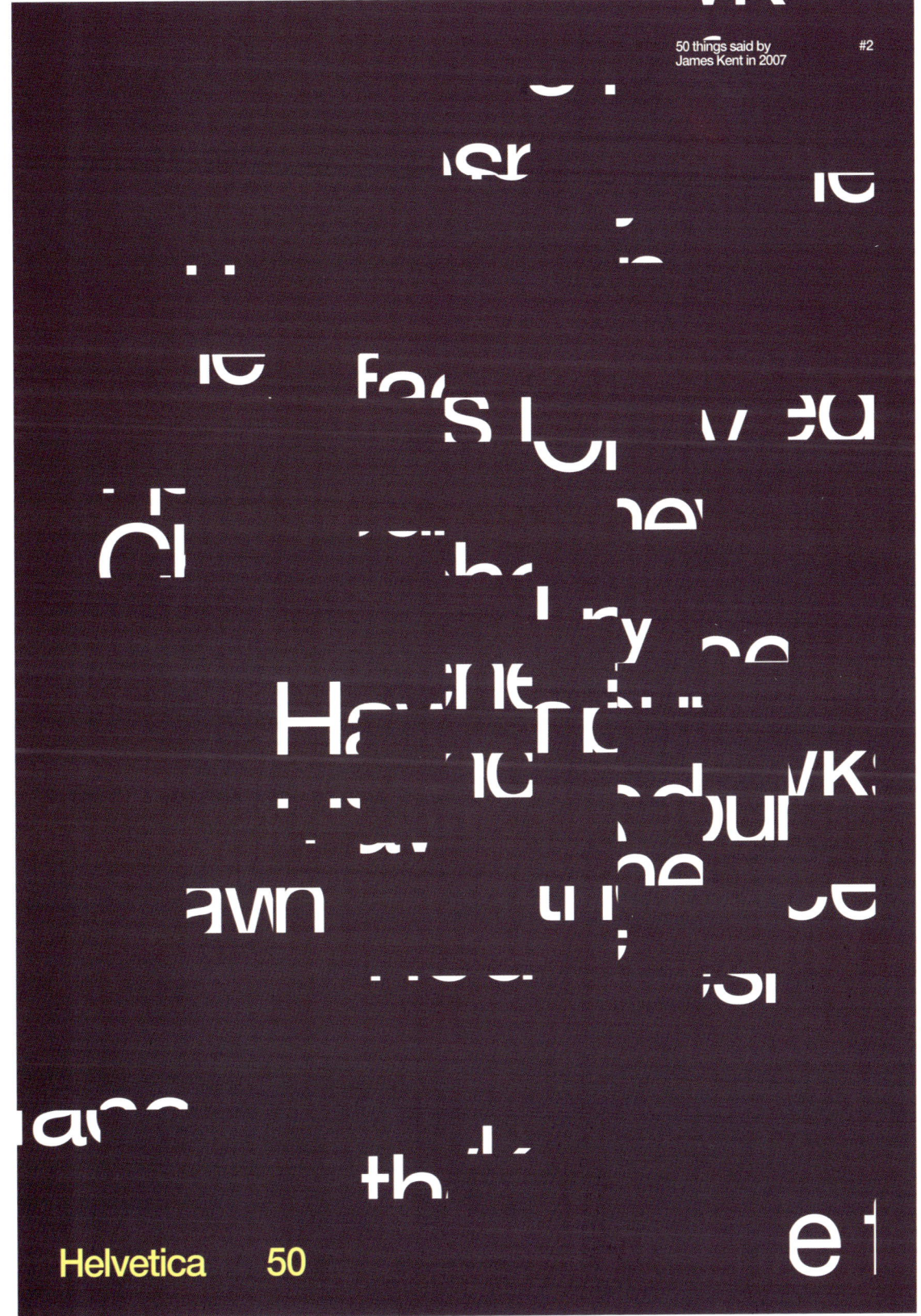

To be honest I can't remember that I was on a such party that was to remember. Last good one was long time ago when I was younger. Anyway, I don't think that it is connected with ages, or maybe so.

Eduard Cehovin

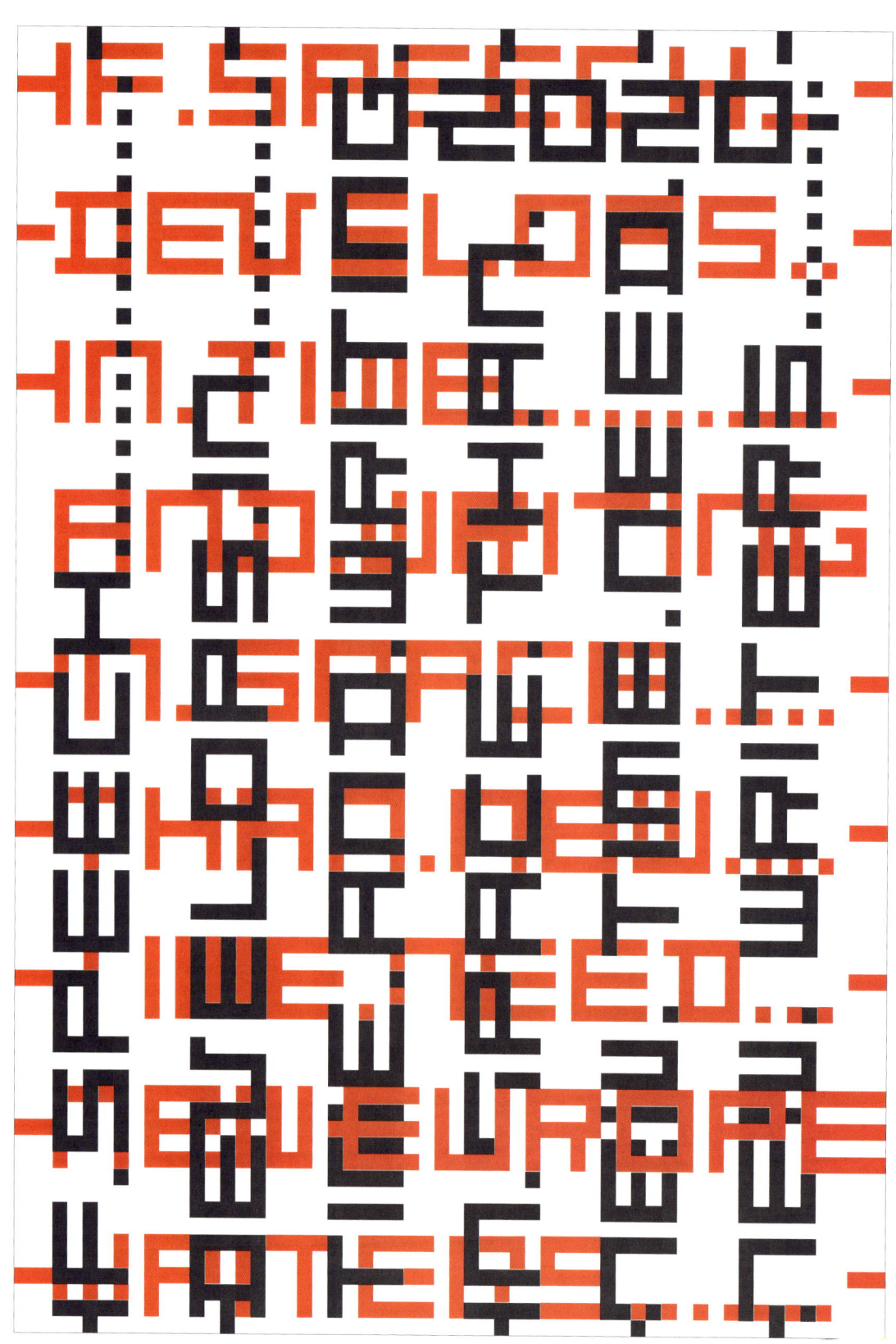

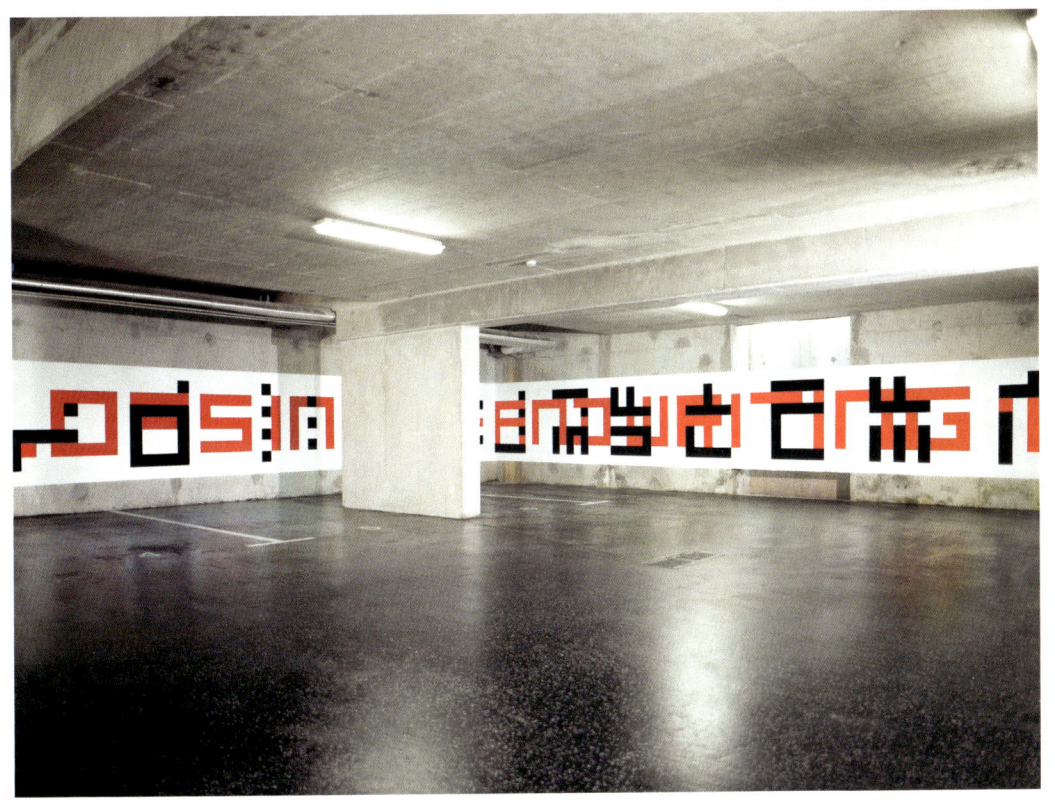

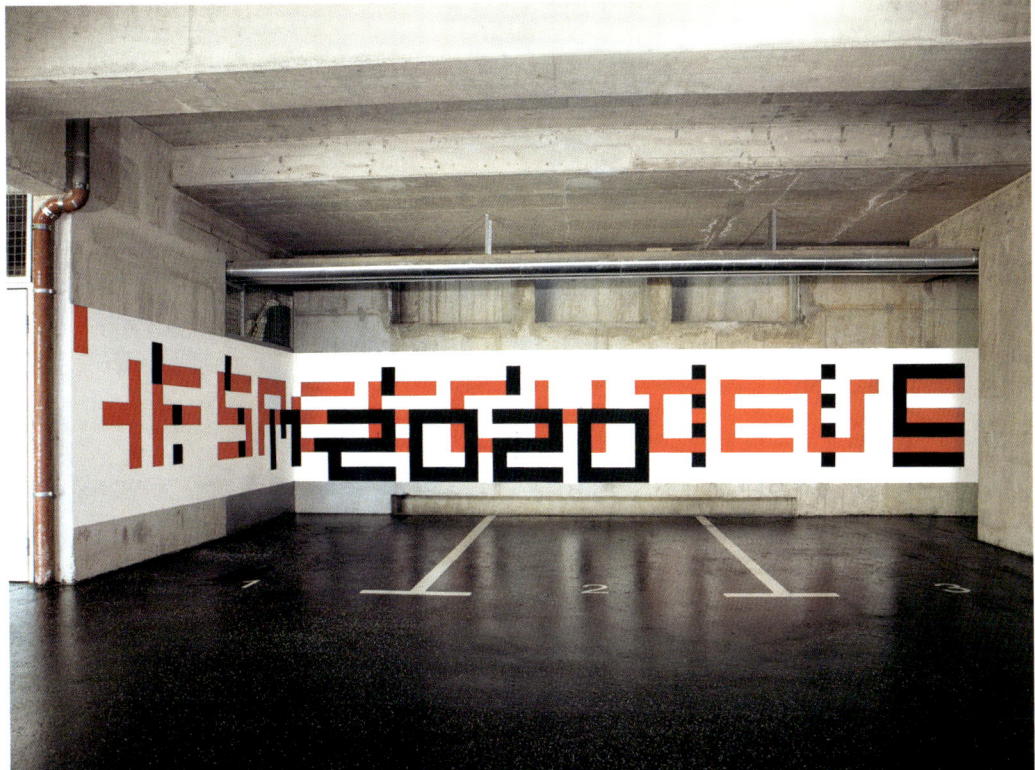

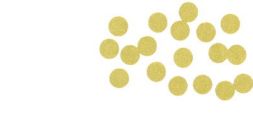

Europe 2020
mural/wall painting | 2004

Eduard Cehovin
www.cehovin.com

With the event *Bled to Europe, Europe to Bled*, the designer proposes this mural. Within its futuristic and urban pattern are the words: "If speaking develops in time and writing in space, then new times need new writers."

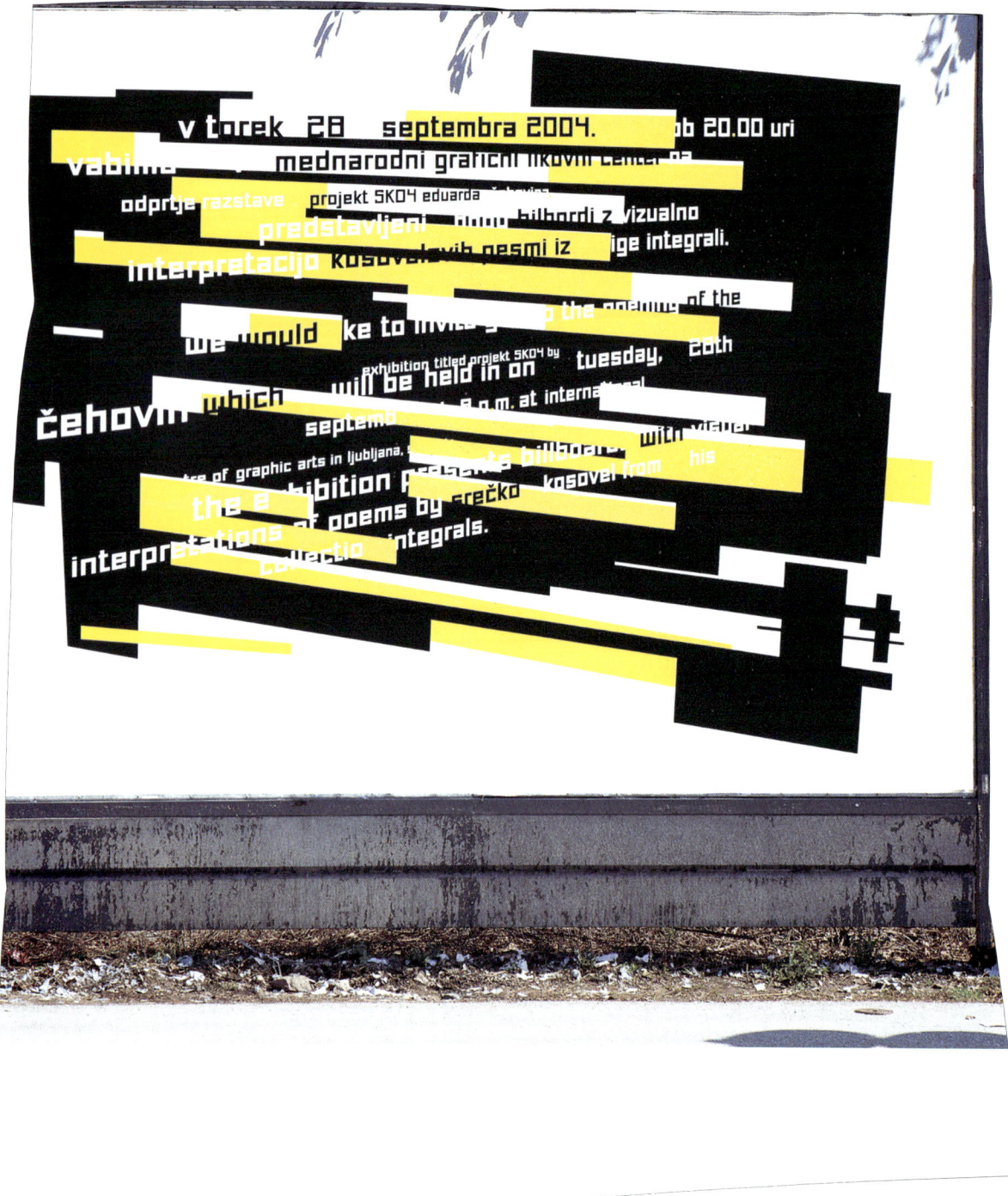

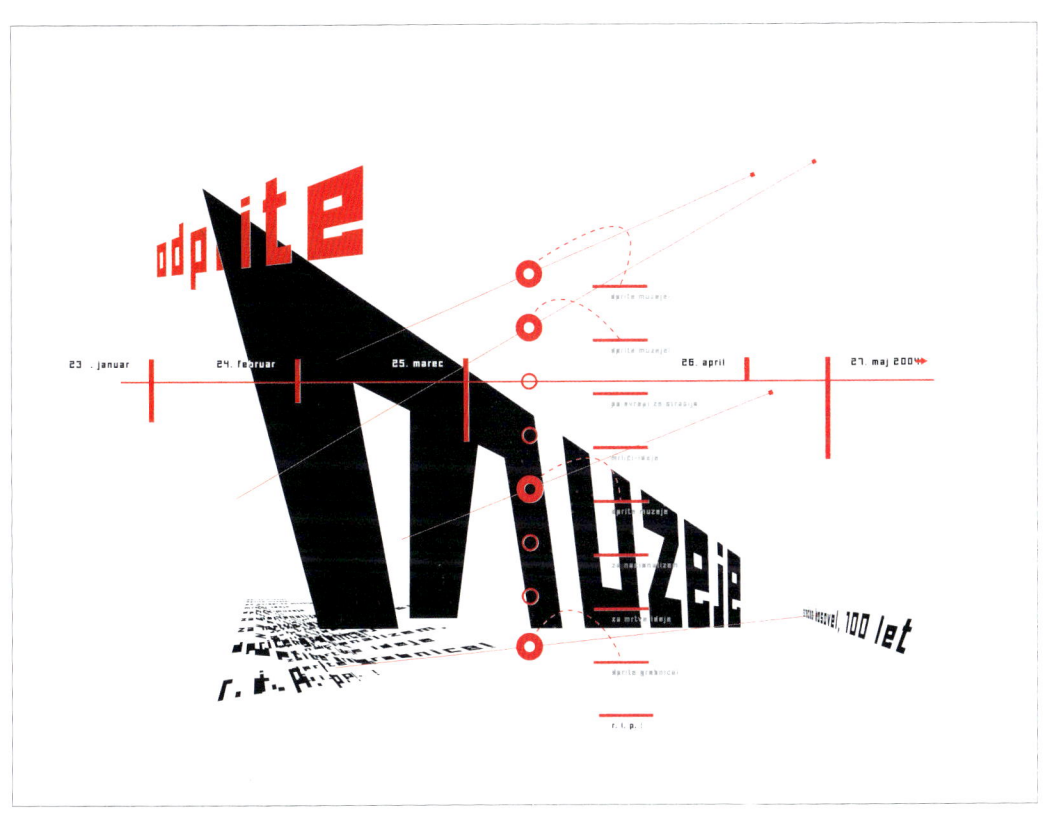

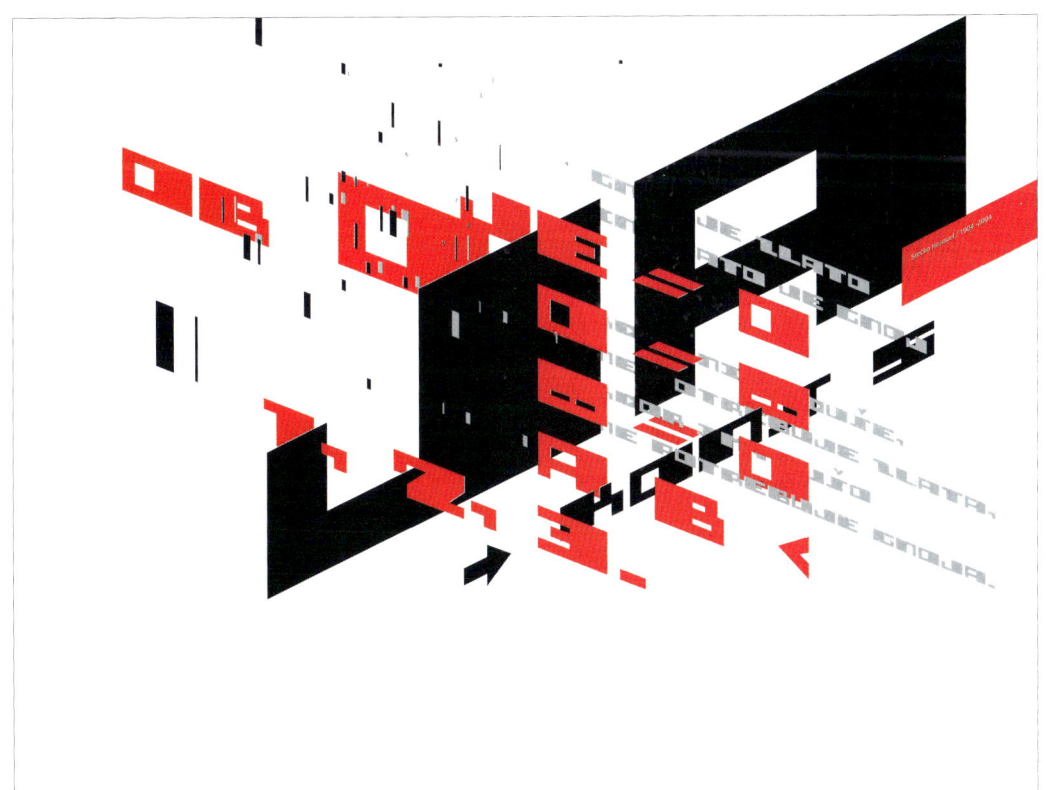

**SK04 / billboard/
invitation for exhibition | 2004**

Eduard Cehovin
www.cehovin.com

A poster to promote an exhibition in Ljubljana (Slovenia) plays with depth. The method: superimposing the planes by way of shadows and tones and the conscious combination of different sizes and diagonals.

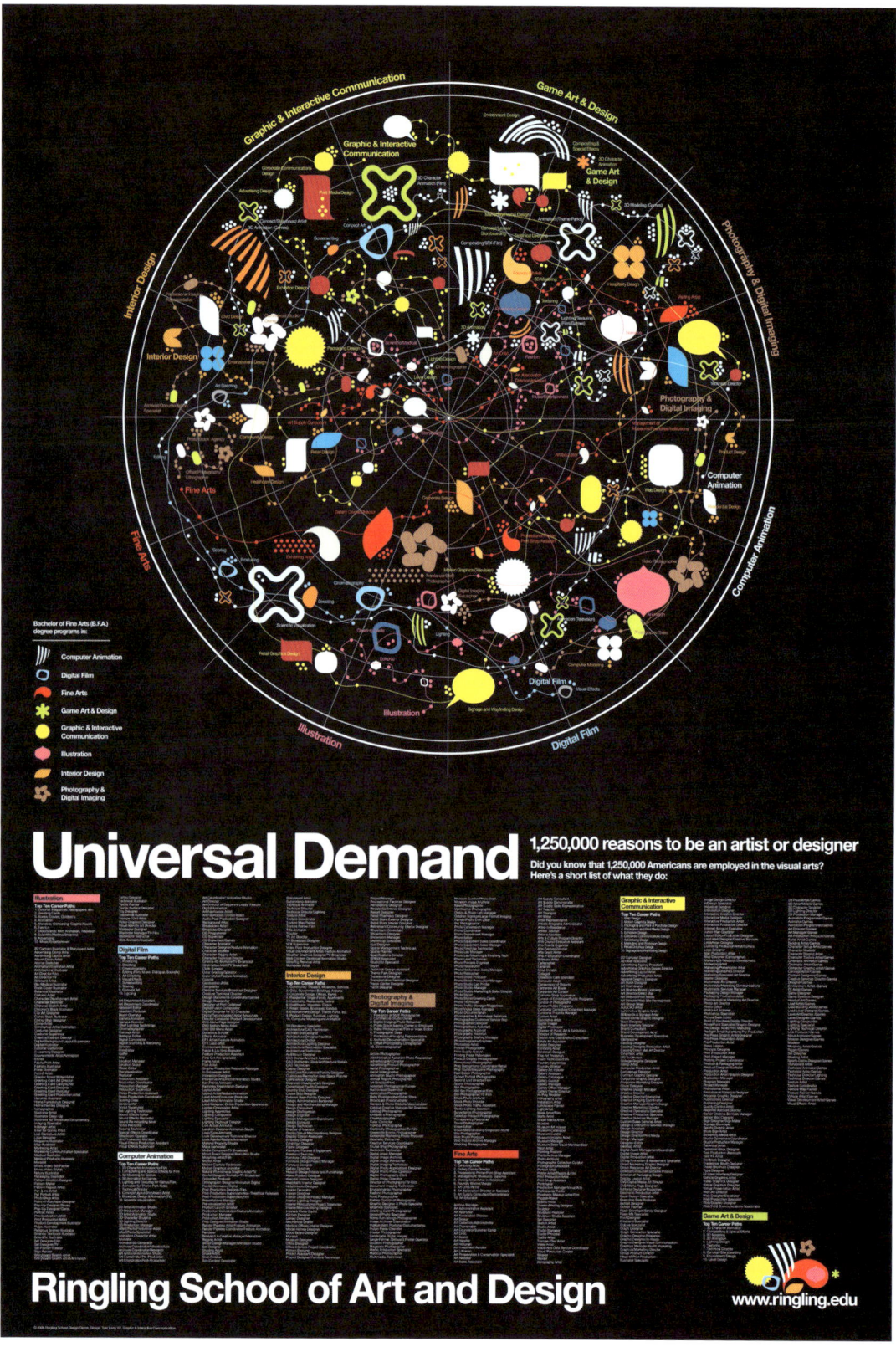

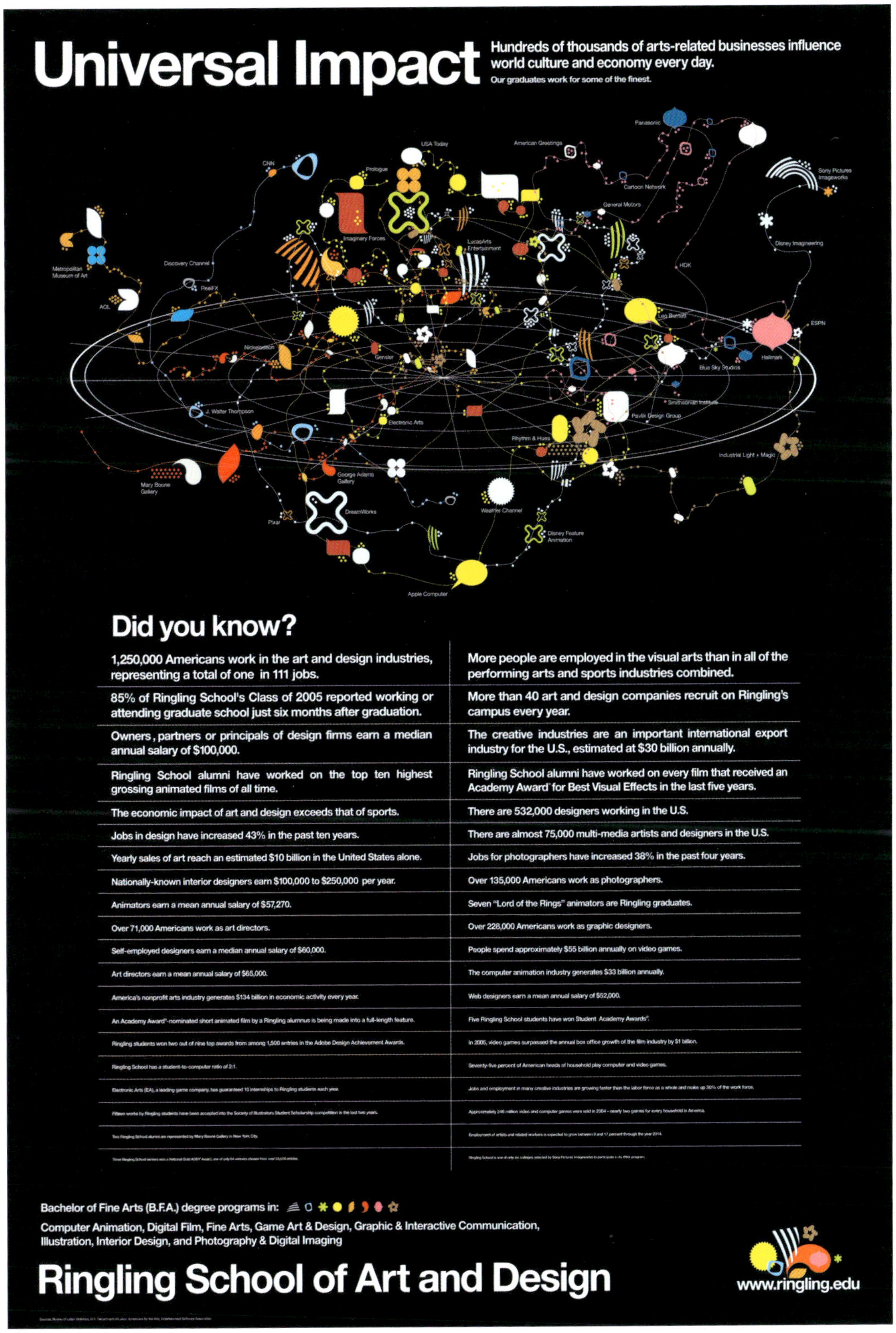

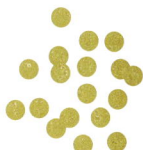

Ringling admissions poster | 2006

Tyler Lang
www.tylerlang.com

Designers and artists are not idle. The poster intends to educate from this perspective. The image represents a global vision of opportunities and complements the idea with facts and reasons to study artistic courses.

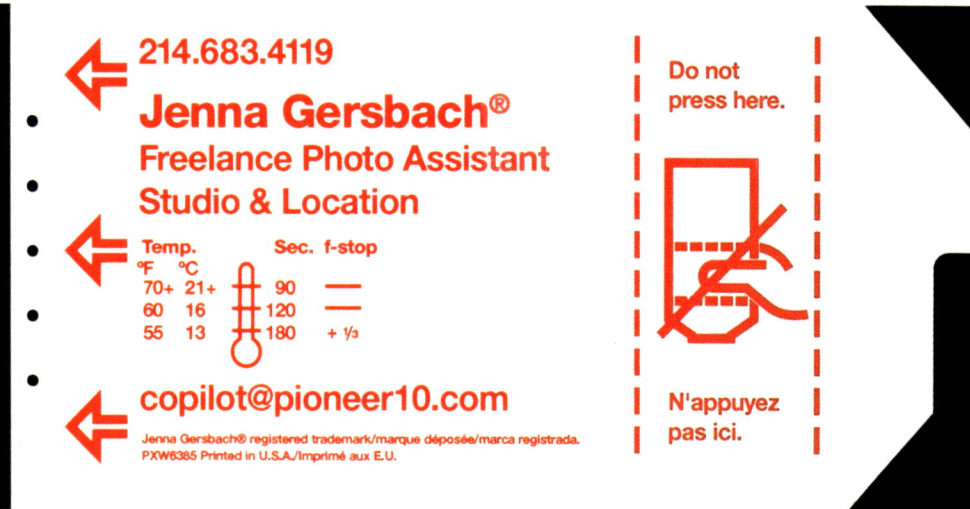

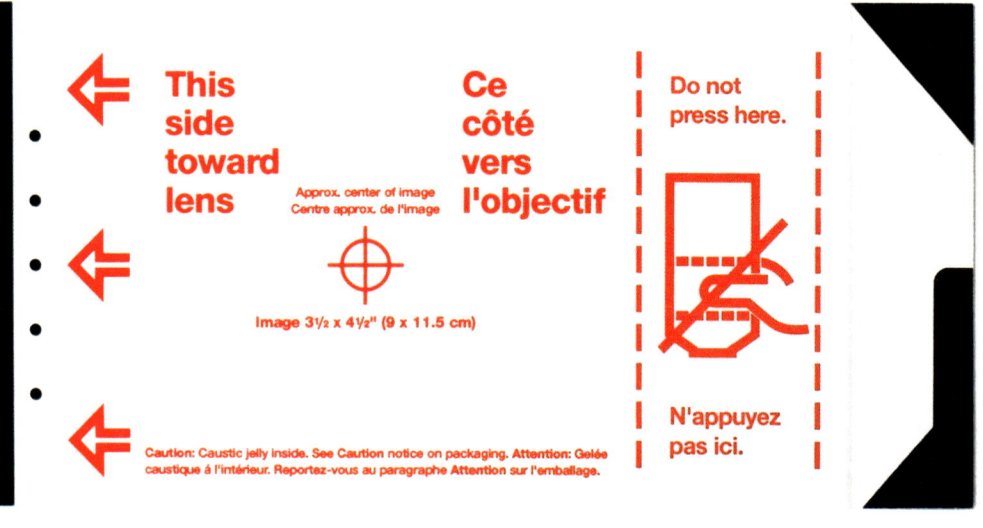

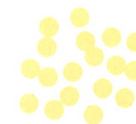

Jenna Gersbach Photography
business card | 2003

Duane King/BBDK
www.bbdk.com

The personal card mimics the appearance and texture of a polaroid, but the strategy does not conceal the visibility of the contact details. For the photographer just a card was necessary to get permanent work.

I was seventeen at secondary school in Aberdeen. A girl in our class had the fortune of a free weekend in her family holiday cottage, at an age where party venues were highly sought after. The minute cottage was host to many young and eager classmates who had traveled the distance by bus (or piled into a newly-licensed-driver's car) with a wide range of drink and smokables. It was a night that seemed to go on for days.

Ewan Robertson

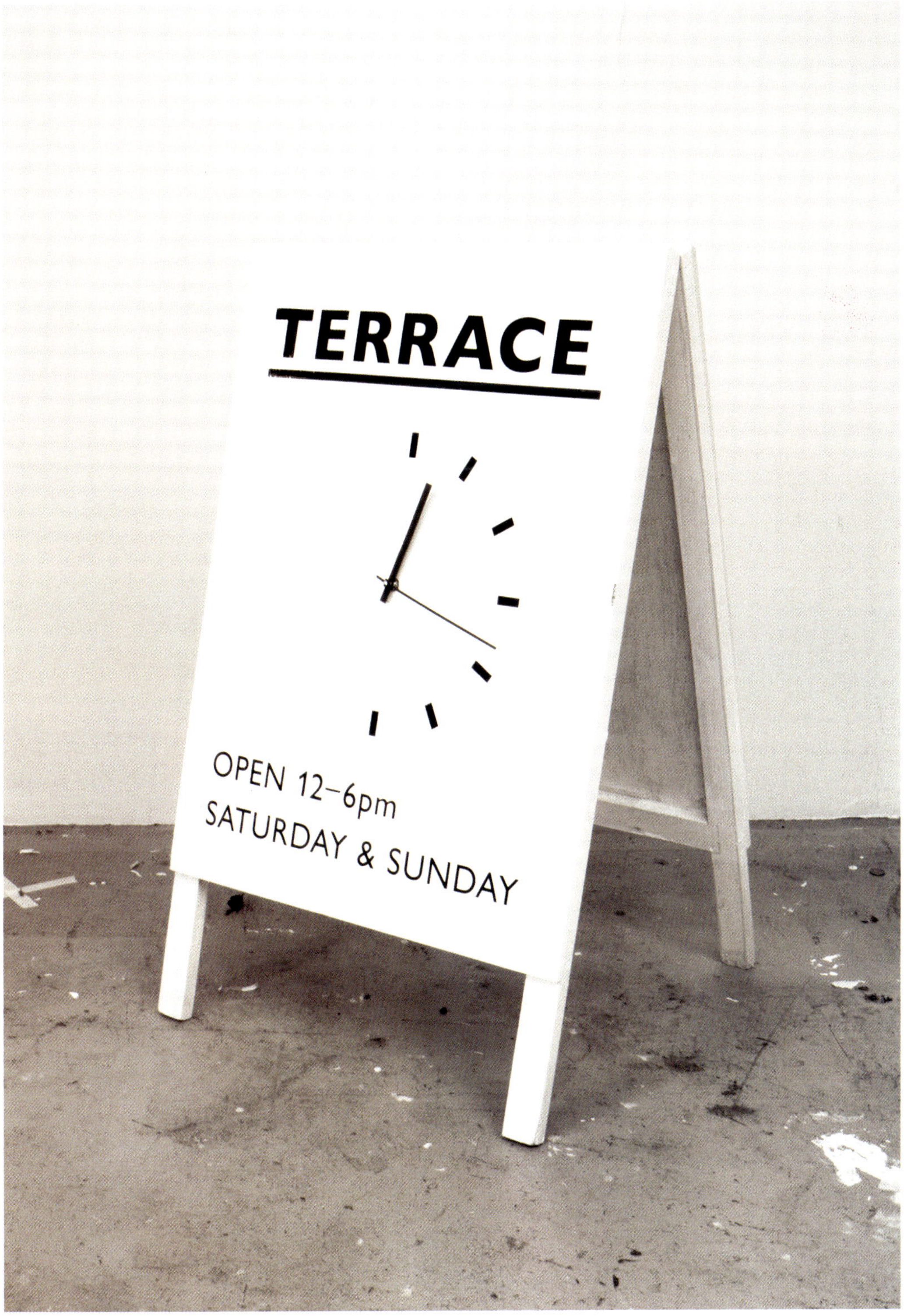

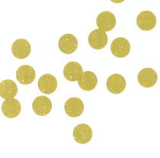

Terrace Sandwich Board | 2007

Ewan Robertson/Oscar & Ewan
www.oscarandewan.co.uk/
terrace.htm

To capture the attention of the pedestrian, the structure of an old poster was copied. The watch in the middle represents the gallery's opening hours, while the hands indicate how much time is left before closing.

2 BIG WAYS 2 WIN BIG! (AGAIN)

>>>

THAT'S RIGHT WE'RE ON THIS RUNAWAY TRAIN CALLED LOVE AND WE AIN'T STOPPIN' FOR NOBODY!

>>>

I

FIRST, SINCE YOU'RE ALREADY HERE, CHECK OUT THE APARTMENT LOVES KOBY, SWEIDAN & FABRICA ("ICING OR CAKE... WEAR YOUR COUCH"), A CRITIQUE CONTEXTUALIZING THE VALUE OF OBJECTS WITHIN THE FRAMEWORK OF THE ICFF. IMAGINED BY OUR FRIENDS BETHANY KOBY AND SELWA SWEIDAN OF FABRICA, BENETTON'S CREATVE THINK TANK IN TREVISO, ITALY, THIS OFF-SITE INSTALLATION EXPLORES THE STORIES OF OBJECTS AND THE RELATIONSHIPS BETWEEN THE DESIGN, THE DESIGNER, THE PRODUCER, THE SHOPKEEPER AND THE CUSTOMER.

II

THEN, GET YOUR COLLECTIVE ASSES ON THE F TRAIN TO CHECK OUT THE APARTMENT LOVES _____, AN EXCLUSIVE EXHIBITION BY CITIZEN: CITIZEN, ARTILLERY, ZOOZOOM AND +81 MAGAZINE. WE HAVE ASSEMBLED A DISTINCTIVE COLLECTION OF OBJECTS THAT RE-PRESENT THE FAMILIAR, OFFERING A NEW SENSE OF BEAUTY AND MEANING THAT CHALLENGES US. THESE ARTISTS ARE INTRIGUED AND IN DIALOGUE WITH THE MEANING, VALUE AND AUTHORSHIP OF OBJECTS. SUBVERTING AND RE-ARTICULATING OUR NOTION OF VALUE, OBJECTIVITY AND CONSUMPTION, AND PLAYING WITH THE TRADITIONS OF THE PAST, CITIZEN SUGGESTS NEW AESTHETIC IDEOLOGIES FOR THE FUTURE.

then go get a vanilla shake and thank us later nobody!

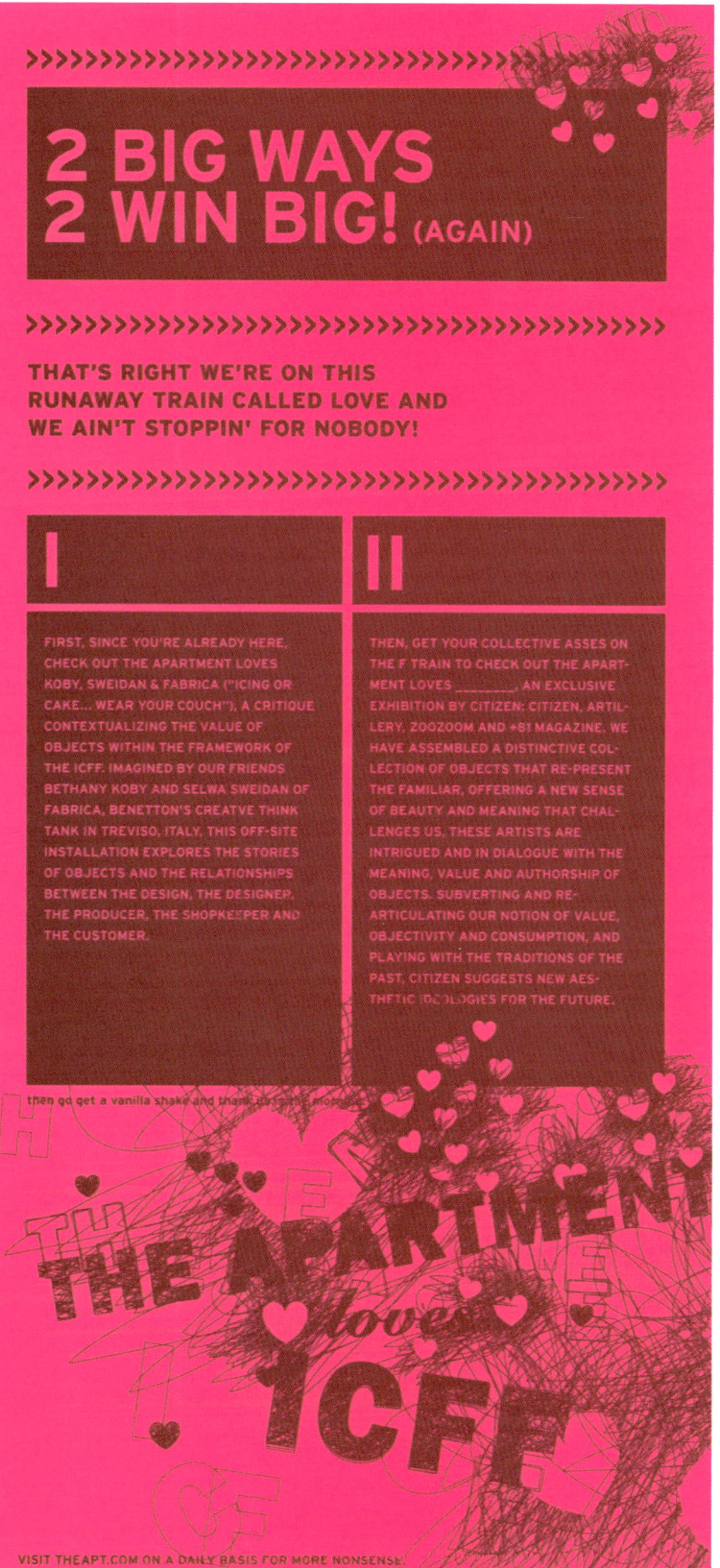

THE APARTMENT loves ICFF!

VISIT THEAPT.COM ON A DAILY BASIS FOR MORE NONSENSE!

WE LIKE TO REMIND YOU THAT THERE IS NO RIGHT OR WRONG SELECTION.

<<<<<<<<<<<<<<<<<<<<<<<<<<<<<<<<<<<<<<<<<<<<<<<

(A)

PERIMETER EDITIONS
WORKS BY JANETTE LAVERRIÈRE, ADRIEN GARDÈRE AND ERIC GIZARD

THE APARTMENT presents the US launch of Perimeter Editions – a new London, Paris-based Furniture and Design Venture that re-edits and reissues furniture by 20th century Modernist masters as well as produces exclusive objects and furniture by contemporary designers. The selection process is based on one guiding principle – original and witty designs in which the design elements never overpower the functionality and comfort of the objects.

>>>

(B)

THE APARTMENT BUILDS AN APARTMENT

THE APARTMENT converts the country's first ymca basketball court into a sprawling 7,500 square foot duplex loft. Exquisitely outfitted with furniture from the world's most exclusive design studios, the space will be exhibited as an extraordinary architectural and cultural showcase. Moreover, THE APARTMENT's philosophy of fine living will be on full display as we attend to every last detail with our signature romantic minimalist approach. Everything, from toiletries and gourmet food products to kitchen appliances and linens, from cleaning products and audio/visual equipments to magazines and dvds, will be a selection of our favorite products. Last but not least, some of new york's most prominent art galleries will contextualize our vision of ideal living by dressing the space with artworks by internationally renowned artists.

with love

The good people from THE APARTMENT

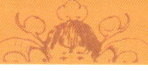 THEAPT.COM

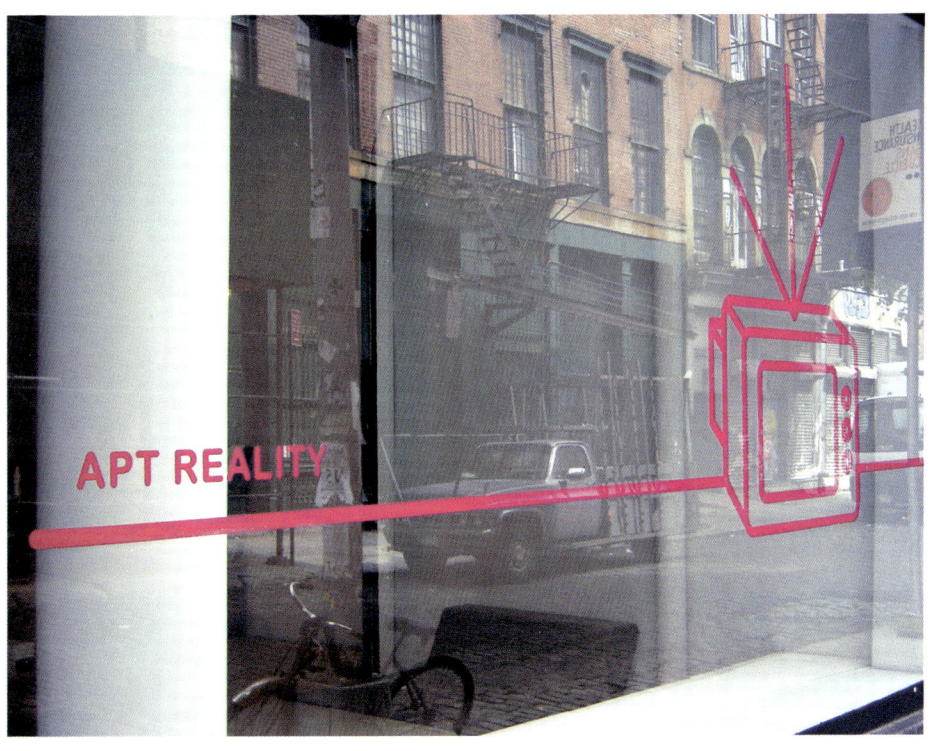

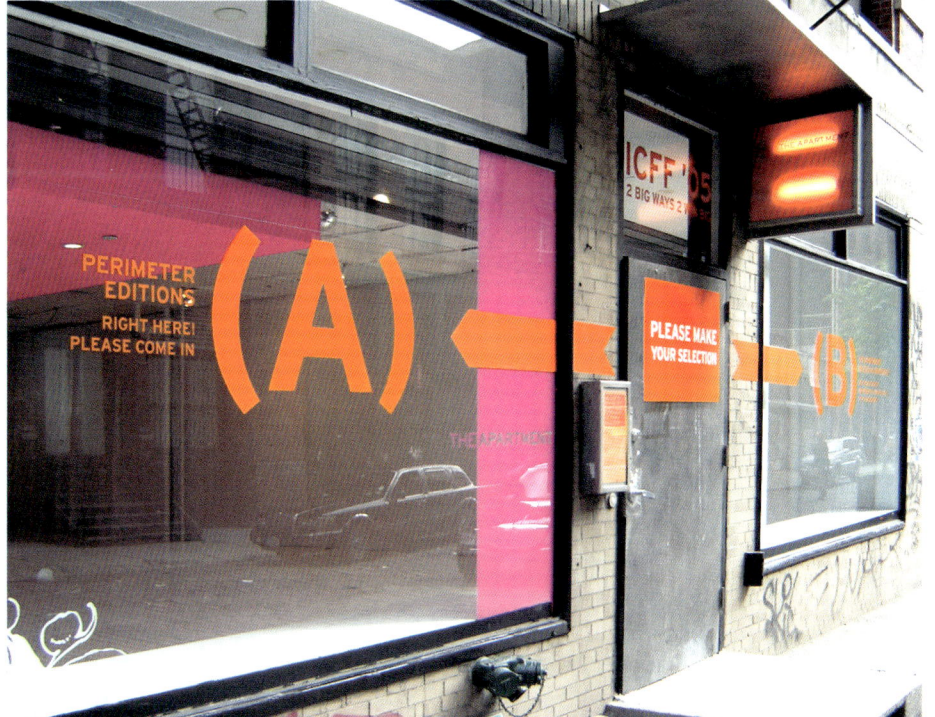

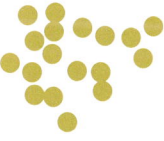

The Apartment
storefront | 2005-2006

Tiziana Haug/The Apartment
www.inthehabit.com

The agency, The Apartment, is located on the ground floor, affording a glimpse of what is going on inside. To avoid the usual confusion of the agency as a shop, there are posters everywhere that indicate its presence.

Great people, great ambience, great music.

Angie Simmonds

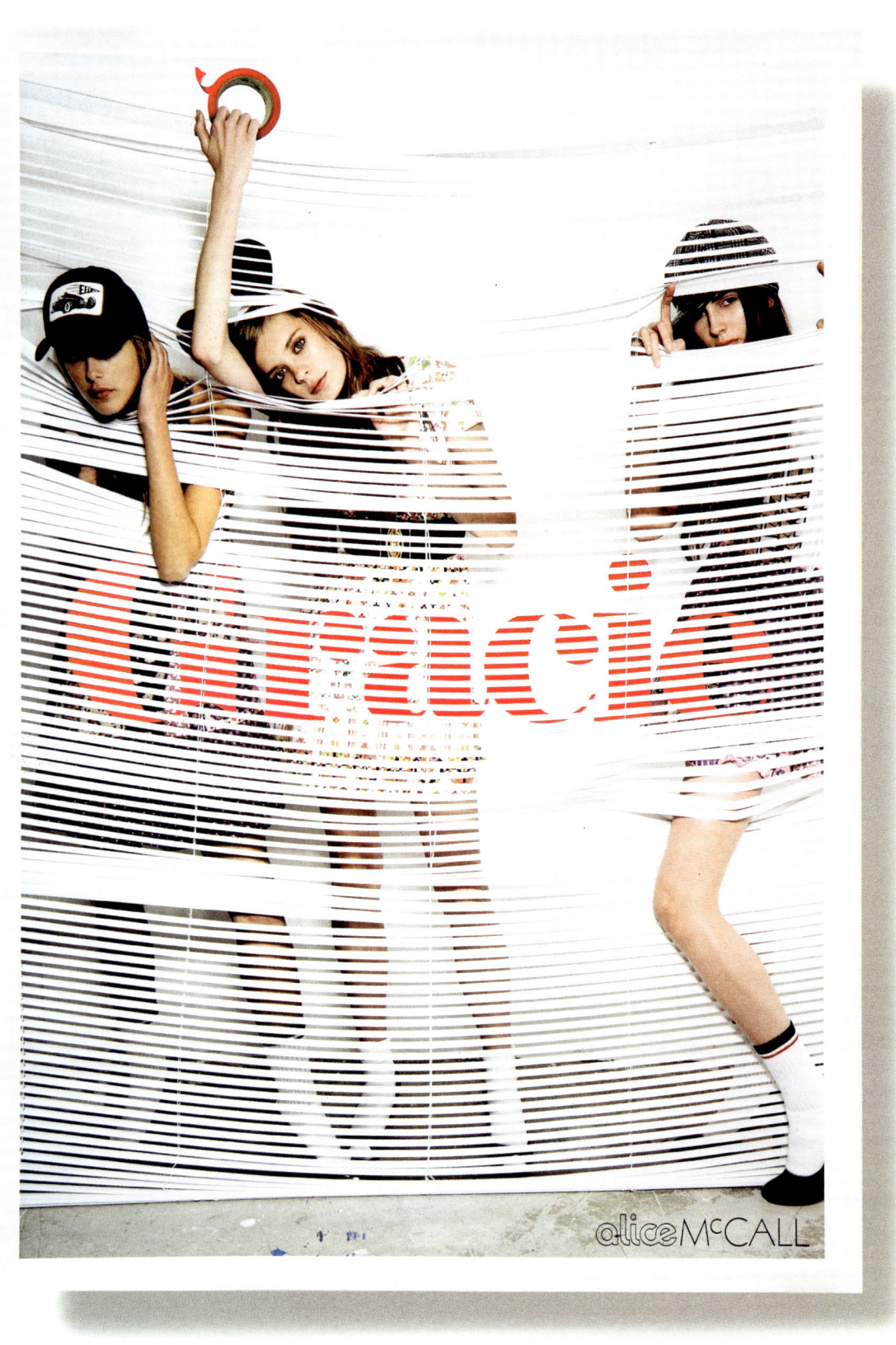

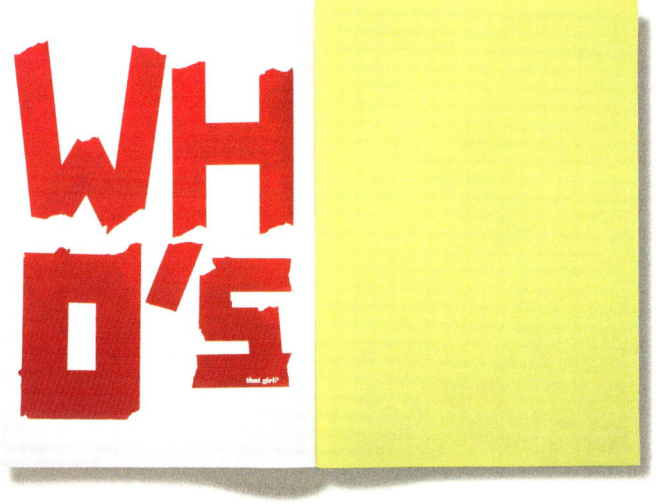
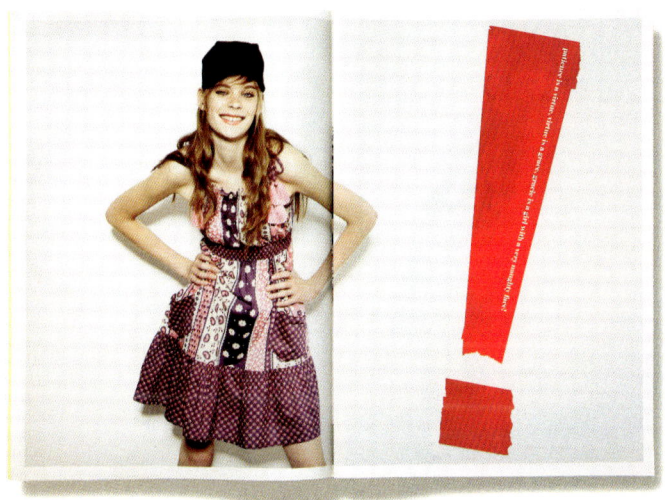
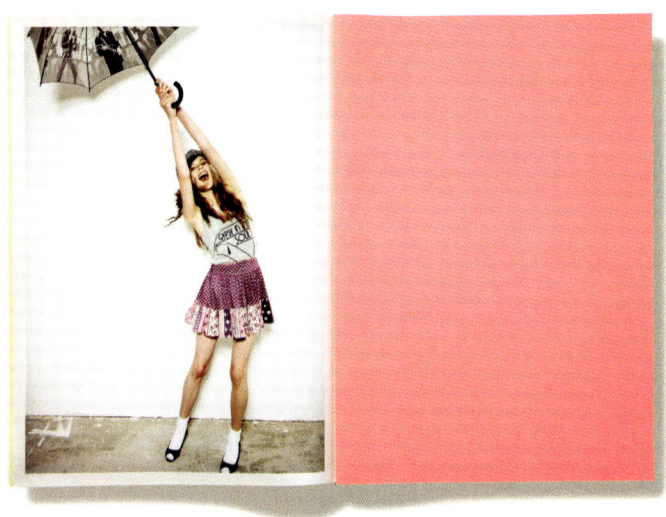
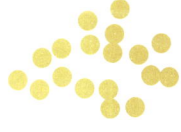

**Gracie by Alice McCall
look book | 2007**

**Caroline Cox, Anthony
Donovan/Frost Design
Design manager: Laura Richardson
www.frostdesign.com.au**

Sticky tape acts as a leitmotif throughout the catalog: it gives shape to the typography and the different signs that are incorporated into the design. The use of Persian blinds is the way in which the horizontal lines from Gracie's logo are integrated.

Singapore creative circle award ceremony in 2001. Kinetic was third in ranking as the most creative agency in Singapore: first and second are MNCs...Locally, we're the first...Plus the fact that my wife found out that she was pregnant on that day...

Kinetic

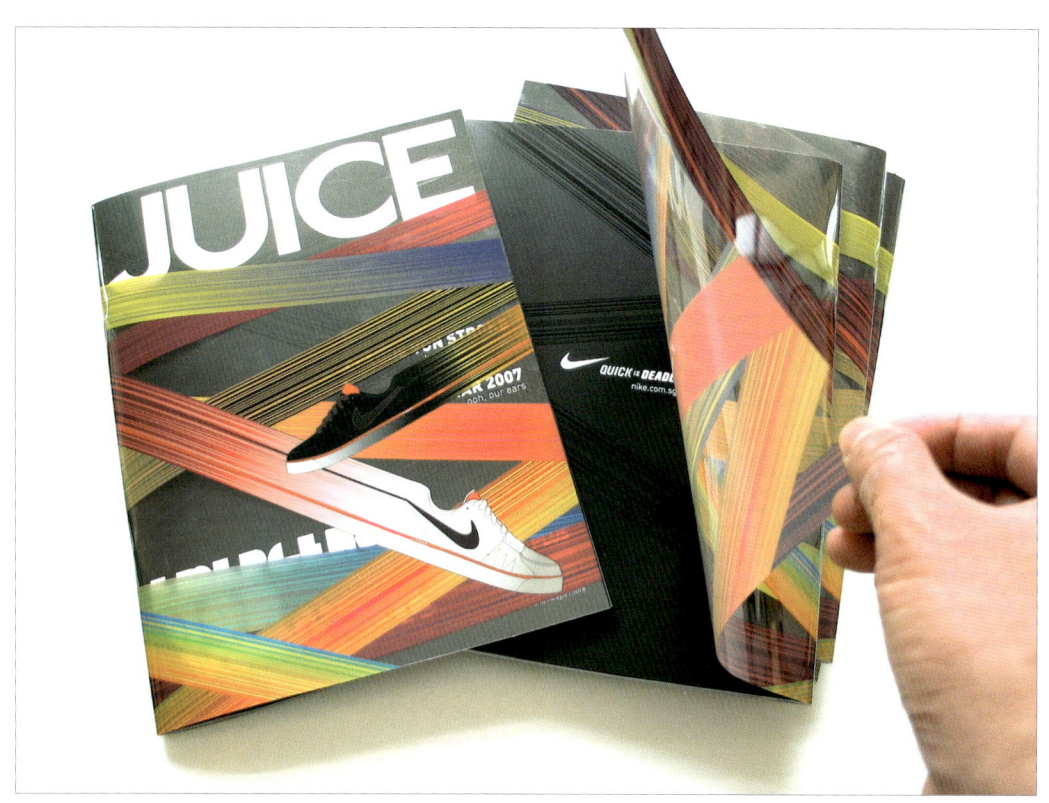

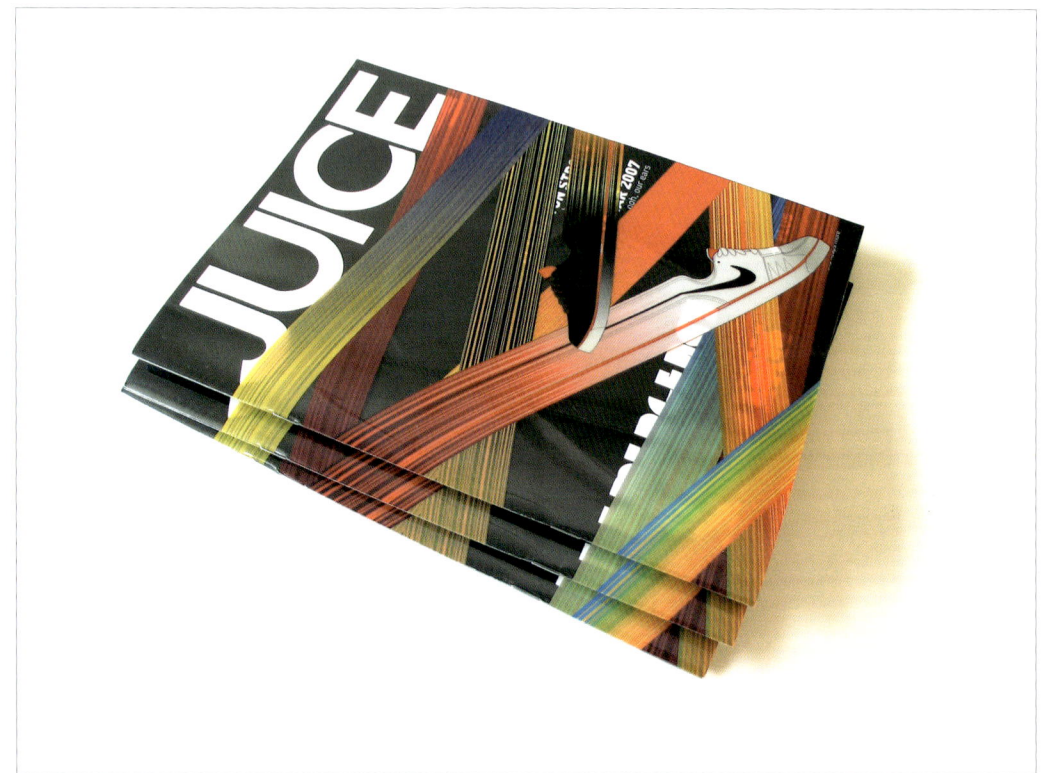

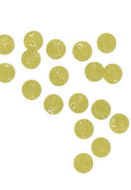

Nike Zoom | 2007

Kinetic
www.kinetic.com.sg

The effect of a zoom is speed, in contrast to the gentle resource of travelling. The promotion of the Nike Zoom is just as dizzying, and so the trainers that penetrate the cover leave a multi-color trail.

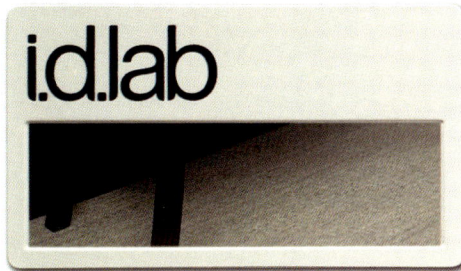
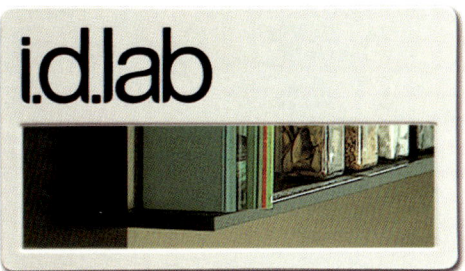
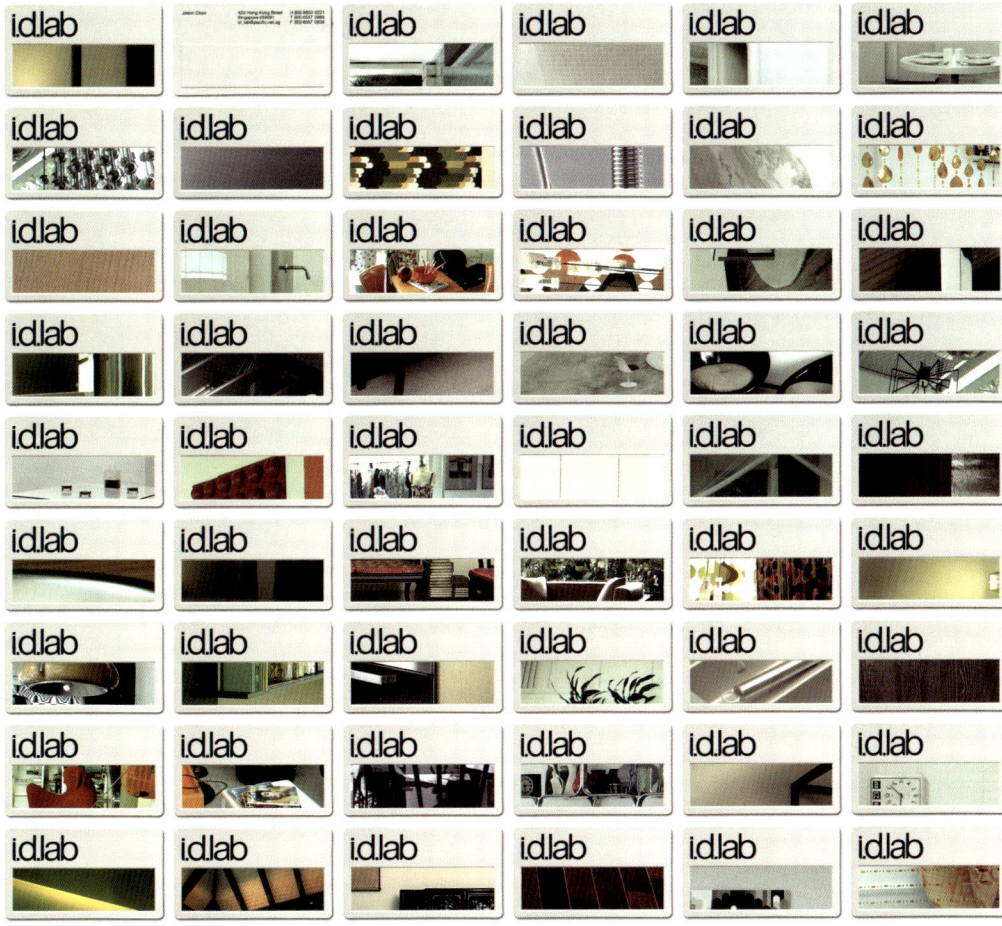

I.D. Lab | 2006

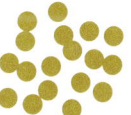

Kinetic
www.kinetic.com.sg

For the business cards of an interior design studio, a photograph has been added to a minimalist design. This personalization indicates the emphasis of the designers on developing different personalities for each commission.

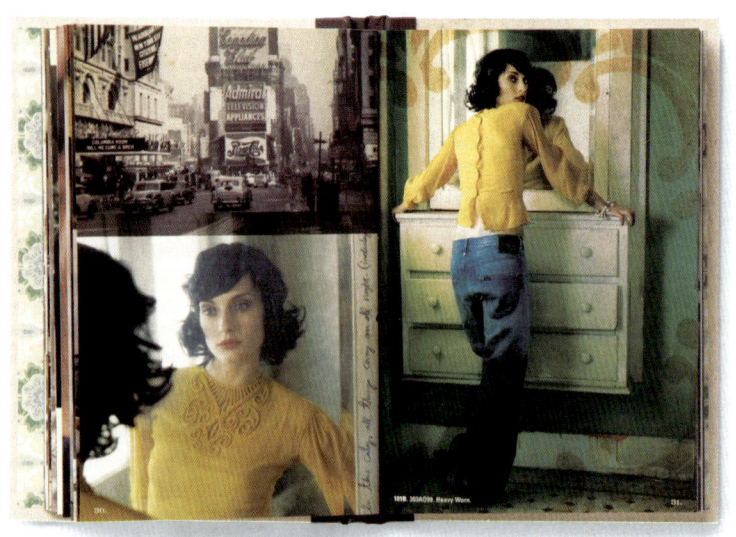
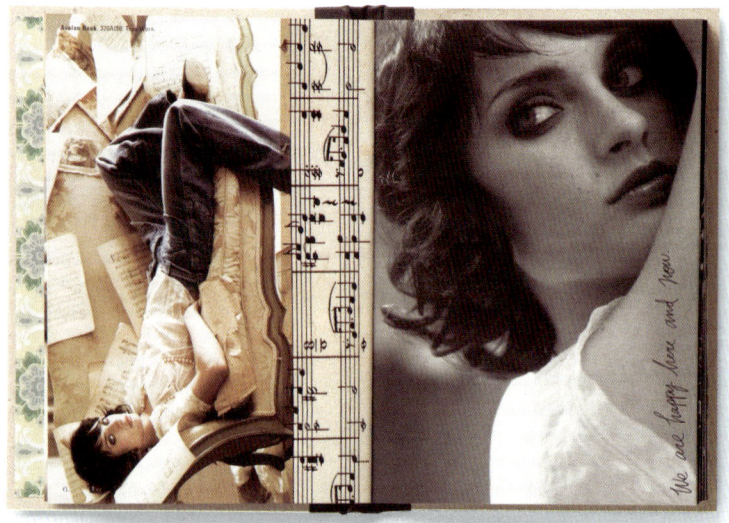
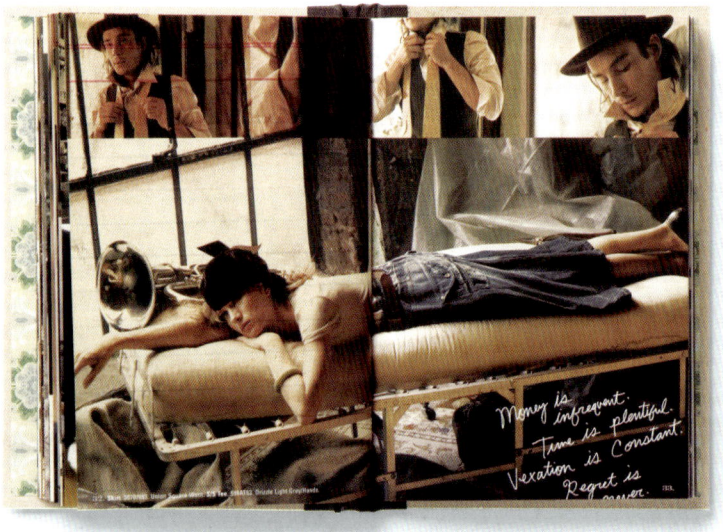
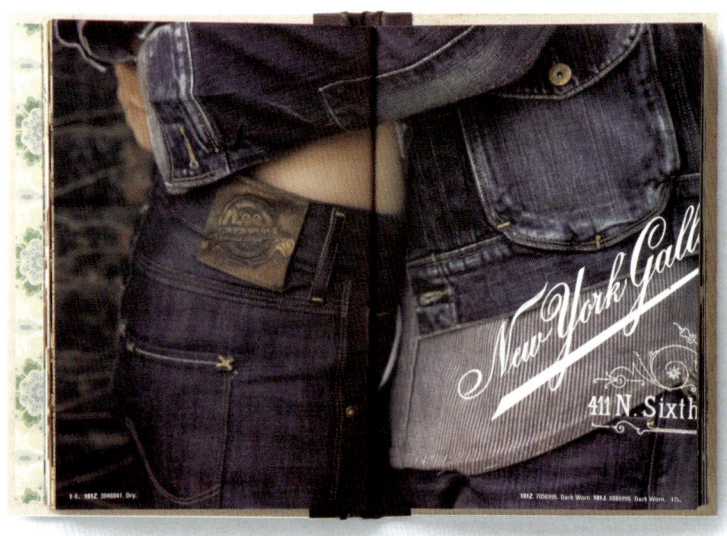

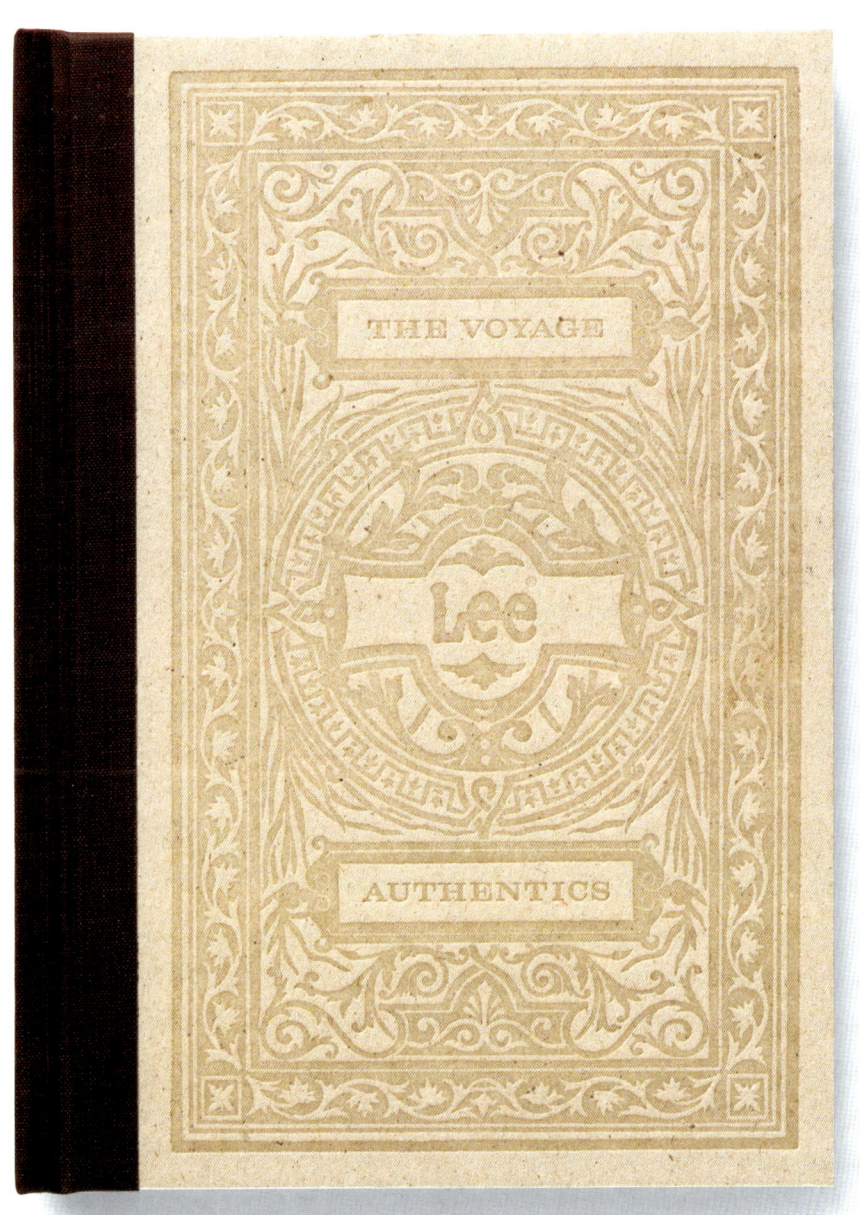

Lee Voyages | 2006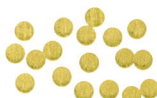

Design Ranch
www.design-ranch.com

This printing kit was sent to fashion magazines and stylists to promote the *Authentics* line of Lee. Inspired by Ellis Island and the American road-trip the proposal makes use of the brand's vintage inheritance.

I prefer a private and quiet setting over crowded scenes. It's more inspiring to me.

Maiko Kuzunishi

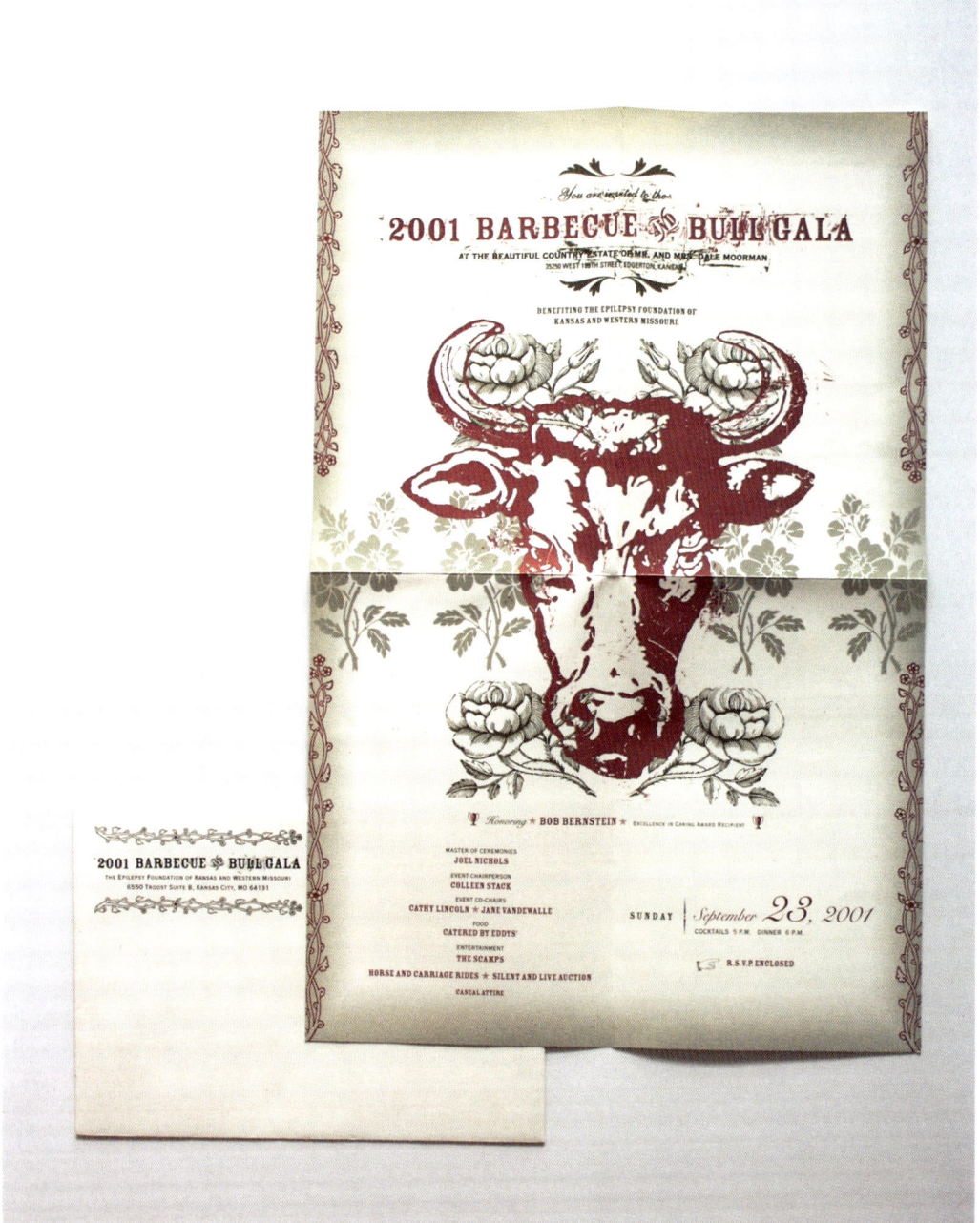

Barbecue and Bull Gala | 2001

Maiko Kuzunishi/Decoylab
www.decoylab.com

Inspired by the name of the event, the poster (that acts as an invitation) uses the figure of the bull. This image sums up the aim of the event and imprints the composition, together with the typographical style, with the coarseness of the West.

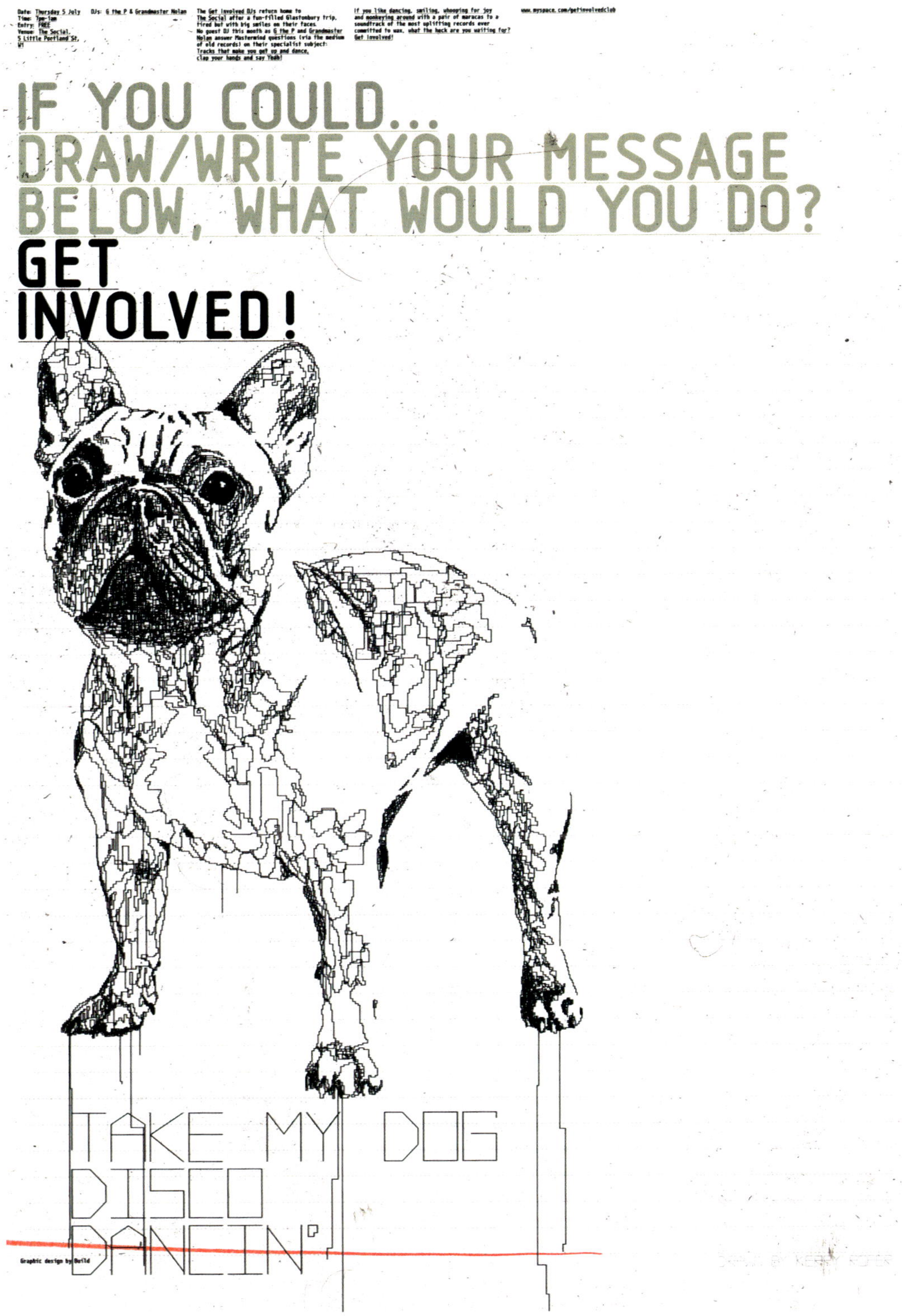

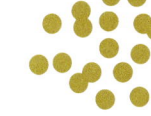

Get Involved
poster | 2007

youarebeautiful, Build
www.youarebeautiful.co.uk

Get Involved is a monthly event that takes place in the London Social Club. Almost like a blank canvas, or even a wall, Build designed a poster that invited the onlooker to participate and get involved.

It would have to be the Leo Burnett party in Cannes 2007: lots of drink and Norman Jay DJ-ing. A very messy night.

Kerry Roper

get Lost

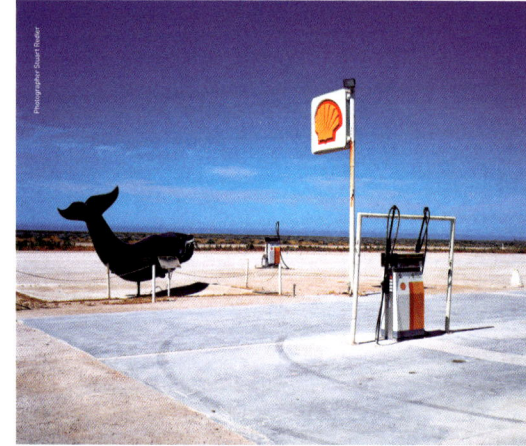

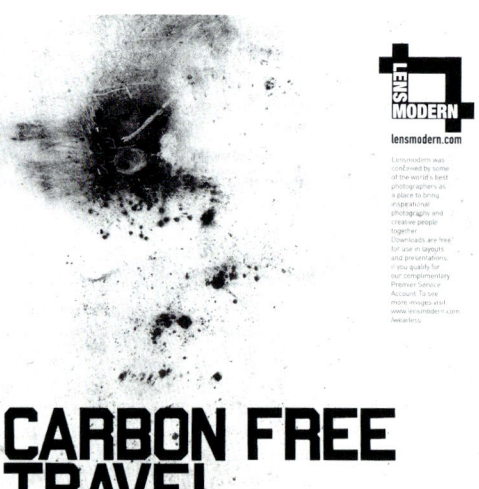

CARBON FREE TRAVEL

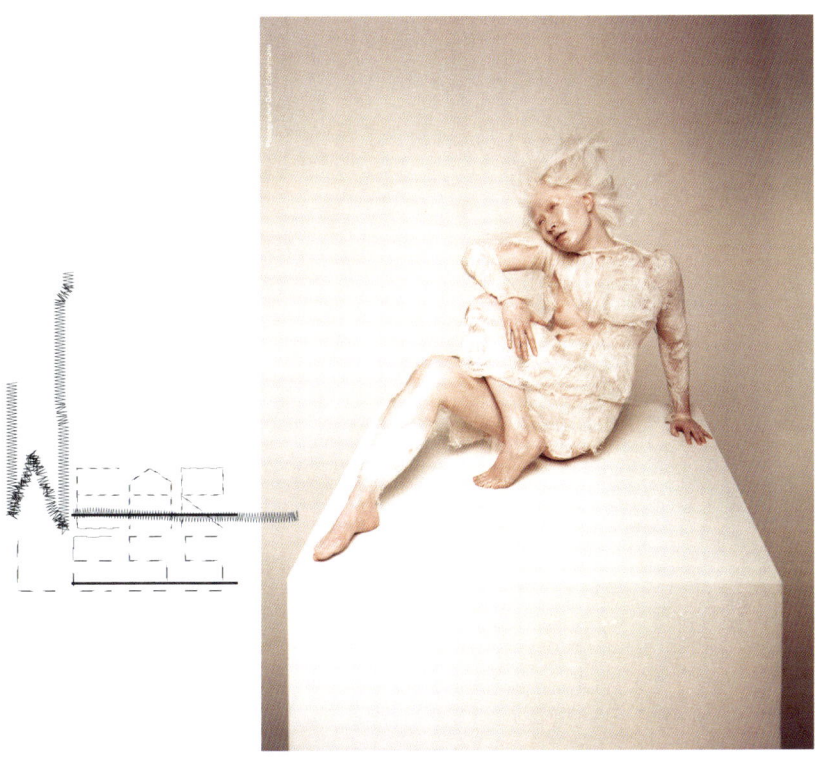
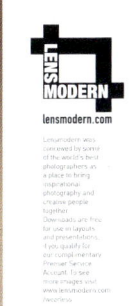
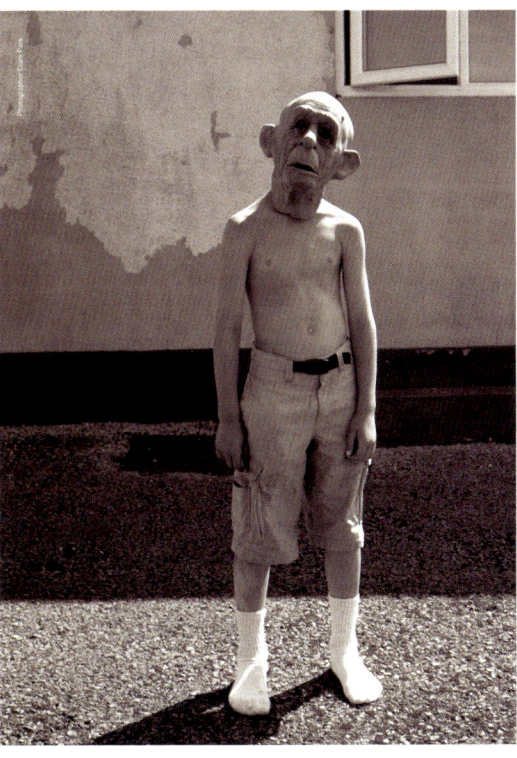
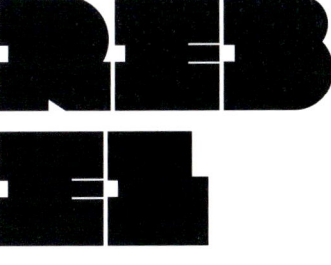
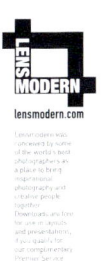
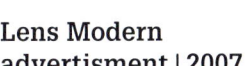

Lens Modern
advertisment | 2007

youarebeautiful, Miles Calcraft
Briginshaw Duffy
www.youarebeautiful.co.uk

Lens Modern is a bookshop that specializes in photography. Focusing on the concept of taking photos, the flyers take a selection of photographs that are presented in a personal way in each of the series.

In the end always the ones that started up the worst.

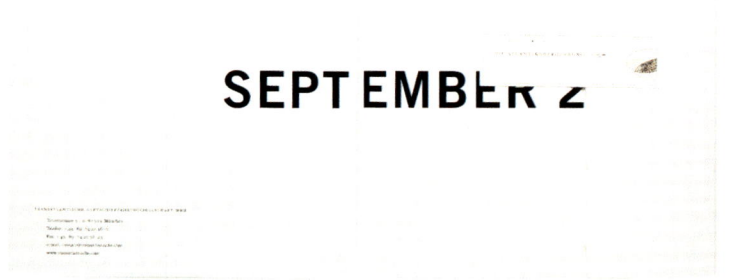

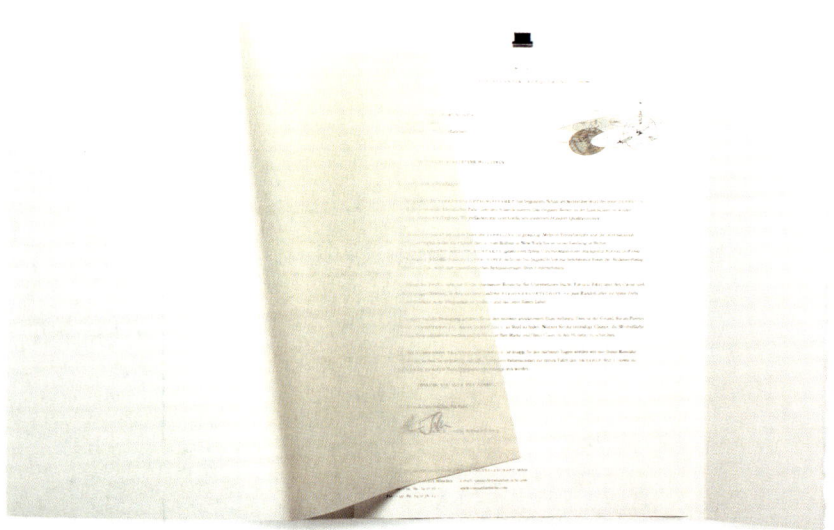

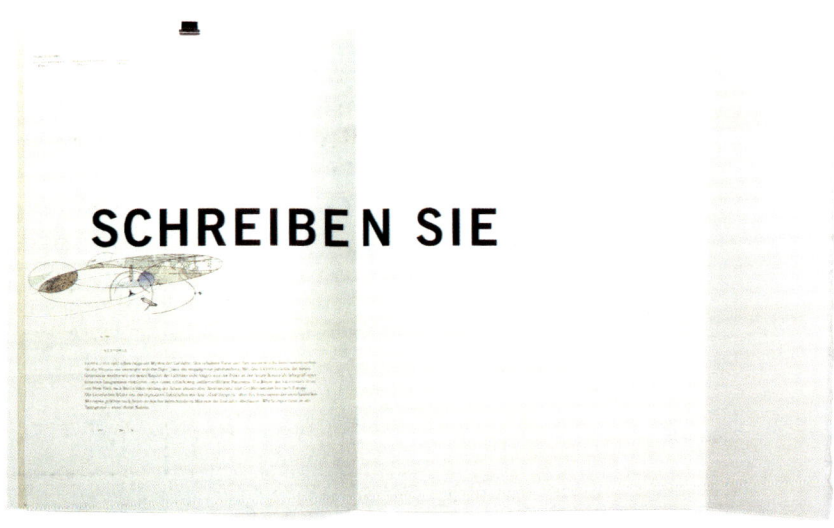

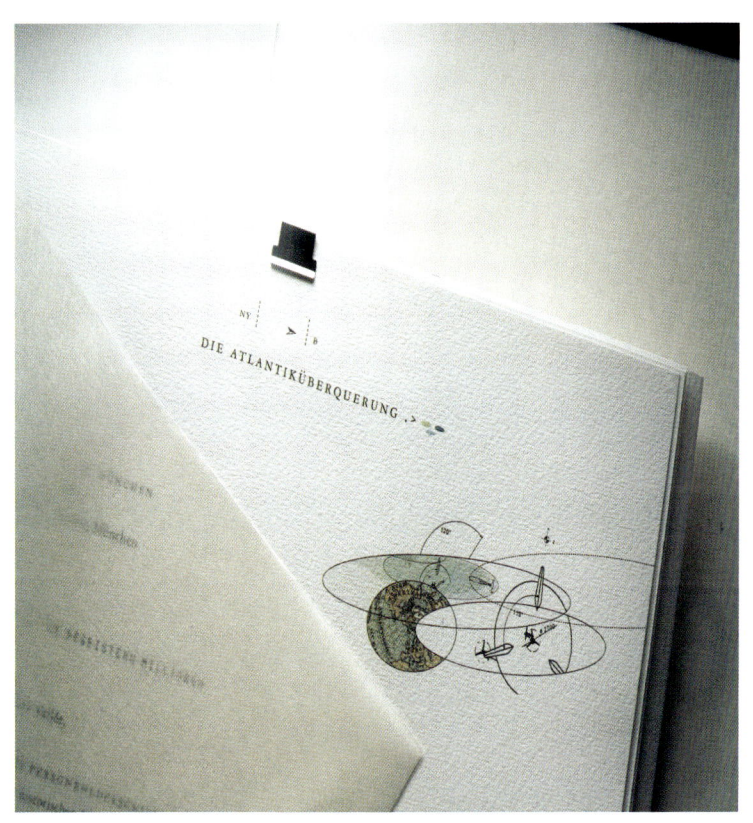

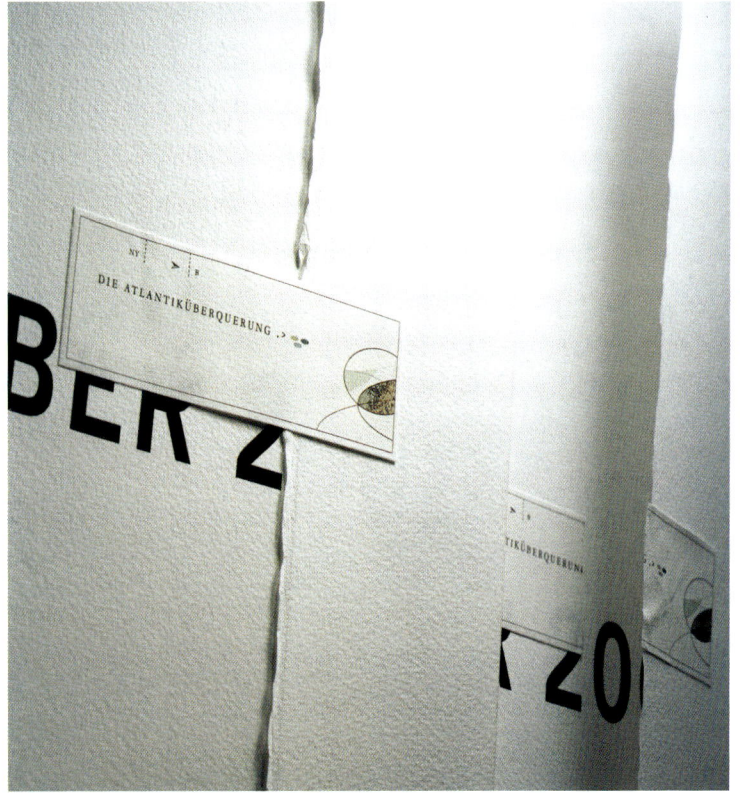

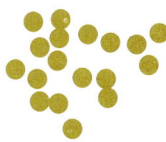

Atlantiküberquerung (Crossing the Atlantic Ocean) | 2000

Sonner, Vallée u. Partner
www.sonnervallee.de

The mailing attempts to capture travelers and promoters of the first voyage by airship across the ocean in the thirties. High-quality materials, classical typographies and a modern design reflect the fascinating connection between the past and the present.

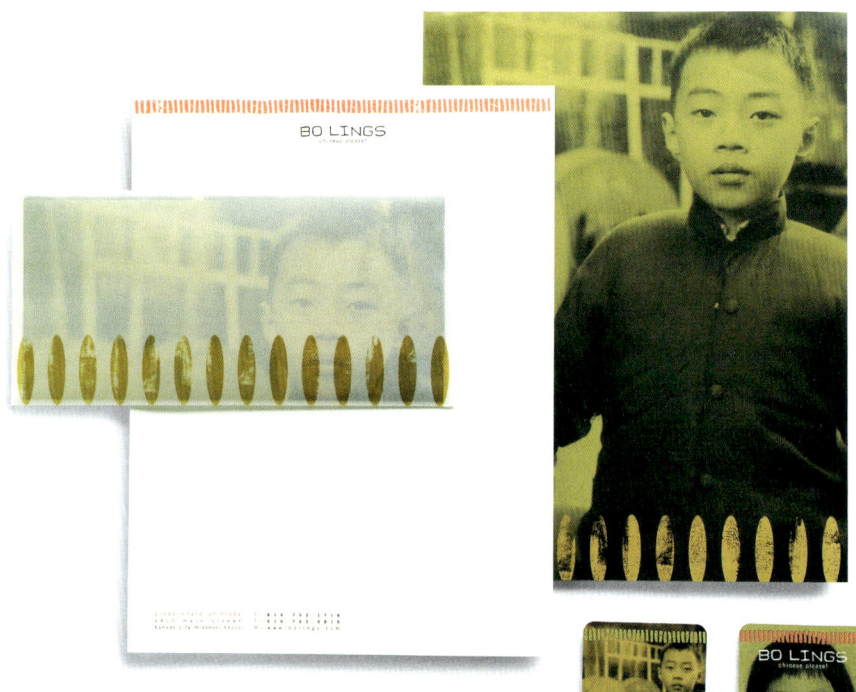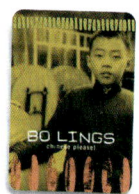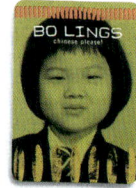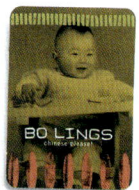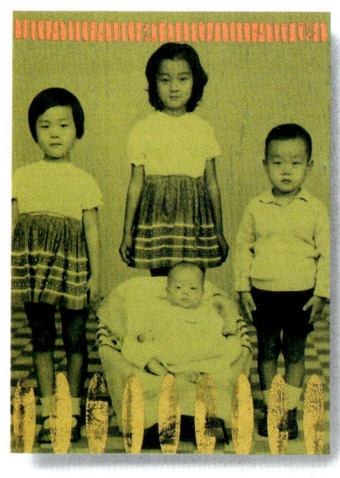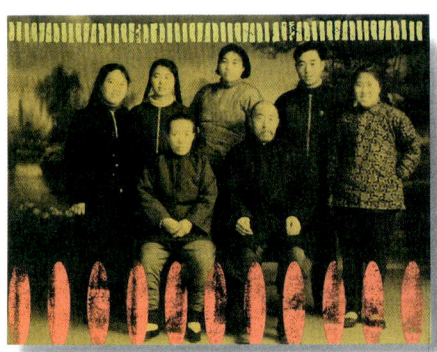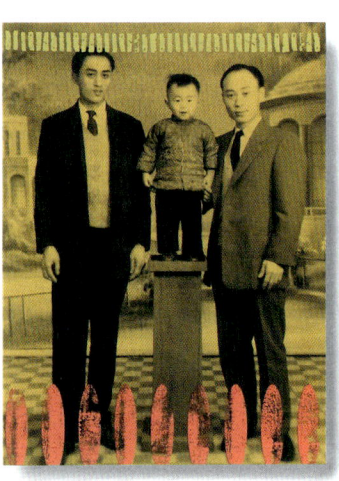

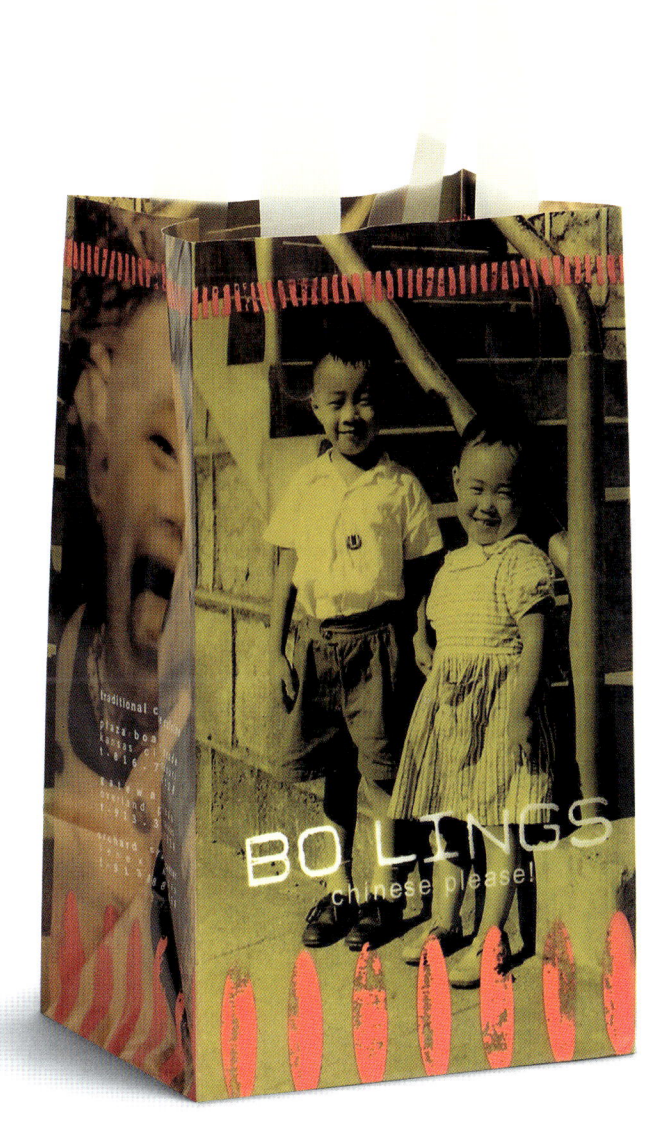

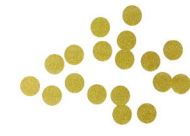

**Bo Lings Chinese
Restaurant | 2002-2005**

Design Ranch
www.design-ranch.com

How can you compete with a chain? With personality. To do this, family photos of the restaurant owner's family were used as well as a traditional color palette and logo, inspired by Chinese food.

One of our favorite party experiences was the opening bash for our design studio Pastille Rose in 2003. Of course the theme was pink. We had bubble gum colored walls, a fridge full of rosé, pink balloons, guests arrived dressed to match and there were many rosy cheeks by the end of the night. It's always fun when people really get into the theme and make an event memorable!

Pastille Rose

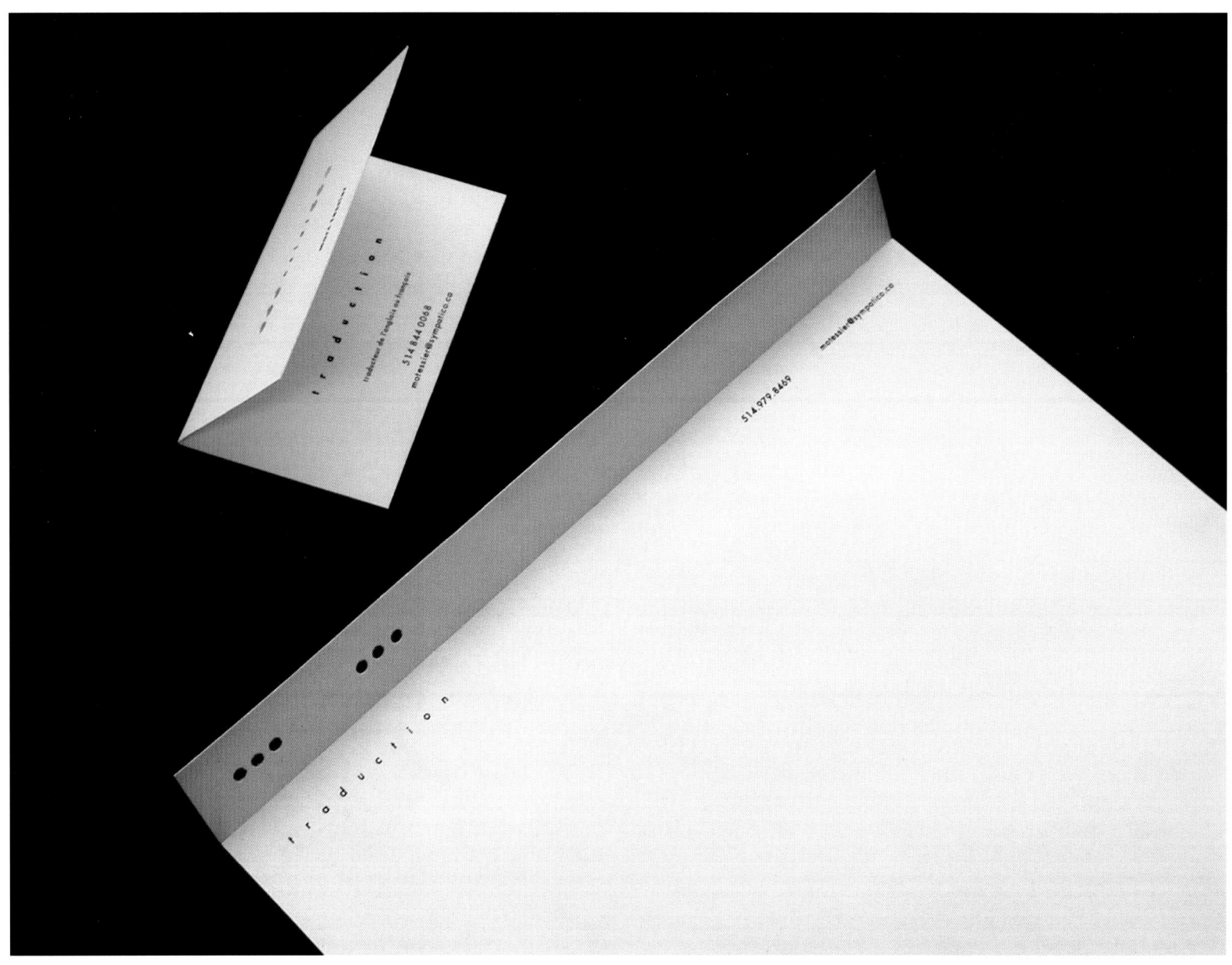

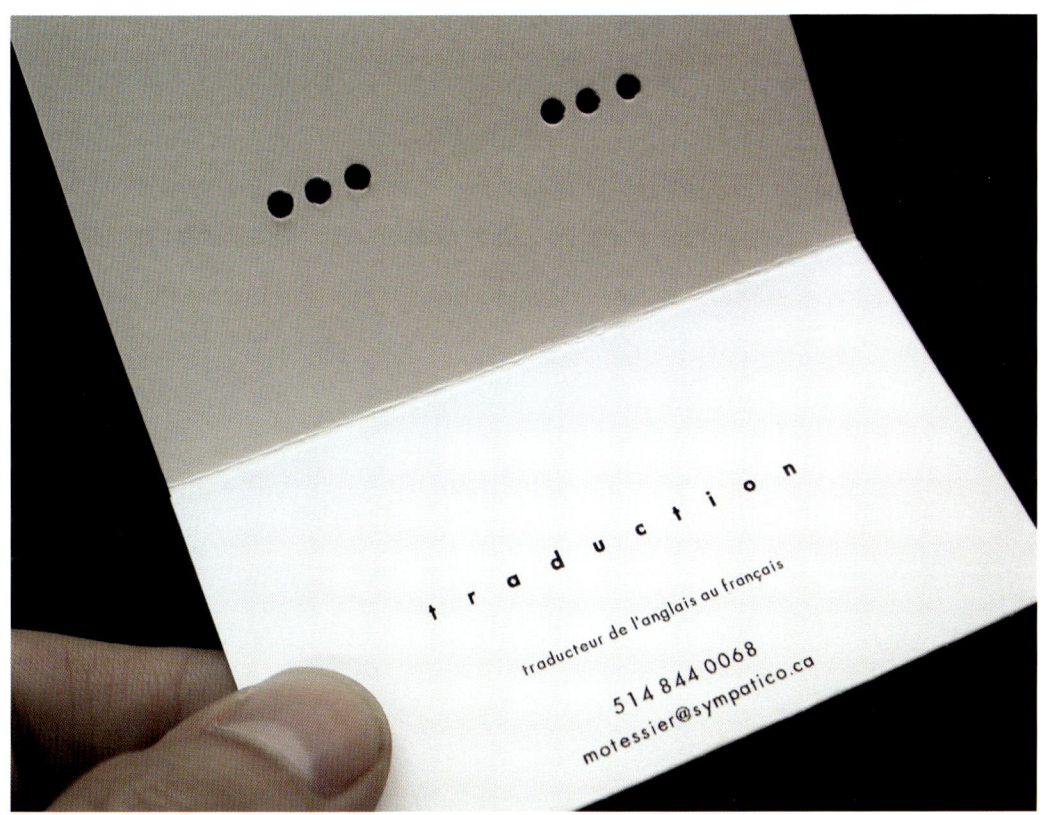

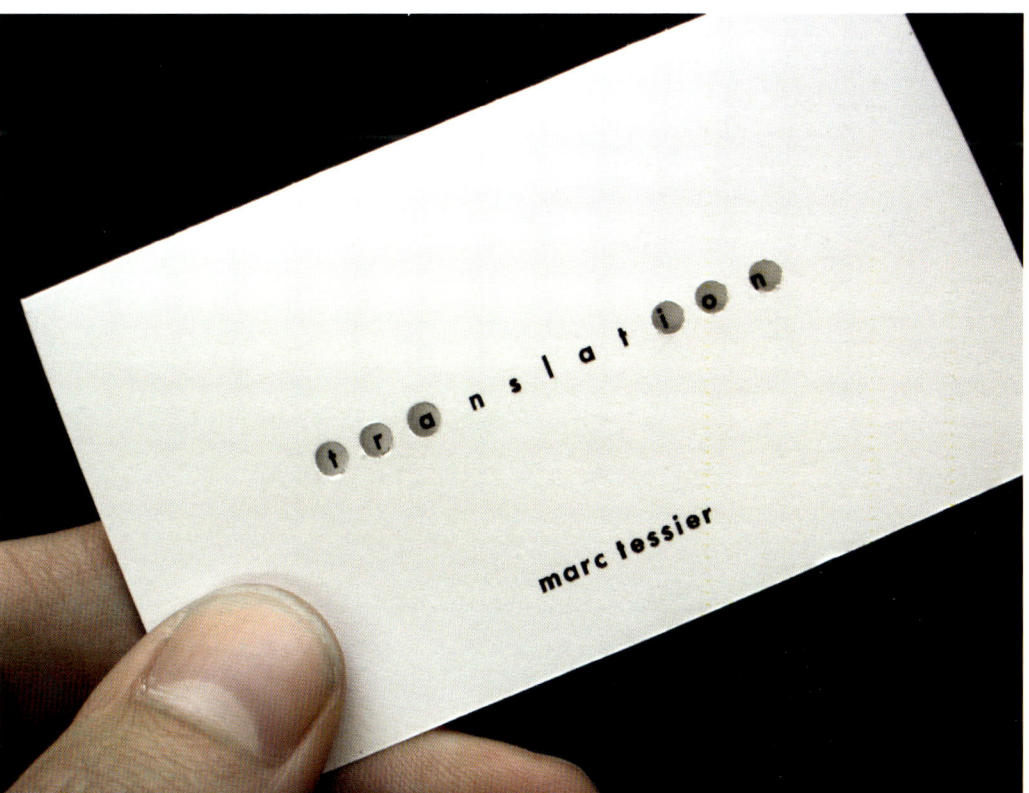

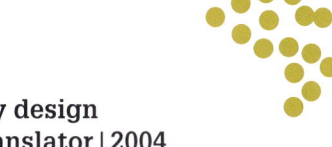

**Identity design
for a translator | 2004**

Ryan Crouchman/Pastille Rose
www.pastillerose.com

This business card physically represents the act of translation. The Futura typeface lends it a corporate touch, and the sharp contrast between black and white emphasizes the idea of duality between two languages.

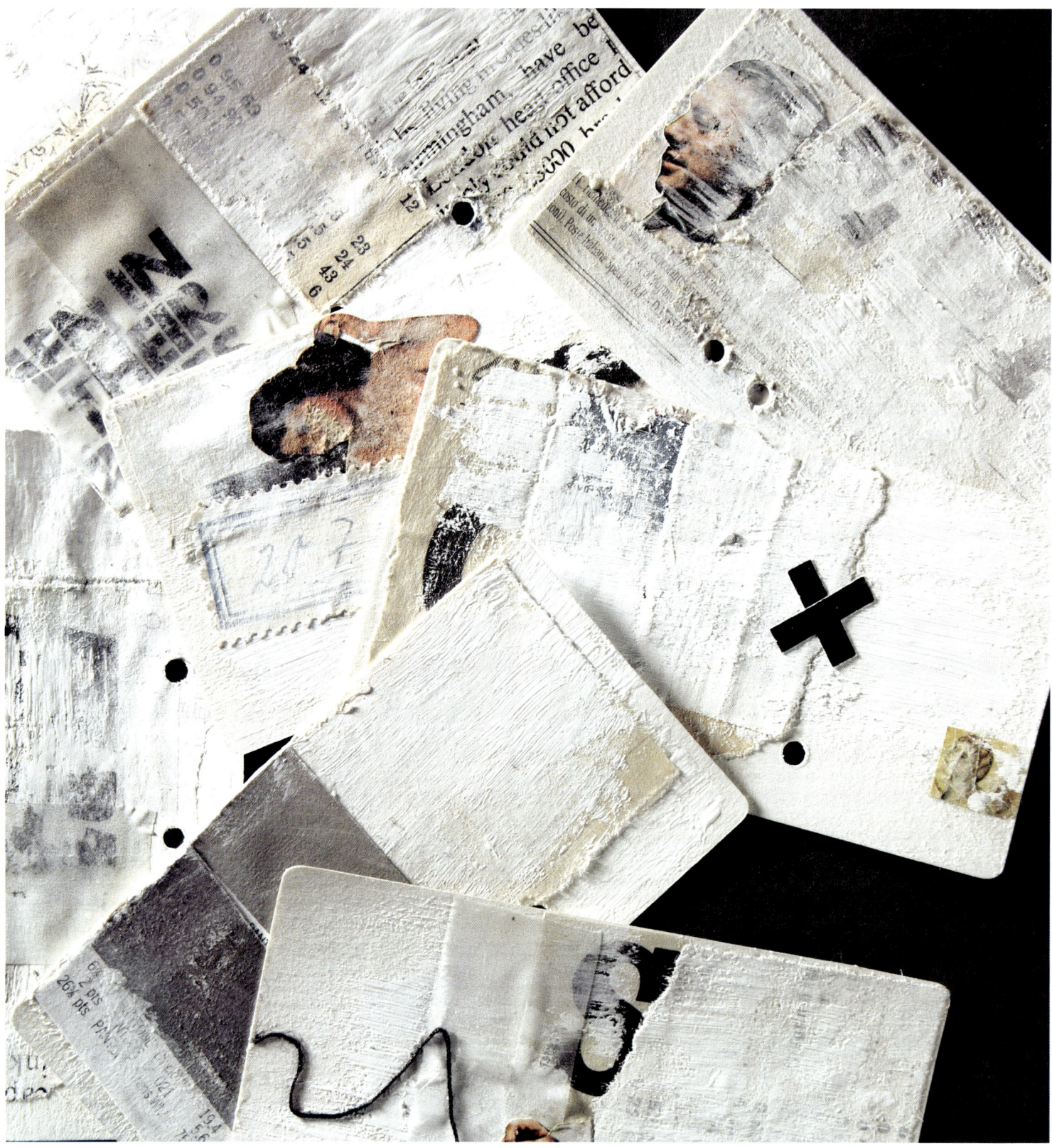

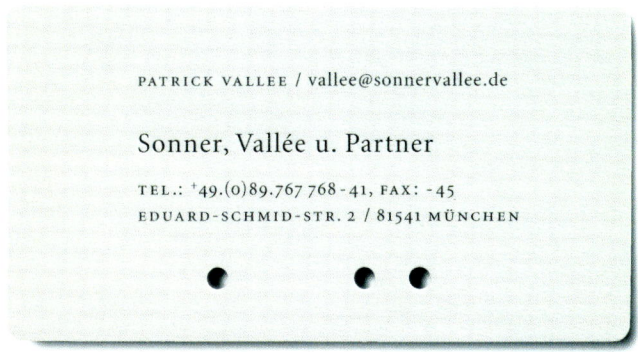
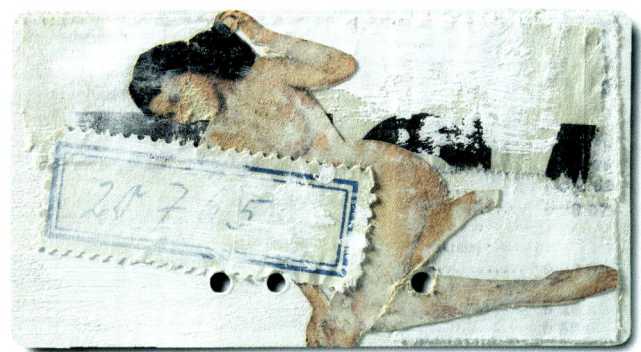
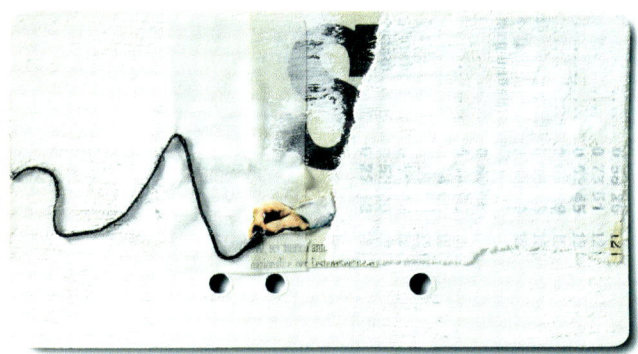
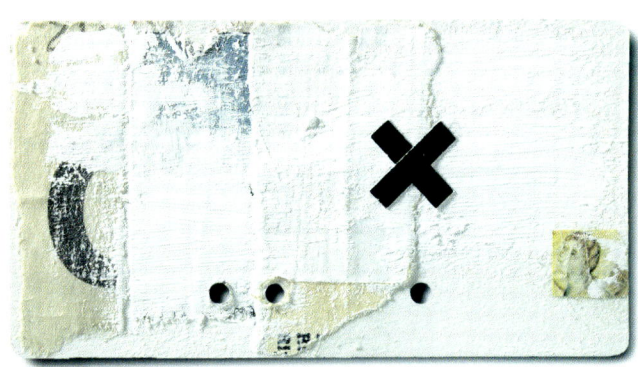

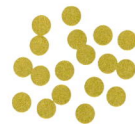

**Sonner, Vallée u. Partner
business cards | 2007**

**Sonner, Vallée u. Partner
www.sonnervallee.de**

A lot of hard work is behind the simple appearance of these business cards: printing on a printing press, cut and a handmade collage. As a limited edition, this card was only given out to clients and special friends.

Our going away party given when we went from working at an agency to working for ourselves! Yippee!

Design Ranch

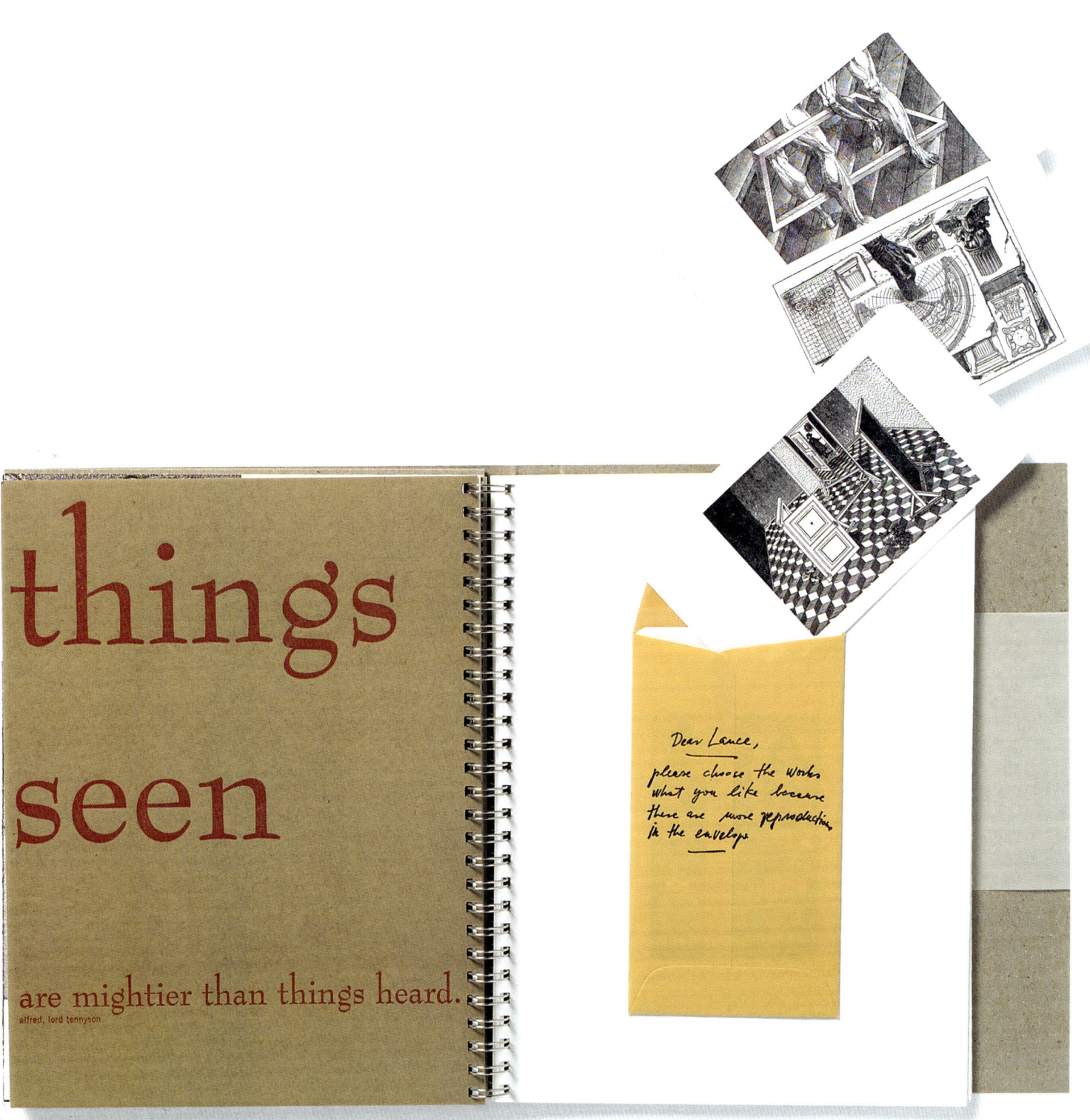

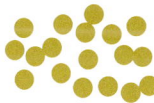

István Orosz exhibition book | 1998

Design Ranch
www.design-ranch.com

This catalog of images coincides with the opening of the artist's gallery. His style, which is reminiscent of Escher, is incorporated into the book so that the vision, the eye and illusion become the work's leitmotif. It includes a poster by the artist.

ISTVÁN OROSZ WAS BORN IN HUNGARY IN 1951. HE WAS TRAINED AS A GRAPHIC DESIGNER AT THE UNIVERSITY OF ARTS AND DESIGN IN BUDAPEST. AFTER GRADUATION IN 1975 HE BEGAN WORKING IN THEATER AS A STAGE DESIGNER (SOMETIMES AS AN ACTOR AS WELL, AND IN FILM AS AN ANIMATOR. LATER, WHEN POSTERS BECAME HIS MAIN INTEREST, OROSZ FOCUSED ON THEATER, MOVIE, AND EXHIBITION POSTERS. INFLUENCED BY EASTERN EUROPEAN DEMOCRATIC CHANGES OROSZ DREW POLITICAL POSTERS AS WELL. OROSZ USES VISUAL PARADOX AND ILLUSIONIST APPROACHES WHILE FOLLOWING TRADITIONAL PRINTING TECHNIQUES SUCH AS WOODCUTTING AND ETCHING. HE ALSO TRIES TO RENEW THE TECHNIQUE OF ANAMORPHOSIS. HE IS A REGULAR PARTICIPANT IN THE MAJOR INTERNATIONAL BIENNIALS OF POSTERS AND GRAPHIC ART (BRNO, WARSAW, TOYAMA, FORT COLLINS, LAHTI) AND HIS WORKS HAVE BEEN SHOWN IN MANY INDIVIDUAL AND GROUP EXHIBITIONS IN HUNGARY AND ABROAD. SEVERAL OF THEM HAVE WON AWARDS. OCCASIONALLY HE PARTICIPATES IN INTERNATIONAL DESIGNER AND ARTIST CONGRESSES (BRAZIL, HOLLAND, CZECH REPUBLIC, MEXICO, ISRAEL, ITALY, AND THE U.S.). HE IS CO-FOUNDER OF D.O.P.P. ARTIST GROUP, FILM DIRECTOR AT THE PANNONIA FILM STUDIO, GUEST TEACHER AT THE UNIVERSITY OF ARTS AND DESIGN IN BUDAPEST, AND MEMBER OF THE HUNGARIAN ART ACADEMY. HE OFTEN USES ΟΥΤΙΣ (No one) AS AN ARTIST'S PSEUDONYM.

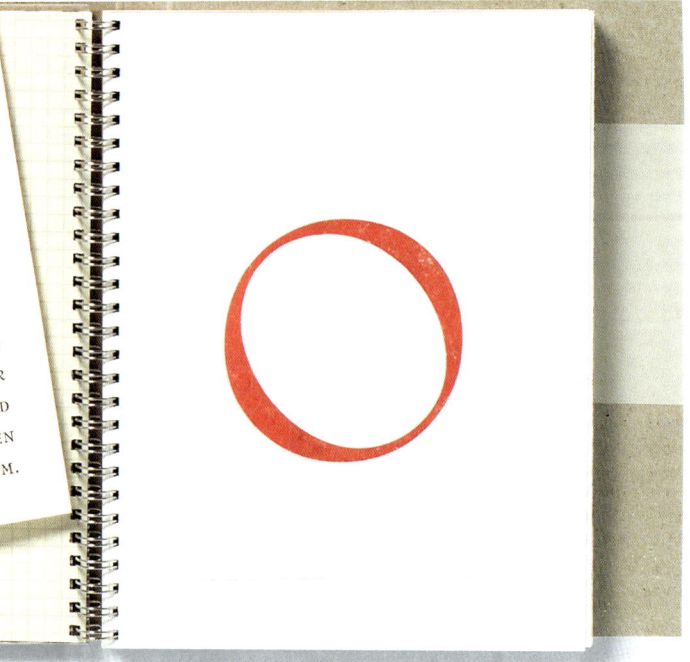

eye

i

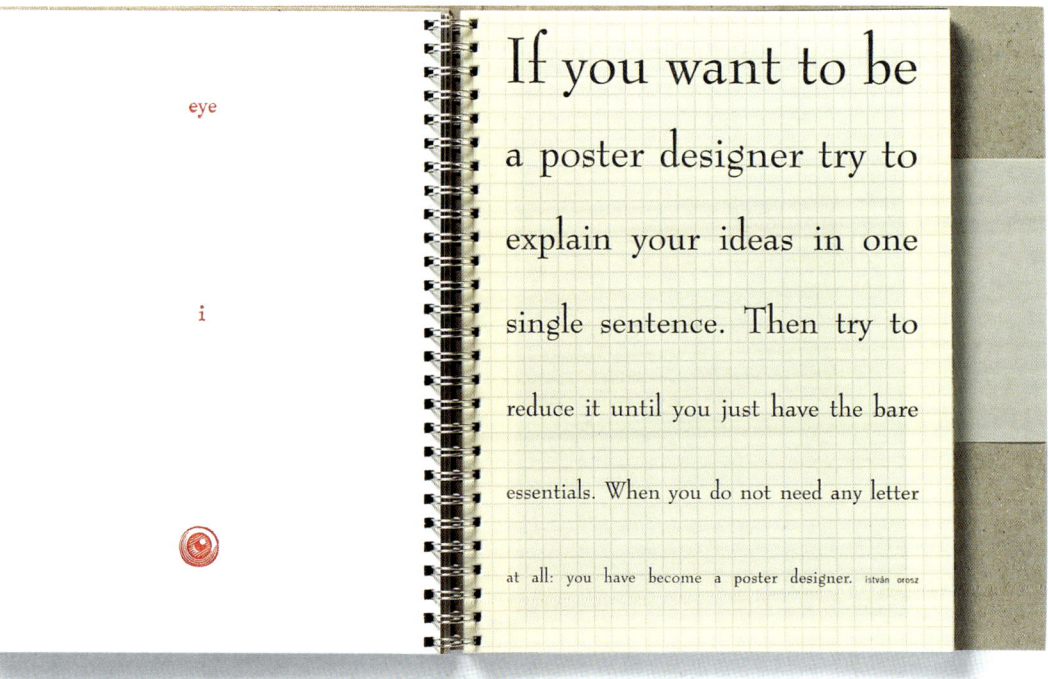

If you want to be a poster designer try to explain your ideas in one single sentence. Then try to reduce it until you just have the bare essentials. When you do not need any letter at all: you have become a poster designer. istván orosz

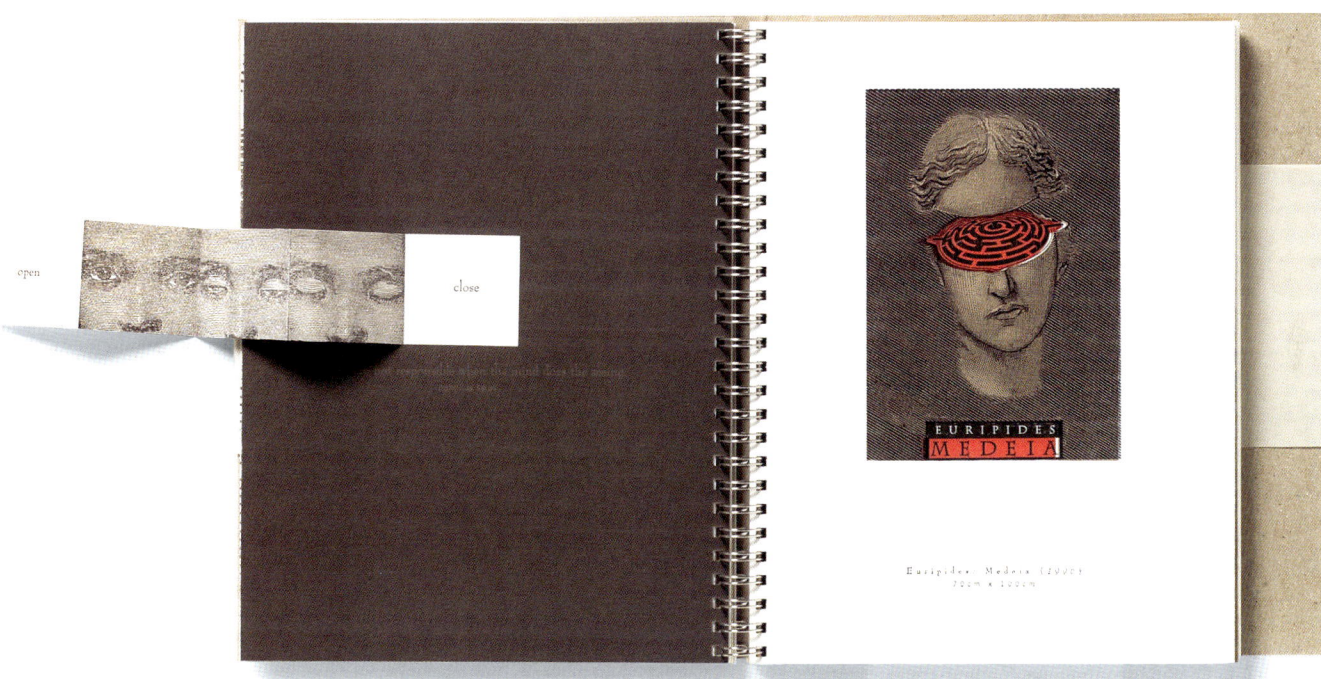

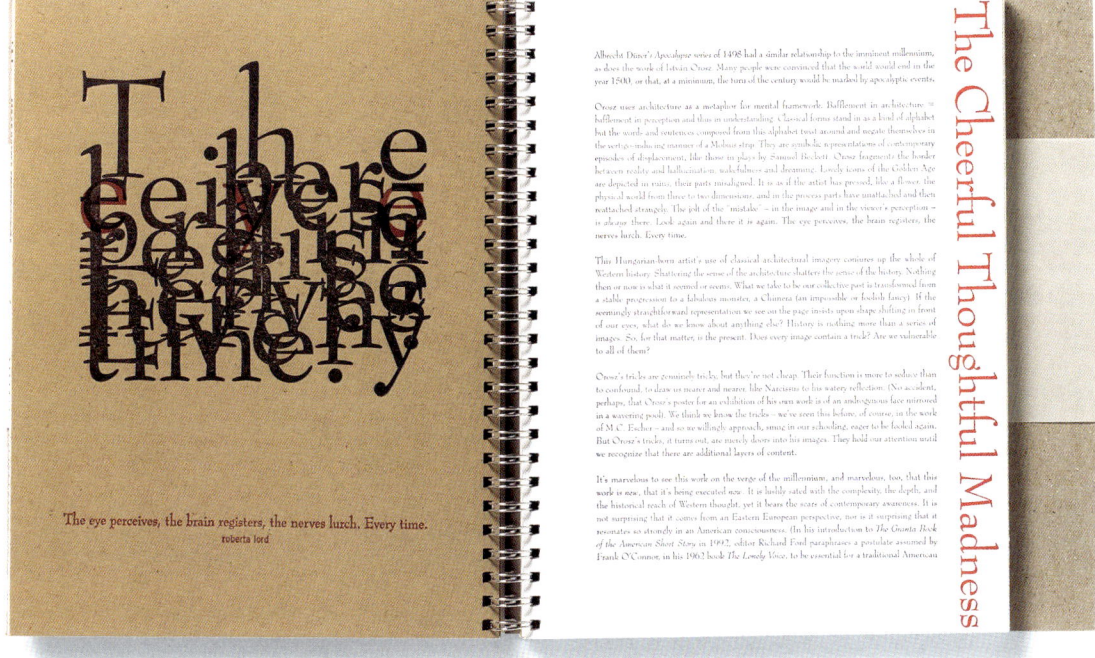

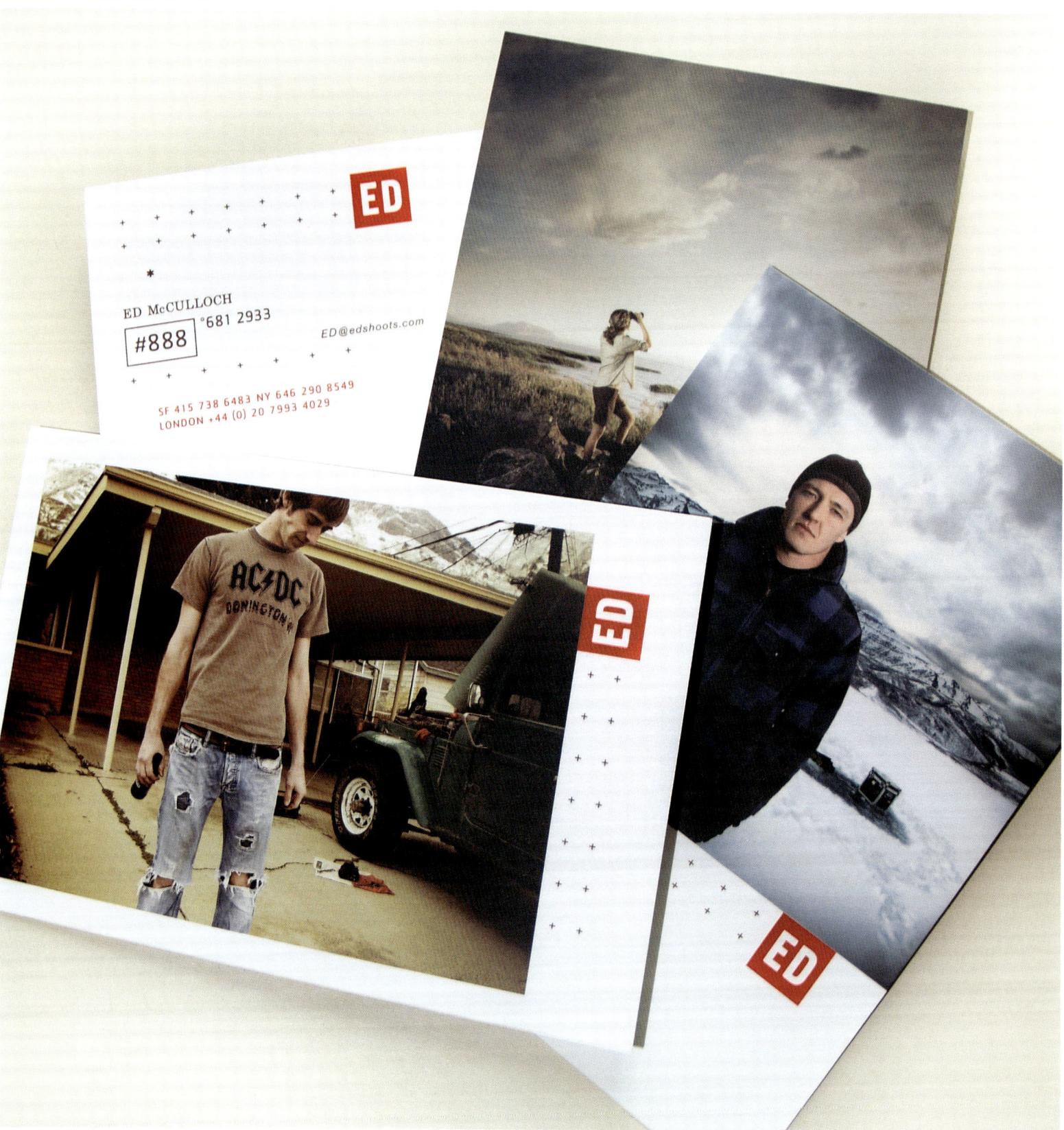

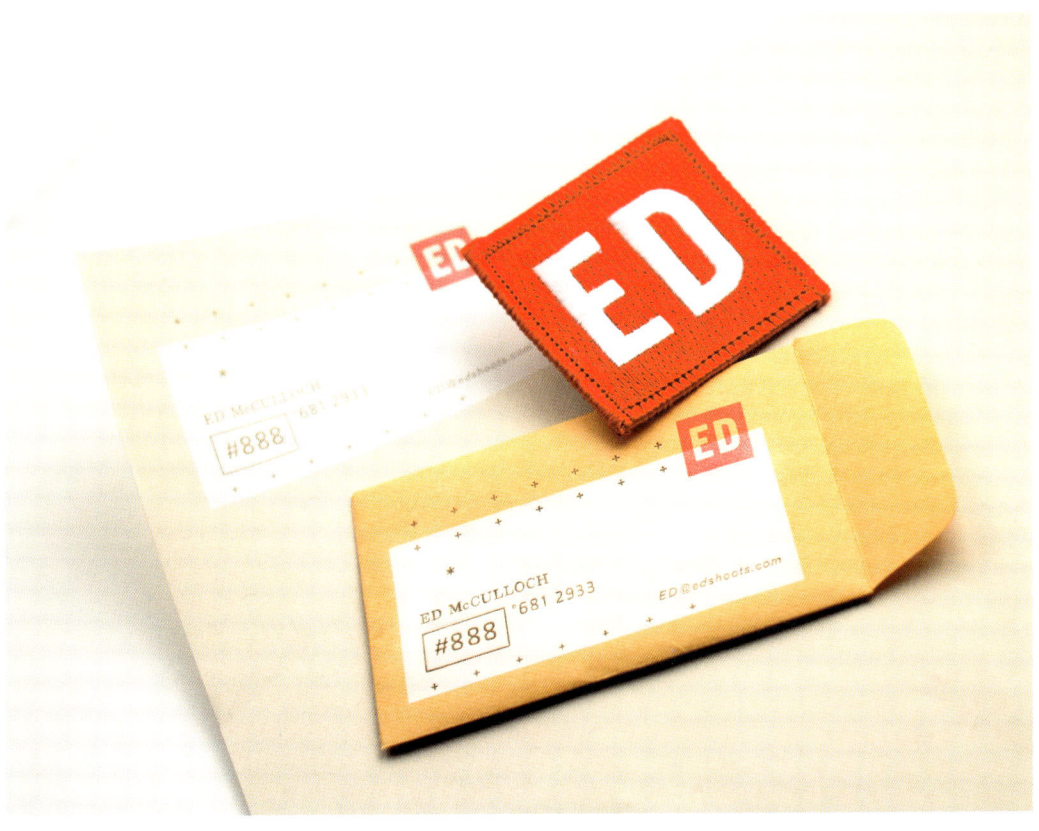

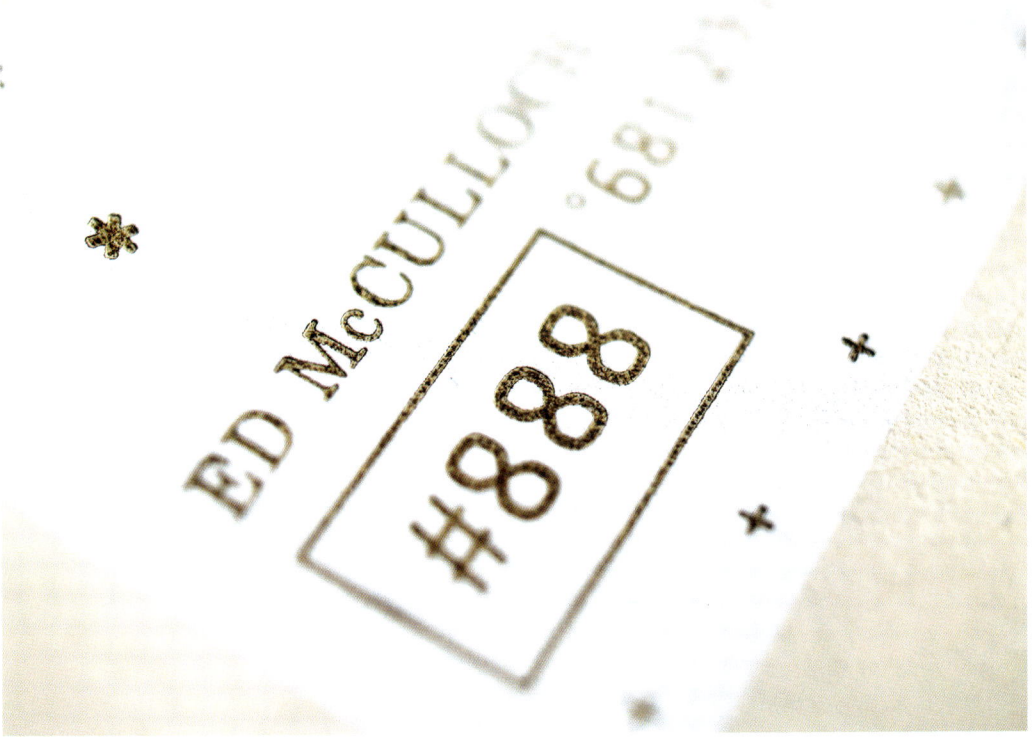

**Ed McCulloch
Photography | 2007**

**Funnel : Eric Kass : Utilitarian +
Commercial + Fine : Art
www.funnel.tv**

The identity designed for the photographer is intended to join the modern with an organic perception of the materials. Thus, the modern aesthetic of the photographs combines with paper in natural colors and tones that make reference to the earth, such as red or brown.

I recently attended and donated a painting to the Evan's Life Foundation Gift Wrapping Party and Fundraiser in Chicago and was amazed by all of the holiday spirit. The old bowling alley turned design firm by SamataMason was packed to the rafters with supporters wrapping donated gifts for less fortunate children while a choir sang and champagne flowed. It was a wonderful holiday experience.

Eric Kass

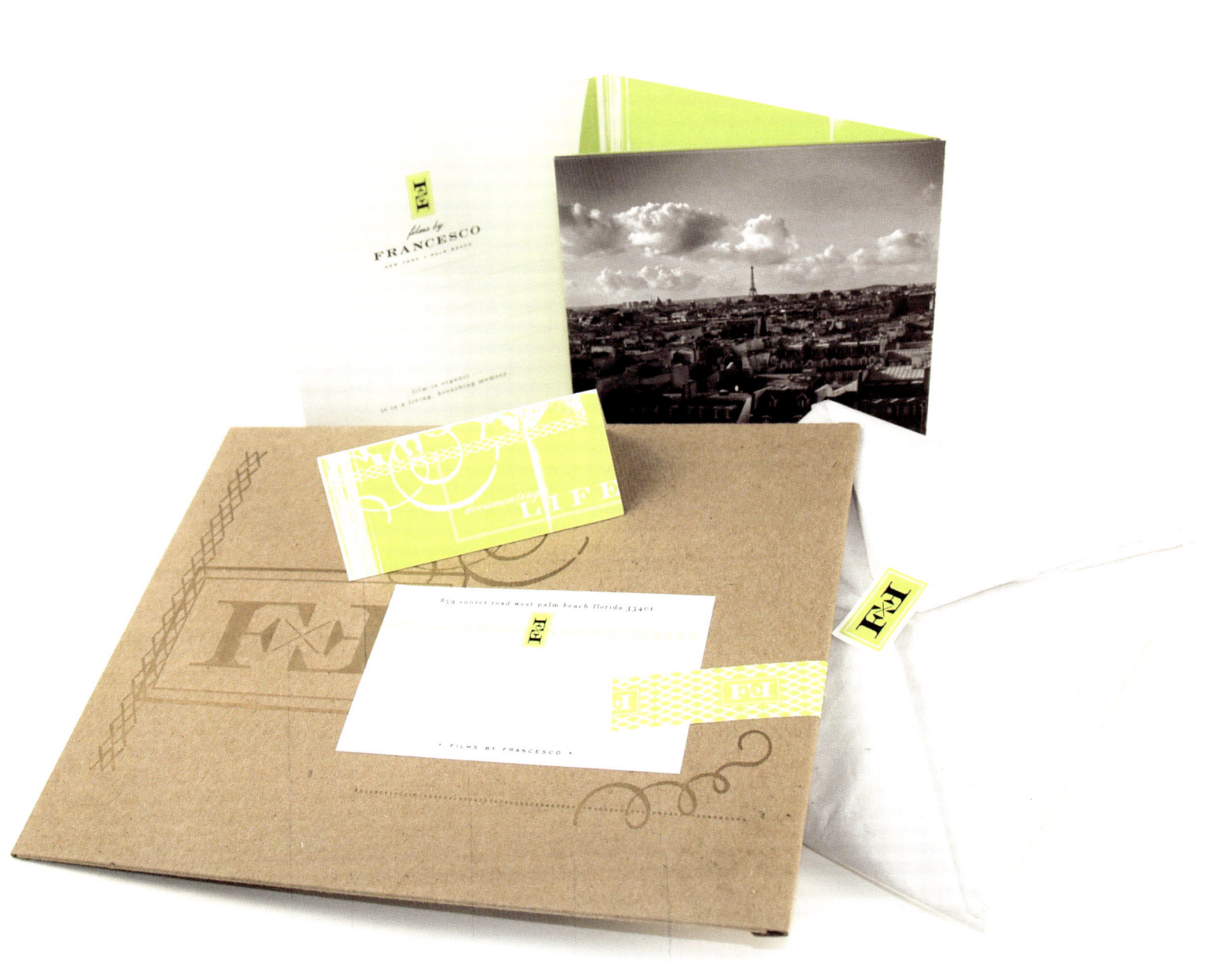

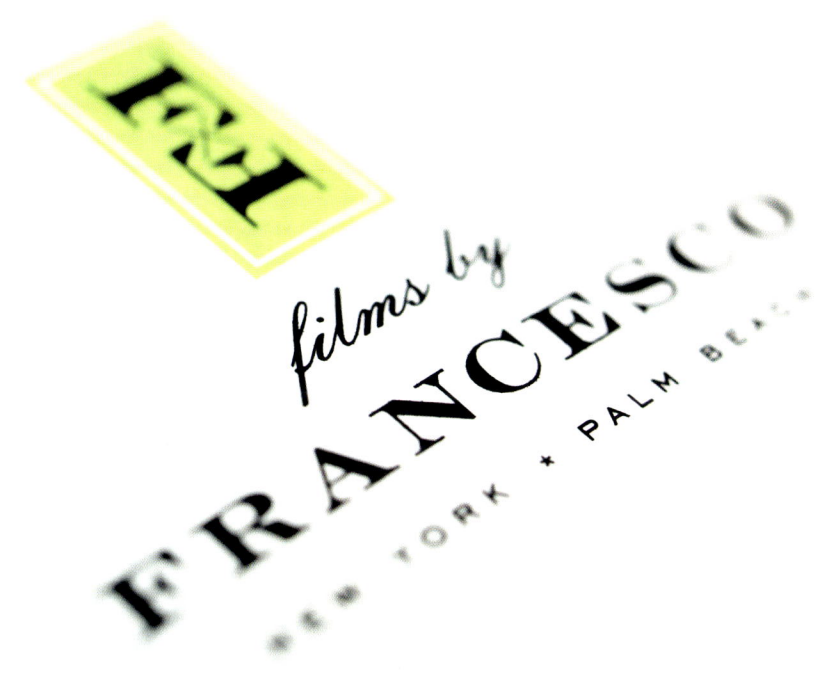

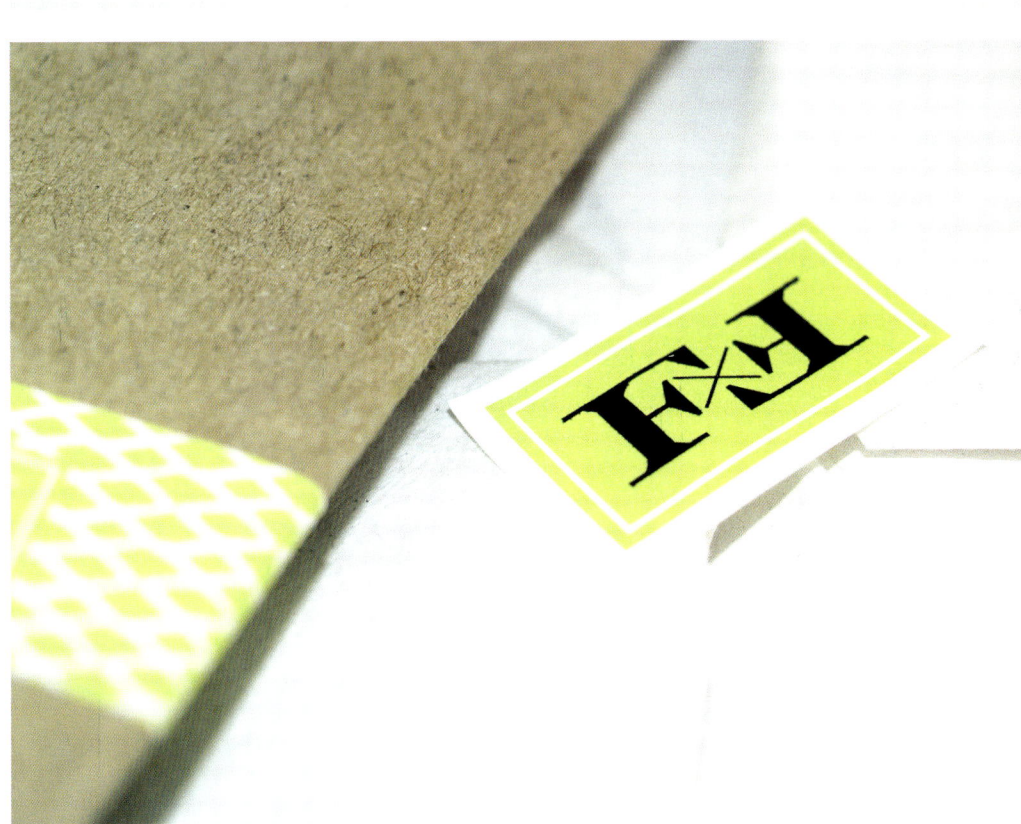

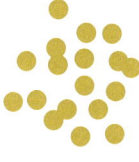

Films by Francesco | 2007

**Funnel : Eric Kass : Utilitarian +
Commercial + Fine : Art
www.funnel.tv**

The proposal of this identity was based on the love for handicrafts, detail and singularity. The different printing techniques (engraving, silkscreen, offset) are intended to emphasize the producer's focus on originality.

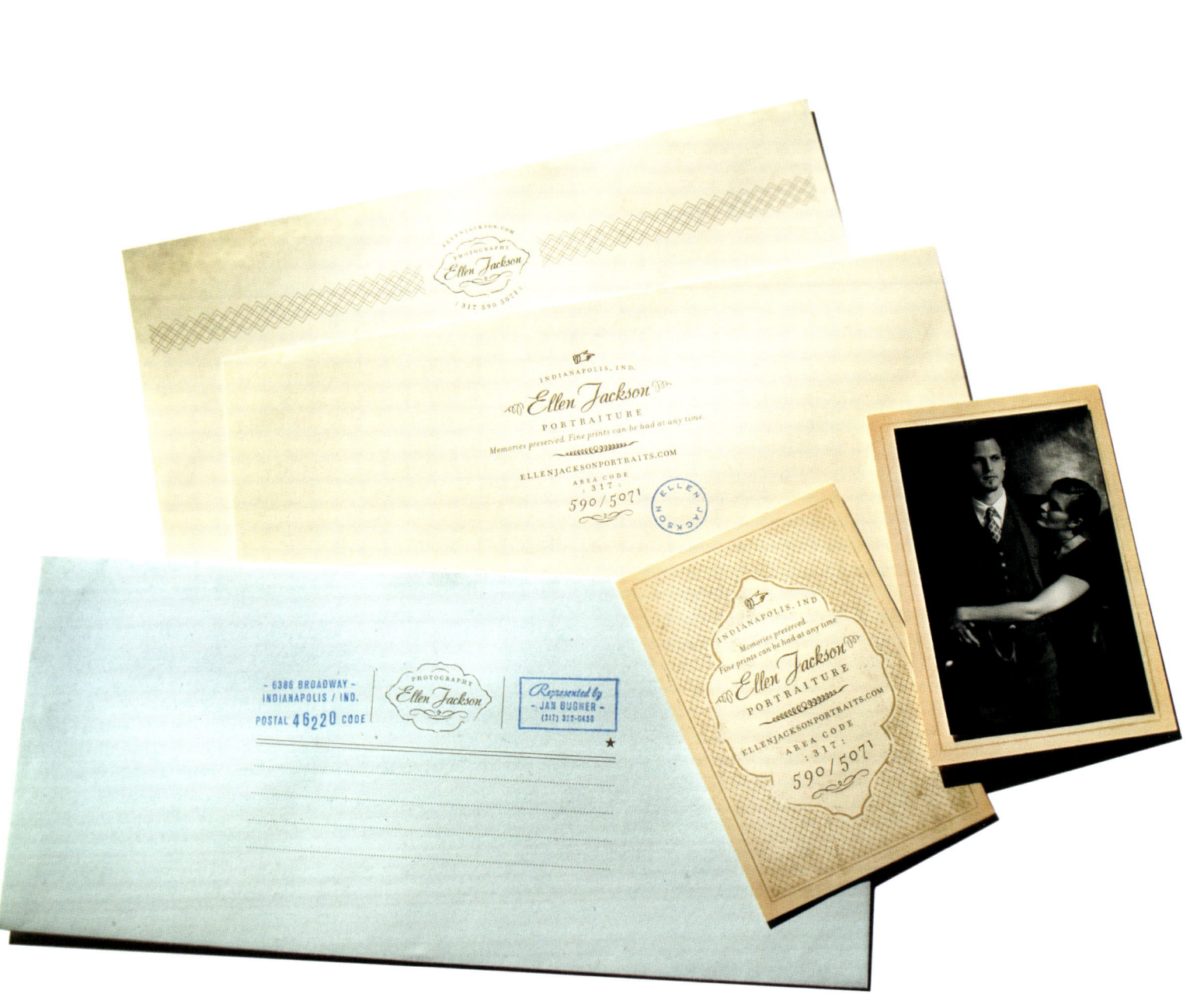

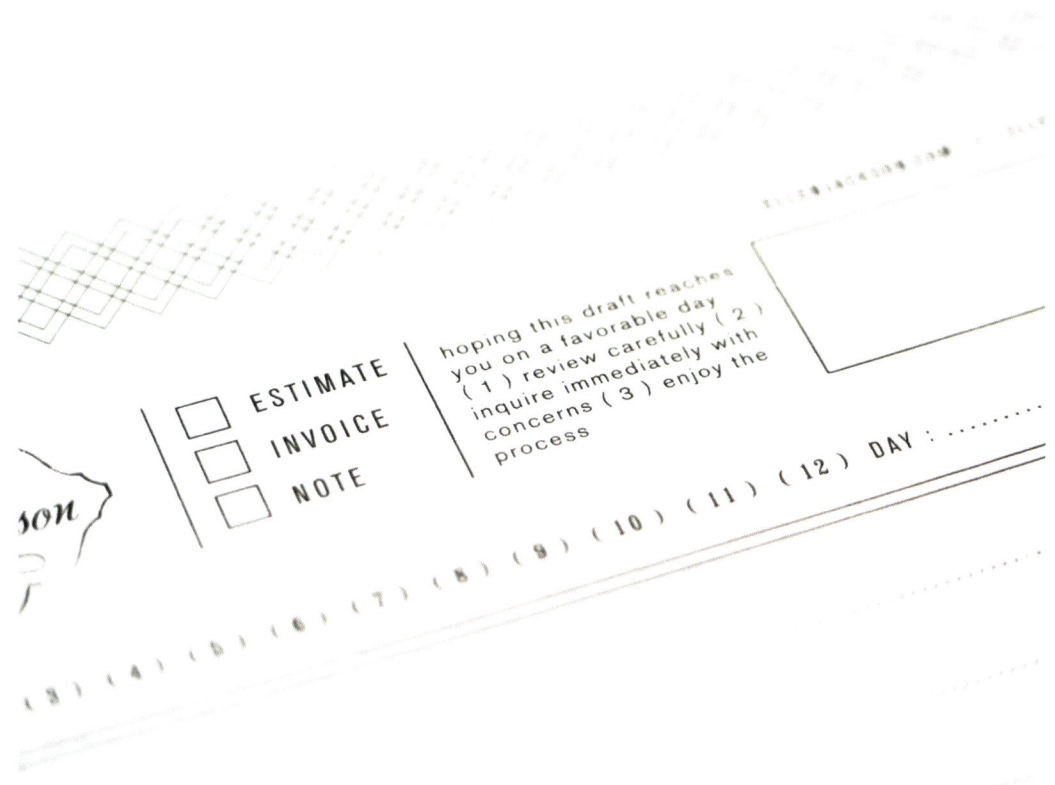

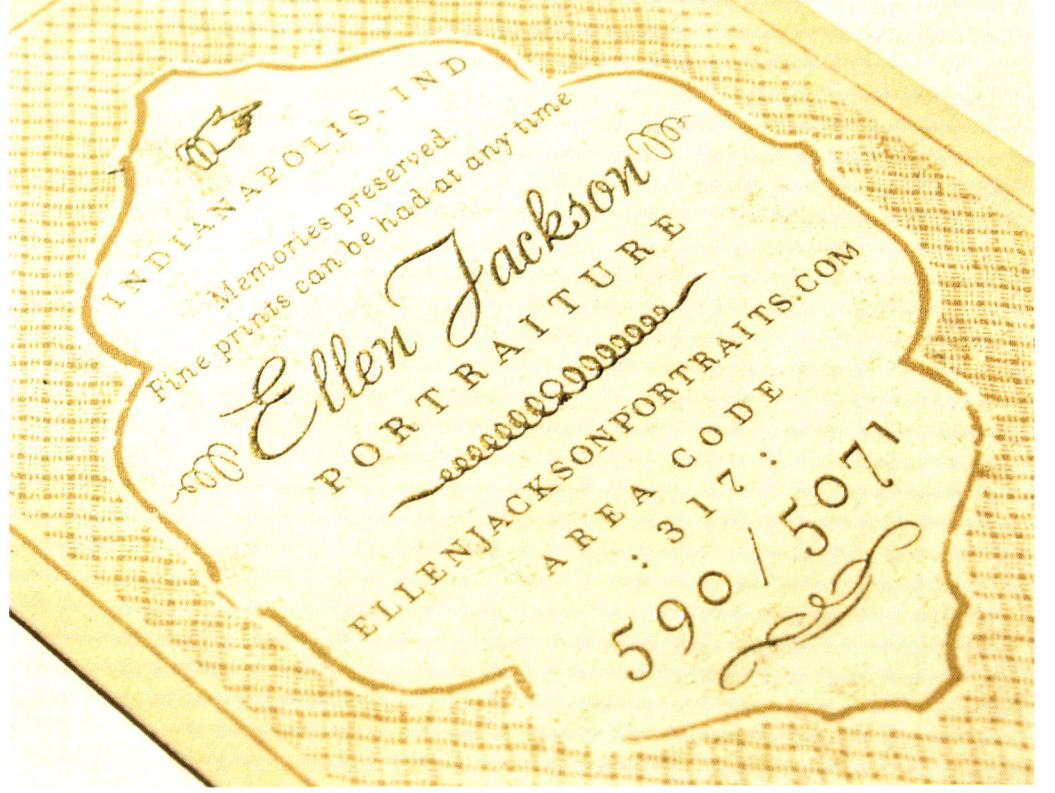

Ellen Jackson Portraiture | 2005

Funnel : Eric Kass : Utilitarian + Commercial + Fine : Art
www.funnel.tv

The photographs of Jackson are reminiscent of days-gone-by. The stationery includes hand-drawn patterns and carvings, which complete the atmosphere of her work, and which are inspired by old business cards of the designer's family.

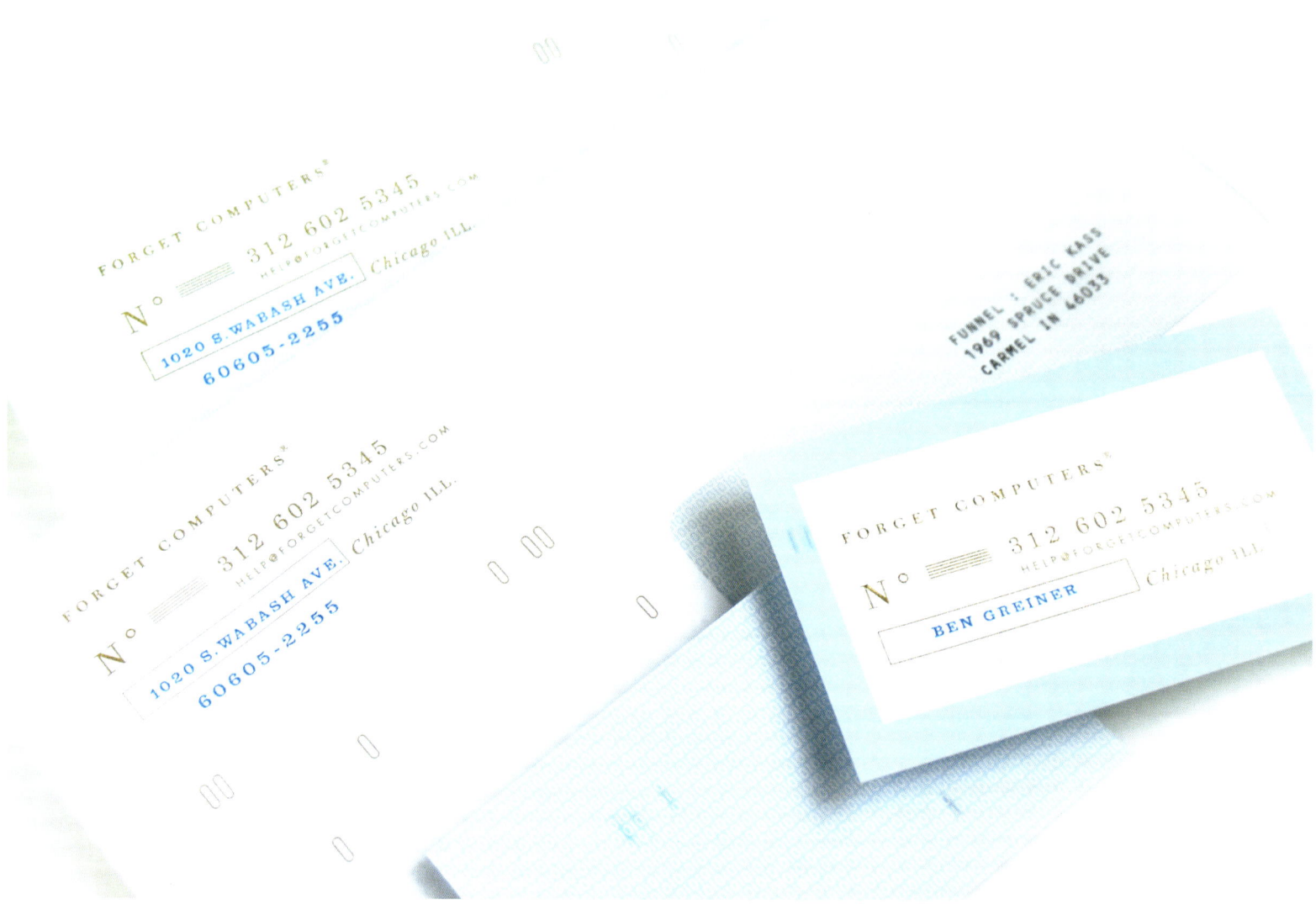

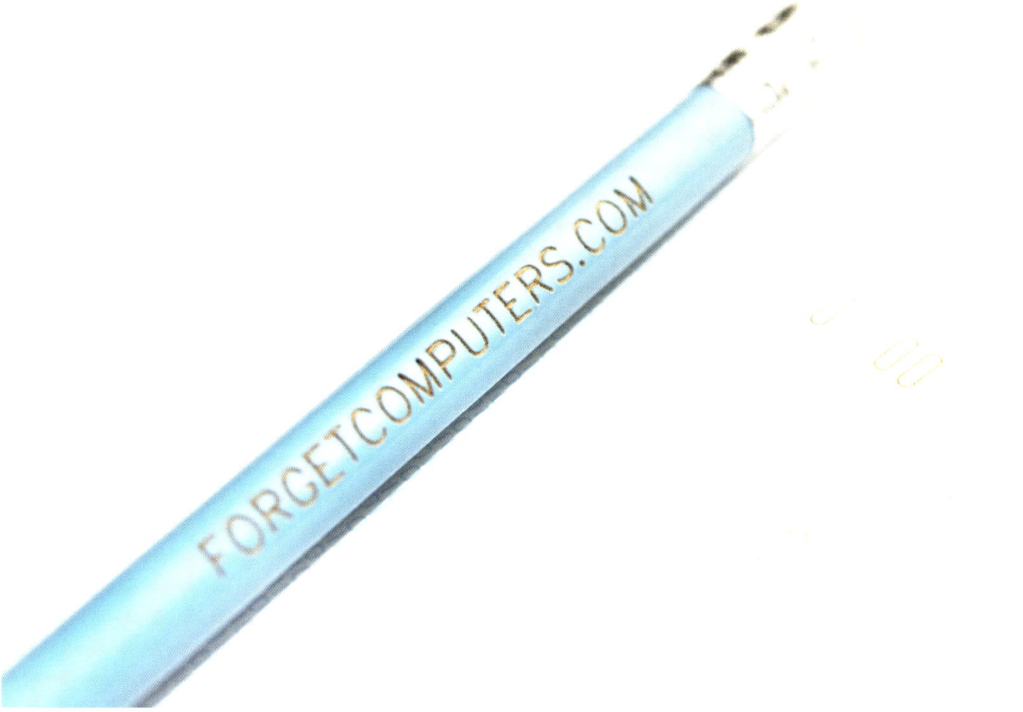

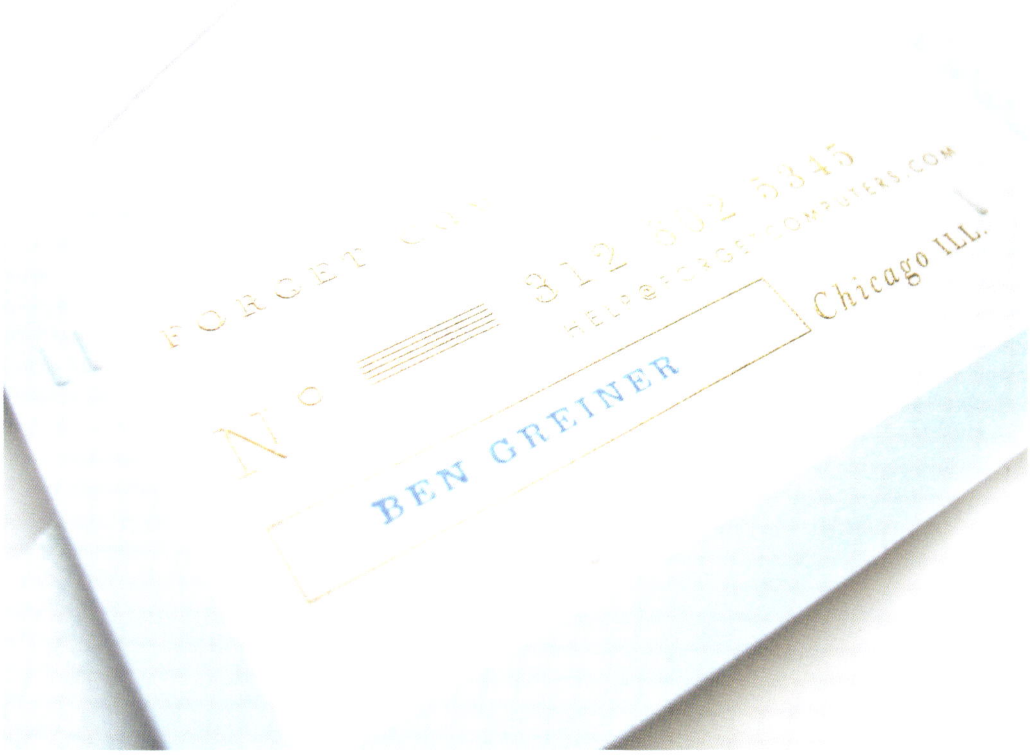

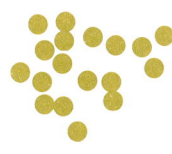

Forget Computers | 2007

Funnel : Eric Kass : Utilitarian + Commercial + Fine : Art
www.funnel.tv

For an Apple computer maintenance service, the stationery uses a vintage look, but with a touch of sophistication provided by the gold inscription. The binary code pattern harps back to the first computers and adds a hint of irony.

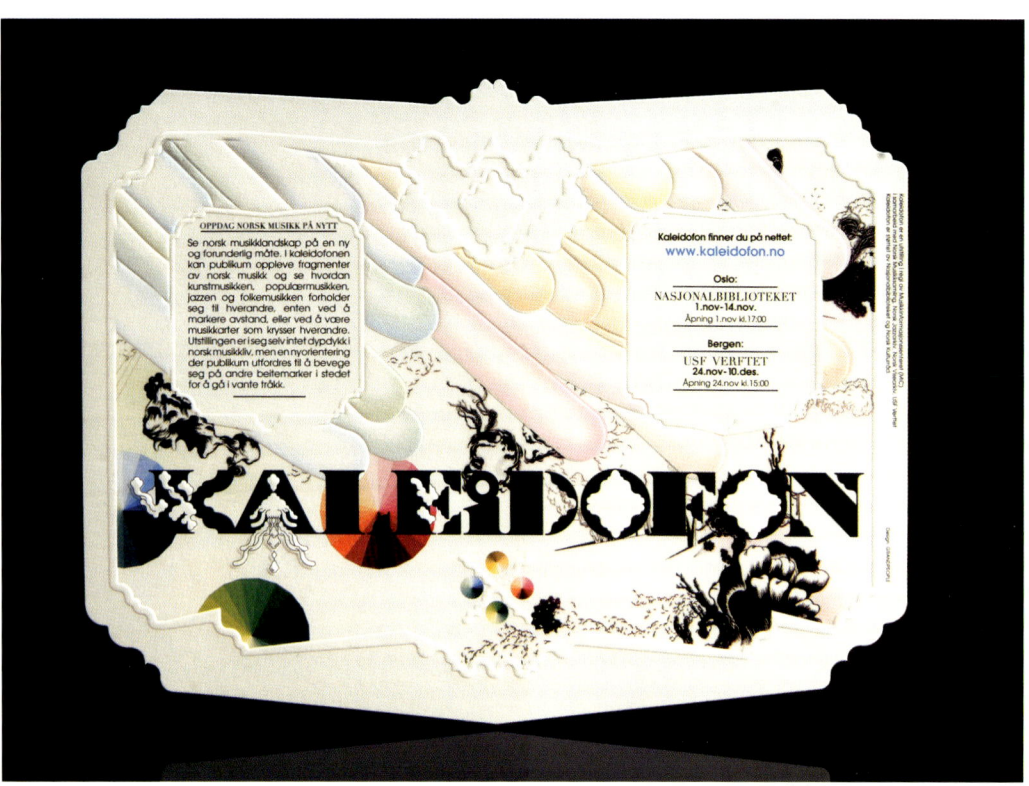

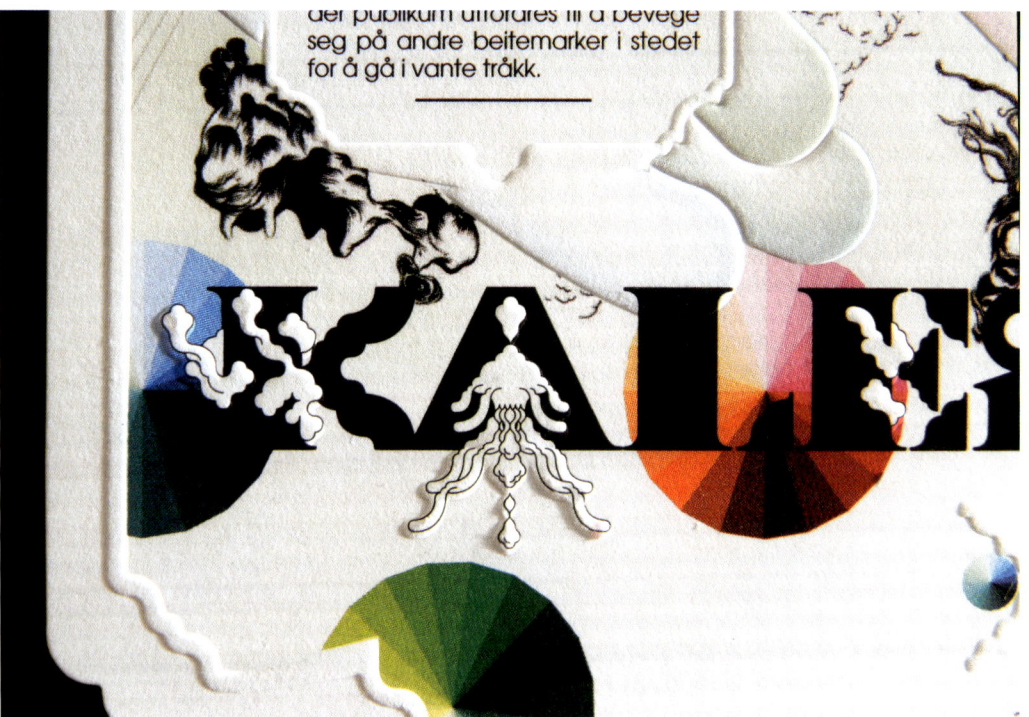

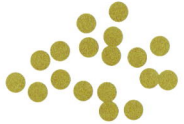

Kaleidofon | 2006

Grandpeople
www.grandpeople.org

Kaleidofon is a web project whose aim is to promote the national collection of contemporary Norwegian music. This business card brings together the delicacy of the reliefs with a modern image produced by the color circles and the variety of shapes.

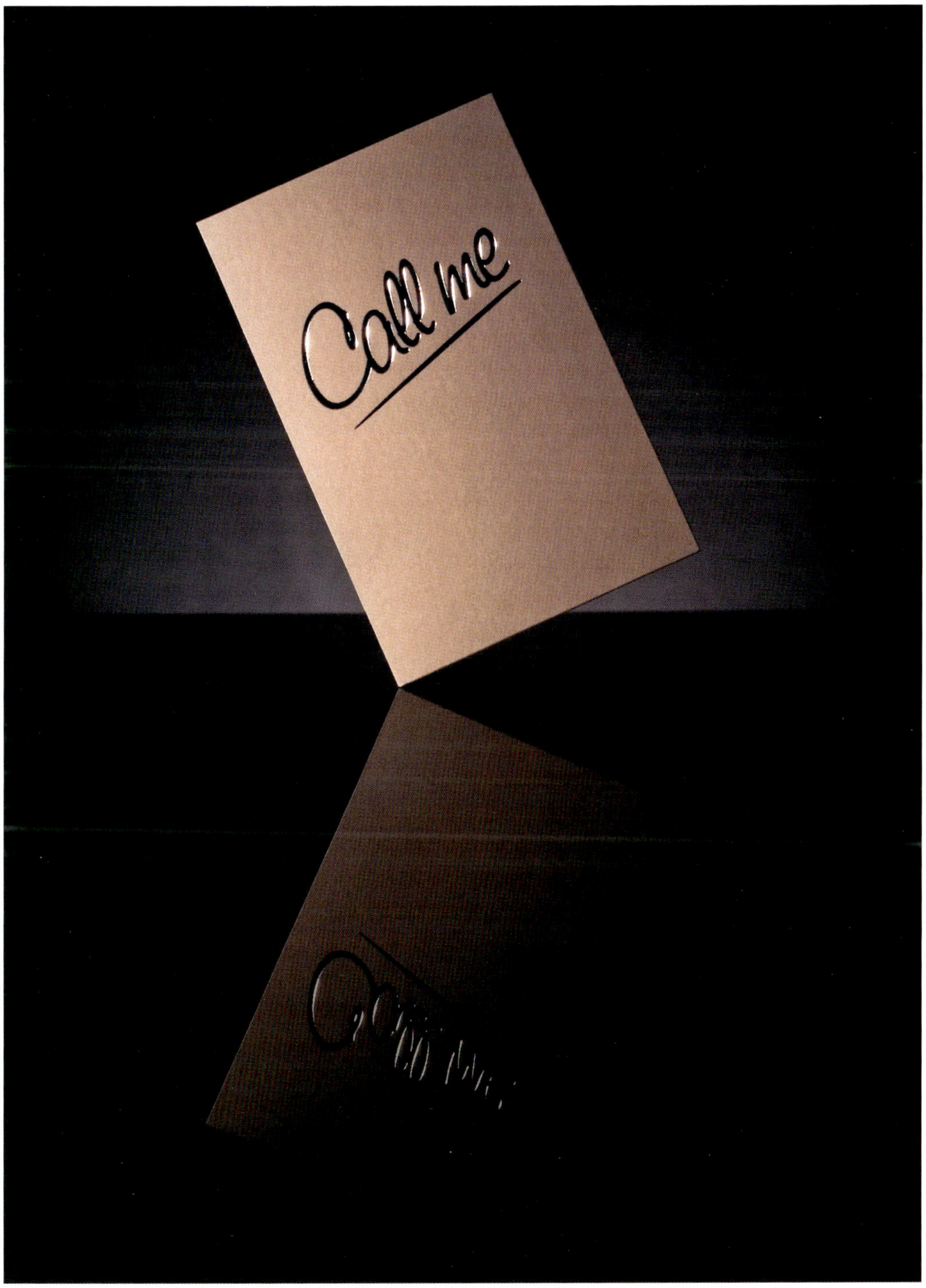

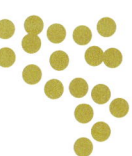

Serial Cut's business card | 2006

Sergio del Puerto/Serial Cut
www.serialcut.com

Designed to be offered to potential clients, the card's function is self-explanatory: to establish contact. Empty on the back, on the front there is just the words "call me" in shiny letters. The typography simulates handwriting.

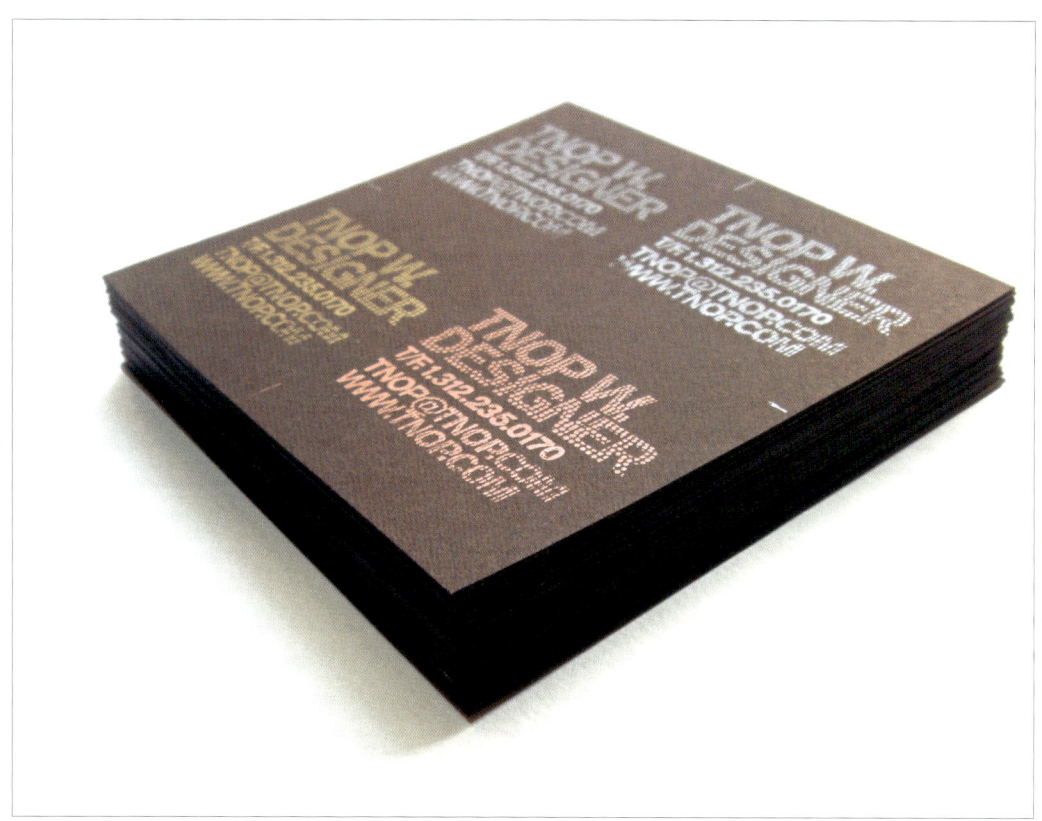

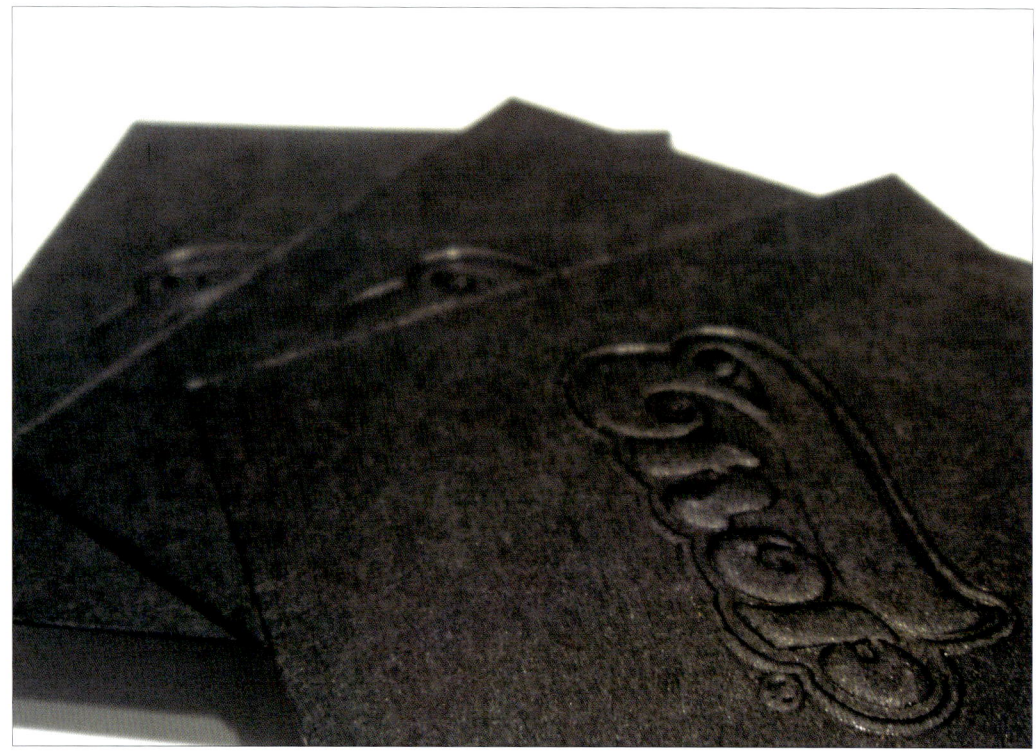

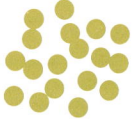

TNOP business cards | 2005-2006

Tnop Wangsillapakun/TNOP design
www.tnop.com

These business cards were produced by hand; from the relief, made by applying hand pressure, to the printing, carried out with a home silk-screen printing kit. The idea was to be able to produce the cards on a low budget.

The 2006 Golden Globes viewing and after party by InStyle magazine was the best party. We have been involved in many grand events, but the final results of this one really blew me away.

Kira Evans

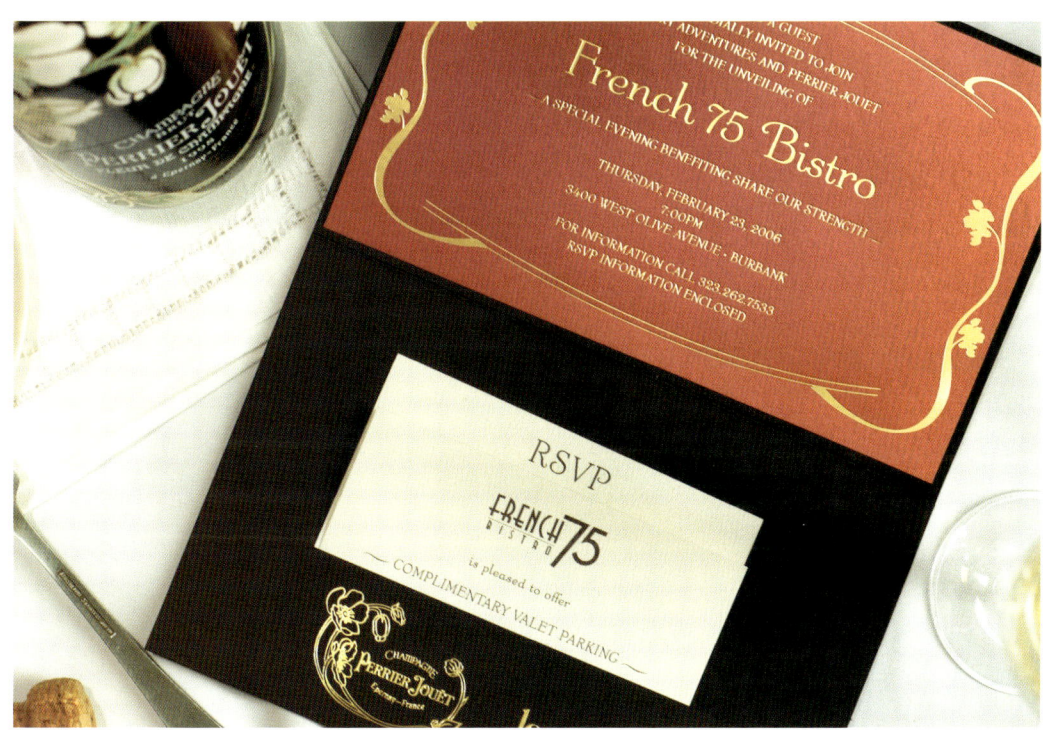

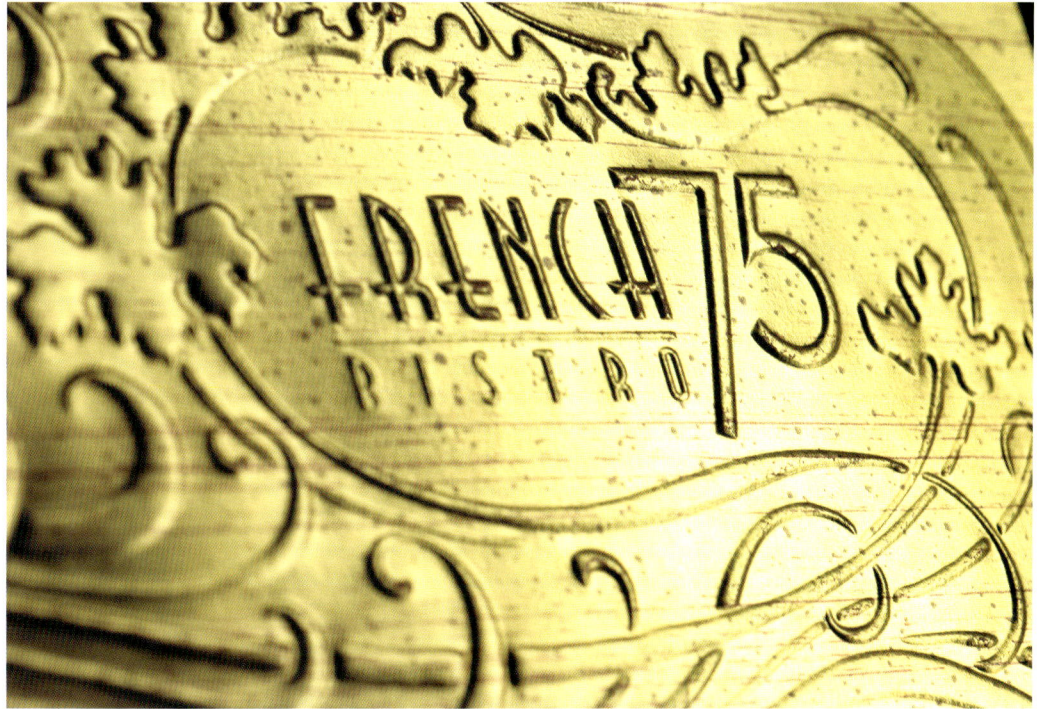

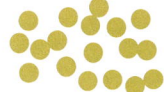

French 75 Bistro
grand opening | 2006

Kira Evans Design
www.kiraevansdesign.com

The restaurant was decorated in an art nouveau style similar to that of *Cheers*. The invitation was based on this interior design to work on paper with a texture similar to plastic and with gold leaves.

I'm someone who believes a good party is that which you remember during the week...And I've been to a lot like that. This holiday period finished in a party in a house with a giant pool, a jacuzzi and a lot of interesting people...I was one of the last to leave when the sun had already come up...I can't talk about the rest, especially in a book on design!

Sergio del Puerto

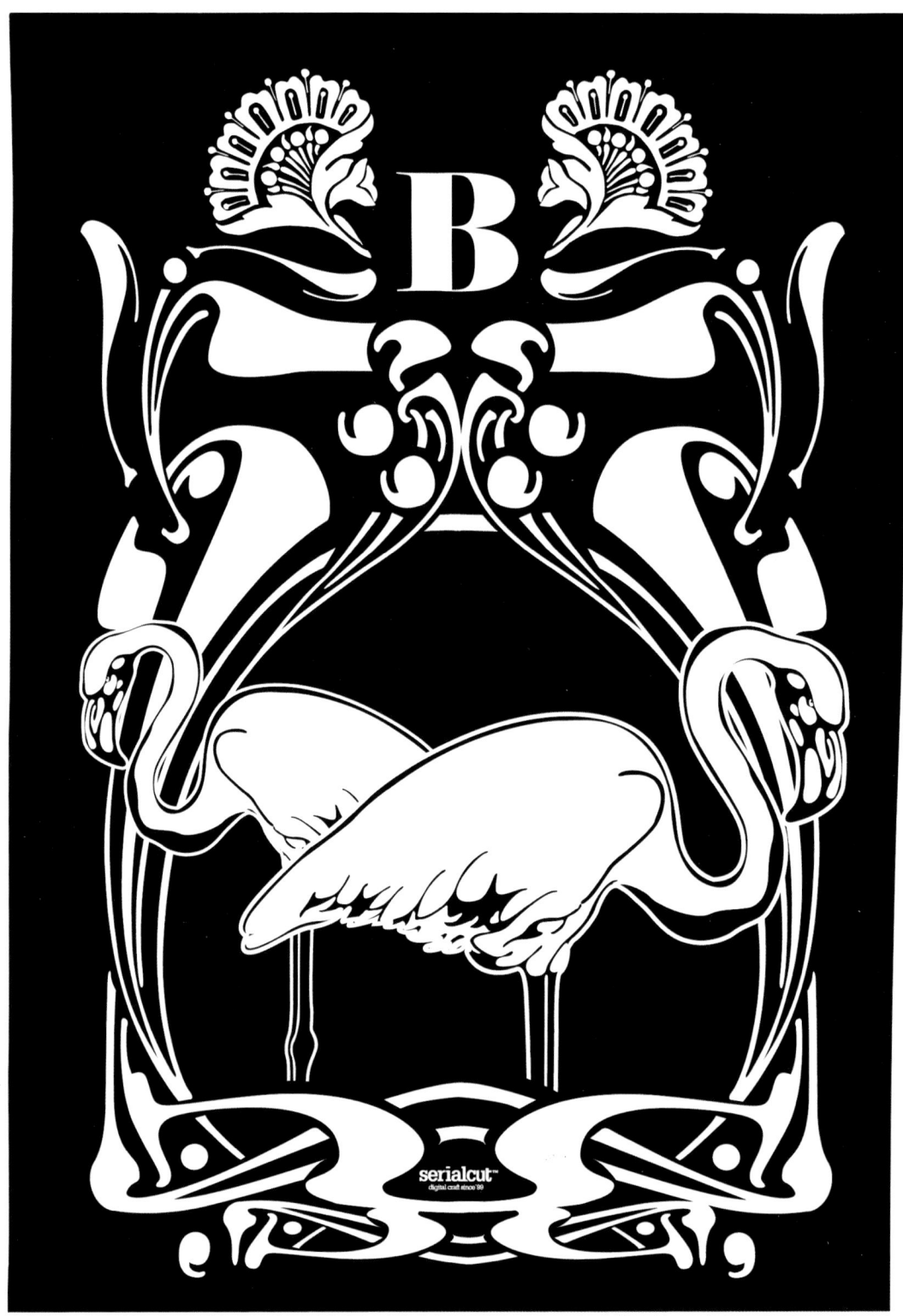

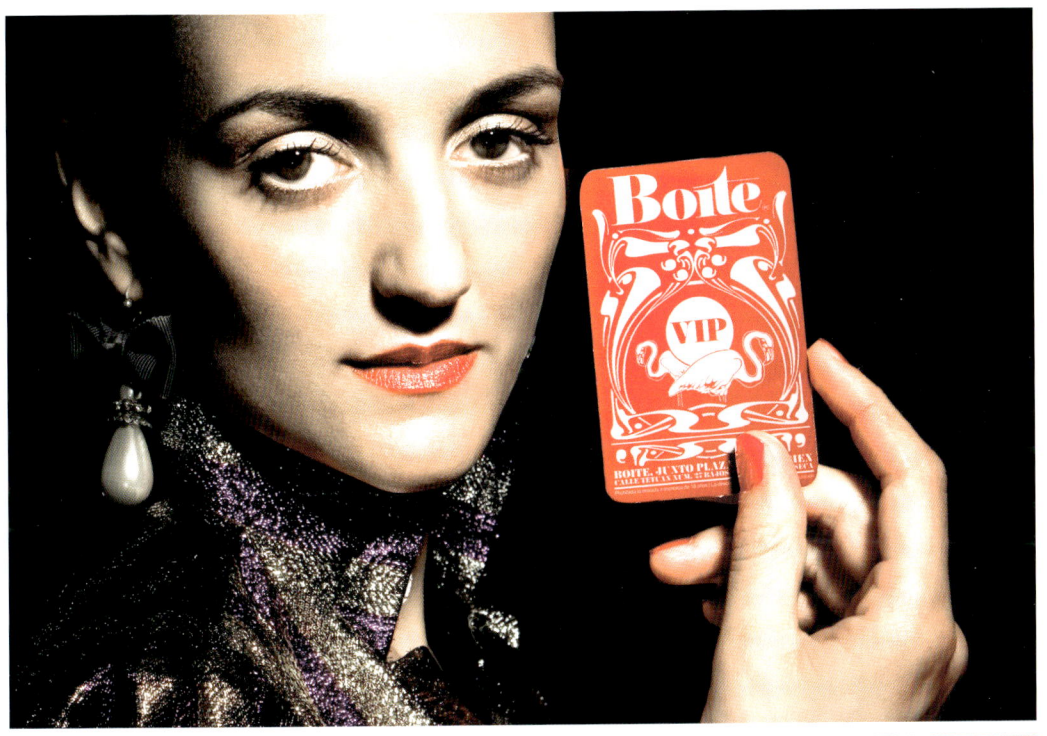

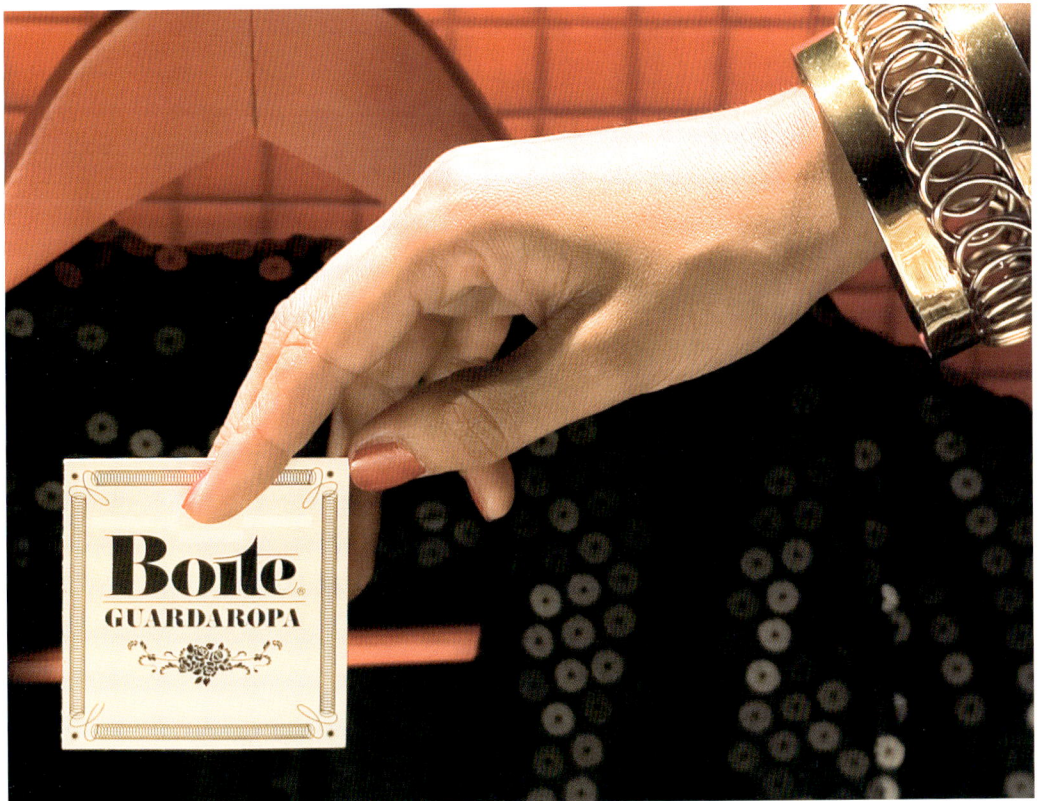

Boite | 2006

Sergio del Puerto/Serial Cut
www.serialcut.com

On the site of this club in Madrid there was previously a traditional ballroom. The logo was inspired by the history of the place. The rest of the graphics were inspired by art nouveau, Monopoly and the West, always combining black, red and white.

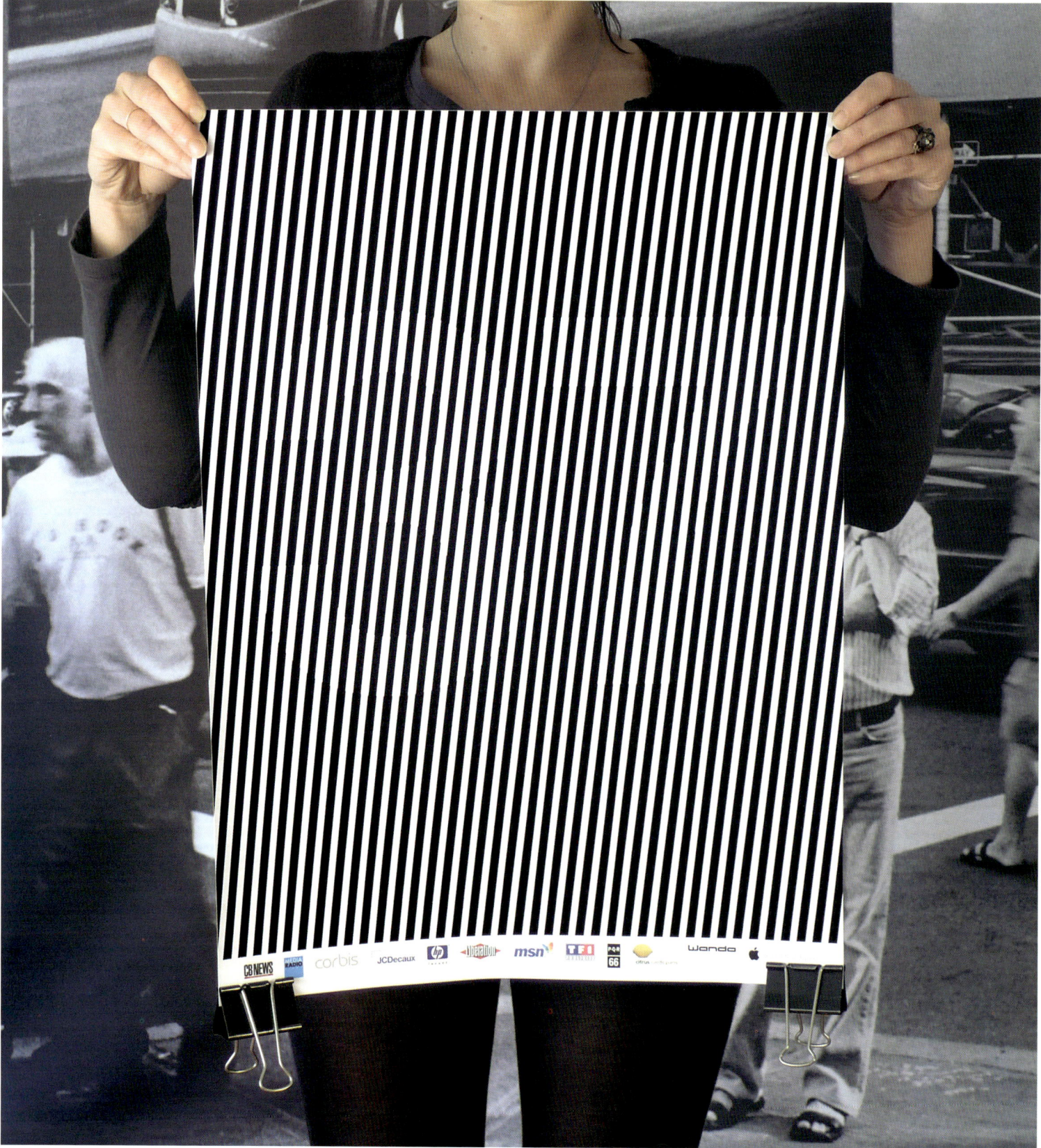

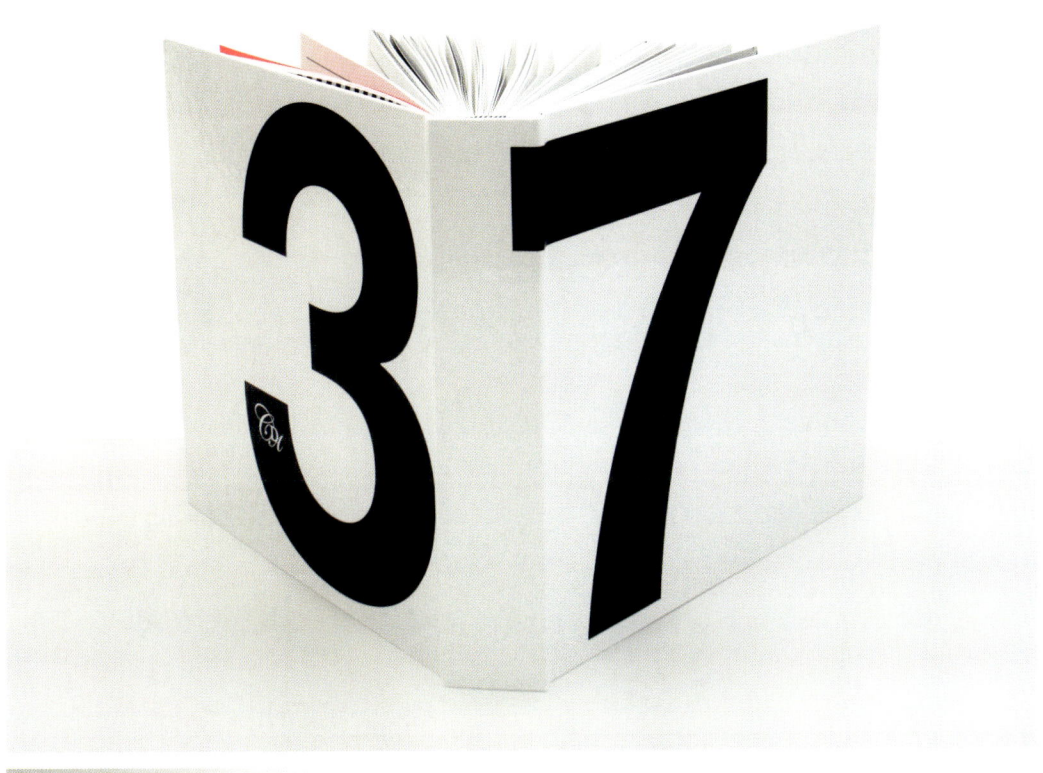
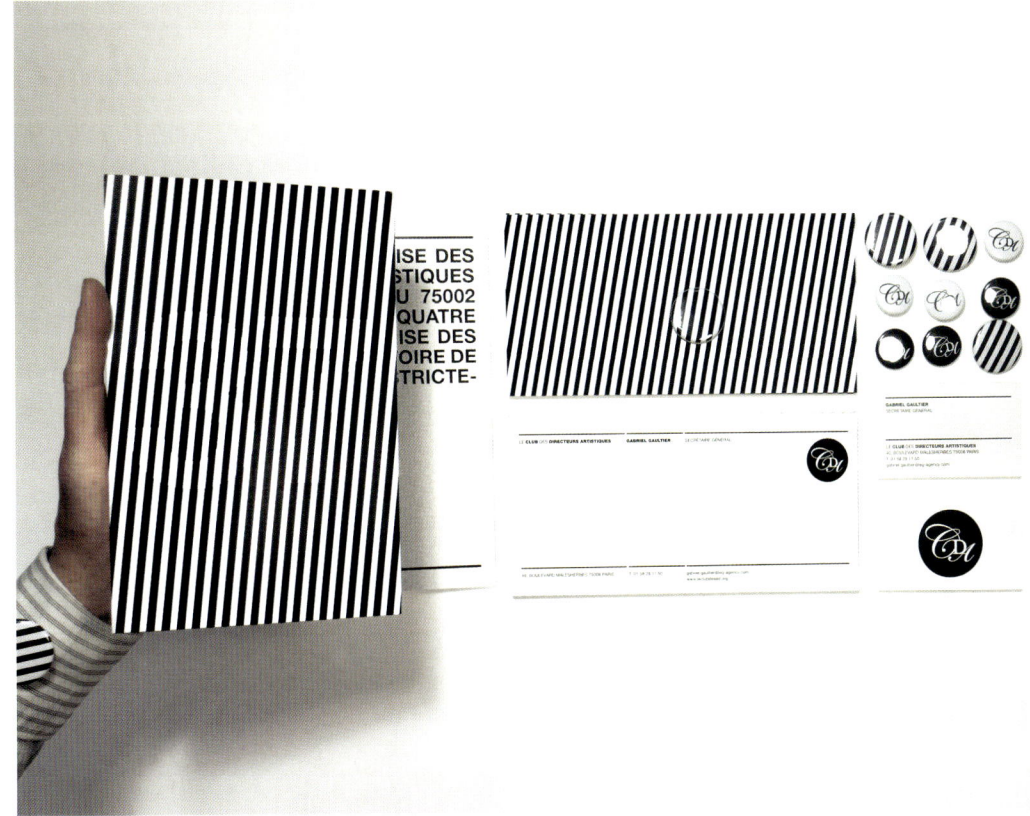

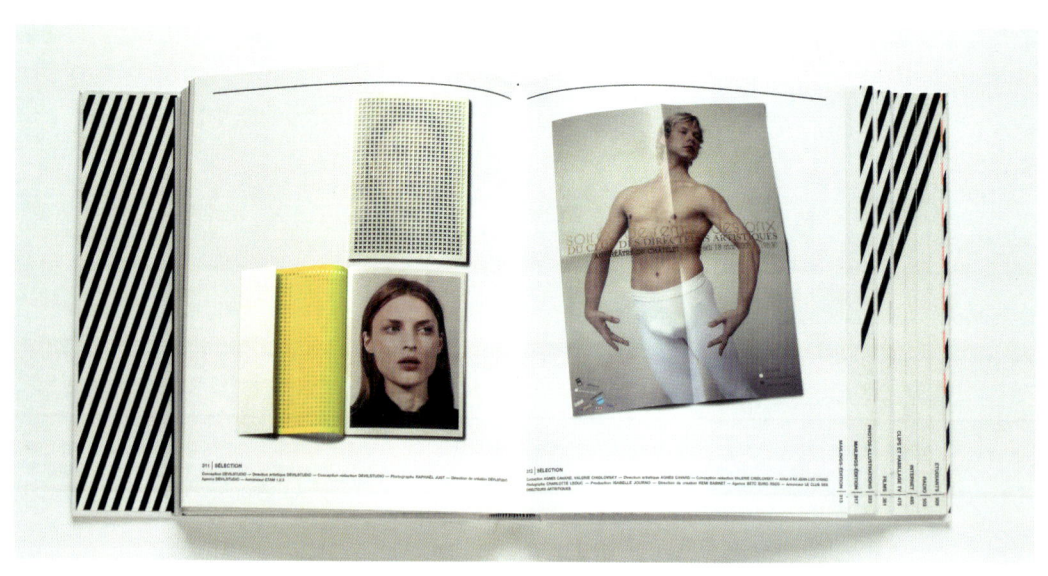
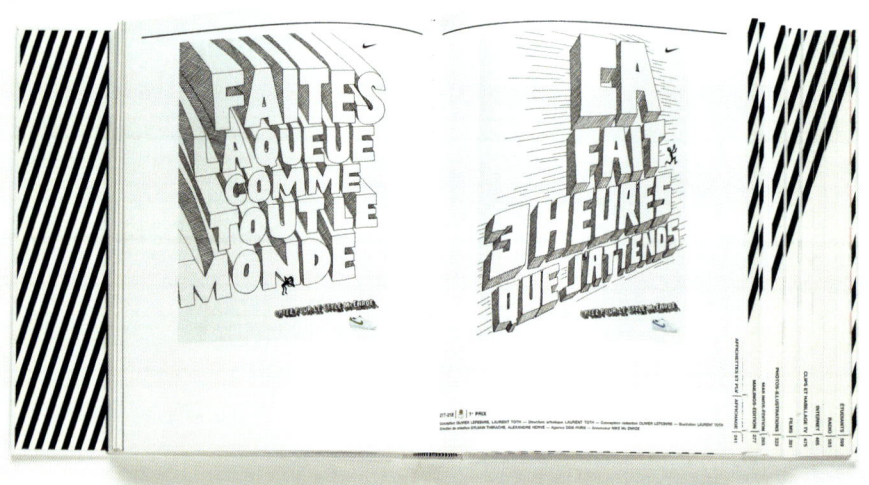
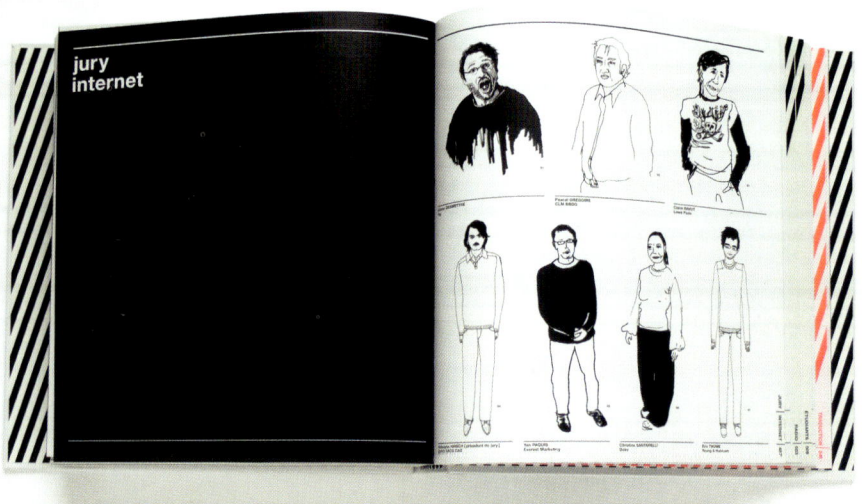

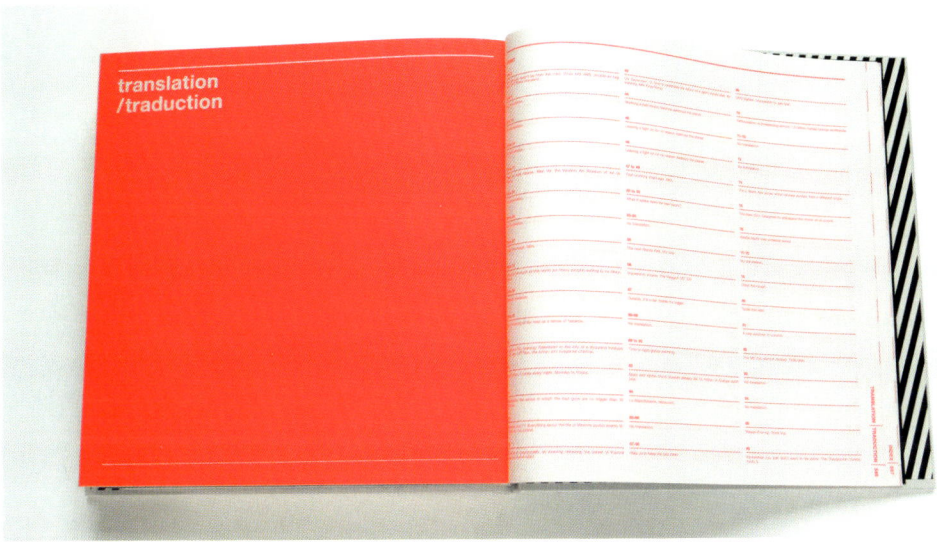

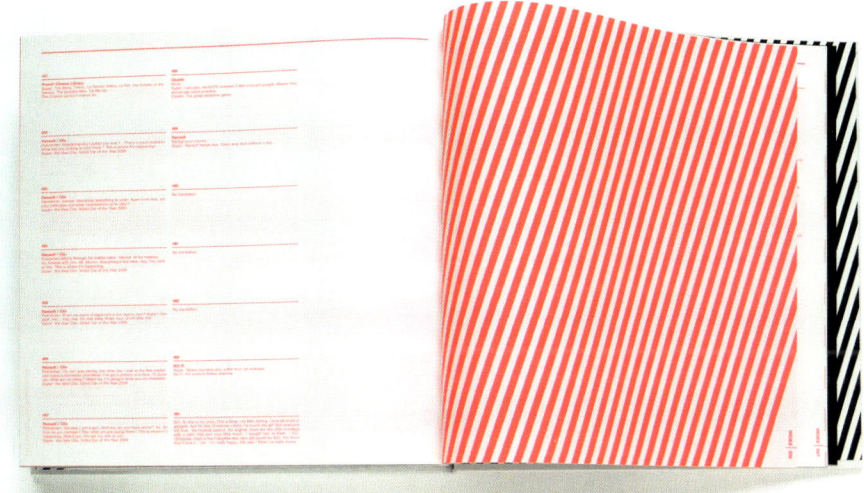

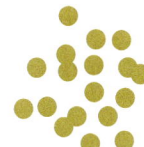

Le club des directeurs
artistiques | 2006

Cleo Charuet/Cleoburo
www.cleoburo.com

The book promotes the most celebrated works of French publicity. To enhance the content, a sober and discrete black and white background was used so as not to detract from the work. Also the distinguished logo was created, which is like a trademark.

It wasn't the best party I've ever been to, but it sure was strange. A bunch of invited people gathered in Stockholm to celebrate the release of the new Adidas Originals Collection. And we found ourselves being served a four-meter-long cake, in the shape of an Adidas shell-toe shoe. Mmmm, yummy!

Jonas Kjellberg

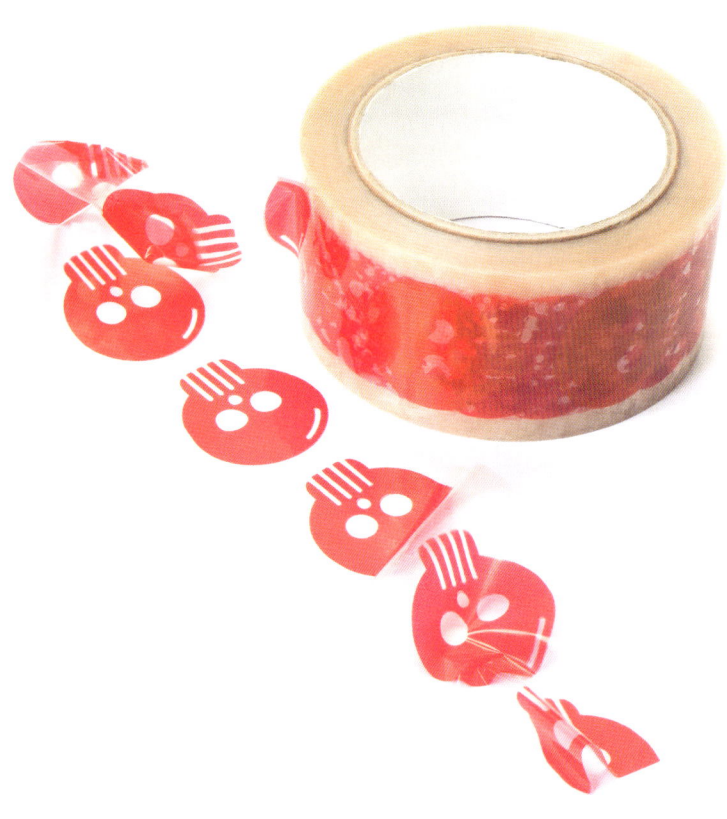

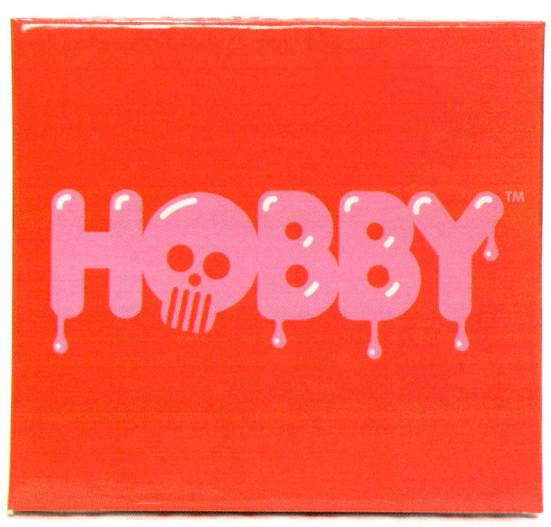

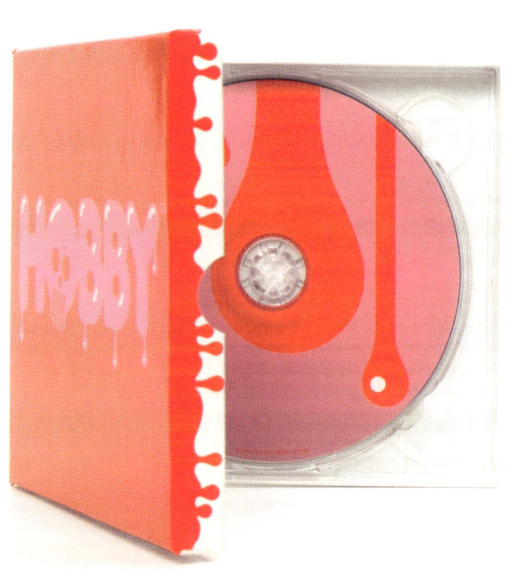

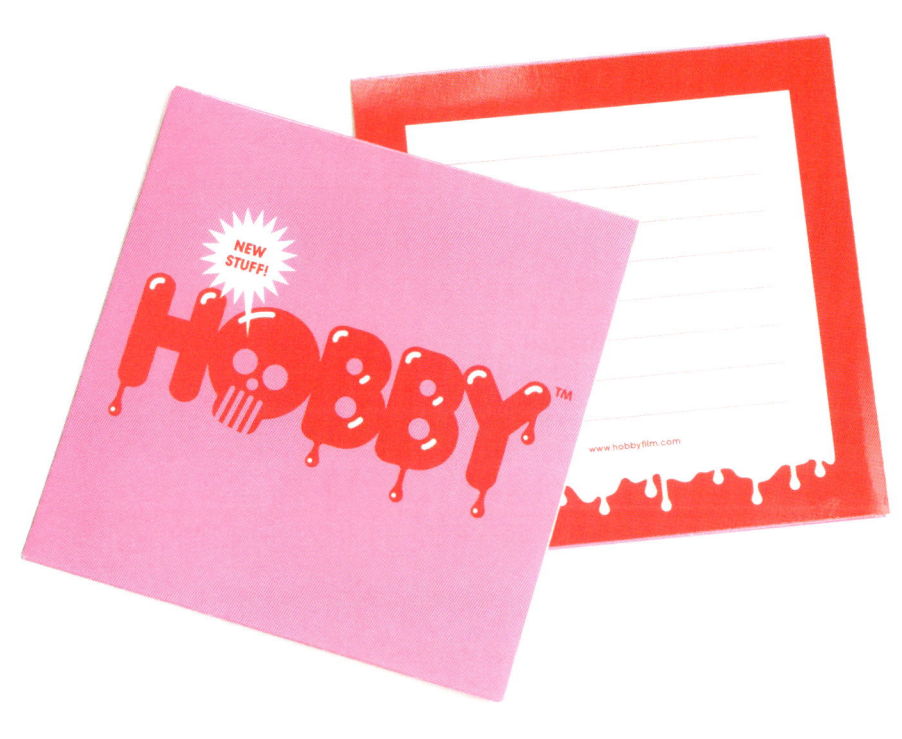

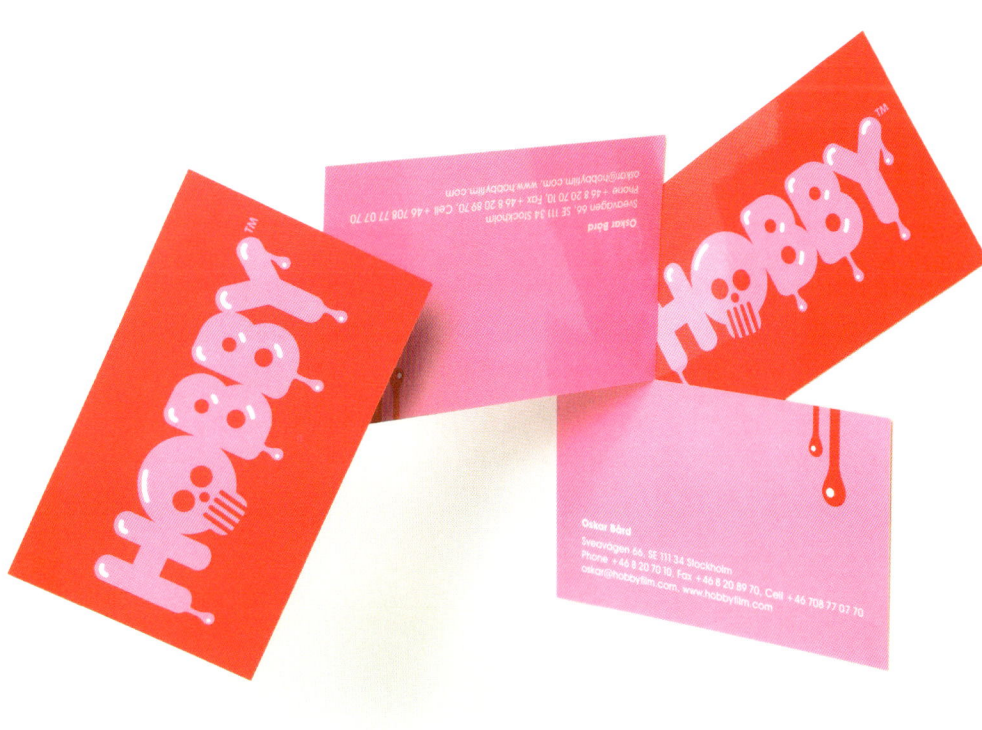

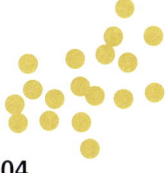

Hobby corporate identity | 2004

Jonas Kjellberg/Zion Graphics
www.ziongraphics.com

The company director wanted something cheerful, which would transmit his almost childish passion for his work, but also wanted to allude to danger. Thus, both concepts were passed through the sieve of caricature.